Applying Ethics:
A Text with Readings

Applying Ethics:
A Text with Readings

Vincent Barry
Bakersfield College

Wadsworth Publishing Company
Belmont, California
A Division of Wadsworth, Inc.

Philosophy Editor: Kenneth King
Production Editor: Carolyn Tanner
Designer: Andrew H. Ogus
Copy Editor: Anne Kelly Draus
Technical Illustrator: Pat Rogondino
Cover: Adriane Bosworth

Printed in the United States of America

3 4 5 6 7 8 9 10—85 84 83

Library of Congress Cataloging in Publication Data

Barry, Vincent E.
  Applying ethics.

  Previously published as: Personal and social ethics. 1978.
  Includes bibliographies and index.
  1. Social ethics.   2. United States—Moral conditions.   I. Title.
HM216.B18   1982   170   81-3058
ISBN 0-534-01000-8   AACR2

ISBN 0-534-01000-8

CONTENTS

7. CAPITAL PUNISHMENT

to Jim Wilson

PREFACE

Instructors face some tough choices in teaching introductory ethics and in selecting a text compatible with their approach. I suppose the basic choice is whether to teach theory, issues, or a combination of both. If theory, does one work with a text, primary sources, or something of each? Compounding the problem, as anyone knows who has struck out on a theory approach, is the real possibility of losing many students in a forest of abstraction.

On the other hand, the issues approach is no jaunt down the yellow brick road. Which issues does one select? Even when that has been decided, how does one approach the issues? With a text, a reader, a combination? The greatest problem with the strict issues approach, I think, is that students have no theoretical basis for structuring, let alone resolving, moral issues. In short, I think that striking a balance between theory and application of the issues remains a foremost challenge for instructors, and certainly for authors who wish to produce a useful instructional tool.

The first edition of this text, entitled *Personal and Social Ethics* (1978), tried to meet this challenge by introducing ethics in a balanced mix of theory and practice, using the text/reader format. It also tried to help students recognize the moral overtones in their own lives; feel the urgency of ethics; and understand, analyze, and resolve moral dilemmas for themselves. This new edition shares these goals. But in addition it brings to readers some of the most important moral issues of our time and, most importantly, tries to help them apply ethical theory to these issues. So influential were these two additional purposes in shaping the contents and structure of this edition that I felt a new title was in order: *Applying Ethics*.

Applying Ethics, then, is a text/reader that integrates theory and application. It is divided into two parts. Part I introduces the study of ethics, including the importance of moral justification and the role that intuition may play in moral decision. The first part also lays out seven important normative theories: egoism, utilitarianism (act and rule), divine command, categorical imperative, prima facie duties, and the maximin principle. Part II considers the following issues: sex outside marriage, pornography, abortion, euthanasia, capital punishment, reverse discrimination, and economic justice and world hunger. In each case, sufficient background material is provided for readers to begin thinking intelligently about the moral aspects of the issues. These issues are then examined within the framework of each ethical theory and further probed in accompanying reading selections (four per chapter).

Several pedagogical devices make *Applying Ethics* especially useful. First, included in each of the chapters on issues are arguments for and against particular propositions (for example, "The rich nations have an obligation to help feed the world's starving masses"). These arguments are presented in dialogue format like conversations people might have every day. The purpose of this format is to air the arguments that surround a moral issue in a way that facilitates understanding, stimulates discussion, and locates the issues in the lives of "ordinary" people.

Second, two case presentations appear at the end of each chapter in Part II. These cases deal with the issues raised. Following each presentation is a number of questions for discussion.

Third, each of the readings is preceded by an introduction that outlines the author's argument. Following each selection are questions for analysis. These questions test not only readers' comprehension but also their ability to integrate what they have read within ethical theory.

Fourth, a bibliography accompanies each chapter. Although these Selections for Further Reading by no means exhaust the topics, they provide a departure point for further study and research.

Finally, *Applying Ethics* is flexible. As indicated, the challenges faced by ethics instructors were uppermost in my mind while writing this new edition. So, I decided very early to structure the book so that it would accommodate as diverse instructional needs as possible. This required not only a text/reader format and an inclusion of theory and issues, but also an integration of these elements in such a way that those who wished could focus on one of these elements exclusively. *Applying Ethics* allows this. While the elements are unified, each is also self-contained. This is a major improvement over the first edition.

I would like to acknowledge those who assisted in developing this new edition: Wadsworth philosophy editor Ken King for the brainstorms that continue to spark the imagination; reviewers Michael A. Foley, Marywood College; W. Murray Hunt, Susquehanna University; Donald L. Jones, Our Lady of the Lake University; Thomas Keene, Our Lady of the Lake University; Peter List, Oregon State University; Thomas Morrow, Carl Albert Junior College; Gregory E. Pence, UAB; and Robert Radford, Oklahoma State University, for their timely suggestions; copy editor Anne Kelly Draus; and Wadsworth production staff Adriane Bosworth and Carolyn Tanner for their careful attention. As always, errors of fact or omission are my responsibility.

Part I
Ethics and Ethical Theories

1
VALUES, ETHICS, JUSTIFICATION

In the late 1950s and early 1960s, America's brew of racial unrest, which had been heating up for so long, finally boiled over. "Justice too long delayed is justice denied"; "We will overcome"; "Freedom now!" These cries for racial equality echoed throughout the land. "Freedom riders," persons who traveled the roads of America's South to demonstrate opposition to racial inequalities, became as commonplace on television screens as the nightly news. So did the face of their leader, the velvet-voiced, inspirational president of the Southern Christian Leadership Conference, the Reverend Martin Luther King, Jr.

At the height of this period of vigorous racial protest, King was arrested in Birmingham, Alabama. The charge: "parading without a permit." The act instantly reminded some of the contrived charges brought against historic figures such as Socrates and Jesus. Others praised the Birmingham commissioner of public safety, Eugene "Bull" Connor, for keeping order and preventing violence. Among those applauding Connor were eight of King's fellow clergymen, who published a statement attacking King's action as unwise and untimely. Confined in the city jail, King responded in what has become known as his "Letter from Birmingham Jail."

In this important document in the history of civil rights, King defends his conduct. It was not only justified, he says, but obligatory. At one point in the long essay, King confronts the central issue of whether it is ever right willfully to break the law. He thinks it is. Here is why:

> You express a great deal of anxiety over our willingness to break laws. This is
> certainly a legitimate concern. Since we so diligently urge people to obey the
> Supreme Court's decision of 1954 outlawing segregation in the public schools, at
> first glance it may seem rather paradoxical for us consciously to break laws. One
> may well ask: "How can you advocate breaking some laws and obeying others?"
> The answer lies in the fact that there are two types of laws: just and unjust. I
> would be the first to advocate obeying just laws. One has not only a legal
> but a moral responsibility to obey just laws. Conversely, one has a moral

responsibility to disobey unjust laws. I would agree with St. Augustine that "an unjust law is no law at all."

Now, what is the difference between the two? How does one determine whether a law is just or unjust? A just law is a man-made code that squares with the moral law or the law of God. An unjust law is a code that is out of harmony with the moral law. To put it in the terms of St. Thomas Aquinas: An unjust law is a human law that is not rooted in eternal law and natural law. Any law that uplifts human personality is just. Any law that degrades human personality is unjust. All segregation statutes are unjust because segregation distorts the soul and damages the personality. It gives the segregator a false sense of superiority and the segregated a false sense of inferiority. Segregation, to use the terminology of the Jewish philosopher Martin Buber, substitutes an "I-it" relationship for an "I-thou" relationship and ends up relegating persons to the status of things. Hence segregation is not only politically, economically, and sociologically unsound, it is morally wrong and sinful. Paul Tillich has said that sin is separation. Is not segregation an existential expression of man's tragic separation, his awful estrangement, his terrible sinfulness. Thus it is that I can urge men to obey the 1954 decision of the Supreme Court, for it is morally right; and I can urge them to disobey segregation ordinances, for they are morally wrong.

Let us consider a more concrete example of just and unjust laws. An unjust law is a code that a numerical or power majority group compels a minority group to obey but does not make binding on itself. This is *difference* made legal. By the same token, a just law is a code that a majority compels a minority to follow and that it is willing to follow itself. This is *sameness* made legal.

Let me give another explanation. A law is unjust if it is inflicted on a minority that, as a result of being denied the right to vote, had no part in enacting or devising the law. Who can say that the legislature of Alabama which set up that state's segregation laws was democratically elected? Throughout Alabama all sorts of devious methods are used to prevent Negroes from becoming registered voters, and there are some counties in which, even though Negroes constitute a majority of the population, not a single Negro is registered. Can any law enacted under such circumstances be considered democratically structured?

Sometimes a law is just on its face and unjust in its application. For instance, I have been arrested on a charge of parading without a permit. Now, there is nothing wrong in having an ordinance which requires a permit for a parade. But such an ordinance becomes unjust when it is used to maintain segregation and to deny citizens the First-Amendment privilege of peaceful assembly and protest.

I hope you are able to see the distinction I am trying to point out. In no sense do I advocate evading or defying the law, as would the rabid segregationist. That would lead to anarchy. One who breaks an unjust law must do so openly, lovingly, and with a willingness to accept the penalty. I submit that an individual who breaks a law that conscience tells him is unjust, and who willingly accepts the penalty of imprisonment in order to arouse the conscience of the community over its injustice, is in reality expressing the highest respect for law.[1]

---

1. From *"Letter from Birmingham Jail, April 16, 1963,"* in Why We Can't Wait *by Martin Luther King, Jr. Copyright ©1963 by Martin Luther King, Jr. Reprinted by permission of Harper & Row, Publishers, Inc.*

Two aspects of King's letter, which are evident even in this short excerpt, make it a lively springboard to our study of ethics. First, it illustrates the moral aspect of an individual's value system. Second, it underscores the importance of justification in moral decision, especially in the public realm.

Both the moral aspect of an individual's value system and the importance of justification in moral decision are focal points of this opening chapter, which introduces the study of ethics, including some basic terms and concepts.

Values and Justification

Although there is much debate about the precise nature of values, let us define *a value simply as an assessment of worth*. Defined as such, values constitute a large part of who we are and how we live. Clearly we humans exhibit all sorts of values, assessments of worth. In automobiles, some of us value low-slung sports models, others conservative sedans. In books, some prefer science fiction, others historical nonfiction. Politically, some people value a democratic form of government, others a constitutional monarchy. Differences in values continue—in religion, art, politics, education, in every area of human affairs. Most importantly, humans seem to be the only animals that can formulate and express a value (notwithstanding ads for cat food).

Where do values come from? How do they arise? Why does one person see beauty in an ocean, while another is unmoved? Why will one person risk life and limb to ensure justice, while another stands detached and indifferent? Our values are generally shaped and formed by experience. Thus, the sea holds little beauty for an individual who has seen a loved one die in it. The person who has felt the sting of racial or sexual discrimination can understandably develop a passion for fair and just treatment, even at great personal risk. In brief, the values we hold, as individuals and as groups, are inseparable from the endlessly changing experiences of our lives.

History reveals that no society has ever been without some value system and that every individual has some code of values. The issue, therefore, is not whether we are to have values but what those values will be.

What we value in the realm of human conduct are called our moral values. Some people, for example, might value justice. They might contend that a person should always do the just thing and refrain from doing what is unjust. Others might value civil order. They might argue that we should always act in a way that promotes civil order and refrain from acting in a way that will produce disorder. Of course, we could speak of other moral values that people hold: honesty, truth, loyalty, love, and so on. But how do we know which values to hold? This is a tough question to answer, perhaps impossible to answer to everyone's satisfaction. The study of ethics partially involves a search for the answer.

Complicating the question of which moral values to hold is the inevitable situation of conflicting values. Martin Luther King was involved in precisely this dilemma. Should he prefer justice or order? By parading without a permit, King clearly stated that in the area of racial equality he valued justice over order. King believed that intentionally breaking the law was the right thing to do in that instance because such behavior would dramatize the inequities of racial injustice. King had chosen a moral value; having chosen it, he acted in accordance with that decision. Thus the King case well illustrates how a personal value can translate into a social position and into subsequent action. Indeed, our positions and actions on the issues of the day take root in the values that we hold for ourselves and our society. Moral positions and conduct cannot be separated from moral values.

But how do we know that King acted right? Can we ever know? Again, this is a difficult question to answer. However, the study of ethics also partially involves a search for what constitutes morally right human conduct.

In defending his action, Martin Luther King realized that it was not enough to express a moral value, to prefer justice to order in the case of racial inequality. He had to justify his position, to demonstrate why racial justice was a superior value to civil order. So often today people hold views without really knowing why. They may be against abortion and capital punishment, for euthanasia and premarital sex, or against censorship and reverse discrimination. On any issue you can find numerous people willing to give you a position. But ask the same people for their reasons, why they believe as they do, and they may not be able to say.

Of course, just because a person cannot give satisfactory reasons for his or her beliefs and positions does not necessarily mean that those viewpoints lack respectability. But if our assessments are to influence others on the significant moral issues of the day, then at some point we must present well reasoned arguments for them. If we want to ensure that our own views are the clearest and most compelling of the alternatives, then we must subject those views to rational analysis.

We shall discuss considerably more about moral justification shortly. But first, let us find out what ethics involves.

Ethics

In the chapters ahead we will focus on values that govern what is called good and bad human conduct. *Ethics is the study of what constitutes good and bad human conduct, including related action and values.*

The term *ethics* is sometimes used synonymously with *morals*. It would be more accurate, though, to use the terms *morals* and *moral* to refer to the conduct itself, and the terms *ethics* and *ethical* to refer to the study of moral conduct or to the code one follows. So, when we use the word *moral*, we refer to an action or person insofar as either is considered right or good. When we use the word *immoral*, we refer to an action or person insofar as either one is considered wrong or bad.

Sometimes in ethics the word *nonmoral* occurs. *Nonmoral* refers to something outside the sphere of moral concern. For example, whether your new sports car will "top out" at 120 or 130 mph is a nonmoral question; it is not a moral issue. But whether you should "top it out" on Main Street on a Wednesday at high noon would probably be a moral question.

In ethics we are concerned with questions of right and wrong, duty and obligation, and moral responsibility. When ethicists use words like *good* or *right* to describe a person or action, they generally mean that the person or action conforms with some moral standard. A good person or action has desirable qualities or possesses qualities desirable to humans. Ethicists often disagree about the nature of these qualities and follow different paths in hopes of discovering them. For purposes of understanding, though, we can view ethics as divided into two fields—normative ethics and nonnormative ethics.

Normative Ethics

Normative ethics involves an attempt to determine precisely what moral standards to follow so that our actions may be morally right or good. There are two normative areas: applied and general. *Applied normative ethics is the attempt to explain and justify positions on specific moral problems,* such as sex outside marriage, capital punishment, euthanasia, reverse discrimination, and so on. This area of· normative ethics is termed *applied* because the ethicist applies or uses the general ethical principles in an attempt to resolve the specific moral problems.

For example, in defending civil disobedience Martin Luther King applied the principles of justice and equality. When such general principles are arranged into an ethical theory, we see the second field of normative ethics, what is called general normative ethics.

General normative ethics is the reasoned search for principles of human conduct, including a critical study of the major theories about what things are good, what acts are right, and what acts are blameworthy. It attempts to determine precisely what moral standards to follow so that our actions may be morally right or good. For most of us, ethical action springs from some standard: "Do unto others as you would have them do unto you"; "Act in such a way that you bring about the greatest good for the greatest number"; "Always act in your own best interests." What principle ought we to adopt? That is partially what general normative ethics tries to discover. It tries to formulate and defend a system of basic ethical principles that presumably are valid for everyone.

Two broad categories of general normative theories can be distinguished: teleological and deontological. Teleological theories maintain that the morality of an action depends on the nonmoral consequences that the action brings about. We will simply call such theories *consequential.* Among the important consequential theories are egoism and utilitarianism. Egoism is concerned with the best consequences for self, utilitarianism with the best consequences for everyone.

In contrast, deontological theories maintain that the morality of an action depends on factors other than consequences. Again, for simplicity, we will refer to deontological theories as *nonconsequential.* Among the important nonconsequential theories are: divine command, categorical imperative, prima facie duties, and maximin principle. Divine command is concerned with acting in such a way that one's action agrees with the laws of God. The categorical imperative is concerned with acting in such a way that one could wish the maxim of one's action to become a universal law. Prima facie duties are concerned with acting in accordance with an overriding obligation as indicated by the circumstances involved. And the maximin principle is concerned with acting in a way that produces for the individual the greatest amount of liberty that is compatible with a like liberty for all. Chapter 2 of this text deals thoroughly with each of these theories.

Nonnormative Ethics

Like normative ethics, nonnormative ethics consists of two fields: scientific and metaethical.

SCIENTIFIC OR DESCRIPTIVE.   *The scientific or descriptive study of morality involves factual investigation of moral behavior.* It is concerned with how people do in fact behave. This approach is used widely in the social sciences. For example, anthropologists and sociologists investigate and describe moral attitudes. They report on how moral attitudes and codes differ from society to society, investigating and describing the values and behaviors of different societies. Thus, anthropologists tell us that Eskimos used to abandon their elderly on the ice and allow them to die of starvation and exposure, and that some African tribes kill infant twins and require that a man marry his brother's widow. The fact that societies often differ markedly in their values and conceptions of right and wrong has led many to advance a doctrine called ethical relativism.

In order to understand ethical relativism, one must first be familiar with ethical absolutism. *Ethical absolutism is the doctrine that there exists one and only one moral code.* Absolutists maintain that this code applies to everyone, at all times, everywhere. What is a duty for me must also be a duty for you. What is a moral duty for an American must also be a moral duty for an Asian, African, European, and aborigine. If euthanasia is wrong, it is wrong for everyone, at all times, everywhere. The fact that a society may see nothing wrong with euthanasia or lying or cannibalism in no way affects the rightness or wrongness of such actions. Ethical absolutists do not necessarily claim that their interpretation of the absolute standard is the true and valid one. But they do insist that there is a true moral code and that this code is the same for all people in all ages.

Ethical relativism is the doctrine that denies that there is a single moral standard that is universally applicable to all people at all times. Relativists deny that there exists only one moral code, law, principle, or standard. They insist that there are many moral codes that take root in diverse social soils and environments. As the name implies, ethical relativists insist that any morality is relative to the time, place, and circumstances in which it occurs. In no way is any moral code absolute.

Ethical relativism is not the same as cultural relativism. Cultural relativism is a sociological fact: Research indicates the existence of many obviously different and often contradictory moral codes. Ethical relativists are not merely saying that what is thought right in one part of the world is frequently thought wrong in another. Scientific or descriptive ethics has established this fact that even absolutists accept. Rather, ethical relativists assert that precisely the same action that is right in one society at one time can be wrong in another. Thus, putting to death anyone over eighty years old can be right in the jungles of New Guinea and wrong in the United States. Such a claim is quite different from saying that putting octogenarians to death is thought to be right in one place and thought to be wrong in another. In brief, ethical relativists believe that what is *thought* right *is* right.

We shall not take the time here to criticize these positions. Whether we agree with absolutism or relativism, we still must decide what we ought to do individually and collectively. Presumably this requires some standard on which we make the decisions. So, whether I am an absolutist or a relativist, the questions remain: How ought I behave and how ought my society behave?

METAETHICS.   The second field of nonnormative ethics is called metaethics. *Metaethics is the highly technical discipline investigating the meaning of ethical terms*, including a critical study of how ethical statements can be verified. Largely the province of philosophers, metaethics is concerned with the meanings of such important ethical terms as *right, obligation,* and *responsibility.* Thus, metaethicists would be more concerned with the meanings of the words *good* or *bad* than with what we think is good or bad. If you maintained, for example, that Martin Luther King's behavior was right, the metaethicist might ask: Just what do you mean by "right"?

Metaethical positions are generally divided into what are sometimes called naturalism, nonnaturalism, and noncognitivism. *Naturalism maintains that ethical statements can be translated into nonethical statements.* One naturalistic position—autobiographical naturalism—contends that an ethical statement simply expresses the approval or disapproval of the speaker. For example, when you say that "King was right," you mean "I approve of King's action." Another naturalistic position—sociological naturalism—contends that an ethical statement simply expresses the approval or disapproval of the majority. For example, "King was right" means "The majority approves of King's action." Still another naturalistic position—theological naturalism—holds that an ethical statement expresses divine approval or disapproval. In that case, "King was right" in effect means that "God (or some equivalent reference) approves of King's action."

Nonnaturalism, in contrast to naturalism, *is the position that an ethical statement defies translation into a nonethical form.* Nonnaturalists insist that at least some ethical words can be defined only in terms of other ethical words. Thus, nonnaturalists might argue that the statement "King was right" can only be translated into other ethical statements, such as "King's action was proper," or "King's action should have been performed," or "King's action was good." They claim that naturalistic translations would be like trying to define *hour* in other than temporal terms, or *inch* in other than spatial terms. It just cannot be done. Clearly, then, nonnaturalists come close to asserting that ethical statements cannot be verified, that they cannot be determined true or false. How then does the nonnaturalist handle ethical statements? One of the foremost nonnaturalists, G. E. Moore, advises that we reflect on them and determine, as well as we can, whether we believe the statements are true. As Moore puts it:

> There is no empirical observation and no mathematical or logical calculation
> which would enable us to discover the truth of ethical propositions. All we can
> do is to distinguish them carefully from all other propositions (especially some

empirical ones with which they are apt to be confused), and then reflect upon them and see whether, after this reflection, we believe that they are true.[2]

In addition to naturalism and nonnaturalism there is a position sometimes called emotivism or noncognitivism. *Emotivism or noncognitivism can be broadly defined as a metaethical position which claims that ethical statements are used to evoke a predetermined response or to encourage a predetermined behavior.* In this view, then, ethical statements can be used, indeed are used, to make someone feel or behave in a certain way. For example, if a teacher says to a student, "Cheating is wrong," the teacher may not be expressing a moral position on cheating but is rather trying to instill in the student a certain attitude toward cheating. The teacher may also be trying to elicit a certain behavior. Ethical statements would therefore amount to commands such as "Don't cheat" or "Don't lie" or "Don't break promises." The essential difference between an autobiographical naturalist and a noncognitivist is that the former believes that ethical statements are subjective and verifiable, while the latter believes that they are subjective but not verifiable.

The chart on the next page organizes all the different fields of normative and nonnormative ethics.

Focus on Normative Ethics

As the title of this text indicates, our emphasis is on applied ethics. The chapters raise issues of contemporary moral importance: sex outside marriage, pornography, abortion, euthanasia, capital punishment, reverse discrimination, world hunger and economic justice. But the book also introduces basic or theoretical ethics. Chapter 2, for example, presents all the normative theories just mentioned, and subsequent chapters apply these theories to the issues raised. Approaching ethics this way, you will rapidly begin to understand the intimacy between theory and application and learn how to apply theoretical ethics to the moral issues that concern you.

There are several reasons for the focus on normative ethics, applied and theoretical. First, most of us approach ethics normatively. In our personal and social lives, we want to determine for ourselves some principles or standards of moral behavior. Although language analysis helps clarify meaning, at some point each of us must investigate normative ethics to determine our principles and standards.

Second, urgent moral issues face us today. These issues cry for resolution that must spring from serious, informed, and extensive debate. In recent years ethicists have indeed recognized the urgency of these issues by rekindling their traditional interest in normative ethics.

The third reason for concentrating on normative ethics deals directly with our next topic for discussion—moral reasoning. As indicated at the outset of this chapter, justification is important in moral decision. And justifying a moral judgment or position inevitably involves appeal to some moral principle or standard. Thus, again we are pitched into normative concerns. This third point will become clearer as we discuss patterns of moral reasoning.

2.   G. E. Moore, *Principia Ethica (London: Cambridge University Press, 1903).*

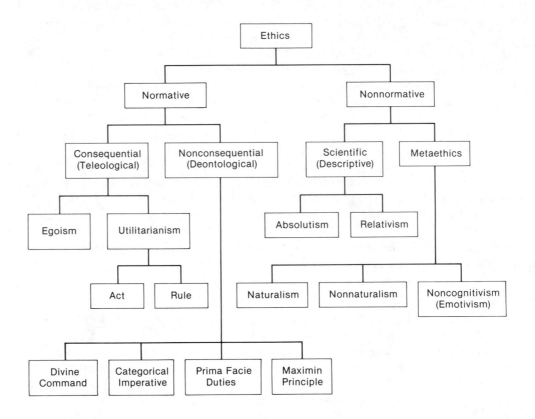

Patterns of Moral Reasoning

Although you are not likely to find among ethicists a consensus of moral opinion on any issue, you will find patterns of moral reasoning. An awareness of these patterns will help you understand what is involved in presenting or criticizing a moral position and also how to begin formulating your own moral positions. Furthermore, you will also be better able to understand the reading selections provided at the end of each chapter.

To begin, it is useful to view patterns of moral reasoning in the context of argument. An argument is a group of statements one of which—the conclusion—is said to follow from the others—the premises. Here is a simple example of an argument:

If a person is a mother, the person is a female.

Fran is a mother.

Therefore, Fran is a female.

Notice that the first two statements, the premises, entail the last statement, the conclusion. In other words, given the first two premises, the conclusion must logically follow.

Regarding civil disobedience, consider these arguments:

If an action violates the law, it is wrong.

Civil disobedience violates the law.

So, civil disobedience is wrong.

If an action violates the will of the majority, the action is wrong.

Civil disobedience violates the will of the majority.

Therefore, it is wrong.

If an action is an expression of one's commitment to a higher law, the action is moral.

Civil disobedience can be an expression of one's commitment to a higher law.

Thus, civil disobedience can be moral.

If an action is the only practical alternative in a situation, the action is right.

Civil disobedience may be the only practical alternative in a situation.

Therefore, civil disobedience may be right.

These represent a wide range of arguments in opposition to or defense of civil disobedience. Notice that each of these contains a particular moral judgment. *A particular moral judgment is a claim about what should be done or what was done by a specific person or group of people in a specific historical situation.* For example, "King's action was good," "King's action was bad," "King was right," and "King was wrong" are all particular moral judgments. Other examples of particular moral judgments are: "The government should allow voluntary euthanasia," "Abortion-on-demand ought not be legalized," "It's right to help feed the world's starving masses." Certain moral words appear in particular moral judgments: *good, bad, right, wrong, should, should not,* and so forth. Although not all judgments using such words are moral judgments (for example, "King was a good speaker" or "Judging from the polls, the President should win the upcoming election"), these words frequently do indicate the presence of particular moral judgments. So do the words *duty, responsibility,* and *obligation.*

Even when moral words are absent, a particular moral judgment may be implied. For example, if the speaker was clearly suggesting moral disapproval in the statement, "King broke the law!" that statement would be expressing a particular moral judgment. So, the context of a statement, its physical and rhetorical surroundings, is important to consider in determining the presence of a particular moral judgment.

Contrasting with particular moral judgments are general moral principles. *General moral principles are claims about what should be done in every case of a certain sort or by everyone in a certain sort of situation.* The first premise in each of the preceding civil disobedience arguments, the "if" premise, may be considered a general moral principle. Sometimes, general moral principles are more global in scope. For example, "One should always treat people as one would want to be treated" or "One should always try to produce the greatest amount of happiness for the greatest number of people."

This distinction between particular moral judgments and general moral principles engenders a feature of defensible moral views that relates directly to our discussion of the patterns of moral reasoning. This feature is: If a particular moral judgment is defensible, then it must be supportable by a defensible general moral principle, usually together with additional facts.[3] *A general moral principle supports a particular moral judgment if the principle, together with facts, logically entails the particular moral judgment.* Thus, if someone argues that abortion-on-demand is wrong but cannot produce a supporting principle when asked, then that person's position is considerably weakened. And if the person does not see any need to support the judgment by appeal to a general principle, then we must conclude that the person simply does not understand how moral concepts are used or is using moral words such as *wrong* in a way much different from their common meaning.

Keeping this feature in mind—that if a particular moral judgment is defensible, then it must be supportable by a defensible general moral principle—will enormously aid your understanding of moral discourse, which can be highly complex and sophisticated. It will also sharpen your own critical faculties and improve your ability to formulate relevant moral arguments. The importance of this feature lies in the fact that much of what occurs in moral debates can be interpreted in the light of the feature itself.

For example, in all the preceding arguments for civil disobedience, someone is trying to defend the morality or immorality of civil disobedience by appeal to a general moral principle and some fact. Once the principle and facts are disclosed, discussion may focus on a number of points. If all parties are willing to grant the general moral principle, then they will concentrate on the factual claims. However, someone may object to the general moral principle; in that case whoever advanced the argument must defend the principle. Usually this defense can be conducted by appeal to an even more general principle, together with more facts, that entails the principle under attack.

Sometimes the proponent of the principle will try to show how the principle entails other particular moral judgments that the opponent accepts. For example, in the following dialogue, Wayne is questioning the moral principle that "if

3. *See: Stephen P. Stitch, "The Recombinant DNA Debate: Some Philosophical Considerations" in* The Recombinant DNA Debate, *ed. David A. Jackson and Stephen P. Stitch (Englewood Cliffs, N.J.: Prentice-Hall, 1979), p. 184.*

an action violates the will of the majority, then the action is wrong." Jami is defending the principle.

Jami: Okay, do you think the government should impose a national reli-
          gion on all Americans?

Wayne: If it tried to, I'd be the first to fight it.

Jami: All right. How do you feel about legalizing pot?

Wayne: I'm against it.

Jami: And using kids in pornography?

Wayne: There are and there should be laws against it.

Jami: But the principle that you're objecting to leads to these judgments
          you agree with.

Of course Jami's argument is by no means a conclusive defense for the general moral principle under discussion. After all, other moral principles could just as easily entail the judgments agreed upon. Wayne points this out.

Wayne: Now wait a minute. I oppose a state religion because it's unconsti-
          tutional, not because it violates the will of the majority. As for grass,
          I'm against legalizing it because we don't know enough about it yet.
          And using kids in pornography is wrong because it involves sexual
          exploitation and exposes kids to a lot of dangers.

Notice that, while Jami's strategy for defending the principle about majority rule proved inconclusive, it did serve to shift the burden of argument to Wayne. It forced him to counter with alternative principles that at least equally well supported the particular moral judgments raised.

In attacking a moral principle a common strategy is first to isolate particular moral judgments that the advocate of the principle rejects and then to demonstrate how the principle plus additional facts actually entail those unacceptable judgments. In the following dialogue, for example, Jami is attacking Wayne's advocacy of the principle that "if an action is an expression of one's commitment to a higher law, then the action is moral."

Jami: What do you think of parents who for religious reasons won't allow
          their children to have necessary medical care?

Wayne: I've heard about that. In fact, there was a couple on our block who
          wouldn't let their kid have a blood transfusion when she needed it.

Jami: You think that's right?

Wayne: Of course not.

> Jami: But they were obeying a "higher law," weren't they? I mean they were probably acting on some religious conviction or on grounds of conscience.
>
> Wayne: Maybe they were, but so what?
>
> Jami: Well, the principle you're defending leads to a judgment you reject. How do you account for that?

At this point, Wayne, or anyone in a similar position, presumably has two alternatives: (1) abandon the principle he is defending, or (2) change his view about the judgment. Wayne must either abandon his view that any action that is an expression of one's commitment to a higher law is moral. Or he can decide that parental denial of necessary medical services for children, on grounds of religion or conscience, is in fact right.

Recognizing thus the patterns of moral reasoning in ethical discourse and the need to support judgments with principles greatly aids in formulating and unravelling ethical arguments. Essential to moral argument, then, is justification. *Justification refers to reasons, the evidence that supports the position. Justification also refers to the reasoning process one follows to arrive at the position.* In justifying our moral positions to others, we must demonstrate that our premises (evidence or reasons) are true and that they logically entail the judgment (the position).

The previously mentioned strategies are common ways that people use to try to justify their moral judgments. However, while a knowledge of these strategies is useful in recognizing and understanding the anatomy of moral arguments, the strategies are not altogether satisfactory for dissecting an argument. In order to analyze an argument, we must first make a study of correct argument. Logic is such a study. Logic provides analytical methodology that enables us to detect flaws in the reasoning process. Obviously this text cannot provide complete logical training. But we can become familiar with some of the emotional and psychological devices people often use to persuade us to their views. These devices are called logical fallacies. A simple acquaintance with these fallacies will help you detect any glaring deficiencies in moral arguments.

Fallacies

Broadly defined, a fallacy is an incorrect way of reasoning. A fallacy is also any attempt to persuade emotionally or psychologically, but not logically. For example, a U.S. senator once voted against the Equal Rights Amendment, which among other things would have forbidden sexual discrimination. He justified his vote by saying that the bill was being sponsored by a "small band of braless bubbleheads." The senator relied not on reason but on name-calling to justify his view. This is a fallacy; it is called the *ad hominem* appeal. *The ad hominem is the fallacy of attacking the person rather than the person's argument.* Instead of attacking weaknesses and shortcomings of the Equal Rights Amendment, the senator attacked some of the sponsors. The ad hominem is one of the many ways that people reason incorrectly. Knowing the more common of these fallacies should help us in analyzing and formulating ethical arguments.

To illustrate some of these fallacies, let us fictionalize a civil disobedience case not too different from the one that involved Martin Luther King. This case concerns the highly controversial subject of forced bussing. Some believe that in order to racially integrate and balance school enrollments, children should be bussed to schools outside their neighborhoods. Others say that this is illegal as well as immoral.

In our fictitious case, Maria Josephson supports forced bussing. So much does she favor it that, like King, she is organizing and planning to lead a demonstration in the heart of a major U.S. city without first obtaining a license to demonstrate. She hopes that by being arrested she and other demonstrators will dramatize to the country the injustice of racially imbalanced schools and the moral obligation to remedy that imbalance through forced bussing. City officials are trying to dissuade Josephson from her proposed course. Charged with this responsibility is the city chief of police, Robert Dillon. The conversation that follows occurs when Dillon visits Josephson in hopes of preventing the demonstration:

Dillon:	I can't impress on you enough, Ms. Josephson, that what you're about to do is wrong.
Josephson:	I disagree with you. Not only is it right, but it is absolutely obligatory.
Dillon:	You realize what will happen to you, don't you?
Josephson:	Of course I do. That doesn't frighten me. I've got right on my side.
Dillon:	And I've got the law on mine.
Josephson:	I disagree. If you really understood it, you would see that the law was on my side.

Unless Maria and the chief quickly start defining their terms, their conversation will rapidly founder for lack of clarity. Terms like *wrong, right,* and *law* all need definition before Dillon and Josephson can hope to reach any accord. Take just one word, *law.* Clearly, by *law* Dillon means statutes, human-made prescriptions for behavior. Josephson may mean the U.S. Constitution, or she may be appealing to some higher law, perhaps what she considers a principle of human rights, perhaps even some kind of divine prescription. It is hard to say. But they seem to be coming from different directions on this one point alone. In short, ambiguity is present.

1. Ambiguity

The fallacy of ambiguity occurs when we use a word or phrase in such a way that its meaning is not clear. Take, for example, the word *wrong* in Dillon's statement

"What you're about to do is wrong." Probably by *wrong* Dillon means "against the law." On the other hand, Josephson understands wrong in a moral context. Undoubtedly she would agree that she is breaking the law, but she would contend that she is not doing "wrong," that is, something immoral. But even used in a moral sense, a word like *wrong* is still ambiguous.

Consider the possible meanings that *wrong* could have in the statement "Civil disobedience is wrong." It may mean that the speaker disapproves of civil disobedience. It may mean that society disapproves of civil disobedience, or possibly it could mean that God, speaking through some pious book like the Bible or the Koran, disapproves of civil disobedience.

So, in evaluating ethical arguments it is important to try to determine what people mean by their ethical terms. Of course, it is just as important to define other terms that may appear in ethical discourse. Thus, if someone argues that abortion is wrong because it is the willful taking of an innocent human life, it is essential to define *human life* and *innocent* before attempting to evaluate that argument. This may seem like a tedious task, but in the long run it is the only way to avoid the fallacy of ambiguity.

2. Invincible Ignorance

Josephson: Do you believe that racial segregation is immoral?

Dillon: Ms. Josephson, I'm not here to debate the merits of your proposed demonstration. My job is merely to enforce the law.

Josephson: But you can't separate law from morality that easily.

Dillon: Perhaps you can't, but that's not the issue.

Josephson: It appears that nothing I can say could convince you that this demonstration may be needed and is right.

Dillon: Nothing at all.

Dillon will not be moved. He is so entrenched in his position that he will not even entertain another view. He is guilty of invincible ignorance.

Perhaps you have heard someone argue, "I don't care what the President has done, he is still the President and therefore should not be impeached," or "No matter what medical authorities say, no one can convince me that cigarette smoking causes lung cancer." Such arguments rely on invincible ignorance. *Invincible ignorance is the fallacy of insisting on the legitimacy of an idea or principle despite contradictory facts.* The attitude of invincible ignorance is captured in the statement: "Don't confuse me with facts. My mind is already made up."

The phrase "I don't care what you say" is a dead giveaway of invincible ignorance. It indicates that the arguer does not wish to confuse the issue with facts. Chief Dillon seems to be taking such a position. He admits that nothing Maria Josephson could say would alter his law enforcement principle, even if the law might be contributing to an unjust or immoral condition. Note, however, that this does not mean that Dillon's position is unjustifiable. It simply means that the way he has attempted to justify it, by relying on invincible ignorance, is fallacious.

Moral arguments frequently rely on invincible ignorance. For example: "I don't care what you say, lying is always wrong"; "It doesn't matter what anyone thinks, abortion isn't right"; "I admit that there are more good reasons to remain sexually faithful than not. But I always do what I feel like."

3. Questionable Claim

Dillon: You're really convinced that what you're doing is right, aren't you?

Josephson: If I weren't, I wouldn't be here.

Dillon: Well, tell me—how can you be so sure?

Josephson: Because racial injustice is wrong and forced bussing is the only way to correct it.

Dillon: The *only* way?

Josephson: That's right.

Dillon: I doubt that.

Dillon doubts that forced bussing is the *only* way to right racial injustice. He probably thinks that Josephson has overstated her case. Frequently people make such expansive claims that they lose credibility. Consider these two advertising claims, for example: "Dial is the most effective deodorant soap you can buy" and "Zest makes you feel cleaner than soap." Each of these statements involves the fallacy of questionable claim. *A questionable claim is one that cannot stand up under investigation because of the breadth of its assertion.* In other words, an argument posited on questionable claim founders for lack of demonstrative evidence. Words like *most* and *best* and other superlatives frequently signal questionable claim fallacies.

In the moral sphere, persons frequently rely on unquestioned assumptions as the foundations of their ethical codes. Thus: "What I believe is right *is* right"; "Whatever the Bible forbids is necessarily wicked"; "Whatever is good for society is always the right thing to do." Obviously these assumptions are morally controversial and need thoughtful examination before acceptance. Without justification, they are questionable claims.

One particular version of the questionable claim fallacy is common. It is the inconsistency. *The fallacy of inconsistency occurs when we contradict ourselves in word or action without justification for the change of mind.* A political example of the inconsistency fallacy occurred during the 1976 presidential primaries. President Ford claimed that Ronald Reagan was too conservative to be president of the United States. Asked afterwards whether he could conceive of Reagan running on the Republican ticket as a vice-presidential candidate, Ford refused to rule out the possibility. How Reagan could be too conservative to be president and yet be put within a ''heartbeat'' of the presidency needed justification. Ford was being inconsistent.

In the moral sphere, parents frequently tell children it is wrong to lie or cheat, and yet they themselves turn around and do precisely that. More seriously, some people seem to act inconsistently when they contend that they believe in the golden rule (doing unto others as you would have them do unto you) while actually operating in their own best interests.

One ethicist, whom we will meet later, so highly regarded logical consistency that he established his ethical code using it as the main principle. Of course, there is no virtue in being consistent for consistency's sake. In the words of a poet, ''a foolish consistency is the hobgoblin of small minds.'' Naturally, when we have good and compelling reasons to change our minds, we obviously should. But when we do not have good reasons or when the reasons are not expressed or apparent, then inconsistency is present.

4. Begging the Question

Josephson: I think the demonstration is right because the goal is right.

Dillon: I don't mean to be rude, Ms. Josephson, but how do you know your goal is right?

Josephson: Chief Dillon, if you have to ask a question like that, you shouldn't be in charge of law enforcement in this city.

Josephson has begged the question. *Begging the question is the fallacy of answering a question with a variation of the very question asked, or of answering a question in such a way that the original question goes unanswered.* When one begs the question, one assumes that the very statement to be proved is true in order to make it look more plausible. Consider this exchange:

A: How do you know God exists?

B: Because it says so in the Bible.

A: But how do you know the Bible speaks the truth?

B: Because it's the inspired word of God.

Notice the circularity in the argument: God exists because it says so in the Bible, which is the inspired word of God. Josephson is guilty of begging the question when she claims that the demonstration is right because the goal is right. But then she must prove that the goal is right. When Dillon asks her to do this, she again begs his question by telling him he should not be a police chief. Whether he should or not is irrelevant to his question, which deserves an answer.

In the moral sphere, circular reasoning frequently undermines arguments. For example:

A: Lying in this instance is the right thing to do because it will produce the most good for the most people.

B: But how do you know that what produces the most good for the most people is the right thing to do?

A: Because that contention is consistent with the greatest happiness principle.

This sounds good until you realize that the greatest happiness principle is that the moral act is the one that produces the most good for the most people. So, what produces the most good for the most people is not only consistent with the greatest happiness principle, it is the principle! Speaker A is guilty of circularity, or begging the question.

5. Argument from Ignorance

Dillon: The fact is that you cannot prove that the demonstration is right.

Josephson: I'm sure I can't in any way that will satisfy you, because you've already made up your mind. But what if I can't? What does that prove?

Dillon: To me it proves that what you're about to do is wrong.

It is tempting to think that because something cannot be proved that it must not be the case. This is Chief Dillon's erroneous conviction, an argument from ignorance. *The argument from ignorance is the fallacy of insisting that a statement is true until proved false or false until proved true.* Perhaps you have heard someone argue like this: "Until you prove that God exists, he does not"; "Since no convincing evidence was brought against the senator, the senator obviously did not break any law"; "Women have never shown themselves to be as fast sprinters as men, so clearly they are not." All of these are arguments from ignorance.

In ethics, the argument from ignorance is tempting because of the seeming nonempirical character of ethical statements. Thus, someone may argue that the doctrine that one should always act in one's own best long-term interests cannot be proven and, therefore, we should reject it. Or, since the doctrine that we have a moral obligation to honor our promises cannot be proved, it is all right to break promises. An even worse argument: Since no moral statement can be empirically verified, then no moral truth exists.

6. False Appeal to Authority

Dillon: Besides, people don't want forced bussing in this city.

Josephson: What does that have to do with it?

Dillon: Everything. It means that the majority of people disagree with you. They don't approve of what you're doing.

Josephson: But I don't see how the views of the people affect the rightness or wrongness of racial integration.

> Dillon: Because this is a democracy. And in a democracy the will of the majority rules.
>
> Josephson: But that doesn't make the will of the majority right.
>
> Dillon: Doesn't it? When an overwhelming number of people are opposed to something, to me that's proof positive that that thing is wrong.

Chief Dillon's appeal is a case of the false appeal to authority. *Authority is an expert source outside the agent and on whom the agent is resting his or her claim to knowledge.* A simple example: "Cigarette smoking is hazardous to health because the surgeon general says so." In this claim to knowledge, the surgeon general is used as the authority, the expert outside the agent making the claim. Here the claim is legitimate, because the authority is indeed an expert in the area and there is general agreement among the experts. When these two criteria are present—expertise and general agreement among experts—you can feel secure in your appeal to authority. But when either is absent, then you have a false appeal to authority.

Suppose, for example, someone is drinking milk because a celebrity has endorsed it. Probably the celebrity is not a nutritionist or in any way qualified to speak about the virtues of milk drinking. So the celebrity is *not* an expert in the field. Moreover, there is disagreement about the value of milk drinking: Milk is not good for everyone. So the claim that you should drink milk because the celebrity endorses milk drinking would be a *false appeal to authority.*

The false appeal to authority frequently crops up in ethics. The following appeals are probably false because of disagreement among experts: "Civil disobedience is an evil practice because civic authorities condemn it"; "Killing is wrong because it says so in the Bible"; "Wiretapping is moral because the President approves of it." Frequently the false appeal to authority takes a version called *popularity,* or *democracy,* as in the conversation here.

The fallacy of popularity, or democracy, is a false appeal to authority that relies on numbers alone to support its claim. For example: "Fifty million people have seen this film. Shouldn't you?"; "This LP has already sold one million copies. Get yours today!" Because we are so influenced by popular appeals, for some people such an appeal may imply a conclusion, as in: "The latest polls indicate that most Americans believe that abortion on demand is right." Possibly implied conclusion: "So it must be!"

Occasionally the false appeal to authority takes the form of the appeal to traditional wisdom. *Traditional wisdom is the fallacy of relying exclusively on the past to justify the present.* The phrase "This is how it has always been done" signals the traditional wisdom appeal. Thus, a woman who insists on keeping her maiden name after marrying might be told that she cannot because it has never been done. In expressing his opposition to the Equal Rights Amendment, Senator Sam Ervin relied on traditional wisdom when he explained that because the bill had lain around Congress for over 40 years without being passed, that was conclusive proof it should not be passed at all. On moral issues, someone might argue, "Traditionally in this society, individuals have always had the right to determine the size of their families. So, it's immoral for the government to tell them how many children they can have."

Undoubtedly, if we pursued the conversation between Maria Josephson and Chief Dillon, we would spot more fallacies. In addition to the ones we have already mentioned, four other fallacies frequently occur.

7. Provincialism

Provincialism is the fallacy of seeing things exclusively through the eyes of your own group, organization, or affiliation. For example: "This automobile must be good because it's made in America." The fallacy of provincialism is especially evident in moral doctrines that insist the good act is the one that a particular group of people approves of. Evident in such reasoning is also an appeal to popularity or democracy.

8. Hasty Conclusion

As its name implies, *the fallacy of hasty conclusion occurs when we make a judgment based on insufficient evidence.* For example: "The last three teachers in the room were males. So all teachers at this college must be males"; "Since only 42 percent of those eligible actually voted, this proves that the majority of voters are apathetic." In ethics, someone may use atypical cases as a basis for a conclusion. For example: "Since it is right to lie if your life is under a direct and immediate threat, it is unwise to hold to a rule that considers lying immoral."

9. Two-Wrongs-Make-a-Right

The fallacy of two-wrongs-make-a-right is the fallacy of defending what is considered wrongdoing by pointing to an instance of similar behavior. Thus, if a traffic officer stops you for speeding, your defense might be: "Why stop me? A Jaguar just passed me as if I were standing still." Perhaps a Jaguar did, but that does not justify your speeding.

Frequently we rely not on a single instance to justify wrongdoing but on a great number of instances. Thus: "Everybody is speeding! I'm just trying to keep up with traffic!" *A person who relies on numbers of instances to justify wrongdoing is guilty of a common-practice appeal.* Here are some examples of the common-practice appeal in moral arguments: "Cheating on your income tax is all right because just about everyone else does it"; "Premarital sex is moral because it has become pretty much an accepted practice"; "Political corruption is not necessarily immoral, for there is such a wide occurrence of it."

10. Slippery Slope

The slippery slope fallacy is the fallacy of objecting to something because you erroneously assume it will inevitably lead to an undesirable consequence. For example, someone argues: "I'm not going to vote for national health insurance, because if that passes then it won't be long before the railroads and steel mills are nationalized and we have out-and-out socialism in the United States.'' The speaker is not objecting to national health insurance as much as to the socialism he or she assumes it will inevitably lead to. But the socialism is not inevitable. The fact is that the passage of national health insurance does not necessitate socializing railroads, steel mills, or anything else for that matter. Each of these is a separate issue and must be advanced independently of a national health insurance program. True, one socialistic program may leave people psychologically disposed toward another socialistic program, but that is another issue.

The way to detect the slippery slope appeal is simply to ask yourself, ''Must A inevitably lead to Z?'' If the answer is no, if the supposedly inevitable chain can be broken at any one link along the way, then the slippery slope fallacy is present.

Sometimes the slippery slope finds its way into moral issues. For example, someone argues, ''Euthanasia should not be legalized because that will lead to the murder of the mentally retarded, the congenitally diseased, the incorrigibly criminal, and all sorts of so-called socially undesirable elements.'' However, legalized mercy deaths for the incurably ill and suffering do not necessarily lead to such morally dubious consequences at all.

Although avoiding these and other fallacies will help us keep ethical discourse on a rational level, avoidance alone does not justify moral positions. Obviously Maria Josephson believes that demonstrating without a permit is in this instance moral, if not legal. But we really do not know why she believes this. Evidently her belief is connected with her conviction that racially imbalanced schools are immoral. She must justify this claim, after which she must then justify that intentionally breaking a law is moral. This she must do without relying on fallacies.

A similar problem faced Martin Luther King and faces all who must make a moral decision. It is one thing to claim, as King did, that segregationist laws are immoral; it is another to justify that claim. Opinions, beliefs, feelings, hunches, even convictions are relatively cheap commodities in the marketplace of ideas. But sound justification for them is rare. King attempted to provide such justification. Since his situation so closely resembles her own, Maria Josephson would do well to consider it. We would as well, for King's thinking exhibits an appreciation of three principles that characterize the moral reasoning and attitude of all ethicists. For simplicity, let's call these the *three don'ts of moral reasoning*.

The Three Don'ts of Moral Reasoning

1. Don't Rely on Emotionalism

With a kind of sweet reasonableness, King in his ''Letter from Birmingham Jail'' outlines for his fellow clergymen the events leading up to Birmingham, how he and his supporters took steps prior to direct action, and why the criticisms of the clergymen are unfounded. It is true that there are moments in the letter when King relies on emotion, as when he recalls the impossibility of explaining to his six-year-old daughter why she cannot go to the public amusement park that has just been advertised on television, and the agony he feels when he sees "tears welling up in her eyes when she is told that Funtown is closed to colored children, and . . . ominous clouds of inferiority beginning to form in her little mental sky."[4] But these emotional moments are rare and, sad to say, based on fact, not fantasy. More important, King uses such dramatic appeal to demonstrate the righteousness of his cause—that racial discrimination poisons a person's self-image and eventually relegates the person to the status of a thing. His is not emotionalism for emotionalism's sake; it is not merely an attempt to win minds by moving hearts.

Emotionalism is poison to almost any argument, certainly to moral ones. When we cast reason aside, we almost always becloud and distort ethical issues. This suggests a curious dimension about ethical judgments. For many of us, ethical judgments precede their reasons, because most of us inherit our moral positions. We generally adopt the moral postures of our parents, religions, societies, peer groups, and other influential social forces without query or quarrel. In this sense, our ethics are based primarily on authorities. The result may be that in effect we are living others' lives; we are living according to a value system that we have never really examined and justified for ourselves. Because these forces are so much a part of our lives, we can very easily emotionalize moral positions that stand against what we have been influenced to believe. And we can just as easily forget the second "don't" of moral reasoning.

2. Don't Rely on Popular Feeling to Determine Morality

We have already mentioned the fallacy of popularity. It bears underscoring. Implied in King's stand is the belief that we must never allow popular feeling or sentiment to decide what is morally right. In the case of segregationist laws, the overwhelming majority, including many church leaders in states practicing discrimination, openly or tacitly favored such laws. But this alone did not make such laws moral. Popular opinion does not determine morality. Neither does a law that may be based on popular consent. We will say more of this shortly.

3. Don't Do Wrong

As do all moralists, King insists that once persons determine what is right they must do it and avoid wrong. Thus he writes, "I have heard numerous southern religious leaders admonish their worshipers to comply with a desegregation decision because it is the law, but I have longed to hear white ministers declare: 'Follow this decree because integration is morally right and because the Negro is your brother.' "[5] So, no matter what people will think of us or how they will treat us, we must never do what is morally wrong.

4. King, "Letter from Birmingham Jail, April 16, 1963," p. 85.

5. King, "Letter from Birmingham Jail, April 16, 1963," p. 86.

These three features seem to characterize all moral reasoning: (1) avoid emotionalism, (2) avoid basing a moral decision only on popular sentiment, and (3) avoid wrong, no matter what the consequences. Admittedly, these are most general. Spelling them out in specific situations is often difficult. Let us see how King does it.

King's Moral Justification of Civil Disobedience

The core of the Martin Luther King case is civil disobedience, his willful breaking of a city ordinance in order to dramatize its inequity and the inequity of racial segregation laws. The question is: Is King morally justified in breaking the ordinance? He believes that he is. More important, he thinks he can justify that belief as indicated in the excerpt presented at the beginning of this chapter.

At the outset King attempts to clarify, to avoid ambiguity. Thus, in providing his justification, King distinguishes between two types of law: just and unjust. He says, "I would be the first to advocate obeying just laws. One has not only a legal but a moral responsibility to obey just laws. Conversely, one has a moral responsibility to disobey unjust laws."[6] At this point, you may wish to question this assumption. If not, you must still wonder what is the difference between a just and an unjust law. This is the crux of the civil disobedience issue. It is a question that Maria Josephson and all engaging in civil disobedience must ultimately answer. King realizes this.

In distinguishing between a just law and an unjust law, King provides four criteria. By so doing he provides grounds for a rational discussion of the civil disobedience issue, which, like most moral questions, could otherwise founder in emotionalism.

First, King contends that the just law is a human-made code that squares with the law of God. An unjust law does not. Again, you might question this contention; certainly you would if you did not believe in God. King further argues that a law that uplifts human personality is just and that a law that degrades human personality is unjust. Since all segregation laws, according to King, degrade human personality, they are unjust. We could construct King's first argument this way:

If a law does not uplift personality, it is unjust.

A segregation law does not uplift personality.

Therefore, a segregation law is unjust.

King further describes a just law as one that a majority compels a minority to obey and also binds itself to obey. Segregation laws are the opposite of this. They bind a minority but not the majority that has formulated them. So, they are unjust. Thus, we can represent King's second argument:

6. King, "Letter from Birmingham Jail, April 16, 1963," p. 86.

If a majority formulates a law to bind a minority but not itself, that law is unjust.

Segregation laws are laws that a majority formulates to bind a minority but not itself.

Therefore, segregation laws are unjust.

In addition, King characterizes an unjust law as one that is inflicted on a minority that, as a result of being denied the right to vote, had no voice in the law's devising or enactment. Again, since segregation laws are of this kind, they are unjust. Thus, King's third argument is:

If a law is inflicted on a minority that, as a result of being denied the right to vote, had no voice in formulating it, then that law is unjust.

Segregation laws are inflicted on a minority that, as a result of being denied the right to vote, had no voice in formulating them.

Therefore, segregation laws are unjust.

Finally, King argues that a just law can be unjust in its application. This is crucial in this case because it is on this basis that he feels justified in willfully breaking the Birmingham ordinance. Remember: King has been arrested on a charge of parading without a permit. There is nothing intrinsically wrong with such an ordinance. But when the ordinance is used to deny citizens the First Amendment privilege of peaceful assembly and protest, and thereby to maintain segregation, then it is unjust. King's argument might be constructed to read:

If a law, which is not intrinsically unjust, is used to deny citizens constitutional rights, then it is an unjust law.

Birmingham's ordinance against parading without a permit is a law that, on its face, is not unjust, but in this case is being used to deny citizens constitutional rights.

Therefore, Birmingham's ordinance against parading without a permit in this case is an unjust law.

Of course, what is implied in King's stand is the third characteristic of all moral reasoning—that we should never do what is wrong. Obviously King believes that what is unjust is wrong. Therefore, he must not obey the law. To do so would be to act immorally. Conversely, to disobey it would be to act morally. Thus, his demonstration.

At this point we may wonder about some of the assumptions King makes. For example, in his first argument King assumes that if a law uplifts personality, then it is just. But why is a law that uplifts personality necessarily just? We could also wonder precisely what *uplifting personality* means. We could ask similar questions about the assumptions King makes in the next three arguments. In doing so we are beginning to wonder how basic ethical judgments and principles are to be justified. After all, the first statement in each of King's arguments is an assumption. On what basis are these assumptions themselves to be justified? If they are not justified, then they are questionable claims.

In his essay it is clear that King is using a law of God as the basis for his assumptions. But not all ethical judgments are so defended. Some ethicists would agree with King's decision, but for different reasons. They might argue that segregation laws are immoral because they are not in the best long-term interests of all people. Others might claim that what King did was immoral because his action was not in his own best long-term interests. Still others might argue that his action was moral because it was in his own best long-term interests. Furthermore, metaethicists would probably wonder precisely what the words *just* and *unjust* mean to begin with. When we raise such questions, we inevitably engage in full-scale philosophical debate about moral issues.

Our coverage so far has emphasized the usefulness of proper reasoning in ethics. It is tempting to infer from our discussion of moral reasoning that right conduct in personal and social affairs always requires explicit thought and analysis, the careful weighing of arguments. Also, one might be tempted to infer that humans in their practical moral decisions must always be able to give a satisfactory account of their reasons and that these reasons be "respectable." Actually, such analysis is only part of moral reasoning, a part that needs a counterweight in order to avoid our overdependence on logic in resolving ethical issues. To provide this balance we will examine briefly the role that intuition may play in moral evaluation.

Intuition

Subjecting moral positions to rational scrutiny surely is useful. Among other things, such analysis helps untangle confusions, minimize prejudice, and avoid superstitions. Probably the more deliberate and methodical our analysis is before a decision and consequent action, the less likely we are to be misled by others' opinions and confused thought. In addition, explicitness in moral reasoning can lead to explicit knowledge for our reasons, which many would say is in itself an intellectual virtue. Indeed, explicit thought is crucial when we must explain, defend, and advocate positions, all inevitable procedures with social issues. For these reasons the theories and issues raised in this text are subjected to critical analysis.

At the same time it's important to recognize that the human consciousness functions in ways other than discursive reasoning to apprehend the world and adjust to it. One of these ways is intuition.

Intuition is generally defined as the function of consciousness that apprehends directly and is not the result of conscious reasoning or of immediate sense perceptions. It is a nonsensuous apprehension, a direct vision of reason, although it does not rely on discursive reasoning. When we reason discursively, we draw conclusions in an orderly, step-by-step way, through logical inferences drawn from premises. When we reason intuitively, we recognize some truth immediately; we see without further evidence that something is true.

Intuition is frequently viewed as analogous to sensation, whereby we apprehend objects through the senses. For example, in seeing the color of the chalk, my eye is directly aware of the chalk. In a like way, the mind or intellect or consciousness can be directly confronted by some object, not a sensuous one but a nonsensuous one. When I know through intuition, I am aware, say, of truth or falsity, rightness or wrongness, not of colors, sounds, smells, tastes, or textures.

To understand precisely how some ethicists view the role of intuition in moral evaluation and judgment, we must be aware of the various positions that philosophers take on intuition generally. For example, some philosophers claim that intuition is present in all knowledge. Thus, intuition may refer to any individual's awareness of the immediate data of consciousness, to the knowledge of oneself that appears present in all knowledge of other objects, to a grasp of the connection between statements in arguments, to an understanding of the axioms of mathematics, or to the recognition of moral and aesthetic standards. Other philosophers hold that intuition is instead the result of subconscious discursive reasoning. Intuition is viewed then as the accumulated experience and thinking, together with persistent labor, which result in an insight into a situation. Still other philosophers believe that intuition is a higher form of knowledge, different in kind from knowledge disclosed by the senses or intellect. Intuition then is a knowledge that may result in a unique vision of reality. Whatever their position on intuition, philosophers agree that there does appear to be an element of intuition in knowledge, moral knowledge included.

Ethicists commonly observe that moral choice involves valuing. Valuing in turn involves an awareness of the pleasant or unpleasant, good or bad, better or worse nature of an object or situation. Such valuing appears to bear the element of intuition. It also may be crucial to our adjustment to life situations. Some philosophers have suggested the possibility that a "feeling" or "valuing" sense is a most important organ of knowledge, that a "feeling" response to a situation may augment knowledge disclosed through the senses and intellect. They connect intuition with basic life interest, as opposed to judgments that are complex. One such basic interest might be romantic love. People "fall in" love on the basis of some unanalyzable, unreconstructible appeal to their feelings. And on this basis they claim to know that they are in love and adopt appropriate courses of action and life style regarding the object of their affection. Valuing in general is much the same; it involves intuition and cannot always be analyzed.

Recognizing this, a number of ethicists espouse *ethical intuitionism*, which views intuition as a reliable source of moral knowledge. However, just as there are various positions on intuition, so there are on ethical intuitionism. Some ethicists believe that a person knows which act is right by an intuition of the act. Thus, when an individual act, such as one that involves hurting another person, is held before the mind, its rightness or wrongness, suitability or unsuitability to a situation, can be grasped by intuition. Other ethicists claim that we intuit the rightness or wrongness not of individual acts but rather of basic moral principles. Such moral principles can take the form of all acts of a specific kind being right or all acts of a specific kind being wrong. We presumably recognize the truth of such moral principles by reflecting on their full meaning; we do not need further evidence to know they are true. When confronted with a particular act, therefore, we can deduce its rightness or wrongness by subsuming the act under the principle. For example, given that I intuit the truth of the moral principle that keeping a promise is right, when faced with an act that involves keeping a promise, I recognize an obligation to keep my promise. Still other ethical intuitionists claim that no such deductions are possible. While agreeing that we intuit moral principles, they claim that we do not infer the correct course of action from the rightness or wrongness of the act as much as from an "educated guess" about the act's morality. In this view, we know by intuition and with certainty the truth of the principle; but we do not know with certainty that a particular course of action is the right one.

Considerably more study must be done on the nature and function of intuition. We simply do not clearly understand what role intuition plays in human consciousness and knowing. It seems indisputable, however, that intuition does play some role. And it is important at least to recognize this element of intuition while studying ethics, not only to understand the philosophical bases for some ethical theories but also to avoid creating a kind of tyranny of the intellect.

Summary and Conclusions

This chapter has dealt with the nature of ethics, moral reasoning, and the role of intuition in moral judgment. Ethics divides into normative and nonnormative fields. Normative ethics includes theory and application; nonnormative includes scientific or descriptive ethics and metaethics. This text will focus on normative ethics, which in part involves the reasoned search for principles of human conduct.

While ethicists rarely form a consensus of moral opinion on any issue, we do find evident patterns of moral reasoning which the professional and nonprofessional ethicists use in trying to argue their positions. The heart of these patterns, and the feature of all defensible moral positions, consists of a moral judgment supported by a general moral principle. This feature allows for a number of strategies in arguing a moral position. Of course, people are not always logical in the way they argue. Frequently they try to persuade by using emotional and psychological devices, called fallacies. A knowledge of these fallacies can help one detect flaws in moral reasoning.

Finally, we tried to balance our discussion of moral reasoning by examining the role of intuition in acquiring moral knowledge. In the last analysis we must strive to effect a balance of the rational and the nonrational, the objective and the subjective.

Selections for Further Reading

Castaneda, H. N. *The Structure of Morality*. Springfield, Ill.: Thomas, 1973.

Grice, G. R. *The Grounds of Moral Judgment*. Cambridge: Cambridge University Press, 1962.

Hampshire, Stuart, et al. *Private and Public Morality*. New York: Cambridge University Press, 1978.

Richards, D. A. *A Theory of Reasons for Actions*. Oxford: Clarendon Press, 1971.

Taylor, Richard. *Good and Evil: A New Direction*. New York: Macmillan, 1970.

Toulmin, Stephen. *An Examination of the Place of Reason in Ethics*. New York: Cambridge University Press, 1950.

2
THEORIES

Frank Grogan wished he had never heard of Icarus Aircraft, let alone JLP-23. Why had he been assigned that particular project? After all, Icarus manufactured a whole fleet of executive aircraft that could keep a young engineer busy for years to come. Why JLP-23?

The irony was that Grogan had first seen the project as a rare opportunity to practice his specialty: aircraft fuselage and airfoil design. But ever since he'd become aware of some potentially dangerous wing-design specifications, the project had become a nightmare.

The whole thing was getting really sticky. Sometimes he wished he hadn't said anything, that he'd kept his mouth shut. But oh no, not him! Not getting any satisfaction below, he had to go right to the top—to President Wendell Kravits himself. Kravits's reaction baffled Grogan. Kravits seemed to think that Grogan knew no more about wing design than a kid assembling a model plane.

"Precipitate." That's what Kravits had termed Grogan's alarm. "Not that I don't commend your vigilance, Frank," he had added, "but the danger you're talking about could materialize only under the most extreme and unrealistic conditions—conditions, in fact, more proper to military flying than civilian."

Maybe Kravits was right, Grogan thought. Kravits certainly had a lot more experience than he himself had. Still, that didn't make Kravits an authority on wing specifications. No, Grogan decided, Kravits was wrong. Given just the right conditions, the wing sections of the JLP-23 could separate from the fuselage.

So now Grogan had to decide whether to drop the whole matter or take it beyond Kravits, maybe to the stockholders or even to the press. More than anything else, he wanted to do the *right* thing. But what was that?

In Chapter 1 we explored the feature of defensible moral views: If a particular moral judgment is defensible, then it must be supportable by a defensible general moral principle. After deliberating, Grogan may decide to drop the whole issue or go to the board of directors or "blow the whistle" on Icarus by revealing the problem to the media. Whatever his judgment and subsequent action, a general moral principle should support them. In other words, if Grogan decides to press the issue no further, he should be able to provide some supporting principle which, together with additional facts, entail his moral judgment. If he cannot produce such a principle or sees no need to, then he simply does not understand how moral concepts are used. Or he is using moral words such as *right* and *wrong*, *good* and *bad*, in a way far different from their common meanings in ethics. Moral principles, therefore, play a fundamental role in Grogan's forming a defensible moral judgment, indeed in forming any defensible moral judgment.

This chapter deals with such principles. Specifically, we will present normative theories that have been most influential in the history of ethical thought. Each theory sets forth principles that are useful in making moral judgments. In discussing the theories, we will use the classification of normative theories previously drawn:

Consequential
    Egoism
    Act and Rule Utilitarianism
Nonconsequential
    Divine Command
    Categorical Imperative
    Prima Facie Duties
    Maximin Principle

Consequential Theories

Traditionally, many theorists contend that the moral rightness of an action can be determined by looking at its consequences. If the consequences are good, the act is right; if bad, the act is wrong. Ethicists who argue this way are called consequentialists (teleologists). *Consequential theories, then, refer to theories that measure the morality of actions on the basis of their nonmoral consequences.* Consequentialists determine what action is right by considering the ratio of good to evil that the action produces. The right act is the one that produces, will probably produce, or is intended to produce at least as great a ratio of good to evil as any other course. The wrong act is the one that does not.

When consequentialists evaluate the nonmoral consequences of an action, they consider what lies outside the realm of morality. For example, if Grogan is a consequentialist, he will evaluate the nonmoral consequences of his choices. Thus, if he speaks out at a stockholders' meeting or talks to the press, he might jeopardize the whole JLP-23 project. Certainly he would hurt subsequent sales of the aircraft and undoubtedly displease his superiors. He might even lose his job and be blackballed in the industry. However, he might be recognized as a conscientious worker. Consumer groups might applaud Grogan's sense of social responsibility. This recognition could improve the public image of Icarus and of the aircraft industry generally. If Grogan chooses not to speak out publicly, the JLP-23 could be completed as proposed. Probably the aircraft would sell very well and Icarus's stockholders would profit handsomely. Of course, if Grogan's fears are accurate, the JLP-23 would pose a threat of injury or death because of its structural weakness. If an accident occurs, the company might be sued. Grogan himself might be held legally accountable.

We need not go on with the consequences. The point is that in determining the morality of an action, consequentialists evaluate its nonmoral consequences and eventually choose the course that would seem to produce the most good.

A fundamental question arises at this point. In deciding what to do, should Grogan consider the consequences only for himself? Or should he consider the consequences for everyone who could be affected? The distinction between consequences for self and for others points up two distinct concepts of consequential ethics: egoism and utilitarianism.

Egoism

Egoism contends that an act is moral when it promotes the individual's best long-term interests. In determining the morality of an action, egoists use their best long-term advantage to measure the action's rightness. If an action produces, will probably produce, or is intended to produce a greater ratio of good to evil for the individual in the long run than any other alternative, then that action is the right one to perform. Indeed, the individual *must* take that course.

Ethicists often distinguish between two kinds of egoism: personal and impersonal. Personal egoists claim that they themselves should pursue their own best long-term interests, but they do not claim that others should necessarily do the same. Impersonal egoists, in contrast, believe that everyone should follow their own best long-term interests.

Several misconceptions haunt egoism. One is that egoists do what they want, that they are believers of "eat, drink, and be merry." Not so. Undergoing unpleasant, even painful experiences is compatible with egoism, providing such temporary sacrifice is consistent with advancing long-term happiness. Another misconception is that egoists necessarily eschew virtues like honesty, generosity, and self-sacrifice. Again, this isn't always so. Whatever is compatible with one's long-term best interests—including self-giving acts—is compatible with egoism. A final misconception is that all egoists are exponents of hedonism, the view that the only good in life worth seeking is pleasure. While it is true that some egoists are hedonistic—as was the ancient Greek philosopher Epicurus (341–270 B.C.)—other egoists identify the good with knowledge, power, or rational self-interest, or with what some modern psychologists call self-actualization. In fact, ethical egoists may hold any theory of what is good and what is bad.

Objections to Egoism

1. *Personal egoism is inconsistent.* The first serious objection to egoism is directed against personal egoism, the position that contends that each individual should act in terms of self-interest but does not say how others should act. Suppose that Grogan is a personal egoist, and that he decides to drop the issue of possible JLP-23 problems because to act otherwise would cause him unnecessary pain. If asked whether others faced with a comparable decision ought to use a pleasure-pain calculus for deciding what to do, Grogan would not be able to say. But why not? If acting in accordance with long-term self-interest is proper for one person, why should it not be proper for all persons? If personal happiness is an ethical standard for one person, it seems that it should be for everyone. By refusing to allow everyone else the same personal pursuit of happiness that they afford themselves, personal egoists seem logically inconsistent. Consequently, personal egoism is not a very popular egoistic position.

More egoists today are impersonal egoists—maintaining that everyone should be egoistic. This was the egoism espoused by thinkers such as Epicurus, Thomas Hobbes (1588–1679), and Friedrich Nietzsche (1844–1900). More recently impersonal egoism has been adopted by philosophers such as Ayn Rand, John Hospers, and Jesse Kalin. However, while impersonal egoism may be more consistent than the personal version, it too has problems.

2. *Whatever its variety, the egoistic standard cannot be verified.* Frequently objectors to egoism claim that ethical egoism cannot be proved, that there is no way of verifying that long-term self-interests should determine human behavior. How can impersonal egoists be sure that individuals ought to consider only their own interests? Egoists reply that individuals will be happier that way. Such an answer is a questionable claim, premised on an unknown fact. Although acting in what he believed was his best long-term interests may have produced happiness for Grogan in the past, he does not really know that it will continue that way. The woman with an ulcer who consumes a spicy pizza, a beer, and a hot fudge sundae may not have felt a twinge of pain the last time she so indulged. But this time, ouch! It seems, therefore, that the egoist can say only that acting out of self-interest will *probably* produce more happiness than not. But even this statement is debatable.

The more complex society becomes, the more interdependent individuals become and the less, it seems, we can act with only our own best interests in mind—or the less we know about what constitutes our best long-term interests. Perhaps, as impersonal egoists maintain, if all acted in their own best interests then collectively there would be more happiness. But in maintaining this, egoists are no longer egoists; they are no longer acting out of self-interest but out of a universal happiness impulse, which moves them closer to utilitarianism, resulting in another evident inconsistency.

Objections to egoism, however, need not be restricted to personal or impersonal egoism. Egoism is open to attack on more general grounds.

3. *Egoism does not provide means for settling conflicts of interest.* Suppose that it is in Grogan's best long-term interests to "blow the whistle" on Icarus, and that it is in Kravits's best long-term interests to silence Grogan. Ethical egoists would have each man do whatever was necessary to promote his own best long-term self-interests. But what Grogan should do is incompatible with what Kravits supposedly should do. Apparently there are two opposing ethical obligations here. Are both right? Egoists insist that egoism is not intended to arbitrate ethical conflicts such as this. Nevertheless, critics likewise insist that a moral code, by definition, must resolve such conflicts. If it cannot, how useful is it?

4. *Egoism introduces inconsistency into moral counsel.* Suppose that Grogan goes to a board member for advice. The board member happens to be an impersonal egoist. Assuming that it is in Grogan's best interests to speak out publicly, the board member advises him to do everything possible to do just that. A few minutes later, Kravits calls the same board member for advice. Again, assuming that it is in Kravits's best interests to silence Grogan, the board member advises Kravits to do everything he can to accomplish that. The board member's counsel hardly seems to indicate a single, consistent attitude. True, the impersonal egoist would maintain that the board member is simply saying that both Grogan and Kravits should try to effect their own best interests and that the board member hopes both will win. But the objection seemingly remains: The board member is recommending as right two conflicting courses of action.

5. *Egoism undermines the moral point of view.* Many ethicists claim that the moral point of view is a necessary part of moral decision making. The moral point of view, according to ethicists, is the attitude of one who sees or tries to see all sides of an issue without being committed to the interests of a particular individual or group. Thus, the moral point of view demands disinterest and impartiality. If we accept the moral point of view, then we must look for it in any proposed ethical standard, including ethical egoism.

But ethical egoists cannot take the moral point of view, for they are always influenced by their own best interests, regardless of the issue, principles, or circumstances involved. Consider in the preceding example the implications of the board member's own egoism. Since she is an egoist, she must advise Grogan and Kravits in *her own* best long-term interests, not theirs. In effect, the board member, as an egoist, must be committed to the narrowest form of moral provincialism.

6. *Egoism ignores blatant wrongs.* This may be the most common objection to egoism, indeed to any consequential ethic. By reducing everything to the standard of the best long-term self-interest, egoism on principle takes no stand against seemingly outrageous acts: murder, unfair discrimination, deliberately false advertising, and so on. All such actions are morally neutral to the egoist until the test of self-interest is applied.

Utilitarianism

While egoism maintains that the promotion of one's own best long-term interests should be the standard of morality, utilitarianism insists that the promotion of the best long-term interests of everyone concerned should be the moral standard. Stated briefly, *the utilitarian doctrine asserts that we should always act so as to produce the greatest possible ratio of good to evil for everyone concerned.* Again, as with all consequential positions, *good* and *evil* are taken to mean nonmoral good and evil.

As developed by John Stuart Mill (1806–1873), utilitarianism maintained that what is intrinsically good is pleasure or happiness. More recent utilitarians, however, view things other than happiness as having intrinsic worth (for example, knowledge, power, beauty, and moral qualities). Their view is termed *pluralistic*, or *ideal*, *utilitarianism* and has attracted thinkers such as G. E. Moore[1] and Hastings Rashdall.[2] But since we will be primarily considering Mill's utilitarianism, we will be using *intrinsic good* to mean happiness. What we will say about Mill's position, however, applies equally to pluralistic utilitarianism, if for *happiness* or *pleasure* the phrase *intrinsic good* is substituted.

Before evaluating the utilitarian doctrine, let's clear up some points about utilitarianism that frequently lead to its misapplication. First, in speaking of right and wrong acts, utilitarians are speaking about those over which we exercise control, those that are voluntary. This does not mean, however, that we must have premeditated the action. For example, suppose that as you are walking down a street you observe a child standing in a driveway as a car is backing up. The child will surely be struck. Without deliberation you rush to the scene and snatch the child away from the path of the car. Although you did not premeditate this action, you could have acted otherwise; you could have chosen not to save the child. This is a voluntary action.

Second, in referring to the "greatest possible ratio of good to evil," utilitarians do not indicate a preference for immediate or remote good. The emphasis is on *greatest*. If the long-term good will be greater than the short-term, we should prefer it, and vice versa. Frequently, however, the long-term good is less certain than the immediate good. In such cases we may prefer the immediate good.

Third, in determining the "greatest possible ratio of good to evil for everyone," we must consider unhappiness or pain as well as happiness. For example, if it were possible to calculate pleasure and pain, then we should subtract from the total happiness our action would produce the total unhappiness it would produce. The result, in theory, will be an accurate measure of the action's worth. So, if an action produces eight units of happiness and four units of unhappiness, its net worth is four units. If a second action produces ten units of happiness and seven units of unhappiness, its net worth is three units. In such a case we should choose the first action over the second. In the event that both acts lead not to happiness but to unhappiness, we should do the one that leads to fewer units of unhappiness.

Fourth, when choosing between two actions, one that you prefer and one that you do not prefer, choose the one that produces the greatest net happiness. Obviously you should not disregard your own preferences, but you should not give them added weight either. Count yourself as just one vote among the many.

Utilitarianism can take one of two forms—act or rule.

1.   G. E. Moore, Principia Ethica *(London: Cambridge University Press, 1903).*

2.   *Hastings Rashdall,* A Theory of Good and Evil: A Treatise on Moral Philosophy, 2 vols. *(New York: Kraus Reprint, reprint of 1924 edition).*

Act Utilitarianism

Act utilitarianism maintains that the right act is the one that produces the greatest ratio of good to evil for all concerned. In performing an action we must ask ourselves what the consequences of this particular act in this particular situation will be for all concerned. If the consequences produce more general good than those of any other alternative, then that action is the right one and the one we should perform.

If Frank Grogan is an act utilitarian, he will consider the consequences of his alternatives not only for himself but for the firm, the aircraft industry, business generally, customers, fellow employees, and society at large. He will let an evaluation of all the consequences to all the parties suggest the course of his action. Under other circumstances, he might act differently, take another course. In short, each situation is considered unique; each new set of circumstances calls for a fresh evaluation.

Act utilitarianism overcomes a number of the objections raised against egoism. First, it provides an objective way to resolve conflicts of self-interest. By proposing a standard outside self-interests, act utilitarianism greatly minimizes and may actually eliminate conflicts of self-interest such as that between Grogan and Kravits. Rather than considering only their own interests, which may conflict, parties appeal to a uniform standard: the general good. Second, act utilitarianism has the logical consistency that personal egoism lacks. And third, act utilitarians are able to take the moral point of view. But act utilitarianism, too, has weaknesses.

Objections to Act Utilitarianism

1. *The consequences of actions are uncertain.* We can never be sure of the consequences of our actions. Evaluation of the morality of those actions on any consequential basis is extremely problematic. Thus, any utilitarian stand seems essentially a questionable claim springing from an unknown fact. Act consequentialists might reply that morality is not so much in what the action produces as in what the agent intends that it produce. For example, if Grogan speaks publicly, it is not so important that he produce the most happiness for all concerned as it is important that he intend his action to do so. It is a safe bet, however, that not one of the Watergate conspirators *intended* his action to lead to what it did. But does this make their actions right? Ironically, in emphasizing intention here, the act utilitarian is not taking a consequential position at all but rather a nonconsequential one.

2. *Some actions are wrong, no matter how much good they produce.* What about actions that in themselves seem questionable? Suppose, for example, that Grogan's calculations lead him to believe that the greatest good will be served if he takes no further action, despite his conviction that the faulty wing design could, in just the right conditions, kill someone. Or suppose that a used-car dealer sets back the odometer on a car in order to get a quick sale. The dealer is certain that the car is in good shape, and is convinced that the odometer reading played no part in setting the sticker price, which in fact is highly competitive. In short, whoever buys the car will undoubtedly get a good deal; indeed, both seller and buyer will get a good deal. Some critics of act utilitarianism would object that such actions, despite their consequences, are in themselves morally objectionable. These critics point out that an act may be wrong because it involves perpetrating an injustice, telling a lie, breaking a promise, or violating a rule. As a result, some ethicists, such as A. C. Ewing, conclude that "act utilitarian principles, logically carried out, would result in far more cheating, lying and unfair action than any good man would tolerate."[3]

3. *The principle of utility may conflict with that of justice.* Critics of utilitarianism have pointed out that mere increase in total happiness is not of itself good. On the contrary, the distribution of happiness is a further and most important question. Surely it is not unreasonable to argue for a state of affairs in which the happy people are those who most deserve to be—even though they may be few in number. This objection relates to the preceding one; in both cases utilitarianism associates justice with efficiency rather than fair play. Utilitarians determine what is just by a calculation of total benefit, not by appeal to merit and desert. If an action is efficient—in the sense that it is calculated to produce more total good than any other alternative—then in the traditional utilitarian view, the action is thereby just. Critics dispute this concept by arguing that the total amount of good is not the most important measure of justice.

Rule Utilitarianism

Rule utilitarianism asserts that we should not consider the consequences of a particular action but rather the consequences of the rule under which the action falls. Reconsider the case of the used-car dealer. Even if the dealer's action produces more happiness than any other alternative, some utilitarians might still consider it wrong. In their evaluation, they would appeal not to the action itself but to the rule under which the action falls. Thus, the rule utilitarian could argue that the rule requiring dealers to represent a car's mileage accurately is a good rule because it generally produces a greater ratio of good to evil than misrepresentation of the mileage. Reasoning thus, they would call the dealer's action immoral, even though in this particular case the greatest good was served.

Rule utilitarians, then, ask us to determine the worth of the rule under which any action falls. If obeying the rule generally produces more total good than violating it, we should obey it, regardless of the consequences in any particular situation. In another example, suppose that the greatest common good would be served by imprisoning someone for a crime the person did not commit. While act utilitarians in theory could condone such an action, rule utilitarians probably could not. Such an action would violate a rule which, if followed, generally produces more good than if violated. The rule: Never imprison an innocent person.

English philosopher George Berkeley (1685–1783) offered one strong argument for rule utilitarianism. Berkeley reasoned that if each time a person must make a moral decision, that person must evaluate the consequences of a pro-

3.　A. C. Ewing, Ethics *(New York: Free Press, 1965), p. 41.*

posed action, then enormous difficulties would arise due to ignorance, prejudice, carelessness, lack of time, or indifference. The result would hardly be in the best interests of the general good. Rules, however, that everyone is aware of and attempts to implement simplify such problems, thereby advancing the common good. Just as we have traffic laws to promote the best interests of all drivers, so rules in the moral realm promote the general good. Although rule utilitarianism seems to resolve some of the problems of act utilitarianism, and today it is vigorously defended by philosophers such as Richard Brandt,[4] it is not an airtight ethical theory.

Objections to Rule Utilitarianism

1. *It is extremely difficult to formulate a satisfactory rule.* One problem that arises in dealing with any rule theory is the formulation of the rule itself. For example, is the rule "Never intentionally deceive anyone" a desirable one? One way to find out is to devise a situation testing its effectiveness.

For example, suppose that someone was holding a pistol to your head and threatened to pull the trigger unless you told the next person who entered the room that your name was something other than what it actually is. Should you in this circumstance deliberately deceive that person who enters the room? It would certainly be a healthy, if not moral thing to do. So, maybe such a rule needs to be qualified to read: "Never intentionally deceive someone *unless your life depends on it.*" But still, problems persist.

Suppose that you have been captured by an enemy who is trying to exact from you vital troop movement information. If you divulge the information, 100 soldiers will most probably perish. If you do not, then you will undoubtedly die. Should you reveal the information? Here your own life may seem less worthy of preservation than the lives of 100 soldiers. So, maybe the rule should be amended again to read: "Never intentionally deceive anyone unless your own life *or someone else's depends on it.*"

The point is that it is difficult to establish rules of moral behavior. True, we can qualify them, but frequently such qualifications so weaken and compromise the rule that the result is more like act utilitarianism than rule.

2. *There is no way to decide between contradictory rules that appear to produce equally desirable results.* For example, one can legitimately argue that the rule "Never intentionally deceive someone unless the truth will deeply pain that person" will produce as great a ratio of good to evil as "Never intentionally deceive anyone even if telling the truth will deeply pain someone else." Which of the two contradictory rules should rule utilitarians choose?

A consummate rule utilitarian supposedly could not prefer one rule to the other. Since both produce equally beneficial results, one rule is not better than the other, even though one appears unjust. If rule utilitarians reply that we must prefer the rule that does not allow the injustice, then they would be inconsistent—they would be introducing nonconsequential factors into their evaluation.

4. *Richard B. Brandt, "In Search of a Credible Form of Rule Utilitarianism," in* Morality and the Language of Conduct, *ed. G. Nakhnikian and H. Castaneda (Detroit: Wayne State University Press, 1961).*

3. *Rule utilitarianism ignores what appear to be blatant wrongs.* We have raised this objection before, in discussing act utilitarianism and egoism. To see how it applies to rule utilitarianism, let us look at another case illustration. Suppose that doctors and scientists could guarantee that they could relieve the suffering of millions of people if they were given a number of experimental patients on whom they would perform agonizingly painful and ultimately fatal operations. Would they be justified in performing these experiments on the "less desirable" and "less productive" members of society (that is, the convicted murderers, the permanently mentally ill, the terminally ill) without their consent? Such experiments would seemingly produce the greatest good for the greatest number. Yet critics of rule utilitarianism argue for the intrinsic worth of the individual human and, consequently, consider any rule that would condone such behavior immoral.

Nonconsequential Theories

Nonconsequentialism (deontology) is the ethical doctrine that denies that the consequences of an action or a rule are the only criteria for determining the morality of an action. Nonconsequentialists insist that some actions are right or wrong, not because they produce a certain ratio of good to evil but because of the nature of the actions themselves. Thus, some nonconsequentialists might argue that lying, breaking a promise, or killing is wrong in itself, not just because it may produce undesirable consequences. A nonconsequentialist determines the morality of an act on grounds that may be arbitrarily decided, divinely revealed, or deducible from metaphysics. So, whereas consequential normative positions argue that we should consider only consequences in evaluating an action, nonconsequential theories maintain that we should consider other factors as well. In some cases nonconsequentialists even contend that we should not consider consequences at all. Like utilitarianism, nonconsequentialism generally takes two forms—act and rule.

Act Nonconsequentialism

Act nonconsequential theories usually maintain that there are no rules or guidelines to govern ethical behavior, that we must evaluate each act as it comes along and determine its rightness or wrongness. Thus, in one context lying may be bad, but in another it may be good; it all depends on the situation. Act nonconsequentialists insist that blanket statements about acts are impossible.

In its extreme form, act nonconsequentialism contends that we can never formulate any rules or guidelines at all, that each situation is fundamentally different from any other; therefore, each situation must be evaluated as a unique ethical dilemma. Of course, extreme act nonconsequentialism would not introduce an action's consequences in determining its morality.

In ancient times Aristotle seems to have espoused this view, and in the eighteenth century Joseph Butler did. Butler advocated that persons about to embark on an ethical course should ask themselves whether the proposed action will be right or wrong. He concluded that the decisions made would be the right ones, providing the persons are "fair minded."[5]

A more moderate act nonconsequential position maintains that general principles or rules of thumb can develop from particular situations and then be used as a basis for making subsequent decisions. This presumes, of course, that recurring situations are sufficiently similar to a prior one to allow application of a rule. For example, suppose that you have determined that the last time you lied to a trusted friend you did the wrong thing. The next time a sufficiently similar situation arises, you have grounds to suspect that it is wrong to lie again. In no case, however, do even moderate act nonconsequentialists claim that a rule would or should override a particular judgment regarding what a person ought to do. In other words, not even a moderate act nonconsequentialist would say *never* lie. As you might expect, there are a number of weaknesses in the act nonconsequential position.

Objections to Act Nonconsequentialism

1. *Act nonconsequentialism provides no ethical direction.* What should Frank Grogan do? Unfortunately, act nonconsequentialism does not seem able to help him. After all, Grogan must consider his situation unique and resolve it accordingly. Extreme act nonconsequentialism cannot even offer general principles such as "Never endanger someone's life" or "Always be loyal to your employer." Each person must rely on intuition, feelings, and inclinations in order to determine the right thing to do. In short, extreme act nonconsequentialism seems to leave each of us in a state of ethical limbo. Act nonconsequentialism extremists argue that the situation should guide the ethical choice. But this appears to be begging the question, for the situation can only provide data and facts that crystallize the choices. The problem remains: Which option does one choose?

2. *Act nonconsequentialism allows feelings to be the guide to moral decisions.* Even moderate act nonconsequentialism does not seem to offer Grogan more help. Although his case is not unique, it is still uncommon enough to make rule-of-thumb formulation difficult. Even if Grogan has some general rules to apply, according to act nonconsequentialists he arrived at them on the basis of intuition or decisions made in the past. But is the way one feels about a certain situation sufficient reason for claiming that what one does is moral? Implied in this objection, of course, is criticism of intuition as a sufficient and legitimate source of moral knowledge.

3. *Act nonconsequentialism precludes the formulation of necessary general ethical rules.* Act nonconsequentialists claim that no two situations are the same and that it is therefore impossible to generalize about moral behavior. But this seems to be a straw man, a weak argument. While it is true that no two situations are ever identical, can any two situations be sufficiently similar to allow moral generalization?

5. *Joseph Butler,* Five Sermons *(New York: Liberal Arts Press, 1949), p. 45.*

For example, suppose Grogan asks you what he should do, and you tell him, "Blow the whistle." Five minutes later he asks you the same question, and this time you say, "Clam up." Assuming that nothing more than the ticking of a clock has occurred in the interim, should you not respond as you did the first time, since the situations are sufficiently similar to warrant the same response? Grogan asks you why you changed your mind and you, as an act nonconsequentialist, reply that the decision you just made bears no connection to the one you made five minutes earlier. Grogan then rightly considers your logic, as well as your ethics, strange, and certainly inconsistent.

When act nonconsequentialists choose to ignore similarities between past and present, they relinquish a most potent tool in inductive reasoning, the analogy. Thus, when someone reasons, "I won't buy another car from Honest Sam the used-car man because the last one I bought was a lemon," the person reasons analogically. If there are enough similarities between the instances and few significant differences, then the analogy is sound. Analogical reasoning is one of the most useful methods we have for maintaining some measure of control over our lives. In ethics, surely when we attribute goodness or badness to an action, we should attribute it to another action that is similar in all relevant respects.

These objections to act nonconsequentialism have led many to adopt a rule nonconsequential position. Let us consider it.

Rule Nonconsequentialism

According to rule nonconsequentialism there are one or more rules to serve as moral standards. For example, some might hold that you should always tell the truth. No matter how good the consequences might be that result from lying, some rule nonconsequentialists might say that to violate the rule of truth telling is always wrong. Unlike moderate act nonconsequentialism, though, rule nonconsequentialism would maintain that these rules are not derived from particular examples or actions but from the nature of the actions themselves. Rule nonconsequentialists divide into two groups: those that espouse one rule and those that espouse more than one rule. Divine command and categorical imperative are single-rule theories; prima facie duties and maximin principle are multiple-rule theories.

Divine Command Theory

An example of a single-rule nonconsequential theory is the rule that says we should always do the will of God. This theory has been termed the *divine command theory*, or *theological voluntarism*. Whatever the situation, the theory goes, if we do what God wills, then we do the right thing; if we do not do what God wills, then no matter what the consequences, we do wrong.

To understand the divine command theory better, it is helpful to see what kinds of thinkers the theory excludes. First, the theory would exclude those who believe that we should obey God's law because by so doing we will promote our own or the general good, or be faithful to some virtuous principles. Perhaps by being obedient to God's law we do accomplish these ends, but those espousing the divine command theory do not justify their actions on any other basis than that God wills a particular action.

Second, the divine command theory excludes those who defend the morality of an action on the basis of some supernatural reward promised to the faithful and denied others. True, maybe the faithful will be rewarded, and behaving righteously is in their best long-term interests. But theological voluntarists would not justify moral actions on these egoistic grounds. Having defined divine command theory and seen two groups of thinkers it excludes, we will now raise some objections to it.

Objections to the Divine Command Theory

1. *We do not know what God has commanded.* One obvious question that arises with theological voluntarism is: How do we know what God has commanded? Frequently voluntarists point to a holy book or scripture as evidence. The Ten Commandments are the likely source for Jews and Christians. Yet we are still left wondering how we know that scriptures represent the inspired word of God. Some would say because it says so in the scriptures. But this is circular reasoning. After all, how do we know that there is a God at all? And if there is, can we be sure that he or she expressed himself or herself in one source and not in another? So, the claim that we know what God has commanded appears questionable.

2. *The divine command theory cannot satisfactorily explain why God commands something.* An even stickier objection is whether God commands something because it is right or whether something is right because God commands it. If God commands something because it is right, then the divine command theory collapses because it contends that something is right *because* God commands it. If something is right because God commands it, then anything God commands must be right. Should God command cruelty, then it seems it would be right—a difficult proposition to accept. Voluntarists often argue that it would contradict God's benevolent nature to do what is patently evil. But this raises other problems. One of them was raised long ago by the Greek philosopher Epicurus: "Is God willing to prevent evil, but not able? Then is he impotent. Is he able, but not willing? Then is he malevolent. Is he both able and willing? Whence then is evil?"

3. *Divine laws are difficult to apply.* Many claim that the commandment not to kill is a divine law. But the same people would say that killing in self-defense or in capital punishment is excepted from this law. Others tolerate no exceptions. Clearly, problems arise in interpreting and applying divine laws. Also, divine laws can conflict. For example, suppose that I could not keep a promise or tell the truth without seriously hurting someone emotionally. Presumably, divine laws direct me to keep promises and tell the truth and also refrain from hurting people. When conflicts such as this arise, how am I to resolve them? Some would answer with a popular expression of the divine command: the golden rule.

The golden rule commands us to treat others as we would want to be treated. If you want to be treated fairly, treat others fairly; if you want to be loved, love others. The core of this principle is impartiality, the doctrine that you should never make an exception of yourself. Do not do to others what you are unwilling to have them do to you. The golden rule has a long history in religious and nonreligious teachings throughout the world. Can it help Grogan?

One problem with the golden rule is that it fails to recognize that inequalities often exist between the parties in an exchange situation. For example, if Grogan applied the rule he might ask himself, "If I were in Kravits's position, would I want an employee to give the public this information?" The answer of course is no. But suppose Grogan asks, "If I were a potential purchaser of the JLP-23, would I want an Icarus employee to reveal publicly such a potentially serious defect?" The answer then is, yes. Even if the golden rule implies that theoretically only one party need object to make an action wrong, it still must address the problem evident here: Parties in an exchange are rarely equal.

An additional problem is that the golden rule falsely assumes we can know how others actually feel and think. Grogan has never been the president of Icarus, or of any other company for that matter. In fact, his present job constitutes the highest level of responsibility he has ever attained. And yet, the golden rule would have him, in effect, step into Kravits's shoes, to imagine how Kravits would see the situation—a very difficult, if not impossible, task. The problem is further compounded by the multitude of "others" who are involved directly and indirectly in the moral decisions any of us must make. In the last analysis, the golden rule asks us to make judgments based on our own perceptions, not on those of others, which we cannot really experience.

Categorical Imperative

One of the most influential thinkers in the history of philosophy was the eighteenth-century German philosopher Immanuel Kant (1724–1804). Kant's ethical theory stands as the premier illustration of a purely deontological theory, one that attempts to exclude a consideration of consequences in moral decision making. To understand Kant's thought as expressed in his important *Foundations of the Metaphysics of Morals,* it is essential to grasp his idea of a good will.[6]

Kant believed that nothing was good in itself except a good will. Contrast this with the utilitarian assertion that only happiness is good in itself. But do not misunderstand Kant. He is not saying that numerous facets of the human personality are not good and desirable, such as intelligence, sensitivity, talent, and so on. But their goodness resides in the will that makes use of them.

By will Kant meant the uniquely human capacity to act according to the concept of law, that is, principles. It is this emphasis on will or intention that decisively sets Kant apart from consequential thinkers. For Kant these laws or principles operate in nature. A good will is one that acts in accordance with nature's law.

In estimating the total worth of our actions, Kant believed that a good will takes precedence over all else. Contained in a good will is the concept of duty.

6. Immanuel Kant, Foundations of the Metaphysics of Morals, *translated by Lewis White (New York: Bobbs-Merrill, 1959).*

Only when we act from duty does our action have moral worth. When we act only out of feeling, inclination, or intended results, our actions—though otherwise identical with ones that spring from a sense of duty—have no true moral worth.

To illustrate, merchants have a duty not to shortchange their customers. But simply because merchants do not shortchange customers, need we say that they are acting from a good will? They may be acting from an inclination to promote business or to avoid legal entanglement. Thus they would be acting in accordance with duty but not *from* duty. In other words, their apparently noble gesture happens to coincide with duty. But they have not willed the action from a sense of duty to be fair and honest. Their action, therefore, would not have true moral worth. For Kant, actions have true moral worth only when they spring from a recognition of a duty and a choice to discharge it.

Still we are left wondering what duties do we have and how do we know them. Suppose that Frank Grogan truly wishes to act from duty. What is his duty? How can he discover it?

Kant believed that through reason alone we can arrive at a moral law, based not on any religious injunctions like the divine command, nor on empirical evidence relating to similar situations or to consequences as in utilitarianism. Just as we know, seemingly through reason alone, that a triangle has three sides and that no triangle is a circle, so by the same kind of reasoning Kant believed that we can arrive at absolute moral truths.

For Kant, an absolute moral truth must be logically consistent, that is, free from internal contradiction. To say, for example, that a triangle has four sides or that a square is a circle is to state a contradiction. Kant aimed to ensure that his absolute moral law would be free from such contradictions. If he could formulate such a rule, he contended, it would oblige everyone without exception to follow it. Kant believed that he formulated such a logically consistent rule in his categorical imperative.

In Kant's view there is just one command or imperative that is categorical, that is, one that presents an action as of itself necessary, regardless of any other considerations. He argued that from this one categorical imperative, this universalizable command, we can derive all commands of duty. *Simply stated, Kant's categorical imperative says that we should act in such a way that we could will the maxim of our action to become a universal law.*

By *maxim*, Kant means the subjective principle of an action, the principle that people in effect formulate in determining their conduct. For example, suppose building contractor John Martin promises to install a sprinkling system in a project but is willing to break that promise if it suits his purposes. His maxim can be expressed: "I'll make promises that I'll break whenever keeping them no longer suits my purposes." This is the subjective principle, the maxim, that directs his action. Kant insisted that the morality of any maxim depends on whether we can wish it to become a universal law. Could Martin's maxim be universally acted upon?

That depends on whether the maxim as law would involve a logical contradiction. In fact, the maxim "I'll make promises that I'll break whenever keeping them no longer suits my purposes" cannot be universally acted upon because it involves a contradiction of will. On the one hand, Martin's willing that it be possible to make promises and have them honored. On the other, if everyone intended to break promises when they desired to, then promises could not be honored in the first place. In other words, it is in the nature of promises that they be believed. A law that allowed promise breaking would contradict the very nature of a promise. This is true even if desirable consequences resulted from breaking the promise.

Note that Kant is not a consequentialist. He is not arguing that the consequences of a universal law condoning promise breaking would be bad and therefore the rule is bad. Instead he is claiming that the rule is self-contradictory, that it is self-defeating, that the institution of promise making would necessarily dissolve if such a maxim were universalized. A closer look at the promise-keeping example reveals three formulations of the categorical imperative.

First, to be a moral rule, the rule of conduct must be consistently universalizable, for Kant's moral rule prescribes categorically, not hypothetically. A hypothetical prescription tells us what we should do if we desire certain consequences. For example, "If we want people to think well of us, we should keep promises." The goodness of promise keeping in a hypothetical prescription depends on consequences. But Kant's imperative is categorical, that is, it commands unconditionally, regardless of consequences. A categorical imperative takes the form "Do this" or "Do not do that," without *if*'s, *and*'s, or *but*'s. Such a command must be universalizable; if it were not, then its worth would be determined on empirical grounds, that is, hypothetically. Stated another way, if a person's only reason for following a moral rule is not that it is a universal law of moral conduct, then that person is allowing empirical conditions to determine the decision. The rule thereby loses its inherent necessity and universality.

Second, Kant also believed that for a rule of conduct to be a moral rule, humans would treat one another as ends in themselves and not just means to ends if they followed the rule. Here we see shades of the golden rule. Kant believed that humans as rational beings would be inconsistent if they did not treat all other humans the way that they want to be treated. And since, according to Kant, rational beings recognize their own inner worth, they would never wish to be used as entities possessing relative worth, that is, as means to ends. For example, Kant would object to the practice of forcing people to be subjects in medical experiments designed to yield a cure for cancer—even though great social benefit might result. The experimenters would be using the individuals as means to a desirable social end. In contrast, treating these individuals as ends in themselves would entail recognition of their rights as human beings to determine the disposition of their own bodies. Thus, in such experiments, Kant would require the subjects' informed consent.

Third and finally, Kant argues that for a rule of conduct to be a moral rule it must allow persons who are universally legislating it to impose it upon themselves. Thus, in the case of racist legislation, for example, when the lawmakers do not bind themselves by the rules that they legislate, then the rules have no moral import.

In making his case for promise keeping and related moral issues, Kant is certainly logically persuasive. But his categorical imperative is not without weaknesses.

Objections to the Categorical Imperative

1. *Kant's principles provide no clear way to resolve conflicts of duties.* Problems arise with the categorical imperative when rules conflict. For example, suppose that by telling someone the truth you would cause that person emotional pain. Presumably, you have obligations both to tell the truth and to avoid causing others pain. Which of these obligations takes precedence when they conflict?

2. *There is no compelling reason for the prohibition against certain actions to be without exception.* Frequently, critics question, even reject Kant's principle of universalizability. They wonder why the prohibition against actions such as lying, promise breaking, killing, and similar actions must function without exception. They charge that Kant failed to distinguish between saying *a person should make no exceptions to a rule* and *the rule itself has no exceptions.*

The statement that a person should make no exceptions to a rule simply means that one should never exclude oneself from a rule's application. Thus, if killing is wrong, it is wrong for me as well as for you. To say that "Killing is wrong, except when I do it" would not be universalizable, for then killing would be right for all to do. But because no one may make of oneself an exception to a rule, it does not follow that the rule itself has no exceptions.

Suppose, for example, we decide that killing is sometimes right, perhaps in self-defense. Thus, the rule becomes "Never kill except in self-defense." Perhaps this rule could be refined, but the point remains: This rule is just as universalizable as "Don't kill." The phrase *except in self-defense* can be viewed not as an exception to the rule but as a qualification of it. Thus, critics of Kant ask why a qualified rule is not just as good as an unqualified one. Recognizing this, we no longer need to state rules in the simple, direct, unqualified manner that Kant did.

So, the apparent problem with Kant's system is the rigidity of the rules that he deduced. There are simply no exceptions to them once they have qualified under the categorical imperative. A more realistic approach, it seems, would be to replace absolute rules (ones that allow no exceptions) with a series of rules, duty to which depends on their relative importance in relation to other relevant rules. This, of course, would entail a rule nonconsequentialism based on more than a single rule. Just such an approach has been taken in the twentieth century by British philosopher William David Ross.

Prima Facie Duties

A half-century ago, British philosopher William David Ross published *The Right and the Good,* in which he presented an ethical theory that can be viewed as an attempt to join aspects of utilitarianism with those of Kantianism.[7]

7. *William David Ross,* The Right and the Good *(Oxford: Clarendon Press, 1930).*

Ross begins his attempt to provide methodology for resolving conflicts of duties by dismissing the consequentialist belief that what makes an act right is solely whether it produces the most good. Frequently, Ross notes, consequences of conflicting behaviors counterbalance each other. Instead of a consequentialism, Ross argues that when deciding among ethical alternatives we must weigh the options to determine what duties we fulfill in performing or in refraining from performing each option. Then we must decide which duty among the alternatives is the most obligatory.

Notice that at least two characteristics of his thinking clearly place Ross in the nonconsequential camp. First, judgment of an action's morality is not solely dependent on its consequences. Second, there are duties or obligations that bind us morally. These duties, presumably, can be stated in rules. How do we know these rules?

Ross claims that we come to know these moral rules or principles by intuition. He holds that the most fundamental part of our moral knowledge is the intuition of certain moral principles. If we reflect on these moral principles, then we stand a better chance of doing what is right than if we did not reflect on them. The form of the intuited moral principles is that either all acts of a certain kind are right or all acts of a certain kind are wrong. For example, "All acts of promise keeping are right," "All acts of injury are wrong." Such principles, says Ross, are known intuitively; if we understand what the principles mean, we recognize their truth. We need no additional evidence to know that the principles are true. Having recognized the truth of a moral principle, we can then reflect on it to determine what we ought to do in a particular situation.

As Ross explains, an act may fall under a number of rules at once. For example, the rule to keep a promise may in a given circumstance conflict with the rule not to do anyone harm. To illustrate, suppose a political candidate promises a wealthy builder that if the builder funds his campaign and he gets elected, he will deliver an attractive government contract to the builder. The politician is subsequently elected and makes good his promise. The fact is that the contractor does good work and his prices are competitive. But, of course, the politician does not even consider any other bids.

On the one hand the politician has certainly fulfilled his promise, which he may have viewed as binding. On the other hand he has violated his duty to society, which trusts that he will not collude with private concerns to advance his own or their own interests, but will always act strictly in the interests of the public good. As a result, we would probably believe that the politician has acted immorally, but not because the consequences of his action were wrong. He acted immorally because we would probably consider the reasons against what he did to count more than the reasons for what he did. In other words, we would have evaluated the conflicting duties and decided in favor of the one we felt to be more morally compelling.

In such a case, as in most others, each act is accompanied by a number of motivational reasons. Each reason in turn appeals to a moral duty—to keep a promise, to be faithful to the people who trust you, to be fair, to be honest. Each of these moral duties provides grounds for doing a particular action, and yet no single one provides sufficient grounds. In other words, simply because the politician has a duty to keep his promise is not grounds enough for delivering the government contract to his supporter. Other reasons appear that impose other duties. Ross is particularly sensitive to cases that involve conflicts of duties. To understand better how he handles them, we must consider his concept of *prima facie* duties.

By prima facie duty Ross is referring to the characteristic an act has because it is a certain kind of act, the characteristic that is self-evident in the act. Ross confesses that the term *prima facie* (a Latin term meaning "on first appearance") is unfortunate because it suggests that "one is speaking only of an appearance which a moral situation presents at first sight, and which may be illusory."[8] What Ross is speaking of is rather "an objective fact involved in the nature of the situation or more strictly in an element of its nature. . . ."[9] He insists that there is nothing arbitrary about *prima facie* duties; one knows them to be true by intuition.

Ross gives two important characteristics to prima facie duties. First, prima facie duties are intuited. Second, prima facie duties are conditional, that is, they can be overridden, although they still retain their character as duties. To illustrate, by intuition I recognize a prima facie duty to keep a promise. There may be times, however, when I feel justified, even obligated, to break a promise, for example in order to prevent injury or pain. In breaking my promise under such conditions, I do not for a minute cease to recognize a prima facie duty to keep a promise. Indeed, in a case with only a single prima facie duty, such as promise keeping, I would be obligated to carry out that duty. Ross gives little attention to such cases, however, because they are not problematic. They pose no real concern to persons who recognize intuitively their duty for example to keep a promise, and realize that their particular case involves, without any conflict, an instance of promise keeping.

So, if promise keeping were the only prima facie duty involved in our earlier case of the politician, then the politician ought to honor the promise. But should he actually keep the promise? Not necessarily—other duties are involved. Ross distinguishes *prima facie* duties from *actual* duties. By *actual duty* Ross means what we actually ought to do in a situation. If there is only one prima facie duty involved, then that is what we actually ought to do. If there are conflicting prima facie duties, our actual duty is what we are obliged to do after we have weighed and considered all the prima facie duties. Unlike prima facie duties, actual duties are *not* intuited. In fact, actual duties are not knowledge at all, in Ross's view. They are more like "educated guesses" or "lucky accidents." Ross cites six categories of prima facie duties.

1. *Duties of fidelity are those that rest on our own prior acts.* Included under duties of fidelity would be the duty not to lie (which Ross views as implied in the act of conversation), the duty to remain faithful to contracts, the duty to keep promises, the duty to repair wrongful acts. Thus, Frank Grogan has a duty of fidelity to honor the terms of his work contract, which includes maximizing stockholders' profits.

8. *Ross,* The Right and The Good, *p. 19.*

9. *Ross,* The Right and The Good, *p. 19.*

2. *Duties of gratitude are those that rest on acts of other people toward the agent.* Ross argues that we are bound by obligations arising from relationships that exist between persons, such as those between friends or between relatives. For example, suppose that you annually contribute one hundred dollars to your favorite charity. The week before you are about to make your yearly contribution, a good friend whom you have not seen in years phones you. You are delighted to hear your friend's voice and fondly recall the many times the person stood by you in times of crisis. Now your friend is in need of one hundred dollars. In this case a duty of gratitude would probably oblige you to give the money to your friend rather than to the charity.

3. *Duties of justice are those that rest on the fact or possibility of a distribution of pleasure or happiness that is not in accordance with the merits of the people concerned; in such cases there is a duty to upset or prevent such a distribution.* Imagine the case of imprisoning a man for something that he did not do, although he is obviously guilty of other crimes for which he has escaped punishment. While removing the man from society would appear to be in everyone's best interests (except his own, perhaps), a duty of justice would oblige us not to imprison him. He does not deserve to be imprisoned for something he did not do, no matter how beneficial the consequences of imprisonment.

4. *Duties of beneficence are those that rely on the fact that there are other people in the world whose virtue, intelligence, or happiness we can improve.* For example, board members of a firm can improve the happiness of the firm's pensionees by voting a cost of living increase in retirement funds, compensation for deferred illnesses directly related to their employment.

5. *Duties of self-improvement are those that rest on the fact that we can improve our own condition of virtue, intelligence, or happiness.* Suppose, for example, that a young woman is exceptionally talented. She plays many musical instruments, paints very well, seems to have a natural language-learning ability, and exhibits high scientific acumen. While the young woman is in the midst of determining her life's goals, a rich relative dies, leaving her so much money that she need not work another day in her life. If she decides to use this inheritance for long-term self-indulgence, making no attempt to cultivate her talents, then the woman would be violating a duty to improve herself.

6. *Duties of nonmaleficence (noninjury) are duties of not injuring others.* Ross includes this obligation to contrast with duties of beneficence. Although not injuring others incidentally means doing them good, Ross interprets the avoidance of injuring others as a more pressing duty than beneficence. Thus, Grogan might do the company more good by keeping quiet. But he risks injuring the innocent, and this imposes an obligation that overrides the beneficence he owes the firm.

In summary, Ross presents six categories of prima facie duties. He does not claim that they represent a complete list of recognizable duties, but he does claim that these are duties we acknowledge and willingly accept without argument. In the case of two conflicting prima facie duties, Ross tells us to fulfill the more obligatory duty. Where more than two duties are involved, our actual duty should be the one with the greatest amount of prima facie rightness over wrongness.

Ross's approach to ethics has two main strengths. First, his list of duties can play an important role in the moral education of individuals. If nothing else, it provides a useful catalogue of duties that one may refer to in particular situations. Second, Ross brings to ethical decisions a utilitarian sensitivity to consequences without ignoring duties of apparently undeniable moral force. Nevertheless, critics have raised objections to his theory.

Objections to Prima Facie Duties

1. *People disagree about moral principles.* How do we know what prima facie duties we have to begin with? How do we know that we have an obligation to tell the truth, to improve ourselves, or not to injure others? Ross claims that these are self-evident truths to anyone of sufficient mental maturity who has given them enough attention. But what if people disagree with Ross's list of duties? Surely we disagree about the relative weight they deserve. Suppose that people did not think they had an obligation to keep a promise, or honor a contract, or accurately represent a product in advertisements? Ross must say that such individuals lack "sufficient mental maturity" or that they did not give the proposition "sufficient attention." But the question arises as to the nature of "sufficient mental maturity." We must also wonder how much is "sufficient" attention to a moral statement. In Ross's view, people have attended sufficiently to a moral proposition when they recognize his list of duties. This argument appears to involve circular reasoning.

2. *It is difficult, if not impossible, to determine the relative weight and merit of conflicting duties.* When faced with a situation that presents one or more conflicting prima facie duties, how do we determine what our actual duty is? In the case of two conflicting prima facie duties, the act is one's duty which is in accord with the more stringent prima facie obligation. In cases of more than two conflicting prima facie duties, the act is one's duty that has the greatest balance of prima facie rightness over prima facie wrongness. But without assigning weights to duties, how can we determine the "most stringent" obligation or "the greatest balance of prima facie rightness over prima facie wrongness"? This is not to belittle or minimize Ross's theory. In numerous cases we in fact face no particular difficulties about resolving conflicts of duties. Thus most people would probably agree that when faced with telling a harmless lie and saving someone from serious injury, we have a more pressing obligation to prevent the injury than to tell the truth. And often in cases where the choice does not appear as clear, thoughtful reflection underscores the efficacy of Ross's approach. But what about other cases when the actual duties are not as clear? Ultimately, it seems that Ross must be judged at best inconclusive about the relative priorities of duties.

Maximin Principle of Justice

We have seen that consequentialists and nonconsequentialists are fundamentally at odds. Specifically utilitarians suggest the greatest happiness principle as the standard of morality, which in theory seems to allow injustices. Kant and Ross, in contrast, make intention and characteristics of acts fundamental moral concerns and emphasize the intrinsic worth of human beings. In 1971 Harvard Professor of Philosophy John Rawls published *A Theory of Justice* in which he proposed a theory of justice that tries to use the strengths of consequential and nonconsequential ethics while avoiding their pitfalls. At the same time, Rawls hoped to offer a workable method for solving problems of social morality. Because his theory attempts to maximize the lot of those minimally advantaged, it's termed the *maximin principle*.

Central to Rawls's theory is the question of establishing principles of justice. What principles will serve as a basis for justice in society? In answering, Rawls asks us to imagine a "natural state," a hypothetical state of nature in which all persons are ignorant of their talents and socioeconomic conditions. He calls this the "original position." Rawls claims that in the original position, people share certain characteristics. The people are mutually self-interested; rational, that is, they more or less accurately know their interests; and similar in their needs, interests, and capacities. Given these assumptions Rawls then asks what people in the original position would be likely to formulate when asked to choose a fundamental principle of justice to be followed. He surmises that they would choose two principles to ensure justice: the liberty principle and the difference principle.

By the *liberty principle* Rawls means that people in the original position would expect each person participating in a practice or affected by it to have an equal right to the greatest amount of liberty that is compatible with a like liberty for all. And by the *difference principle* Rawls means that people in the original position would allow inequality only insofar as it serves each person's advantage and arises under conditions of equal opportunity.

Before examining these concepts further, we should mention that by *person* Rawls means not only particular human beings but also collective agencies. And by *practice* he means any form of activity that a system of rules specifies, such as offices, roles, rights, and duties. Now let us examine the heart of Rawls's theory: the principles of equal liberty and difference.

Equality means that all persons are to be treated the same. Specifically, by *equality* Rawls means the impartial and equitable administration and application of rules that define a practice. The equal liberty principle expresses this concept.

When Rawls terms equality "impartial," he is referring to the spirit of disinterestedness that should characterize the distribution of goods and evils, to the fact that no person should receive preferred consideration. When he speaks of "equitable administration," Rawls seems to mean that the distribution must be fair and just to begin with. Let us apply these two characteristics of equality to a concrete situation.

Suppose a firm draws up job specifications for a particular position. The equal liberty principle decrees that everybody be judged by these criteria. The rule would not be impartially administered if the firm made an exception for an applicant. Nor would it be equitably administered if it excluded candidates from consideration on non-job-related criteria, perhaps on grounds of color or sex. Remember that Rawls is defining liberty with reference to the pattern of rights, duties, powers, and liabilities established by a practice. In this case, anyone applying for the job has a right to expect equal treatment insofar as the job specifications will be applied and to expect that the distribution is fair and equal to begin with.

But Rawls's equal liberty principle expresses the idea of equality in another, more important way. An intrinsic part of all regulations is that they infringe on personal liberty. Suppose, for example, the job specifications in question call for a college education. Those persons lacking a college education therefore cannot compete equally for the job. In his equal liberty principle, Rawls recognizes this inherent characteristic of all laws and other practices: By nature they encroach on the equal liberty of those subject to them. Thus when a bus company will not consider anyone older than 35 years for the position of bus driver, it infringes on the equal liberty of the many persons older than 35 who may not only wish to apply for such a job but, in fact, are capable of doing the work required. Some argue that justice would only require an equal liberty, that is, as long as everyone over 35 is denied consideration by the bus company, justice is being served. Or, as long as college education is required of everyone applying for a job, then such a requirement is just.

Rawls appears more philosophically perceptive on this point, however, than his opponents appear to be. He notes that if a more extensive liberty were possible for all without loss, damage, or conflict, then it would be irrational to settle upon a lesser liberty. In the bus company case, for example, an argument could be made for a more extensive liberty than is allowed by the 35-year-old age cut-off. Indeed, such an argument partially has contributed to the extension of the mandatory retirement age, and in some cases (for example, California) to its abolition.

Crucial to any theory of social justice is the determination of when inequality is permissible. After all, a just society is not one in which all are equal, but one in which inequalities are justifiable. Rawls addresses this problem with his difference principle.

Rawls's difference principle defines what kinds of inequalities are permissible. It specifies under what conditions the equal liberty principle may be violated.

For Rawls, equality is not contingent. It does not depend on something else, such as on the greatest happiness for the most people, for its justification. For Rawls, equality is fundamental and self-justifying. This does not mean that equality can never be violated. It means that inequality is permissible only if in all likelihood the practice involving the inequality works to the advantage of every individual affected or to the advantage of the least well-off. In other words, Rawls arranges inequalities so that ideally they benefit all affected or at least those most in need. Suppose, for example, that the bus company establishes a minimum corrected vision level for all bus drivers. Although this works against those who cannot reach the minimum, the standard can be justified by showing how such a rule works to the advantage of all concerned, even those excluded. (After all, they will not be in a position of risking their own safety or of having it risked by others.)

Although such a rationale may appear to be a case of the greatest happiness principle, it is not. The difference principle, in fact, does not allow inequalities generally justified on utilitarian grounds, that is, on the grounds that the disadvantages of persons in one position are outweighed by the advantages of those in another. On the contrary, the difference principle allows inequality ideally only when it works to *everyone's* advantage. Thus the key point in the hypothetical example: Even those excluded from consideration are advantaged by the inequality. The fundamental difference, then, between utilitarianism and Rawls's theory of justice is in their concepts of justice. In utilitarianism, the concept of justice rests on some notion of efficiency.

In contrast to these consequential concepts of justice, Rawls's is best described by his own word *reciprocity*. Reciprocity is the principle that requires that a practice be such that all members who fall under it could and would accept it and be bound by it. It requires the possibility for mutual acknowledgment of principles by free people, having no authority over one another; this makes the idea of reciprocity fundamental to justice and fairness. Without this acknowledgment, Rawls claims, there can be no basis for a true community. Thus a fair business contract would be one in which all affected can and will accept it and be bound by it.

In effect, then, where there is conflict between his two principles, Rawls relies on his first principle of justice, the equal liberty principle. He insists that it is logically prior to the difference principle. In contrast, the utilitarian sees liberty as contingent on social productivity; in other words, liberty is desirable insofar as it produces the most happiness for the most people. Obviously, the utilitarian position does not allow the loss of liberty if the greatest number are not served. But Rawls would argue that any position that even allows the possibility of the loss of equal liberty is unacceptable. As Rawls puts it, "Each person possesses an inviolability founded on justice that even the welfare of society as a whole cannot override. . . . Therefore . . . the rights secured by justice are not subject to political bargaining or to the calculus of social interests."[10]

Besides agreeing on these basic principles of justice, Rawls claims that people in the original position would also recognize "natural duties" that generate one's obligations to another. The duties that Rawls lists are identical with those noted in discussing Ross's prima facie duties. Moreover, Rawls acknowledges the need to rank these as being of higher and lower obligations, although he does not undertake this task, presumably because his primary concern is with justice in social institutions.

Finally, Rawls recognizes the legitimacy of paternalism. By *paternalism* he means that occasions arise when people are not in a position to make decisions

10.   *John Rawls*, A Theory of Justice *(Cambridge, Mass.: Harvard University Press, 1971), p. 4.*

for themselves, that others must make the decisions for them. In business decisions, for example, consumers still exercise little influence over the planning, manufacturing, and marketing of goods and services. Rawls's recognition of paternalism requires that those in a decision-making capacity introduce the concerns, interests, and values of those who will be affected by decisions but do not have any substantive input to make their feelings known.

Objections to the Maximin Principle

Since its formulation in 1971, Rawls's maximin principle has been the center of a highly technical philosophical debate. At this point it is impossible to isolate objections that all critics would share. But three criticisms recur often enough to bear mentioning.

1. *Rawls's theory is based on several questionable assumptions.* Recall that according to Rawls, when we don the veil of ignorance we are mutually self-interested, that is, we establish practices normally on the basis of self-advantage. But this is so only because Rawls assumes that humans would be rational. When Rawls describes people as rational, he implies a great many things that seem questionable: (a) that we more or less know our own interests, (b) that we can trace the likely consequences of one course over another and resist temptation of personal gain, (c) that we are not greatly bothered by the perceptible difference between our own condition and someone else's. Rawls also assumes that people have similar enough needs, interests, and capacities so that fruitful cooperation among people is possible. At the same time, he conceals from people in the original position any knowledge of their interests, talents, purposes, plans, and conceptions of the good. How can people so ignorant of these important aspects of their identities and personalities agree on principles to regulate their lives? But even conceding these assumptions, we can detect other weaknesses in Rawls's theory.

2. *Rawls's principle brings a measure of whim to moral decision making.* Although Rawls is clear about the primacy of the equal liberty principle, differences in emphasis and interpretation might elevate the difference principle to the position of whim and thus lead to a contrasting moral decision. Take, for example, the case of sexual discrimination in employment practices. Under ideal conditions—those that Rawls describes as part of his definition of rationality—no one would agree to introduce the practice of sexual discrimination into employment for fear of being victimized by it. But this seems certain only if we assume a kind of germ-free, vacuum-like decision-making context; we must assume that there is no sexual discrimination to begin with.

But what would occur if you asked those same rational, self-interested, uncoerced people how they would redress already existing discriminatory employment practices? Perhaps they might emphasize the need to redress this injustice as quickly as possible through a program of preferential hiring that favored the discriminated-against group over the non-discriminated-against one. In so doing, they might employ Rawls's difference principle, by arguing that this temporary discrimination in employment would ultimately benefit all and therefore was permissible. But would it be altogether *irrational* for someone to object that such a defense is purely speculative, that in fact there are bound to be individual persons who will find themselves decidedly worse off under such a practice than not under it? Is it unthinkable that, reasoning this way, at least some people would refuse to be bound by a preferential hiring program?

It does not seem to be stretching a point for such people to invoke Rawls's equal liberty principle by claiming that preferential hiring programs on face value violate this principle. Unless we have warped Rawls's position, it appears that reasonable people could disagree on their interpretations and emphasis of Rawls's theory of justice. This evident weakness suggests another one.

Summary and Conclusions

This completes our overview of major normative ethical theories. We have viewed these theories in two categories: consequential and nonconsequential. Under consequentialism, we discussed egoism, and act and rule utilitarianism. Under nonconsequentialism, we discussed the divine command, the categorical imperative, prima facie duties, and the maximin principle. Although each of these theories has weaknesses, they nonetheless have a wide range of application for moral decision making, as we will see in the chapters ahead.

A question inevitably arises here: Which theory, if any, ought I endorse? There is no principle that we can apply in choosing from among the smorgasbord of ethical principles. So, perhaps the whole enterprise of trying to formulate and justify moral principles is futile and should be abandoned. While such a reaction is understandable—especially from those beginning a study of ethics— there are good reasons not to act on this impulse of despair. After all, to say that an ethical theory is imperfect is not to say that it is empty or that the search for a satisfactory theory is futile. Human relationships present a tangled web of frequently subtle, ill-defined problems. It is little wonder that we do not have a single theory that wins everyone's acceptance.

Each ethical theory discussed has an impressive range of application. In criticizing each theory, philosophers inevitably focus on its weaknesses. This approach is consistent with the philosophical enterprise of pursuing truth and certainty. Philosophers cite cases that tend to break the theory down, that test its strength at the most fundamental levels. Failing to grasp this aspect of the philosophical enterprise, one could conclude that there is little worth in these ethical theories. This judgment would be a gross overstatement that not even the theories' harshest critics would agree with. It would be as indefensible as scrapping the theory of biological evolution or of quantum mechanics because these are incomplete or unsatisfactory in important ways. As in the world of science, so in the realm of human relationships which ethics deals with, we face complex realities that by nature seem to preclude total success.

Granted that these theories, though imperfect, are extremely useful, is not a selection of one theory ultimately arbitrary? Since none can be proved correct, does it matter which one we choose? Again, such a reaction is totally understandable, but before deciding that the choice of an ethical theory is arbitrary, we should reflect on the meaning of that word.

It probably would be an arbitrary decision to conclude that, since all ethical codes generally agree on basic ideals, it does not matter which code is followed. This position would be incorrect because each code commits us to different principles. The thoughtful person recognizes these differences and chooses. Such a choice, rooted as it is in a consideration of the alternatives, cannot be arbitrary. Instead it is based on the best available evidence, on a consideration of everything it could possibly be founded on. In other words:

> To describe such ultimate decisions as arbitrary . . . would be like saying that a complete description of the universe was utterly unfounded, because no further fact could be called upon in corroboration of it. This is not how we use the words "arbitrary" and "unfounded." Far from being arbitrary, such a decision would be the most well-founded of decisions, because it would be based upon a consideration of everything upon which it could possibly be founded.[11]

The selection of an ethical theory is only arbitrary for frivolous and unthinking people who have never undertaken a serious investigation into ethical theory. For those persons who have, the choice—far from being arbitrary—is often slow, methodical, and agonizing. The process suggests not the impudence of those who say it does not matter but the courage of those who say it does. It is an individual choice, not an arbitrary one.

Finally, we should note that the fundamental worth of studying and understanding ethical thought is not that we thereby have definitive guides to moral conduct. Rather, the value lies in becoming aware of the moral options available to us, of the general paradigm within which moral inquiry can take place as concrete human beings grapple with real-life issues. Individual moral choices are frequently not between obvious right or wrong, good or bad, but between actions and values that contain elements of both. The challenge, then, is not so much one of finding an ethical standard to use, but of applying a defensible standard in a specific instance.

The chapters that follow are designed to help meet this challenge. They not only raise specific issues, but they also show how these theories might be applied to the issues. We will see that all theories are of some use, but that some prove more useful than others in particular situations. Such a study will prove valuable in helping us recognize the various kinds of ethical systems that may be employed in given situations and in determining what values override others in a conflict.

Selections for Further Reading

Broad, C. D. *Five Types of Ethical Theory*. New York: Harcourt, Brace, 1930.

Frankena, William. *Ethics*. 2nd ed. Englewood Cliffs, N.J.: Prentice-Hall, 1973.

11.   *R. M. Hare,* The Language of Morals *(Oxford: Clarendon Press, 1952), p. 69.*

Fried, Charles. *An Anatomy of Values: Problems of Personal and Social Choice.* Cambridge, Mass.: Harvard University Press, 1970.

Kant, Immanuel. *Foundations of the Metaphysics of Morals.* Lewis White Beck, Trans. New York: Bobbs-Merrill, 1959.

Ladd, J. *Ethical Relativism.* Belmont, Calif.: Wadsworth, 1973.

Mill, John Stuart. *Utilitarianism.* New York: Bobbs-Merrill, 1957.

Muller, Herbert J. *The Children of Frankenstein.* Bloomington: Indiana University Press, 1970.

Nietzsche, Friedrich. *Genealogy of Morals.* F. Golffing, trans. Garden City, N.Y.: Doubleday, 1956.

Oraison, Mafe. *Morality for Moderns.* J. F. Bernard, Trans. New York: Doubleday, 1972.

Plato. *The Republic.* Benjamin Jowett, Trans. New York: Random House, 1957.

Ramsey, Paul. *Basic Christian Ethics.* New York: Scribner's, 1950.

Rawls, John. *A Theory of Justice.* Cambridge, Mass.: Harvard University Press, 1971.

Ross, W. D. *Foundations of Ethics.* New York: Oxford University Press, 1954.

Stace, W. T. *The Concept of Morals.* New York: Macmillan, 1965.

Warnock, Mary. *Existential Ethics.* New York: St. Martin's Press, 1968.

Part II

Issues

3
SEX OUTSIDE MARRIAGE

Perhaps no people have changed as much as Americans have in the past 25 years. Nowhere is the change more apparent than in our sexual ethics.

One can hardly go anywhere in the United States today without hearing people talk of the "new morality," the "sexual revolution," and the "permissive society." In the midst of this seeming break with our puritanical heritage, people react in different ways. Some fully savor the newfound sexual freedom. Others remain on the sidelines, curious, even envious, but still too inhibited to be anything more than rapt onlookers. Still others, ever mindful of past legendary downfalls, prophesy moral decay or worse.

One facet of the so-called sexual revolution is the dramatic increase in sex outside marriage. *"Sex outside marriage"* in this text *means any sexual relation other than between marital partners.* Such relations include sex between unmarried people, and sex between persons who are not married to each other, but one of whom is married. Studies indicate that well over 50 percent of the women and 75 percent of the men in America have sex outside marriage.

The increasing incidence of and opportunities for sex outside marriage present a number of problems for people today, particularly for young unmarried people. Dealing with peer pressure, reconciling the new sexual morality with a more conventional upbringing, handling emotions that often accompany sexual intimacies, maintaining a healthful self-image, coping with the insecurities that the absence of marital bonding can cause, managing the fear or reality of venereal disease, dealing with the uncertainties of birth control devices, reconciling feelings of guilt and shame—these are only some of the many concerns.

The changes in sexual morality have ushered in a host of related psychological and sociological problems. But even more important, the changes seem to have forced many individuals to take a good long look at sexual values generally and to answer for themselves a question whose answer heretofore often was glibly given them by religion, parents, and society. That question is: Is sex outside marriage always morally objectionable?

This question is the primary concern of Chapter 3. Before considering how the ethical theories might approach it and what some scholars in sexual ethics have written about it, we should briefly sketch some related material. Among the material that serves as useful background to any discussion of sexual ethics are: the determinants of sexual behavior, the difference between public and private morality, and the components of a sexual standard.

Determinants of Sexual Behavior

There are at least three determinants of sexual behavior: biological, psychological, and sociological. Biological determinants generally have been based on some concept of instinct. For example, one explanation relates sexual behavior to the need to reproduce. In this sense sexual behavior is part of a deep-seated biological incentive for animals to reproduce their kind and perpetuate their species.

Another biological explanation is that animals engage in sex because it is pleasurable. The incentive then is not in the consequences of the sexual behavior (reproduction) but in sex itself. In this sense sex originates in a psychological "drive" associated with sensory pleasure; the reproductive consequences are a by-product.

Still another biological explanation relates sex to hormonal influence. Hormones, which begin to exert their influence even before birth, are known to be vital in sexual development, though relatively dispensable for sexual functioning in the mature adult. The precise connection between hormones and sexual behavior remains uncertain.

In discussing the psychological determinants, it is helpful to distinguish at least two sorts of explanations. The first position considers the psychological facts as reflections and manifestations of underlying biological processes. A good example of this view can be seen in the psychoanalytic theory of Sigmund Freud (1856–1939). Freud argued that the sex drive, termed the *libido*, is the psychological representation of a biological instinct. Thus, he considered sexual behavior a representation or an extension of a biological drive.

Contrasting with this psychoanalytic view is the second position that claims sexual behavior is largely acquired through a variety of psychological and social mechanisms. Sexual behavior in this view is associated with learned patterns of behavior rather than with biological factors. In brief, each of us behaves sexually as we do because that is how we have learned to behave.

The psychological and emotional purposes and aims of sexual behavior have also been a subject of study. Some think that sex carries an affective component: It is not engaged in for its own sake but assumes added significance as an expression of affection or love for a partner. Others have looked on sex as a means for obtaining love. Still others have viewed sex as contributing to one's self-esteem and self-concept, and as figuring prominently in one's moral or spiritual identity. All these are among the purposes or aims of sex that are commonly catalogued.

The third determinant of sexual behavior involves social factors. While the distinction between the psychological and the social is fuzzy, generally the social or cultural view emphasizes the interpersonal over the intrapsychic, and group processes over internal ones. In the social view, sexuality is a cohesive force that binds the family unit together. It also functions as a form of communication, symbolizes status, and is a vehicle for aesthetic self-expression. Sex also can be an outlet for aggression.

In studying these determinants of sexual behavior, it is important to see them as complementary and integrated, rather than mutually exclusive. A choice of one factor over the others as the predominant explanation seems neither necessary nor desirable, although admittedly this observation is debatable. In the last analysis, all behavior, including sexual, appears to be the interactional outcome of all three influences.

Despite the complementary nature of these determinants, each of them can and does serve as a basis for a comprehensive sexual morality. We must acknowledge this if we are to unearth the underlying assumptions of both our own standards on sex and those of others.

Connection Between Determinants and Sexual Standards

To see how an emphasis on a certain determinant of sexual behavior can affect one's view of sexual morality, consider the strict association of sex with procreation. This viewpoint has served as the basis for condemning sexual behavior other than that intended to reproduce the species and also various methods of birth control. In Christianity and Judaism, for example, the procreative emphasis, together with a recognition of sex as a cohesive force that binds the family unit together, traditionally has led to the condemnation of sex outside marriage.

Even if one disregards procreation as the primary function of sex and emphasizes just the social determinant, one might draw a similar moral judgment about sex outside marriage. Sex outside marriage might produce offspring that society ultimately might have to maintain. Or, if birth control measures are taken, one might still condemn sex outside marriage on the basis that it discourages marrying and having children, and so undermines the foundations of society.

As another example of the connection between determinant emphasis and sexual standards, consider a view that emphasizes the psychological aims or purposes that sex serves. One might be inclined to approve of sex between unmarried consenting adults in cases where the self-esteem and sense of identity of both persons are served, where sex is an expression of mutual love, or where "nobody gets hurt." In contrast, a strictly procreative view or a view that subordinates sex to a social role might consider sex immoral even under these conditions.

The point is that no moral judgment—certainly not one in so complex an area as sexual behavior—stands unsupported. In sexual morality, deep-seated explanations about the origins of sexuality inevitably undergird moral judgments about specific sexual behaviors. In formulating defensible moral judgments about sex, then, we should be aware of these explanations, the influence they exert on our judgments, and the weight of evidence they have. This requires continual reading, study, and research about the nature of human sexuality.

Private vs. Public Morality

In discussions of sexual morality, the issue of private vs. public morality unavoidably arises. In sexual matters, private morality refers to sexual behavior that is not conducted before others and does not violate the rights of others. Public morality refers to sexual behavior that is carried out before others or violates others' individual rights. We make this distinction for several reasons.

First, how we classify sexual behavior can affect our moral judgment of it. For example, college sophomore Marcie considers any sexual behavior conducted by consenting married adults in private to be morally unobjectionable. In her view, if a married couple willingly engage in the sexual act, derive pleasure from it, do not hurt themselves or anybody else by it, then it is all right. However, Marcie objects to any act of coitus performed in public because it invades the privacy rights of others. Notice that the basis for her moral distinction here is not the act but its public performance. As Marcie puts it: "It's not what they do, it's where they do it."

A second reason for making the distinction between private and public sexual morality is that traditionally the state has exercised the right to regulate public sexual behavior. Thus, rape and the seduction of the sexually naive minor are criminal offenses, and morally objectionable by virtually all moral standards. If we assume that the state does have the right to regulate public sexual behavior, then specific sexual acts must be properly designated. Otherwise the state will end up unjustifiably invading individual privacy and constraining personal liberty. In fact, many people today, including members of the American Law Institute, think that most of the laws pertaining to sexual behavior are unconstitutional because they attempt to regulate what are essentially acts of private sexual morality.

For example, in most parts of the United States homosexual acts that conform to the designation of private are still criminal offenses. What's more, in many states premarital sex, oral-genital contacts, intercourse with prostitutes, and extramarital sex are also illegal. Even a cursory look at the U.S. penal code indicates that, generally speaking, such laws are not directed to "the preservation of public order," as most criminal laws are. Rather they embody an ethical viewpoint that is rooted in the assumption that sex is primarily for procreation. This philosophical bias is understandable when one realizes that most legislators shared this viewpoint when the laws were written. Thus, homosexuality, masturbation, and oral sex were designated as criminal offenses, even when they conformed to the definition of private sexual acts. In recent years such laws have become repugnant to enough lawyers and lawmakers alike that the American

Law Institute in preparing its Model Penal Code (1955) recommended the abolition of all laws governing sex activities performed in private between consenting
adults.

The point in raising this issue is certainly not to equate legality with morality. Nor is it to argue that all sex acts conforming to the definition of private
morality are thereby moral. This claim would be patently absurd, for private
sexual behavior involves basic moral principles such as freedom, justice, and
honesty that will enter into the moral evaluation of it. Rather, the point is that
private and public sexual morality must be distinguished in order to facilitate
moral evaluation of specific sexual behavior.

Sexual Standards

Given the confusion about private and public morality; the uncertainties
about the explanations, aims, and purposes of sexual behavior; and the radical
changes in sexual values and conduct, how ought we behave sexually? For
some, like Marcie's parents, the answer lies in a strictly legalistic code of "do's"
and "don't's." Others prefer to cast off sexual "shackles," to be free of traditional restraints. In effect, they adopt the "Ernest Hemingway" ethic. Asked
once what he thought was "right," Hemingway replied: Whatever you feel good
after doing. Still others take a midway position between these two extremes.
They try to temper permissiveness with concern. Thus, for Marcie's boyfriend
Steve, sexual behavior that hurts someone is wrong; if it does not hurt and gives
pleasure to all, then it is right.

There are both advantages and disadvantages in these approaches to sexual
standards. The legalistic approach certainly is decisive. Following her parents'
dicta would leave little doubt in Marcie's mind about how she ought to behave.
She would never have to agonize over sexual decisions. But Marcie considers
such an approach overly directive. As she says, "It treats every sex act outside
marriage the same way." In other words, this approach does not take into
consideration special circumstances which, for many, may make an act of sex
outside marriage all right.

The permissive approach has the advantage of being flexible and not inhibit-
ing what is spontaneous, imaginative, and exciting in sex. But it provides little
more direction than a pleasure principle would allow. Indeed, it can callously
disregard the potential harm, especially the emotional and psychological harm,
that sexual involvements can produce.

The intermediate position allows consideration for situational nuances,
while at the same time providing some direction for sexual judgments. But still,
it leaves us the problem of determining whether a particular sexual behavior will
harm someone. Whom should we consider in the evaluation—just the individuals involved, or also those indirectly affected, such as relatives, friends, and
society as a whole? In addition, the whole concept of harm is ambiguous.
Undoubtedly people can be harmed in ways other than physically or emotionally. For example, they can be treated unjustly, or their freedom restrained
illegitimately. The intermediate approach generally disregards such basic moral

concerns as justice and freedom, viewing these as philosophical abstractions. Yet, such "abstractions" often play a crucial role in particular sexual acts.

Faced with the necessity of choosing a sexual standard, and the apparent inadequacies of the prevailing ones, what are we to do? One useful thing is to try to isolate some realistic components of a fundamental standard of sexual behavior, some basic criteria that a sexual standard must meet.

Components of a Fundamental Sexual Standard

There is no agreement about what a fundamental sexual standard should contain. But there are a number of components that arise frequently enough to be presented here. Herant Katchadourian and Donald Lunde in their incisive work on human sexuality[1] lay out five of them, which are at least worth considering.

First, our sexual standard might begin with an acceptance of sexual realities. Such realities include a recognition of biological facts about the sexual organs and their functions. More important, sexual realities include an acceptance of sexual feelings as legitimate biological and psychological manifestations, rather than afflictions, weaknesses, or curses. Acceptance of sexual realities also includes a willingness to accept behavioral facts about sex—a recognition of how people behave sexually, regardless of how we think they should behave. Finally, and most important, acceptance of sexual realities includes facing up to our own thoughts and feelings. If we fail to confront our own sexuality, we cannot possibly come to terms with ourselves on sexual issues. Indeed, we invite dishonesty into our sexual relations.

Second, a sexual standard might provide for the enhancement of sexuality. Sexuality, after all, is as much a potential that we are born with as are intellectual and artistic capabilities. As with all potentialities, sexuality must be developed and cultivated. This requires a nutritive milieu, which includes warm contacts with other people. In short, a fundamental standard for sexual behavior apparently should accept the basic value of sex. A standard that in effect claims that we can do no wrong sexually so long as we do nothing at all treats sex not as a value but as a necessary evil. Similarly, a standard that does not view sex as something to be enhanced makes sex a strictly mechanical operation at best, not a potential that, when fully developed, can produce physical, intellectual, emotional, and spiritual growth.

Third, a fundamental sexual standard should integrate sexuality into life as a whole. Certainly individual sexual needs vary. Maybe for Steve sex is the focal point of life. But for others, sex seems hardly to matter at all. Probably for most of us the importance of sex falls somewhere in between. The influence of sex in our overall lives obviously varies from person to person, depending on genetic predispositions, the environment we were raised in, and the societal values we were exposed to. But ultimately a standard that does not make sense of sex in the context of one's whole life has limited application.

Fourth, a fundamental standard should address the relation between sex

---

1. *Herant A. Katchadourian and Donald T. Lunde,* Fundamentals of Human Sexuality *(New York: Holt, Rinehart and Winston, 1975).*

and marriage. Whether sex ought to occur within or outside marriage is the most frequently discussed concern regarding heterosexual intercourse. In Western culture, the traditional expectation has been that sex should be confined to marriage. But clearly many depart from this belief. Both premarital and extramarital sex appear to be occurring more frequently, although the incidence varies widely among social groups. Sex outside marriage raises fundamental concerns not only about the interests of the individuals involved but about society generally, since sexual problems continue to be a common cause of marital discord. Similarly, marital sex can raise questions about the integrity of the family unit and society in general, as well as about the marriage partners themselves. So, any standard that ignores the relation of sex to marriage fails to address a basic aspect of heterosexual sex.

Fifth, a fundamental standard must consider the relation of sex to love. The connection between the two continues to be hotly debated. The Western ideal has tried to combine sex, love, and marriage. But not many seem able to attain this ideal. As a result, many today consider love, but not marriage, a necessary condition for sex. Some do not even view love as necessary for sex. The separation of sex from love and marriage is seen by some as sexual depravity, by others as sexual liberation.

There is no question that love is a complex emotion and acts of love can have different components. Psychologist Rollo May, for example, distinguishes several kinds of love, among which are: sex (or lust), eros (the urge toward higher states of being and relationships), philia (friendship or brotherly love), and agape (selfless love as exemplified in the love of God for man). Clearly, then, we can love without sex. But sex is equally complex. Perhaps, like love, sex too should be viewed as an entity in itself. If we can have love without sex, why not sex without love? Each of us inevitably faces this question in our sexual relations. Therefore, a standard that fails to address the relation of sex and love ignores a most important aspect of sexual relations.

The foregoing remarks about the determinants of sex, public and private morality, and the components of a sexual standard provide useful background for discussions of sexual morality. With this background, we can now turn to a few of the more common moral issues of human sexuality: homosexuality, extramarital sex, and the issue with the widest appeal—premarital sex.

Homosexuality

Initial Considerations

In the most general sense, *a homosexual is a person whose dominant sexual preference is for a person of the same sex.* In everyday language, *homosexual* designates a male whose preference is for a male; *lesbian* designates a female with a preference for a female.

The monumental 1948 Kinsey study on male sexuality revealed the prevalence of homosexual acts in American society.[2] Excluding prepuberty homosexual behavior (which about 60 percent of the males in the study had experienced), Kinsey found that by age 45, 37 percent of the males in the study had had at least one homosexual experience leading to orgasm. Such experiences were far more common among single people of both sexes than among married people. Thus, by 45 about 50 percent of the single males and 26 percent of the single females in the study had had such a homosexual encounter. In contrast, by age 45 about 10 percent of the married males and 3 percent of the married females had had a similar experience.

Kinsey's data, which indicated that about 2 to 4 percent of the adult population was homosexual, have been subsequently strengthened by other studies in the United States, Sweden, and Germany. Further confirming evidence comes from the U.S. Armed Forces, which rejects or discharges about 1 percent of their inductees because of homosexuality. (Presumably there are more homosexuals in the armed services who have been undetected.) The incidence of lesbianism appears to be about one-third that of male homosexuality.

It should be noted that Kinsey's data continue to be rejected by some people, even though his critics have not provided quantitative information of their own. Since Kinsey was tolerant of homosexuals, some critics claim that a disproportionately large number of homosexuals volunteered for his study. While Kinsey's findings cannot be taken as representative of the United States as a whole or as a current picture of homosexuality in the United States, they still represent the most extensive data available. Indeed, some would claim that Kinsey's statistics on the homosexual population must be considered conservative estimates of today's homosexual population.

Although the American Psychiatric Association has rejected the designation of homosexuality as an illness, many professionals hold different views. Freudian psychoanalysts, for example, claim that homosexuals suffer from stunted psychosexual development or develop their sexual preferences through conditioned responses to inappropriate sexual objects. More current research on homosexuality views it from a biological point, focusing on physical examination, chromosome and endocrine studies. So far such research has failed to identify any particular biological difference between homosexuals and heterosexuals.

Even more recent studies have concentrated on the family relations homosexual men had as young boys. These findings are consistent with the general observations about the childhoods of many homosexuals—the essential pattern is one of a dominant mother and a passive father.

In the midst of all this research, many homosexuals insist that they have freely chosen a homosexual life style. They do not view their homosexual proclivities as an illness. Indeed, if anyone is ill, they say, it is society which suffers from narrow-mindedness and intolerance. Given the inconclusiveness of the data available, it is probably best to view homosexual acts as similar to other

2. A. C. Kinsey, W. B. Pomeroy, and C. E. Martin, Sexual Behavior in the Human Male (Philadelphia: W. B. Saunders Co., 1948).

sexual acts, that is, as the result of an interaction of biological, psychological, and social forces.

Moral Assessments

While explanations for homosexuality are inconclusive, many have made moral judgments about homosexual behavior. For example, some claim that homosexuality is unnatural. They draw this conclusion by assuming that procreation is the primary function of sex. Since homosexual acts cannot result in procreation, homosexual behavior in this view is unnatural, and those engaging in such acts are thereby considered immoral.

The argument against this judgment is that procreation is not, in fact, the primary function of sex, or at least not exclusively so. Pleasure and love are also important components of sex. When either of these is taken as a function at least coequal with procreation, then homosexual acts intended to foster pleasure or love are not unnatural. And thus, those engaging in them are not immoral.

Others claim that homosexuality is wrong because many people find it repugnant. Perhaps they do. But this would only argue for the conclusion that *public* homosexual acts should be prohibited. What about homosexual acts conducted privately between consenting adults? Such private acts cannot be said to offend public taste. In fact, those who argue on behalf of the morality of homosexuality insist that regulation of private homosexual acts is an unjustifiable invasion of privacy and an unfair restraint on personal liberty.

Others claim that homosexuality is an abomination of God's law. Not only do specific sections of both the Old Testament and the New Testament prohibit homosexual behavior, most of the world's religions reject it as evil. But, one may ask, is this not a false appeal to authority? After all, religious laws have force only for those who subscribe to the religion, or to the belief in a God who has authored moral law. In addition, religious adherents themselves disagree on this issue. Some ministers of religion not only condone homosexuality but openly profess it as a personal life style which, they believe, is consistent with the law of God.

Still others object to homosexuality because it is a threat to the young. These critics claim that homosexuals set a bad example for children, openly proselyte for homosexuality and thus undermine traditional cultural values, or even prey on children. But "setting a bad example" is really an objection that begs the question, for the issue is whether or not homosexuality is bad to begin with. Those defending homosexuality point out that the life style of any adult can serve as a model for a young person. The issue is whether or not the life style of a homosexual is moral.

Regarding the alleged proselyting aspect of homosexual behavior, homosexuals and many nonhomosexuals alike have called the charge spurious. There is no evidence, they say, to support such a claim. In fact, the so-called gay liberation movement has been aimed almost exclusively at winning societal tolerance of, not adherence to, homosexuality. But even if homosexuals do proselyte for homosexuality, why does that necessarily pose a threat to society? The thrust of such a fear is that once we let homosexuality "out of the closet," then youth will march in lockstep to the beat of the homosexual drum. But such an assumption ignores the origins of homosexuality, which appear to be extremely complex.

In answer to the claim that homosexuals prey on children, it is true that some homosexuals have molested children. No one would seriously argue that this is anything but morally reprehensible. But homosexual child molesters are atypical of the whole population of homosexuals. To infer that all or most or even a large number of homosexuals represent a clear and present danger to children on the basis of the behavior of a few homosexuals is, to say the least, a hasty conclusion. Besides, apologists for homosexuality often point out, statistics show that most child molesters are heterosexual; generally, they are adult males who prey on female children.

Extramarital Sex

Initial Considerations

Extramarital sex, often termed adultery, *refers to having sexual intercourse with someone other than one's marriage partner.* Although extramarital sex traditionally has been condemned in Western society, it continues to flourish. Current estimates indicate that by the time they reach 45, about 50 percent of married men and about 25 percent of married women eventually commit adultery. But among young women the rate is quickly approaching the male rate, as the "double standard," which traditionally has tolerated male but not female indiscretions, slowly dissolves.

The *Playboy* magazine survey of sexual behavior (1974)[3] revealed several findings that bear on traditional moral assessments of extramarital sex. First, in most cases the partner engaging in the extramarital sex attempts to conceal it from the spouse. Second, extramarital affairs continue to result in conflict, often guilt, as the Kinsey study indicated 30 years ago. Finally, extramarital sex seems to be less gratifying than marital sex and often involves sexual malfunction.

Why do people engage in extramarital sex? In some cases, the reasons are practical: length of separation from spouse, debilitating illness of spouse, lack of interest, sexual malfunction. In other cases, marital sex is available but inadequate, unexciting, or unfulfilling. In still other cases, individuals simply eschew traditional marital expectations that marriage partners can be all things to each other. Whatever the reason for the extramarital sex, in most cases far more than the sexual act appears to be involved. Much extramarital behavior can be traced to certain psychological events in a person's life or to particular time intervals in the marriage.

Moral Assessments

One of the strongest arguments proposed against extramarital sex is that it violates the contract that the partners have entered into. Implied in the conven-

3. *M. Hunt,* Sexual Behavior in the 1970's *(Chicago: Playboy Press, 1974).*

tional marriage contract is a pledge of sexual exclusivity. Since extramarital sex violates this pledge, it is wrong.

Those defending the morality of at least some acts of extramarital sex claim that if the relation is kept secret, then the partner does not get hurt. But noninjury is really irrelevant, because the agreement is still violated. A more pertinent response, therefore, introduces marriages that do not involve even an implied pledge of sexual exclusivity—for example, the so-called "open marriage." Such an arrangement seems to meet the violation-of-trust objection to extramarital sex.

But many condemn extramarital sex even in cases of "open marriage." They argue that extramarital sex can injure the betrayed partner emotionally and psychologically. In the final analysis, extramarital sex implies rejection of one spouse by the other. However sophisticated the partners think they are or claim to be, feelings of inadequacy, dissatisfaction, and failure are bound to creep in. In fact, the *Playboy* survey indirectly supports this claim. Of the couples surveyed, 80 to 90 percent found the prospect of marital infidelity by a spouse unacceptable. Still, there may be instances in which a spouse may be genuinely unaffected by the extramarital relations of the partner. A blanket condemnation of extramarital sex ignores these cases, as few as they may be.

But even when injury to a spouse is not a significant factor, critics often argue that extramarital sex remains a mockery to the traditional concept of marriage. True, dishonesty and deception may not be involved in the adultery, nor injury to the spouse for that matter. But marriage has a social component that extramarital sex flouts. In short, extramarital sex does injury to the institution of marriage by sullying its traditional meaning, significance, and function. But, skeptics have asked, is this not just an appeal to traditional wisdom? Indeed, some have advocated a reassessment of the marital institution, including a reevaluation of the conventional roles that spouses play and the propriety of what is expected of them.

Premarital Sex

Initial Considerations

Premarital sex continues to be the major issue in sexual morality. Since those involved usually are young, parents and society traditionally have discouraged premarital encounters in order to protect adolescents from damage to personality, career, marital prospects, and so on. Of course, the overriding concern and fear used to be pregnancy. However, social attitudes are changing, largely due to the variety of contraceptives, especially the "pill," which social scientist Ashley Montagu ranks in social significance with the discovery of fire, learning how to make tools, and the harnessing of nuclear energy.[4]

Several studies conducted over the past ten years indicate that the incidence of premarital sex is increasing, especially among the young. For example,

4. *Ashley Montagu,* Sex, Man and Society *(New York: Tower Publications, 1969), p. 11.*

Kantner and Zelnik reported that in 1971 nearly 28 percent of the never-married female population aged 15 to 19 had had some coital experience. Their survey also indicated that intercourse was beginning at younger ages and that its extent among teenagers was increasing.[5]

The *Playboy* survey (1974) cited earlier indicated that the percentage of married persons between the ages of 18 and 24 who had sexual intercourse prior to marriage was 95 percent for males and 81 percent for females. Similarly, a survey conducted by Sorenson in 1973 showed that of the sampled adolescents between ages 13 and 19, 52 percent had had some premarital intercourse (50 percent of the boys, 45 percent of the girls). Of this group 13 percent (17 percent boys, 7 percent girls) had their first experience at age 12 or younger. By age 15, 71 percent of the boys and 56 percent of the girls in the nonvirgin group had engaged in coitus.[6]

The remarkable apparent increase in the prevalence of premarital sex, especially among the young, testifies to the marked changes that have occurred since Kinsey conducted his monumental investigation of sexual behavior. But in one very important respect things have not changed much at all: The majority of premarital sexual acts continues to occur between those who hope to marry. Kinsey found this to be so; so do all recent surveys.

What effect, if any, does premarital sex have on later marriage? Does premarital sex increase one's chances of a successful marriage? Does it help produce compatible marital partners? Undoubtedly the connection between premarital sex and marriage is important sociologically. It is also important morally, arising often in debates about the morality of premarital sex. So far, however, research has failed to turn up any significant connection between premarital sex and marriage.

With these preliminary considerations behind us, we now turn to the common arguments for and against premarital sex. We will present these arguments in a dialogue format: One imaginary person makes a point and another responds with a counterpoint. The tone of these exchanges is informal, even colloquial at times. This is intentional. The tone should brighten up what could otherwise be the dreary task of reading formal argument after formal argument. We will use this format throughout the remainder of the text.

Arguments Against Premarital Sex

1. *It is against God's law.*

POINT: "It's fashionable today to speak of 'affairs,' 'relationships,' 'involvements,' and even 'things' when what we really mean is *sex*. Let's stop kidding ourselves. There's a term for premarital sex no matter who it involves, where it goes on, or what the reasons are. *Fornication. Fornication* is a Biblical term for sex that goes on before marriage. And we all know what the Bible says

5. *J. F. Kantner and M. Zelnik, "Sexual Experience of Young Unmarried Women in the United States,"* Family Planning Perspectives, 4 *(October 1972), pp. 9–18.*

6. *R. C. Sorenson,* Adolescent Sexuality in Contemporary America (The Sorensen Report) *(New York: World Publishing Co., 1973).*

about fornication: It's wrong. No *if*'s, *and*'s or *but*'s about it. Fornication by any other name is still sinful.''

COUNTERPOINT: ''What you say probably carries a lot of weight with people who believe like you do. But I don't. Before you can persuade me that premarital sex violates the law of God, you're going to have to convince me that God exists, that the Bible is the inspired word of God, and that the Bible absolutely prohibits every act of premarital sex. Now that's a tall order. But if you expect me to take you seriously, you're just going to have to fill it.''

2. *It undermines marriage.*

POINT: ''Let's face it, premarital sex torpedoes the whole institution of marriage. After all, who's going to get married if they can sample all the 'goodies' with none of the headaches? Not many. And if marriage breaks down, what happens to the family? It collapses, that's what happens. And with it goes our whole society because, as everybody knows, the family is the cornerstone of society. Why is premarital sex wrong? I'll tell you in a nutshell: It destroys marriage, the family, and society.''

COUNTERPOINT: ''You make it sound like no one who has premarital sex will ever marry. That's just not true. Check the record: People are marrying as much as ever, even those who have premarital sex. Who knows, premarital sex may even help marriages out. But there's no evidence that it discourages people from marrying.''

3. *Unwanted children can result.*

POINT: ''The only foolproof contraceptive is abstinence. Don't kid yourself: Anybody who 'does it' risks a pregnancy. When couples are married, they can properly take care of offspring. But when they're not, they can't. So what do they do? Have an abortion or bring a kid into the world under really insecure conditions. Either way, they act immorally.''

COUNTERPOINT: ''You know as well as I that most of us who have premarital sex believe in the 'better-safe-than-sorry' philosophy. We use contraceptives; and while they're not foolproof, they're pretty safe. But even if kids do result, what makes you so sure they won't be loved and cared for just as much as if the parents were married? Plenty of mothers, and fathers too, do a beautiful job raising kids on their own. I don't know why you assume that children can only or best be raised in a so-called traditional family. You have no way of knowing that, since society has never seriously allowed any other alternative.''

4. *Premarital sex encourages transitory relationships and promiscuity.*

POINT: ''We're living in a time when men and women enter into relationships with each other very lightly, and discard them just as casually. These kinds of relationships are bittersweet at best. Often they're really damaging to the participants; they leave them emotional wrecks whose pieces society must eventually pick up. One of the big reasons for these transitory relationships is that too many people are looking out only for themselves. The fact is that premarital sex encourages people to pursue only their own pleasures, without accepting responsibility for their actions and how they affect others. And if that weren't enough, it also encourages promiscuity by saying to people: Go ahead; have sex anytime you feel like with whoever you want. Promiscuous people aren't happy; and they're not solid members of society. So the bottom line is that premarital sex is wrong because it encourages transitory relationships and promiscuity, neither of which is good for individuals or society."

COUNTERPOINT: "I don't doubt that lots of men and women have short-lived relationships and that there seem to be more of these relationships than ever. I don't even doubt that as a result society is quickly getting populated with an army of the walking wounded. But at the same time plenty of unmarried men and women have mature, long-term, and thoroughly enriching relationships that happen to involve sex without marriage. Some of these relationships even lead to marriage. Certainly you can't call such relationships transitory. And you can't call them promiscuous—if by promiscuity you mean the frequent changing of one's sexual partners. Sure, some people who have premarital sex are promiscuous. But so are some married people. What are you going to conclude then—that marriage encourages promiscuity?"

Arguments for Premarital Sex

1. *Premarital sex is strictly a private matter.*

POINT: "When all's said and done, the key point is that premarital sex is strictly a private matter. If two individuals freely consent to have sex with each other before marriage, fully aware of each other's intentions and motives, then it's strictly their own affair. The only moral issue is that they be honest with each other and respectful of each other's feelings. But whether or not they should have sex—that's their own affair, no one else's."

COUNTERPOINT: "You overlook many aspects of premarital sex that make it more than the participants' 'own affair.' One of these is disease. Statistics show a direct correlation between an increase in premarital sex and an increase in V.D. Even you would admit that society has a legitimate interest in controlling V.D. Another aspect of premarital sex is the ever-present danger of an unwanted pregnancy. What happens then? The woman has either an abortion or the child. Abortion is more than a private affair, you know. Society has a stake in just how we're going to consider and treat fetal life. And what about the fetus itself? You can bet that if it could speak, it would have something to say on its own behalf. If the woman has the child, who will care for it if she and the father can't or won't? Whose name will it have? If the couple decides to marry just to give the child a name, what effect will this have on the marriage and on the child when he or she later finds out? Sure, these questions are intensely personal. But they're of social concern, too. And those who have premarital sex have to recognize the social implications of their acts. They also have to see that in violating society's norms they hurt society itself. Traditionally our society has frowned on premarital sex;

it has considered sex something to be reserved for the sanctity and stability of a marital relationship. Whether you agree with this standard or not is really irrelevant. In flouting it you do harm to society. So, far from being strictly a personal matter, premarital sex raises serious social questions.

  2. *To expect celibacy is unrealistic, unreasonable, and unfair.*

POINT: "Everybody knows how much our society emphasizes sex. Films, T.V., books, commercials—they're all full of it. We're bombarded with *sex-sell* from the time we're kids. Then when we get old enough to do something about it, society says, "Uh-uh, look but don't touch. Save it for marriage." But at the same time we have to delay marriage because of the demands for professional education. So, the average Joe and Jane are expected to remain chaste during their most sexually active period, between puberty and marriage—and to do it after society has worked them up to a sexual fever pitch! This is not only the height of hypocrisy; it's also unrealistic, unreasonable, and unfair. The fact that many of us have premarital sex points to the almost irresistible sex drive that most normal humans feel. Prolonged sublimation of these urges can actually blunt one's sexuality. But even if it doesn't, it's totally unreasonable to expect someone to deny 'what comes naturally.' "

COUNTERPOINT: "Why do you insist on viewing human sexual passion as simply a blind and immensely powerful force? Don't you realize that in so doing you portray human sexuality as akin to animal sexuality? What you overlook is the human significance of sex, which is essentially bound up with love. When you deny the human significance of sex, you dehumanize human sex, as well as humans themselves. You talk about what's 'unrealistic' and 'unreasonable.' Well, what's so unrealistic about expecting humans to exercise a uniquely human behavioral characteristic, self-control? What's so unreasonable about expecting humans to put sex in a human perspective? Humans can make choices, you know. You make it appear as if they can't, that we're all compelled to act on the basis of some 'irresistible drive.' There's nothing at all irresistible about the sex drive, unless you happen to be a rabbit. Quite the opposite. What makes human sexuality unique is that it's subject to control and direction. To deny this is to deny what's fundamentally human."

  3. *Premarital sex promotes sexual compatibility.*

POINT: "One of the old saws of our society is that sexual behavior is just as natural as falling off a log. Nobody needs any practice, skills, or techniques to perform sexually. This attitude reduces sex to biological coupling. But a sexual relationship is far more than that. It's a complex phenomenon and requires a great deal of knowledge, ability, and compatibility. To perform sexually, and not just couple, we have to feel comfortable sexually with ourselves and others. To say that people can or should learn all they need to know about sexual per- formance after marrying is to minimize the importance of sex in marriage. It's one thing to find out your spouse doesn't like chopped liver or the opera; it's another to discover your spouse is a dud in bed. Of course sex isn't the only thing in marriage. But it's a really important part of it. People who intend to marry owe it to themselves and their partners to find out as much about themselves sexually as they can *before* marrying. Marriage holds enough surprises without making sex one of them!"

COUNTERPOINT: "I can't believe you! Listening to you, a person would swear that the only place to learn about sex is on a waterbed! Aren't you aware of the spate of readily available material that makes what you say highly doubtful? All the books and classes on sex, marriage, and family make personal sexual experience far less important than it was in the past. What's more, by stressing sexual knowledge and compatibility, you make sexual attraction the sole basis for a relationship. But anyone who's married knows that marriage entails a lot more than sex. Plenty of married couples who, by your standards, are 'sexually incompatible' are nonetheless fulfilled in marriage in many other ways. If they used premarital sexual compatibility as a standard, they probably never would have married. But beyond this, even granting that premarital sex can be an invaluable source of one's own and others' sexuality, think about all the risks that are involved: the instability of the relationship, the reduction of each other to sex objects, the possibility of pregnancy. Then there's one obvious fact you overlook: Premarital sexual compatibility does not guarantee marital sexual compatibility, let alone successful marriages. Plenty of couples who successfully experiment before marriage discover sexual problems after they marry—because marriage presents a whole set of unique problems that can affect sex. For example, many married couples have sex problems as a direct result of financial or occupational problems. Before they married they didn't have to deal with these problems, or at least not in the same way they did after marriage. So, premarital relations don't serve as a valid test of marital sexual compatibility."

Ethical Theories

Egoism

For egoists, the morality of any act of sex outside marriage would depend on a calculation of the long-term consequences for the self. The calculation would include such consequential considerations as the possibility of pregnancy, the emotional and psychological benefits and risks, the sexual knowledge of oneself that might be acquired, the sexual experience one might derive, and the sexual proficiency one could develop. Essentially nonconsequential considerations such as obeying the law of God, maintaining the institution of marriage, and respecting the inherent privacy of the act generally would not figure in the egoist's calculation (although an egoist with a strong religious background might wonder about subsequent feelings of guilt and remorse). Similarly, essentially utilitarian considerations such as the effects of premarital sex on the institution of marriage or on society as a whole would be largely irrelevant to the egoist, unless of course they could be shown to affect one's own long-term happiness.

In the final analysis, if the calculation indicated that more long-term happiness for self would accrue from engaging in premarital sex than in refraining from it, then the egoist would consider such an act not only justifiable but obligatory.

Act Utilitarianism

Utilitarians would consider the issue of sex outside marriage from the view of social utility. Act utilitarians would consider what, if anything, makes an act of sex outside marriage right. If the specific act was more productive of the social good than any other alternative, then it would be right; if not, then it would be wrong. The act utilitarian's calculation would include the likely physical, emotional, and intellectual impact of the act on the participants and on significant others in their lives—spouses, children, parents, close friends. But also considered would be the potential impact on other affiliations of the engaging parties, such as professional, business, or religious associations. In addition, act utilitarians would consider the likely effect of the behavior on the morals of society at large, for example on the value that people place on marital fidelity.

The key factor from the act utilitarian's viewpoint is that, while specific acts of sex outside marriage are to be isolated from other similar acts in the moral calculation, they are not exclusively private, but also social in nature. In short, for the act utilitarian the morality of a particular act of sex outside marriage would depend on particular social conditions, on an independent calculation of social desirability. It is conceivable, of course, that by this standard, sex outside marriage could be morally justifiable. Thus the act utilitarian would reject the proposition that sex outside marriage is always morally objectionable.

Rule Utilitarianism

Rule utilitarians would ask whether the act of sex outside marriage conforms with or violates a rule that is justifiable on the basis of utility. Unlike act utilitarians, rulists would not be concerned with whether or not the particular act of sex outside marriage would produce the greatest amount of social good. Rather, rulists would look at the rule under which the act fell and whether that rule was productive of the most social good. If the rule was, then the act would be justifiable. Thus, is the rule that prohibits sex outside marriage productive of more social good than its contradiction, which would allow for at least some sex outside marriage? Is the proposed rule useful for an individual to accept and a society to sanction?

Traditionally, the rule prohibiting sex outside marriage has received a social utility defense as follows. Family stability is vital to the rearing of children and the consequent welfare of society. Marital fidelity is necessary for establishing and maintaining stable family units. Sex confined to marriage cements the relationship between husband and wife that is necessary for producing stable family units. Furthermore, the unavailability of sex outside marriage will likely keep marriages solid, indeed encourage people to get married. Thus, the rule that enjoins people from having sex outside marriage seems firmly based on considerations of social utility. At the same time, in theory, rule utilitarianism allows for rules to be qualified, so long as the qualifications do not make the rule inordinately complex or impractical. What these qualifications might be in this case is hard to say, and perhaps should be left to the professional rule utilitarian to specify. Without such qualifications, it seems that rule utilitarianism would more likely than not endorse the proscription against sex outside marriage.

Divine Command

Divine command theorists would determine whether an act of sex outside marriage corresponds with the law of God. Western religious tradition generally has taken the primary function of sex to be the insemination of wives by husbands—procreation. Sex also has a secondary, nonprocreative, companionate function, which is usually held to be achievable only within marriage. But even if this companionate function is achievable outside marriage, only the marital state is proper to the main function of sex—procreation. Thus, in keeping with God's will, individuals should confine sex to the marital state and, by implication, society ought to discourage sex outside marriage. It seems, then, the divine command would support the contention that sex outside marriage is always morally objectionable.

Categorical Imperative

An application of Kant's categorical imperative suggests the same conclusions as warranted by divine command. To see this we must first ask whether the maxim, "Sex outside marriage is always morally objectionable," is universalizable. Like divine command theorists, Kant would look on sex as functioning mainly for procreation. Yes, he would agree, sex in many instances is pleasurable, but pleasure is not its primary function. Therefore, to have intercourse while obstructing the possibility of procreation would be to act inconsistently with the primary, natural function of sex.

Of course, such a conclusion addresses only the issue of contraception. While many acts of sex outside marriage involve contraception and could be viewed as wrong on that basis, many do not. How would Kant's theory judge, for example, the unmarried couple who engages in sex fully intending to procreate? Can the maxim that sanctions sex outside marriage so long as the sex is intended for procreation be universalized?

Building on the point that the natural primary function of sex is to preserve the species, Kant would argue that preservation of the species involves more than just biological reproduction. It extends to the proper rearing of children, which presumably includes ensuring their physical, intellectual, and moral welfare. Essential to this and to the nature of society as a whole are stable family units. The limitation of sex to marriage is a necessary condition of forming and maintaining stable family units. Thus, the maxim that would allow sex outside marriage logically is incompatible with the institution of marriage and is, therefore, not universalizable. In brief, according to Kant's categorical imperative, sex outside marriage is never morally justifiable. Society should not condone it; individuals ought not engage in it.

Prima Facie Duties

The issue of sex outside marriage raises numerous prima facie duties that must be considered in order to determine one's actual duty. For example, adulterous relationships bring up duties of fidelity and noninjury to the spouse. Indeed, any act of sex outside marriage inevitably raises profound questions of emotional and psychological injury due to the psychological bonds that sex commonly forges. At the same time, one might recognize duties of self-improvement and beneficence in acts of sex outside marriage. For example, some psychiatrists point out that serious sexual dysfunctions afflict a large number of marriages. Such problems often can be traced to prohibitions against early childhood sexual experimentation and adolescent sexual intercourse. It is conceivable, then, that based on such observations, one might argue a duty of self-improvement in at least some acts of sex outside marriage. In addition, it is at least possible that some acts of sex outside marriage are beneficent in that they dislodge sexual blocks that are preventing individuals from functioning in a personally fulfilling way. In such instances, refusal to engage in sexual acts could further damage those individuals.

Apparently, then, Ross's prima facie duties do not provide such clear-cut direction on the issue of sex outside marriage as, say, divine command and the categorical imperative do. Figuring prominently in Ross's calculation, however, would be duties of noninjury. In a multiple-duty situation, one always has an obligation to prevent injury to another if injury is possible. While it is true that in some instances one could be injuring another by not having sex, in many more cases one risks injuring self and others by having sex outside marriage. Physical, emotional, psychological, or moral injury—any of these can easily be present in any act of sex outside marriage. So, Ross's duty of nonmaleficence (noninjury) would be given scrupulous attention by a prima facie duty theorist considering the issue of sex outside marriage. But, admittedly, when all the prima facie duties involved have been thoroughly scrutinized, one's actual duty may be to have sex outside marriage. Thus, Ross's theory would support neither the proposition that sex outside marriage is always morally objectionable nor, by implication, a social prohibition of sex outside marriage.

Maximin Principle

In addition to his two basic principles of justice, Rawls is aware of the need for principles that bind and guide individuals as moral decision makers. Thus, he offers his "natural duties," which, in effect, are identical to Ross's prima facie duties. A consideration of these duties would be just as important for Rawls as for Ross. Unfortunately, neither theorist ranks the duties, with the exception of giving noninjury a standing priority. So, while Rawls would certainly introduce natural duties, such as noninjury and promise keeping, into an evaluation of sex outside marriage, his list of natural duties does not in itself provide a decisive position on the issue.

Rawls's equal liberty principle, however, does seem to reject a prohibition against all acts of sex outside marriage. Given the original position, rational, self-interested people, who are aware of their needs and interests, surely would not bind themselves by such a policy that would proscribe sex outside marriage. Their reason would be recognition that marriage simply may not be an acceptable life style for them. They would realize, too, that they might never want to marry, or never be fortunate enough to succeed at it. At the same time, people in the original position would be aware of their sexual needs, interests, and capacities, and expect to have the greatest amount of freedom to pursue their sexual desires that is consistent with a like freedom for all. A prohibition against sex outside marriage seems incompatible with this equal liberty principle.

Thus, Rawls's theory leads us to conclude that at least some acts of sex outside marriage are morally justifiable, and that society would not be morally justified in proscribing all sexual acts outside marriage. On the personal level, Rawls, like Ross, would pay particular attention to those natural duties that generally regulate our conduct as individual moral agents. And, again like Ross, Rawls would give special consideration to the duty of noninjury in evaluating the morality of individual acts of sex outside marriage.

If our interpretations are correct, we are left with a curious mix of moral views regarding the personal and social dimensions of sex outside marriage. Divine command and the categorical imperative seemingly agree that on the personal and social levels sex outside marriage is always morally objectionable. Rule utilitarianism is not so absolutistic, but it does seem inclined to support the injunction against sex outside marriage. Act utilitarianism, however, rejects the prohibition, as do egoism, prima facie duty ethics, and maximin principle. The latter two decisively reject it on the social level, while cautioning individuals about duties in this area on the personal level.

Sex Without Love

Albert Ellis

In the following selection from his book Sex Without Guilt, *psychotherapist and marriage counselor Albert Ellis argues that love is not necessary for sex. He claims that while affectional sex (sex with love) may be more desirable than nonaffectional sex (sex without love), the former is not at all necessary.*

Ellis offers several reasons for his view. Among them are the facts that many individuals do enjoy nonaffectional sex, that in its biological phase sex is essentially nonaffectional, and that many people have no capacity for affection or love. What about those individuals in society, especially many women, who say they enjoy sex only when it is accompanied by affection? Such people are kidding themselves, says Ellis. If they were honest with themselves, they would acknowledge that sex without love is pleasurable.

Ellis also responds to his critics, those who argue against nonaffectional love. One of their arguments is what we would call an egoistic consideration. Thus, those who criticize nonaffectional

---

sex sometimes claim that individuals who have nonloving instead of loving sex are opting for immediate gratification at the expense of long-term enjoyment. Ellis admits that this might be true but only if these individuals generally restrict their sex relations to the nonaffectional kind. If they have nonaffectional sex only occasionally, and otherwise engage in sex with love, then in his view they are giving up very little, if any, enjoyment. They might even be gaining some.

In addition, those opposing nonaffectional sex claim that by deferring sex relations until affectional sex comes along, one will have greater pleasure. Ellis finds no evidence to support this claim. But even if individuals do "save" themselves for sex with love, Ellis questions whether their total satisfaction necessarily will be greater.

A further argument advanced by those against sex without love is essentially utilitarian. They claim that if society openly permitted sex without love, it would drive out affectional sex (with, presumably, disastrous consequences for marriage, the family, and society as a whole). But Ellis finds no evidence to support this hypothesis. In fact, his clinical experience shows that those who are capable of affectional sex seek and find it: Those who remain nonaffectional in their sex relations generally are incapable of sex with love.

Ellis's essay is well worth study because it raises questions about the connection between love and sex. As we saw earlier in this chapter, the relation between love and sex is something that any fundamental standard for sexual behavior should address.

A scientific colleague of mine, who holds a professorial post in the department of sociology and anthropology at one of our leading universities, recently asked me about my stand on the question of human beings having sex relations without love. Although I have taken something of a position on this issue in my book, *The American Sexual Tragedy*, I have never quite considered the problem in sufficient detail. So here goes.

In general, I feel that affectional, as against nonaffectional, sex relations are *desirable* but not *necessary*. It is usually desirable that an association between coitus and affection exist—particularly in marriage, because it is often difficult for two individuals to keep finely tuned to each other over a period of years, and if there is not a good deal of love between them, one may tend to feel sexually imposed upon by the other.

The fact, however, that the coexistence of sex and love may be desirable does not, to my mind, make it necessary. My reasons for this view are several:

1. Many individuals—including, even, many married couples—*do* find great satisfaction in having sex relations without love. I do not consider it fair to label these individuals as criminal just because they may be in the minority.

Moreover, even if they are in the minority (as may well *not* be the case), I am sure that they number literally millions of men and women. If so, they constitute a sizeable subgroup of humans

whose rights to sex satisfaction should be fully acknowledged and protected.

2. Even if we consider the supposed majority of individuals who find greater satisfaction in sex-love than in sex-sans-love relations, it is doubtful if all or most of them do so for *all* their lives. During much of their existence, especially their younger years, these people tend to find sex-without-love quite satisfying, and even to prefer it to affectional sex.

When they become older, and their sex drives tend to wane, they may well emphasize coitus with rather than without affection. But why should we condemn them *while* they still prefer sex to sex-love affairs?

3. Many individuals, especially females in our culture, who say that they only enjoy sex when it is accompanied by affection are actually being unthinkingly conformist and unconsciously hypocritical. If they were able to contemplate themselves objectively, and had the courage of their inner convictions, they would find sex without love eminently gratifying.

This is not to say that they would *only* enjoy nonaffectional coitus, nor that they would always find it *more* satisfying than affectional sex. But, in the depths of their psyche and soma, they would deem sex without love pleasurable *too*.

And why should they not? And why should we, by our puritanical know-nothingness, force these individuals to drive a considerable portion of their sex feelings and potential satisfactions underground?

If, in other words, we view sexuo-amative relations as desirable rather than necessary, we sanction the innermost thoughts and drives of many of our fellowmen and fellowwomen to have sex *and* sex-love relations. If we take the opposing view, we hardly destroy these innermost thoughts and drives, but frequently tend to intensify them while denying them open and honest outlet. This, as Freud pointed out, is one of the main (though by no means the only) source of rampant neurosis.

4. I firmly believe that sex is a biological, as well as a social, drive, and that in its biological phases it is essentially nonaffectional. If this is so, then we can expect that, however we try to civilize the sex drives—and civilize them to *some* degree we certainly must—there will always be an underlying tendency for them to escape from our society-inculcated shackles and to be still partly felt in the raw.

When so felt, when our biosocial sex urges lead us to desire and enjoy sex without (as well as with), love, I do not see why we should make their experiences feel needlessly guilty.

5. Many individuals—many millions in our society, I am afraid—have little or no capacity for affection or love. The majority of these individuals, perhaps, are emotionally disturbed, and should preferably be helped to increase their affectional propensities. But a large number are not particularly disturbed, and instead are neurologically or cerebrally deficient.

Mentally deficient persons, for example, as well as many dull normals (who, together, include several million citizens of our nation) are notoriously shallow in their feelings, and probably intrinsically so. Since these kinds of individuals—like the neurotic and the organically deficient—are for the most part, in our day and age, *not* going to be properly treated and *not* going to overcome their deficiencies, and since most of them definitely *do* have sex desires, I again see no point in making them guilty when they have nonloving sex relations.

Surely these unfortunate individuals are sufficiently handicapped by their disturbances or impairments without our adding to their woes by anathematizing them when they manage to achieve some nonamative sexual release.

6. Under some circumstances—though these,

I admit, may be rare—some people find more satisfaction in nonloving coitus even though, under other circumstances, these *same* people may find more satisfaction in sex-love affairs. Thus, the man who *normally* enjoys being with his girlfriend because he loves as well as is sexually attracted to her, may occasionally find immense satisfaction in being with another girl with whom he has distinctly nonloving relations.

Granting that this may be (or is it?) unusual, I do not see why it should be condemnable.

7. If many people get along excellently and most cooperatively with business partners, employees, professors, laboratory associates, acquaintances, and even spouses for whom they have little or no love or affection, but with whom they have certain specific things in common, I do not see why there cannot be individuals who get along excellently and most cooperatively with sex mates with whom they may have little else in common.

I personally can easily see the tragic plight of a man who spends much time with a girl with whom he has nothing in common but sex: since I believe that life is too short to be well consumed in relatively one-track or intellectually low-level pursuits. I would also think it rather unrewarding for a girl to spend much time with a male with whom she had mutually satisfying sex, friendship, and cultural interests but no love involvement. This is because I would like to see people, in their 70-odd years of life, have maximum rather than minimum satisfactions with individuals of the other sex with whom they spend considerable time.

I can easily see, however, even the most intelligent and highly cultured individuals spending a *little* time with members of the other sex with whom they have common sex and cultural but no real love interests. And I feel that, for the time expended in this manner, their lives may be immeasurably enriched.

Moreover, when I encounter friends or psychotherapy clients who become enamored and spend considerable time and effort thinking about and being with a member of the other sex with whom they are largely sexually obsessed, and for whom they have little or no love, I mainly view these sexual infatuations as one of the penalties of their being human. For humans are the kind of animals who are easily disposed to this type of behavior.

I believe that one of the distinct inconveniences or tragedies of human sexuality is that it endows us, and perhaps particularly the males among us, with a propensity to become exceptionally involved and infatuated with members of the other sex whom, had we no sex urges, we would hardly notice. That is too bad; and it might well be a better world if it were otherwise. But it is *not* otherwise, and I think it is silly and pernicious for us to condemn ourselves because we are the way that we are in this respect.

We had better *accept* our biosocial tendencies, or our fallible humanity—instead of constantly blaming ourselves and futilely trying to change certain of its relatively harmless, though still somewhat tragic, aspects.

For reasons such as these, I feel that although it is usually—if not always—*desirable* for human beings to have sex relations with those they love rather than with those they do not love, it is by no means *necessary* that they do so. When we teach that it *is* necessary, we only needlessly condemn millions of our citizens to self-blame and atonement.

The position which I take—that there are several good reasons why affectional, as against nonaffectional, sex relations are desirable but not necessary—can be assailed on several counts. I shall now consider some of the objections to this position to see if they cannot be effectively answered.

It may be said that an individual who has nonloving instead of loving sex relations is not necessarily wicked but that he is self-defeating because, while going for immediate gratification, he will miss out on even greater enjoyments. But this would only be true if such an individual (whom we shall assume, for the sake of discussion, *would* get greater enjoyment from affectional sex relations than from nonaffectional ones) were *usually* or *always* having nonaffectionate coitus. If he were *occasionally* or *sometimes* having sex without love, and the rest of the time having sex with love, he would be missing out on very little, if any, enjoyment.

Under these circumstances, in fact, he would normally get *more* pleasure from *sometimes* having sex without love. For the fact remains, and must not be unrealistically ignored, that in our present-day society sex without love is *much more frequently* available than sex with love.

Consequently, to ignore nonaffectional coitus when affectional coitus is not available would, from the standpoint of enlightened self-interest, be sheer folly. In relation both to immediate *and* greater enjoyment, the individual would thereby be losing out.

The claim can be made of course that if an individual sacrifices sex without love *now* he will experience more pleasure by having sex with love in the future. This is an interesting claim; but I find no empirical evidence to sustain it. In fact, on theoretical grounds it seems most unlikely that it will be sustained. It is akin to the claim that if an individual starves himself for several days in a row he will greatly enjoy eating a meal at the end of a week or a month. I am sure he will—provided that he is then not too sick or debilitated to enjoy anything! But, even assuming that such an individual derives enormous satisfaction from his one meal a week or a month, is his *total* satisfaction greater than it would have been had he enjoyed three good meals a day for that same period of time? I doubt it.

So with sex. Anyone who starves himself sexually for a long period of time—as virtually everyone who rigidly sticks to the sex with love doctrine must—will (perhaps) *ultimately* achieve greater satisfaction when he does find sex with love than he would have had, had he been sexually freer. But, even assuming that this is so, will his *total* satisfaction be greater?

It may be held that if both sex with and without love are permitted in any society, the nonaffectional sex will drive out affectional sex, somewhat in accordance with Gresham's laws of currency. On the contrary, however, there is much reason to believe that just because an individual has sex relations, for quite a period, on a nonaffectional basis, he will be more than eager to replace it, eventually, with sex with love.

From my clinical experience, I have often found that males who most want to settle down to having a single mistress or wife are those who have tried numerous lighter affairs and found them wanting. The view that sex without love eradicates the need for affectional sex relationships is somewhat akin to the ignorance is bliss theory. For it virtually says that if people never experienced sex with love they would never realize how good it was and therefore would never strive for it. Or else the proponents of this theory seem to be saying that sex without love is so greatly satisfying, and sex with love so intrinsically difficult and disadvantageous to attain, that given the choice between the two, most people would pick the former. If this is so, then by all means let them pick the former: with which, in terms of their greater and total happiness, they would presumably be better off.

I doubt however, that this hypothesis *is* factually sustainable. From clinical experience, again, I can say that individuals who are capable of sex with love usually seek and find it; while those who remain nonaffectional in their sex affairs generally are not particularly capable of sex with love and need psychotherapeutic help before they can become thus capable.

Questions for Analysis

1. *Pick out one example each of provincialism, false appeal to authority, ambiguity, and the straw man in Ellis's essay. Can you spot any other fallacies?*

2. *Do you think that Ellis successfully refutes the claim of those who say they enjoy only affectional sex (argument 3)?*

3. *Which determinant of sex, if any, does Ellis seem particularly mindful of?*

4. *Ellis says, "When we teach that it is necessary [love for sex], we only needlessly condemn millions of our citizens to self-blame and atonement." Do you agree? Is this argument essentially a utilitarian one?*

5. *Ellis's theory is that love, while perhaps desirable, is not necessary for sex. Is this claim compatible with divine command? With the categorical imperative? With the maximin principle?*

The Human Venture in Sex, Love and Marriage

Peter A. Bertocci

In contrast with Ellis's position is the position held by philosophy professor Peter A. Bertocci, who defends the human significance of sex in love. In this selection from his book The Human Venture in Sex, Love and Marriage, *Bertocci begins by attacking the egoistic position that associates sex exclusively with self-satisfaction. In Bertocci's view, sex that has self-satisfaction as its primary goal is not as fulfilling as sex dedicated to other objectives.*

Bertocci takes issue with those who view human life, including sex, as essentially no different from the life of higher animals. In such a view, the sexual behavior of humans is as automatic and mechanical as it is in other animals. Thus, from this strictly biological viewpoint, the only relevant arguments against, say, premarital sex relate to the physical effects of sexual promiscuity, the danger of sexual diseases, and the possibility of pregnancy. But Bertocci feels that this biological perspective neglects the human significance of sex, which must take into consideration the human's total psychological being. When the total human is taken into account, then a whole cluster of other arguments against sex outside marriage arise.

The thrust of Bertocci's argument is that the meaning and value of sex cannot be divorced from the meaning and value of life itself. For Bertocci, love, marriage, and family are among the

From Peter A. Bertocci, The Human Venture in Sex, Love and Marriage *(Chicago: Association Press/Follett Publishing Company, 1949), pp. 61–71, 95–106, 110–115. Reprinted by permission of Follett Publishing Company, a division of Follett Corporation.*

"supreme values of human existence." Thus, he feels that sex must be viewed and understood within the context of love, marriage, and family.

Bertocci goes on to develop a "love progression," in which love leads to marriage, marriage to family, family to social responsibility. He feels that sex lust (or nonaffectional sex, to use Ellis's term), while pleasurable and seemingly satisfactory in itself, is ultimately inadequate because it does not tap into this love progression, which brings completeness, growth in character and personality, and a sense of social responsibility. Indeed, sex love (or affectional sex) without marriage is inadequate for the same reasons.

In short, love, marriage, family, and social responsibility are the highest values of human existence, according to Bertocci. If sex is to provide its deepest, most lasting, and most profound satisfaction, it must symbolically express these other values.

The Significance of Sexual Intercourse in Married Life

In trying to give Harry and Judith a reasonable answer [to the question of why it may be wrong for two persons who care for each other to have intercourse before marriage] we must assume that the basic motive behind their desire for premarital sexual intercourse is love. Judith and Harry are not in lust with each other, but in love with each other. The main motive is not exploitation, not the pleasure of satisfying sexual desire as such, but the desire to express in a physical way the unity that they feel spiritually. The sexual act would here symbolize the yearning of each person to unite himself more completely with the beloved; it becomes one of the best ways of saying, "I love you."

It is because we believe that this motive is psychologically and ethically sound that we wish to elaborate further what seems to be the profoundest meaning of the sexual act, before trying to show that sexual intercourse before marriage endangers that meaning. We cannot take the argument on its own ground without evaluating the place of sex in the marriage of lovers.

The act of sexual intercourse between a man and a woman gives pleasure at the purely biological level. As the expression of feelings that involve their whole psychophysical being, especially when they are stirred to a high emotional pitch, it is highly satisfying. The psychological satisfaction is deepest when the couple experience orgasm together, when in these brief rhythmic moments of mutual physiological response, both persons reach the climax of their emotional expression at the same time. If human beings were simply physiological organisms, and if this act could be dissociated from other human needs, the physiological and psychological pleasure and satisfaction involved in it would justify it as an end in itself. *But because human beings are more than physiological reactions, because these responses mean more than they themselves as actions in intercourse are, sexual intercourse can seldom, if ever, be an isolated experience of satisfaction.* This physiological transaction can become a source either of much mental discontent, moral guilt, and aesthetic disgust, or of profound mental peace, moral satisfaction, and aesthetic delight, not to mention the possibilities of religious value.

Here, for human beings, is the crux of the sexual problem in life. Sex is a means of communicating a variety of meanings; it objectifies or symbolizes a variety of feelings and ideas that human beings have about themselves and others. It can mean simply, "I'm sexually hungry and I want satisfaction through you." It can mean, "I love you and I want to be identified as far as possible with you." Or it can mean, "We love each other. Life means so much to us that we want children to share its creative joy and values." There are other meanings, of course—as many meanings as the mates find possible in and through each other. These three stages need not exclude each other though the first may endanger the next two. But for two persons who love each other, and therefore find life's meaning heightened and focused in that love, there can hardly be conceived a more expressive symbol of the yearning for unity than a mutual, harmonious orgasm. Two persons find their deepest satisfaction not in mere self-satisfaction, but in making it possible for the loved one to express his feelings in and through his own contribution to a harmonious act.

The testimony of married persons who have

found it possible so to discipline their reaction as to find mutuality in orgasm gives clear corroboration at this point. To feel that one's partner encourages and enjoys one's own activity and responses, to feel that one can meet the needs of the person one loves even as one expresses the intensity and meaning of one's own desires, is, indeed, a human experience worth cherishing. We cannot emphasize enough the qualitative enjoyment and meaning of this experience. What two lovers experience, especially in simultaneous orgasm, is not so much physiological simultaneity but the meanings that they, as two human beings dedicated to each other, so want to express. No wonder lovers who have experienced exhaustion in the psychological and physical release of their tension can continue to embrace each other in the afterglow of mental peace, physiological relaxation, and grateful appreciation. How clearly this act can symbolize what the marriage of two loving persons means, the dedication of one's being to the growing happiness of another.

This is an experience that does work creatively in the lives of two persons, for it renews confidence and infuses new meaning. The amazing fact about it is that it can, on the same physiological base, go on being a source of renewal. Youth, middle age, and maturity find different levels of meaning and renewal thereby. This would hardly be so were it not that through sexual intercourse the lovers who are now parents (or the lovers who are now the center of responsibilities and joys in family and civic life, or the lovers who are now older physically but more mature as persons) go on using it to communicate meanings that never find adequate expression in words.

If what I have been saying is true, it is clear that both the harmony of sex experience and the expressive significance of that unity are such sources of strength and enjoyment in married life that they deserve the needed preparation and protection. Violins cannot create music if they are not tuned, or if the violinist cannot control his feelings, thoughts, and muscles to suit his meaning. If there is no "music" in the violinist, even the greatest skill in playing will not produce "music with a soul." To carry this figure further, violinists cannot create music when they are not playing the same score or when they have not been able to synchronize their playing in accordance with their respective parts in the musical whole. Harmony,

physiological and spiritual, requires more than good will; it requires careful discriminating thought, sensitive and sincere feeling, and self-discipline that subordinates tensions for the sake of the whole.

It may seem that we are making too much of the unity of intercourse, but if that be an error it is one that needs underscoring since we are purposely insisting upon the quality of the experience. Sexual intercourse has its greatest value when the minds and actions of two persons communicate their meanings. From this viewpoint, it is unfortunate that so many persons, in and out of marriage, are forfeiting such a high quality of experience, frequently without realizing that they are doing so. They are expressing lust, decreasing sexual tension, experiencing different depths of pleasure. But they are usually sacrificing, or jeopardizing, richer values otherwise open to them.

Let us pause here and attempt to avoid misunderstanding.

We are not saying that young men and women, for whom sex has been simply a pleasurable outlet, or who have been unable, for differing reasons, to live controlled sexual lives, are inevitably barred from mutuality in orgasm (or that those who have remained virginal will by that very fact have guaranteed mutuality). But other things being equal, a personal history of relative promiscuity and a loss of self-confidence and adequate self-control are not conducive to achievement of mutuality. While it is important to realize that many other psychological factors will enter into the achievement of mutual orgasm at any one point in married life, we fly in the face of all we know about psychological habits and associations if we allow ourselves to think that a relatively undisciplined past, with all its associations and psychological effects upon the individual, will not become an obstacle—not necessarily insuperable to be sure—to mutuality.

To continue, part of our central thesis is that human beings have been and are, in fact, losing much of the joy possible in sex and love because they are thinking too much of sex expression and not enough about expressing values through sex and in love. We cannot be said to be educating persons with regard to sex until we are as much concerned about the objectives of complete sexual experience as we have been about removing inhibitions. Sex expression is not self-expression. And self-expression is not necessarily the expression of love. We have taken too little cognizance of the probable fact that multitudes of men and women are disappointed with their sexual experience; it becomes, like ordinary eating, a means of regularly satisfying an otherwise discomforting need. The less persons understand about the meaning that sex can have in their lives, the more likely are they to find the most direct means of expression.[1] The very fact that the physical pleasure of releasing tension is theirs blinds them to higher values that would both intensify the physiological pleasure and also lead to more complete fulfillment of their total being.

From this point of view of quality in sex experience, there is very little value in Kinsey's data with regard to the relation of premarital intercourse and sexual effectiveness in marriage. He says:

> It is sometimes asserted that all persons who have premarital intercourse subsequently regret the experience, and that such regrets may constitute a major cloud on their lives. There are a few males whose histories seem to indicate that they have so reacted to their premarital experience, but a high proportion of the thousands of experienced males whom we have questioned on this point indicated that they did not regret having had such an experience, and that the premarital intercourse had not caused any trouble in their subsequent marital adjustments (p. 562).[2]

As Kinsey realizes, even at this level of description one needs accurate data from the wives. But the ambiguous words in his statement are "trouble" and "regret." If "no trouble" means simply that there were no special inhibitions, or feelings of guilt that hindered physiological reaction, or that no serious disunity between the partners was involved, the crux of the problem is not touched. Assuming—what we doubt can be assumed—that "experienced males" would admit that they had been deceived by their desires, what we need to know (and cannot find out probably from men habituated to satisfy desires conveniently) is the effect upon the quality of their marital relation, both sexually and as a whole. Did it make for greater loyalty, for deeper appreciation and respect, both of oneself, one's partner, and the act itself?

When Kinsey continues, "It is notable that most of the males who did regret the experience were individuals who had had very little premarital intercourse, amounting in most cases to not more than one or two experiences" (p. 563), is the conclusion to be drawn that if they had further indulged they would have ceased being disturbed? Or does this also suggest that some persons expected more from themselves and from the sexual experience, and that they realized how little sex as a merely biological or even sociable experience had to contribute to their lives? Obviously, there are no definite conclusions to be drawn from such data.

But Kinsey goes so far in trying to avoid any generalization condemning premarital experience that he makes "the significance of premarital intercourse" depend "upon the situations under which it is had" (p. 561), upon whether the experience is free from fear or "satisfying." This again begs the real question of the kind of fear and the quality of satisfaction. The whole problem is: Can a person outside of married love find the most that sex can bring to human life? Can experiences in which one's fundamental concern is the satisfaction of one's own desire become the psychological basis for an experience in which concern for another's complete well-being is symbolized in the sexual act? Can ego-centered habituation, in idea, in motive, in emotion, in action, be a help in establishing a relation in which another human being, a home, and children call for self-mastery?

A little reflection, then, will make clear the task before any two married persons. It will be evident that much discipline may be required if mutuality is to be realized at the psychophysiological level. Even assuming that past experience with sex has been without serious conflict, so that both persons are emotionally free and are ready to discover the full meaning of sex in their relations to each other, they cannot be sure that the experience of unity will readily be theirs. The sexual responsiveness of the male and female orgasm is by no means the same, and every couple has to work out the modes of mutual response suited to their own particular natures.

At this point of physiological unity one cannot dogmatize about the prerequisites in terms of past sexual experience. As already suggested, one cannot universalize the statement that habits of response derived from premarital experience will interfere necessarily with present adjustment to one's partner. A person's attitude toward his or her past experience, the effect of it upon his emotional life, the attitude of the mate, the total import of the other values in a marriage are always probably more important than the mere fact of abstinence or nonabstinence. But even from the point of view of physiological unity, are not the probabilities on our side when we say that, other things being normal, the chances of harmonizing responses are much greater when two lovers come together who have a history of self-mastery and confidence with regard to sex? Will not "a past of pleasure" be a threat to the more important psychological, moral, aesthetic, and religious overtones—those which transform physical notes into a human symphony.

We need not here go into the different physical and psychological causes that might well lead to an initial disharmony and to a long struggle to achieve the kind of mental freedom and control necessary for increasing sexual harmony. Suffice it to say that one of the greatest misconceptions that young people bring to marriage is that there will be no sex problem in marriage. The fact is that marriage may create as many sex problems as it solves. Too many honeymoons have found two persons who loved each other not a little disturbed, and sometimes shocked, by inability to enjoy the kind of sexual harmony for which their spirits were prepared. To repeat, then, any couple that looks forward to married life needs to face honestly and resolutely the fact that the finest psychophysical expression of their love may have to await the patient discipline and understanding for which their particular response patterns call. Fortunately their meaning to each other, the unity they feel, can be expressed in other ways as they work for greater unity in the sexual satisfaction of their love.

One of the strongest reasons for urging that a person come through adolescence feeling that he is in control of sex (and not sex in control of him) should now be clear. For the less he can control his mind and body, the more difficult his readjustment to his beloved may be at the very time he is most anxious to succeed. The more he is conditioned to a certain form of sexual progression, the more habituated he has become to certain modes of response, the greater the variety of thoughts and associations that come crowding into his mind now that he is trying to meet the needs of

his life partner, the harder it is to make the new adjustment that has to be made to his loved one. The person whose past experience with sex has been that of the hungry animal, or that of the egotistic philanderer who has thought of his partner essentially as a means to his enjoyment, will not have an easy time meeting a new situation in which his highest nature wants expression for the sake of his beloved. From the point of view of married life as a whole, the person who has learned to think of human beings as "males" or "females" who can be "used" may indeed find and create more trouble than he can imagine.

It would be tragic to underemphasize the importance of such psychological influences. Let two persons bring wandering thoughts, feelings of insecurity and guilt, desires for self-aggrandizement, or any other expectations foreign to the unique problem of welding two lives together, and the marriage of their spirits will have this much more to overcome.

Are Not Our Sexual Standards Artificial?

We must now turn to another lingering doubt, which is related to what we have been saying about the conflict between the sex desire and the social code. For I am sure that someone will say: In other societies, where no one expects young people to abstain from the satisfaction of their sexual desires, and where the element of fear and social ostracism is reduced to a minimum, there are no bad results, and people seem to be healthier in their attitudes toward sex. May it not be, then, that in developing our social codes and laws we have created problems for young people that did not have to arise at all? Indeed, if a person just does not care about what society thinks, if he has no moral compunctions and, therefore, no resultant sense of guilt about his free sexual life, that person does not seem to suffer any of the disturbances associated with sexual repression.

And my reader might add: Are you sure that all the fuss you are making about sexual control, yes, even as a means to a fuller love relation, is worth the bother? Since sex is so recurrent in human life, would it not be better to remove the bars at this point and let individuals (and society) use the energy now spent in combatting "sexual license" for other desirable personal and social objectives? If we are actually pitting individuals against a drive that in their ripening years is a constant thorn in their sides, are we not really flagellating them unnecessarily? Why not make legal and acceptable what so many people are now doing covertly, and at the expense of an artificially created bad conscience?

Indeed, why not be sensible and scientific, and provide persons from adolescence on with knowledge of contraceptives and prophylactics so that they will be able to enjoy sexual relations with a minimum of fear and with a maximum of birth control? If, as they come into marriage, a couple did not expect premarital abstinence any more than they expect abstinence from other forms of social relations, it would not bother them, and marriage would not be undermined. After all, remember that a great many people even now are breaking the social code, for they reject the moral conception on which it is based. They do not seem to be worse for it. Is it not our problem, then, really to recognize that our present moral and legal codes, developed in earlier stages of socioeconomic-religious development, are no longer applicable and are, in fact, creating more problems today than they solve?

Thus many a thoughtful young person will argue. Remembering our own prolonged collegiate harangues and bull sessions, we can honestly say that this line of argument still strikes a sympathetic chord, especially when we note the great amount of time and energy young and old alike, in and out of family, spend in worrying about maintaining chastity. There are many difficult theoretical questions here, and we can no more than hint at an approach to them.

1. Let us not fool ourselves that we would minimize our social problems by making knowledge of prophylactics and contraceptives more available. Such knowledge and the medical attention necessary should be available as soon as possible, but not because in this way unwanted births might be decreased. There are no methods of contraception that are foolproof (aside from medical operations that keep sperm and ovum from making contact). Errors in adjustment and imperfection in the materials—let alone carelessness or even failure to use them—would certainly occur many times. Unless we were to make provision for an enormous program of legal abortions, a multitude of children would be born when neither father nor mother were mature enough or economically able to take care of their children.

Let us make no mistake about the choices before us. If our psychological and sociological investigations have told us much about the sex urge, they have also emphasized the need that infants and children have for feeling wanted and loved. The constant feeling of insecurity makes deeper inroads on healthy living than the frustration of sex as such. Parents must be psychologically and morally mature to help children meet their problems as they grow up. Our central obligation, therefore, is to preserve the kind of parental care that will enable children to feel at home in their world. To suppose that removal of social restraints regarding sexual control would take us nearer to this goal is to be blind to the many problems with which society would then be beset. Are we willing to have many more children born than can receive adequate care psychologically and morally? We might, indeed, decrease the number of sexual disturbances that are (supposedly) due to sexual inhibition, and increase the many other problems that occur when the life ventures of children and adults are rendered insecure and unstable.

Our choice is not between black and white, and any system will work hardship on many persons. But, surely, any suggestions that would tend to increase the number of inadequately cared-for children, let alone endanger the stability that monogamous marriage provides, cannot compare even with our present imperfect system. A main reason why those who now indulge in premarital sex experience, or even extramarital sex experience, can enjoy the supposed benefits of their "freedom" is that there are enough other human beings left who, despite their imperfections, stand by the system that does give the social stability needed. Let the order of the day emphasize not control but convenience, not long-range planning but "doing what I want when I want it," and it will not take long for physical and social decay to set in. Would this be more "natural" than the kind of system we have? Can those who live by such parasitism honestly encourage others to join them as they "use" and endanger the lives of other persons in order to guarantee their own pleasures?

2. We might remind ourselves, before passing to the next point, that what recommends the idea

of birth control is not that there may be a limitation in the number of children, but that birth of children can be controlled in a manner designed to ensure the most adequate care of the number of children a given family can absorb and support. We do not face the facts if we allow ourselves to forget that, the imperfections of contraceptives from the point of safety aside, they are aesthetically obnoxious, to say the least, to a large number of married people who use them only because they do want to limit their families or adequately space their children. The purpose of birth control is to help enrich the experience of sexual love by reducing the probability of pregnancy, and to increase the possibilities of health and education in a given family. The goal of birth control is to help improve the quality of adult life and the opportunities of children for sensitive nurture. To consider the use of contraceptives simply as a way of providing individuals with pleasure minus responsibility is to encourage the dilution of the meaning of sexual intercourse.

3. But these considerations are not so important as those pointed out earlier in discussing the sexual progression and the place of self-control in the complete enjoyment of sex experience itself. To express sex as sex with different "congenial" partners is to establish certain modes and tempos of response, many mental and emotional associations, that cannot be sloughed off at will. If we remember that sex itself is not the cause of love (though it is certainly a factor in love), but that love is a profound cause of sexual intimacy in human experience, we are confronted with another stubborn fact of our psychological nature that forces us to make a choice.

Let us assume that Dick and Jane have, as the supporter of sexual freedom would advocate, moved through their adolescence and early youth indulging their sexual urge discreetly and prudently. Since they have felt no rigorous moral compunctions or morbid sense of guilt, they are not vulnerable to mental disease, and, let us grant, they have enjoyed good, clean, fun on the sexual level. For they have experienced the release of sexual tension when they were really bothered, and they have been fortunate enough to find suitable partners with whom they shared normal, companionable relations and friendships. Let us make their case even stronger by assuming that

their attitudes throughout their varied experience were not dominated by an abnormal, aggressive desire for mastery.

With this psychological orientation to men and women and sex, let us suppose that Dick and Jane meet each other and fall in love. They now *fall in love*, but their past experience has been of *falling in lust*. They now no longer anticipate a good-for-a-while relationship, but a lifelong partnership in which they may share as much of life's meaning as possible with each other and make each other the home base for all adventures in value. Two persons like these (whatever their past, I am assuming) want to be one; they want to feel unified in every way. For them the sexual experience, even if they had never had it before, would now be an opportunity demanded by the total impetus of their love and not merely their lust. This love dictates loyalty to each other, for it represents the fact that the other is valued above all others.

Is it now more serious psychologically and spiritually to disappoint the natural desires of sex than the natural desires of love for loyalty and concentrated devotion? What Dick and Jane want now supremely is love; and, speaking objectively, what they need is love if their lives are to have the quality and inspiration that love contributes to life. Yet the Dick-and-Jane-in-love are confronted by the Dick-and-Jane-in-lust, and the habits of the past—such as finding the attractive physical specimen to share the pleasure of lust, such as desiring sexual experience every so often and in a certain manner or mode—now assert themselves. Here, let us emphasize, *it is not society that is making artificial laws which cause conflict and make them unhappy; it is the psychological laws of their natures as human beings.* Lust and the habit of lust stand in conflict with love and the demands of love. The past of life, enhanced and strengthened by habit, stands in defiance of the development of life as a whole. Dick and Jane want each other completely, dependably, forever. They do not want to feel that the sexual habits of the past may break up something which they now so wholly approve. They dread the thought that their past may threaten the foundations of their happiness together as central units of a family. If Jane and Dick are honest with themselves and with each other, they may well pause and face the fact that, much as they wish to follow the high, broad avenue of growth, because of their past habits they are better fitted to travel the lower, narrower streets of sexual satisfaction.

Let us now assume that, having become engaged, they find it impossible because of established habits to refrain from sexual intercourse. But the sexual intercourse they now want is more than the satisfaction of a strong urge. They want to express their love by the very actions which in the past have expressed lust. They want so much to have this experience say what they cannot say in words. They want everything to be perfect. But now past habits of response, and many past associations with this act, crowd in upon the activity of mind and body, barring the way to the kind of unity and satisfaction their love calls for. It is not society which is barring their way to joy and peace now, but their own past in conflict with the present. Society and its laws did not artificially create this situation. It is the psychological structure of Jane and Dick—the way their natures work out once they have made certain choices. The problem they have—the struggle between self-satisfying lust and other-regarding love—is one their natures would develop in *any* social situation (assuming the value of love). They may, indeed, after a kind of discipline they are not used to, be able to make their way to a harmonious unity of confident love, but the struggle before them is not artificially created by society.

It will not be forgotten, of course, that two other persons, Harry and Judith, despite their controlled psychological past, may have difficulty in achieving the kind of sexual unity that will adequately recreate their bodies and minds. But, we hold out much more hope for their achievement of this unity and for the prolongation and enrichment of this love than we do for Jane and Dick. And happily it cannot be asserted that Jane and Dick may not under the incentive and inspiration of their love find their way with patience, mutual forgiveness, and persistent self-discipline to the kind of unity, mutual confidence, and loyalty to which their love aspires. Nevertheless, the moral attitudes and psychological habits of Dick and Jane may well stand in the way of the present satisfaction of their love. These attitudes and habits may destroy more than one moment of peace and trust, especially when the other tensions of married partnership and home building come into their lives. Once more, then, we come back to a question we have been asking over and over in these

pages: When we are honest with the facts of our lives, and when we consider what we desire from life as a whole, is the satisfaction of sex lust along the way worth it? Do we not, in fact, endanger or sacrifice our unique heritage of love for a mess of pottage by thinking that we have solved the sex problem by convenient expression?

In a society where people came together physically and separated whenever they pleased, one might be tempted to think that artificial frustrations would be avoided. But how sure could we be that both persons would find it convenient to separate at the same time? The one who gets caught by love suffers. In the midst of their enjoyment can they keep from being haunted by the knowledge that on their principle of action one or the other may change his mind when he pleases? These are not problems society's codes create. They are snares into which our human nature falls once we play fast and loose with it.

4. Before closing this section, we must dwell a little longer on another aspect of the suggestion that it is society which makes all the trouble by imposing unnatural standards of conduct on the young. When we talk this way, we seem to assume that our forebears had somehow discovered and forced upon their children a group of moral edicts that had no intimate relation to their needs. Now, it is certainly true that this attitude of the law enforcer has been present in a great deal of societal restriction on human beings. No doubt many laws have been enforced that took little or no account of the needs and desires of the persons who were expected to live by them. They do reflect a slave morality.

Some philosophical and theological theories of law easily lend themselves to manipulation of persons rather than to a regard for the growth of persons. Against them let us assert quite vigorously that human beings are not to be considered the playthings of the gods or, for that matter, of fate, let alone of society or state or church. But it is a great calamity that persons whom study should have at least rendered more cautious make the puerile assertion that the restrictions upon sexual behavior have been imposed only by the philosophical rationalizations of ascetic kill-joys who had little regard for the normal enjoyments of normal persons. It is true that sexual restraint has been advocated in the name of, and as the will of, God. But let it be remembered that God was usually considered not the torturer of little children, but the lover of men. If more of the truth be known, we suspect that the will of God was indeed called in to back up what was shrewdly observed to be a law of the human nature—which, incidentally, God had made that way! This is not the place to review and refute different theories, for the question is an involved one. But it seems fair to say that it is erroneous to maintain that the grounds of sexual control lie not in the nature of human experience and experiment, but in artificial restraints imposed without any realistic justification by society.

That there must be some control of sexual activity is patent in any reflective analysis of the problem of human beings as they come together. Different societies may exercise different controls in order to preserve their form of social organization. Sometimes the controls may be to encourage persons to have more sexual experience, more wives or husbands, and more children. However, we make serious mistakes in the study of values when we compare a mode of behavior in one society with a similar mode of behavior in another without carefully evaluating each mode in the light of the total pattern of values and customs in each society. The fact is that each society must pay in some way or other for the controls that it seeks to enforce on sex, or on property, education, or anything else, for that matter.

The real question, therefore, is: What form of society, what kind of institutions will help human beings in their situations to complete their lives and fulfill their potentialities in the richest possible manner and with the minimum of fruitless frustration? One part of this large question seems clear, namely, that a monogamous home built about confident, controlled love is the best kind of insurance for the growth of human beings and the symphonic satisfaction of human drives.

We can imagine societies in which ideological, economic, and social problems would be such that the kind of love and home we have in mind is beyond present reach and grasp. Theirs, then, would have to be a different form of social code, and that code might work better for them without home-building possibilities than it would for us. But it does not mean that they too would not be better off if they could pay the price for the kind of human love and nurture that joins two lovers and their progeny in a common pursuit of creative

living. The problem every person and every society has to face is: Do we want to protect the experience of love even more than the experience of sex? If we agree that the experience of love, given the structure of human beings, is endangered by the expression of sex as an end in itself, then we must organize our institutions and educational efforts to encourage love. And we must discipline sex for the sake of love. . . .

Is Sexual Guilt Not an Artificial Barrier?

If boy or girl were not taught to inhibit their sexual desires, and if as young people they felt no moral guilt or anxiety about it, would it have any bad effect on their lives? The answer is: If, indeed, they had no moral compunctions about free sexual expression, it would not produce mental disturbance, for no real conflict would be set up in their lives. But if these persons ever decided to move into the area of love, they might well expect conflict, and then other disturbances would have to be faced. No one could predict the outcome.

But when we say that some sexual promiscuity will not have a bad effect, I suspect we have in mind mental disorder rooted in the sex-conscience conflict. It is unfortunate that so many of us have got into the habit of thinking that if we do not develop a neurosis we are not being badly affected. But here we really misinterpret what our psychology does in fact teach us. As might be expected, we know the diseased extreme better than we understand what makes for the most effective and enduring health.

Does the fact that a person does not develop a neurosis, owing to the fact that he has no moral compunctions about premarital or extramarital sex-expression, mean that he is better off because he is expressing sex? Study that person's life carefully—his attitudes toward himself, his sense of responsibility for the needs of others—and you may well discover a weakness of moral fiber, of capacity to get the most out of himself despite hardship and sacrifice. What does such a person do in the presence of frustration now? What will he do if he ever undertakes a vocation and marriage, in which there will be great need for willingness to forego present personal pleasures for the sake of later satisfactions? The person who can pleasurably indulge in sexual intercourse owing to his freedom from moral guilt may escape a "complex" or specific mental disorder, but when the total quality of his life is analyzed, when his human sensitiveness and his capacity to forego self-indulgence for the sake of others is evaluated, the deficit in his personality may be more serious than he realizes.

One other fact of experience must be emphasized in relation to this question. I have listened frequently to young men and women, some of them engaged, who because of their thwarted desires for sexual intercourse have wished that they had never been brought up to think it's "bad." And some have concluded that "since we only think it's bad and it really isn't, there really is no good reason why we shouldn't express our desires." Many young people who have gone this way have discovered, to their dismay and undiminished sense of guilt, that their conscience would not keep quiet just because they told it that it was all wrong.

We cannot here discuss the whole problem of conscience, though we must protest the oversimplified and superficially "scientific" accounts of it given by those who reduce it merely to the watchdog voice of society in us. Whatever final theoretical position we take, the fact cannot be forgotten that it does no good to try to laugh off a "conscience," and it frequently does much harm. Laughing the conscience off is hardly the way to get rid of it, any more than laughing away sex or any other strong desire exiles it. It is not impossible to change the content of one's conscience so that it will take account of the present actualities of life as well as of the past. A person whose conscience tells him that every manifestation of sex is bad may be suffering from a distasteful emotional experience in childhood which he then illogically generalized. It will take him time and effort of thought and will to feel differently about that verdict and change his conscience at that point. During the interlude, when his conscience is changing, he will experience the uncertainty that goes with any new development. One does not, however, make a new conscience simply by breaking the old one. The redirection calls for painstaking insight and effort if it is going to represent a real, unified growth of the personality.

Let us apply this fact to the question before us. Too many young people are sure that, in view of the strength of their desire for each other, they can dismiss the conscientious scruples which have been exerting themselves, enter into sex experience, enjoy it thoroughly, and never feel any aftereffects. "After all," they may say, "this conscience about sex is just a fairy tale I picked up in my childhood, like the idea of Santa Claus." But then they find that the experience does not take up the whole mind, that they did not enjoy it quite as much as they thought they would. Later they find that they do keep on feeling guilty about it. Both the possibility of premarital sex experience and the whole idea of sex experience now evoke guilt. Thus, when the sex experience is later to be used as an expression of marital love, it comes into mind with the guilt feeling attached, to destroy what might otherwise be a communication of undivided devotion and love.

This kind of effect was quite clear in the experience of Arthur and Ethel. Arthur had been brought up on the idea that sex should express love and that it should be a bond in married love only. The war came on when he was a sophomore in college and interrupted his life and the normal course of an excellent relation with Ethel. On one of his three-day leaves Ethel met him half-way across the country, so that they could be together longer. They had earlier discussed the possibility of sexual experience, and we suspect that under normal peacetime conditions they would have abstained from sexual intercourse despite their strong love for each other. Now, however, they convinced each other at their hotel that those compunctions they had been feeling about "going all the way" were silly residuals of childhood. They met each other on several other occasions and shared their love with each other.

The last time we saw Ethel she said that soon after Arthur had returned to college, his work (he had been a college leader and an excellent scholar) had gone to pieces, he had broken his engagement and had written her excoriating letters filled with bitterness and the feeling that she had allowed him to make a mess of his life. Anyway, he was no longer any good. We are afraid that Arthur's conscience is still barking, and that the guilt he has been feeling at this point is so heavy upon him that he has allowed it to seep into other areas of his life. And now Ethel, whose conscience "didn't feel too bad" earlier, is miserable, not only about the breaking of the engagement, but also about his attitude toward himself and toward her. This is only one instance of a truth we need to remember, that our conscience, whatever its ultimate nature, has a way of staying with us, and that we are being more than careless when we think we can change it *simply by breaking it.*

In a chapter in which we have been considering lingering doubts, we must not leave the impression of being satisfied with the present status of morality or custom on these problems. It has been our concern to suggest rather the direction in which we need to go in our thinking. What is really disturbing is the fact that so few people are getting from sex the profound, creative experience possible through it. People are cheating themselves of the deeper possibilities sex experience can open to them *if* it symbolically binds together two personalities committed to each other, to their God, their children, and their civil responsibilities. Comparatively speaking, persons are at present experiencing jazz when they might know the stirring themes of symphonies. Our task is not so much to control sex as it is to increase every opportunity for understanding and for growth of personality. Crusades against sex will not do what we really need to do—work with intelligent commitment to the kind of living in which love for others and respect for self are the magnetic poles.

From the cradle to the grave, literally, our task is to develop appreciation for the enriching responsibilities and activities of human experience and, within these, the meaning of sex and love. And we need, as part of this total conception, to change our attitude toward those who have failed to meet their social responsibilities from one of vindictive punishment to one of understanding redirection. Only thus may such persons re-enter, as far as possible for them, into their heritage of sex, love, and family. We do not protect society simply by penalizing its weaker members, especially when this frequently means hurting their children more than they need to be hurt. We help society—indeed, we prove that we have the highest and most stable type of society—when we can help those who fall by the way to rediscover their good potentialities and rebuild them.

Notes

1. This statement finds support in Kinsey's statistics with regard to the differences both in freedom of sex expression and mode of sex expression in persons with little school education—and, one assumes, what that means to the development of human understanding.

2. From A. C. Kinsey, W. B. Pomeroy, and C. E. Martin, *Sexual Behavior in the Human Male* (Philadelphia: W. B. Saunders Co., 1948).

Questions for Analysis

1. *Bertocci's key assumption is that "love, marriage and the home are among the supreme values of human existence; that the human beings who cannot enjoy the blessings that love, marriage, and the home bestow are relatively poverty-stricken." Do you agree with this assumption or do you find it questionable? Are there other values that you would suggest are coequal with love, marriage, and the home?*

2. *With which, if any, of the chief determinants of sex would you identify Bertocci's view?*

3. *What, according to Bertocci, is the most important component of a fundamental sexual standard?*

4. *What does Bertocci mean when he says: "The deception in the progression of love is just the opposite that in the sexual progression"?*

5. *Which of the theoretical views on sex outside marriage does Bertocci's viewpoint most resemble?*

Is Adultery Immoral?

Richard Wasserstrom

The following essay "Is Adultery Immoral?" by philosopher and legal scholar Richard Wasserstrom is a good example of how we might start thinking about sexual morality. Wasserstrom focuses on one kind of behavior that, as we have seen, frequently is considered a case of sexual immorality: adultery. Specifically, he reviews some of the arguments against adultery and the issues they leave unresolved.

One common argument is that adultery is wrong because it involves breaking a promise, an act that is always prima facie *wrong. But adultery is worse than the typical cases of promise breaking because it almost always involves injury to the nonadulterous spouse.*

A second argument ties adultery to deception, which is taken to be always immoral. Adultery can involve active deception, in which the adulterous spouse might deliberately lie to the nonadulterous spouse; or passive deception, in which the adulterous spouse simply says nothing about the adulterous relationship. Either way deception is involved. And since deception is always wrong, so is adultery.

Wasserstrom, however, develops an argument claiming that adultery might involve a more pervasive deception. Generally, our society associates sexual intercourse with deep feelings of affection, even love. By cultural convention sex is the most authoritative way of communicating to another the nature and degree of one's affections. When adulterous spouses do not actually have these feelings for extramarital partners but pretend they do, then they are deceiving the extramarital partners. If, however they are sincere in their feelings for the extramarital partners but do not have appropriate feelings for their spouses, then they are likely deceiving the spouses. Since these feelings of affection that ought to accompany sexual intercourse can be held toward only one person at a time, adulterous spouses are always guilty of deception and, therefore, always act immorally.

This sort of pervasive deception connected with adultery is, however, open to criticism. First, it could be argued that such a claim represents an inaccurate account of the connection between sex and affection. Second, the account is based on the questionable assumption that it is desirable for sexual intercourse to carry the meaning ascribed to it.

As Wasserstrom points out, the underlying and most important issue in this facet of pervasive deception in adultery is the connection between sex and love. He shows how those advocating sexual liberation sometimes want to separate love and sex, and other times want to sever the link between love and exclusivity. If either of these permissive views is accepted, does it necessarily follow that adultery would not involve either promise breaking or deception?

Take, for example, the case of an open marriage, in which the partners willingly agree to sever love from exclusivity. Can this possibly involve deception? Some would say that by such an open agreement a couple could no longer be properly described as married to one another. But Wasserstrom points out that a compelling argument cannot be made for a commitment to exclusivity as a necessary condition for marriage. Others would argue that adultery, even in an open marriage, is wrong because it undermines marriage as a social institution. Wasserstrom considers this argument incomplete because it does not demonstrate that marriage is, in fact, a desirable and just social institution.

From Richard Wasserstrom, "Is Adultery Immoral?" in Today's Moral Problems *(New York: Macmillan, 1975). Reprinted by permission of the author.*

As the foregoing synopsis indicates, Wasserstrom's essay involves intricate moral analysis. This is its chief value. It does not resolve the adultery issue but shows how any of us might approach an issue involving sexual morality.

Many discussions of the enforcement of morality by the law take as illustrative of the problem under consideration the regulation of various types of sexual behavior by the criminal law. It was, for example, the Wolfenden Report's recommendations concerning homosexuality and prostitution that led Lord Devlin to compose his now famous lecture, "The Enforcement of Morals." And that lecture in turn provoked important philosophical responses from H. L. A. Hart, Ronald Dworkin, and others.

Much, if not all, of the recent philosophical literature on the enforcement of morals appears to take for granted the immorality of the sexual behavior in question. The focus of discussion, at least, is whether such things as homosexuality, prostitution, and adultery ought to be made illegal even if they are immoral, and not whether they are immoral.

I propose in this paper to think about the latter, more neglected topic, that of sexual morality, and to do so in the following fashion. I shall consider just one kind of behavior that is often taken to be a case of sexual immorality—adultery. I am interested in pursuing at least two questions. First, I want to explore the question of in what respects adulterous behavior falls within the domain of morality at all. For this surely is one of the puzzles one encounters when considering the topic of sexual morality. It is often hard to see on what grounds much of the behavior is deemed to be either moral or immoral, for example, private homosexual behavior between consenting adults. I have purposely selected adultery because it seems a more plausible candidate for moral assessment than many other kinds of sexual behavior.

The second question I want to examine is that of what is to be said about adultery, without being especially concerned to stay within the area of morality. I shall endeavor, in other words, to identify and to assess a number of the major arguments that might be advanced against adultery. I believe that they are the chief arguments that would be given in support of the view that adultery is immoral, but I think they are worth considering even

if some of them turn out to be nonmoral arguments and considerations.

A number of the issues involved seem to me to be complicated and difficult. In a number of places I have at best indicated where further philosophical exploration is required without having successfully conducted the exploration myself. The paper may very well be more useful as an illustration of how one might begin to think about the subject of sexual morality than as an elucidation of important truths about the topic.

Before I turn to the arguments themselves there are two preliminary points that require some clarification. Throughout the paper I shall refer to the immorality of such things as breaking a promise, deceiving someone, etc. In a very rough way, I mean by this that there is something morally wrong that is done in doing the action in question. I mean that the action is, in a strong sense, of *"prima facie"* prima facie wrong or unjustified. I do not mean that it may never be right or justifiable to do the action; just that the fact that it is an action of this description always does count against the rightness of the action. I leave entirely open the question of what it is that makes actions of this kind immoral in this sense of "immoral."

The second preliminary point concerns what is meant or implied by the concept of adultery. I mean by "adultery" any case of extramarital sex, and I want to explore the arguments for and against extramarital sex, undertaken in a variety of morally relevant situations. Someone might claim that the concept of adultery is conceptually connected with the concept of immorality, and that to characterize behavior as adulterous is already to characterize it as immoral or unjustified in the sense described above. There may be something to this. Hence the importance of making it clear that I want to talk about extramarital sexual relations. If they are always immoral, this is something that must be shown by argument. If the concept of adultery does in some sense entail or imply immorality, I want to ask whether that connection is a rationally based one. If not all cases of extramarital sex are immoral (again, in the sense described above), then the concept of adultery should either be weakened accordingly or restricted to those classes of extramarital sex for which the predication of immorality is warranted.

One argument for the immorality of adultery might go something like this: What makes adultery immoral is that it involves the breaking of a promise, and what makes adultery seriously wrong is that it involves the breaking of an important promise. For, so the argument might continue, one of the things the two parties promise each other when they get married is that they will abstain from sexual relationships with third persons. Because of this promise both spouses quite reasonably entertain the expectation that the other will behave in conformity with it. Hence, when one of the parties has sexual intercourse with a third person he or she breaks that promise about sexual relationships which was made when the marriage was entered into, and defeats the reasonable expectations of exclusivity entertained by the spouse.

In many cases the immorality involved in breaching the promise relating to extramarital sex may be a good deal more serious than that involved in the breach of other promises. This is so because adherence to this promise may be of much greater importance to the parties than is adherence to many of the other promises given or received by them in their lifetime. The breaking of this promise may be much more hurtful and painful than is typically the case.

Why is this so? To begin with, it may have been difficult for the nonadulterous spouse to have kept the promise. Hence that spouse may feel the unfairness of having restrained himself or herself in the absence of reciprocal restraint having been exercised by the adulterous spouse. In addition, the spouse may perceive the breaking of the promise as an indication of a kind of indifference on the part of the adulterous spouse. If you really cared about me and my feelings—the spouse might say—you would not have done this to me. And third, and related to the above, the spouse may see the act of sexual intercourse with another as a sign of affection for the other person and as an additional rejection of the nonadulterous spouse as the one who is loved by the adulterous spouse. It is not just that the adulterous spouse does not take the feelings of the spouse sufficiently into

account, the adulterous spouse also indicates through the act of adultery affection for someone other than the spouse. I will return to these points later. For the present, it is sufficient to note that a set of arguments can be developed in support of the proposition that certain kinds of adultery are wrong just because they involve the breach of a serious promise which, among other things, leads to the intentional infliction of substantial pain by one spouse upon the other.

Another argument for the immorality of adultery focuses not on the existence of a promise of sexual exclusivity but on the connection between adultery and deception. According to this argument, adultery involves deception. And because deception is wrong, so is adultery.

Although it is certainly not obviously so, I shall simply assume in this paper that deception is always immoral. Thus the crucial issue for my purposes is the asserted connection between extramarital sex and deception. Is it plausible to maintain, as this argument does, that adultery always does involve deception and is on that basis to be condemned?

The most obvious person on whom deceptions might be practiced is the nonparticipating spouse; and the most obvious thing about which the nonparticipating spouse can be deceived is the existence of the adulterous act. One clear case of deception is that of lying. Instead of saying that the afternoon was spent in bed with A, the adulterous spouse asserts that it was spent in the library with B, or on the golf course with C.

There can also be deception even when no lies are told. Suppose, for instance, that a person has sexual intercourse with someone other than his or her spouse and just does not tell the spouse about it. Is that deception? It may not be a case of lying if, for example, the spouse is never asked by the other about the situation. Still, we might say, it is surely deceptive because of the promises that were exchanged at marriage. As we saw earlier, these promises provide a foundation for the reasonable belief that neither spouse will engage in sexual relationships with any other persons. Hence the failure to bring the fact of extramarital sex to the attention of the other spouse deceives that spouse about the present state of the marital relationship.

Adultery, in other words, can involve both active and passive deception. An adulterous spouse may just keep silent or, as is often the fact, the spouse may engage in an increasingly complex way of life devoted to the concealment of the facts from the nonparticipating spouse. Lies, half-truths, clandestine meetings, and the like may become a central feature of the adulterous spouse's existence. These are things that can and do happen, and when they do they make the case against adultery an easy one. Still, neither active nor passive deception is inevitably a feature of an extramarital relationship.

It is possible, though, that a more subtle but pervasive kind of deceptiveness is a feature of adultery. It comes about because of the connection in our culture between sexual intimacy and certain feelings of love and affection. The point can be made indirectly at first by seeing that one way in which we can, in our culture, mark off our close friends from our mere acquaintances is through the kinds of intimacies that we are prepared to share with them. I may, for instance, be willing to reveal my very private thoughts and emotions to my closest friends or to my wife, but to no one else. My sharing of these intimate facts about myself is from one perspective a way of making a gift to those who mean the most to me. Revealing these things and sharing them with those who mean the most to me is one means by which I create, maintain, and confirm those interpersonal relationships that are of most importance to me.

Now in our culture, it might be claimed, sexual intimacy is one of the chief currencies through which gifts of this sort are exchanged. One way to tell someone—particularly someone of the opposite sex—that you have feelings of affection and love for them is by allowing to them or sharing with them sexual behaviors that one doesn't share with the rest of the world. This way of measuring affection was certainly very much a part of the culture in which I matured. It worked something like this. If you were a girl, you showed how much you liked someone by the degree of sexual intimacy you would allow. If you liked a boy only a little, you never did more than kiss—and even the kiss was not very passionate. If you liked the boy a lot and if your feeling was reciprocated, necking, and possibly petting, was permissible. If the attachment was still stronger and you thought it might even become a permanent relationship, the sexual activity was correspondingly more intense and more intimate, although whether it would ever lead to sexual intercourse depended on whether the parties (and particularly the girl) accepted fully the prohibition on nonmarital sex. The situation for the boy was related, but not exactly the same. The assumption was that males did not naturally link sex with affection in the way in which females did. However, since women did, males had to take this into account. That is to say, because a woman would permit sexual intimacies only if she had feelings of affection for the male and only if those feelings were reciprocated, the male had to have and express those feelings, too, before sexual intimacies of any sort would occur.

The result was that the importance of a correlation between sexual intimacy and feelings of love and affection was taught by the culture and assimilated by those growing up in the culture. The scale of possible positive feelings toward persons of the other sex ran from casual liking at the one end to the love that was deemed essential to and characteristic of marriage at the other. The scale of possible sexual behavior ran from brief, passionless kissing or hand-holding at the one end to sexual intercourse at the other. And the correlation between the two scales was quite precise. As a result, any act of sexual intimacy carried substantial meaning with it, and no act of sexual intimacy was simply a pleasurable set of bodily sensations. Many such acts were, of course, more pleasurable to the participants because they were a way of saying what the participants' feelings were. And sometimes they were less pleasurable for the same reason. The point is, however, that in any event sexual activity was much more than mere bodily enjoyment. It was not like eating a good meal, listening to good music, lying in the sun, or getting a pleasant back rub. It was behavior that meant a great deal concerning one's feelings for persons of the opposite sex in whom one was most interested and with whom one was most involved. It was among the most authoritative ways in which one could communicate to another the nature and degree of one's affection.

If this sketch is even roughly right, then several things become somewhat clearer. To begin with, a possible rationale for many of the rules of conventional sexual morality can be developed. If, for example, sexual intercourse is associated with the kind of affection and commitment to another that is regarded as characteristic of the marriage relationship, then it is natural that sexual intercourse should be thought properly to take place between persons who are married to each other. And if it is thought that this kind of affection and commitment is only to be found within the marriage relationship, then it is not surprising that sexual intercourse should only be thought to be proper within marriage.

Related to what has just been said is the idea that sexual intercourse ought to be restricted to those who are married to each other as a means by which to confirm the very special feelings that the spouses have for each other. Because the culture teaches that sexual intercourse means that the strongest of all feelings for each other are shared by the lovers, it is natural that persons who are married to each other should be able to say this to each other in this way. Revealing and confirming verbally that these feelings are present is one thing that helps to sustain the relationship; engaging in sexual intercourse is another.

In addition, this account would help to provide a framework within which to make sense of the notion that some sex is better than other sex. As I indicated earlier, the fact that sexual intimacy can be meaningful in the sense described tends to make it also the case that sexual intercourse can sometimes be more enjoyable than at other times. On this view, sexual intercourse will typically be more enjoyable where the strong feelings of affection are present than it will be where it is merely "mechanical." This is so in part because people enjoy being loved, especially by those whom they love. Just as we like to hear words of affection, so we like to receive affectionate behavior. And the meaning enhances the independently pleasurable behavior.

More to the point, moreover, an additional rationale for the prohibition on extramarital sex can now be developed. For given this way of viewing the sexual world, extramarital sex will almost always involve deception of a deeper sort. If the adulterous spouse does not in fact have the appropriate feelings of affection for the extramarital partner, then the adulterous spouse is deceiving that person about the presence of such feelings. If, on the other hand, the adulterous spouse does have the corresponding feelings for the extramarital partner but not toward the nonparticipating

spouse, the adulterous spouse is very probably deceiving the nonparticipating spouse about the presence of such feelings toward that spouse. Indeed, it might be argued, whenever there is no longer love between the two persons who are married to each other, there is deception just because being married implies both to the participants and to the world that such a bond exists. Deception is inevitable, the argument might conclude, because the feelings of affection that ought to accompany any act of sexual intercourse can only be held toward one other person at any given time in one's life. And if this is so, then the adulterous spouse always deceives either the partner in adultery or the nonparticipating spouse about the existence of such feelings. Thus extramarital sex involves deception of this sort and is for this reason immoral even if no deception vis-à-vis the occurrence of the act of adultery takes place.

What might be said in response to the foregoing arguments? The first thing that might be said is that the account of the connection between sexual intimacy and feelings of affection is inaccurate. Not inaccurate in the sense that no one thinks of things that way, but in the sense that there is substantially more divergence of opinion than that account suggests. For example, the view I have delineated may describe reasonably accurately the concepts of the sexual world in which I grew up, but it does not capture the sexual *weltanschauung* of today's youth at all. Thus, whether or not adultery implies deception in respect to feelings depends very much on the persons who are involved and the way they look at the "meaning" of sexual intimacy.

Second, the argument leaves to be answered the question of whether it is desirable for sexual intimacy to carry the sorts of messages described above. For those persons for whom sex does have these implications, there are special feelings and sensibilities that must be taken into account. But it is another question entirely whether any valuable end—moral or otherwise—is served by investing sexual behavior with such significance. That is something that must be shown and not just assumed. It might, for instance, be the case that substantially more good than harm would come from a kind of demystification of sexual behavior: one that would encourage the enjoyment of sex more for its own sake and one that would reject the centrality both of the association of sex with love and of love with only one other person.

I regard these as two of the more difficult, unresolved issues that our culture faces today in respect to thinking sensibly about the attitudes toward sex and love that we should try to develop in ourselves and in our children. Much of the contemporary literature that advocates sexual liberation of one sort or another embraces one or the other of two different views about the relationship between sex and love.

One view holds that sex should be separated from love and affection. To be sure sex is probably better when the partners genuinely like and enjoy each other. But sex is basically an intensive, exciting sensuous activity that can be enjoyed in a variety of suitable settings with a variety of suitable partners. The situation in respect to sexual pleasure is no different from that of the person who knows and appreciates fine food and who can have a very satisfying meal in any number of good restaurants with any number of congenial companions. One question that must be settled here is whether sex can be so demystified; another, more important question is whether it would be desirable to do so. What would we gain and what might we lose if we all lived in a world in which an act of sexual intercourse was no more or less significant or enjoyable than having a delicious meal in a nice setting with a good friend? The answer to this question lies beyond the scope of this paper.

The second view seeks to drive the wedge in a different place. It is not the link between sex and love that needs to be broken; rather, on this view, it is the connection between love and exclusivity that ought to be severed. For a number of the reasons already given, it is desirable, so this argument goes, that sexual intimacy continue to be reserved to and shared with only those for whom one has very great affection. The mistake lies in thinking that any "normal" adult will only have those feelings toward one other adult during his or her lifetime—or even at any time in his or her life. It is the concept of adult love, not ideas about sex, that, on this view, needs demystification. What are thought to be both unrealistic and unfortunate are the notions of exclusivity and possessiveness that attach to the dominant conception of love between adults in our and other cultures. Parents of four, five, six, or even ten children can certainly claim and sometimes claim correctly that they love all of their children, that they love them all equally, and that it is simply untrue to their feelings to insist that the numbers involved diminish either the quantity or the quality of their love. If this is an idea that is readily understandable in the case of parents and children, there is no necessary reason why it is an impossible or undesirable ideal in the case of adults. To be sure, there is probably a limit to the number of intimate, "primary" relationships that any person can maintain at any given time without the quality of the relationship being affected. But one adult ought surely be able to love two, three, or even six other adults at any one time without that love being different in kind or degree from that of the traditional, monogomous, lifetime marriage. And as between the individuals in these relationships, whether within a marriage or without, sexual intimacy is fitting and good.

The issues raised by a position such as this one are also surely worth exploring in detail and with care. Is there something to be called "sexual love" which is different from parental love or the nonsexual love of close friends? Is there something about love in general that links it naturally and appropriately with feelings of exclusivity and possession? Or is there something about sexual love, whatever that may be, that makes these feelings especially fitting here? Once again the issues are conceptual, empirical, and normative all at once: What is love? How could it be different? Would it be a good thing or a bad thing if it were different?

Suppose, though, that having delineated these problems we were now to pass them by. Suppose, moreover, we were to be persuaded of the possibility and the desirability of weakening substantially either the links between sex and love or the links between sexual love and exclusivity. Would it not then be the case that adultery could be free from all of the morally objectionable features described so far? To be more specific, let us imagine that a husband and wife have what is today sometimes characterized as an "open marriage." Suppose, that is, that they have agreed in advance that extramarital sex is—under certain circumstances—acceptable behavior for each to engage in. Suppose, that as a result there is no impulse to deceive each other about the occurrence or nature of any such relationships, and that no deception in fact occurs. Suppose, too, that there is no deception in respect to the feelings involved between the adulterous spouse and the extramarital partner. And suppose, finally, that one or the other or both of the spouses then has sexual intercourse in circumstances consistent with these understandings. Under this description, so the agreement might conclude, adultery is simply not immoral. At a minimum, adultery cannot very plausibly be condemned either on the ground that it involves deception or on the ground that it requires the breaking of a promise.

At least two responses are worth considering. One calls attention to the connection between marriage and adultery; the other looks to more instrumental arguments for the immorality of adultery. Both issues deserve further exploration.

One way to deal with the case of the "open marriage" is to question whether the two persons involved are still properly to be described as being married to each other. Part of the meaning of what it is for two persons to be married to each other, so this argument would go, is to have committed oneself to have sexual relationships only with one's spouse. Of course, it would be added, we know that that commitment is not always honored. We know that persons who are married to each other often do commit adultery. But there is a difference between being willing to make a commitment to marital fidelity, even though one may fail to honor that commitment, and not making the commitment at all. Whatever the relationship may be between the two individuals in the case described above, the absence of any commitment to sexual exclusivity requires the conclusion that their relationship is not a marital one. For a commitment to sexual exclusivity is a necessary although not a sufficient condition for the existence of a marriage.

Although there may be something to this suggestion, as it is stated it is too strong to be acceptable. To begin with, I think it is very doubtful that there are many, if any, *necessary* conditions for marriage; but even if there are, a commitment to sexual exclusivity is not such a condition.

To see that this is so, consider what might be taken to be some of the essential characteristics of a marriage. We might be tempted to propose that the concept of marriage requires the following: a formal ceremony of some sort in which mutual

obligations are undertaken between two persons of the opposite sex; the capacity on the part of the persons involved to have sexual intercourse with each other; the willingness to have sexual intercourse only with each other; and feelings of love and affection between the two persons. The problem is that we can imagine relationships that are clearly marital and yet lack one or more of these features. For example, in our own society, it is possible for two persons to be married without going through a formal ceremony, as in the common-law marriages recognized in some jurisdictions. It is also possible for two persons to get married even though one or both lacks the capacity to engage in sexual intercourse. Thus, two very elderly persons who have neither the desire nor the ability to have intercourse can, nonetheless, get married, as can persons whose sexual organs have been injured so that intercourse is not possible. And we certainly know of marriages in which love was not present at the time of the marriage, as, for instance, in marriages of state and marriages of convenience.

Counterexamples not satisfying the condition relating to the abstention from extramarital sex are even more easily produced. We certainly know of societies and cultures in which polygamy and polyandry are practiced, and we have no difficulty in recognizing these relationships as cases of marriages. It might be objected, though, that these are not counterexamples because they are plural marriages rather than marriages in which sex is permitted with someone other than with one of the persons to whom one is married. But we also know of societies in which it is permissible for married persons to have sexual relationships with persons to whom they were not married, for example, temple prostitutes, concubines, and homosexual lovers. And even if we knew of no such societies, the conceptual claim would still, I submit, not be well taken. For suppose all of the other indicia of marriage were present: Suppose the two persons were of the opposite sex. Suppose they had the capacity and desire to have intercourse with each other; suppose they participated in a formal ceremony in which they understood themselves voluntarily to be entering into a relationship with each other in which substantial mutual commitments were assumed. If all these conditions were satisfied, we would not be in any doubt about whether or not the two persons were married even though they had not taken on a commitment of sexual exclusivity and even though they had expressly agreed that extramarital sexual intercourse was a permissible behavior for each to engage in.

A commitment to sexual exclusivity is neither a necessary nor a sufficient condition for the existence of a marriage. It does, nonetheless, have this much to do with the nature of marriage: Like the other indicia enumerated above, its presence tends to establish the existence of a marriage. Thus, in the absence of a formal ceremony of any sort, an explicit commitment to sexual exclusivity would count in favor of regarding the two persons as married. The conceptual role of the commitment to sexual exclusivity can, perhaps, be brought out through the following example. Suppose we found a tribe which had a practice in which all the other indicia of marriage were present but in which the two parties were *prohibited* ever from having sexual intercourse with each other. Moreover, suppose that sexual intercourse with others was clearly permitted. In such a case we would, I think, reject the idea that the two were married to each other and we would describe their relationship in other terms, for example, as some kind of formalized, special friendship relation—a kind of heterosexual "blood-brother" bond.

Compare that case with the following. Suppose again that the tribe had a practice in which all of the other indicia of marriage were present, but instead of a prohibition on sexual intercourse between the persons in the relationship there was no rule at all. Sexual intercourse was permissible with the person with whom one had this ceremonial relationship, but it was no more or less permissible than with a number of other persons to whom one was not so related (for instance, all consenting adults of the opposite sex). Although we might be in doubt as to whether we ought to describe the persons as married to each other, we would probably conclude that they were married and that they simply were members of a tribe whose views about sex were quite different from our own.

What all of this shows is that *a prohibition* on sexual intercourse between the two persons involved in a relationship is conceptually incompatible with the claim that the two of them are married. The *permissibility* of intramarital sex is a necessary part of the idea of marriage. But no such incompatibility follows simply from the added permissibility of extramarital sex.

These arguments do not, of course, exhaust the arguments for the prohibition on extramarital sexual relations. The remaining argument that I wish to consider—as I indicated earlier—is a more instrumental one. It seeks to justify the prohibition by virtue of the role that it plays in the development and maintenance of nuclear families. The argument, or set of arguments, might, I believe, go something like this.

Consider first a farfetched nonsexual example. Suppose a society were organized so that after some suitable age—say, 18, 19, or 20—persons were forbidden to eat anything but bread and water with anyone but their spouse. Persons might still choose in such a society not to get married. Good food just might not be very important to them because they have underdeveloped taste buds. Or good food might be bad for them because there is something wrong with their digestive system. Or good food might be important to them, but they might decide that the enjoyment of good food would get in the way of the attainment of other things that were more important. But most persons would, I think, be led to favor marriage in part because they preferred a richer, more varied, diet to one of bread and water. And they might remain married because the family was the only legitimate setting within which good food was obtainable. If it is important to have society organized so that persons will both get married and stay married, such an arrangement would be well suited to the preservation of the family, and the prohibitions relating to food consumption could be understood as fulfilling that function.

It is obvious that one of the more powerful human desires is the desire for sexual gratification. The desire is a natural one, like hunger and thirst, in the sense that it need not be learned in order to be present within us and operative upon us. But there is in addition much that we do learn about what the act of sexual intercourse is like. Once we experience sexual intercourse ourselves—and in particular once we experience orgasm—we discover that it is among the most intensive, short-term pleasures of the body.

Because this is so, it is easy to see how the prohibition upon extramarital sex helps to hold marriage together. At least during that period of life when the enjoyment of sexual intercourse is one of the desirable bodily pleasures, persons will wish to enjoy those pleasures. If one consequence of being married is that one is prohibited from having sexual intercourse with anyone but one's spouse, then the spouses in a marriage are in a position to provide an important source of pleasure for each other that is unavailable to them elsewhere in the society.

The point emerges still more clearly if this rule of sexual morality is seen as of a piece with the other rules of sexual morality. When this prohibition is coupled, for example, with the prohibition on nonmarital sexual intercourse, we are presented with the inducement both to get married and to stay married. For if sexual intercourse is only legitimate within marriage, then persons seeking that gratification which is a feature of sexual intercourse are furnished explicit social directions for its attainment; namely marriage.

Nor, to continue the argument, is it necessary to focus exclusively on the bodily enjoyment that is involved. Orgasm may be a significant part of what there is to sexual intercourse, but it is not the whole of it. We need only recall the earlier discussion of the meaning that sexual intimacy has in our own culture to begin to see some of the more intricate ways in which sexual exclusivity may be connected with the establishment and maintenance of marriage as the primary heterosexual, love relationship. Adultery is wrong, in other words, because a prohibition on extramarital sex is a way to help maintain the institutions of marriage and the nuclear family.

Now I am frankly not sure what we are to say about an argument such as this one. What I am convinced of is that, like the arguments discussed earlier, this one also reveals something of the difficulty and complexity of the issues that are involved. So, what I want now to do—in the brief and final portion of this paper—is to try to delineate with reasonable precision what I take several of the fundamental, unresolved issues to be.

The first is whether this last argument is an argument for the *immorality* of extramarital sexual intercourse. What does seem clear is that there are differences between this argument and the ones considered earlier. The earlier arguments condemned adulterous behavior because it was be-

havior that involved breaking of a promise, taking unfair advantage, or deceiving another. To the degree to which the prohibition on extramarital sex can be supported by arguments which invoke considerations such as these, there is little question but that violations of the prohibition are properly regarded as immoral. And such a claim could be defended on one or both of two distinct grounds. The first is that things like promise-breaking and deception are just wrong. The second is that adultery involving promise-breaking or deception is wrong because it involves the straightforward infliction of harm on another human being— typically the nonadulterous spouse—who has a strong claim not to have that harm so inflicted.

The argument that connects the prohibition on extramartial sex with the maintenance and preservation of the institution of marriage is an argument for the instrumental value of the prohibition. To some degree this counts, I think, against regarding all violations of the prohibition as obvious cases of immorality. This is so partly because hypothetical imperatives are less clearly within the domain of morality than are categorical ones, and even more because instrumental prohibitions are within the domain of morality only if the end they serve or the way they serve it is itself within the domain of morality.

What this should help us see, I think, is the fact that the argument that connects the prohibition on adultery with the preservation of marriage is at best seriously incomplete. Before we ought to be convinced by it, we ought to have reasons for believing that marriage is a morally desirable and just social institution. And this is not quite as easy or obvious a task as it may seem to be. For the concept of marriage is, as we have seen, both a loosely structured and a complicated one. There may be all sorts of intimate, interpersonal relationships which will resemble but not be identical with the typical marriage relationship presupposed by the traditional sexual morality. There may be a number of distinguishable sexual and loving arrangements which can all legitimately claim to be called *marriages*. The prohibitions of the traditional sexual morality may be effective ways to maintain some marriages and ineffective ways to promote and preserve others. The prohibitions of the traditional sexual morality may make good psychological sense if certain psychological theories are true, and they may be purveyors of immense psychological mischief if other psychological theories are true. The prohibitions of the traditional sexual morality may seem obviously correct if sexual intimacy carries the meaning that the dominant culture has often ascribed to it, and they may seem equally bizarre when sex is viewed through the perspective of the counterculture. Irrespective of whether instrumental arguments of this sort are properly deemed moral arguments, they ought not to fully convince anyone until questions like these are answered.

Questions for Analysis

1. *What does Wasserstrom mean by calling promise breaking and deception "prima facie wrong"? Does his description of prima facie wrong accord with Ross's?*

2. *Explain how one can argue that certain kinds of adultery are wrong because they involve the intentional breaking of a promise.*

3. *Explain how the culturally based connection between sex and love can provide a rationale for the rules of conventional sexual morality, for restricting sexual intercourse to those who are married to each other, for saying that some sex is better than other sex, and for claiming that adultery always involves deception.*

4. *Wasserstrom offers essentially four arguments against adultery—state them. Which of these arguments is strictly consequential?*

5. *Which of the arguments do you think Kant would find appealing? Why?*

The Morality of Homosexual Behavior

Ronald Atkinson

On what grounds, if any, could private, harmless homosexual acts between consenting adults be held immoral? This is the question that philosophy professor Ronald Atkinson addresses in "The Morality of Homosexual Behavior."

In responding to the question, Atkinson cites several common objections to homosexual acts: (1) that they are objectionable on prudential grounds, (2) that they present such morally objectionable features as seduction and the exploitation of the young, (3) that they fall well short of the ideal form of human relationship. Atkinson attempts to refute each of these.

Since many object to homosexuality on grounds that it is "unnatural," Atkinson at some length tries to make sense of the notions of "nature" and "natural," as these concepts apply to sexual morality, especially to homosexuality. Some people equate "unnatural" with "disgusting." Thus, since they find homosexuality disgusting, they consider it unnatural. But, as Atkinson points out, no connection necessarily exists between what is disgusting and what is unnatural. (In terms of informal logic, such an argument relies exclusively on an appeal to provincialism to justify its conclusion.)

Many people, however, associate naturalness in sex with procreation. Sex, then, that cannot or is not intended to procreate is unnatural. But by this account, sexual intercourse between a married couple who permanently practice birth control would be unnatural.

In Atkinson's view most of the arguments that claim homosexuality is immoral are based on theological, not empirical premises. Since theological premises are always matters of dispute, the conclusions that they entail are questionable. Yes, homosexuality may be unnatural. But the traditional arguments advanced to establish this conclusion are either inconsistent, based on questionable premises, or both. Consequently, there are currently no sound reasons that compel adherence to the conclusion that homosexuality is unnatural, and therefore immoral.

The Wolfenden Committee did not spend much time on the question of morality of homosexual behavior. Possibly they felt that in any way to question its immorality would only arouse opposition to their recommendation concerning the attitude to be taken to it by the law. They are emphatic that, in staking a claim for a sphere of private morality and immorality beyond the reach of the law, they do not wish to be understood as condoning private immorality. Moreover, in so far as the concern is with *positive* morality, the received code of behavior such as it is, there is no doubt at all that homosexual activity is immoral. But can one avoid asking the question whether positive morality is right on this matter? Suppose, as the Wolfenden Committee thought, that there may be homosexual acts which do no harm to nonconsenting nonadults, and which, being private, are no affront to public decency—on what grounds could they be held to be morally wrong?

Not on utilitarian grounds, obviously; nor, leaving out of account the present state of the law and public opinion, on prudential grounds either. People do not choose to become homosexuals, they rather find that they are: And even if they should then want to change the direction of their sexual inclinations, which they may not, there would at present seem to be no certainty that this can be successfully accomplished. To deny one's sexual nature all physical expression, still ignoring the consequences homosexuals may suffer from law and public opinion, goes beyond, if not contrary to, the demands of prudence.

It may be that, in fact, many homosexual relationships present morally objectionable features: They may involve seduction, and exploitation of the young. But the evidence noticed above suggests that most do not, and that the risk of a homosexual who practices with fellow adults turning to boys is comparatively small. It is, moreover, relevant to the assessment of the moral importance of such risk as there is to point out that the harm done by seduction, or even assault, to young boys can easily be exaggerated—as can the damage done by heterosexual interference with small girls. In both cases the extreme reactions of parents, understandable though they may be, tend to increase the harm. And the likelihood of a boy being turned into a homosexual by seduction would not seem to be very great, as home influences are more important than outside encounters in determining one's sexual orientation. Most men who engage in homosexual activity in special circumstances—school, prison, the army—appear to abandon it when heterosexual opportunities become available. Some, much, even most homosexual activity may be morally exceptionable: So too is a good deal of heterosexual activity. In neither case is this necessarily so. Nor does it appear that homosexual relationships in themselves are necessarily more objectionable than heterosexual ones. I can see no good reason to doubt that it is possible for a homosexual to conduct his sexual life with prudence, beneficence, fairness and responsibility. If he does, there is no ground for moral complaint.

Another claim that is often made is that homosexual relationships are apt to be morally worthless or of little worth, to fall very far short of the ideal form of human relationship. (It is important to distinguish this complaint from the previous one. *That* was to the effect that they offended against, so to say, "basic morality": *This* is to the effect that they are not ideal. . . .) Homosexual relations seem normally to be of brief duration, and homosexual promiscuity to be common. They seem, that is to say, to resemble those heterosexual relationships which are held to be least worth while. This sort of contention has great rhetorical force. It purports to make a lavish concession, to allow, as, of course, many people do not, that homosexual relationships are to be judged on the *same footing* as heterosexual ones, and yet still contrives to find them objectionable. How far must we go along with it?

Two comments are in place. The first, and less important one, is that the unworthwhile features manifested by some homosexual relationships may largely be the result of the public attitude to them. The result of, and hence not the justification for, that attitude. Stable relationships are hardly possible when all homosexual associations are condemned out of hand. The more important point is that, low though casual sexual encounters may be on the heterosexual's scale of preference, they may still be the best or only form of sexual association available to the homosexuals involved. The basic morality of avoiding harm and unfairness to others we may reasonably demand of everybody: Our ideals in so far as they go beyond this are for the guidance of our own, not other people's, conduct. In general we do not blame people, or hold them to be wicked or immoral, for not sharing our ideals; at worst we may hold them misguided or mistaken, or that they are "missing something." It is doubtful, in fact, whether even such mild criticisms or commiserations fit the case of the homosexual, who has not chosen his condition and probably cannot change it.

It may further be noted that from the point of view of the morality of personal relationships, which was considered in a different connection above . . . , homosexual associations as such cannot be held to be immoral. The authors of the Quaker pamphlet recognise this with characteristic candor:

> . . . we see no reason why the physical nature of a sexual act should be the criterion by which the question whether it is moral should be decided. An act which (for example) expresses true affection between two individuals and gives pleasure to them both, does not seem to us to be sinful by reason *alone* of the fact that it is homosexual. The same criteria seem to us to apply whether a relationship is heterosexual or homosexual [p. 36].

I expressed some doubt above about the responsibility of viewing heterosexual associations exclusively from the agent-centered ethic of personal relationships. This seemed to me to take insufficient account of the possibility of children being conceived. This consideration does not arise where homosexual associations are concerned.

It is true, of course, that many people find the thought of homosexual practice deeply disgusting. It is sometimes suggested that this is the result of overcompensation for their own latent homosexuality, but whatever the explanation of it, the fact remains. One cannot, however, allow any simple inference from the disgusting to the immoral. In fact, surely, in this case the movement of thought is the other way. Homosexual practices are felt to be peculiarly disgusting because they are held to be exceptionally sinful or immoral. They disgust because they are "unnatural."

No one who thinks like this will be induced to improve his view of homosexual activity by such claims as that made by Chesser (*Live and Let Live*, pp. 30–1) that the most abominated homosexual act, anal intercourse, is probably commoner among married than homosexual couples. The act is felt to be abominable whenever and between whomsoever it occurs. What puts homosexuals utterly beyond the pale is that *all* their physical sexual activities are necessarily unnatural in some degree, even if not in the very highest.

It is, as already suggested . . . , a matter of great difficulty to grasp the rationale of this way of thinking, to make sense of the notions of *nature* and *the natural* involved. As a beginning one has to suppose that the purpose or function of sex is mainly procreation. It would seem to follow that heterosexual intercourse which is intended to be fertile is the ideally natural sexual act. This is not, however, exactly the conclusion usually desired, for such intercourse clearly could take place outside marriage or even a loving relationship. Consequently sex has to be allowed a second, nonprocreative, "relational" or companionate purpose, which may then be held to be achievable only within marriage. Provided not too much is made of the relational purpose, provided that it is kept firmly subordinate to the procreational one, homosexual activity is still bound to come out as unnatural—it cannot fulfill procreational purposes at all. But . . . there are snags in emphasizing the importance of the procreational purpose. Suppose we want to allow deliberately infertile heterosexual intercourse within marriage. Even in this case it is still possible to pay some regard to the claims of procreation by insisting that couples should not refuse to have children altogether, even though they may use contraceptives for a large proportion of their married life. This is a typically Anglican attitude, expressed for instance by Dr. D. S. Bailey in his "Homosexuality and Christian Morals" (in Rees & Usill). From this point of view homosexual activity can still consistently be held to be unnatural. I do not, however, see how it can be by anyone prepared to allow permanently childless marriages, or intentionally infertile heterosexual relationships outside marriage.

It is, in my opinion, *possible* consistently to hold homosexual activity to be unnatural. Much care and ingenuity are, however, required, and I suspect that many people who do regard it as unnatural are, in fact, inconsistent at one point or another. Nor, rare though it is, is consistency enough. The *truth* of the premises concerning the purposes of sex, and the relative importance of the purposes assigned, is crucial too. And yet, as observed above, it is very difficult to see how it is to be ascertained. They are not empirical premises, of which the truth could be assessed by some sort of morally neutral scientific enquiry—biological, psychological, sociological, or whatever it might be. The relevant form of enquiry is, perhaps, theological—but whether there is a subject-matter for theology is itself a controversial question. There is no ground, even in principle, for expecting reasonable men to agree on matters of theology, as there is on matters of biology, psychology and sociology. The credentials of theology as a subject are in dispute. And the propositions of natural theology are just as uncertain as those of revealed.

Accordingly, to the unbeliever, arguing to moral conclusions from theologically based premises about the nature or purpose of sex seems to be little more than a matter of arbitrarily selecting those premises which yield the moral conclusions desired. If you want to condemn contraception and homosexuality you have to emphasize the procreational purpose. If you want to permit contraception you must give greater weight to nonprocreational purposes. To the believer, on the other hand, it does not seem like this at all. He must believe that questions about the nature and purpose of sex relate to matters of (nonempirical) fact. He will not see himself as arbitrarily choosing answers that are in line with moral judgments he has reached on other grounds, but rather, when he differs from his predecessors in moral theology, as correcting their mistakes of emphasis. These mistakes he may see as the result of prejudices resulting from local and temporary features of his predecessors' situation. If they attributed undue importance to procreation this will be because they did not write from the vantage point of a potentially overpopulated world. The truth will never change, but our view of it does, perhaps getting nearer to it all the time.

I have myself no enthusiasm at all for appraising human conduct as natural or unnatural. I have, however, tried to draw attention to the *complexity* of the notion of the natural employed by moral theologians, mainly in order to show how different it is from that implicit in the popular condemnation of homosexual behavior as unnatural. In the popular view the unnatural and the disgusting are closely connected, and judging something to be unnatural is felt to be the simple, direct, inevitable reaction of the "healthy" mind to it. But there can be nothing simple in any notion of the natural which will admit of application over the whole range of sexual behavior, which will serve as the key idea in a comprehensive sexual morality. Nor will there be any necessary connection between the corresponding notion of the *unnatural* and the disgusting.

Questions for Analysis

1. Atkinson says that harmless and private homosexual acts between consenting adults "obviously" cannot be considered immoral on utilitarian grounds. Why "obviously"?

2. Why can such acts not be considered immoral on "prudential grounds"?

3. Is the argument that such acts present morally objectionable features a consequential or nonconsequential one? Explain. How does Atkinson try to refute this argument?

4. *Atkinson says that those who claim that homosexual relationships fall far short of ideal human relationships appear to make a "lavish concession" to the debate about the morality of homosexuality. What is this "lavish concession"? How does Atkinson reply to the claim?*

5. *Atkinson claims that most of the arguments calling homosexuality "unnatural" are not based on empirical premises and, therefore, are questionable. Explain what he means.*

6. *Show how Kant would object to homosexuality on the grounds that it is unnatural.*

CASE PRESENTATION
Sex and the Single Man

"Trust me, trust me, trust me," Marcus Aurelius Markam, III, was saying to his pal Chuck as they left the science building and headed for the cafeteria. "In matters of sex, honesty is the best policy."

"I thought all was fair in love and war," Chuck said, puzzled.

"Not any more," Mark told him. "At least not in sex anyway. No, today the watchword is *candor*. Be open, direct, and frank with today's woman, and she will melt into your arms like butter in a hot pan." Then he looked imperiously down his long nose at Chuck and asked, "That *is* what you want Kathy to do, isn't it—melt?"

Chuck nodded weakly.

"Well, then, be up front with her."

A deep worry line formed between Chuck's blue eyes. He tugged at his right earlobe, a habit of his whenever he was nervous. "You really think so, huh?"

"Absolutely!" Mark assured him, slicing the air for emphasis with a red-white-and-blue Bic ballpoint pen.

Confusion washed over Chuck's freckled face. "I would have thought . . ."

"That deception, deceit, and duplicity get girls into bed, right?"

"Something like that, I guess," said Chuck.

Mark smiled. "A common misconception," he said. Then he draped an arm over Chuck's shoulders and whispered, "Would you believe I've gotten more girls into bed with the unvarnished truth than with barefaced lies?"

"The truth?"

Mark slapped a bony hand over Chuck's mouth to silence him, and again whispered, "The truth!"

When Mark removed his hand, all Chuck could say was, "Amazing!" which he repeated several times before they reached the cafeteria.

"The thing about it is," Chuck said to Mark over hamburgers and fries, "I'm torn between wanting Kathy and not wanting to hurt her. Does that make any sense?"

"Perfect sense, perfect sense," Mark replied, smothering his burger with raw onions. "That's precisely why you must be up front with her. Anything less and you'll never be able to live with yourself, believe me."

Chuck put down his milk carton long enough to tug at his ear. "But how can you expect a girl to go to bed with you after you've told her you don't love her?"

"Well, well, well," said Mark, carefully positioning his burger on a plate full of onion rings. "Now it comes out."

"What?"

Mark dabbed the corners of his mouth before saying, "I had no idea that my best friend was *so* naive."

"Naive? What're you talking about?"

"No offense intended, but it's true. Little did I think that anyone I knew, let alone numbered among my friends, still believed that girls needed to be lied to before they . . . well, I'm speechless. Pass me the relish, will ya?"

"So you think I should be up front with her, huh?" Chuck said later to Mark as they passed the library.

"I think you should tell her you want to sleep with her with no strings attached—unless, of course, she's kind of kinky, in which case she may want strings."

"Tell her right out, huh? Just like that?"

"She'll respect you for it."

"But I want her to go to bed with me!"

"That will follow, that will follow."

"You really think so?"

"Trust me, trust me."

Questions for Analysis

1. *Would you agree that the morality of premarital sex depends largely, if not exclusively, on honestly and thoroughly communicating your feelings to your partner? Stated another way, do you think that the only immorality of harmless and private premarital sex between consenting adults is deception by one toward the other regarding one's actual feelings or the meaning that one attaches to the act of sexual intercourse?*

2. *Suppose that Chuck follows Mark's advice and Kathy agrees to have sex with him. They use contraceptives and enjoy a sexual relationship, with the understanding that whenever one or the other of them wishes to end the relationship, the relationship is over. What possible grounds would there be for claiming that sex under such conditions is immoral?*

3. *Mark professes honesty in all heterosexual relationships. Kant would commend his concern with honesty, but would not consider Mark has a genuine commitment to honesty, that is, acts from a duty to be honest. Explain.*

4. *Suppose that you were Chuck and you knew that Mark was an egoist. Would you be skeptical of his advice? If so, why?*

CASE PRESENTATION
Making It with a Perfect Stranger

"Don't you ever just want to make it with a perfect stranger?"

Meg remembered how shocked she was when Joan had asked her that. No, not shocked—incredulous! Why, she couldn't even imagine doing it with anyone but Ty, her husband.

Meg and Ty had been happily married for three years. Early in their marriage, they had decided to postpone having a family in order to pursue careers, he in banking, she in sales. The arrangement had worked out beautifully. Both were very successful, which seemed only to enrich their marriage.

But Meg's job kept her on the road a lot. In the beginning she didn't have time to feel lonely. The travel was too stimulating. New places, new faces, new challenges—it was all great fun. It still was. But increasingly Meg felt the need and desire for male company, maybe even for a "fling."

"God!" she thought to herself over a martini in the lounge of some dreary hotel in a nondescript city she happened to be working. "I'm actually contemplating a one-night stand!" Recalling Joan's words, she smiled softly and thought, "Well, what do you know!"

"So what canary have you swallowed?"

"What?" said Meg, startled by the male voice.

A tall, slim man with a shock of wavy black hair stood by her table, half-filled tumbler in hand. "You're smiling like the proverbial cat that swallowed the canary," he said pleasantly.

Meg could feel her face flush. Even in the lounge's dim light, she knew the stranger could see it turn beet-red. "I'm very sorry," he said in a sincere tone. "I didn't mean to embarrass you, I really didn't." And with that, he turned to walk off.

He hadn't taken more than two steps when Meg said, "Oh, you didn't embarrass me." The man turned, faced her squarely, flashed a winning smile, and asked if he could join her. "Why not?" said Meg, matter-of-factly.

They never even exchanged names. Meg wanted it that way. And they didn't feed each other any well-oiled lines or swap addresses or phone numbers. They did have a few drinks, enjoyed a good meal, and shared a bed. In the morning they parted with a brief kiss and didn't even promise to get together again when next in town.

And what did Meg make of it all? It was far too early to say. Although she now knew what it was like to make it with a perfect stranger, she didn't know what to make of making it.

Questions for Analysis

1. *What possible objections would there be to the morality of an adulterous relation under these circumstances?*

2. *Do you think that Meg has a moral obligation to tell Ty what happened?*

3. *Meg subsequently confessed her indiscretion to Joan, who told her: "Whatever you do, you shouldn't tell Ty." Do you think Meg has a moral obligation not to tell Ty? Explain. Do you think she was wrong in telling Joan? Explain.*

4. *According to Ross's theory, what prima facie duties might Meg have considered in deciding to have extramarital sex?*

5. *At Meg's insistence, she and the stranger exchanged no personal information. Do you think that this bears on the morality of the adulterous relation, or is it immaterial?*

Selections for Further Reading

Baker, Robert, and Frederick Elliston. *Philosophy and Sex.* Buffalo, N.Y.: Prometheus Books, 1975.

Benson, R. O. D. *In Defense of Homosexuality: Male and Female.* New York: Julian Press, 1955.

Duvall, Evelyn M. *Why Wait Until Marriage?* New York: Association Press, 1965.

Geddes, D. P., Ed. *An Analysis of the Kinsey Reports on Sexual Behavior in the Human Male and Female.* New York: New American Library, 1962.

Guyon, Rene. *Sexual Freedom.* Eden and Cedar Paul, Trans. New York: Knopf, 1950.

Hoffman, Martin. *The Gay World: Male Homosexuality and the Social Creation of Evil.* New York: Basic Books, 1968.

Reiss, Ira L. *Premarital Sexual Standards in America.* New York: Free Press, 1960.

Roy, R. *Honest Sex.* New York: New American Library, 1968.

Russell, Bertrand. *Marriage and Morals.* New York: Liveright, 1929.

Vinck, Jose De. *The Virtue of Sex.* New York: Hawthorn Books, 1966.

Whiteley, C. H., and W. M. Whiteley. *Sex and Morals.* New York: Basic Books, 1967.

4
PORNOGRAPHY

Pornography is a big business. Estimates of the trade in pornographic and obscene materials in the United States alone run as high as several billion dollars a year. Many individuals, institutions, and agencies have become alarmed by the increasing traffic in pornographic magazines, books, films, and other materials.

Among those concerned is the U.S. Congress, which has labeled traffic in pornographic materials a matter of national concern. Responding to these developments, in 1966 the Congress established the Commission on Obscenity and Pornography. The Commission's responsibility was to make recommendations concerning pornographic and obscene materials based on a thorough study of them. In 1970, the Commission submitted its report to the President and the Congress. It recommended that legislation prohibiting the sale, exhibition, and distribution of sexual material to consenting adults be repealed.

The Commission's report met with widespread executive, legislative, and popular disapproval. In fact, the Commission itself was divided: Six of the eighteen members did not support the Commission's recommendation. As a result, implementation of the recommendation has been sporadic.

Whether or not there should be laws restricting the consenting adult's access to pornography is a key moral question in the pornography issue. But an even more basic question—and one that often intrudes on the discussions of the morality of restrictive pornography legislation—is whether or not there is anything morally objectionable about pornographic materials.

In this chapter we shall consider both questions: the morality of pornographic materials and the morality of restrictive pornography laws. Central to both questions is the definition of pornography. Thus, we shall begin our discussion by considering the problem of defining pornography. Having done that, we will then air some of the arguments relative to the two main moral concerns that the pornography issue involves.

The Meaning of Pornography

What is pornographic? Or, precisely, what material is rightly considered pornographic and why? The exact meanings of *pornographic* and *pornography* are a principal issue in the debate on the morality both of pornography and of the laws that would restrict its production and discrimination.

Generally, pornography refers to literature, art, or photography that is "obscene." To understand the meaning of *pornography*, then, one must understand what *obscene* means.

The *Random House Dictionary* defines *obscene* as: "1. offensive to modesty or decency; 2. intended to cause sexual excitement or lust; 3. abominable or disgusting." Clearly such a definition is loaded with words that imply value judgments: "offensive," "abominable," "disgusting," and so forth. Such descriptions refer to feelings or reactions in those who experience pornographic material. This is an important point because it suggests that "obscenity" is not a property inherent in a book, film, or photograph, but a tendency that the work may have to elicit feelings of revulsion in those who experience it.

Thus, the claim that the X-rated movie *Deep Throat* depicts various human sexual behavior can be verified by observing the film. To call the same film "obscene" or "pornographic" is to express a personal evaluation the legitimacy of which depends, at least in part, on the perspective of the person or group making the judgment. If beauty is in the eye of the beholder, then obscenity and pornography seem to be, too.

Of course, perceptions change. To illustrate, few if any people today would consider Mark Twain's *Huckleberry Finn* an "obscene" piece of literature. And yet, at the time of its publication, this American classic was condemned as obscene. So was Nathaniel Hawthorne's *The Scarlet Letter*, which today continues to be assigned reading for many high school students.

We could add more examples, but there is no need. The point is that our reasons for calling something obscene or pornographic cannot be divorced from where and when we live. Moreover, our own personal judgments of pornography are as much subject to change as those of the society in which we live. Thus, it is not at all uncommon to find oneself firmly convinced that a film or book is obscene or pornographic only to find oneself wondering, some time afterward, what was ever considered so objectionable about the material. And, of course, the reverse is possible, too: What once did not even make a person blink, subsequently elicits a disapproving scowl.

Because of the highly idiosyncratic nature of judgments about pornography, many argue that it is impossible to assign any meaningful definition to the terms *obscene* and *pornographic*. Not everyone agrees, however. In the landmark case, *Roth* v. *United States* (1957), the U.S. Supreme Court laid down a definition of obscenity that for more than two decades has been applied in cases of alleged pornography.

In defining obscene and pornographic material, the Court cited four basic characteristics. First, the material must be considered in terms of its appeal to "the average person." This contrasted sharply with earlier definitions that included material which might affect only those susceptible to it. Second, the material must be "patently offensive because it affronts contemporary community standards relating to the description or representation of sexual matters." Third, the work must be taken as a whole, not piecemeal; the dominant theme must be taken into account rather than material taken out of context. Thus, the terms *pornographic* or *obscene* may be applied only to material whose *theme* satisfies the other elements of the definition. Fourth, the material must be a strict appeal to "prurient interest." It must be totally lacking in any social value or importance. By the Court's account, then, a work is obscene or pornographic if, considered in terms of its appeal to the average person, it offends community standards because its theme, taken as a whole, appeals to prurient interests and is without social value.

Is such a definition operational? No, say its detractors. They point out, first, that "average person" is a hopelessly vague phrase. Who, after all, is this so-called "average person"? And even if we could isolate such a creature, we could not bottle him or her in such a way as to ensure that the person's attitude, outlooks, and appetites never changed.

The Court's critics see similar operational problems in the phrase "contemporary community standards." Just what "community" should we have in mind? The village, town, city, county, state, region, country? And even if we could agree on the "community," can we really determine what the community's standards are? Perhaps some citizens group should represent the view of the community. Or maybe each member of the community should be polled: If more individuals think a work obscene than not, then by the community's standards it is. Of course, we would have no way of knowing that the people judged the work pornographic on "legitimate" grounds: on its appeal to the average person, on its appeal to prurience, on its lack of social value.

In addition, critics argue that any judgment about a work's "prurience" is so subjective as to be useless. In the last analysis, they say, all such judgments will be little more than expressions of someone's beliefs.

Finally, there is the matter of "social value." Who can say what has social value? Sometimes what appears to have no social value turns out to be extremely worthwhile. In a dynamic, evolving society such as ours, it is very difficult, if at all possible, to say with assurance what has value and what does not. Might not a reasonable criterion for judging whether material has any redeeming value be whether or not it "plays," that is, whether or not it finds any audience? If it does, then it serves some social purpose; it has some social value. Moreover, the fact that what is repugnant to the vast majority of people can still find a niche in society may itself be a social value in reaffirming the full and open nature of our society.

Of course, the Supreme Court's definition is a legal one. But other definitions have been proposed. In a religious vein, some have argued that any material calculated to arouse sexual passion is obscene. But such a definition ignores the nature of the material itself. Is overtly asexual material to be taken as pornographic so long as it was *intended* to arouse sexual passion? By the same token, is material not pornographic that has a high sexual content but that was not intended to arouse sexual passion? From a psychological viewpoint, other definitions try to distinguish pornography from what is often termed "erotic realism." The latter supposedly provides an accurate picture of sex as a basic aspect of life. Pornography, on the other hand, is thought to lack such realism, often exaggerating the sexuality of the people it portrays, focusing exclusively on the physiological responses of the participants, and frequently presenting what is widely considered deviant sexual behavior. Still, such a distinction seems to raise just as many questions of interpretation as it intends to dispel.

Still other definitions would view pornography in terms of dehumanization and depersonalization. An obscene work—as distinguished from an artistic one—presents a disgusting picture of human life, not for the reader's or viewer's contemplation, but for their enjoyment, even participation. In effect, while erotic works of art present sexual material for the spectator's consideration and edification, pornography invites them to wallow in it. Maybe so. But by what criteria are we to distinguish the work which invites contemplation from that which invites sheer sexual indulgence?

Finally, there are those who, while admitting they cannot define pornography, nonetheless say they can recognize it. In the words of Supreme Court Justice Potter Stewart: "I know it when I see it." Thus, in 1974, the Court, after due deliberation, ruled that the film *Carnal Knowledge* was not obscene, but that *The Illustrated Presidential Report of the Commission on Obscenity and Pornography* was.

Moral Issues

Pornography and obscenity raise numerous moral questions, two of which concern us here. The first may be phrased: Are pornographic materials in and of themselves morally objectionable, or are they not? We will call the various arguments connected with this question "Arguments Against Pornographic Materials" and "Arguments for Pornographic Materials." The second question, which concerns the legality of pornography, may be stated: Is it right for the state to limit the consenting adult's access to obscene and pornographic material? In responding to this question, we will present "Arguments for Censorship" and "Arguments Against Censorship."

It is most important to distinguish these two questions. Whether or not pornography is moral is a separate and distinct question from whether or not consenting adults should be allowed access to it. One could argue consistently that pornography is morally objectionable, but that the state has no right to limit an adult's access to it. Or one might argue consistently that pornography is not morally objectionable, but that the state ought to limit an adult's access to it.

There is another reason to keep the two issues separate. Often arguments for censorship assume that pornography is morally objectionable and, therefore, should be suppressed. Perhaps what is immoral ought to be suppressed, perhaps not. Whatever the view—and there are grounds for reasonable debate—the issue is strictly academic until it is established that pornography is, in fact, immoral. But often this is ignored; pornography is assumed to be immoral, and the argument moves inexorably toward its censorship.

So, keep in mind the distinction between the morality of pornographic material and the morality of laws that restrict the adult's access to pornographic materials. While obviously related by common subject, these important questions for the individual and society are significantly different, as we will see in the arguments connected with them.

Arguments Against Pornographic Materials

1. *Pornography degrades humans.*

POINT: "Nobody can deny that every piece of pornography shares one thing with every other piece of pornography: It degrades humans. It presents in graphic detail a depraved picture of human life; it portrays humans functioning in a way less than human, wallowing around on some animal level of lust and depravity, and inviting the spectators to join them. What's wrong with pornography? It affronts human dignity; in its portrayal of humans, it dehumanizes them."

COUNTERPOINT: "Now don't tell me you've never had a lustful thought. Why even a U.S. President once admitted to having lusted in his heart. Let's not kid ourselves: Lust is as much a human emotion as fear, anger, or hatred. And, whether we like to admit it or not, some people do act in depraved ways—and, at times, a lot more than in the average 'porno' flick. So, frankly, I don't see what's so 'dehumanizing' about portraying these aspects of the human personality. Sure, I'd probably agree that they aren't as uplifting as showing the human in its finest hour, reaching the pinnacle of human achievement or extending the bounds of human endurance. But that's really irrelevant. We're not judging art here, but morality. I might also agree that some people are scandalized, maybe even 'dehumanized' by pornography. But that speaks more of their reaction to the material than to any feature of the material itself. Some people are amused by 'porn,' others bored by it. So, what are we to say—that there's something inherently amusing or boring about pornography? No, simply that some people react to pornography in a bored or amused way."

2. *Pornography separates sexual passion from affection or love.*

POINT: "In our culture, sexual intimacies generally have been associated with the most profound affection that one human being can show toward another. While it's true that sex doesn't always carry that symbolic meaning, our society still recognizes that it should. And individuals in many cases still expect sex to carry that affectionate, caring, loving aspect. But you'll never find this side of sex in pornography. Quite the opposite. Every effort is made in pornography to separate sex from affection, caring, and love. 'Impersonal lust' is the order of the day. In the real world, sex that doesn't have love as its senior partner is objectionable. It's no less objectionable when portrayed that way on the screen or in a book.''

COUNTERPOINT: ''Sure, sex with affection may be more enjoyable than affectionless sex. It may even be an ideal. But what falls short of the ideal isn't necessarily wrong. Nor is it wrong to portray what is less than the ideal. In fact, some people would say that without such portrayals we'd lose sight of the ideal. But for the sake of argument, let's assume that affectionless sex is wrong. Even so, it doesn't necessarily follow that to portray affectionless sex, even pornographically, is also wrong. Lots of things are wrong—kidnapping, rape, murder. That doesn't mean that it's wrong to portray these subjects in film or literature. Sure, you might say that a presentation that 'sympathizes' or 'glorifies' these things, a presentation that does not categorically condemn them, is wrong. But what constitutes a 'sympathetic' or 'glorifying' presentation? At what point does a film, for example, not only cease to portray sexual passion with affection and begin to portray it as a depersonalized sexual desire, but also glorify that presentation? I don't know; I don't think anybody does. I'm not even sure what criteria you'd use to make such a judgment. So how can you call something wrong when you can't even pin down what it is you're judging objectionable?''

3. *Pornography is anti-female.*

POINT: ''Anyone who's seen even one pornographic film or read one obscene book realizes that the pornographic view is an anti-female view. Pornographic material generally portrays women as things, not persons; as objects, not creatures. They are playthings of a male, machinery to be tinkered with and manipulated. Why, pornography is as much a kind of group defamation as is Nazi propaganda, which degrades Jews. Just as we find anti-Semitic material objectionable on the grounds that it degrades a group of human beings and lessens the inherent respect and dignity they deserve, so we should object to pornography. After all, pornography undercuts respect for women, reinforces cultural prejudices, and encourages acts of violence against women.''

COUNTERPOINT: ''First of all, there's a big difference in intent between pornographic and anti-Semitic material. The latter is motivated by hate and aims not only to degrade Jews, but to incite others to join a verminous, genocidal cause. But hate isn't the impulse behind pornography. Money usually is, sometimes notoriety, even sheer pleasure. But not hate, and certainly not hate of women. Look at the material, study it. I think you'll find that if it does 'dehumanize,' it plays no favorites. Males are 'depersonalized' as much as females. And second, you don't have to get very far into anti-Semitic material before you find examples of viciously cruel, overt defamation. You never find that in pornography. And you won't find any singling out of a vulnerable minority group. On the contrary, 'porn' deals with humans across the board: male and female, black and white, Jew and Gentile. And it certainly doesn't invite the sort of violence against women that anti-Semitic propaganda does against Jews. In fact, there's no evidence of a correlation between pornography and violence directed at women.''

4. *Pornography breaks down protective barriers.*

POINT: "Our society subjects us to extensive conditioning on matters of sex. And for good reason: Sex is a most powerful appetite, which, if not carefully controlled, can produce a lot of hardship for ourselves and others. No wonder our families, schools, and churches take such pains in helping us develop constructive attitudes toward sex and deal with sexual feelings and fantasies which, if pursued, would hurt us and society. If this process is effective, then by the time we're adults we have learned to channel our sexual drives properly and have developed certain barriers to help us do that. But pornography breaks down those barriers; it loosens the wildest of sexual feelings and fantasies. The result is behavior that is neither in the interest of the individual nor in the interest of society. So, what makes pornography objectionable is that it threatens to undo the control that individuals exercise over their sexuality and leads to self-destructive and antisocial behavior."

COUNTERPOINT: "You make it sound like anybody who enjoys pornography will turn into some sort of sex fiend! That's absurd. In fact, there's some reason to believe that pornography can be healthful for some people and for society. But beyond this, you blithely assume that society's conditional process is above reproach, even that we must ensure that nothing occurs to 'undo' it. Did it ever occur to you that society's sexual values and the way they're taught may in part explain the great popularity of pornography?"

Arguments for Pornographic Materials

1. *Pornography can be beneficial.*

POINT: "Not only is pornography not necessarily degrading, it can actually be beneficial. Obviously, those who produce and willingly participate in it feel neither degraded nor exploited. In fact, they often enjoy considerable financial and professional success as a result. They may even feel that they're contributing something worthwhile to society. But beyond this, pornographic material can be a useful source of information about human sexuality. Even more important, it can serve as a sexual release for those in society who, for one reason or another, can't find or have difficulty finding sexual fulfillment in the absence of such materials. Given these benefits, and that there's no solid evidence that pornography harms anyone, there's no reason to object to it."

COUNTERPOINT: "The fact that pornography may benefit the people involved with it says very little about the morality of pornography. Robbery, murder, and skyjacking also benefit the participants, but that doesn't make those activities moral. Likewise, lots of people would enjoy the spectacle of a duel with pistols at dawn, but that doesn't make dueling right. As for those poor souls who can find sexual release only through pornography, don't you think it would make more sense for society to identify and help those individuals in ways that are more meaningful for both them and society? But even granting your 'benefits,' they don't nearly begin to offset the liabilities of pornography, including its depraved view of human sexuality and dehumanization of men and women.''

2. *Sexually explicit material is morally neutral.*

POINT: ''The word *pornography* is loaded. As soon as you use it, you're making a pejorative judgment. That's why I'd prefer to talk about 'sexually explicit material.' That phrase describes the material under discussion but doesn't judge it as offensive or disgusting, thereby biasing a moral evaluation of it. Now it seems to me that the only way someone can find such material in and of itself objectionable is by finding human sexuality or human sexual passion morally objectionable, because this is what 'sexually explicit material' deals with. As far as I'm concerned, there's nothing dirty, sinful or evil about sex. Like eating, exercising, or watching T.V., sex is morally neutral. Certainly it can raise moral concerns, and so can 'explicit sexual material.' For example, if people were forced to view such material or to participate in it, I'd consider that a violation of their civil rights and therefore wrong. But the material itself is neither good nor bad. It's morally inert. Everything depends on how it's used: when, by whom, and with what results. But to call sexually explicit material in and of itself morally objectionable doesn't make sense.''

COUNTERPOINT: ''You conveniently forget, or ignore, that 'explicit sexual material' serves up more than just human sexuality and sexual passion. It packages sex, and that package, more often than not, is colored by dehumanization, human exploitation, sadism, masochism, and all other forms of behavior that degrade human sexuality and human beings. Also, sexually explicit material has a viewpoint, and part of the viewpoint usually is an invitation to the spectator to join the fun. Who are we kidding? 'Sexually explicit material,' as you use that term, is inseparable from debasing forms of sexual behavior. So, when you say that such material is in itself morally neutral or inert, you're sadly mistaken. Its content *always* raises serious moral questions about the proper concept of human sexuality, the dignity of human beings, and the treatment that individuals accord one another.''

Arguments for Censorship

1. *Pornography leads to crime.*

POINT: ''Let's be clear about one thing: Pornography leads to crime. Take, for example, the case of the unstable young man who raped a girl after he'd been aroused by lurid scenes in an obscene comic book. Such cases could multiply. Why the Gebhard study (1965) confirmed reports of police officers that sex offenders often have pornography in their possession or admit to having seen pornographic materials. If you're still not convinced, just use a little common sense. If good literature can have a salutary effect on readers, then why can't obscene and pornographic material have a harmful effect? It can. And that's why the state must regulate pornography—to help reduce the incidence of crimes.''

COUNTERPOINT: "I agree that there's a large body of knowledge dealing with the relation between pornography and sex crimes. But—and it's a big 'but'—no cause-and-effect relation has ever been found. In fact, in the Gebhard studies the use of pornography by sex offenders was compared to the experiences of a control group of normal, nonoffender males, and to those of a group of prisoners who weren't sex offenders. Guess what. There was *no* difference among the groups in their use, possession of, or exposure to pornography. If there were any correlations to be drawn, they would be between the use of and exposure to pornography and the individual's age, socioeconomic class and educational level. And as if that weren't enough, consider this: The study found that sex offenders weren't prone to any greater sexual arousal from viewing pornography than were other groups of males."

2. *The community has the right and obligation to enforce its moral standards.*

POINT: "Like it or not, most people today find pornography repugnant. Sure there are some people who aren't offended by the obscene; and there are those who even enjoy it. But so what? Society is run by majority rule. When the consensus supports a moral standard, the community has every right to enforce that standard. Indeed, it has an obligation to."

COUNTERPOINT: "For a government to impose conventional moral standards on the individual amounts to a tyranny of the majority. In fact, nothing is more repugnant than to impose the moral standards of the community on all its members, even those who disagree with those decisions. It was the recognition of this fact that led the founding fathers to incorporate the Bill of Rights into the Constitution, and specifically to draft the First Amendment, which provides that 'Congress shall make no law . . . abridging the freedom of speech, or of the press.' 'No law abridging' means *no* law abridging, not even laws we happen to agree with, or anti-obscenity laws. What could be more clear? The supreme law of the land has fixed its own value on freedom of speech and press by putting these freedoms beyond the reach of federal power to abridge."

3. *The government has the right and duty to suppress views that are incompatible with the security and well-being of the community.*

POINT: "Nobody objects when the government polices individuals who don't maintain standards of health and who threaten society. By the same token, why shouldn't the government be concerned with the moral health of individuals, since this too can affect societal well-being? We all know that pornographic materials have the effect of preoccupying men and women with gratification of their own sensual desires. It also leads to impersonal expressions of sexuality, the destruction of love, and the psychological deprivation of children unfortunate enough to be under the guardianship of adults who indulge in pornography. Since all this can undermine the moral foundations of society, it seems clear to me that government has the right and duty to regulate pornographic and obscene materials."

COUNTERPOINT: "Sure, government has the right, even the obligation to secure and protect its citizens from physical harm. But physical threats are quite different from what you term moral threats; and the physical health of society differs markedly from its moral health. Yes, a government ought to ensure that diseases aren't spread by indifferent or uncaring individuals; it's justified in quarantining, even imposing treatment on certain individuals in order to protect society. But 'pornography' isn't smallpox; it's not a disease which, if unchecked, will rage and consume the population. The litany of 'effects' that you say pornography produces just doesn't wash. Of course, viewing or reading erotic materials is sexually arousing for a large number of people, especially males. In your view, such sexual stimulation presumably will lead the normal individual to all sorts of unspeakable, unhealthful acts. But there's no reason, not one iota of evidence, for believing that the sexual stimulation of normal individuals leads to anything other than fantasies and normal sexual activity. Now, I find nothing inherently wrong with fantasies, even sexual ones; nor do I find anything objectionable about normal sexual activity."

4.   *People need standards of decency and direction in sexual matters.*

POINT: "Generally speaking, people need direction, standards of decency, particularly regarding sex. The home, church, and school are unable to provide this necessary guidance alone. Law is needed. Law must hold up an authoritative standard for guidance of opinion and judgment. So, laws that regulate pornography and obscenity perform a needed educative function. They alert people to the fact that the organized community draws a line between the decent and the indecent. In effect, such laws say: 'This is what we believe is decent, and this is what we believe is indecent; this is what's right, and this is what's wrong; this is what our community will permit, and this is what it will not permit.' The beneficial, long-term effect of such standards on people's moral values and attitudes can't be underestimated. By the same token, there's no calculating the negative long-term impact on values and attitudes in the absence of legal guidelines."

COUNTERPOINT: "Frankly, I resent the paternalistic cut of your argument. There's more than a hint of: 'Now don't worry, folks, we're doing this for your own good.' Thank you, but no thanks. Certainly government has a right and duty to intervene in matters where there's a clear and present threat of harm. But in the case of pornography, there is none. Thus, the government has no right to restrict one's access to pornographic material, even for one's own good. Individuals should be the judge of what's for their own good, not government. In a word, I find the paternalistic principle you propose unacceptable justification for limiting personal liberty."

Arguments Against Censorship

1.   *No operationally meaningful definition of* obscene *is possible.*

POINT: "It's obvious that individuals bring to a film or a book their own concepts of offensiveness, which may differ from time to time in the same individuals. Also, there's no way of knowing the impact of materials on the public because of all the variables involved. What's more, in trying to define obscenity, one inevitably tries to do so in terms of the 'average person.' The fact is there is no such animal, and so any definition or description of the obscene that ties it to an 'average person' is simply foolish. Another definitional problem arises in trying to define the 'community' whose standards we're supposed to use. Finally, it's impossible to determine with anything that even approaches objectivity which works have 'redeeming social value,' presumably a criterion for exempting material from censorship. The bottom line is that we don't have any meaningfully operational definition of *obscene* and *pornographic.* If you can't even define these terms, how can you write laws about them? You can't and you shouldn't."

COUNTERPOINT: "The problem with your argument is that it fails to distinguish between the impossibility of formulating a definition and the difficulty of applying one. I grant you that even the Supreme Court's definition of what's obscene may pose operational problems. But this isn't an uncommon problem in law. Law is, in part, based on a set of definitional assumptions. Whether or not a particular phenomenon falls within that definitional assumption always involves some interpretation. Certainly this is true of obscenity and pornography. Sometimes there's very little difficulty in applying the definition; other times considerably more interpretation is involved. If a law is difficult to interpret and apply, then we should refine it. But we shouldn't conclude that an operational difficulty proves that it's impossible to define terms in any meaningfully operational way and, therefore, that a law can't and shouldn't be formulated."

2. *Governmental abuse will follow such legislation.*

POINT: "Asking government to serve as censor to our films and literature is like asking a wolf to guard the chicken house. Why, if government is allowed to oversee what people can read and view in sexual matters, there's no telling what government will attempt to regulate next—and it won't wait to be asked either. Invite government in, and don't be at all surprised if it then proceeds to constrain our religious and political freedoms, using, again, deviations from the standards of the nonexistent 'average' person and 'the community' as its justification."

COUNTERPOINT: "Oh, come now, you know as well as I that the passage of anti-smut laws doesn't at all mean the end of our religious and political freedoms. There's no reason whatever to suspect that government will invade any other aspects of people's reading or viewing, as, for example, by censoring politically 'unorthodox' material. Don't you realize that during World War II the government was given wide-ranging liberty-limiting powers? Certainly it had far greater censorship prerogatives than it would under proposed obscenity and pornography legislation. What better opportunity did government have to extend these powers than it had after the war? But it never happened. In the end, each of your fears poses a separate and distinct issue from pornography and obscenity legislation. If the time ever came when political or religious censorship was a serious social consideration, then it would have to be debated on its own merits. In no way would it, or should it, necessarily be tied to anti-smut laws."

3.   *Censorship raises insurmountable operational problems.*

POINT: "Think about the operational problems that censorship raises. The chief one is: Which works won't be censored? Some have said that the 'classics' will and should be exempt from censorship. Okay, but what's a 'classic'? Any traditional definition probably would exclude new works, since a work usually can't be recognized as a classic until some time after its release. Fine, but what does that mean? It means that the censor must determine which works will become classics—an absurdly impossible task. As a result, censors will have little choice but to ban these 'nonclassics' that smack of smut. You probably think this is an idle fear. Is it? Plenty of works of art and literature that today are considered classics once were banned. Works by Chaucer, Shakespeare, Swift, and Twain, just to mention a few. And more recently William Faulkner, Ernest Hemingway, and James Joyce found their works banned. Just imagine what creative artists would suffer, who must compose with the specter of the censor haunting their every move. One of the world's greatest writers, Leo Tolstoy, said it all. 'You would not believe,' wrote the Russian novelist, 'how from the very commencement of my activity that horrible censor question has tormented me. I wanted to write what I felt; but at the same time it occurred to me that what I wrote would not be permitted and involuntarily I had to abandon the work. I abandoned and went on abandoning and meanwhile the years passed away.' "

COUNTERPOINT: "As a sensitive, intelligent person, who's interested in the arts generally and literature in particular; and as one who's sensitive to the state of the artist in society, I share your concerns. Like you, I don't want an atmo-sphere that inhibits our artists, nor do I want simpletons censoring works of merit. Furthermore, I don't for a minute deny that some abuses have accompa-nied anti-obscenity laws. Despite all that, let me ask you this: What law ever has been free from potential abuse at the hands of the overzealous, the narrow-minded, the ill-informed, and, yes, the lame-brained? My point is that the objections you raise really speak to the implementations of anti-obscenity laws and not to the justifiability of the laws themselves. To me what you say is like arguing against capital punishment legislation because capital punishment laws are unfairly applied. If there is inequity in the application of the law, then let's correct that. But let's not abolish the law. The problem isn't with the law, but with how it's implemented."

4.   *Government has no right to limit liberty where there is no danger of harm.*

POINT: "When is a government justified in limiting individual liberty? When there's evidence of harm to others. But there's no evidence that pornog-raphy presents a clear and present danger to members of society. So, the government has no right to pass laws restricting an adult's access to pornography."

COUNTERPOINT: "I disagree that pornography presents no danger to society. Even if we are uncertain that pornography leads to crime, why assume that it doesn't? It seems to me more prudent to assume that it does, until the overwhelming weight of evidence proves otherwise. After all, assuming that pornography is innocuous is far riskier than assuming that it is harmful. Actually, I think there's pretty good reason for assuming that pornography probably is harmful. At the very least it often deals with things like exhibitionism, voyeurism, prostitution, sadism, child molestations, and other forms of sexual perversions, many of which involve harm to people. Besides, much of the stuff portrayed is illegal. So in trafficking in this smut, pornography encourages disrespect for and even disobedience of the law. Surely, this is a threat to a peaceful society. But all this aside, I think that, freed of censorship, pornography poses a direct and immediate threat to the style and quality of life that we want and value. To say, then, that pornography poses no threat or harm to society is to be wrong. On the contrary, pornography threatens the peace, security, and values of our society. The government has a right and duty to prevent such harm through the passage of anti-obscenity laws."

5. *Pornography can be beneficial.*

POINT. "Much that is positive may be said on behalf of pornography. For one thing, it can aid normal sexual development. For another, it can invigorate flagging sexual relations. Why it's even been used successfully in sex therapy sessions, to treat various sexual dysfunctions. And there's little question that pornographic materials can provide some people release from sexual tensions. It can provide an acceptable sexual substitute for those who might otherwise be sexually frustrated. Finally, it's at least possible that exposure to pornography has prevented people from acting in a harmful way, perhaps from committing sex crimes."

COUNTERPOINT: "Regarding your last claim—that exposure to pornography may actually prevent antisocial acts—I suggest you read the minority report offered by several members of the Commission on Obscenity and Pornography. It mentions a study that finds the group reporting the highest excitation to masturbation rates by pornography were rapists. Now, surely you can't say that pornography served as an adequate catharsis for these people. If it had, why did they go out and rape someone? In still another study, 39 percent of sex offenders reported that pornography had something to do with their committing the sex offense. As for your claim that pornography serves as a 'release' for some people, perhaps it does. But what kind of release? Escape might be a better term—escape from reality into fantasy and narcissism. Some release! Who knows that the darkly private, short-lived release you speak of doesn't eventuate in greater tension, frustration and, worst of all, despair and self-hate?

Ethical Theories

Egoism

Is pornographic material morally objectionable? Egoists would not find anything morally objectionable about pornography *per se*. Their only issue would be its effects on the individual using it, as considered from the individual's own vantage point. Thus, if as an egoist I calculate that I personally will derive more long-term pleasure from using pornographic material than from not using it, then I should indulge. Egoists would not be concerned with such essentially nonconsequential concerns as that pornography is degrading or separates love from affection. Nor would they be especially mindful of the argument that pornography can harm society, except insofar as such harm might have an impact on themselves. They would agree that explicit sexual material is morally neutral. Whether or not its use is moral ultimately depends on the likely long-term effects on the individual using it as determined by that individual.

Egoists would evaluate proposed pornography legislation in a similar manner. Is the law likely to produce the most long-term happiness for me? If so, it is moral; if not, it is immoral. On the one hand, restrictive legislation would limit the individual's freedom of choice and, thus, limit the individual's opportunities to maximize personal happiness. On the other hand, if virtually unrestricted access to pornography would have serious negative social consequences, then these would concern the egoist, whose happiness obviously is somewhat tied up with the integrity and stability of society as a whole. It seems that egoists would be much more comprehensive in their weighing the probable consequences of a law than in determining the probable consequences of an isolated act that they themselves might perform. But of course, in the final analysis the morality of either is determined by appeal to long-term self-interest.

Act Utilitarianism

Like egoists, the act utilitarian would not find anything objectionable about pornography in itself, but would subject any act of pornography usage to the principle of utility. If the act likely will produce the most total good, then it is right. Figuring prominently in such a calculation, of course, would be the likely social impact of using pornography. Even if it was shown that pornography generally has a harmful effect on society in, say, breeding crime and sullying values, the act utilitarian still could condone individual acts involving pornography if such acts would likely produce the most common good.

An act utilitarian could support restrictive legislation, providing that the legislation was necessary to prevent harm to others. Obviously, this means that pornography must first be proved a harm to others. If it was, and the proposed law clearly would prevent this harm (without, of course, causing even more harm), then the act utilitarian would consider the law justified. At the same time, the act utilitarian could *still* support individual acts involving pornography as morally right and justifiable.

In the absence of any hard evidence that pornography does, in fact, present a clear and present danger to society, the act utilitarian would have no basis for supporting anti-pornography legislation. The act utilitarian probably would argue that, in such an instance, society would be better served by tolerating all expressions of individual liberty that do not harm others, although they harm the individuals themselves. As John Stuart Mill states in *On Liberty*: ". . . There are many acts which, being directly injurious only to the agents themselves, ought not be legally interdicted, but which, if done publicly, are a violation of good manners, and, coming thus within the category of offenses against others, may rightfully be prohibited."[1]

Rule Utilitarianism

The rule utilitarian would be concerned with the likely consequences of practicing a rule such as: People ought never use pornography. If followed, would this rule or a rule like it, produce the most total good? The answer is not clear. Foremost in the rule utilitarian's calculation would be the alleged connection between pornography and social harm. In the absence of a proven causal connection, the rule utilitarian could not very well endorse such a rule. After all, subscription to the rule could easily involve a restriction of free choice (for example, I would like to see a pornographic film but I should not because people ought not use pornography). Thus, if there is no connection between pornography and social harm, the grounds for limiting personal liberty dissolve.

The same point applies to the subject of proposed pornography legislation. For the rule utilitarian, such legislation would be justified if, and only if, pornography poses a real threat to the welfare of others. If it does not, or has not been shown to, then the rule utilitarian would object to restrictive legislation as abridging individuals' freedom and thus their opportunity to maximize the common good. The "fly in the ointment" in this case is the word *harm*. Would *offense* fall within the definition of *harm*? Does *offense* in, say, "That movie *offends* me," fall within the category of *harm*? This issue is important because, if harm includes offense, then one can consider material "offensive" to the vast majority of society to be "harmful." In that event, the rule utilitarian might have a basis for restricting an adult's access to pornographic and obscene materials. Where there is no established harm to others, the rule utilitarian probably would not approve such legislation. Where harm is determined, then they could support restrictive legislation.

Divine Command

There are a number of aspects about pornography that most divine command theorists could object to. They might charge, for example, that pornographic or obscene material is calculated to arouse venereal pleasure, sexual passion. Since any voluntary stimulation of the sex organs outside marriage generally is considered contrary to God's will, then any material that provides such stimulation is inherently evil. But, of course, this argument says nothing of

---

1. *John Stuart Mill,* On Liberty *(London: J. M. Dent, 1910), p. 78.*

pornography used in a marital context. The more frequently heard objection based on divine command is that pornography degrades humans, women in particular, and separates sexual passion from affection or love. Since anything that reduces the inherent dignity and worth of human beings is contrary to God's will, pornographic material is therefore evil. Similarly, divine command theorists argue that by God's decree sex has a primary function of procreation and a companionate function of expressing love and commitment within the context of security that marriage provides. In its portrayal of men and women disporting themselves in all manners of sexual perversions, pornography is an abomination of the will of God.

Divine command theorists generally would also hold that the state has the right and duty to translate the will of God into law. Thus, the state is justified in limiting individual liberty in order to prevent immorality. In this way the divine command theory could support restrictive pornography legislation. Of course, divine command theorists might also capitalize on the claim that pornography leads to crime and social instability. Since the state has the right to protect society from such harm, it is justified in passing anti-pornography laws.

Categorical Imperative

If the arguments against pornography have any legitimacy, Kant could object to several aspects of pornography. If pornography does indeed degrade humans, then it would affront the Kantian principle that people ought to be treated with dignity and respect. Again, if pornography dehumanizes women and treats them as playthings, then again that would violate the injunction to treat humans with respect. And if pornography does effectively separate sex from procreation, affection, and love, and portray sex as governed exclusively by the pleasure principle, then this would undercut the function of sex and subordinate duty to pleasure. In a more subtle way, Kant could argue that pornography brings what should be a profoundly private aspect of human relations more and more into the public domain. Literary critic George Steiner, writing about pornography, develops this very point:

> Sexual relations are or should be one of the citadels of privacy, the night place where we must be allowed to gather the splintered, harried elements of our consciousness into some kind of inviolate order and repose. It is in sexual experience that a human being alone, and two human beings in that attempt at total communication, which is also communion, can discover the unique best of their identity.[2]

If Steiner is correct, then pornography seems to invade this "last, vital privacy" in a way that is ugly and demeaning, and is a threat to freedom.

Clearly there are many *if*'s in the foregoing analysis, and those conditions obviously must be established before the Kantian position against pornography could be inferred.

Much the same can be said of Kant's likely reaction to proposed restrictive

---

2.   George Steiner, "Night Words," in The New Criticism, ed. P. Nobile (New York: Random House, 1970), p. 131.

pornography legislation. In the presence of the conditions catalogued, then the state would seem justified in restricting the adult's access to obscene and pornographic materials. But in the absence of those conditions, then such laws would be an unjustifiable invasion of privacy and personal liberty. They would be denying individuals the autonomy that they are entitled to.

Prima Facie Duties

In evaluating pornography, Ross would consider the variety of prima facie duties that use of pornography raises. On the one hand, since it is claimed that pornography leads to crime, social instability, and casual, even perverted sexual relations, there is the duty to avoid injury to consider. Also, since it is claimed that pornography flouts the dignity that people deserve, and that it is particularly unfair, even pernicious, in its portrayal of women, there is the duty to justice to consider. On the other hand, since it is claimed that pornography can be beneficial, there is the duty of beneficence and self-improvement to consider. In the last analysis, Ross does not provide a clear judgment about pornography and its use. Whether one has an actual duty to avoid pornography depends on an evaluation of all the prima facie duties evident in a particular situation, and a judgment about which is the overriding duty.

If it were certain that pornography is a clear and present threat to society, then Ross probably would support restrictive pornography legislation, since the government's overriding obligation would be to prevent injury and harm to members of society. But the connection between pornography and harm is by no means certain. In the absence of any clear connection, it seems that restrictive legislation would not be justified under Ross's theory. Presumably, the justification for such legislation (assuming harm to others is not a question) would be the prevention of immoral behavior and/or the protection of individuals from themselves. But Ross probably would object, as Kant might, that the state has no right to limit moral freedom in order to prevent what it considers immoral behavior. In so acting, the government would be honoring the duty of beneficence at the expense of justice and noninjury. As for protecting people from themselves, while Ross does allow for paternalism, he would not extend it to the point where government is making decisions about what is morally good and bad, right and wrong for adults in strictly personal and private matters. So, it would appear that whether or not Ross would support restrictive pornography legislation depends largely on the connection between pornography and social harm.

Maximin Principle

Much of what Rawls would say about pornography would depend on the merit of the common arguments advanced for and against it and restrictive legislation. For example, if it were certain that pornography did lead to crime and serious social problems, then rational, self-interested creatures in the original position probably would agree, for their own protection, to be bound by a rule that prohibits pornography. But lacking a definite connection between pornography and social harm, we can conjecture that occupants of the original position would recognize that pornography might just be their only or primary source of sexual release and satisfaction. And if their use of pornography affected no one but themselves, then they would not likely bind themselves to a rule that would undercut their chances of sexual gratification. The key point here is the privacy and social harmlessness of the act.

Whether restrictive pornography legislation is justifiable would depend largely on the same sort of analysis. Rawls certainly would recognize harm to others as a liberty-limiting principle; he would even recognize the state's right to act paternalistically, that is, to prevent one from harming oneself. But legislation passed to enforce the moral views or the tastes of the majority is another matter. After all, what would rational, self-interested people in the original position think of a law designed to impose the values and moral standards of the majority on the minority? They would probably bristle, for they would realize that they easily could be in the minority. So, again, an application of Rawls's ethics to the morality of restrictive pornography legislation seems to hinge on whether, in fact, pornography causes harm to others or self.

Making the World Safe for Pornography

Edward J. Mishan

As we have seen in this chapter, various arguments have been offered on behalf of pornography. For example, some claim that pornography has positive effects on the personality, that it increases a person's capacity for enjoyment, and that, in general, it is harmless. But economist Edward J. Mishan considers such claims at best inconclusive or unconvincing.

In "Making the World Safe for Pornography," Mishan observes a sexually permissive trend that, if left unchecked, will result in what he terms the "Pornographic Society." By his account, such a society would be one in which all existing restraints on obscenity and pornography had vanished. What might be the effects of such a society? Would it be compatible with anyone's definition of the "Good Life"? Mishan thinks not.

Taking a utilitarian viewpoint, Mishan foresees dire social consequences if all restraints on pornography are lifted. Among the consequences, he believes, would be damage to the emotional health of children, the quality of love, and the stability of society. Indeed, according to Mishan, it is not at all farfetched to speculate about the end of civilization as we know it, should current permissive trends continue.

Familiar arguments, used to persuade us that the growth of sexual permissiveness has wholesome effects on the personality, and increases the capacity for enjoyment, are, to say the least, inconclusive, while those attempting to persuade us that, no matter what the degree of depravity in a work, it cannot really harm anyone, are wholly unconvincing. It is time, therefore, to bring some thought to bear on the harmful consequences society may suffer if current trends toward increasing pornography continue.

I begin by acknowledging the fact that not all those favoring the abolition of censorship are equally comfortable at the turn of events. Some are

From Edward J. Mishan, "Making the World Safe for Pornography," Encounter, March 1972. Reprinted by permission of the publisher.

prepared to admit that things have gone "too far," or far enough. Yet, as indicated, they continue for the most part to rest their hopes for containment, or improvement, on some eventual recoil from current excesses, or on some re-assertion of an imagined natural law that is latent in liberal democracies, or, in the last resort, on the gradual onset of ennui. However, since there is no evidence at present of any slackening in the growth of the market in pornography, hard or soft, it is just possible that—unless the state takes action—our innocent Sex Lobbyists will be proved wrong by events. If so, the question of the consequences for Western societies of an unarrested trend toward increased public pornography becomes very pertinent. In addressing myself to so large a question, I admittedly enter the realm of speculation though without, I hope, forsaking the conventions of reasoned discourse.

In order to avoid tedious qualifications at every turn in the argument, let us project existing trends and think in terms of an emergent "Pornographic Society," one in which all existing restraints have vanished. There are no legal checks on any form of erotic experience, "natural" or "unnatural," and no limit with respect to place, time, scale, or medium, in the depiction of what today would be called the carnal and lascivious. Neither are there any limits placed on the facilities for auto-eroticism, or for participating in any activity, heterosexual, homosexual, bestial, or incestuous, sado-masochistic, fetishistic, or just plain cruel. Provided actors, audience, and participants are willing, provided there is a market for the "product," no objection is entertained.

Any who would accuse me of being an alarmist merely for proposing the concept as an aid to enquiry would surely be revealing also that, were such a society to come into being, there would indeed be grounds for alarm. Since, however, they would reject this possible outcome (in the absence of state action) it would be of some interest if they could be more articulate on the nature and strength of the forces they believe can be depended upon to stem the tide. It would be of further interest to know just how far they expect society to travel along the primrose path to all-out pornography. How far would they themselves wish to travel along this road or, to be more fastidious, what existing or possible features would

they wish to admit or prohibit, extend or contract? In short, where would they wish to "draw the line," and, having drawn it, on what principles would they defend it, and by what sanctions? Finally, if they could be persuaded that the forces they once relied upon to restore some sort of equilibrium are too weak to operate, what measures would they favor now in order to stay the pace of movement toward the pornographic society? . . .

It is time to turn about in our minds some of the facets of the problem posed by the concept of the Pornographic Society; namely, whether such a society is compatible with the Good Life, *any* good life.

First, allowing that family life will continue in such a society, what are we to make of the effect on the child's psychology of his apprehension of a society obsessed with carnal indulgence? It has been alleged, occasionally, that children are immune to pornography; that, up to a certain age, it does not signify. Though this allegation cannot draw on any evidence since they are not in fact exposed, when young, to sexual circuses, we need not pursue this controversial question here because, presumably, there does come an age when they begin to understand the significance of what is happening about them. It is appropriate, then, to question the effect on the child's emotional life, in particular his regard and feelings for his parents.

Is it not just possible that the child needs not only to love his parents but to esteem them? In his first gropings for order and security in a world of threatening impulse, does he not need to look up to beings who provide assurance, who appear to him as "good" and wise and just? Will such emotional needs not be thwarted in a society of uninhibited sexual device? I do not pretend to know the answers to these questions, but no one will gainsay their importance. In view of the possibly very grave consequences on our children's children, would it not be an act of culpable negligence to allow current trends toward an increasingly promiscuous society to continue without being in sight of the answers?

Consider next the quality of love in such a society. Three closely related questions arise.

Treated simply as a physical exploit with another body, and divorced from the intrusion of sentiment, is sexual fulfillment possible?[1] David

Holbrook, for one, has doubts whether this is possible. Indeed, he concludes that the so-called sexual revolution is "placing limits on people's capacities to develop a rich enjoyment of sexual love by reducing it to sexuality."[2] Nor has Irving Kristol any brief for the more visible manifestations of the sexual revolution:

> There are human sentiments . . . involved in this animal activity. But when sex is public the viewer does not—cannot—see the sentiments. . . . He can only see the animal coupling. And that is why, when men and women make love, as we say, they prefer to be alone—because it is only when you are alone that you can make love, as distinct from merely copulating in an animal and casual way.

The second question that comes to mind in this connection is whether romantic love will become obsolete in a society of unfettered sexual recourse.

The "savage" in Aldous Huxley's brilliant satire, *Brave New World,* who commits suicide in despair, tried for romantic love but could obtain only instant sex. There might well continue to be sexual friendships, sexual rivalries, sexual jealousies. But the sublimation of sex, thought to be the wellspring of creative imagination and of romantic love, would be no more. One of the great sources of inspiration of poetry and song, of chivalry and dedication, throughout the ages would have dried up. To the denizens of the pornographic society the story of Abelard and Heloise or even the theories of Stendhal *On Love* would be implausible, if not incomprehensible.

The third related question is about the quality of love in general that can be expected to emerge along the road to such a society. One wonders if it would really be possible to love other people very much, or to care for them as persons very much in a world without opportunity for sublimation. Can such virtues as loyalty, honor, compassion, sacrifice, charity, or tenderness, flourish in an environment of uninhibited public exhibitionism and pornography?

Taking a wider perspective of the scene, one wonders whether it is possible to unite unchecked public sexual indulgence with the continued progress of any civilization—thinking of civilization in terms not merely of increasing scientific advance and technological innovation but in those, also, of a refinement of taste and sensibility. Let the reader ponder on the question at his leisure, bearing in mind the reflection that whereas the emergence in the past of a new civilization, or of a new age within the matrix of an existing civilization, has indeed always been associated with a rapid displacement of old conceptions, values, and purposes by new ones, it has never been associated with a mass movement toward unbridled sexual licentiousness. For, aside from the sexually neurotic elements at large in Western societies, there are in each of us—among "normal" people, that is—infantile and regressive elements that are for the most part dormant though deeply imbedded. "Emotional maturity" is a frail plant that can sustain itself only by clinging to an appropriate social structure. Familiar taboos that place a variety of constraints on freedom of sexual practices reflect a society's desire to guard against the activation of such elements. Until recently the laws of all Western societies sanctioned and reinforced taboos against an unlimited sexual freedom that, if actively sought, could be destructive of organized society.

Thus, a first experiment of this kind just might be the last experiment ever. Goaded on by the predatory forces of commercial opportunism, expectations of carnal gratification—aroused by increasingly salacious spectacles, and increasing facilities for new sexual perversions—would soar beyond the physical limits of attainments. In the unrelenting search for the uttermost in orgiastic experience, cruel passions might be unleashed, impelling humanity into regions beyond barbarism. One has only to recall the fantastic sadistic barbarities of the Nazi era—and to recall also that in 1941 the Nazis were within an ace of winning the War—to accept this conjecture as neither farfetched nor fanciful, and to recognize that civilization is indeed but skin-deep. . . .

Such questions need not be regarded as merely rhetorical. They may be thought of as genuine questions. But unless the answers to them are quite other than what I suspect they are, there are clear and present dangers in the current drift toward increased sexual permissiveness.

Notes

1. In order to avoid turning the question into a semantic issue, it could be rephrased more precisely as follows: Does suspension of sentiment *vis-à-vis* the sexual partner strengthen the physical sensations of pleasure or does it weaken them?

2. See his review of the books written by Dr. Viktor Frankl, *The Doctor and the Soul* and *Psychotherapy and Existentialism,* and that written by Dr. Rollo May, *Love and the Will,* in *The Times,* 20 March 1971.

Questions for Analysis

1. *Do you agree with Mishan that arguments for the wholesome effects of sexual permissiveness are "inconclusive" or "wholly unconvincing"?*

2. *Describe some of the conditions present in the "Pornographic Society."*

3. *Do you think that Mishan is an alarmist for proposing the concept of the Pornographic Society?*

4. *Specify the psychological threat that the Pornographic Society would pose for children.*

5. *What evidence, if any, does Mishan provide for suggesting that in the Pornographic Society sexual fulfillment would be impossible, romantic love would become obsolete, and the quality of love would be tarnished? Do you think the evidence offered, if any, warrants the conclusions?*

6. *Mishan's final charge is that permissive sex threatens to unravel the very fabric of organized civilization. Explain what he means. Why does he have this fear? Do you think his fear is well-founded or not?*

Beyond the (Garbage) Pale or Democracy, Censorship and the Arts

Walter Berns

About ten years ago, political scientist Walter Berns wrote an essay which alluded to an editorial that appeared in The New York Times *(1 April 1969) entitled "Beyond the (Garbage) Pale." In effect, the editorial called for the censorship of explicit portrayal of sexual intercourse on the stage. Thus, the title of Berns's essay, a part of which appears here.*

While Berns's argument for censorship of pornography is not a new one, it is not the most common in contemporary procensorship literature. Pruned to its essentials, the argument goes something like this. Pornography can have political consequences, intended or not. The chief political consequence is that it makes us "shameless." Indeed, one of the purposes of pornography seems to be to convince us that shame is unnatural. But, in Berns's view, shame is not only natural, it is necessary for the proper functioning and stability of society. Without shame, individuals are "unruly and unrulable." Having lost all measure of self-restraint, individuals will have to be ruled by tyrants. Thus, tyranny, not democracy, is the proper government for the shameless and

---

From Walter Berns, "Beyond the (Garbage) Pale or Democracy, Censorship and the Arts," in Censorship and Freedom of Expression, *Harry M. Clor, ed. (Chicago: Rand McNally, 1971). Reprinted by permission of Harry M. Clor.*

self-indulgent. Since pornography induces shamelessness and self-indulgence, it undercuts democracy.

In support of his contention, Berns refers to a number of "thoughtful men" who were familiar with this censorship argument at the time modern democracies were being constituted. He, and presumably they, claim that censorship is not only compatible with a democracy, it is a necessary part of it.

The case for censorship is at least as old as the case against it, and, contrary to what is usually thought today, has been made under decent and democratic auspices and by intelligent men. To the extent to which it is known today, however, it is thought to be pernicious or, at best, irrelevant to the enlightened conditions of the twentieth century. It begins from the premise that the laws cannot remain indifferent to the manner in which men amuse themselves, or to the kinds of amusement offered them. "The object of art," as Lessing put the case, "is pleasure, and pleasure is not indispensable. What kind and what degree of pleasure shall be permitted may justly depend on the law-giver."[1] Such a view, especially in this uncompromising form, appears excessively Spartan and illiberal to us; yet Lessing was one of the greatest lovers of art who ever lived and wrote.

We turn to the arts—to literature, films and the theatre, as well as to the graphic arts which were the special concern of Lessing—for the pleasure to be derived from them, and pleasure has the capacity to form our tastes and thereby to affect our lives, and the kind of people we become, and the lives of those with whom and among whom we live. Is it politically uninteresting whether men and women derive pleasure from performing their duties as citizens, parents, and spouses or, on the other hand, from watching their laws and customs and institutions ridiculed on the stage? Whether the passions are excited by, and the affections drawn to, what is noble or what is base? Whether the relations between men and women are depicted in terms of an eroticism wholly divorced from love and calculated to destroy the capacity for love and the institutions, such as the family, that depend on love? Whether a dramatist uses pleasure to attach man to what is beautiful or to what is ugly? We may not be accustomed to thinking of these things in this manner, but it is not strange that so much of the obscenity from which so many of us derive our pleasure today has an avowed political purpose.[2] It would seem that these pornographers know intuitively what liberals—for example, Morris Ernst—have forgotten, namely, that there is indeed a "causal relationship . . . between word or pictures and human behavior." At least they are not waiting for behavioral science to discover this fact.

The purpose is sometimes directly political and sometimes political in the sense that it will have political consequences intended or not. This latter purpose is to make us shameless, and it seems to be succeeding with astonishing speed. Activities that were once confined to the private scene—to the "ob-scene," to make an etymological assumption—are now presented for our delectation and emulation in center stage. Nothing that is appropriate to one place is inappropriate to any other place. No act, we are to infer, no human possibility, no possible physical combination or connection, is shameful. Even our lawmakers now so declare. "However plebian my tastes may be," Justice Douglas asked somewhat disingenuously in the *Ginzburg* case, "who am I to say that others' tastes must be so limited and that others' tastes have no 'social importance'?" Nothing prevents a dog from enjoying sexual intercourse in the marketplace, and it is unnatural to deprive man of the same pleasure, either actively or as voyeurs in the theatre. Shame itself is unnatural, a convention devised by hypocrites to inhibit the pleasures of the body. We must get rid of our "hangups."

But what if, contrary to Freud and to what is generally assumed, shame is natural to man in the sense of being an original feature of human existence, and shamelessness unnatural in the sense of having to be acquired? What if the beauty that we are capable of knowing and achieving in our lives with each other derives from the fact that man is naturally a "blushing creature," the only creature capable of blushing? Consider the case of voyeurism, a case that, under the circumstances, comes quickly to mind. Some of us—I have even known students to confess to it—experience discomfort watching others on the stage or screen performing sexual acts, or even the acts preparatory to sexual acts, such as the disrobing of a woman by a man. This discomfort is caused by shame or is akin to shame. True, it could derive from the fear of being discovered enjoying what society still sees as a forbidden game. The voyeur who experiences shame in this sense is judging himself by the conventions of his society and, according to the usual modern account, the greater the distance separating him from his society in space or time, the less he will experience this kind of shame. This shame, which may be denoted as concealing shame, is a function of the fear of discovery by one's own group. The group may have its reasons for forbidding a particular act, and thereby leading those who engage in it to conceal it—to be ashamed of it—but these reasons have nothing to do with the nature of man. Voyeurism, according to this account, is a perversion only because society says it is, and a man guided only by nature would not be ashamed of it.

According to another view, however, not to be ashamed—to be a shameless voyeur—is more likely to require explanation, for voyeurism is by nature a perversion.

> Anyone who draws his sexual gratification from looking at another lives continuously at a distance. If it is normal to approach and unite with the partner, then it is precisely characteristic of the voyeur that he remains alone, without a partner, an outsider who acts in a stealthy and furtive manner. To keep his distance when it is essential to draw near is one of the paradoxes of his perversion. The looking of the voyeur is of course also a looking at and, as such, is as different from the looks exchanged by lovers as medical palpation from the gentle caress of the hand.[3]

From this point of view, voyeurism is perversion not merely because it is contrary to convention, but because it is contrary to nature. Convention here follows nature. Whereas sexual attraction brings man and woman together seeking a unity that culminates in the living being they together create, the voyeur maintains a distance; and because he maintains a distance he looks at, he does not communicate; and because he looks at he objectifies, he makes an object of that with which it is

natural to join. Objectifying, he is incapable of uniting and therefore of love. The need to conceal voyeurism—the concealing shame—is a corollary of the protective shame, the shame that impels lovers to search for privacy and for an experience protected from the profane and the eyes of the stranger. The stranger is ''at odds with the shared unity of the [erotic couple], and his mere presence tends to introduce some objectification into every immediate relationship.''[4] Shame, both concealing and protective, protects lovers and therefore love. And a polity without love—without the tenderness and the charming sentiments and the poetry and the beauty and the uniquely human things that depend on it and derive from it—a polity without love would be an unnatural monstrosity.[5]

To speak in a manner that is more obviously political, such a polity may even be impossible, except in a form unacceptable to free men. There is a connection between self-restraint and shame, and therefore a connection between shame and self-government or democracy. There is therefore a danger in promoting shamelessness and the fullest self-expression or indulgence. To live together requires rules and a governing of the passions, and those who are without shame will be unruly and unrulable; having lost the ability to restrain themselves by observing the rules they collectively give themselves, they will have to be ruled by others. Tyranny is the mode of government for the shameless and self-indulgent who have carried liberty beyond any restraint, natural and conventional.

Such was the argument made prior to the twentieth century, when it was generally understood that democracy, more than any other form of government, required self-restraint, which it would inculcate through moral education and impose on itself through laws, including laws governing the manner of public amusements. It was the tyrant who could usually allow the people to indulge themselves. Indulgence of the sort we are now witnessing did not threaten his rule, because his rule did not depend on a citizenry of good character. Anyone can be ruled by a tyrant, and the more debased his subjects the safer his rule. A case can be made for complete freedom of the arts among such people, whose pleasures are derived from activities divorced from their labors and any duties associated with citizenship. Among them a theatre, for example, can serve to divert the search for pleasure from what the tyrant regards as more dangerous or pernicious pursuits.[6]

Such an argument was not unknown among thoughtful men at the time modern democracies were being constituted. It is to be found in Jean-Jacques Rousseau's *Letter to M. d'Alembert on the Theatre*. Its principles were known by Washington and Jefferson, to say nothing of the antifederalists, and later on by Lincoln, all of whom insisted that democracy would not work without citizens of good character; and until recently no justice of the Supreme Court and no man in public life doubted the necessity for the law to make at least a modest effort to promote that good character, if only by protecting the effort of other institutions, such as the church and the family, to promote and maintain it. The case for censorship, at first glance, was made wholly with a view to the political good, and it had as its premise that what was good for the arts and sciences was *not* necessarily good for the polity.

Notes

1. *Laocoön* (New York: Noonday Press), ch. 1, p. 10.

2. *Che!* and *Hair*, for example, are political plays. . . .

3. Erwin W. Straus, *Phenomenological Psychology* (Basic Books, New York, 1966), p. 219. I have no doubt that it is possible to want to observe sexual acts for reasons unrelated to voyeurism. Just as a physician has a clinical interest in the parts of the body, philosophers will have an interest in the parts of the soul, or in the varieties of human things which are manifestations of the body and the soul. Such a "looking" would not be voyeurism and would be unaccompanied by shame; or the desire to see and

to understand would require the "seer" to overcome shame. (Plato, *Republic*, 439e) In any event, the case of the philosopher is politically irrelevant, and aesthetically irrelevant as well.

4. *Straus*, p. 221.

5. It is easy to prove that shamefulness is not the only principle governing the question of what may properly be presented on the stage; shamefulness would not, for example, govern the case of a scene showing the copulating of a married couple who love each other very much. That is not intrinsically shameful—on the contrary—yet it ought not to be shown. The principle here is, I think, an aesthetic one: Such a scene is dramatically weak because the response of the audience would be characterized by prurience and not by a sympathy with what the scene is intended to portray, a beautiful love. This statement can be tested by joining a collegetown movie audience; it is confirmed unintentionally by a defender of nudity on the stage. . . .

6. The modern tyrant does not encourage passivity among his subjects; on the contrary, they are expected by him to be public-spirited: to work for the State, to exceed production schedules, to be citizen soldiers in the huge armies, and to love Big Brother. Indeed, in Nazi Germany and the Soviet Union alike, the private life was and is discouraged, and with it erotic love and the private attachments it fosters. Censorship in a modern tyrannical state is designed to abolish the private life to the extent that this is possible. George Orwell understood this perfectly. This severe censorship that characterizes modern tyranny, and distinguishes it sharply from premodern tyranny, derives from the basis of modern tyrannical rule: Both Nazism and Communism have roots in theory, and more precisely, a kind of utopian theory. The modern tyrant parades as a political philosopher, the heir of Nietzsche or Marx, with a historical mission to perform. He cannot leave his subjects alone.

Questions for Analysis

1. *Do you agree with Berns that what is good for the arts and sciences is not necessarily good for society?*

2. *Do you agree that one of the purposes of pornography is to make us shameless?*

3. *Why does Berns believe that shame is necessary for the protection of lovers and love, and what does that have to do with the justification of censorship?*

4. *Would you call Berns's argument essentially utilitarian or not? Could his argument be termed Kantian? Explain.*

5. *In what sense could Berns's argument be said to "fly in the face of" popular conceptions of democracy?*

Dissenting Opinion in *United States* v. *Roth*

Judge Jerome Frank

A man named Roth conducted a business in New York in the publication of books, photographs, and magazines. He used sexually explicit circulars and advertising material to solicit sales. Charges were brought against him of mailing obscene circulars and advertising and of mailing an obscene book, all in violation of the federal obscenity statute. He was convicted by a jury in the District Court for the Southern District of New York upon four counts of a 26-count indictment. In 1956, his conviction was affirmed by the Court of Appeals for the Second Circuit, and subsequently upheld by the U.S. Supreme Court.

What follows is the dissenting opinion in the Court of Appeals ruling, penned by Judge Jerome Frank. Frank's comprehensive opinion is often regarded as a classic statement against censorship of obscenity. Although written prior to the Supreme Court's disposition of the First Amendment issue and legal definition of obscenity in United States v. *Roth (354 U.S. 476, 1957), Frank's viewpoint remains highly influential. It deals with a wide range of pertinent issues, and continues to furnish supporting material for those who claim that censorship of pornography is unconstitutional, unwise, or immoral.*

Here Frank's opinion has been edited to less than half its original length. Most footnotes have been deleted, the remainder renumbered.

I agree with my colleagues that, since ours is an inferior court, we should not hold invalid a statute which our superior has . . . often said is constitutional (albeit without any full discussion). Yet I think it not improper to set forth, as I do in the Appendix, considerations concerning the obscenity statute's validity with which, up to now, I think the Supreme Court has not dealt in any of its opinions. I do not suggest the inevitability of the conclusion that the statute is unconstitutional. I do suggest that it is hard to avoid that conclusion, if one applies to that legislation the reasoning the Supreme Court has applied to other sorts of legislation. Perhaps I have overlooked conceivable compelling contrary arguments. If so, maybe my Appendix will evoke them.

To preclude misunderstanding of my purpose in stirring doubts about this statute, I think it well to add the following:

(a) As many of the publications mailed by defendant offend my personal taste, I would not cross a street to obtain them for nothing; I happen not to be interested in so-called "pornography"; and I think defendant's motives obnoxious. But if the statute were invalid, the merit of those publications would be irrelevant. . . . So, too, as to defendant's motives: "Although the defendant may be the worst of men . . . the rights of the best of men are secure only as the rights of the vilest and most abhorrent are protected."[1]

(b) It is most doubtful (as explained in the Appendix) whether anyone can now demonstrate that children's reading or looking at obscene matter has a probable causal relation to the children's antisocial conduct. If, however, such a probable causal relation could be shown, there could be little doubt, I think, of the validity of a statute (if so worded as to avoid undue ambiguity) which specifically prohibits the distribution by mail of obscene publications for sale to young people. But discussion of such legislation is here irrelevant, since, to repeat, the existing federal statute is not thus restricted.

(c) Congress undoubtedly has wide power to protect public morals. But the First Amendment severely limits that power in the area of free speech and free press. . . .

(e) The First Amendment, of course, does not prevent any private body or group (including any church) from instructing, or seeking to persuade, its adherents or others not to read or distribute obscene (or other) publications. That constitutional provision—safeguarding a principle indispensable in a true democracy—leaves unhampered all nongovernmental means of molding public opinion about not reading literature which some think undesirable; and, in that respect, experience teaches that democratically exercised censorship by public opinion has far more potency, and is far less easily evaded, than censorship by government. The incessant struggle to influence public opinion is of the very essence of the democratic process. A basic purpose of the First Amendment is to keep that struggle alive, by not permitting the dominant public opinion of the present to become embodied in legislation which will prevent the formation of a different dominant public opinion in the future.

(f) At first glance it may seem almost frivolous to raise any question about the constitutionality of the obscenity statute at a time when many seemingly graver First Amendment problems confront the courts. But (for reasons stated in more detail in the Appendix) governmental censorship of writings, merely because they may stimulate, in the reader, sexual thoughts the legislature deems undesirable, has more serious implications than appear at first glance: We have been warned by eminent thinkers of the easy path from any apparently mild governmental control of what adult citizens may read to governmental control of adults' political and religious reading. John Milton, Thomas Jefferson, James Madison, John Stuart Mill and Alexis de Tocqueville have pointed out that any paternalistic guardianship by government of the thoughts of grown-up citizens enervates their spirit, keeps them immature, all too ready to adopt towards government officers the attitude that, in general, "Papa knows best." If the government possesses the power to censor publications which arouse sexual thoughts, regardless of whether those thoughts tend probably to transform themselves into antisocial behavior, why may not the government censor political and religious publications regardless of any causal relation to probably dangerous deeds? And even if we confine attention to official censorship of publications tending to stimulate sexual thoughts, it should be asked why, at any moment, that censorship cannot be extended to advertisements and true reports or photographs, in our daily press, which, fully as much, may stimulate such thoughts?

(g) Assuming, *arguendo*, that a statute aims at an altogether desirable end, nevertheless its desirability does not render it constitutional. . . .

Appendix

In 1799, eight years after the adoption of the First Amendment, Madison, in an address to the General Assembly of Virginia,[2] said that the "truth of opinion" ought not to be subject to "imprisonment, to be inflicted by those of a different opinion"; he there also asserted that it would subvert the First Amendment to make a "distinction between the freedom and the licentiousness of the press." Previously, in 1792, he wrote that "a man has property in his opinions and free communication of them," and that a government which "violates the property which individuals have in their opinion . . . is not a pattern for the United States."[3] Jefferson's proposed Constitution for Virginia (1776) provided: "Printing presses shall be free, except so far as by commission of private injury cause may be given of private action."[4] In his Second Inaugural Address (1805), he said:

> No inference is here intended that the laws provided by the State against false and defamatory publications should not be enforced. . . . The press, confined to truth, needs no other restraint . . . ; and no other definite line can be drawn between the inestimable liberty of the press and demoralizing licentiousness. If there still be improprieties which this rule would not restrain, its supplement must be sought in the censorship of public opinion.

. . . Jefferson, in 1798, quoting the First Amendment, said it guarded "in the same sentence, and under the same words, the freedom of religion, of speech, and of the press; insomuch, that whatever violates either throws down the sanctuary which covers the others."[5] In 1814, he wrote in a letter,

> I am really mortified to be told that in the United States of America, a fact like this (the sale of a book) can become a subject of inquiry, and of criminal inquiry too, as an offense against religion; that (such) a question can be carried before the civil magistrate. Is this then our freedom of religion? And are we to have a censor whose imprimatur shall say what books may be sold and what we may buy? . . . Whose foot is to be the measure to which ours are all to be cut or stretched?[6]

Those utterances highlight this fact: Freedom to speak publicly and to publish has, as its inevitable and important correlative, the private rights to hear, to read, and to think and to feel about what one hears and reads. The First Amendment protects those private rights of hearers and readers. . . .

The question therefore arises whether the courts, in enforcing the First Amendment, should interpret it in accord with the views prevalent among those who sponsored and adopted it or in accord with subsequently developed views which would sanction legislation more restrictive of free speech and free press.

So the following becomes pertinent: Some of those who in the twentieth century endorse legislation suppressing "obscene" literature have an attitude toward freedom of expression which does not match that of the framers of the First Amendment (adopted at the end of the eighteenth century) but does stem from an attitude toward writings dealing with sex which arose decades later, in the midnineteenth century, and is therefore labeled—doubtless too sweepingly—"Victorian." It was a dogma of "Victorian morality" that sexual misbehavior would be encouraged if one were to "acknowledge its existence or at any rate to present it vividly enough to form a lifelike image of it in the reader's mind"; this morality rested on a "faith that you could best conquer evil by shutting your eyes to its existence,"[7] and on a kind of word magic.[8] The demands at that time for "decency" in published words did not comport with the actual sexual conduct of many of those who made those demands: "The Victorians, as a general rule, managed to conceal the 'coarser' side of their lives so thoroughly under a mask of respectability that we often fail to realize how 'coarse' it really was. . . ." Could we have recourse to the vast unwritten literature of bawdry, we should be able to form a more veracious notion of life as it (then) really was. The respectables of those days often, "with unblushing license," held "high revels" in "night houses."[9] Thanks to them, Mrs. Warren's profession flourished, but it was considered sinful to talk about it in books.[10] Such a prudish and purely verbal moral code, at odds (more or less hypocritically) with the actual conduct of its adherents was (as we have seen) not the moral code of those who framed the First Amendment. One would suppose, then, that the courts should interpret and enforce that Amendment according to the views of those framers, not according to the later "Victorian" code. . . .

The Statute, as Judicially Interpreted, Authorizes Punishment for Inducing Mere Thoughts, and Feelings, or Desires

For a time, American courts adopted the test of obscenity contrived in 1868 by L. J. Cockburn, in *Queen* v. *Hicklin*, L.R. 3 Q.B. 360: "I think the test of obscenity is this, whether the tendency of the matter charged as obscenity is to deprave and corrupt those whose minds are open to such immoral influences, and into whose hands a publication of this sort might fall." He added that the book there in question "would suggest . . . thoughts of a most impure and libidinous character."

The test in most federal courts has changed: They do not now speak of the thoughts of "those whose minds are open to . . . immoral influences" but, instead, of the thoughts of average adult normal men and women, determining what these thoughts are, not by proof at the trial, but by the standard of "the average conscience of the time," the current "social sense of what is right."

Yet the courts still define obscenity in terms of the assumed average normal adult reader's sexual thoughts or desires or impulses, without reference to any relation between those "subjective" reactions and his subsequent conduct. The judicial opinions use such key phrases as this: "suggesting lewd thoughts and exciting sensual desires," "arouse the salacity of the reader," "allowing or implanting . . . obscene, lewd, or lascivious thoughts or desires," "arouse sexual desires." The judge's charge in the instant case reads accordingly: "It must tend to stir sexual impulses and lead to sexually impure thoughts." Thus the statute, as the courts construe it, appears to provide criminal punishment for inducing no more than thoughts, feelings, desires.

No Adequate Knowledge Is Available Concerning the Effects on the Conduct of Normal Adults of Reading or Seeing the "Obscene"

Suppose we assume, *arguendo*, that sexual thoughts or feelings, stirred by the "obscene," probably will often issue into overt conduct. Still it does not at all follow that that conduct will be antisocial. For no sane person can believe it socially harmful if sexual desires lead to normal, and not antisocial, sexual behavior since, without such behavior, the human race would soon disappear.

Doubtless, Congress could validly provide punishment for mailing any publications if there were some moderately substantial reliable data showing that reading or seeing those publications probably conduces to seriously harmful sexual conduct on the part of normal adult human beings. But we have no such data.

Suppose it argued that whatever excites sexual longings might *possibly* produce sexual misconduct. That cannot suffice: Notoriously, perfumes sometimes act as aphrodisiacs, yet no one will suggest that therefore Congress may constitutionally legislate punishment for mailing perfumes. It may be that among the stimuli to irregular sexual conduct, by normal men and women, may be almost anything—the odor of carnations or cheese, the sight of a cane or a candle or a shoe, the touch of silk or a gunnysack. For all anyone now knows, stimuli of that sort may be far more provocative of such misconduct than reading obscene books or seeing obscene pictures. Said John Milton, "Evil manners are as perfectly learnt, without books, a thousand other ways that cannot be stopped."

Effect of "Obscenity" on Adult Conduct

To date there exist, I think, no thoroughgoing studies by competent persons which justify the conclusion that normal adults' reading or seeing of the "obscene" probably induces antisocial conduct. Such competent studies as have been made do conclude that so complex and numerous are the causes of sexual vice that it is impossible to assert with any assurance that "obscenity" represents a ponderable causal factor in sexually deviant adult behavior. "Although the whole subject of obscenity censorship hinges upon the unproved assumption that 'obscene' literature is a significant factor in causing sexual deviation from the community standard, no report can be found of a single effort at genuine research to test this assumption by singling out as a factor for study the effect of sex literature upon sexual behavior."[11] What little competent research has been done points definitely in a direction precisely opposite to that assumption.

Alpert reports[12] that, when, in the 1920s, 409 women college graduates were asked to state in writing what things stimulated them sexually, they answered thus: 218 said men; 95 said books;

40 said drama; 29 said dancing; 18 said pictures; 9 said music. Of those who replied "that the source of their sex information came from books, not one specified a 'dirty' book as the source. Instead, the books listed were: The Bible, the dictionary, the encyclopedia, novels from Dickens to Henry James, circulars about venereal diseases, medical books, and Motley's *Rise of the Dutch Republic*." Macaulay, replying to advocates of the suppression of obscene books, said: "We find it difficult to believe that in a world so full of temptations as this, any gentleman whose life would have been virtuous if he had not read Aristophanes or Juvenal, will be vicious by reading them." Echoing Macaulay, Jimmy Walker, former mayor of New York City, remarked that he had never heard of a woman seduced by a book. New Mexico has never had an obscenity statute; there is no evidence that, in that state, sexual misconduct is proportionately greater than elsewhere.

Effect on Conduct of Young People

. . . Judge Clark[13] speaks of "the strongly held views of those with competence in the premises as to the very direct connection" of obscenity "with the development of juvenile delinquency." . . . One of the cited writings is a report, by Dr. [Marie] Jahoda and associates, entitled "The Impact of Literature: A Psychological Discussion of Some Assumptions in the Censorship Debate" (1954). I have read this report (which is a careful survey of all available studies and psychological theories). I think it expresses an attitude quite contrary to that indicated by Judge Clark. In order to avoid any possible bias in my interpretation of that report, I thought it well to ask Dr. Jahoda to write her own summary of it, which, with her permission, I shall quote.

Dr. Jahoda's summary reads as follows:

Persons who argue for increased censorship of printed matter often operate on the assumption that reading about sexual matters or about violence and brutality leads to antisocial actions, particularly to juvenile delinquency. An examination of the pertinent psychological literature has led to the following conclusions:

1. There exists no research evidence either to prove or to disprove this assumption definitely.

2. In the absence of scientific proof two lines of psychological approach to the examination of the assumption are possible: (a) a review of what is known on the causes of juvenile delinquency; and (b) a review of what is known about the effect of literature on the mind of the reader.

3. In the vast research literature on the causes of juvenile delinquency there is no evidence to justify the assumption that reading about sexual matters or about violence leads to delinquent acts. Experts on juvenile delinquency agree that it has no single cause. Most of them regard early childhood events, which precede the reading age, as a necessary condition for later delinquency. At a later age, the nature of personal relations is assumed to have much greater power in determining a delinquent career than the vicarious experiences provided by reading matter. Juvenile delinquents as a group read less, and less easily, than nondelinquents. Individual instances are reported in which so-called "good" books allegedly influenced a delinquent in the manner in which "bad" books are assumed to influence him.

Where childhood experiences and subsequent events have combined to make delinquency psychologically likely, reading could have one of two effects: It could serve a trigger function releasing the criminal act or it could provide for a substitute outlet of aggression in fantasy, dispensing with the need for criminal action. There is no empirical evidence in either direction.

4. With regard to the impact of literature on the mind of the reader, it must be pointed out that there is a vast overlap in content between all media of mass communication. The daily press, television, radio, movies, books and comics all present their share of so-called "bad" material, some with great realism as reports of actual events, some in clearly fictionalized form. It is virtually impossible to isolate the impact of one of these media on a population exposed to all of them. Some evidence suggests that the particular communications which arrest the attention of an individual are in good part a matter of choice. As a rule, people do not expose themselves to everything that is offered, but only to what agrees with their inclinations. Children, who have often not yet crystallized their preferences and have more unspecific curiosity than many adults, are therefore perhaps more open to accidental influences from literature. This may present a danger to youngsters who are insecure or maladjusted who find in reading (of "bad" books as well as of "good" books) an escape from reality which they do not dare face. Needs which are not met in the real world are gratified in a fantasy world. It is likely, though not fully demonstrated, that excessive reading of comic books will intensify in children those qualities which drove them to the comic book world to begin with: an inability to face the world, apathy, a belief that the individual is hopelessly impotent and driven by uncontrollable forces and, hence, an acceptance of violence and brutality in the real world.

It should be noted that insofar as causal sequence is implied, insecurity and maladjustment in a child must precede this exposure to the written word in order to lead to these potential effects. Unfortunately, perhaps, the reading of Shakespeare's tragedies or of Andersen's and Grimm's fairy tales might do much the same.

Maybe someday we will have enough reliable data to show that obscene books and pictures do tend to influence children's sexual conduct adversely. Then a federal statute could be enacted which would avoid constitutional defects by authorizing punishment for using the mails or interstate shipments in the sale of such books and pictures to children.

It is, however, not at all clear that children would be ignorant, in any considerable measure, of obscenity, if no obscene publications ever came into their hands. Youngsters get a vast deal of education in sexual smut from companions of their own age. A verbatim report of conversations among young teen-age boys (from average respectable homes) will disclose their amazing proficiency in obscene language, learned from other boys. Replying to the argument of the need for censorship to protect the young, Milton said: "Who shall regulate all the . . . conversation of our youth . . . appoint what shall be discussed . . . ?" Most judges who reject that view are long past their youth and have probably forgotten the conversational ways of that period of life: "I remember when I was a little boy," said Mr. Dooley, "but I don't remember how I was a little boy."

The Obscenity Statute and the Reputable Press

Let it be assumed, for the sake of the argument, that contemplation of published matter dealing with sex has a significant impact on children's conduct. On that assumption, we cannot overlook the fact that our most reputable newspapers and periodicals carry advertisements and photographs displaying women in what decidedly are sexually alluring postures, and at times emphasizing the importance of "sex appeal." That women are there shown scantily clad increases "the mystery and allure of the bodies that are hidden," writes an eminent psychiatrist. "A leg covered by a silk stocking is much more attractive than a naked one; a bosom pushed into shape by a brassiere is more alluring than the pendant realities."[14] Either, then, the statute must be sternly applied to prevent the mailing of many reputable newspapers and periodicals containing such ads and photographs, or else we must acknowledge that they have created a cultural atmosphere for children in which, at a maximum, only the most trifling additional effect can be imputed to children's perusal of the kind of matter mailed by the defendant. . . .

Da Capo: Available Data Seem Wholly Insufficient to Show That the Obscenity Statutes Come Within Any Exception to the First Amendment

I repeat that because that statute is not restricted to obscene publications mailed for sale to minors, its validity should be tested in terms of the evil effects of adult reading of obscenity on adult conduct. With the present lack of evidence that publications probably have such effects, how can the government discharge its burden of demonstrating sufficiently that the statute is within the narrow exceptions to the scope of the First Amendment? One would think that the mere possibility of a causal relation to misconduct ought surely not be enough. . . .

If the Obscenity Statute Is Valid, Why May Congress Not Validly Provide Punishment for Mailing Books Which Will Provoke Thoughts It Considers Undesirable About Religion or Politics?

If the statute is valid, then, considering the foregoing, it would seem that its validity must rest on this ground: Congress, by statute, may constitutionally provide punishment for the mailing of books evoking mere thoughts or feelings about sex, if Congress considers them socially dangerous, even in the absence of any satisfactory evidence that those thoughts or feelings will tend to bring about socially harmful deeds. If that be correct, it is hard to understand why, similarly, Congress may not constitutionally provide punishment for such distribution of books evoking mere thoughts or feelings about religion or politics which Congress considers socially dangerous, even in the absence of any satisfactory evidence that those thoughts or feelings will tend to bring about socially dangerous deeds.

The Judicial Exception of the "Classics"

As I have said, I have no doubt the jury could reasonably find, beyond a reasonable doubt, that many of the publications mailed by defendant were obscene within the current judicial definition of the term as explained by the trial judge in his charge to the jury. But so, too, are a multitude of recognized works of art found in public libraries. Compare, for instance, the books which are exhibits in this case with Montaigne's *Essay on Some Lines of Virgil* or with Chaucer. Or consider the many nude pictures which the defendant transmitted through the mails, and then turn to the reproductions in the articles on paintings and sculptures in the *Encyclopaedia Britannica* (14th edition). Some of the latter are no less "obscene" than those which led to the defendant's conviction. Yet these Encyclopedia volumes are readily accessible to everyone, young or old, and, without let or hindrance, are frequently mailed to all parts of the country. Catalogues of famous art museums, almost equally accessible and also often mailed, contain reproductions of paintings and sculpture, by great masters, no less "obscene."

To the argument that such books (and such reproductions of famous paintings and works of sculpture) fall within the statutory ban, the courts have answered that they are "classics,"—books of "literary distinction" or works which have "an accepted place in the arts," including, so this court has held, Ovid's *Art of Love* and Boccacio's *Decameron*. There is a "curious dilemma" involved in this answer that the statute condemns "only books which are dull and without merit," that in no event will the statute be applied to the "classics," that is, books "of literary distinction."[15] The courts have not explained how they escape that dilemma, but instead seem to have gone to sleep (although rather uncomfortably) on its horns.

. . . No one can rationally justify the judge-made exception. The contention would scarcely pass as rational that the "classics" will be read or seen solely by an intellectual or artistic elite; for, even ignoring the snobbish, undemocratic nature of this contention, there is no evidence that the elite has a moral fortitude (an immunity from moral corruption) superior to that of the "masses." And if the exception, to make it rational, were taken as meaning that a contemporary book is exempt if it equates in "literary distinction" with the "classics," the result would be amazing: Judges would have to serve as literary critics; jurisprudence would merge with aesthetics; authors and publishers would consult the legal digests for legal-artistic precedents; we would some day have a Legal Restatement of the Canons of Literary Taste. . . .

How Censorship Under the Statute Actually Operates

Prosecutors, as censors, actually exercise prior restraint. Fear of punishment serves as a powerful restraint on publication, and fear of punishment often means, practically, fear of prosecution. For most men dread indictment and prosecution; the publicity alone terrifies, and to defend a criminal action is expensive. If the definition of obscenity had a limited and fairly well-known scope, that fear might deter restricted sorts of publications only. But on account of the extremely vague judicial definition of the obscene, a person threatened with prosecution if he mails (or otherwise sends in interstate commerce) almost any book which deals in an unconventional, unorthodox manner with sex, may well apprehend that, should the threat be carried out, he will be punished. As a result, each prosecutor becomes a literary censor (dictator) with immense unbridled power, a virtually uncontrolled discretion. A statute would be invalid which gave the Postmaster General the power, without reference to any standard, to close the mails to any publication he happened to dislike. Yet, a federal prosecutor, under the federal obscenity statute, approximates that position: Within wide limits, he can (on the advice of the Postmaster General or on no one's advice) exercise such a censorship by threat without a trial, without any

judicial supervision, capriciously and arbitrarily. Having no special qualifications for that task, nevertheless, he can, in large measure, determine at his will what those within his district may not read on sexual subjects. In that way, the statute brings about an actual prior restraint of free speech and free press which strikingly flouts the First Amendment. . . .

The Dangerously Infectious Nature of Governmental Censorship of Books

Governmental control of ideas or personal preferences is alien to a democracy. And the yearning to use governmental censorship of any kind is infectious. It may spread insidiously. Commencing with suppression of books as obscene, it is not unlikely to develop into official lust for the power of thought-control in the areas of religion, politics, and elsewhere. Milton observed that "licensing of books . . . necessarily pulls along with it so many other kinds of licensing." Mill noted that the "bounds of what may be called moral police" may easily extend "until it encroaches on the most unquestionably legitimate liberty of the individual." We should beware of a recrudescence of the undemocratic doctrine uttered in the seventeenth century by Berkeley, Governor of Virginia: "Thank God there are no free schools or preaching, for learning has brought disobedience into the world, and printing has divulged them. God keep us from both."

The People as Self-Guardians: Censorship by Public Opinion, Not by Government

Plato, who detested democracy, proposed to banish all poets; and his rulers were to serve as guardians of the people, telling lies for the people's good, vigorously suppressing writings these guardians thought dangerous. Governmental guardianship is repugnant to the basic tenet of our democracy: According to our ideals, our adult citizens are self-guardians, to act as their own fathers, and thus become self-dependent. When our governmental officials act towards our citizens on the thesis that "Papa knows best what's good for you," they enervate the spirit of the citizens: To treat grown men like infants is to make them infantile, dependent, immature.

So have sagacious men often insisted. Milton, in his *Areopagitica*, denounced such paternalism:

"We censure them for a giddy, vicious and un-guided people, in such sick and weak (a) state of faith and discretion as to be able to take down nothing but through the pipe of a licensor." "We both consider the people as our children," wrote Jefferson to Dupont de Nemours, "but you love them as infants whom you are afraid to trust without nurses, and I as adults whom I freely leave to self-government." Tocqueville sagely remarked: "No form or combination of social policy has yet been devised to make an energetic people of a community of pusillanimous and enfeebled citizens." "Man," warned Goethe, "is easily accustomed to slavery and learns quickly to be obedient when his freedom is taken from him." Said Carl Becker, "Self-government, and the spirit of freedom that sustains it, can be maintained only if the people have sufficient intelligence and honesty to maintain them with a minimum of legal compulsion. This heavy responsibility is the price of freedom."[16] The "great art," according to Milton, "lies to discern in what the law is to bid restraint and punishment, and in what things persuasion only is to work." So, we come back, once more, to Jefferson's advice: The only completely democratic way to control publications which arouse mere thoughts or feelings is through nongovernmental censorship by public opinion.

The Seeming Paradox of the First Amendment

Here we encounter an apparent paradox: The First Amendment, judicially enforced, curbs public opinion when translated into a statute which restricts freedom of expression (except that which will probably induce undesirable conduct). The paradox is unreal: The Amendment ensures that public opinion—the "common conscience of the time"—shall not commit suicide through legislation which chokes off today the free expression of minority views which may become the majority public opinion of tomorrow.

Private Persons or Groups May Validly Try to Influence Public Opinion

The First Amendment obviously has nothing to do with the way persons or groups, not a part of government, influence public opinion as to what constitutes "decency" or "obscenity." The Catholic Church, for example, has a constitutional right to persuade or instruct its adherents not to read designated books or kinds of books.

The Fine Arts Are Within the First Amendment's Protection

"The framers of the First Amendment," writes Chafee, "must have had literature and art in mind, because our first national statement on the subject of freedom of the press, the 1774 address of the Continental Congress to the inhabitants of Quebec, declared, 'The importance of this (freedom of the press) consists, beside the advancement of truth, science, morality and *arts* in general, in its diffusion of liberal sentiments on the administration of government.' "[17] One hundred and sixty-five years later, President Franklin Roosevelt said, "The arts cannot thrive except where men are free to be themselves and to be in charge of the discipline of their own energies and ardors. The conditions for democracy and for art are one and the same. What we call liberty in politics results in freedom of the arts."[18] The converse is also true.

In our industrial era when, perforce, economic pursuits must be, increasingly, governmentally regulated, it is especially important that the realm of art—the noneconomic realm—should remain free, unregimented, the domain of free enterprise, of unhampered competition at its maximum. An individual's taste is his own private concern. *De gustibus non disputandum* represents a valued democratic maxim.

Milton wrote: "For though a licenser should happen to be judicious more than the ordinary, yet his very office . . . enjoins him to let pass nothing but what is vulgarly received already." He asked, "What a fine conformity would it starch us all into? We may fall . . . into a gross conformity stupidly. . . ." In 1859 Mill, in his essay *On Liberty*, maintained that conformity in taste is not a virtue, but a vice. "The danger," he wrote, "is not the excess but the deficiency of personal impulses and preferences. By dint of not following their own nature (men) have no nature to follow . . . Individual spontaneity is entitled to free exercise. . . . That so few men dare to be eccentric marks the chief danger of the time." Pressed by the demand for conformity, a people degenerate into "the deep slumber of a decided opinion," yield a "dull and torpid consent" to the accustomed. "Mental despotism" ensues. For "whatever crushes individuality is despotism by whatever name it be called. . . . It is not by wearing down into uniformity all that is individual in themselves, but by cultivating it, and calling it forth, within the limits imposed by the rights and interests of others, that human beings become a noble and beautiful object of contemplation; and as the works partake the character of those who do them, by the same process human life also becomes rich, diversified, and animating. . . . In proportion to the development of his individuality, each person becomes more valuable to himself, and is therefore capable of being more valuable to others. There is a greater fullness of life about his own existence, and when there is more life in the units there is more in the mass which is composed of them."

To vest a few fallible men—prosecutors, judges, jurors—with vast powers of literary or artistic censorship, to convert them into what Mill called a "moral police," is to make them despotic arbiters of literary products. If one day they ban mediocre books as obscene, another day they may do likewise to a work of genius. Originality, not too plentiful, should be cherished, not stifled. An author's imagination may be cramped if he must write with one eye on prosecutors or juries; authors must cope with publishers who, fearful about the judgments of governmental censors, may refuse to accept the manuscripts of contemporary Shelleys or Mark Twains or Whitmans.

Some few men stubbornly fight for the right to write or publish or distribute books which the great majority at the time consider loathsome. If we jail those few, the community may appear to have suffered nothing. The appearance is deceptive. For the conviction and punishment of these few will terrify writers who are more sensitive, less eager for a fight. What, as a result, they do not write might have been major literary contributions. "Suppression," Spinoza said, "is paring down the state till it is too small to harbor men of talent."

Notes

1. Judge Cuthbert Pound dissenting in *People* v. *Gitlow*, 234 N.Y. 132, 158, 136 N.E. 317, 327.
2. Padover, *The Complete Madison* (1953), pp. 295–296.
3. Padover, *The Complete Madison* (1953), pp. 267, 268–269.
4. Padover, *The Complete Jefferson* (1943), p. 109.
5. Padover, *The Complete Jefferson* (1943), p. 130.
6. Padover, *The Complete Jefferson* (1943), p. 889.
7. Winfield-Stratford, *Those Earnest Victorians* (1930), p. 151.
8. See Kaplan, "Obscenity as an Esthetic Category," 20 *Law and Contemporary Problems* (1955), pp. 544, 550: "In many cultures, obscenity has an important part in magical rituals. In our own, its magical character is betrayed in the puritan's supposition that words alone can work evil, and that evil will be averted if only the words are not uttered."
9. Wingfield-Stratford, *Victorians*, pp. 296–297.
10. Paradoxically, this attitude apparently tends to "create" obscenity, for the foundation of obscenity seems to be secrecy and shame: "The secret becomes shameful because of its secrecy." Kaplan, "Obscenity as an Esthetic Category," 20 *Law and Contemporary Problems* (1955), pp. 544, 556.
11. Lockhart and McClure, "Obscenity and the Courts," 20 *Law and Contemporary Problems* (1955), pp. 587, 595.
12. Alpert, "Judicial Censorship and the Press," 52 *Harvard Law Review* (1938), pp. 40, 72.
13. The majority opinion upholding Roth's conviction was delivered by Chief Judge Clark, U.S. Court of Appeals, Second Circuit. [The Editor]
14. Myerson, *Speaking of Man* (1950), p. 92.
15. *Roth* v. *Goldman*, 2 Cir., 172 F.2d 788.
16. Becker, *Freedom and Responsibility in the American Way of Life* (1945), p. 42.
17. Chafee, *Government and Mass Communication* (1947), p. 53.
18. Message at dedicating exercises of the New York Museum of Modern Art, May 8, 1939.

Questions for Analysis

1. What evidence does Frank offer for the claim that: "Freedom to speak publicly and to publish has, as its inevitable and important correlative, the private right to hear, to read, and to think about what one hears and reads"? Do you agree?

2. Do you agree that pro-censorship views can be traced to Victorian influences?

3. *On what grounds does Frank dispute the claim that there is a connection between pornography and conduct?*

4. *Would it be accurate to say that Frank would oppose even pornography aimed at minors?*

5. *Do you think, as Frank claims, that a prohibition against the dissemination of sexual materials would logically justify a prohibition against other things considered "socially dangerous"?*

6. *Frank contends that government control of ideas or personal preferences is alien to a democracy. Contrast this view with Walter Berns's view in "Beyond the (Garbage) Pale or Democracy, Censorship and the Arts."*

7. *Distinguish the consequential from the nonconsequential considerations that make up Frank's argument.*

Pornography Without Prejudice

G. L. Simons

In the following selection from his book Pornography Without Prejudice, *British sexologist G. L. Simons begins by conceding that harm may result from pornography. But he feels that is hardly grounds for limiting the consenting adult's access to it. Quite the contrary, Simons feels that anti-pornographers must first prove that pornography actually causes harm and that the harm is considerable.*

Following this initial observation, Simons catalogues what he believes are some of the benefits of pornography. Included in these benefits are: that pornography gives pleasure to many people, that it sometimes aids sexual development, and that it can substitute for sexual activity. Moreover, pornography may have a cathartic effect; that is, its availability may neutralize "aberrant" sexual tendencies and thereby reduce the incidence of sex crimes.

Like Mishan's, Simons's argument is essentially utilitarian. He defends his thesis by appeal to the likely net benefit that will result from making pornography available.

It is not sufficient, for the objectors' case, that they demonstrate that some harm has flowed from pornography. It would be extremely difficult to show that pornography had *never* had unfortunate consequences, but we should not make too much of this. Harm has flowed from religion, patriotism, alcohol and cigarettes without this fact impelling people to demand abolition. The harm, if established, has to be weighed against a variety of considerations before a decision can be reached as to the propriety of certain laws. Of the British Obscenity Laws the Arts Council Report comments[1] that "the harm would need to be both indisputable and very dire indeed before it could be judged to outweigh the evils and anomalies inherent in the Acts we have been asked to examine."

The onus therefore is upon the anti-pornographers to demonstrate not only that harm is caused by certain types of sexual material but that the harm is considerable: If the first is difficult the second is necessarily more so, and the attempts to date have not been impressive. It is even possible to argue that easily available pornography has a number of benefits. Many people will be familiar with the *catharsis* argument whereby pornography

From G. L. Simons, Pornography without Prejudice *(London: Abelard–Schuman Limited). Reprinted by permission of the publisher.*

is said to cut down on delinquency by providing would-be criminals with substitute satisfactions. This is considered later but we mention it here to indicate that access to pornography may be socially beneficial in certain instances, and that where this is possible the requirement for anti-pornographers to *justify* their objections must be stressed.

The general conclusion[2] of the U.S. Commission was that no adequate proof had been provided that pornography was harmful to individual or society—"if a case is to be made out against 'pornography' [in 1970] it will have to be made on grounds other than demonstrated effects of a damaging personal or social nature." . . .

The heresy (to some ears) that pornography is harmless is compounded by the even greater impiety that it may be beneficial. Some of us are managing to adjust to the notion that pornography is unlikely to bring down the world in moral ruin, but the idea that it may actually do good is altogether another thing. When we read of Professor Emeritus E. T. Rasmussen, a pioneer of psychological studies in Denmark, and a government adviser, saying that there is a possibility "that pornography can be beneficial," many of us are likely to have *mixed* reactions, to say the least. In fact this thesis can be argued in a number of ways.

The simplest approach is to remark that people enjoy it. This can be seen to be true whether we rely on personal testimony or the most respectable index of all in capitalist society— "preparedness to pay." The appeal that pornography has for many people is hardly in dispute, and in a more sober social climate that would be justification enough. Today we are not quite puritan enough to deny that *pleasure* has a worthwhile place in human life: not many of us object to our food being tasty or our clothes being attractive. It was not always like this. In sterner times it was *de rigueur* to prepare food without spices and to wear the plainest clothes. The cult of puritanism reached its apotheosis in the most fanatical asceticism, where it was fashionable for holy men to wander off into a convenient desert and neglect the body to the point of cultivating its lice as "pearls of God." In such a bizarre philosophy pleasure was not only condemned in its sexual manifestations but in all areas where the body could conceivably take satisfaction. These days we

are able to countenance pleasure in most fields but in many instances still the case for *sexual* pleasure has to be argued.

Pleasure is not of course its own justification. If it clearly leads to serious malaise, early death, or the *dis*pleasure of others, then there is something to be said against it. But the serious consequences have to be demonstrated: It is not enough to condemn certain forms of pleasurable experience on the grounds of *possible* ill effect. With such an approach *any* human activity could be censured and freedom would have no place. In short, if something is pleasurable and its bad effects are small or nonexistent then it is to be encouraged: Opposition to such a creed should be recognized as an unwholesome antipathy to human potential. Pleasure is a good except where it is harmful (and where the harmfulness is *significant*). . . .

That pornography is enjoyable to many people is the first of the arguments in its favor. In any other field this would be argument enough. It is certainly sufficient to justify many activities that have—unlike a taste for pornography—demonstrably harmful consequences. Only in a sexually neurotic society could a tool for heightening sexual enjoyment be regarded as reprehensible and such as to warrant suppression by law. The position is well summarized[3] in the *first* of the Arts Council's twelve reasons for advocating the repeal of the Obscenity Publications Acts:

> It is not for the State to prohibit private citizens from choosing what they may or may not enjoy in literature or art unless there were incontrovertible evidence that the result would be injurious to society. There is no such evidence.

A further point is that availability of pornography may *aid*, rather than frustrate normal sexual development. Thus in 1966, for example, the New Jersey Committee for the Right to Read presented the findings of a survey conducted among nearly a thousand psychiatrists and psychologists of that state. Amongst the various personal statements included was the view that "sexually stimulating materials" might help particular people develop a normal sex drive.[4] In similar spirit, Dr. John Money writes[5] that pornography "may encourage normal sexual development and broadmindedness," a view that may not sound well to the anti-pornographers. And even in circumstances where possible dangers of pornography are pointed out conceivable good effects are sometimes acknowledged. In a paper issued[6] by The Danish Forensic Medicine Council it is pointed out that neurotic and sexually shy people may, by reading pornographic descriptions of normal sexual activity, be freed from some of their apprehension regarding sex and may thereby attain a freer and less frustrated attitude to the sexual side of life. . . .

One argument in favor of pornography is that it can serve as a substitute for actual sexual activity involving another person or other people. This argument has two parts, relating as it does to (1) people who fantasize over *socially acceptable* modes of sexual involvement, and (2) people who fantasize over types of sexual activity that would be regarded as illegal or at least immoral. The first type relates to lonely and deprived people who for one reason or another have been unable to form "normal" sexual contacts with other people; the second type are instances of the much quoted *catharsis* argument.

One writer notes[7] that pornography can serve as a substitute for both the knowledge of which some people have been deprived and the pleasure in sexual experience which they have not enjoyed. One can well imagine men or women too inhibited to secure sexual satisfaction with other adults and where explicit sexual material can alleviate some of their misery. It is facile to remark that such people should seek psychiatric assistance or even "make an effort": The factors that prevent the forming of effective sexual liaisons are just as likely to inhibit any efforts to seek medical or other assistance. Pornography provides sex *by proxy*, and in such usage it can have a clear justification.

It is also possible to imagine circumstances in which men or women—for reasons of illness, travel or bereavement—are unable to seek sexual satisfaction with spouse or other loved one. Pornography can help here too. Again it is easy to suggest that a person abstain from sexual experience, or, if having *permanently* lost a spouse, seek out another partner. Needless to say such advice is often quite impractical—and the alternative to pornography may be prostitution or adultery. Montagu notes that pornography can serve the same purpose as "dirty jokes," allowing a person to discharge harmlessly repressed and unsatisfied sexual desires.

In this spirit, Mercier (1970) is quoted by the U.S. Commission:

> . . . it is in periods of sexual deprivation— to which the young and the old are far more subject than those in their prime—that males, at any rate, are likely to reap psychological benefit from pornography.

And also Kenneth Tynan (1970):

> For men on long journeys, geographically cut off from wives and mistresses, pornography can act as a portable memory, a welcome shortcut to remembered bliss, relieving tension without involving disloyalty.

It is difficult to see how anyone could object to the use of pornography in such circumstances, other than on the grounds of a morbid anti-sexuality.

The *catharsis argument* has long been put forward to suggest that availability of pornography will neutralize "aberrant" sexual tendencies and so reduce the incidence of sex crime or clearly immoral behavior in related fields. (Before evidence is put forward for this thesis it is worth remarking that it should not be necessary to demonstrate a *reduction* in sex crime to justify repeal of the Obscenity Laws. It should be quite sufficient to show that an *increase* in crime will not ensue following repeal. We may even argue that a small increase may be tolerable if other benefits from easy access to pornography could be shown: But it is no part of the present argument to put this latter contention.)

Many psychiatrists and psychologists have favored the catharsis argument. Chesser, for instance, sees[8] pornography as a form of voyeurism in which—as with sado-masochistic material—the desire to hurt is satisfied passively. If this is so and the analogy can be extended we have only to look at the character of the voyeur—generally furtive and clandestine—to realize that we have little to fear from the pornography addict. Where consumers are preoccupied with fantasy there is little danger to the rest of us. Karpman (1959), quoted by the U.S. Commission, notes that people reading "salacious literature" are less likely to become sexual offenders than those who do not since the reading often neutralizes "aberrant sexual interests." Similarly the Kronhausens have argued that "these 'unholy' instruments" may be a safety-valve for the sexual deviate and potential sex offender. And Cairns, Paul and Wishner (1962) have remarked that *obscene materials* provide a way of releasing strong sexual urges without doing harm to others.

It is easy to see the plausibility of this argument. The popularity of all forms of sexual literature—from the superficial, *sexless*, sentimentality of the popular women's magazine to the clearest "hard-core" porn—has demonstrated over the ages the perennial appetite that people have for fantasy. To an extent, a great extent with many single people and frustrated married ones, the fantasy constitutes an important part of the sex-life. The experience may be vicarious and sterile but it self-evidently fills a need for many individuals. If literature, as a *symbol* of reality, can so involve human sensitivities it is highly likely that when the sensitivities are *distorted* for one reason or another the same sublimatory function can occur: The "perverted" or potentially criminal mentality can gain satisfaction, as does the lonely unfortunate, in sex *by proxy*. If we wanted to force the potential sex criminal on to the streets in search of a human victim perhaps we would do well to deny him his sublimatory substitutes: Deny him fantasy and he will be forced to go after the real thing. . . .

The importance of this possibility should be fully faced. If a causal connection *does* exist between availability of pornographic material and a *reduction* in the amount of sex crime—and the evidence is wholly consistent with this possibility rather than its converse—then people who deliberately restrict pornography by supporting repressive legislation are prime architects of sexual offences against the individual. The anti-pornographers would do well to note that their anxieties may be driving them into a position the exact opposite of the one they explicitly maintain—their commitment to reduce the amount of sexual delinquency in society.

The most that the anti-pornographers can argue is that at present the evidence is inconclusive—a point that would be taken by Kutschinsky *et al.* But if the inconclusive character of the data is once admitted then the case for repressive legislation falls at once. For in a *free* society, or one supposedly aiming after freedom, social phenomena are, like individuals, innocent until proven guilty—and an activity will be permitted unless there is clear evidence of its harmful consequences. This point was well put—in the specific connection with pornography—by

Bertrand Russell, talking[9] when he was well over 90 to Rupert Crawshay-Williams.

After noting how people beg the question of causation in instances such as the Moors murders (where the murders and the reading of de Sade *may* have a common cause), Russell ("Bertie") said that on the whole he disapproved of sadistic pornography being available. But when Crawshay-Williams put the catharsis view, that such material might provide a harmless release for individuals who otherwise may be dangerous, Russell said at once—"Oh, well, if that's true, then I don't see that there is anything against sadistic pornography. In fact it should be encouraged. . . ." When it was stressed that there was no preponderating evidence either way Russell argued that we should fall back on an overriding principle—"in this case the principle of free speech."

Thus in the absence of evidence of harm we should be permissive. Any other view is totalitarian. . . .

If human enjoyment *per se* is not to be condemned then it is not too rash to say that we *know* pornography does good. We can easily produce our witnesses to testify to experiencing pleasure. If in the face of this—and no other favorable argument—we are unable to demonstrate a countervailing harm, then the case for easy availability of pornography is unassailable. If, in such circumstances, we find some people unconvinced it is futile to seek out further empirical data. Once we commit ourselves to the notion that the evil nature of something is axiomatic we tacitly concede that evidence is largely irrelevant to our position. If pornography never fails to fill us with predictable loathing then statistics on crime, or measured statements by careful specialists, will not be useful: Our reactions will stay the same. But in this event we would do well to reflect on what our emotions tell us of our own mentality. . . .

Notes

1. *The Obscenity Laws*, André Deutsch, 1969, p. 33.
2. *The Report of the Commission on Obscenity and Pornography*, Part Three, II, Bantam Books, 1970, p. 169.
3. *The Obscenity Laws*, André Deutsch, 1969, p. 35.
4. Quoted by Isadore Rubin, 'What Should Parents Do About Pornography?' *Sex in the Adolescent Years*, Fontana, 1969, p. 202.

5.   John Money, contribution to "Is Pornography Harmful to Young Children?" *Sex in the Childhood Years*, Fontana, 1971, p. 181–5.

6.   Paper from The Danish Forensic Medicine Council to The Danish Penal Code Council, published in The Penal Code Council Report on Penalty for Pornography, Report No. 435, Copenhagen, 1966, pp. 78–80, and as appendix to *The Obscenity Laws*, pp. 120–4.

7.   Ashley Montagu, "Is Pornography Harmful to Young Children?" *Sex in the Childhood Years*, Fontana, 1971, p. 182.

8.   Eustace Chesser, *The Human Aspects of Sexual Deviation*, Arrow Books, 1971, p. 39.

9.   Rupert Crawshay-Williams, *Russell Remembered*, Oxford University Press, 1970, p. 144.

Questions for Analysis

1.   *What was the key finding of the U.S. Commission on pornography (1970)?*

2.   *Does Simons believe that pleasure alone can justify pornography?*

3.   *Under what conditions is pleasure a good? How does this relate to the use of pornography?*

4.   *Is the evidence Simons provides that pornography may aid rather than frustrate sexual development sufficient to warrant the claim?*

5.   *What are the two parts of the argument for pornography as proxy sexual activity?*

6.   *State the "catharsis" argument. Do you think there is enough evidence to support it?*

7.   *Explain why Simons's argument is utilitarian.*

CASE PRESENTATION
Bunny Running

Clarence O'Dell, the bookstore manager, had a nickname—"The Rabbit." Why was he called "The Rabbit"? Oh, that's hard to say. Maybe because of the incessant twitching of his nostrils that gave him the appearance of constantly sniffing the air the way rabbits do. Or maybe it was the way he carried his arms, close to his sides and bent at the elbows, in the posture of supplication. Some thought it was because he once wrote a letter to the editor of the local paper deploring as "obscene and abhorrent" a practice called "bunny running." In bunny running, you pursue a rabbit on your dirt bike until the creature's heart literally bursts in its chest. Bunny running was a rather popular pastime of some of the local boys and men. Whatever the reasons, the man who ran the college bookstore with a quiet efficiency had been called "The Rabbit" for as long as anyone could remember.

True to his nickname, The Rabbit avoided even the hint of danger, preferring instead to bury himself in the bramble of books, stationery and sundry supplies that was the bookstore's stockroom. But things have a way of crowding in, of flushing out even the most ensconced of us.

Playboy. Playgirl. Penthouse. Dude. Pretty racy stuff, a lot of people thought the morning The Rabbit laid these magazines out on the shelves next to *Scientific American, Quest, Ebony, Esquire,* and the other periodicals he sold. But The Rabbit didn't see the move as at all bold or controversial. For him it was simply good business. "Besides," The Rabbit told a reporter for *Whipsaw,* the college paper, "compared with a lot of things around today, this is pretty tame stuff."

But not everyone agreed. In fact, Abner Massey, a psychology professor, charged into the bookstore that very afternoon and demanded to see The Rabbit. After some minutes, The Rabbit finally emerged from the stockroom; with cautious little steps and nostrils aquiver, he approached his adversary, who, everyone agreed, had come loaded for bear.

Well, the professor raged about how such filthy magazines had no place in any public display, let alone on the same shelf as the *Reader's Digest.* He even impugned The Rabbit's character and sense of morality and threatened to lead a boycott of the store. And how did The Rabbit respond to these charges and threats? Well, in a trembling voice no louder than a whisper, he kept saying: "If you can buy 'em in the Safeway, why can't you buy 'em here?"

But Clarence O'Dell was certainly no crusader rabbit. No sooner had a citizen's group calling itself Citizens Against Filth (CAF) formed and pressured the college authorities to do something, than The Rabbit caved in. He promised to remove the objectionable material *posthaste.*

No way—by then a student counter group, clamoring for free choice and freedom of the press, threatened reprisals if the magazines were withdrawn. The nature of the reprisals were unspecified.

So, there was The Rabbit, in the middle of a crossfire. To be sure, nature hadn't equipped him for such stress. The Rabbit couldn't sleep, and he only nibbled at his food. Weak with worry, wrung out with anxiety, he groped for a solution. And then, when things seemed darkest, inspiration struck him.

Why not remove the magazines from the shelves and place them behind the counter? They'd still be available for purchase, but they wouldn't be on display.

Well, like any compromise, The Rabbit's didn't wholly satisfy either side. There were grumbles of displeasure, bleats of indignation; but in the end both sides went along, albeit begrudgingly.

And so the greatest personal controversy in "Rabbit" O'Dell's life came to a conclusion. A successful conclusion, some said. Maybe so. But not too many months later, the man they called The Rabbit was found in the stockroom slumped over a stack of civics texts. It seems he suffered a massive heart attack, or in the words of earthy old Doc Wilcox: "The Rabbit's heart just kind of exploded in his chest."

Questions for Analysis

1. *Would you consider magazines such as* Playboy *and* Penthouse *pornographic? Explain.*

2. *Assuming that the materials in question were obscene, do you think that a college should prohibit their sale in the campus bookstore or not?*

3. *Do you think that the college should abide by community standards in this matter or not?*

4. *Do you think the difference between inconspicuously selling the magazines and displaying them is morally significant?*

5. *In selling the magazines "under the counter," is the bookstore violating any of the publishers' rights?*

6. *If you were the manager of the bookstore, to whom would you owe the greatest allegiance: the students, the faculty, the college administrators, the community?*

CASE PRESENTATION
The Little Tenderloin

SCENE: *The passenger section of a plane that has landed for a brief layover in a small nondescript town before continuing to some big city beyond the horizon. Two passengers, Sig and Sy, are reacting to a full-page ad for "adult entertainment" that appears in the local newspaper.*

Sig: Wow!

Sy: Incredible!

Sig: Wow!!

Sy: Unbelievable!

Sig: What's the name of this burg anyway?

Sy: Beats me.

Sig: Geez, it looks like such a sleepy little place, doesn't it?

Sy: A regular Sleepy Hollow.

Sig: Why, look at that old twin-engine over there.

Sy: Yeah, isn't that something?

Sig: Makes you pine for the old days, doesn't it?

Sy: You said it.

Sig: But you didn't have stuff like *this* around in the old days.

Sy: Not in burgs like this you didn't.

Sig: No way . . . I mean this is really hot stuff, you know?

Sy: I know it.

Sig: I mean who would have thought it?

Sy: In a place like this, no less.

Sig: Makes you wonder, you know?

Sy: Yeah.

Sig: About "Middle America."

Sy: "Middle America." Yeah, right.

Sig: I mean a backwater like this that's into this kind of heavy action.

Sy: I know what you're saying. Makes you wonder where it's all going to end.

Sig: Where it's all going to end—*that's* the question. What's the country coming to? I mean New York, San Francisco, I can understand. But a way station like this . . . I don't know. I just don't know anymore.

Sy: It's hard to figure.

Sig: I'll say . . . Well, I'll be!

Sy: What's that?

Sig: Get a load of this!

Sy: What? What?

Sig: It's a full-page, open letter to the Mayor of this joint.

Sy: You're kiddin'.

Sig: No, here, look for yourself.

An Open Letter to the Mayor and the City Council

Mr. Mayor and members of the Council, an intolerable infringement on our CIVIL RIGHTS is growing within our city and we must publicly call it to your attention. We law-abiding, God-fearing, decent-living citizens are being subjected to highly obscene and pornographic materials in the section of our city popularly known as Little Tenderloin.

There one can find all kinds of lewd "adult" stores and theaters that cater to the sexually degenerate. It's shameful enough that such a district even exists, but now it threatens to spread its moral malignancy two blocks to the north and thus further blight our community.

Where will it stop? At our playgrounds? In our schoolyards? Or will it not stop even there? Likely as not some apostle of civil rights will defend the smut merchant's right to peddle his verminous wares even on our doorstep!

But what about OUR civil rights? Don't we have a right to the kind of community we think is decent and proper for ourselves and our children? Don't we have a right to be protected from the degrading, the depraved, and the utterly offensive? Don't we, the overwhelming majority, have a right to say: "NO. WE DON'T WANT THIS VILENESS IN OUR COMMUNITY!"?

We can almost hear the replies now: "Nobody is asking you to go into Little Tenderloin"; "What you don't see won't hurt you." To this we say, respectfully, "BALDERDASH!"

Little Tenderloin, like any other neighborhood or landmark, is an expression and extension of the community. It's a symbol, as much as our art gallery, city park, or library. It says: "This is what the people of this town respect and stand for. This is what they value and cherish." Well, WE DON'T! LITTLE TENDERLOIN IS A MONSTROUS DECEIT! We deserve better. WE DEMAND BETTER!

Sig:	Wow!
Sy:	Incredible!
Sig:	Wow!!
Sy:	Unbelievable!
Sig:	What'd you say the name of this joint was?
Sy:	Beats me.
Sig:	Geez, but it looks like such a sleepy little place, doesn't it?
Sy:	A regular Sleepy Hollow.
Sig:	How do you like that for . . . what? Repression. Am I right?
Sy:	That is definitely repression.
Sig:	Fascism, even. . . . You think that's too strong?
Sy:	You kidding? Look at that guard out there by the gate.
Sig:	Yeah, you're right—a real fascist if I ever saw one.
Sy:	A stormtrooper.
Sig:	Makes you wonder, you know.
Sy:	You said it.
Sig:	"Middle America." What's happened to Middle America? You know, the source of everything we cherish—our strength, our bedrock values, our moral fiber.
Sy:	I hear you, I hear you!
Sig:	I mean if Middle America is into this kind of heavy repression . . . wow!
Sy:	That's the thing I like about a big city, you know?
Sig:	Tolerance.
Sy:	Exactly.

Sig: Live and let live.

Sy: There you go.

Sig: Different strokes for different folks.

Sy: Hey, speaking of different strokes—I mean *really* different strokes—there's this bizarre, I mean *bizarre*, joint in Cleveland. . . .

Sig: Cleveland!? You're kidding!

Sy: No, seriously. Kinky—I mean *kinky*. Let me tell you about this place.

Sig: Yeah, go ahead. You got the address?

Questions for Analysis

1. *Is the community justified in enforcing its moral standards?*

2. *If you were the owner of a shop in Little Tenderloin, what would you say in defense of yourself and your business? What rights would you appeal to?*

3. *Do you think that the following maxim is universalizable: "A community should enforce its moral standards even on those who disagree with them"? Explain.*

4. *Do you think the maximin principle would endorse or reject a rule that permitted a community to impose its moral standards on all community members? Explain.*

Selections for Further Reading

Boyer, Paul S. *Purity in Print.* New York: Scribner's, 1968.

Clor, Harry M. *Obscenity and Public Morality: Censorship in a Liberal Society.* Chicago: University of Chicago Press, 1969.

Comstock, Anthony. *Traps for the Young.* Cambridge, Mass.: Harvard University Press, 1967.

Emerson, Thomas I. *The System of Freedom of Expression.* New York: Random House, 1970.

————. *Toward a General Theory of the First Amendment.* New York: Random House, 1966.

Gerber, Albert. *Sex, Pornography, and the Law.* 2nd rev. ed. New York: Ballantine, 1964.

Gilmore, Donald H. *Sex, Censorship and Pornography.* San Diego: Greenleaf Classics, 1969.

Holbrook, David, Ed. *The Case Against Pornography.* New York: The Library Press, 1973.

Hoyt, Olga G., and Edwin P. Hoyt. *Censorship in America.* New York: Seabury Press, 1962.

Marcuse, Ludwig. *Obscene: The History of an Indignation.* New York: Fernhill House, 1965.

Rembar, Charles. *The End of Obscenity.* New York: Simon and Schuster, 1970.

St. John-Stevas, Norman. *Obscenity and The Law.* London: Secker and Warburg, 1956.

Sharp, Donald B., Ed. *Commentaries on Obscenity.* Metuchen, N.J.: Scarecrow Press, 1970.

5
ABORTION

Jane Roe was an unmarried pregnant woman who wished to have an abortion, an intentional termination of a pregnancy by inducing the loss of the fetus. Unfortunately for Ms. Roe, she lived in Texas, where abortion statutes forbade abortion except to save the life of the mother. So, she went to court to prove that the statutes were unconstitutional.

The three-judge district court ruled that Jane Roe had reason to sue, that the Texas criminal abortion statutes were void on their face, and, most importantly, that the right to choose whether to have children was protected by the Ninth through the Fourteenth Amendments. Since the district court denied a number of other aspects of the suit, the case went to the United States Supreme Court. On 22 January 1973, in the now famous *Roe* v. *Wade* decision, the Supreme Court affirmed the district court's judgment.[1]

Expressing the views of seven members of the Court, Justice Blackmun pointed out that the right to privacy applies to a woman's decision on whether to terminate her pregnancy, but that her right to terminate is not absolute. Her right may be limited by the state's legitimate interests in safeguarding the woman's health, in maintaining proper medical standards, and in protecting human life. Blackmun went on to point out that the unborn are not included within the definition of *person* as used in the Fourteenth Amendment. Most importantly, he indicated that prior to the end of the first trimester of pregnancy, the state may not interfere with or regulate an attending physician's decision, reached in consultation with his patient, that the patient's pregnancy should be terminated. After the first trimester and until the fetus is viable, the state may regulate the abortion procedure only for the health of the mother. After the fetus becomes viable, the state may prohibit all abortions except those necessary to preserve the health or life of the mother.

In dissenting, Justices White and Rehnquist said that nothing in the lan-

1. *See* U.S. Supreme Court Reports, *October Term 1972, lawyers' edition (Rochester, N.Y.: Lawyers' Cooperative Publishing, 1974), p. 147.*

guage or history of the U.S. Constitution supported the Court's judgment, that the Court had simply manufactured a new constitutional right for pregnant women. The abortion issue, they said, should have been left with the people and the political processes they had devised to govern their affairs.

Thus, for the time being at least, the abortion question has been resolved legally. But the issue is hardly dead. A number of anti-abortion movements have surfaced, a fact that not only indicates that some people think abortion should be illegal, but that many believe it is wrong. Abortion, whether legal or not, still remains a most personal moral concern for those who must confront it. Obviously its legality provides options that may not have been present before, but these can make the moral dilemma that much thornier; in the past one could always rationalize away the possibility of an abortion on the basis of its illegality.

Some say an abortion is right if (1) it is therapeutic, that is, when it is necessary to preserve the physical or mental health of the woman; (2) it prevents the birth of a severely handicapped child; or (3) it ends a pregnancy resulting from some criminal act of sexual intercourse. Others say that even therapeutic abortions are immoral. Still others argue that any restrictive abortion legislation is wrong and must be liberalized to allow a woman to have an abortion on demand, that is, at the request of her and her physician, regardless or even in the absence of reasons. In order to evaluate such claims, it is helpful to have some biological background and to consider what sort of entities the unborn are and whether they have rights.

Biological Background

Since most of the controversy that surrounds the abortion issue concerns precisely when a human life is considered to exist, it is important to have some background about the development of the human fetus, and familiarity with the terms that designate the various developmental stages. Conception or fertilization occurs when a female germ cell termed an *ovum* is penetrated by a male germ cell called a *spermatozoon*. The result is a single cell containing a full genetic code of 46 chromosomes called the *zygote*. The zygote then journeys down the fallopian tube, which carries ova from the ovary to the uterus. This passage generally takes two or three days. During the journey the zygote begins a process of cellular division that increases its size. Occasionally, the zygote ends its journey in the fallopian tube where it continues to develop. Because the tube is so narrow, such a pregnancy generally must be terminated by surgery.

When the multicell zygote reaches the uterus, it floats free in the intrauterine fluid and develops into what is termed a *blastocyst*, a ball of cells surrounding a fluid-filled cavity. By the end of the second week, the blastocyst implants itself in the uterine wall. From the end of the second week until the end of the eighth week, the unborn entity is termed an *embryo*. In the interim (four to five weeks) organ systems begin to develop, and the embryo takes on distinctly human external features.

The eighth week is important in the biological development and in a discussion of abortion, because it is then that brain activity generally becomes detectable. From this point until birth, the embryo is termed a *fetus*, although in common parlance *fetus* is used to designate the unborn entity at whatever stage.

Two other terms that designate events in fetal development are worth noting because they sometimes arise in abortion discussions. One is *quickening*, a term that refers to the point at which the mother begins to feel the movements of the fetus. This occurs somewhere between the thirteenth and twentieth weeks. The second term is *viability*, the point at which the fetus is capable of surviving outside the womb. The fetus ordinarily reaches viability around the twenty-fourth week. Generally, then, events during pregnancy unfold as follows:

Developmental Timetable

zygote: day 1 through day 3
blastocyst: day 4 through week 2
embryo: week 3 through week 8
fetus: week 9 until birth
quickening: between weeks 13 and 20
viability: around week 24

Should the unborn entity be terminated at any point in this timetable, an abortion is said to occur. Thus, *abortion simply refers to the termination of a pregnancy*.

Abortions can happen for a number of reasons. Sometimes the abortion occurs "spontaneously," that is, because of internal biochemical factors or because of an injury to the woman. Such spontaneous abortions are ordinarily termed *miscarriages*.

Abortions also can result directly from human intervention, which can occur in a variety of ways. Sometimes it happens very early, as when a woman takes a drug such as the "morning-after pill" in order to prevent the blastocyst from implanting in the uterine wall. Subsequent intervention during the first trimester (through week 12) usually takes one of two forms: (1) uterine or vacuum aspiration, (2) dilation and curettage.

In *uterine or vacuum aspiration* the narrow opening of the uterus, termed the *cervix*, is dilated. A small tube is then inserted into the uterus, and its contents are vacuumed or emptied by suction. In *dilation and curettage* (D&C), the cervix is again widened. But this time its contents are scraped out by means of a spoon-shaped surgical instrument called a curette. These two procedures can sometimes be done through week 16, but after that the fetus is generally too large to make the procedures practical.

The most common abortion technique after week 16 is called *saline injection*. In this procedure the amniotic fluid (the fluid in the amnion, which is a membrane sac surrounding the fetus) is drawn out through a hollow needle and replaced by a solution of salt and water. This leads to a miscarriage.

Another but far rarer method after the sixteenth week is the *hysterotomy*. This is a surgical procedure whereby the fetus is removed from the uterus through an incision. This procedure is generally called a Caesarean section and is rarely performed for an abortion. Thus, we can list the various abortion possibilities as follows:

1. Internally induced:

    a. Spontaneous abortion: anytime

2. Externally induced:

    a. Drug such as "morning-after pill": immediately following intercourse

    b. Uterine or vacuum aspiration: through week 12

    c. Dilation and curettage: through week 12

    d. Saline injection: after week 16

    e. Hysterotomy (extremely rare): after week 16

With this biological background, we can now turn to the chief moral problem that abortion raises.

The Moral Problem

The key moral problem of abortion is: Under what conditions, if any, is abortion morally justifiable? In answer to this question, three positions are broadly identifiable.

First, the so-called conservative view holds that abortion is never morally justifiable, or, at most, justifiable only when the abortion is necessary to save the mother's life. This view is commonly associated with Roman Catholics, although they are certainly not the only persons who espouse it. In contrast is the second position, the so-called liberal view, which holds that abortion is always morally justifiable, regardless of the reasons or the time in fetal development. Most recently, this view has been advanced by women's rights advocates, who focus on the woman's right to make decisions that will affect her body. But again, this position has adherents outside the sphere of the female liberation movement. Third and finally, the so-called intermediate or moderate views consider abortion morally acceptable up to a certain point in fetal development and/or claim that some reasons, not all, provide a sufficient justification for abortion.

While there is no consensus on the moral acceptability of abortion, there is agreement that any answer to the question depends on (1) one's view of what sort of entities fetuses are and (2) whether such entities have rights. These two important problems generally are referred to as the ontological and moral status of the fetus.

The Ontological Status
of the Fetus

In philosophy the term *ontology* refers to the theory and nature of being and existence. When we speak of the ontological status of the fetus, we mean the kind of entity the fetus is. Determining the ontological status of fetuses bears directly on the issue of fetal rights and, subsequently, on permissible treatment of the fetus.

Actually, the problem of ontological status embraces a number of questions, such as: (1) whether the fetus is an individual organism; (2) whether the fetus is biologically a human being; (3) whether the fetus is psychologically a human being; (4) whether the fetus is a person.[2] Presumably, to affirm question (2) attributes more significant status to the fetus than affirming question (1); and affirming question (3) assigns even greater status. To affirm question (4), that the fetus is a person, probably is to assign the most significant status to the fetus, although this, as well as the other presumptions, depends on the precise meaning of the concepts involved.

Complicating the question of the fetus's ontological status is the meaning of the expression *human life*. The concept of "human life" can be used in at least two different ways. On the one hand, it can refer to *biological* human life, that is, to a set of biological characteristics that distinguish the human species from other nonhuman species. In this sense, "human life" may be coextensive with "individual organism," as in question (1). On the other hand, "human life" may refer to *psychological* human life, that is, to life that is characterized by the properties that are distinctly human. Among these properties might be the abilities to use symbols, to think, and to imagine. Abortion discussions can easily founder when these distinctions are not made. For example, many who would agree that abortion involves the taking of human life in the biological sense would deny that it involves taking human life in the psychological sense. Moreover, they might see nothing immoral about taking life exclusively in the biological sense, although they would consider taking life in the psychological sense morally unacceptable. Thus, they find nothing morally objectionable about abortion. Of course, at the root of this judgment is an assumption about the meaning of *human life*.

Intertwined with one's concept of human life is one's concept of "personhood." The concept of personhood may or may not differ from either the biological or the psychological sense of "human life." Thus, some would argue that to be a person is simply to have the biological and/or psychological properties that make an organism human. However, others would propose additional conditions for personhood, such as consciousness, self-consciousness, rationality, even the capacities for communication and moral judgment. In this view, an entity must satisfy some or all of these criteria, even additional ones, to be a person. Still other theorists would extend the concept of personhood to include properties bestowed by human evaluation, in addition to the factual properties possessed by a person. Thus, they might argue that a person must be the bearer of legal rights and social responsibilities, and must be capable of being assigned moral responsibility, of being praised or blamed.

Clearly the conditions that one believes are necessary for "person" status directly affect the ontological status of the fetus. For example, if the condition is

2.   *Tom L. Beauchamp and Le Roy Walters,* Contemporary Issues in Bioethics *(Belmont, Calif.: Dickenson, 1978), p. 188.*

only of an elementary biological nature, then the fetus can more easily qualify as a person than if the conditions include a list of factual properties. Further, if "personhood" must be analyzable in terms of properties bestowed by human evaluation, then it becomes infinitely more difficult for the fetus to qualify as a person.

In the final analysis, the ontological status of fetuses remains an open issue. But some viewpoint ultimately underpins any position on the morality of abortion. Thus, whether conservative, liberal, or moderate, one must be prepared eventually to defend one's view of the ontological status of fetuses.

When Ontological Status Is Attained

Further complicating the problem of the ontological status is the question of when in fetal development the fetus gains full ontological status. Whether one claims the fetus is an individual organism, a biological human being, a psychological human being, or a full-fledged person, one must specify at what point in its biological development the fetus attains this status. Thus, it is one thing to say what status the fetus has; it is another to say *when* it has attained such status. A judgment about *when* the fetus has the status bears as directly on abortion views as does a judgment of the status itself.

We can identify a number of positions on when status is attained. An extreme conservative position would argue that the fetus has full ontological status from conception. Thus, at the time of conception the fetus must be regarded as an individual person. In direct contrast to this view is the extreme liberal position, which holds that the fetus never achieves ontological status.

Viewing these as polar positions, we can identify a cluster of moderate views that fall between them. In every instance, the moderate view tries to pinpoint full ontological status somewhere between conception and birth. For example, some would draw the line when brain activity is first present; others draw it at quickening; still others would draw the line at viability.

The Moral Status of the Unborn

The issue of moral status of the unborn is generally, but not always, discussed in terms of the unborn's rights. What rights, if any, does the unborn have? Any position on abortion must at some point address this question, and all seriously argued positions do, at least by implication.

Various views on the moral status of the unborn are currently circulating. Each view can be associated with one or another of the views on the unborn's ontological status. For example, claiming that the unborn has full ontological status at conception, the extreme conservative view also holds that the unborn has full moral status at the same stage. Thus, whether zygote, blastocyst, embryo, or fetus, the unborn entity enjoys the same rights that we attribute to any adult human. In this view, abortion would be a case of denying the unborn the right to life. Therefore, abortion could never be undertaken without reasons sufficient to override the unborn's claim to life. In other words, only conditions that would justify the killing of an adult human—for example, self-defense—would morally justify an abortion.

Liberals similarly derive their view of moral status from their theory of ontological status. The extreme liberal view would deny the unborn any moral status. In this view abortion is not considered comparable to killing an adult person. Indeed, abortion may be viewed as little more than removing a mass of organic material, not unlike an appendectomy. Its removal raises no serious moral problems. A somewhat less liberal view, while granting the unborn ontological status as being biologically human, claims it is not human in any significant moral sense and thus has no significant rights.

Likewise, moderates would assign moral status to the unborn at the point that the entity attained full ontological status. Thus, if brain activity is taken as the point of ontological status, then abortions conducted before that time would not raise serious moral questions; those conducted subsequent to that development would. Currently, viability seems to be an especially popular point at which to assign ontological status. And so, many moderate theorists today insist that abortion raises significant moral questions only *after* the unborn has attained viability. This view is reflected in some of the opinions delivered in the *Roe* v. *Wade* case.

It is important to note that granting the unborn moral status does not at all deny moral status to the woman. Indeed the question of whose rights should take precedence when a conflict develops raises thorny questions, especially for conservatives and moderates. For example, while granting the unborn full moral status, some conservatives nonetheless approve of therapeutic abortions—abortions performed to save the woman's life or to correct some life-threatening condition. These are often viewed as cases of self-defense or justifiable homicide. Since self-defense and justifiable homicide commonly are considered justified grounds for killing an adult person, they are also taken as moral justification for killing the unborn. But other conservatives disapprove of even therapeutic abortions.

Similarly, while moderates grant the unborn moral status at some point in fetal development, they too must arbitrate cases of conflicting rights. They must determine just what conditions are sufficient for allowing the woman's right to override the fetus's right to life. Here the whole gamut of conditions involving the pregnancy must be evaluated, including rape, incest, fetal deformity, and of course physical or psychological harm to the woman.

Pro-Life Arguments (Against Abortion)

1. *Abortion is murder.*

POINT: "You don't have to be a lawyer to know what murder means: the intentional killing of an innocent human life. Who can imagine an uglier and more outrageous act? Well, I can think of at least one: abortion. At least when you kill adults, they usually have a chance to defend themselves. But what chance does a fetus have? None. Try as you will, you can't escape the inevitable fact that abortion is murder."

COUNTERPOINT: "You make it sound like fetuses can go out and buy ice cream cones whenever they want, as well as think, imagine, wonder, hope, dream, and create. Why, a fetus isn't any more a 'human being' than cake batter is a cake. Certainly murder is a terrible thing—the murder of a full-fledged walking, talking human being, not of a glob of protoplasm."

2.   *Abortion sets a dangerous precedent.*

POINT: "Everybody would agree that any action leading to a casual attitude toward life is wrong. But that's just what abortion is. And that includes therapeutic abortion. As for abortions committed in the case of severely deformed fetuses, why they're no more than the first step to 'putting away' the severely handicapped, the dysfunctional, the senile, and the incurably ill in our society. No, abortion leads to a shabby attitude toward life; it opens a Pandora's box of unspeakable affronts to human dignity and worth. Remember: The Holocaust under Hitler began with the legalization of abortion. Every abortion that's demanded or performed takes us one step closer to a systematic recognition of abortion, and everything that implies."

COUNTERPOINT: "Why do you assume that the practice of abortion inevitably will lead to disrespect for life and usher in an age of nightmarish inhumanity? You and I both know that issues dealing with the severely handicapped or incurably ill are separate and distinct questions from abortion, and must be examined on their own merits. As for your Hitler reference, that has nothing to do with the question of whether abortion's right or wrong. It's outrageously irrelevant. Besides, legal abortion didn't produce the Holocaust; Hitler's madness and those who cooperated with it did. Even if your point had any merit, it really argues against *allowing* abortions, and not their morality."

3.   *Abortion involves psychological risks for the woman.*

POINT: "Let's face it: A woman and the child she's bearing are about as close as any two humans can ever get. And I don't mean just biologically, but emotionally and psychologically, too. Ask any mother—she'll tell you. For a woman to intentionally harm her unborn violates the deepest levels of her unconscious needs, impulses, and desires. And she's bound to pay a big price for this psychologically. Plenty of women already have—ask the psychologists. There's no question about it: The woman who has an abortion not only kills her unborn, she also seriously damages herself."

COUNTERPOINT: "If there was an annual award for sweeping generalizations, you'd certainly get it. Why, you talk of 'women' as if they were all the same. Sure, lots of women, maybe even most, want to carry their unborn to term. But *lots* and *most* don't mean *all*. Who knows what lurks in the so-called unconscious mind? Maybe a woman who outwardly wants to bear children secretly doesn't. Ask the psychologists, you say. All right, ask them. And while you're at it, ask about child abuse, post- and neonatal trauma, and nervous breakdowns. What makes you think every woman is suited to be a mother? Some women discover only after giving birth that they genuinely *don't* want the child. They assumed they did largely because of environmental conditioning which, as you well illustrated, has been scrupulous about heaping hot coals of guilt on the poor woman who might honestly admit she does not want to carry, bear, and rear children. It's time we put aside these stereotypes about women for good. And while we're at it, let's not confuse what women actually want to do with what we believe they *should* want to do."

4.   *Alternatives to abortion are available.*

POINT: "All this talk about unwanted pregnancies and bringing undesired and unloved children into the world just won't cut it. Who are we kidding? There are countless individuals and couples who are dying to have kids but can't. If a woman doesn't want to carry a child to term, that's no reason to abort it. Just put it up for adoption at birth. As for the tragically deformed infant that no one may want to adopt, there are plenty of institutions and agencies set up for those pitiful souls."

COUNTERPOINT: "Sure there are plenty of people willing and able to adopt. But even if the child will be adopted, the woman still has to carry it for nine months. And she may be either unwilling or unable to do that. What's more, giving up your child for adoption is no emotional picnic, you know. And often it's no easier on the child. Plenty of adoptees anguish over unresolved feelings of parental rejection. As for the deformed, why make society foot the bill for someone else's responsibility? I for one don't want my hard-earned tax dollars spent caring for someone else's problems that easily could have been prevented in the first place."

5.   *The woman must be responsible for her sexual activity.*

POINT: "No woman *has* to get pregnant. You don't have to be the 'happy hooker' to know that there are plenty of readily available contraceptives. When a woman doesn't practice some form of birth control, she takes responsibility for what happens. For a woman to sacrifice an innocent human life just because she's been careless, ignorant, or indiscreet is the height of sexual and moral irresponsibility."

COUNTERPOINT: "Come now, everybody knows that there's no surefire birth control method, except abstinence. Any woman who has sex stands the same chance of getting pregnant as a driver of having an accident. Why, even if a driver drives recklessly and has a serious accident, we allow them the opportunity to repair the damage to themselves and others, don't we? In fact, we help them do it! To make a woman bear a child out of some warped sense of 'personal responsibility' is like turning our back on a torn and bloody motorist because 'he got what he deserved.' Such an attitude reflects more vindictiveness and punishment than commitment to the principle of personal responsibility. No matter why a woman gets pregnant, she still has the right to dispose of her pregnancy as she sees fit. Sure, she may have been irresponsible, but that's a separate issue from what she then chooses to do about the result of her indiscretion.''

Pro-Choice Arguments (For Abortion)

1.   *Pregnancies are dangerous for the woman.*

POINT: ''There are very few adults, if any, who haven't had a direct or indirect experience that shows how dangerous pregnancies can be to the life and health of women. Let those without such knowledge look at the record. They'll see that in some cases the woman's life is actually on the line. In other cases, the woman must endure heroic suffering and hardship during the term. In still other cases, the woman must endure lifelong health problems that are the direct result of the pregnancy. Given these possible risks, women should have the say about whether they want to run them or not.''

COUNTERPOINT: ''Your argument would be very persuasive if this were the nineteenth century. But it's not. Where have you been for the last 30 years? Don't you realize that modern medicine has, in effect, wiped out the dangers connected with pregnancy? Sure, there remain some cases where the woman's life is in jeopardy. But even in those cases, why assume that her life must be saved at all costs? There's another human life at stake, you know. As for your long-term ill-effects of pregnancy, what did you have in mind—varicose veins, hemorrhoids, and an aching back? When such 'horrors' become justification for abortion, we're really in trouble. What will be acceptable justification next—a ski trip to Aspen which, unluckily for the fetus, pops up in the seventh month?''

2.   *Many unborn are unwanted or deformed.*

POINT: ''Everybody knows that society has serious population, pollution, and poverty problems—not to mention crime, disease, and world hunger. The problems already are taxing our financial capacity to deal with them. One way we can begin to deal with these problems is to make sure that every child that's brought into the world is wanted and healthy. Ignoring this we just worsen the world's problems. Fortunately, we've got lots of ways to ensure that unwanted and unhealthy children are never born. Contraceptives are one way. But for one reason or another, some people don't play it safe, and it's usually those who can least afford to maintain children physically and emotionally. Such people need an alternative form of birth control: abortion. Abortion's especially necessary in the case of monstrously deformed fetuses. If a woman is willing and able to bear and care for the deformed or unintended child, fine. But if she isn't willing or can't, then it's unfair to make the rest of us pay the price for the problem that she's created and the responsibility she's shirked.''

COUNTERPOINT: ''Your thinking is really mind-boggling. You make it sound like the unloved or the deformed are responsible for every social or global problem we have; or if we can just keep these 'undesirables' from being born, then all our headaches will vanish. Sure, we have considerable problems, but lots of things account for them, including human mismanagement of resources, inadequate or misguided technology, nearsighted and unimaginative leadership, as well as the age-old conditions of human greed, prejudice, and downright stupidity. The idea that abortions can help improve these conditions is exactly the kind of mindless proposal that contributes to our problems. It's unfair, you say, to make society pay the price for maintaining the unwanted or deformed child. What's so unfair about it? I always thought that part of a society's function was to provide for those least able to fend for themselves. What would you suggest we do with our mental health services and facilities? Discontinue them, I guess. How about simply exterminating the mentally defective? That would really save us a bundle. And how about just executing criminals instead of incarcerating them? You shouldn't find that objectionable. After all, what could be more 'unfair' by your standard than making society pay the price for maintaining those who have flouted society's conventions?''

3. *Some pregnancies result from rape or incest.*

POINT: "There's no more heinous a crime committed against a woman than rape or incest. To oblige a woman morally to bear the child of such an outrage goes beyond adding insult to injury. It's brutally barbaric. Nothing short of the woman's free choice would morally justify going through with a rape or incest pregnancy.''

COUNTERPOINT: "Agreed, rape and incest are ugly. But pregnancies resulting from them are rare. You're so concerned with not punishing the woman who has already been sexually abused. Well, by the same token, why punish the unborn by making them give up their lives? If making a woman carry to term a fetus that's resulted from rape or incest is a case of making the innocent suffer, then how much more innocent suffering is terminating the life of the fetus? Besides, nobody is asking the woman to raise a child she doesn't want or can't maintain. There are plenty of individuals and institutions who'll do that if she's unwilling or unable.''

4. *Women have rights over their own bodies.*

POINT: "Women bear the full and exclusive burden of carrying a fetus to term. They must endure the physical and emotional risks, the discomfort, the disruptions of career and routine living. Given this burden, they have the right to decide whether or not they want to go through with a pregnancy. But beyond this, the unborn is a part of the woman's body, and she should have absolute say over whether or not it's going to remain in her body and be allowed to be born. To deny her that right is about as crude and basic a violation of free choice as anything imaginable.''

COUNTERPOINT: "Of course women have certain rights over their own bodies. But having basic rights doesn't mean that those rights are absolute and take precedence over all others' rights. My right to free speech doesn't justify my yelling 'Fire!' in a crowded theater when, in fact, there is no fire. Nor does the woman's right over her own body mean she's justified in taking the life of the unborn. As soon as a woman gets pregnant, a relationship exists between her and the unborn. And like any other relationship, this one must involve a careful defining, assigning, and setting the priorities of rights and responsibilities. This is especially important in pregnancies because the unborn are in no position to argue for or defend their own rights. Let the woman who's so concerned about her own body make sure she doesn't get pregnant in the first place. But once she gets pregnant, her right takes a back seat to the unborn's right to life, certainly so long as the unborn's life doesn't threaten the woman's life.''

Legal Considerations

We began this chapter by referring to a landmark abortion ruling. It is important to recognize that the question of whether a woman ought to have a legal right to an abortion is related to, but different from, the question of whether an abortion is ever morally justifiable.

Naturally, the morality of abortion can and does bear on the morality of restrictive abortion legislation. Thus, people who believe that abortion is in and of itself morally objectionable often object to nonrestrictive legislation. And those who reject the notion that abortion is inherently repugnant often support nonrestrictive legislation. But it is also perfectly consistent to object to abortion while opposing restrictive abortion legislation because, say, such laws would abridge the individual's right to free choice. And it is perfectly consistent, and common, to argue that individual acts of abortion may be moral, even obligatory, while opposing a loosening of abortion laws because, for example, such a systematic policy may lead to abuses. In short, one can be opposed to abortion but also opposed to restrictive abortion legislation; or in favor of individual acts of abortion but against nonrestrictive legislation.

Any of the pro-life arguments can be marshalled in support of restrictive legislation; and any of the pro-choice arguments can be marshalled on behalf of nonrestrictive legislation. Thus, one could argue that since abortion is murder, the state has a moral obligation to protect its citizens by preventing their murder; or, since abortion involves risks for women, the state has an obligation to protect its citizens—women, in this case—from such risks. A person could also argue that the state has an obligation to relieve society's burden of caring for the unwanted or deformed unborn by making abortions possible for women; or that the state has an obligation to minimize the profound hardship that a rape or incest pregnancy causes a woman by allowing her to have an abortion.

Ethical Theories

Egoism

Egoism would not necessarily be committed to any specific position on the ontological or moral status of the fetus. Thus, conservative, liberal, or moderate theories could be consistent with an egoistic view.

For egoists the moral acceptability of any act of abortion depends on an evaluation of the long-term consequences for self. The egoistic pregnant woman, therefore, would determine whether or not an abortion is justified by carefully assessing the likely long-term advantages and disadvantages of having the child. Among the considerations would be the physical, psychological, and financial effects of bearing and subsequently raising the child. If, after this calculation, she thought it was in her best long-term interests to have the child, then she would be morally obliged to do so. But if the calculation indicated greater disadvantages for her, then she would be morally obligated to terminate the pregnancy. At no point in the evaluation would the egoist be concerned with any of the pro-life arguments except insofar as these might have an impact on the psychology of the woman and, thus, could affect her emotionally. By the same token, egoists would not heed the nonconsequential pro-choice claim that women have a right over their own bodies. In the last analysis, egoism can serve as a theoretical basis for either having an abortion or not having one, or for either supporting or opposing restrictive abortion legislation.

Act Utilitarianism

Like egoists, act utilitarians would not necessarily be committed to any particular theory of the ontological and moral status of the fetus. An act utilitarian could consistently espouse a conservative view and at the same time endorse a particular act of abortion. Thus, an act utilitarian might decide that treating the unborn as a full person from the time of conception produces more total good than any other position. The same act utilitarian might consider an individual act of abortion morally justifiable because it likely will produce more total good in a particular situation than allowing the pregnancy to continue. So, even if the unborn is considered a person, the principle of utility may still justify an abortion, because killing a person is not considered necessarily wrong. The morality of an act of abortion, then, depends on an evaluation of the likely consequences for all who will be affected. This would include a consideration of the consequences for the unborn, which would be particularly important in the cases of deformed fetuses whose birth might usher in profound suffering and hardship for the child, family, and society generally. As for abortion legislation, the act utilitarian would evaluate it on the basis of its social effects. If particular abortion laws would likely advance the general happiness of society, then they would be justifiable. Otherwise, they would not.

Rule Utilitarianism

All the foregoing discussion about act utilitarianism also applies to rule utilitarianism, with the exception that the rule utilitarian would be concerned with the consequences of the rule under which an act of abortion falls, and not with the consequences of the act itself. The rule utilitarian possibly would view an unqualified prohibition of abortion as a rule with consequences that would be less socially beneficial than the consequences of a less restrictive rule allowing therapeutic abortions. At the same time the rule utilitarian might argue that a rule preventing elective abortion or abortion on demand could produce more total unhappiness than a rule forbidding it. Figuring in the calculation would be the same categories of consequences that concern the act utilitarian. But, whereas the act utilitarian might condone one act of elective abortion but disapprove of another, the rule utilitarian could not allow such latitude, after establishing that forbidding elective abortion will produce more happiness than permitting it. The rule utilitarian would apply the same logic to abortion legislation. Ultimately, the morality of such laws would be determined by appeal to the utility principle.

Divine Command

Of central importance in applying divine command to the abortion issue is the traditional religious view that the unborn has full ontological and moral status from conception. Divine command theorists generally have viewed the unborn as a person from conception to birth. A good example of how such a view affects subsequent positions on abortion is the Roman Catholic outlook, which inevitably appears in discussions on abortion and abortion legislation. The Roman Catholic position is that the fetus is an innocent person. Even when a pregnancy is due to rape or incest, the fetus may not be held accountable and made to suffer through its death. According to Roman Catholics, then, direct abortion is never morally justifiable, and there should be laws that acknowledge and protect the rights of fetuses. Laws permitting direct abortion would be immoral.

Notice the word *direct* in the preceding example. While, according to Roman Catholic moral theology, the fetus may never be deliberately killed, it may be allowed to die as a consequence of an action that is intended to save the life of the mother. For example, suppose that a pregnant woman is found to have a malignant uterus. In order to save the woman's life, the uterus must be removed and, as a result, the fetus will be lost. Such an operation would be morally permissible.

Not all applications of divine command, however, are as restrictive as the Roman Catholic view. Indeed, some moralists who consider themselves squarely in the tradition of sound Christian morality and theology take a rather liberal stand on abortion. For example, Christian moralist Joseph Fletcher has argued that unselfish love, *agape,* is the one unexceptional principle in Christian ethics. In effect, according to Fletcher, we do what God wants us to do if and only if we act out of loving concern, that is, in a way characterized by love of God and neighbor. By this interpretation even elective abortion could be morally permissible so long as it serves love. In fact, in his *Situation Ethics,* Fletcher says: "No unwanted and unintended baby should ever be born."[3] But Fletcher's Christian version of act utilitarianism does not by any means represent mainstream religious views on abortion, which generally are quite conservative.

3.   *Joseph Fletcher,* Situation Ethics: The New Morality *(Philadelphia: Westminster Press, 1966), p. 39.*

Categorical Imperative

The key issue in applying Kantian ethics to the question of abortion is the status of the unborn, and Kant's thought is open to interpretation on this. If the unborn is a person, then the unborn has the inherent worth that any person has and must be treated with the same consideration and respect. Thus, only the reasons that could justify taking the life of an adult person could justify taking the life of the unborn. Self-defense certainly would be such a reason. Indeed, Kant would argue that a woman was not only morally justified but also obliged to have an abortion if the unborn was directly threatening her life. To act otherwise would be literally self-defeating. Similarly, destroying a seriously deformed fetus might be a way of recognizing the unborn's dignity. By sparing the unborn fetus a life of suffering and indignity, we would be treating the fetus as any rational being would want to be treated. Also, assuming the unborn is a person, Kant would argue for laws that recognize and protect the rights of fetuses, because they would ensure that fetuses, like any other persons, were treated with the dignity and respect that they deserve.

But so long as the status of the fetus is in doubt, the legitimacy of such laws is uncertain. One could then argue that the laws would simply function to restrict the autonomous, self-directed nature of rational beings; that is, they would deny the woman the right to choose. If the status of the fetus is in doubt, then the woman's right over her own body would be the overriding Kantian consideration. Clearly, then, the status of the fetus is the most important determinant in an application of Kantian ethics to abortion.

Prima Facie Duties

Abortion is no less complicated an issue for Ross. Again, the morality of abortion would depend on the status of the unborn. If the unborn is considered a person, then the unborn has rights that must be acknowledged. Certainly the basic right would be the right to life. While therapeutic abortions might be justified, it seems that nontherapeutic abortions would never be because they would subordinate the prima facie duty of noninjury to lesser duties, such as self-improvement. Similarly, Ross, like Kant, would endorse laws that acknowledge and protect the rights of the unborn. But the matter changes dramatically if the status of the fetus is in doubt. Then the issue of injuring a "person" dissolves. Not recognizing the person status of the unborn, however, would not necessarily justify all or even most abortions, because a variety of situational prima facie duties still would have to be considered before one determined one's actual duty. But should the fetus's status be in doubt, the prima facie duty ethicist could overcome the most significant moral objections to abortion. Moreover, the ethicist might consider restrictive abortion legislation unjust. Again, like Kant's, Ross's nonconsequential view leaves the status of the fetus open to interpretation, and thus his position on the abortion issue is unclear.

Maximin Principle

Trying to apply Rawls's maximin principle to the abortion issue raises many of the same problems apparent in the discussion of Kant and Ross. Again, the major question involves the status of the fetus. If the unborn fetus is a person, then the unborn has the right to life. Certainly no one in the original position would agree to a policy that would allow a life to be taken for reasons of personal convenience or happiness. Thus, nontherapeutic abortions would be unjustified. By the same token, rational, self-interested creatures behind the veil of ignorance surely would agree to be bound to a self-defense principle. Thus, therapeutic abortions would be justified. Furthermore, Rawls could use his principle of paternalism to justify legislation intended to protect the rights of the unborn who, of course, are in no position to protect themselves.

But again, as with the other nonconsequential views, the issue grows complicated when the status of the fetus is in doubt. Then nontherapeutic abortions could be moral. And restrictive abortion legislation could be a violation of the equal liberty principle; in denying a woman the right to choose, it would not be allowing the greatest amount of freedom consistent with a like freedom for all.

An Almost Absolute Value in History

John T. Noonan

Like many authors on the subject of abortion, law professor John T. Noonan locates the central issue in the ontological status of the unborn. In his essay, "An Almost Absolute Value in History," Noonan assigns the unborn full ontological status at the moment of conception.

Noonan not only puts this view in the context of traditional Christian theology, he also tests its strength compared with the other distinctions of ontological status that are commonly made: viability, experience, quickening, attitude of parents, and social visibility. Noonan shows why he thinks each of these distinctions is unsound.

In addition to the unique problems that each of these distinctions has, Noonan believes that they share one overriding problem: They are distinctions that appear to be arbitrary. Noonan feels that if distinctions that lead to moral judgments are not to appear arbitrary, then they should relate to some real difference in probabilities. He argues that his position passes this test, because it recognizes the fact that 80 percent of the zygotes formed (the conceptus) will develop into new beings. For Noonan this probability is a most compelling reason for granting the conceptus full ontological status.

In short, conception is the decisive moment of humanization, for it is then that the unborn receives the genetic code of the parents. These arguments lead Noonan to condemn abortion, except in cases of self-defense.

The most fundamental question involved in the long history of thought on abortion is: How do you determine the humanity of a being? To phrase the question that way is to put in comprehensive hu-

From John T. Noonan, "An Almost Absolute Value in History," in Morality of Abortion: Legal and Historical Perspectives, *John T. Noonan, ed. (Harvard University Press, 1970). Reprinted by permission.*

manistic terms what the theologians either dealt with as an explicitly theological question under the heading of "ensoulment" or dealt with implicitly in their treatment of abortion. The Christian position as it originated did not depend on a narrow theological or philosophical concept. It had no relation to theories of infant baptism. It appealed to no special theory of instantaneous ensoulment. It took the world's view on ensoulment as that view changed from Aristotle to Zacchia. There was, indeed, theological influence affecting the theory of ensoulment finally adopted, and, of course, ensoulment itself was a theological concept, so that the position was always explained in theological terms. But the theological notion of ensoulment could easily be translated into humanistic language by substituting "human" for "rational soul"; the problem of knowing when a man is a man is common to theology and humanism.

If one steps outside the specific categories used by the theologians, the answer they gave can be analyzed as a refusal to discriminate among human beings on the basis of their varying potentialities. Once conceived, the being was recognized as man because he had man's potential. The criterion for humanity, thus, was simple and all-embracing: If you are conceived by human parents, you are human.

The strength of this position may be tested by a review of some of the other distinctions offered in the contemporary controversy over legalizing abortion. Perhaps the most popular distinction is in terms of viability. Before an age of so many months, the fetus is not viable, that is, it cannot be removed from the mother's womb and live apart from her. To that extent, the life of the fetus is absolutely dependent on the life of the mother. This dependence is made the basis of denying recognition to its humanity.

There are difficulties with this distinction. One is that the perfection of artificial incubation may make the fetus viable at any time: It may be removed and artificially sustained. Experiments with animals already show that such a procedure is possible. This hypothetical extreme case relates to an actual difficulty: there is considerable elasticity to the idea of viability. Mere length of life is not an exact measure. The viability of the fetus depends on the extent of its anatomical and functional development. The weight and length of the fetus are better guides to the state of its development than age, but weight and length vary. Moreover, different racial groups have different ages at which their fetuses are viable. Some evidence, for example, suggests that Negro fetuses mature more quickly than white fetuses. If viability is the norm, the standard would vary with race and with many individual circumstances.

The most important objection to this approach is that dependence is not ended by viability. The fetus is still absolutely dependent on someone's care in order to continue existence; indeed a child of one or three or even five years of age is absolutely dependent on another's care for existence; uncared for, the older fetus or the younger child will die as surely as the early fetus detached from the mother. The unsubstantial lessening in dependence at viability does not seem to signify any special acquisition of humanity.

A second distinction has been attempted in terms of experience. A being who has had experience, has lived and suffered, who possesses memories, is more human than one who has not. Humanity depends on formation by experience. The fetus is thus "unformed" in the most basic human sense.

This distinction is not serviceable for the embryo which is already experiencing and reacting. The embryo is responsive to touch after eight weeks and at least at that point is experiencing. At an earlier stage the zygote is certainly alive and responding to its environment. The distinction may also be challenged by the rare case where aphasia has erased adult memory: Has it erased humanity? More fundamentally, this distinction leaves even the older fetus or the younger child to be treated as an unformed inhuman thing. Finally, it is not clear why experience as such confers humanity. It could be argued that certain central experiences such as loving or learning are necessary to make a man human. But then human beings who have failed to love or to learn might be excluded from the class called man.

A third distinction is made by appeal to the sentiments of adults. If a fetus dies, the grief of the parents is not the grief they would have for a living child. The fetus is an unnamed "it" till birth, and is not perceived as personality until at least the fourth month of existence when movements in the womb manifest a vigorous presence demanding joyful recognition by the parents.

Yet feeling is notoriously an unsure guide to

the humanity of others. Many groups of humans have had difficulty in feeling that persons of another tongue, color, religion, sex, are as human as they. Apart from reactions to alien groups, we mourn the loss of a ten-year-old boy more than the loss of his one-day-old brother or his 90-year-old grandfather. The difference felt and the grief expressed vary with the potentialities extinguished, or the experience wiped out; they do not seem to point to any substantial difference in the humanity of baby, boy, or grandfather.

Distinctions are also made in terms of sensation by the parents. The embryo is felt within the womb only after about the fourth month. The embryo is seen only at birth. What can be neither seen nor felt is different from what is tangible. If the fetus cannot be seen or touched at all, it cannot be perceived as man.

Yet experience shows that sight is even more untrustworthy than feeling in determining humanity. By sight, color became an appropriate index for saying who was a man, and the evil of racial discrimination was given foundation. Nor can touch provide the test; a being confined by sickness, "out of touch" with others, does not thereby seem to lose his humanity. To the extent that touch still has appeal as a criterion, it appears to be a survival of the old English idea of "quickening"—a possible mistranslation of the Latin *animatus* used in the canon law. To that extent touch as a criterion seems to be dependent on the Aristotelian notion of ensoulment, and to fall when this notion is discarded.

Finally, a distinction is sought in social visibility. The fetus is not socially perceived as human. It cannot communicate with others. Thus, both subjectively and objectively, it is not a member of society. As moral rules are rules for the behavior of members of society to each other, they cannot be made for behavior toward what is not yet a member. Excluded from the society of men, the fetus is excluded from the humanity of men.

By force of the argument from the consequences, this distinction is to be rejected. It is more subtle than that founded on an appeal to physical sensation, but it is equally dangerous in its implications. If humanity depends on social recognition, individuals or whole groups may be dehumanized by being denied any status in their society. Such a fate is fictionally portrayed in *1984* and has actually

been the lot of many men in many societies. In the Roman empire, for example, condemnation to slavery meant the practical denial of most human rights; in the Chinese Communist world, landlords have been classified as enemies of the people and so treated as nonpersons by the state. Humanity does not depend on social recognition, though often the failure of society to recognize the prisoner, the alien, the heterodox as human has led to the destruction of human beings. Anyone conceived by a man and a woman is human. Recognition of this condition by society follows a real event in the objective order, however imperfect and halting the recognition. Any attempt to limit humanity to exclude some group runs the risk of furnishing authority and precedent for excluding other groups in the name of the consciousness or perception of the controlling group in the society.

A philosopher may reject the appeal to the humanity of the fetus because he views "humanity" as a secular view of the soul and because he doubts the existence of anything real and objective which can be identified as humanity. One answer to such a philosopher is to ask how he reasons about moral questions without supposing that there is a sense in which he and the others of whom he speaks are human. Whatever group is taken as the society which determines who may be killed is thereby taken as human. A second answer is to ask if he does not believe that there is a right and wrong way of deciding moral questions. If there is such a difference, experience may be appealed to: To decide who is human on the basis of the sentiment of a given society has led to consequences which rational men would characterize as monstrous.

The rejection of the attempted distinctions based on viability and visibility, experience and feeling, may be buttressed by the following considerations: Moral judgments often rest on distinctions, but if the distinctions are not to appear arbitrary fiat, they should relate to some real difference in probabilities. There is a kind of continuity in all life, but the earlier stages of the elements of human life possess tiny probabilities of development. Consider for example, the spermatozoa in any normal ejaculate: There are about 200,000,000 in any single ejaculate, of which one has a chance of developing into a zygote. Consider the oocytes which may become ova: There are

100,000 to 1,000,000 oocytes in a female infant, of which a maximum of 390 are ovulated. But once spermatozoon and ovum meet and the conceptus is formed, such studies as have been made show that roughly in only 20 percent of the cases will spontaneous abortion occur. In other words, the chances are about 4 out of 5 that this new being will develop. At this stage in the life of the being there is a sharp shift in probabilities, an immense jump in potentialities. To make a distinction between the rights of spermatozoa and the rights of the fertilized ovum is to respond to an enormous shift in possibilities. For about twenty days after conception the egg may split to form twins or combine with another egg to form a chimera, but the probability of either event happening is very small.

It may be asked, What does a change in biological probabilities have to do with establishing humanity? The argument from probabilities is not aimed at establishing humanity but at establishing an objective discontinuity which may be taken into account in moral discourse. As life itself is a matter of probabilities, as most moral reasoning is an estimate of probabilities, so it seems in accord with the structure of reality and the nature of moral thought to found a moral judgment on the change in probabilities at conception. The appeal to probabilities is the most commonsensical of arguments, to a greater or smaller degree all of us base our actions on probabilities, and in morals, as in law, prudence and negligence are often measured by the account one has taken of the probabilities. If the chance is 200,000,000 to 1 that the movement in the bushes into which you shoot is a man's, I doubt if many persons would hold you careless in shooting; but if the chances are 4 out of 5 that the movement is a human being's, few would acquit you of blame. Would the argument be different if only one out of ten children conceived came to term? Of course this argument would be different. This argument is an appeal to probabilities that actually exist, not to any and all states of affairs which may be imagined.

The probabilities as they do exist do not show the humanity of the embryo in the sense of a demonstration in logic any more than the probabilities of the movement in the bush being a man demonstrate beyond all doubt that the being is a man. The appeal is a "buttressing" consideration,

showing the plausibility of the standard adopted. The argument focuses on the decisional factor in any moral judgment and assumes that part of the business of a moralist is drawing lines. One evidence of the nonarbitrary character of the line drawn is the difference of probabilities on either side of it. If a spermatozoon is destroyed, one destroys a being which had a chance of far less than 1 in 200 million of developing into a reasoning being, possessed of the genetic code, a heart and other organs, and capable of pain. If a fetus is destroyed, one destroys a being already possessed of the genetic code, organs, and sensitivity to pain, and one which had an 80 percent chance of developing further into a baby outside the womb who, in time, would reason.

The positive argument for conception as the decisive moment of humanization is that at conception the new being receives the genetic code. It is this genetic information which determines his characteristics, which is the biological carrier of the possibility of human wisdom, which makes him a self-evolving being. A being with a human genetic code is man.

This review of current controversy over the humanity of the fetus emphasizes what a fundamental question the theologians resolved in asserting the inviolability of the fetus. To regard the fetus as possessed of equal rights with other humans was not, however, to decide every case where abortion might be employed. It did decide the case where the argument was that the fetus should be aborted for its own good. To say a being was human was to say it had a destiny to decide for itself which could not be taken from it by another man's decision. But human beings with equal rights often come in conflict with each other, and some decision must be made as whose claims are to prevail. Cases of conflict involving the fetus are different only in two respects: the total inability of the fetus to speak for itself and the fact that the right of the fetus regularly at stake is the right to life itself.

The approach taken by the theologians to these conflicts was articulated in terms of "direct" and "indirect." Again, to look at what they were doing from outside their categories, they may be said to have been drawing lines or "balancing values." "Direct" and "indirect" are spatial metaphors: "line-drawing" is another. "To weigh" or "to balance" values is a metaphor of a more complicated mathematical sort hinting at the process which goes on in moral judgments. All the metaphors suggest that, in the moral judgments made, comparisons were necessary, that no value completely controlled. The principle of double effect was no doctrine fallen from heaven, but a method of analysis appropriate where two relative values were being compared. In Catholic moral theology, as it developed, life even of the innocent was not taken as an absolute. Judgments on acts affecting life issued from a process of weighing. In the weighing, the fetus was always given a value greater than zero, always a value separate and independent from its parents. This valuation was crucial and fundamental in all Christian thought on the subject and marked it off from any approach which considered that only the parents' interests needed to be considered.

Even with the fetus weighed as human, one interest could be weighed as equal or superior: that of the mother in her own life. The casuists between 1450 and 1895 were willing to weigh this interest as superior. Since 1895, that interest was given decisive weight only in the two special cases of the cancerous uterus and the ectopic pregnancy. In both of these cases the fetus itself had little chance of survival even if the abortion were not performed. As the balance was once struck in favor of the mother whenever her life was endangered, it could be so struck again. The balance reached between 1895 and 1930 attempted prudentially and pastorally to forestall a multitude of exceptions for interests less than life.

The perception of the humanity of the fetus and the weighing of fetal rights against other human rights constituted the work of the moral analysts. But what spirit animated their abstract judgments? For the Christian community it was the injunction of Scripture to love your neighbor as yourself. The fetus as human was a neighbor; his life had parity with one's own. The commandment gave life to what otherwise would have been only rational calculation.

The commandment could be put in humanistic as well as theological terms: Do not injure your fellow man without reason. In these terms, once the humanity of the fetus is perceived, abortion is never right except in self-defense. When life must be taken to save life, reason alone cannot say that a mother must prefer a chid's life to her own. With this exception, now of great rarity, abortion violates the rational humanist tenet of the equality of human lives.

For Christians the commandment to love had received a special imprint in that the exemplar proposed of love was the love of the Lord for his disciples. In the light given by this example, self-sacrifice carried to the point of death seemed in the extreme situations not without meaning. In the less extreme cases, preference for one's own interests to the life of another seemed to express cruelty or selfishness irreconcilable with the demands of love.

Questions for Analysis

1. *Do you agree that considering the unborn a person from the moment of conception poses fewer problems than any of the alternative views?*

2. *What problems does Noonan see in distinctions based upon: (a) viability, (b) experience, (c) feelings of adults, (d) social visibility?*

3. *Explain how Noonan used "biological probabilities" to buttress his view of the unborn as a person from the moment of conception? Is his argument persuasive?*

4. *On what grounds does Noonan object to abortion?*

5. *Is it accurate to say that Noonan finds abortion always impermissible?*

Abortion and Infanticide

Michael Tooley

In "Abortion and Infanticide" philosophy professor Michael Tooley addresses the question of what property a thing must possess in order to have a serious right to life. Tooley's answer: A thing has a serious right to life only if it possesses the concept of a self as a continuing subject of experiences and other mental states, and believes that it is itself such a continuing entity.

Tooley's basic argument in support of this claim is what he calls the self-consciousness requirement. Essentially, it goes as follows. Having a right to life presupposes that one is capable of wanting to continue existing as a subject of experiences and other mental states. But this, in turn, presupposes that one has the concept of such a continuing entity and that one believes that one is oneself such an entity. An entity that lacks such consciousness of itself as a continuing subject of mental states would have no serious right to life.

It follows from this analysis that not only do the unborn have no serious right to life, but some of the born may not either. Thus, infanticide, as well as abortion, would be morally permissible.

A key question that arises from Tooley's analysis is: At what point does an organism come to possess the concept of a self as a continuing subject of experiences and other mental states, together with the belief that it is itself such a continuing entity? Tooley concedes that the matter requires considerable psychological investigation. Nonetheless, he believes that everyday observation makes it "perfectly clear" that a newborn baby does not possess this concept.

This essay deals with the question of the morality of abortion and infanticide.[1] The fundamental ethical objection traditionally advanced against these practices rests on the contention that human fetuses and infants have a right to life. It is this claim which will be the focus of attention here. The basic issue to be discussed, then, is what properties a thing must possess in order to have a serious right to life. My approach will be to set out and defend a basic moral principle specifying a condition an organism must satisfy if it is to have a serious right to life. It will be seen that this condition is not satisfied by human fetuses and infants, and thus that they do not have a right to life. So unless there are other substantial objections to abortion and infanticide, one is forced to conclude that these practices are morally acceptable ones. In contrast, it may turn out that our treatment of adult members of other species—cats, dogs, polar bears—is morally indefensible. For it is quite possible that such animals do possess properties that endow them with a right to life.

I. Abortion and Infanticide

One reason the question of the morality of infanticide is worth examining is that it seems very difficult to formulate a completely satisfactory liberal position on abortion without coming to grips with the infanticide issue. The problem the liberal encounters is essentially that of specifying a cutoff point which is not arbitrary: At what stage in the development of a human being does it cease to be morally permissible to destroy it? It is important to be clear about the difficulty here. The conservative's objection is not that since there is a continuous line of development from a zygote to a newborn baby, one must conclude that if it is seriously wrong to destroy a newborn baby it is also seriously wrong to destroy a zygote or any intermediate stage in the development of a human being. His point is rather that if one says it is wrong to destroy a newborn baby but not a zygote or some intermediate stage in the development of a human being, one should be prepared to point to a *morally relevant* difference between a newborn baby and the earlier stage in the development of a human being.

Precisely the same difficulty can, of course, be raised for a person who holds that infanticide is morally permissible. The conservative will ask what morally relevant differences there are between an adult human being and a newborn baby. What makes it morally permissible to destroy a baby, but wrong to kill an adult? So the challenge remains. But I will argue that in this case there is an extremely plausible answer.

Reflecting on the morality of infanticide forces one to face up to this challenge. In the case of abortion a number of events—quickening or viability, for instance—might be taken as cutoff points, and it is easy to overlook the fact that none of these events involves any morally significant change in the developing human. In contrast, if one is going to defend infanticide, one has to get very clear about what makes something a person, what gives something a right to life.

One of the interesting ways in which the abortion issue differs from most other moral issues is that the plausible positions on abortion appear to be extreme positions. For if a human fetus is a person, one is inclined to say that, in general, one would be justified in killing it only to save the life of the mother.[2] Such is the extreme conservative position.[3] On the other hand, if the fetus is not a person, how can it be seriously wrong to destroy it? Why would one need to point to special circumstances to justify such action? The upshot is that there is no room for a moderate position on the issue of abortion such as one finds, for example, in the Model Penal Code recommendations.[4]

Aside from the light it may shed on the abortion question, the issue of infanticide is both interesting and important in its own right. The theoretical interest has been mentioned: It forces one to face up to the question of what makes something a person. The practical importance need not be labored. Most people would prefer to raise children who do not suffer from gross deformities or from severe physical, emotional, or intellectual handicaps. If it could be shown that there is no moral objection to infanticide the happiness of society could be significantly and justifiably increased.

Infanticide is also of interest because of the strong emotions it arouses. The typical reaction to infanticide is like the reaction to incest or cannibalism, or the reaction of previous generations to masturbation or oral sex. The response, rather than appealing to carefully formulated moral principles, is primarily visceral. When philosophers themselves respond in this way, offering no arguments, and dismissing infanticide out of hand, it is reasonable to suspect that one is dealing with a taboo rather than with a rational prohibition.[5] I shall attempt to show that this is in fact the case.

II. Terminology: "Person" versus "Human Being"

How is the term "person" to be interpreted? I shall treat the concept of a person as a purely moral concept, free of all descriptive content. Specifically, in my usage, the sentence "X is a person" will be synonymous with the sentence "X has a (serious) moral right to life."

This usage diverges slightly from what is perhaps the more common way of interpreting the term "person" when it is employed as a purely moral term, where to say that X is a person is to say that X has rights. If everything that had rights had a right to life, these interpretations would be extensionally equivalent. But I am inclined to think that it does not follow from acceptable moral principles that whatever has any rights at all has a right to life. My reason is this. Given the choice between being killed and being tortured for an hour, most adult humans would surely choose the latter. So it seems plausible to say it is worse to kill an adult human being than it is to torture him for an hour. In contrast, it seems to me that while it is not seriously wrong to kill a newborn kitten, it is seriously wrong to torture one for an hour. This *suggests* that newborn kittens may have a right not to be tortured without having a serious right to life. For it seems to be true that an individual has a right to something whenever it is the case that, if he wants that thing, it would be wrong for others to deprive him of it. Then if it is wrong to inflict a certain sensation upon a kitten if it doesn't want to experience that sensation, it will follow that the kitten has a right not to have sensation inflicted upon it.[6] I shall return to this example later. My point here is merely that it provides some reason for holding that it does not follow from acceptable moral principles that if something has any rights at all, it has a serious right to life.

There has been a tendency in recent discussions of abortion to use expressions such as "person" and "human being" interchangeably. B. A. Brody, for example, refers to the difficulty of determining "whether destroying the fetus constitutes the taking of a human life," and suggests it is very plausible that "the taking of a human life is an action that has bad consequences for him whose life is being taken."[7] When Brody refers to something as a human life he apparently construes this as entailing that the thing is a person. For if every living organism belonging to the species homo sapiens counted as a human life, there would be no difficulty in determining whether a fetus inside a human mother was a human life.

The same tendency is found in Judith Jarvis Thomson's article, which opens with the statement: "Most opposition to abortion relies on the premise that the fetus is a human being, a person, from the moment of conception."[8] The same is true of Roger Wertheimer, who explicitly says: "First off I should note that the expressions 'a human life,' 'a human being,' 'a person' are virtually interchangeable in this context."[9]

The tendency to use expressions like "person" and "human being" interchangeably is an unfortunate one. For one thing, it tends to lend covert support to antiabortionist positions. Given such usage, one who holds a liberal view of abortion is put in the position of maintaining that fetuses, at least up to a certain point, are not human beings. Even philosophers are led astray by this usage. Thus Wertheimer says that "except for monstrosities, every member of our species is indubitably a person, a human being, at the very latest at birth."[10] Is it really *indubitable* that newborn babies are persons? Surely this is a wild contention. Wertheimer is falling prey to the confusion naturally engendered by the practice of using "person" and "human being" interchangeably. Another example of this is provided by Thomson: "I am inclined to think also that we shall probably have to agree that the fetus has already become a human person well before birth. Indeed, it comes as a surprise when one first learns how early in its life it begins to acquire human characteristics. By the tenth week, for example, it already has a face, arms and legs, fingers and toes; it has

internal organs, and brain activity is detectable."[11] But what do such physiological characteristics have to do with the question of whether the organism is a person? Thomson, partly, I think, because of the unfortunate use of terminology, does not even raise this question. As a result she virtually takes it for granted that there are some cases in which abortion is "positively indecent."[12]

There is a second reason why using "person" and "human being" interchangeably is unhappy philosophically. If one says that the dispute between pro- and anti-abortionists centers on whether the fetus is a human, it is natural to conclude that it is essentially a disagreement about certain facts, a disagreement about what properties a fetus possesses. Thus Wertheimer says that "if one insists on using the raggy fact-value distinction, then one ought to say that the dispute is over a matter of fact in the sense in which it is a fact that the Negro slaves were human beings."[13] I shall argue that the two cases are not parallel, and that in the case of abortion what is primarily at stake is what moral principles one should accept. If one says that the central issue between conservatives and liberals in the abortion question is whether the fetus is a person, it is clear that the dispute may be either about what properties a thing must have in order to be a person, in order to have a right to life—a moral question—or about whether a fetus at a given stage of development as a matter of fact possesses the properties in question. The temptation to suppose that the disagreement must be a factual one is removed.

It should now be clear why the common practice of using expressions such as "person" and "human being" interchangeably in discussions of abortion is unfortunate. It would perhaps be best to avoid the term "human" altogether, employing instead some expression that is more naturally interpreted as referring to a certain type of biological organism characterized in physiological terms, such as "member of the species Homo sapiens." My own approach will be to use the term "human" only in contexts where it is not philosophically dangerous.

III. The Basic Issue: When Is a Member of the Species Homo Sapiens a Person?

Settling the issue of the morality of abortion and infanticide will involve answering the following questions: What properties must something have to be a person, i.e., to have a serious right to life? At what point in the development of a member of the species Homo sapiens does the organism possess the properties that make it a person? The first question raises a moral issue. To answer it is to decide what basic [14] moral principles involving the ascription of a right to life one ought to accept. The second question raises a purely factual issue, since the properties in question are properties of a purely descriptive sort.

Some writers seem quite pessimistic about the possibility of resolving the question of the morality of abortion. Indeed, some have gone so far as to suggest that the question of whether the fetus is a person is in principle unanswerable: "We seem to be stuck with the indeterminateness of the fetus' humanity."[15] An understanding of some of the sources of this pessimism will, I think, help us to tackle the problem. Let us begin by considering the similarity a number of people have noted between the issue of abortion and the issue of Negro slavery. The question here is why it should be more difficult to decide whether abortion and infanticide are acceptable than it was to decide whether slavery was acceptable. The answer seems to be that in the case of slavery there are moral principles of a quite uncontroversial sort that settle the issue. Thus most people would agree to some such principle as the following: No organism that has experiences, that is capable of thought and of using language, and that has harmed no one, should be made a slave. In the case of abortion, on the other hand, conditions that are generally agreed to be sufficient grounds for ascribing a right to life to something do not suffice to settle the issue. It is easy to specify other, purportedly sufficient conditions that will settle the issue, but no one has been successful in putting forward considerations that will convince others to accept those additional moral principles.

I do not share the general pessimism about the possibility of resolving the issue of abortion and infanticide because I believe it is possible to point to a very plausible moral principle dealing with the question of *necessary* conditions for something's having a right to life, where the conditions in question will provide an answer to the question of the permissibility of abortion and infanticide.

There is a second cause of pessimism that

should be noted before proceeding. It is tied up with the fact that the development of an organism is one of gradual and continuous change. Given this continuity, how is one to draw a line at one point and declare it permissible to destroy a member of Homo sapiens up to, but not beyond, that point? Won't there be an arbitrariness about any point that is chosen? I will return to this worry shortly. It does not present a serious difficulty once the basic moral principles relevant to the ascription of a right to life to an individual are established.

Let us turn now to the first and most fundamental question: What properties must something have in order to be a person, i.e., to have a serious right to life? The claim I wish to defend is this: An organism possesses a serious right to life only if it possesses the concept of a self as a continuing subject of experiences and other mental states, and believes that it is itself such a continuing entity.

My basic argument in support of this claim, which I will call the self-consciousness requirement, will be clearest, I think, if I first offer a simplified version of the argument, and then consider a modification that seems desirable. The simplified version of my argument is this. To ascribe a right to an individual is to assert something about the prima facie obligations of other individuals to act, or to refrain from acting, in certain ways. However, the obligations in question are conditional ones, being dependent upon the existence of certain desires of the individual to whom the right is ascribed. Thus if an individual asks one to destroy something to which he has a right, one does not violate his right to that thing if one proceeds to destroy it. This suggests the following analysis: "A has a right to X" is roughly synonymous with "If A desires X, then others are under a prima facie obligation to refrain from actions that would deprive him of it."[16]

Although this analysis is initially plausible, there are reasons for thinking it not entirely correct. I will consider these later. Even here, however, some expansion is necessary, since there are features of the concept of a right that are important in the present context, and that ought to be dealt with more explicitly. In particular, it seems to be a conceptual truth that things that lack consciousness, such as ordinary machines, cannot have rights. Does this conceptual truth follow from the above analysis of the concept of a right? The answer depends on how the term "desire" is interpreted. If one adopts a completely behavioristic interpretation of "desire," so that a machine that searches for an electrical outlet in order to get its batteries recharged is described as having a desire to be recharged, then it will not follow from this analysis that objects that lack consciousness cannot have rights. On the other hand, if "desire" is interpreted in such a way that desires are states necessarily standing in some sort of relationship to states of consciousness, it will follow from the analysis that a machine that is not capable of being conscious, and consequently of having desires, cannot have any rights. I think those who defend analyses of the concept of a right along the lines of this one do have in mind an interpretation of the term "desire" that involves reference to something more than behavioral dispositions. However, rather than relying on this, it seems preferable to make such an interpretation explicit. The following analysis is a natural way of doing that: "A has a right to X" is roughly synonymous with "A is the sort of thing that is a subject of experiences and other mental states, A is capable of desiring X, and if A does desire X, then others are under a prima facie obligation to refrain from actions that would deprive him of it."

The next step in the argument is basically a matter of applying this analysis to the concept of a right to life. Unfortunately the expression "right to life" is not entirely a happy one, since it suggests that the right in question concerns the continued existence of a biological organism. That this is incorrect can be brought out by considering possible ways of violating an individual's right to life. Suppose, for example, that by some technology of the future the brain of an adult human were to be completely reprogrammed, so that the organism wound up with memories (or rather, apparent memories), beliefs, attitudes, and personality traits completely different from those associated with it before it was subjected to reprogramming. In such a case one would surely say that an individual had been destroyed, that an adult human's right to life had been violated, even though no biological organism had been killed. This example shows that the expression "right to life" is misleading, since what one is really concerned about is not just the continued existence of a biological

organism, but the right of a subject of experiences and other mental states to continue to exist.

Given this more precise description of the right with which we are here concerned, we are now in a position to apply the analysis of the concept of a right stated above. When we do so we find that the statement "A has a right to continue to exist as a subject of experiences and other mental states" is roughly synonymous with the statement "A is a subject of experiences and other mental states, A is capable of desiring to continue to exist as a subject of experiences and other mental states, and if A does desire to continue to exist as such an entity, then others are under a prima facie obligation not to prevent him from doing so."

The final stage in the argument is simply a matter of asking what must be the case if something is to be capable of having a desire to continue existing as a subject of experiences and other mental states. The basic point here is that the desires a thing can have are limited by the concepts it possesses. For the fundamental way of describing a given desire is as a desire that a certain proposition be true.[17] Then, since one cannot desire that a certain proposition be true unless one understands it, and since one cannot understand it without possessing the concepts involved in it, it follows that the desires one can have are limited by the concepts one possesses. Applying this to the present case results in the conclusion that an entity cannot be the sort of thing that can desire that a subject of experiences and other mental states exist unless it possesses the concept of such a subject. Moreover, an entity cannot desire that it itself *continue* existing as a subject of experiences and other mental states unless it believes that it is now such a subject. This completes the justification of the claim that it is a necessary condition of something's having a serious right to life that it possess the concept of a self as a continuing subject of experiences, and that it believe that it is itself such an entity.

Let us now consider a modification in the above argument that seems desirable. This modification concerns the crucial conceptual claim advanced about the relationship between ascription of rights and ascription of the corresponding desires. Certain situations suggest that there may be exceptions to the claim that if a person doesn't desire something, one cannot violate his right to it.

There are three types of situations that call this claim into question: (i) situations in which an individual's desires reflect a state of emotional disturbance; (ii) situations in which a previously conscious individual is temporarily unconscious; (iii) situations in which an individual's desires have been distorted by conditioning or by indoctrination.

As an example of the first, consider a case in which an adult human falls into a state of depression which his psychiatrist recognizes as temporary. While in the state he tells people he wishes he were dead. His psychiatrist, accepting the view that there can be no violation of an individual's right to life unless the individual has a desire to live, decides to let his patient have his way and kills him. Or consider a related case in which one person gives another a drug that produces a state of temporary depression; the recipient expresses a wish that he were dead. The person who administered the drug then kills him. Doesn't one want to say in both these cases that the agent did something seriously wrong in killing the other person? And isn't the reason the action was seriously wrong in each case the fact that it violated the individual's right to life? If so, the right to life cannot be linked with a desire to live in the way claimed above.

The second set of situations are ones in which an individual is unconscious for some reason—that is, he is sleeping, or drugged, or in a temporary coma. Does an individual in such a state have any desires? People do sometimes say that an unconscious individual wants something, but it might be argued that if such talk is not to be simply false it must be interpreted as actually referring to the desires the individual *would* have if he were now conscious. Consequently, if the analysis of the concept of a right proposed above were correct, it would follow that one does not violate an individual's right if one takes his car, or kills him, while he is asleep.

Finally, consider situations in which an individual's desires have been distorted, either by inculcation of irrational beliefs or by direct conditioning. Thus an individual may permit someone to kill him because he has been convinced that if he allows himself to be sacrificed to the gods he will be gloriously rewarded in a life to come. Or an individual may be enslaved after first having been conditioned to desire a life of slavery. Doesn't one want to say that in the former case an individual's right to life has been violated, and in the latter his right to freedom?

Situations such as these strongly suggest that even if an individual doesn't want something, it is still possible to violate his right to it. Some modification of the earlier account of the concept of a right thus seems in order. The analysis given covers, I believe, the paradigmatic cases of violation of an individual's rights, but there are other, secondary cases where one also wants to say that someone's right has been violated which are not included.

Precisely how the revised analysis should be formulated is unclear. Here it will be sufficient merely to say that, in view of the above, an individual's right to X can be violated not only when he desires X, but also when he *would* now desire X were it not for one of the following: (i) he is in an emotionally unbalanced state; (ii) he is temporarily unconscious; (iii) he has been conditioned to desire the absence of X.

The critical point now is that, even given this extension of the conditions under which an individual's right to something can be violated, it is still true that one's right to something can be violated only when one has the conceptual capability of desiring the thing in question. For example, an individual who would now desire not to be a slave if he weren't emotionally unbalanced, or if he weren't temporarily unconscious, or if he hadn't previously been conditioned to want to be a slave, must possess the concepts involved in the desire not to be a slave. Since it is really only the conceptual capability presupposed by the desire to continue existing as a subject of experiences and other mental states, and not the desire itself, that enters into the above argument, the modification required in the account of the conditions under which an individual's rights can be violated does not undercut my defense of the self-consciousness requirement.[18]

To sum up, my argument has been that having a right to life presupposes that one is capable of desiring to continue existing as a subject of experiences and other mental states. This in turn presupposes both that one has the concept of such a continuing entity and that one believes that one is oneself such an entity. So an entity that lacks such a consciousness of itself as a continuing subject of mental states does not have a right to life.

It would be natural to ask at this point whether satisfaction of this requirement is not only necessary but also sufficient to ensure that a thing has a right to life. I am inclined to an affirmative answer. However, the issue is not urgent in the present context, since as long as the requirement is in fact a necessary one we have the basis of an adequate defense of abortion and infanticide. If an organism must satisfy some other condition before it has a serious right to life, the result will merely be that the interval during which infanticide is morally permissible may be somewhat longer. Although the point at which an organism first achieves self-consciousness and hence the capacity of desiring to continue existing as a subject of experiences and other mental states may be a theoretically incorrect cutoff point, it is at least a morally safe one: Any error it involves is on the side of caution.

IV. Some Critical Comments on Alternative Proposals

I now want to compare the line of demarcation I am proposing with the cutoff points traditionally advanced in discussions of abortion. My fundamental claim will be that none of these cutoff points can be defended by appeal to plausible, basic moral principles. The main suggestions as to the point past which it is seriously wrong to destroy something that will develop into an adult member of the species Homo sapiens are these: (a) conception; (b) the attainment of human form; (c) the achievement of the ability to move about spontaneously; (d) viability; (e) birth.[19] The corresponding moral principles suggested by these cutoff points are as follows: (1) It is seriously wrong to kill an organism, from a zygote on, that belongs to the species Homo sapiens. (2) It is seriously wrong to kill an organism that belongs to Homo sapiens and that has achieved human form. (3) It is seriously wrong to kill an organism that is a member of Homo sapiens and that is capable of spontaneous movement. (4) It is seriously wrong to kill an organism that belongs to Homo sapiens and that is capable of existing outside the womb. (5) It is seriously wrong to kill an organism that is a member of Homo sapiens that is no longer in the womb.

My first comment is that it would not do simply to omit the reference to membership in the species Homo sapiens from the above principles, with the exception of principle (2). For then the principles would be applicable to animals in general, and one would be forced to conclude that it was seriously wrong to abort a cat fetus, or that it was seriously wrong to abort a motile cat fetus, and so on.

The second and crucial comment is that none of the five principles given above can plausibly be viewed as a basic moral principle. To accept any of them as such would be akin to accepting as a basic moral principle the proposition that it is morally permissible to enslave black members of the species Homo sapiens but not white members. Why should it be seriously wrong to kill an unborn member of the species Homo sapiens but not seriously wrong to kill an unborn kitten? Difference in species is not per se a morally relevant difference. If one holds that it is seriously wrong to kill an unborn member of the species Homo sapiens but not an unborn kitten, one should be prepared to point to some property that is morally significant and that is possessed by unborn members of Homo sapiens but not by unborn kittens. Similarly, such a property must be identified if one believes it seriously wrong to kill unborn members of Homo sapiens that have achieved viability but not seriously wrong to kill unborn kittens that have achieved that state.

What property might account for such a difference? That is to say, what basic moral principles might a person who accepts one of these five principles appeal to in support of his secondary moral judgment? Why should events such as the achievement of human form, or the achievement of the ability to move about, or the achievement of viability, or birth serve to endow something with a right to life? What the liberal must do is to show that these events involve changes, or are associated with changes, that are morally relevant.

Let us now consider reasons why the events involved in cutoff points (b) through (e) are not morally relevant, beginning with the last two: viability and birth. The fact that an organism is not physiologically dependent upon another organism, or is capable of such physiological independence, is surely irrelevant to whether the organism has a right to life. In defense of this contention, consider a speculative case where a fetus is able to learn a language while in the womb. One would surely not say that the fetus had no right to life until it emerged from the womb, or until it was capable of existing outside the womb. A less speculative example is the case of Siamese twins who have learned to speak. One doesn't want to say that since one of the twins would die were the two to be separated, it therefore has no right to life. Consequently it seems difficult to disagree with the conservative's claim that an organism which lacks a right to life before birth or before becoming viable cannot acquire this right immediately upon birth or upon becoming viable.

This does not, however, completely rule out viability as a line of demarcation. For instead of defending viability as a cutoff point on the ground that only then does a fetus acquire a right to life, it is possible to argue rather that when one organism is physiologically dependent upon another, the former's right to life may conflict with the latter's right to use its body as it will, and moreover, that the latter's right to do what it wants with its body may often take precedence over the other organism's right to life. Thomson has defended this view: "I am arguing only that having a right to life does not guarantee having either a right to the use of or a right to be allowed continued use of another person's body—even if one needs it for life itself. So the right to life will not serve the opponents of abortion in the very simple and clear way in which they seem to have thought it would."[20] I believe that Thomson is right in contending that philosophers have been altogether too casual in assuming that if one grants the fetus a serious right to life, one must accept a conservative position on abortion.[21] I also think the only defense of viability as a cutoff point which has any hope of success at all is one based on the considerations she advances. I doubt very much, however, that this defense of abortion is ultimately tenable. I think that one can grant even stronger assumptions than those made by Thomson and still argue persuasively for a semiconservative view. What I have in mind is this. Let it be granted, for the sake of argument, that a woman's right to free her body of parasites which will inhibit her freedom of action and possibly impair her health is stronger than the parasite's right to life, and is so even if the parasite has as much right to life as an adult human. One can still argue that abortion ought not to be permitted. For

if A's right is stronger than B's, and it is impossible to satisfy both, it does not follow that A's should be satisfied rather than B's. It may be possible to compensate A if his right isn't satisfied, but impossible to compensate B if his right isn't satisfied. In such a case the best thing to do may be to satisfy B's claim and to compensate A. Abortion may be a case in point. If the fetus has a right to life and the right is not satisfied, there is certainly no way the fetus can be compensated. On the other hand, if the woman's right to rid her body of harmful and annoying parasites is not satisfied, she can be compensated. Thus it would seem that the just thing to do would be to prohibit abortion, but to compensate women for the burden of carrying a parasite to term. Then, however, we are back at a (modified) conservative position.[22] Our conclusion must be that it appears unlikely there is any satisfactory defense either of viability or of birth as cutoff points.

Let us now consider the third suggested line of demarcation, the achievement of the power to move about spontaneously. It might be argued that acquiring this power is a morally relevant event on the grounds that there is a connection between the concept of an agent and the concept of a person, and being motile is an indication that a thing is an agent.[23]

It is difficult to respond to this suggestion unless it is made more specific. Given that one's interest here is in defending a certain cutoff point, it is natural to interpret the proposal as suggesting that motility is a necessary condition of an organism's having a right to life. But this won't do, because one certainly wants to ascribe a right to life to adult humans who are completely paralyzed. Maybe the suggestion is rather that motility is a sufficient condition of something's having a right to life. However, it is clear that motility alone is not sufficient, since this would imply that all animals, and also certain machines, have a right to life. Perhaps, then, the most reasonable interpretation of the claim is that motility together with some other property is a sufficient condition of something's having a right to life, where the other property will have to be a property possessed by unborn members of the species Homo sapiens but not by unborn members of other familiar species.

The central question, then, is what this other property is. Until one is told, it is very difficult to evaluate either the moral claim that motility together with that property is a sufficient basis for ascribing to an organism a right to life or the factual claim that a motile human fetus possesses that property while a motile fetus belonging to some other species does not. A conservative would presumably reject motility as a cutoff point by arguing that whether an organism has a right to life depends only upon its potentialities, which are of course not changed by its becoming motile. If, on the other hand, one favors a liberal view of abortion, I think that one can attack this third suggested cutoff point, in its unspecified form, only by determining what properties are necessary, or what properties sufficient, for an individual to have a right to life. Thus I would base my rejection of motility as a cutoff point on my claim, defended above, that a necessary condition of an organism's possessing a right to life is that it conceive of itself as a continuing subject of experiences and other mental states.

The second suggested cutoff point—the development of a recognizably human form—can be dismissed fairly quickly. I have already remarked that membership in a particular species is not itself a morally relevant property. For it is obvious that if we encountered other "rational animals," such as Martians, the fact that their physiological makeup was very different from our own would not be grounds for denying them a right to life.[24] Similarly, it is clear that the development of human form is not in itself a morally relevant event. Nor do there seem to be any grounds for holding that there is some other change, associated with this event, that is morally relevant. The appeal of this second cutoff point is, I think, purely emotional.

The overall conclusion seems to be that it is very difficult to defend the cutoff points traditionally advanced by those who advocate either a moderate or a liberal position on abortion. The reason is that there do not seem to be any basic moral principles one can appeal to in support of the cutoff points in question. We must now consider whether the conservative is any better off.

V. Refutation of the Conservative Position

Many have felt that the conservative's position is more defensible than the liberal's because the conservative can point to the gradual and continuous development of an organism as it changes from a zygote to an adult human being. He is then in a position to argue that it is morally arbitrary for the liberal to draw a line at some point in this continuous process and to say that abortion is permissible before, but not after, that particular point. The liberal's reply would presumably be that the emphasis upon the continuity of the process is misleading. What the conservative is really doing is simply challenging the liberal to specify the properties a thing must have in order to be a person, and to show that the developing organism does acquire the properties at the point selected by the liberal. The liberal may then reply that the difficulty he has meeting this challenge should not be taken as grounds for rejecting his position. For the conservative cannot meet this challenge either; the conservative is equally unable to say what properties something must have if it is to have a right to life.

Although this rejoinder does not dispose of the conservative's argument, it is not without bite. For defenders of the view that abortion is always wrong have failed to face up to the question of the basic moral principles on which their position rests. They have been content to assert the wrongness of killing any organism, from a zygote on, if that organism is a member of the species Homo sapiens. But they have overlooked the point that this cannot be an acceptable *basic* moral principle, since difference in species is not in itself a morally relevant difference. The conservative can reply, however, that it is possible to defend his position—but not the liberal's—*without* getting clear about the properties a thing must possess if it is to have a right to life. The conservative's defense will rest upon the following two claims: first, that there is a property, even if one is unable to specify what it is, that (i) is possessed by adult humans, and (ii) endows any organism possessing it with a serious right to life. Second, that if there are properties which satisfy (i) and (ii) above, at least one of those properties will be such that any organism potentially possessing that property has a serious right to life even now, simply by virtue of that potentiality, where an organism possesses a property potentially if it will come to have that property in the normal course of its development. The second claim—which I shall refer to as the potentiality principle—is critical to the conservative's defense. Because of it he is able to defend his position without deciding what properties a thing must possess in order to have a right to life. It is enough to know that adult members of Homo sapiens do have such a right. For then one can conclude that any organism which belongs to the species Homo sapiens, from a zygote on, must also have a right to life by virtue of the potentiality principle.

The liberal, by contrast, cannot mount a comparable argument. He cannot defend his position without offering at least a partial answer to the question of what properties a thing must possess in order to have a right to life.

The importance of the potentiality principle, however, goes beyond the fact that it provides support for the conservative's position. If the principle is unacceptable, then so is his position. For if the conservative cannot defend the view that an organism's having certain potentialities is sufficient grounds for ascribing to it a right to life, his claim that a fetus which is a member of Homo sapiens has a right to life can be attacked as follows. The reason an adult member of Homo sapiens has a right to life, but an infant ape does not, is that there are certain psychological properties which the former possesses and the latter lacks. Now, even if one is unsure exactly what these psychological properties are, it is clear that an organism in the early stages of development from a zygote into an adult member of Homo sapiens does not possess these properties. One need merely compare a human fetus with an ape fetus. What mental states does the former enjoy that the latter does not? Surely it is reasonable to hold that there are no significant differences in their respective mental lives—assuming that one wishes to ascribe any mental states at all to such organisms. (Does a zygote have a mental life? Does it have experiences? Or beliefs? Or desires?) There are, of course, physiological differences, but these are not in themselves morally significant. If one held that potentialities were relevant to the ascription of a right to life, one could argue that the physiological differences, though not morally significant in themselves, are morally significant by virtue of their causal consequences: They will lead to later psychological differences that are morally relevant, and for this reason the physiological differences are themselves morally significant. But if the potentiality principle is not available, this line of argument cannot be used, and there will then be

no differences between a human fetus and an ape fetus that the conservative can use as grounds for ascribing a serious right to life to the former but not to the latter.

It is therefore tempting to conclude that the conservative view of abortion is acceptable if and only if the potentiality principle is acceptable. But to say that the conservative position can be defended if the potentiality principle is acceptable is to assume that the argument is over once it is granted that the fetus has a right to life, and, as was noted above, Thomson has shown that there are serious grounds for questioning this assumption. In any case, the important point here is that the conservative position on abortion is acceptable *only if* the potentiality principle is sound.

One way to attack the potentiality principle is simply to argue in support of the self-consciousness requirement—the claim that only an organism that conceives of itself as a continuing subject of experiences has a right to life. For this requirement, when taken together with the claim that there is at least one property, possessed by adult humans, such that any organism possessing it has a serious right to life, entails the denial of the potentiality principle. Or at least this is so if we add the uncontroversial empirical claim that an organism that will in the normal course of events develop into an adult human does not from the very beginning of its existence possess a concept of a continuing subject of experiences together with a belief that it is itself such an entity.

I think it best, however, to scrutinize the potentiality principle itself, and not to base one's case against it simply on the self-consciousness requirement. Perhaps the first point to note is that the potentiality principle should not be confused with principles such as the following: The value of an object is related to the value of the things into which it can develop. This "valuation principle" is rather vague. There are ways of making it more precise, but we need not consider these here. Suppose now that one were to speak not of a right to life, but of the value of life. It would then be easy to make the mistake of thinking that the valuation principle was relevant to the potentiality principle—indeed, that it entailed it. But an individual's right to life is not based on the value of his life. To say that the world would be better off if it contained fewer people is not to say that it would be right to achieve such a better world by killing some of the present inhabitants. *If* having a right to life were a matter of a thing's value, then a thing's potentialities, being connected with its expected value, would clearly be relevant to the question of what rights it had. Conversely, once one realizes that a thing's rights are not a matter of its value, I think it becomes clear that an organism's potentialities are irrelevant to the question of whether it has a right to life.

But let us now turn to the task of finding a direct refutation of the potentiality principle. The basic issue is this. Is there any property J which satisfies the following conditions: (1) There is a property K such that any individual possessing property K has a right to life, and there is a scientific law L to the effect that any organism possessing property J will in the normal course of events come to possess property K at some later time. (2) Given the relationship between property J and property K just described, anything possessing property J has a right to life. (3) If property J were not related to property K in the way indicated, it would not be the case that anything possessing property J thereby had a right to life. In short, the question is whether there is a property J that bestows a right to life on an organism *only because* J stands in a certain causal relationship to a second property K, which is such that anything possessing that property ipso facto has a right to life.

My argument turns upon the following critical principle: Let C be a causal process that normally leads to outcome E. Let A be an action that initiates process C, and B be an action involving a minimal expenditure of energy that stops process C before outcome E occurs. Assume further that actions A and B do not have any other consequences, and that E is the only morally significant outcome of process C. Then there is no moral difference between intentionally refraining from performing action A, assuming identical motivation in both cases. This principle, which I shall refer to as the moral symmetry principle with respect to action and inaction, would be rejected by some philosophers. They would argue that there is an important distinction to be drawn between "what we owe people in the form of aid and what we owe them in the way of non-interference,"[25] and that the latter, "negative duties," are duties that it is more serious to neglect than the former, "posi-

tive" ones. This view arises from an intuitive response to examples such as the following. Even if it is wrong not to send food to starving people in other parts of the world, it is more wrong still to kill someone. And isn't the conclusion, then, that one's obligation to refrain from killing someone is a more serious obligation than one's obligation to save lives?

I want to argue that this is not the correct conclusion. I think it is tempting to draw this conclusion if one fails to consider the motivation that is likely to be associated with the respective actions. If someone performs an action he knows will kill someone else, this will usually be grounds for concluding that he wanted to kill the person in question. In contrast, failing to help someone may indicate only apathy, laziness, selfishness, or an amoral outlook: The fact that a person knowingly allows another to die will not normally be grounds for concluding that he desired that person's death. Someone who knowingly kills another is more likely to be seriously defective from a moral point of view than someone who fails to save another's life.

If we are not to be led to false conclusions by our intuitions about certain cases, we must explicitly assume identical motivations in the two situations. Compare, for example, the following: (1) Jones sees that Smith will be killed by a bomb unless he warns him. Jones's reaction is: "How lucky, it will save me the trouble of killing Smith myself." So Jones allows Smith to be killed by the bomb, even though he could easily have warned him. (2) Jones wants Smith dead, and therefore shoots him. Is one to say there is a significant difference between the wrongness of Jones's behavior in these two cases? Surely not. This shows the mistake of drawing a distinction between positive duties and negative duties and holding that the latter impose stricter obligations than the former. The difference in our intuitions about situations that involve giving aid to others and corresponding situations that involve not interfering with others is to be explained by reference to probable differences in the motivations operating in the two situations, and not by reference to a distinction between positive and negative duties. For once it is specified that the motivation is the same in the two situations, we realize that inaction is as wrong in the one case as action is in the other.

There is another point that may be relevant. Action involves effort, while inaction usually does not. It usually does not require any effort on my part to refrain from killing someone, but saving someone's life will require an expenditure of energy. One must then ask how large a sacrifice a person is morally required to make to save the life of another. If the sacrifice of time and energy is quite large it may be that one is not morally obliged to save the life of another in that situation. Superficial reflection upon such cases might easily lead us to introduce the distinction between positive and negative duties, but again it is clear that this would be a mistake. The point is not that one has a greater duty to refrain from killing others than to perform positive actions that will save them. It is rather that positive actions require effort, and this means that in deciding what to do a person has to take into account his own right to do what he wants with his life, and not only the other person's right to life. To avoid this confusion, we should confine ourselves to comparisons between situations in which the positive action involves minimal effort.

The moral symmetry principle, as formulated above, explicitly takes these two factors into account. It applies only to pairs of situations in which the motivations are identical and the positive action involves minimal effort. Without these restrictions, the principle would be open to serious objection; with them, it seems perfectly acceptable. For the central objection to it rests on the claim that we must distinguish positive from negative duties and recognize that negative duties impose stronger obligations than positive ones. I have tried to show how this claim derives from an unsound account of our moral intuitions about certain situations.

My argument against the potentiality principle can now be stated. Suppose at some future time a chemical were to be discovered which when injected into the brain of a kitten would cause the kitten to develop into a cat possessing a brain of the sort possessed by humans, and consequently into a cat having all the psychological capabilities characteristic of adult humans. Such cats would be able to think, to use language, and so on. Now it would surely be morally indefensible in such a situation to ascribe a serious right to life to members of the species Homo sapiens without also ascribing it to cats that have undergone such a process of development: There would be no morally significant differences.

Secondly, it would not be seriously wrong to refrain from injecting a newborn kitten with the special chemical, and to kill it instead. The fact that one could initiate a causal process that would transform a kitten into an entity that would eventually possess properties such that anything possessing them ipso facto has a serious right to life does not mean that the kitten has a serious right to life even before it has been subjected to the process of injection and transformation. The possibility of transforming kittens into persons will not make it any more wrong to kill newborn kittens than it is now.

Thirdly, in view of the symmetry principle, if it is not seriously wrong to refrain from initiating such a causal process, neither is it seriously wrong to interfere with such a process. Suppose a kitten is accidentally injected with the chemical. As long as it has not yet developed those properties that in themselves endow something with a right to life, there cannot be anything wrong with interfering with the causal process and preventing the development of the properties in question. Such interference might be accomplished either by injecting the kitten with some "neutralizing" chemical or simply by killing it.

But if it is not seriously wrong to destroy an injected kitten which will naturally develop the properties that bestow a right to life, neither can it be seriously wrong to destroy a member of Homo sapiens which lacks such properties, but will naturally come to have them. The potentialities are the same in both cases. The only difference is that in the case of a human fetus the potentialities have been present from the beginning of the organism's development, while in the case of the kitten they have been present only from the time it was injected with the special chemical. This difference in the time at which the potentialities were acquired is a morally irrelevant difference.

It should be emphasized that I am not here assuming that a human fetus does not possess properties which in themselves, and irrespective of their causal relationships to other properties, provide grounds for ascribing a right to life to whatever possesses them. The point is merely that if it is seriously wrong to kill something, the reason cannot be that the thing will later acquire properties that in themselves provide something with a right to life.

Finally, it is reasonable to believe that there are properties possessed by adult members of Homo sapiens which establish their right to life, and also that any normal human fetus will come to possess those properties shared by adult humans. But it has just been shown that if it is wrong to kill a human fetus, it cannot be because of its potentialities. One is therefore forced to conclude that the conservative's potentiality principle is false.

In short, anyone who wants to defend the potentiality principle must either argue against the moral symmetry principle or hold that in a world in which kittens could be transformed into "rational animals" it would be seriously wrong to kill newborn kittens. It is hard to believe there is much to be said for the latter moral claim. Consequently one expects the conservative's rejoinder to be directed against the symmetry principle. While I have not attempted to provide a thorough defense of that principle, I have tried to show that what seems to be the most important objection to it—the one that appeals to a distinction between positive and negative duties—is based on a superficial analysis of our moral intuitions. I believe that a more thorough examination of the symmetry principle would show it to be sound. If so, we should reject the potentiality principle, and the conservative position on abortion as well.

VI. Summary and Conclusions

Let us return now to my basic claim, the self-consciousness requirement: An organism possesses a serious right to life only if it possesses the concept of a self as a continuing subject of experiences and other mental states, and believes that it is itself such a continuing entity. My defense of this claim has been twofold. I have offered a direct argument in support of it, and I have tried to show that traditional conservative and liberal views on abortion and infanticide, which involve a rejection of it, are unsound. I now want to mention one final reason why my claim should be accepted. Consider the example mentioned in section II—that of killing, as opposed to torturing, newborn kittens. I suggested there that while in the case of adult humans most people would consider it

worse to kill an individual than to torture him for an hour, we do not usually view the killing of a newborn kitten as morally outrageous, although we would regard someone who tortured a newborn kitten for an hour as heinously evil. I pointed out that a possible conclusion that might be drawn from this is that newborn kittens have a right not to be tortured, but do not have a serious right to life. If this is the correct conclusion, how is one to explain it? One merit of the self-consciousness requirement is that it provides an explanation of this situation. The reason a newborn kitten does not have a right to life is explained by the fact that it does not possess the concept of a self. But how is one to explain the kitten's having a right not to be tortured? The answer is that a desire not to suffer pain can be ascribed to something without assuming that it has any concept of a continuing self. For while something that lacks the concept of a self cannot desire that a self not suffer, it can desire that a given sensation not exist. The state desired—the absence of a particular sensation, or of sensations of a certain sort—can be described in a purely phenomenalistic language, and hence without the concept of a continuing self. So long as the newborn kitten possesses the relevant phenomenal concepts, it can truly be said to desire that a certain sensation not exist. So we can ascribe to it a right not to be tortured even though, since it lacks the concept of a continuing self, we cannot ascribe to it a right to life.

This completes my discussion of the basic moral principles involved in the issue of abortion and infanticide. But I want to comment upon an important factual question, namely, at what point an organism comes to possess the concept of a self as a continuing subject of experiences and other mental states, together with the belief that it is itself such a continuing entity. This is obviously a matter for detailed psychological investigation, but everyday observation makes it perfectly clear, I believe, that a newborn baby does not possess the concept of a continuing self, any more than a newborn kitten possesses such a concept. If so, infanticide during a time interval shortly after birth must be morally acceptable.

But where is the line to be drawn? What is the cutoff point? If one maintained, as some philosophers have, that an individual possesses concepts only if he can express these concepts in language, it would be a matter of everyday observation whether or not a given organism possessed the concept of a continuing self. Infanticide would then be permissible up to the time an organism learned how to use certain expressions. However, I think the claim that acquisition of concepts is dependent on acquisition of language is mistaken. For example, one wants to ascribe mental states of a conceptual sort—such as beliefs and desires—to organisms that are incapable of learning a language. This issue of prelinguistic understanding is clearly outside the scope of this discussion. My point is simply that *if* an organism can acquire concepts without thereby acquiring a way of expressing those concepts linguistically, the question of whether a given organism possesses the concept of a self as a continuing subject of experiences and other mental states, together with the belief that it is itself such a continuing entity, may be a question that requires fairly subtle experimental techniques to answer.

If this view of the matter is roughly correct, there are two worries one is left with at the level of practical moral decisions, one of which may turn out to be deeply disturbing. The lesser worry is where the line is to be drawn in the case of infanticide. It is not troubling because there is no serious need to know the exact point at which a human infant acquires a right to life. For in the vast majority of cases in which infanticide is desirable, its desirability will be apparent within a short time after birth. Since it is virtually certain that an infant at such a stage of its development does not possess the concept of a continuing self, and thus does not possess a serious right to life, there is excellent reason to believe that infanticide is morally permissible in most cases where it is otherwise desirable. The practical moral problem can thus be satisfactorily handled by choosing some period of time, such as a week after birth, as the interval during which infanticide will be permitted. This interval could then be modified once psychologists have established the point at which a human organism comes to believe that it is a continuing subject of experiences and other mental states.

The troubling worry is whether adult animals belonging to species other than Homo sapiens may not also possess a serious right to life. For once one says that an organism can possess the concept of a continuing self, together with the belief that it is itself such an entity, without having any way of expressing that concept and that belief linguistically, one has to face up to the question of whether animals may not possess properties that bestow a serious right to life upon them. The suggestion itself is a familiar one, and one that most of us are accustomed to dismiss very casually. The line of thought advanced here suggests that this attitude may turn out to be tragically mistaken. Once one reflects upon the question of the *basic* moral principles involved in the ascription of a right to life to organisms, one may find himself driven to conclude that our everyday treatment of animals is morally indefensible, and that we are in fact murdering innocent persons.

A Postscript

June 1973

The key to the question of the moral permissibility of abortion is, I think, the insight that there is a conceptual connection between the possession of a particular right and the capacity to have the corresponding desire. The claim that there is such a conceptual connection was supported by an analysis of the concept of a right and an account of the conditions under which an individual's right to something can be violated. The simplest suggestion as to the nature of this conceptual connection is that an action cannot violate an individual's right to something unless he has, at the time the action is performed, a desire for that thing. This account is, however, exposed to obvious counterexamples, and as a result I suggested that "an individual's right to X can be violated not only when he desires X, but also when he *would* now desire X were it not for one of the following: (i) he is in an emotionally unbalanced state; (ii) he is temporarily unconscious; (iii) he has been conditioned to desire the absence of X."

I believe that the basic contentions and the supporting arguments advanced in my defense of abortion and infanticide are essentially correct. However, it may be helpful to indicate very briefly the more important changes and additions I would make if I were revising the essay. A more detailed discussion of these points can be found in my response to criticisms in the Summer 1973 issue of *Philosophy & Public Affairs* ["Michael Tooley Replies," Vol. 2, 419–432.].

The clauses dealing with emotionally unbalanced individuals and with individuals who have been subjected to conditioning which has "distorted" their desires are perhaps fair enough, for these are clearly exceptional cases, and it is not obvious exactly what account they should receive. But in the case of the temporarily unconscious individual one feels that it is an *ad hoc* modification simply to add a clause which says that an action can violate such an individual's right to something, even though he does not at the time have any desire for the thing. It would seem that a satisfactory account of rights should make clear the underlying rationale. If one fails to do this, a critic may well ask why one should make an exception of temporarily unconscious adults, but not of infants and fetuses.

I think that this problem can be dealt with by setting out a slightly more subtle account of the conditions under which an individual's rights can be violated. Such an account differs from that offered above by incorporating explicit reference to past and future desires. Leaving aside cases in which an individual's desires have been affected by lack of relevant information, or by emotional imbalance, or by his being subjected to abnormal physiological or psychological factors, one could then say that an individual's rights can be violated either by violating a corresponding desire which he now has, or, in appropriate circumstances, by violating a corresponding desire which he had at some time in the past, or will have at some time in the future.

The need to take into account past and future desires is shown by the fact that some present actions may violate, on the one hand, the rights of a dead person, and, on the other, the rights of future generations. For not only do these individuals fail to have the corresponding desire at the time the action is performed; they do not even exist.

Given this more complex but, I think, very natural account of the conceptual connection between rights and desires, the case of the temporarily unconscious individual becomes clear. If one kills such an individual one violates his right to life because one violates a desire he had before becoming unconscious: the desire to continue to exist as a subject of experiences and other mental states. The temporarily unconscious adult thus contrasts sharply with a human fetus or newborn infant,

since the latter has not had, at any time past or present, a desire to continue to exist as a subject of experiences and other mental states. Consequently abortion and infanticide do not involve the violation of anyone's right to life.

The above revision also necessitates a slight change in the self-consciousness requirement which something must satisfy in order to have a right to life. In revised form, the self-consciousness requirement will state that an organism cannot have a serious right to life unless it either now possesses, or did possess at some time in the past, the concept of a self as a continuing subject of experiences and other mental states together with the belief that it is itself such an entity.

The other main revisions involve my discussion of the conservative position on abortion. First, there is a slight inaccuracy in my argument against the conservative position. I contended that the conservative position on abortion is defensible only if the potentiality principle is correct. The potentiality principle states that if there are properties possessed by normal adult human beings that endow any organism possessing them with a serious right to life, then at least one of those properties is such that any organism potentially possessing it has a serious right to life, simply by virtue of that potentiality. This conflicts with the account of rights offered earlier. A fertilized human egg cell has never had a desire to continue to exist as a subject of experiences and other mental states, nor is it the case that it would have had such a desire had it not been deprived of relevant information or subjected to abnormal influences. Therefore on the account of rights, it has no right to life, but on the potentiality principle, it appears to have such a right.

This problem can be avoided by revising the potentiality principle slightly. The principle should say, not that an organism that potentially possesses the relevant property has a right to life, but merely that in virtue of its potentiality, to kill such an organism is seriously wrong. (It is true that many people might be unwilling to accept this modification, since it implies that some actions are seriously wrong even though they do not violate anyone's right. This makes the question of *why* it is seriously wrong to kill a fetus a pressing one.)

This change does not substantially affect my objection to the conservative position. For the argument that I offer against the original version of the potentiality principle, based upon the moral symmetry principle, can easily be modified so that it is also an argument against the revised version.

It should be mentioned, however, that the original statement of my argument against the potentiality principle was somewhat imprecise at one point. Let me briefly restate the initial stages of the argument. Suppose that one has a special chemical that will, when injected into a kitten, slowly change its brain into one that is comparable to a human brain, and hence transform the kitten into an animal with all the psychological capabilities characteristic of normal adult human beings. It then follows from the moral symmetry principle that if one has a kitten which has been injected with the special chemical, but which has not had the time to develop the relevant psychological properties, it is no more seriously wrong to inject the kitten with some "neutralizing" chemical that will interfere with the process and thus prevent the kitten from developing the properties in question, than it would be to intentionally refrain from injecting a kitten with the special chemical.

What deserves emphasis is that it is not being assumed here that neither action is seriously wrong. What follows from the moral symmetry principle is simply that one action is no more wrong than the other. My original formulation of the argument was unclear and potentially misleading on this point.

The argument now proceeds as follows. Compare a kitten that has been injected with the special chemical, and then had the chemical neutralized before it could take effect, with a kitten that has not been injected with the special chemical. It is clear that it is no more seriously wrong to kill the former than to kill the latter. For although their bodies have undergone different processes in the past, this difference is morally irrelevant, and there need be no other differences between them, with respect either to present properties or potentialities.

Next, consider two kittens, one of which has been injected with the chemical, but has not yet developed those properties that in themselves would give it a right to life, and the other of which has not been injected with the chemical. It follows from the previous two steps in the argument that the combined action of injecting the first kitten with a neutralizing substance and then killing it is no more seriously wrong than the combined action of intentionally refraining from injecting the second kitten with the chemical, and then killing it. From this point on the argument will proceed as originally set out.

Finally, let me propose a second objection to the potentiality principle both in its original and revised versions. I believe that if one accepts the potentiality principle, one ought also to accept a generalized version of it. The generalized potentiality principle states that it is not only wrong to destroy *organisms* which have the appropriate potentialities, it is also seriously wrong to prevent *systems of objects*, which would normally develop the morally relevant properties in question, from doing so. For the contention would be that whether the potentialities reside in a single organism or in a system of interrelated objects is morally irrelevant. What matters is only that one is dealing with something that will, if not interfered with, develop the morally significant properties in question. To accept either the original or the revised version of the potentiality principle, while rejecting the generalized version of it, would seem to be an indefensible position.

If, however, one accepts the generalized potentiality principle, one will be forced to conclude that some methods of contraception are seriously wrong. It is true that some people who defend an extreme conservative position on abortion will find this a cheering conclusion. But I think that there are many more people who are conservatives on abortion who would want to reject, as completely unacceptable, the view that artificial contraception is seriously wrong. If my second argument is correct, such a combination of positions cannot successfully be defended. One must either accept the claim that some methods of contraception are seriously wrong, or else abandon the conservative position on abortion.

Notes

1. I am grateful to a number of people, particularly the Editors of *Philosophy & Public Affairs*, Rodelia Hapke, and Walter Kaufmann, for their helpful comments. It should not, of course, be inferred that they share the views expressed in this paper.

2. Judith Jarvis Thomson has argued with great force and ingenuity that this conclusion is mistaken. I will comment on her argument later. [See Judith Jarvis

Thomson, "A Defense of Abortion," *Philosophy and Public Affairs* 1 (1971): 47–66. Reprinted in Marshall Cohen *et al.* ed., *The Rights and Wrongs of Abortion.* Princeton, N.J.: Princeton University Press, 1974, pp. 3–22. Page references are to the reprint.]

3. While this is the position conservatives tend to hold, it is not clear that it is the position they ought to hold. For if the fetus is a person it is far from clear that it is permissible to destroy it to save the mother. Two moral principles lend support to the view that it is the fetus which should live. First, other things being equal, should not one give something to a person who has had less rather than to a person who has had more? The mother has had a chance to live, while the fetus has not. The choice is thus between giving the mother more of an opportunity to live while giving the fetus none at all and giving the fetus an opportunity to enjoy life while not giving the mother a further opportunity to do so. Surely fairness requires the latter. Secondly, since the fetus has a greater life expectancy than the mother, one is in effect distributing more goods by choosing the life of the fetus over the life of the mother.

  The position I am here recommending to the conservative should not be confused with the official Catholic position. The Catholic Church holds that it is seriously wrong to kill a fetus directly even if failure to do so will result in the death of *both* the mother and the fetus. This perverse value judgment is not part of the conservative's position.

4. Section 230.3 of the American Law Institute's *Model Penal Code* (Philadelphia, 1962). There is some interesting, though at times confused, discussion of the proposed code in *Model Penal Code—Tentative Draft No. 9* (Philadelphia, 1959), pp. 146–162.

5. A clear example of such an unwillingness to entertain seriously the possibility that moral judgments widely accepted in one's own society may nevertheless be incorrect is provided by Roger Wertheimer's superficial dismissal of infanticide on pages 25–26. [See Roger Wertheimer, "Understanding the Abortion Argument," *Philosophy and Public Affairs* 1 (1971): 67–95. Reprinted in Marshall Cohen *et al.* ed., *The Rights and Wrongs of Abortion.* Princeton, N.J.: Princeton University Press, 1974, pp. 23–51. Page references are to the reprint.]

6. Compare the discussion of the concept of a right offered by Richard B. Brandt in his *Ethical Theory* (Englewood Cliffs, N.J., 1959), pp. 434–441. As Brandt points out, some philosophers have maintained that only things that can *claim* rights can have rights. I agree with Brandt's view

that "inability to claim does not destroy the right" (p. 440).

7. B. A. Brody, "Abortion and the Law," *Journal of Philosophy*, LXVIII, no. 12 (17 June 1971): 357–369. See pp. 357–358.

8. P. 3.

9. P. 25.

10. *Ibid.*

11. Pp. 3–4.

12. P. 21.

13. P. 34.

14. A moral principle accepted by a person is *basic for him* if and only if his acceptance of it is not dependent upon any of his (nonmoral) factual beliefs. That is, no change in his factual beliefs would cause him to abandon the principle in question.

15. Wertheimer, p. 44.

16. Again, compare the analysis defended by Brandt in *Ethical Theory*, pp. 434–441.

17. In everyday life one often speaks of desiring things, such as an apple or a newspaper. Such talk is elliptical, the context together with one's ordinary beliefs serving to make it clear that one wants to eat the apple and read the newspaper. To say that what one desires is that a certain proposition be true should not be construed as involving any particular ontological commitment. The point is merely that it is sentences such as "John wants it to be the case that he is eating an apple in the next few minutes" that provide a completely explicit description of a person's desires. If one fails to use such sentences one can be badly misled about what concepts are presupposed by a particular desire.

18. There are, however, situations other than those discussed here which might seem to count against the claim that a person cannot have a right unless he is conceptually capable of having the corresponding desire. Can't a young child, for example, have a right to an estate, even though he may not be conceptually capable of wanting the estate? It is clear that such situations have to be carefully considered if one is to arrive at a satisfactory account of the concept of a right. My inclination is to say that the correct description is not that the child now has a right to the estate, but that he will come to have such a right when he is mature, and that in the meantime no one else has a right to the estate. My reason for saying that the child does not now have a right to the estate is that he cannot now do things with the estate, such as selling it or giving it away, that he will be able to do later on.

19. Another frequent suggestion as to the cutoff point not listed here is quickening. I omit it because it seems clear that if abortion after quickening is wrong, its wrongness must be tied up with the motility of the fetus, not with the mother's awareness of the fetus' ability to move about.

20. P. 12.

21. A good example of a failure to probe this issue is provided by Brody's "Abortion and the Law."

22. Admittedly the modification is a substantial one, since given a society that refused to compensate women, a woman who had an abortion would not be doing anything wrong.

23. Compare Wertheimer's remarks, p. 35.

24. This requires qualification. If their central nervous systems were radically different from ours, it might be thought that one would not be justified in ascribing to them mental states of an experiential sort. And then, since it seems to be a conceptual truth that only things having experiential states can have rights, one would be forced to conclude that one was not justified in ascribing any rights to them.

25. Philippa Foot, "The Problem of Abortion and the Doctrine of the Double Effect," *The Oxford Review* 5 (1967): 5–15. See the discussion on pp. 11ff.

Questions for Analysis

1. *How can infanticide shed light on the abortion question?*

2. *Why does Tooley consider infanticide an interesting and important question in its own right?*

3. *Tooley believes an organism possesses a serious right to life only if it possesses self-consciousness. What does he mean by "self-consciousness"?*

4. *Trace the steps in Tooley's argument that lead him to pose self-consciousness as a requirement for person status.*

5. *Explain Tooley's criticism of both the liberal and the conservative views regarding their positions on the status of the unborn and, consequently, on abortion.*

6. *Why does Tooley suggest that our everyday treatment of animals may be morally indefensible?*

Abortion: Law, Choice, and Morality

Daniel Callahan

Philosopher Daniel Callahan's viewpoint regarding the status of the fetus is positioned somewhere between the two extremes of Noonan and Tooley. In Callahan's view, as developed in his Abortion: Law, Choice and Morality, *the unborn is neither just a mass of protoplasm nor a full-fledged person. As a result, Callahan believes it is equally improper to deny the fetus any moral status or to assign it full moral status.*

Essentially, Callahan believes that an abortion choice is a private choice: Individuals ought to be allowed to make their own decisions. But he quickly points out that a legal freedom to choose does not dissolve the serious moral questions that an abortion choice always raises.

The thrust of Callahan's essay, therefore, addresses the question of how a woman ought to go about making an abortion choice, if her action is to be considered moral. He isolates a number of

---

factors to consider in any serious and responsible evaluation of an abortion choice: the biological evidence, the philosophical assumptions implied in the term human, *a philosophical theory of biological analysis, the social consequences of the different analyses of and the meaning of the word* human, *and consistency of meaning and use. He especially warns against making a personal choice easy either through intellectual ignorance or by appeal to personal convenience.*

In the last analysis, Callahan suggests that the woman who faces an abortion choice keep foremost in mind the sanctity of life and the fact that abortion always involves a violation of that sanctity. In that way she will remain sensitive to the moral gravity of an abortion decision and weigh her reasons for wanting an abortion accordingly.

The strength of pluralistic societies lies in the personal freedom they afford individuals. One is free to choose among religious, philosophical, ideological and political creeds; or one can create one's own highly personal, idiosyncratic moral code and view of the universe. Increasingly, the individual is free to ignore the morals, manners and mores of society. The only limitations are upon those actions which seem to present clear and present dangers to the common good, and even there the range of prohibited actions is diminishing as more and more choices are left to personal and private decisions. I have contended that, apart from some regulatory laws, abortion decisions should be left, finally, up to the women themselves. Whatever one may think of the morality of abortion, it cannot be established that it poses a clear and present danger to the common good. Thus society does not have the right decisively to interpose itself between a woman and the abortion she wants. It can only intervene where it can be shown that some of its own interests are at stake *qua* society. Regulatory laws of a minimal kind therefore seem in order, since in a variety of ways already mentioned society will be affected by the number, kind and quality of legal abortions. In short, with a few important stipulations, what I have been urging is tantamount to saying that abortion decisions should be private decisions. It is to accept, in principle, the contention of those who believe that, in a free, pluralistic society, the woman should be allowed to make her own moral choice on abortion and be allowed to implement that choice.

But pluralistic societies also lay a few traps for the unwary. It is not a large psychological step from saying that individuals should be left free to make up their own minds on some crucial moral issues (of which abortion is one) to an adoption of the view that one personal decision is as good as another, that any decision is a good one as long as it is honest or sincere, that a free decision equals a correct decision. However short the psychological step, the logical gap is very large. An absence of cant, hypocrisy and coercion may prepare the way for good personal decisions. But that is only to clean the room, and something must then be put in it. The hazard is that, once cleaned, it will be filled with capriciousness, sentimentality, a thinly disguised conformity to the reigning moral taste, or strongly felt but inadequately analyzed moral opinions. This is a particular danger in affluent pluralistic societies, heavily dominated by popular tastes, communication media and the absence of shared values. Philosophically, the view that all values are equally good and all private moral choices on a par is all but dead; but it still has a strong life at the popular level, where there is a tendency to act as if, once personal freedom is legally and socially achieved, moral questions cease to exist.

A considerable quantity of literature exists in the field of ethics concerned with such problems as subjective and objective values, the meaning and use of ethical principles and moral rules, the role of intentionality. That literature need not be reviewed here. But it is directly to the point to observe that a particular failing of the abortion-on-request literature is that it persistently scants the moral problem of how a woman, if granted the desired legal freedom to make her own decision about abortion, should go about making that decision. Up to a point, this deficiency is understandable. The immediate tactical problem has been to get the laws changed or repealed; that has been the burden of the public struggle, which has concentrated on statutes and legislators rather than on the moral contents and problems of personal decision-making. It is reasonable and legitimate to say that a woman should be left free to make the decision in the light of her own personal values; that is, I believe, the best legal solution. But it leaves totally untouched the question of how, once freedom is achieved, she ought to go about the personal business of forming a coherent, rational, sensitive moral perspective and opinion on abortion. After freedom, what then? Society may have no right to demand that a woman give it good reasons why she should have an abortion before permitting it. But this does not entail that the woman should not, as a morally responsible person, have good reasons to justify her desires or acts in her own eyes.

This is only to say that a solution of the legal problem is not the same as a solution to the moral problem. That the moral struggle is transferred from the public to the private sphere should not be taken to mean that the moral problem has been solved; only its public aspect, under a permissive law or a repeal of all laws, has been dealt with. The personal problem will remain.

Some women will be part of a religious group or ethical tradition which they freely choose and which can offer them something, possibly very much, in the way of helpful moral insight consistent with that tradition. The obvious course in that instance is for them to turn to their tradition to see what it has to offer them on the particular problem of abortion. But what of those who have no tradition to repair to or those who find their tradition wanting on this problem? One way or another, they will have to find some way of developing a set of ethical principles and moral rules to help them act responsibly, to justify their own conduct in their own eyes. To press the problem to a finer point, what ought they to think about as they try to work out their own views on abortion?

Only a few suggestions will be made here, taking the form of arguing for an ethic of personal responsibility which tries, in the process of decision-making, to make itself aware of a number of things. The biological evidence should be considered, just as the problem of methodology must be considered; the philosophical assumptions implicit in different uses of the word "human" need to be considered; a philosophical theory of biological analysis is required; the social consequences of different kinds of analyses and different meanings of the word "human" should be thought through;

consistency of meaning and use should be sought to avoid *ad hoc* and arbitrary solutions.

It is my own conviction that the "developmental school" offers the most helpful and illuminating approach to the problem of the beginning of human life, avoiding, on the one hand, a too narrow genetic criterion of human life and, on the other, a too broad and socially dangerous social definition of the "human." Yet the kinds of problems which appear in any attempt to decide upon the beginning of life suggest that no one position can be either proved or disproved from biological evidence alone. It becomes a question of trying to do justice to the evidence while, at the same time, realizing that how the evidence is approached and used will be a function of one's way of looking at reality, one's moral policy, the values and rights one believes need balancing, and the type of questions one thinks need to be asked. At the very least, however, the genetic evidence for the uniqueness of zygotes and embryos (a uniqueness of a different kind than that of the uniqueness of sperm and ova), their potentiality for development into a human person, their early development of human characteristics, their genetic and organic distinctness from the organism of the mother, appear to rule out a treatment even of zygotes, much less the more developed stages of the conceptus, as mere pieces of "tissue," of no human significance or value. The "tissue" theory of the significance of the conceptus can only be made plausible by a systematic disregard of the biological evidence. Moreover, though one may conclude that a conceptus is only potential human life, in the process of continually actualizing its potential through growth and development, a respect for the sanctity of life, with its bias in favor even of undeveloped life, is enough to make the taking of such life a moral problem. There is a choice to be made and it is a moral choice. In the near future, it is likely that some kind of simple, safe abortifacient drug will be developed, which either prevents implantation or destroys the conceptus before it can develop. It will be tempting then to think that the moral dilemma has vanished, but I do not believe it will have.

It is possible to imagine a huge number of situations where a woman could, in good and sensitive conscience, choose abortion as a moral solution to her personal or social difficulties. But, at the very least, the bounds of morality are overstepped when either through a systematic intellectual negligence or a willful choosing of that moral solution most personally convenient, personal choice is deliberately made easy and problem-free. Yet it seems to me that a pressure in that direction is a growing part of the ethos of technological societies; it is easily possible to find people to reassure us that we need have no scruples about the way we act, whether the issue is war, the suppression of rebellion and revolution, discrimination against minorities or the use of technological advances. Pluralism makes possible the achieving of freer, more subtle moral thinking; but it is a possibility constantly endangered by cultural pressures which would simplify or dissolve moral doubts and anguish.

The question of abortion "indications" returns at the level of personal choice. I have contended that the advent of permissive laws should not mean a cessation of efforts to explore the problem of "indications." When a woman asks herself, as she ought, whether her reasons for wanting an abortion are sound reasons—which presumes abortion is a serious enough moral issue to warrant the need to provide oneself with good reasons for choosing it—she will be asking herself about justifiable indications. Thus, transposed from the legal to the personal level, the kinds of concerns adumbrated in the earlier chapters on indications remain fully pertinent. It was argued in those chapters that, with the possible exception of exceedingly rare instances of a direct threat to the physical life of the mother, one cannot speak of general categories of abortion indications as *necessitating* an abortion. In a number of circumstances, abortion may be a wise and justifiable solution to a distressed pregnancy. But when the language of necessity is used, the implication is that no other conceivable alternative is available. It may be granted, willingly enough, that some set of practical circumstances in some (possibly very many) concrete cases may indicate that abortion is the only feasible option open. But these cases cannot readily be determined in advance, and, for that reason, it is necessary to say that no formal indication as such (e.g., a psychiatric indication) entails a necessary, predetermined choice in favor of abortion.

The word "indication" remains the best word,

suggesting that a number of given circumstances will bring the possibility or desirability of abortion to the fore. But to escalate the concept of an indication into that of a required procedure is to go too far. Abortion is *one* way to solve the problem of an unwanted or hazardous pregnancy (physically, psychologically, economically or socially), but it is rarely the only way, at least in affluent societies (I would be considerably less certain about making the same statement about poor societies). Even in the most extreme cases—rape, incest, psychosis, for instance—alternatives will usually be available and different choices, open. It is not necessarily the end of every woman's chance for a happy, meaningful life to bear an illegitimate child. It is not necessarily the automatic destruction of a family to have a seriously defective child born into it. It is not necessarily the ruination of every family living in overcrowded housing to have still another child. It is not inevitable that every immature woman would become even more so if she bore a child or another child. It is not inevitable that a gravely handicapped child can hope for nothing from life. It is not inevitable that every unwanted child is doomed to misery. It is not written in the essence of things, as a fixed law of human nature, that a woman cannot come to accept, love and be a good mother to a child who was initially unwanted. Nor is it a fixed law that she could not come to cherish a grossly deformed child. Naturally, these are only generalizations. The point is only that human beings are as a rule flexible, capable of doing more than they sometimes think they can, able to surmount serious dangers and challenges, able to grow and mature, able to transform inauspicious beginnings into satisfactory conclusions. Everything in life, even in procreative and family life, is not fixed in advance; the future is never wholly unalterable.

Yet the problem of personal question-asking must be pushed a step farther. The way the questions are answered will be very much determined by a woman's way of looking at herself and at life. A woman who has decided, as a personal moral policy, that nothing should be allowed to stand in the way of her own happiness, goals and self-interest will have no trouble solving the moral problem. For her, an unwanted pregnancy will, by definition, be a pregnancy to be terminated. But only by a Pickwickian use of words could this form of reasoning be called moral. It would preclude any need to consult the opinion of others, any need to examine the validity of one's own viewpoint, any need to, for instance, ask when human life begins, any need to interrogate oneself in any way, intellectually or morally; will and desire would be king.

Assuming, however, that most women would seek a broader ethical horizon than that of their exclusively personal self-interest, what might they think about when faced with an abortion decision? A respect for the sanctity of human life should, I believe, incline them toward a general and strong bias against abortion. Abortion is an act of killing, the violent, direct destruction of potential human life, already in the process of development. That fact should not be disguised, or glossed over by euphemism and circumlocution. It is not the destruction of a human person—for at no stage of its development does the conceptus fulfill the definition of a person, which implies a developed capacity for reasoning, willing, desiring and relating to others—but it is the destruction of an important and valuable form of human life. Its value and its potentiality are not dependent upon the attitude of the woman toward it; it grows by its own biological dynamism and has a genetic and morphological potential distinct from that of the woman. It has its own distinctive and individual future. If contraception and abortion are both seen as forms of birth limitation, they are distinctly different acts; the former precludes the possibility of a conceptus being formed, while the latter stops a conceptus already in existence from developing. The bias implied by the principle of the sanctity of human life is toward the protection of all forms of human life, especially, in ordinary circumstances, the protection of the right to life. That right should be accorded even to doubtful life; its existence should not be wholly dependent upon the personal self-interest of the woman.

Yet she has her own rights as well, and her own set of responsibilities to those around her; that is why she may have to choose abortion. In extreme situations of overpopulation, she may also have a responsibility for the survival of the species or of a people. In many circumstances, then, a decision in favor of abortion—one which overrides the right to life of that potential human being she carries within—can be a responsible moral decision, worthy neither of the condemnation of others nor of self-condemnation. But the bias of the principle of the sanctity of life is against a routine, unthinking employment of abortion; it bends over backwards not to take life and gives the benefit of the doubt to life. It does not seek to diminish the range of responsibility toward life—potential or actual—but to extend it. It does not seek the narrowest definition of life, but the widest and the richest. It is mindful of individual possibility, on the one hand, and of a destructive human tendency, on the other, to exclude from the category of "the human" or deny rights to those beings whose existence is or could prove burdensome to others.

The language used to describe abortion will have an important bearing on the sensitivities and imagination of those women who must make abortion decisions. Abortion can be talked about in the language of medical technology and technique—as, say, "a therapeutic procedure involving the emptying of the uterine contents." That language is neutral, clinical, unemotional. Or abortion can be talked about in the emotive language of relieving woman from suffering, or meeting the need for freedom among women, or saving a nation from a devastating overpopulation. Both kinds of language have their place, for abortion has more than one result and meaning and abortion can legitimately be talked about in more than one way. What is objectionable is a conscious manipulation of language to incite an irrational emotional response, to allay doubts or to mislead the imagination. Particularly misleading is one commonly employed mixture of rhetorical modes by advocates of abortion on request. That is the use of a detached, clinical language to describe the actual operation itself combined with an emotive rhetoric to evoke the personal and social goods which an abortion can bring about. Thus, when every effort is made to suggest that emotion and feeling are perfectly appropriate to describe the social and personal goals of abortion, but that a clinical language only is appropriate when the actual technique and medical objective of an abortion is described, then the moral imagination is being misled.

Any human act can be described in impersonal, technological language, just as any act can be described in emotive language. What is wanted is an equity in the language. It is fair enough and to the point to say that in many circumstances abortion will save a woman's health or her family. It only becomes misleading when the act itself, as distinguished from its therapeutic goal, is talked about in an entirely different way. For, abortion is not just an "emptying of the uterine contents." It is also an act of killing; there will be no abortion unless the conceptus is killed (or its further existence made impossible, which amounts to the same thing). If it is appropriate to evoke the imagination and elicit sympathy for those women in a distressed pregnancy who could be helped by abortion, it is no less appropriate to evoke the imagination about what actually occurs in an abortion "procedure."

Imagination should also come into play at another point. It is often argued by proponents of abortion that there is no need for a woman ever to take any chances in a distressed pregnancy, particularly in the instance of an otherwise healthy woman who, if she has an abortion on one occasion, could simply get pregnant again on another, more auspicious occasion. This might be termed the "replacement theory" of abortion indications: since fetus "x" can be replaced by fetus "y," then there is no reason why a woman should have any scruples about such a replacement. This way of conceiving the choices effectively dissolves them; it becomes important only to know whether a woman can get pregnant again when she wants to. But this strategy can be employed only at the price of convincing oneself that there is no difference whatever among embryos or fetuses, that they all have exactly the same potentiality. But even the sketchiest knowledge of the genetic uniqueness of each conceptus (save in the instance of monozygotic twins), and thus the different genetic potentialities of each, should raise doubts on that point. Yet, having said that, I would not want to deny that the possibility of a further pregnancy could have an important bearing on the moral reasoning of a woman whose present pregnancy was threatening. If, out of a sense of responsibility toward her present children or her present life situation, a woman decided that an abortion was the wisest, most moral course, then the possibility

that she could become pregnant later, when these responsibilities would be less pressing, would be a pertinent consideration.

The goal of these remarks is to keep alive in the consciences of women who have an abortion choice a moral tension; and it is to hope that they will be willing to bear the pain and the uncertainty of having to make a moral choice. It is the automatic, unthinking and unimaginative personal solution of abortion questions which women themselves should be extremely wary of, either for or against an abortion. A woman can, with little trouble, find both people and books to reassure her that there is no problem about abortion at all; or people and books to convince her that she would be a moral monster if she chose abortion. A woman can choose in advance the views she will listen to and thus have her predispositions confirmed. Yet a willingness to keep alive a moral tension, and to be wary of precipitous solutions, presupposes two things. First, that the woman herself wants to do what is right, realizing that what is right may not always be that which is most convenient, most easy or most immediately apt to solve a pressing problem. It is simply not the case that what one wants to do, or would like to do, or is predisposed to do is necessarily the right thing to do. A willingness seriously to entertain that moral perception—which, of course, does not in itself imply a decision for or against an abortion— is one sign of moral seriousness.

Second, moral seriousness presupposes one is concerned with the protection and furthering of life. This means that, out of respect for human life, one bends over backwards not to eliminate human life, not to desensitize oneself to the meaning and value of potential life, not to seek definitions of the "human" which serve one's self-interest only. A desire to respect human life in all of its forms means, therefore, that one voluntarily imposes upon oneself a pressure against the taking of life; that one demands of oneself serious reasons for doing so, even in the case of a very early embryo; that one use not only the mind but also the imagination when a decision is being made; that one seeks not to evade the moral issues but to face them; that one searches out the alternatives and conscientiously entertains them before turning to abortion. A bias in favor of the sanctity of human life in all of its forms would include a bias against abortion on the part of women; it would be the last rather than the first choice when unwanted pregnancies occurred. It would be an act to be avoided if at all possible.

A bias of this kind, voluntarily imposed by a woman upon herself, would not trap her; for it is also part of a respect for the dignity of life to leave the way open for an abortion when other reasonable choices are not available. For she also has duties toward herself, her family and her society. There can be good reasons for taking the life even of a very late fetus; once that also is seen and seen as a counterpoise in particular cases to the general bias against the taking of potential life, the way is open to choose abortion. The bias of the moral policy implies the need for moral rules which seek

to preserve life. But, as a policy which leaves room for choice—rather than entailing a fixed set of rules—it is open to flexible interpretation when the circumstances point to the wisdom of taking exception to the normal ordering of the rules in particular cases. Yet, in that case, one is not genuinely taking exception to the rules. More accurately, one would be deciding that, for the preservation or furtherance of other values or rights—species-rights, person-rights—a choice in favor of abortion would be serving the sanctity of life. That there would be, in that case, conflict between rights, with one set of rights set aside (reluctantly) to serve another set, goes without saying. A subversion of the principle occurs when it is made out that there is no conflict and thus nothing to decide.

Questions for Analysis

1. What does Callahan mean by a "pluralistic society"?

2. When are regulatory laws justifiable? Is this a utilitarian justification?

3. Callahan says that ". . . a solution of the legal problem is not the same as a solution to the moral problem." What does this mean? How does it apply to an abortion choice?

4. What is the "tissue theory" and why does Callahan reject it?

5. Callahan claims that a woman's abortion decision will very much be determined by her way of looking at herself and at life. What does he mean, and do you agree?

6. In Callahan's view are there any formal indications that entail a necessary choice in favor of an abortion? How does his view relate to his cautions about abortion decisions?

7. What does Callahan mean by keeping alive a "moral tension" in the conscience of a woman who faces an abortion choice?

8. Would it be accurate to say that Callahan considers some acts of abortion morally justifiable? If so, under what conditions would such abortions be justifiable?

A Defense of Abortion

Judith Jarvis Thomson

In 1971 philosopher Judith Jarvis Thomson wrote an essay entitled "A Defense of Abortion." In the decade since, Thomson's article has become a classic in the literature of abortion.

What makes her treatment of the pro-choice position unique is that it begins by conceding, for the sake of argument, that the fetus is a person from the moment of conception. This concession is significant because, as Thomson points out, most opposition to abortion builds on this assumption that the unborn has person status and rights from the moment of conception.

Thomson focuses her essay on an important question: Granted that the unborn is a person from the moment of conception, does it necessarily follow that abortion is always wrong? She thinks not. Relying primarily on a series of analogies, she attacks the argument that the immorality of abortion is entailed by the premise that asserts the person status of the unborn.

Toward the end of her essay, Thomson admits that anti-abortionists might object that the immorality of abortion follows not so much from the fact that the unborn is a person as from the special relationship between the unborn and the mother. Thus, anti-abortionists claim that the unborn is a person for whom the woman has a unique kind of responsibility because she is the mother.

In responding to this claim, Thomson argues that we have no responsibility for another person unless we have assumed it. If parents do not take any birth control measures, if they do not elect an abortion, if they choose to take the child home with them from the hospital, then certainly they have a responsibility to and for the child. For they then have assumed responsibility, implicitly and explicitly, in all their actions. But if a couple has taken measures to prevent conception, this implies quite the opposite of any "special responsibility" for the unintended and unwanted fetus. Thus, in Thomson's view, the woman has no special responsibility to the unborn simply because of a biological relationship.

Ironically, as Thomson points out, many pro-choice advocates object to her argument for a couple of reasons. First, while Thomson argues that abortion is not impermissible, she does not think that it is always permissible. There may be times, for example, when carrying the child to term requires only minimal inconvenience; in such cases the woman would be required by "Minimally Decent Samaritanism" to have the child. Those supporting abortion on demand object to such a limitation of choice.

Second, while Thomson, like act utilitarians, would sanction some acts of abortion, she is not arguing for the right to kill the unborn child. That is, removing a nonviable fetus from the mother's body and thereby guaranteeing its death is not the same as removing a viable fetus from the mother's body and then killing it. In Thomson's view, the former may be permissible; the latter never is. Again, some pro-choice advocates object to this limitation of choice.

Most opposition to abortion relies on the premise that the fetus is a human being, a person, from the moment of conception. The premise is argued for, but, as I think, not well. Take, for example, the most common argument. We are asked to notice that the development of a human being from conception through birth into childhood is continuous; then it is said that to draw a line, to choose a point in this development and say "before this point the thing is not a person, after this point it is

From Judith Jarvis Thomson, "A Defense of Abortion," Philosophy and Public Affairs, 1, no. 1 (Fall 1971). Copyright ©1971 by Princeton University Press. Reprinted by permission of Princeton University Press. Ms. Thomson acknowledges her indebtedness to James Thomson for discussion, criticism, and many helpful suggestions.

a person'' is to make an arbitrary choice, a choice for which in the nature of things no good reason can be given. It is concluded that the fetus is, or anyway that we had better say it is, a person from the moment of conception. But this conclusion does not follow. Similar things might be said about the development of an acorn into an oak tree, and it does not follow that acorns are oak trees, or that we had better say they are. Arguments of this form are sometimes called ''slippery slope arguments''—the phrase is perhaps self-explanatory—and it is dismaying that opponents of abortion rely on them so heavily and uncritically.

I am inclined to agree, however, that the prospects for ''drawing a line'' in the development of the fetus looks dim. I am inclined to think also that we shall probably have to agree that the fetus has already become a human person well before birth. Indeed, it comes as a surprise when one first learns how early in its life it begins to acquire human characteristics. By the tenth week, for example, it already has a face, arms and legs, fingers and toes; it has internal organs, and brain activity is detectable.[1] On the other hand, I think that the premise is false, that the fetus is not a person from the moment of conception. A newly fertilized ovum, a newly implanted clump of cells, is no more a person than an acorn is an oak tree. But I shall not discuss any of this. For it seems to me to be of great interest to ask what happens if, for the sake of argument, we allow the premise. How, precisely, are we supposed to get from there to the conclusion that abortion is morally impermissible? Opponents of abortion commonly spend most of their time establishing that the fetus is a person, and hardly any time explaining the step from there to the impermissibility of abortion. Perhaps they think the step too simple and obvious to require much comment. Or perhaps instead they are simply being economical in argument. Many of those who defend abortion rely on the premise that the fetus is not a person, but only a bit of tissue that will become a person at birth; and why pay out more arguments than you have to? Whatever the explanation, I suggest that the step they take is neither easy nor obvious, that it calls for closer examination than it is commonly given, and that when we do give it this closer examination we shall feel inclined to reject it.

I propose, then, that we grant that the fetus is a person from the moment of conception. How does the argument go from here? Something like this, I take it. Every person has a right to life. So the fetus has a right to life. No doubt the mother has a right to decide what shall happen in and to her body; everyone would grant that. But surely a person's right to life is stronger and more stringent than the mother's right to decide what happens in and to her body, and so outweighs it. So the fetus may not be killed; an abortion may not be performed.

It sounds plausible. But now let me ask you to imagine this. You wake up in the morning and find yourself back to back in bed with an unconscious violinist. A famous unconscious violinist. He has been found to have a fatal kidney ailment, and the Society of Music Lovers has canvassed all the available medical records and found that you alone have the right blood type to help. They have therefore kidnapped you, and last night the violinist's circulatory system was plugged into yours, so that your kidneys can be used to extract poisons from his blood as well as your own. The director of the hospital now tells you, ''Look, we're sorry the Society of Music Lovers did this to you—we would never have permitted it if we had known. But still, they did it, and the violinist now is plugged into you. To unplug you would be to kill him. But never mind, it's only for nine months. By then he will have recovered from his ailment, and can safely be unplugged from you.'' Is it morally incumbent on you to accede to this situation? No doubt it would be very nice of you if you did, a great kindness. But do you *have* to accede to it? What if it were not nine months, but nine years? Or longer still? What if the director of the hospital says, ''Tough luck, I agree, but you've now got to stay in bed, with the violinist plugged into you, for the rest of your life. Because remember this. All persons have a right to life, and violinists are persons. Granted you have a right to decide what happens in and to your body, but a person's right to life outweighs your right to decide what happens in and to your body. So you cannot ever be unplugged from him.'' I imagine you would regard this as outrageous, which suggests that something really is wrong with that plausible-sounding argument I mentioned a moment ago.

In this case, of course, you were kidnapped;

you didn't volunteer for the operation that plugged the violinist into your kidneys. Can those who oppose abortion on the ground I mentioned make an exception for a pregnancy due to rape? Certainly. They can say that persons have a right to life only if they didn't come into existence because of rape; or they can say that all persons have a right to life, but that some have less of a right to life than others, in particular, that those who came into existence because of rape have less. But these statements have a rather unpleasant sound. Surely the question of whether you have a right to life at all, or how much of it you have, shouldn't turn on the question of whether or not you are the product of a rape. And in fact the people who oppose abortion on the ground I mentioned do not make this distinction, and hence do not make an exception in the case of rape.

Nor do they make an exception for a case in which the mother has to spend the nine months of her pregnancy in bed. They would agree that would be a great pity, and hard on the mother; but all the same, all persons have a right to life, the fetus is a person, and so on. I suspect, in fact, that they would not make an exception for a case in which, miraculously enough, the pregnancy went on for nine years, or even the rest of the mother's life.

Some won't even make an exception for a case in which continuation of the pregnancy is likely to shorten the mother's life; they regard abortion as impermissible even to save the mother's life. Such cases are nowadays very rare, and many opponents of abortion do not accept this extreme view. All the same, it is a good place to begin: A number of points of interest come out in respect to it.

1. Let us call the view that abortion is impermissible even to save the mother's life "the extreme view." I want to suggest first that it does not issue from the argument I mentioned earlier without the addition of some fairly powerful premises. Suppose a woman has become pregnant, and now learns that she has a cardiac condition such that she will die if she carries the baby to term. What may be done for her? The fetus, being a person, has a right to life, but as the mother is a person too, so has she a right to life. Presumably they have an equal right to life. How is it supposed to come out that an abortion may not be performed? If mother and child have an equal right to life,

shouldn't we perhaps flip a coin? Or should we add to the mother's right to life her right to decide what happens in and to her body, which everybody seems to be ready to grant—the sum of her rights now outweighing the fetus' right to life?

The most familiar argument here is the following. We are told that performing the abortion would be directly killing[2] the child, whereas doing nothing would not be killing the mother, but only letting her die. Moreover, in killing the child, one would be killing an innocent person, for the child has committed no crime, and is not aiming at his mother's death. And then there are a variety of ways in which this might be continued. (1) But as directly killing an innocent person is always and absolutely impermissible, an abortion may not be performed. Or, (2) as directly killing an innocent person is murder, and murder is always and absolutely impermissible, an abortion may not be performed.[3] Or, (3) as one's duty to refrain from directly killing an innocent person is more stringent than one's duty to keep a person from dying, an abortion may not be performed. Or, (4) if one's only options are directly killing an innocent person or letting a person die, one must prefer letting the person die, and thus an abortion may not be performed.[4]

Some people seem to have thought that these are not further premises which must be added if the conclusion is to be reached, but that they follow from the very fact that an innocent person has a right to life.[5] But this seems to me to be a mistake, and perhaps the simplest way to show this is to bring out that while we must certainly grant that innocent persons have a right to life, the theses in (1) through (4) are all false. Take (2), for example. If directly killing an innocent person is murder, and thus is impermissible, then the mother's directly killing the innocent persons inside her is murder, and thus is impermissible. But it cannot seriously be thought to be murder if the mother performs an abortion on herself to save her life. It cannot seriously be said that she *must* refrain, that she *must* sit passively by and wait for her death. Let us look again at the case of you and the violinist. There you are, in bed with the violinist, and the director of the hospital says to you, "It's all most distressing, and I deeply sympathize, but you see this is putting an additional strain on your kidneys, and you'll be dead within the month. But you *have* to stay where you are all the same. Because unplug-ging you would be directly killing an innocent violinist, and that's murder, and that's impermis-sible." If anything in the world is true, it is that you do not commit murder, you do not do what is impermissible, if you reach around to your back and unplug yourself from that violinist to save your life.

The main focus of attention in writings on abortion has been on what a third party may or may not do in answer to a request from a woman for an abortion. This is in a way understandable. Things being as they are, there isn't much a woman can safely do to abort herself. So the ques-tion asked is what a third party may do, and what the mother may do, if it is mentioned at all, is deduced, almost as an afterthought, from what it is concluded that third parties may do. But it seems to me that to treat the matter in this way is to refuse to grant to the mother that very status of person which is so firmly insisted on for the fetus. For we cannot simply read off what a person may do from what a third party may do. Suppose you find yourself trapped in a tiny house with a grow-ing child. I mean a very tiny house, and a rapidly growing child—you are already up against the wall of the house and in a few minutes you'll be crushed to death. The child on the other hand won't be crushed to death; if nothing is done to stop him from growing he'll be hurt, but in the end he'll simply burst open the house and walk out a free man. Now I could well understand it if a bystander were to say, "There's nothing we can do for you. We cannot choose between your life and his, we cannot be the ones to decide who is to live, we cannot intervene." But it cannot be concluded that you too can do nothing, that you cannot at-tack it to save your life. However innocent the child may be, you do not have to wait passively while it crushes you to death. Perhaps a pregnant woman is vaguely felt to have the status of house, to which we don't allow the right of self-defense. But if the woman houses the child, it should be remembered that she is a person who houses it.

I should perhaps stop to say explicitly that I am not claiming that people have a right to do anything whatever to save their lives. I think, rather, that there are drastic limits to the right of self-defense. If someone threatens you with death unless you torture someone else to death, I think

you have not the right, even to save your life, to do so. But the case under consideration here is very different. In our case there are only two people involved, one whose life is threatened, and one who threatens it. Both are innocent: The one who is threatened is not threatened because of any fault, the one who threatens does not threaten because of any fault. For this reason we may feel that we bystanders cannot intervene. But the per-son threatened can.

In sum, a woman surely can defend her life against the threat to it posed by the unborn child, even if doing so involves its death. And this shows not merely that the theses in (1) through (4) are false; it shows also that the extreme view of abor-tion is false, and so we need not canvass any other possible ways of arriving at it from the argument I mentioned at the outset.

2. The extreme view could of course be weakened to say that while abortion is permissible to save the mother's life, it may not be performed by a third party, but only by the mother herself. But this cannot be right either. For what we have to keep in mind is that the mother and the unborn child are not like two tenants in a small house which has, by an unfortunate mistake, been rent-ed to both: The mother *owns* the house. The fact that she does adds to the offensiveness of deduc-ing that the mother can do nothing from the sup-position that third parties can do nothing. But it does more than this: It casts a bright light on the supposition that third parties can do nothing. Cer-tainly it lets us see that a third party who says "I cannot choose between you" is fooling himself if he thinks this is impartiality. If Jones has found and fastened on a certain coat, which he needs to keep him from freezing, but which Smith also needs to keep him from freezing, then it is not impartiality that says "I cannot choose between you" when Smith owns the coat. Women have said again and again "This body is *my* body!" and they have reason to feel angry, reason to feel that it has been like shouting into the wind. Smith, after all, is hardly likely to bless us if we say to him, "Of course it's your coat, anybody would grant that it is. But no one may choose between you and Jones who is to have it."

We should really ask what it is that says "no one may choose" in the face of the fact that the body that houses the child is the mother's body. It may be simply a failure to appreciate this fact. But it may be something more interesting, namely the sense that one has a right to refuse to lay hands on people, even where it would be just and fair to do so, even where justice seems to require that somebody do so. Thus justice might call for somebody to get Smith's coat back from Jones, and yet you have a right to refuse to be the one to lay hands on Jones, a right to refuse to do physical violence to him. This, I think, must be granted. But then what should be said is not "no one may choose," but only "*I* cannot choose," and indeed not even this, but "*I* will not *act*," leaving it open that somebody else can or should, and in particular that anyone in a position of authority, with the job of securing people's rights, both can and should. So this is no difficulty. I have not been arguing that any given third party must accede to the mother's request that he perform an abortion to save her life, but only that he may.

I suppose that in some views of human life the mother's body is only on loan to her, the loan not being one which gives her any prior claim to it. One who held this view might well think it impartiality to say "I cannot choose." But I shall simply ignore this possibility. My own view is that if a human being has any just, prior claim to anything at all, he has a just, prior claim to his own body. And perhaps this needn't be argued for here anyway, since, as I mentioned, the arguments against abortion we are looking at do grant that the woman has a right to decide what happens in and to her body.

But although they do grant it, I have tried to show that they do not take seriously what is done in granting it. I suggest the same thing will reappear even more clearly when we turn away from cases in which the mother's life is at stake, and attend, as I propose we now do, to the vastly more common cases in which a woman wants an abortion for some less weighty reason than preserving her own life.

3. Where the mother's life is not at stake, the argument I mentioned at the outset seems to have a much stronger pull. "Everyone has a right to life, so the unborn person has a right to life." And isn't the child's right to life weightier than anything other than the mother's own right to life, which she might put forward as ground for an abortion?

This argument treats the right to life as if it were unproblematic. It is not, and this seems to me to be precisely the source of the mistake.

For we should now, at long last, ask what it comes to, to have a right to life. In some views having a right to life includes having a right to be given at least the bare minimum one needs for continued life. But suppose that what in fact *is* the bare minimum a man needs for continued life is something he has no right at all to be given? If I am sick unto death, and the only thing that will save my life is the touch of Henry Fonda's cool hand on my fevered brow, then all the same, I have no right to be given the touch of Henry Fonda's cool hand on my fevered brow. It would be frightfully nice of him to fly in from the West Coast to provide it. It would be less nice, though no doubt well meant, if my friends flew out to the West Coast and carried Henry Fonda back with them. But I have no right at all against anybody that he should do this for me. Or again, to return to the story I told earlier, the fact that for continued life that violinist needs the continued use of your kidneys does not establish that he has a right to be given the continued use of your kidneys. He certainly has no right against you that *you* should give him continued use of your kidneys. For nobody has any right to use your kidneys unless you give him such a right; and nobody has the right against you that you shall give him this right—if you do allow him to go on using your kidneys, this is a kindness on your part, and not something he can claim from you as his due. Nor has he any right against anybody else that *they* should give him continued use of your kidneys. Certainly he had no right against the Society of Music Lovers that they should plug him into you in the first place. And if you now start to unplug yourself, having learned that you will otherwise have to spend nine years in bed with him, there is nobody in the world who must try to prevent you, in order to see to it that he is given something he has a right to be given.

Some people are rather stricter about the right to life. In their view, it does not include the right to be given anything, but amounts to, and only to, the right not to be killed by anybody. But here a related difficulty arises. If everybody is to refrain from killing that violinist, then everybody must refrain from doing a great many different sorts of things. Everybody must refrain from slitting his throat, everybody must refrain from shooting him—and everybody must refrain from unplugging you from him. But does he have a right against everybody that they shall refrain from unplugging you from him? To refrain from doing this is to allow him to continue to use your kidneys. It could be argued that he has a right against us that *we* should allow him to continue to use your kidneys. That is, while he had no right against us that we should give him the use of your kidneys, it might be argued that he anyway has a right against us that we shall not now intervene and deprive him of the use of your kidneys. I shall come back to third-party interventions later. But certainly the violinist has no right against you that *you* shall allow him to continue to use your kidneys. As I said, if you do allow him to use them, it is a kindness on your part, and not something you owe him.

The difficulty I point to here is not peculiar to the right of life. It reappears in connection with all the other natural rights; and it is something which an adequate account of rights must deal with. For present purposes it is enough just to draw attention to it. But I would stress that I am not arguing that people do not have a right to life—quite to the contrary, it seems to me that the primary control we must place on the acceptability of an account of rights is that it should turn out in that account to be a truth that all persons have a right to life. I am arguing only that having a right to life does not guarantee having either a right to be given the use of or a right to be allowed continued use of another person's body—even if one needs it for life itself. So the right to life will not serve the opponents of abortion in the very simple and clear way in which they seem to have thought it would.

4. There is another way to bring out the difficulty. In the most ordinary sort of case, to deprive someone of what he has a right to is to treat him unjustly. Suppose a boy and his small brother are jointly given a box of chocolates for Christmas. If the older boy takes the box and refuses to give his brother any of the chocolates, he is unjust to him, for the brother has been given a right to half of them. But suppose that, having learned that otherwise it means nine years in bed with that violinist, you unplug yourself from him. You surely are not being unjust to him, for you gave him no right to use your kidneys, and no one else can have given him any such right. But we have to notice that in unplugging yourself, you are killing

him; and violinists, like everybody else, have a right to life, and thus in the view we were considering just now, the right not to be killed. So here you do what he supposedly has a right you shall not do, but you do not act unjustly to him in doing it.

The emendation which may be made at this point is this: The right to life consists not in the right not to be killed, but rather in the right not to be killed unjustly. This runs a risk of circularity, but never mind: It would enable us to square the fact that the violinist has a right to life with the fact that you do not act unjustly toward him in unplugging yourself, thereby killing him. For if you do not kill him unjustly, you do not violate his right to life, and so it is no wonder you do him no injustice.

But if this emendation is accepted, the gap in the argument against abortion stares us plainly in the face: It is by no means enough to show that the fetus is a person, and to remind us that all persons have a right to life—we need to be shown also that killing the fetus violates its right to life, i.e., that abortion is unjust killing. And is it?

I suppose we may take it as a datum that in the case of pregnancy due to rape the mother has not given the unborn person a right to the use of her body for food and shelter. Indeed, in what pregnancy should it be supposed that the mother has given the unborn person such a right? It is not as if there were unborn persons drifting about the world, to whom a woman who wants a child says "I invite you in."

But it might be argued that there are other ways one can have acquired a right to the use of another person's body than by having been invited to use it by that person. Suppose a woman voluntarily indulges in intercourse, knowing of the chance it will issue in pregnancy, and then she does become pregnant; is she not in part responsible for the presence, in fact the very existence, of the unborn person inside? No doubt she did not invite it in. But doesn't her partial responsibility for its being there itself give it a right to the use of her body?[6] If so, then her aborting it would be more like the boy's taking away the chocolates, and less like your unplugging yourself from the violinist—doing so would be depriving it of what it does have a right to, and thus would be doing it an injustice.

And then, too, it might be asked whether or

not she can kill it even to save her own life: If she voluntarily called it into existence, how can she now kill it, even in self-defense?

The first thing to be said about this is that it is something new. Opponents of abortion have been so concerned to make out the independence of the fetus, in order to establish that it has a right to life, just as its mother does, that they have tended to overlook the possible support they might gain from making out that the fetus is *dependent* on the mother, in order to establish that she has a special kind of responsibility for it, a responsibility that gives it rights against her which are not possessed by any independent person—such as an ailing violinist who is a stranger to her.

On the other hand, this argument would give the unborn person a right to its mother's body only if her pregnancy resulted from a voluntary act, undertaken in full knowledge of the chance a pregnancy might result from it. It would leave out entirely the unborn person whose existence is due to rape. Pending the availability of some further argument, then, we would be left with the conclusion that unborn persons whose existence is due to rape have no right to the use of their mothers' bodies, and thus that aborting them is not depriving them of anything they have a right to and hence is not unjust killing.

And we should also notice that it is not at all plain that this argument really does go even as far as it purports to. For there are cases and cases, and the details make a difference. If the room is stuffy, and I therefore open a window to air it, and a burglar climbs in, it would be absurd to say, "Ah, now he can stay, she's given him a right to the use of her house—for she is partially responsible for his presence there, having voluntarily done what enabled him to get in, in full knowledge that there are such things as burglars, and that burglars burgle." It would be still more absurd to say this if I had had bars installed outside my windows, precisely to prevent burglars from getting in, and a burglar got in only because of a defect in the bars. It remains equally absurd if we imagine it is not a burglar who climbs in, but an innocent person who blunders or falls in. Again, suppose it were like this: Peopleseeds drift about in the air like pollen, and if you open your windows, one may drift in and take root in your carpets or upholstery. You don't want children, so you fix up your windows with fine mesh screens, the very best you

can buy. As can happen, however, and on very, very rare occasions does happen, one of the screens is defective; and a seed drifts in and takes root. Does the personplant who now develops have a right to the use of your house? Surely not—despite the fact that you voluntarily opened your windows, you knowingly kept carpets and upholstered furniture, and you knew that screens were sometimes defective. Someone may argue that you are responsible for its rooting, that it does have a right to your house, because after all you *could* have lived out your life with bare floors and furniture, or with sealed windows and doors. But this won't do—for by the same token anyone can avoid a pregnancy due to rape by having a hysterectomy, or anyway by never leaving home without a (reliable!) army.

It seems to me that the argument we are looking at can establish at most that there are *some* cases in which the unborn person has a right to the use of its mother's body, and therefore *some* cases in which abortion is unjust killing. There is room for much discussion and argument as to precisely which, if any. But I think we should sidestep this issue and leave it open, for at any rate the argument certainly does not establish that all abortion is unjust killing.

5. There is room for yet another argument here, however. We surely must all grant that there may be cases in which it would be morally indecent to detach a person from your body at the cost of his life. Suppose you learn that what the violinist needs is not nine years of your life, but only one hour: All you need do to save his life is spend one hour in that bed with him. Suppose also that letting him use your kidneys for that one hour would not affect your health in the slightest. Admittedly you were kidnapped. Admittedly you did not give anyone permission to plug him into you. Nevertheless it seems to me plain you *ought* to allow him to use your kidneys for that hour—it would be indecent to refuse.

Again, suppose pregnancy lasted only an hour, and constituted no threat to life or death. And suppose that a woman becomes pregnant as a result of rape. Admittedly she did not voluntarily do anything to bring about the existence of a child. Admittedly she did nothing at all which would give the unborn person a right to the use of her body. All the same it might well be said, as in the newly emended violinist story, that she *ought* to allow it to remain for that hour—that it would be indecent in her to refuse.

Now some people are inclined to use the term "right" in such a way that it follows from the fact that you ought to allow a person to use your body for the hour he needs, that he has a right to use your body for the hour that he needs, even though he has not been given that right by any person or act. They may say that it follows also that if you refuse, you act unjustly toward him. This use of the term is perhaps so common that it cannot be called wrong; nevertheless it seems to me to be an unfortunate loosening of what we would do better to keep a tight rein on. Suppose that box of chocolates I mentioned earlier had not been given to both boys jointly, but was given only to the older boy. There he sits, stolidly eating his way through the box, his small brother watching enviously. Here we are likely to say "You ought not to be so mean. You ought to give your brother some of those chocolates." My own view is that it just does not follow from the truth of this that the brother has any right to any of the chocolates. If the boy refuses to give his brother any, he is greedy, stingy, callous—but not unjust. I suppose that the people I have in mind will say it does follow that the brother has a right to some of the chocolates, and thus that the boy does act unjustly if he refuses to give his brother any. But the effect of saying this is to obscure what we should keep distinct, namely the difference between the boy's refusal in this case and the boy's refusal in the earlier case, in which the box was given to both boys jointly, and in which the small brother thus had what was from any point of view clear title to half.

A further objection to so using the term "right" that from the fact that A ought to do a thing for B, it follows that B has a right against A that A do it for him, is that it is going to make the question of whether or not a man has a right to a thing turn on how easy it is to provide him with it; and this seems not merely unfortunate, but morally unacceptable. Take the case of Henry Fonda again. I said earlier that I had no right to the touch of his cool hand on my fevered brow, even though I needed it to save my life. I said it would be frightfully nice of him to fly in from the West Coast to provide me with it, but that I had no right against him that he should do so. But suppose he isn't on the West Coast. Suppose he has only to walk across the room, place a hand briefly on my brow—and lo, my life is saved. Then surely he ought to do it, it would be indecent to refuse. Is it to be said, "Ah, well, it follows that in this case she has a right to the touch of his hand on her brow, and so it would be an unjustice in him to refuse"? So that I have a right to it when it is easy for him to provide it, though no right when it's hard? It's rather a shocking idea that anyone's right should fade away and disappear as it gets harder and harder to accord them to him.

So my own view is that even though you ought to let the violinist use your kidneys for the one hour he needs, we should not conclude that he has a right to do so—we should say that if you refuse, you are, like the boy who owns all the chocolates and will give none away, self-centered and callous, indecent in fact, but not unjust. And similarly, that even supposing a case in which a woman pregnant due to rape ought to allow the unborn person to use her body for the hour he needs, we should not conclude that he has a right to do so; we should conclude that she is self-centered, callous, indecent, but not unjust, if she refuses. The complaints are no less grave; they are just different. However, there is no need to insist on this point. If anyone does wish to deduce "he has a right" from "you ought," then all the same he must surely grant that there are cases in which it is not morally required of you that you allow that violinist to use your kidneys, and in which he does not have a right to use them, and in which you do not do him an injustice if you refuse. And so also for mother and unborn child. Except in such cases as the unborn person has a right to demand it—and we were leaving open the possibility that there may be such cases—nobody is morally *required* to make large sacrifices, of health, of all other interests and concerns, of all other duties and commitments, for nine years, or even for nine months, in order to keep another person alive.

6. We have in fact to distinguish between the two kinds of Samaritan: the Good Samaritan and what we might call the Minimally Decent Samaritan. The story of the Good Samaritan, you will remember, goes like this:

> A certain man went down from Jerusalem to
> Jericho, and fell among thieves, which
> stripped him of his raiment, and wounded
> him, and departed, leaving him half dead.
> And by chance there came down a certain

priest that way; and when he saw him, he passed by on the other side.

And likewise a Levite, when he was at the place, came and looked on him, and passed by on the other side.

But a certain Samaritan, as he journeyed, came where he was; and when he saw him he had compassion on him.

And went to him, and bound up his wounds, pouring in oil and wine, and set him on his own beast, and brought him to an inn, and took care of him.

And on the morrow, when he departed, he took out two pence, and gave them to the host, and said unto him, "Take care of him; and whatsoever thou spendest more, when I come again, I will repay thee."

(Luke 10:30–35)

The Good Samaritan went out of his way, at some cost to himself, to help one in need of it. We are not told what the options were, that is, whether or not the priest and the Levite could have helped by doing less than the Good Samaritan did, but assuming they could have, then the fact they did nothing at all shows they were not even Minimally Decent Samaritans, not because they were not Samaritans, but because they were not even minimally decent.

These things are a matter of degree, of course, but there is a difference, and it comes out perhaps most clearly in the story of Kitty Genovese, who, as you will remember, was murdered while thirty-eight people watched or listened, and did nothing at all to help her. A Good Samaritan would have rushed out to give direct assistance against the murderer. Or perhaps we had better allow that it would have been a Splendid Samaritan who did this, on the ground that it would have involved a risk of death for himself. But the thirty-eight not only did not do this, they did not even trouble to pick up a phone to call the police. Minimally Decent Samaritanism would call for doing at least that, and their not having done it was monstrous.

After telling the story of the Good Samaritan, Jesus said, "Go, and do thou likewise." Perhaps he meant that we are morally required to act as the Good Samaritan did. Perhaps he was urging people to do more than is morally required of them. At all events it seems plain that it was not morally required of any of the thirty-eight that he rush out to give direct assistance at the risk of his own life, and that it is not morally required of anyone that he give long stretches of his life—nine years or nine months—to sustaining the life of a person who has no special right (we were leaving open the possibility of this) to demand it.

Indeed, with one rather striking class of exceptions, no one in any country in the world is *legally* required to do anywhere near as much as this for anyone else. The class of exceptions is obvious. My main concern here is not the state of the law in respect to abortion, but it is worth drawing attention to the fact that in no state in this country is any man compelled by law to be even a Minimally Decent Samaritan to any person; there is no law under which charges could be brought against the thirty-eight who stood by while Kitty Genovese died. By contrast, in most states in this country women are compelled by law to be not merely Minimally Decent Samaritans, but Good Samaritans to unborn persons inside them. This doesn't by itself settle anything one way or the other, because it may well be argued that there should be laws in this country—as there are in many European countries—compelling at least Minimally Decent Samaritanism.[7] But it does show that there is a gross injustice in the existing state of the law. And it shows also that the groups currently working against liberalization of abortion laws, in fact working toward having it declared unconstitutional for a state to permit abortion, had better start working for the adoption of Good Samaritan laws generally, or earn the charge that they are acting in bad faith.

I should think, myself, that Minimally Decent Samaritan laws would be one thing, Good Samaritan laws quite another, and in fact highly improper. But we are not here concerned with the law. What we should ask is not whether anybody should be compelled by law to be a Good Samaritan, but whether we must accede to a situation in which somebody is being compelled—by nature, perhaps—to be a Good Samaritan. We have, in other words, to look now at third-party interventions. I have been arguing that no person is morally required to make large sacrifices to sustain the life of another who has no right to demand them, and this even where the sacrifices do not include life itself; we are not morally required to be Good Samaritans or anyway Very Good Samaritans to one another. But what if a man cannot extricate himself from such a situation? What if he appeals to us to extricate him? It seems to me plain that there are cases in which we can, cases in which a Good Samaritan would extricate him. There you are, you were kidnapped, and nine years in bed with that violinist lie ahead of you. You have your own life to lead. You are sorry, but you simply cannot see giving up so much of your life to the sustaining of his. You cannot extricate yourself, and ask us to do so. I should have thought that—in light of his having no right to the use of your body—it was obvious that we do not have to accede to your being forced to give up so much. We can do what you ask. There is no injustice to the violinist in our doing so.

7. Following the lead of the opponents of abortion, I have throughout been speaking of the fetus merely as a person, and what I have been asking is whether or not the argument we began with, which proceeds only from the fetus' being a person, really does establish its conclusion. I have argued that it does not.

But of course there are arguments and arguments, and it may be said that I have simply fastened on the wrong one. It may be said that what is important is not merely the fact that the fetus is a person, but that it is a person for whom the woman has a special kind of responsibility issuing from the fact that she is its mother. And it might be argued that all my analogies are therefore irrelevant—for you do not have that special kind of responsibility for that violinist, Henry Fonda does not have that special kind of responsibility for me. And our attention might be drawn to the fact that men and women both *are* compelled by law to provide support for their children.

I have in effect dealt (briefly) with this argument in section 4 above; but a (still briefer) recapitulation now may be in order. Surely we do not have any such "special responsibility" for a person unless we have assumed it, explicitly or implicitly. If a set of parents do not try to prevent pregnancy, do not obtain an abortion, but rather take it home with them, then they have assumed responsibility for it, they have given it rights, and they cannot *now* withdraw support from it at the cost of its life because they now find it difficult to go on providing for it. But if they have taken all reasonable precautions against having a child, they do not simply by virtue of their biological relationship to the child who comes into existence have a special

responsibility for it. They may wish to assume responsibility for it, or they may not wish to. And I am suggesting that if assuming responsibility for it would require large sacrifices, then they may refuse. A Good Samaritan would not refuse—or anyway, a Splendid Samaritan, if the sacrifices that had to be made were enormous. But then so would a Good Samaritan assume responsibility for that violinist; so would Henry Fonda, if he is a Good Samaritan, fly in from the West Coast and assume responsibility for me.

8. My argument will be found unsatisfactory on two counts by many of those who want to regard abortion as morally permissible. First, while I do argue that abortion is not impermissible, I do not argue that it is always permissible. There may well be cases in which carrying the child to term requires only Minimally Decent Samaritanism of the mother, and this is a standard we must not fall below. I am inclined to think it a merit of my account precisely that it does *not* give a general yes or a general no. It allows for and supports our sense that, for example, a sick and desperately frightened fourteen-year-old schoolgirl, pregnant due to rape, may of *course* choose abortion, and that any law which rules this out is an insane law. And it also allows for and supports our sense that in other cases resort to abortion is even positively indecent. It would be indecent in the woman to request an abortion, and indecent in a doctor to perform it, if she is in her seventh month, and wants the abortion just to avoid the nuisance of postponing a trip abroad. The very fact that the arguments I have been drawing attention to treat all cases of abortion, or even all cases of abortion in which the mother's life is not at stake, as morally on a par ought to have made them suspect at the outset.

Secondly, while I am arguing for the permissibility of abortion in some cases, I am not arguing for the right to secure the death of the unborn child. It is easy to confuse these two things in that up to a certain point in the life of the fetus it is not able to survive outside the mother's body; hence removing it from her body guarantees its death. But they are importantly different. I have argued that you are not morally required to spend nine months in bed, sustaining the life of that violinist; but to say this is by no means to say that if, when you unplug yourself, there is a miracle and he survives, you then have a right to turn around and slit his throat. You may detach yourself even if this costs him his life; you have no right to be guaranteed his death, by some other means, if unplugging yourself does not kill him. There are some people who will feel dissatisfied by this feature of my argument. A woman may be utterly devastated by the thought of a child, a bit of herself, put out for adoption and never seen or heard of again. She may therefore want not merely that the child be detached from her, but more, that it die. Some opponents of abortion are inclined to regard this as beneath contempt—thereby showing insensitivity to what is surely a powerful source of despair. All the same, I agree that the desire for the child's death is not one which anybody may gratify, should it turn out to be possible to detach the child alive.

At this place, however, it should be remembered that we have only been pretending throughout that the fetus is a human being from the moment of conception. A very early abortion is surely not the killing of a person, and so is not dealt with by anything I have said here.

Notes

1. Daniel Callahan, *Abortion: Law, Choice and Morality* (New York, 1970), p. 373. This book gives a fascinating survey of the available information on abortion. The Jewish tradition is surveyed in David M. Feldman, *Birth Control in Jewish Law* (New York, 1963), part 5, the Catholic tradition in John T. Noonan, Jr., "An Almost Absolute Value in History," in *The Morality of Abortion*, ed. John T. Noonan, Jr. (Cambridge, Mass., 1970).

2. The term "direct" in the arguments I refer to is a technical one. Roughly, what is meant by "direct killing" is either killing as an end in itself, or killing as a means to some end, for example, the end of saving someone else's life. See note 5 on this page, for an example of its use.

3. Cf. *Encyclical Letter of Pope Pius XI on Christian Marriage*, St. Paul Editions (Boston, n.d.), p. 32: "However much we may pity the mother whose health and even life is gravely imperiled in the performance of the duty allotted to her by nature, nevertheless what could ever be a sufficient reason for excusing in any way the direct murder of the innocent? This is precisely what we are dealing with here." Noonan (*The Morality of Abortion*, p. 43) reads this as follows: "What cause can ever avail to excuse in any way the direct killing of the innocent? For it is a question of that."

4. The thesis in (4) is in an interesting way weaker than those in (1), (2), and (3): They rule out abortion even in cases in which both mother *and* child will die if the abortion is not performed. By contrast, one who held the view expressed in (4) could consistently say that one needn't prefer letting two persons die to killing one.

5. Cf. the following passage from Pius XII, *Address to the Italian Catholic Society of Midwives:* "The baby in the maternal breast has the right to life immediately from God. —Hence there is no man, no human authority, no science, no medical, eugenic, social, economic or moral 'indication' which can establish or grant a valid juridical ground for a direct deliberate disposition of an innocent human life, that is a disposition which looks to its destruction either as an end or as a means to another end perhaps in itself not illicit. —The baby, still not born, is a man in the same degree and for the same reason as the mother" (quoted in Noonan, *The Morality of Abortion*, p. 45).

6. The need for a discussion of this argument was brought home to me by members of the Society for Ethical and Legal Philosophy, to whom this paper was orginally presented.

7. For a discussion of the difficulties involved, and a survey of the European experience with such laws, see *The Good Samaritan and the Law*, ed. James M. Ratcliffe (New York, 1966).

Questions for Analysis

1. *Does the belief that abortion is always impermissible necessarily result from the argument that the unborn is a person from the moment of conception? If not, what additional premises are necessary?*

2. *Why does Thomson conclude that "a woman surely can defend her life against the threat to it posed by the unborn child, even if doing so involves its death"?*

3. *How does Thomson answer the claim that the unborn's right to life weighs more (in the moral sense) than anything other than the mother's own right to life?*

4. *Does Thomson feel that there may be cases in which it would be wrong for a woman to have an abortion? Explain.*

5. *Distinguish between a "Good Samaritan" and a "Minimally Decent Samaritan."*

CASE PRESENTATION
A Bundle of Grief

"But can't you tell for sure?" the young woman asked the doctor desperately.

The doctor shook his head and said, "Not for sure."

The woman buried her head in her hands and sobbed. The doctor did what he could to comfort her, but she seemed inconsolable.

Finally, her face wet with tears and her voice breaking, the woman muttered, "It's really ironic, isn't it?" Then she laughed bitterly.

She didn't have to explain. The doctor knew what she meant. For some time the woman who sat before him—33-year-old Fran Jeffries—and her 40-year-old husband Bill had been trying to have a baby. It was important to them, not only because they had no children but because they were quickly reaching the age when, for a number of medical and nonmedical reasons, having a family simply wouldn't be prudent. And now, at long last, Fran was pregnant. But what should have been a moment of great exaltation was in fact a time of grief, worry, and despair.

"If only—" Fran began.

Before she could go on, the doctor interrupted her. "Now you must stop berating yourself, Fran," he said firmly. "You had no control over what happened."

Of course she hadn't. She had by chance been in the wrong place at the wrong time. As a result she'd been raped. Fran had told no one except the doctor, and him only when she learned she was pregnant, a fact that she was still concealing from Bill.

"I don't know what to do," Fran kept saying, twisting a tissue until it was only dust in her lap.

"The first thing you must do is tell Bill everything," the doctor said.

Fran smiled. "He wants a baby more than anything else in the world," she said. "Who knows—maybe this will be our only opportunity."

"So what are you saying?" the doctor asked. "That it's better to let him believe the baby's his?"

"It could be, couldn't it?"

The doctor nodded. "Still," he said, "don't you think Bill should have a voice in the decision?"

"But what if he says no?"

"If both of you want to abort the pregnancy, we can do that."

Fran thought for awhile before saying, "What's there to be gained by telling him? Isn't it enough that one of us has to agonize over this?"

"Maybe you have a point," the doctor agreed. "But I don't see why you should have to shoulder the whole burden."

The young woman smiled. "The burden is the price I pay for the only certainty in this whole sordid affair."

"What's that?" the doctor asked her.

"That I'm the mother," she said.

Questions for Analysis

1. Do you think that an abortion is justified in cases of rape?

2. Do you think that Fran would act morally if she had an abortion without informing Bill of anything?

3. Suppose that Fran informs Bill. Together they decide Fran should have the abortion. Do you think the abortion would then be morally justified?

4. Do you think Fran would be acting immorally if she goes ahead with the pregnancy while allowing Bill to believe that he is without doubt the father?

5. Do you think that fathers have any rights in abortion decisions? If they do, do you think that their rights are as morally significant as the mother's? Would you say that a father's right to decide the disposition of the unborn overrides the mother's right when a conflict exists between their wishes?

6. Suppose Fran refuses to inform Bill. Do you think that the doctor would have a moral obligation to inform him?

7. In many states a physician must report a minor's request for an abortion to the girl's parents or guardians. Do you think such a law is morally justified?

CASE PRESENTATION
Setting Priorities

Gail Belle was a dental hygienist. Her husband Mike was a chemical engineer. Both were in their twenties and had been married four years. Early in their marriage, Gail and Mike had decided that their careers and the opportunities for travel and personal enrichment that two salaries would afford were more important to them than having a family. They couldn't have been happier with their way of life.

Then Gail got pregnant. The Belles assumed that it had happened during the time that Gail was off the pill and using a diaphragm. But, as the Belles well knew, how it happened was immaterial. The question was, what should they do?

Immediately on learning of her pregnancy, Gail decided she wanted an abortion. Mike agreed. But it wasn't long before doubts set in.

"Maybe a child wouldn't be such a bad idea," Gail thought at one point.

Mike didn't dispute that, but he did catalogue all the things that would change were they to have a child. Gail didn't like that part of it at all.

The upshot of their uncertainty was that about four-and-a-half months passed before the Belles made up their minds to have the abortion.

"I can and will do it," Gail's doctor told her, "but first I want you to be interviewed by a counselor."

"Don't you think I know my own mind?" Gail asked.

"Of course I do," the doctor assured her. "It's just routine in abortion cases."

The interview wasn't at all bad. In fact, it helped to crystallize for the Belles the reasons they were having the abortion. First, they faced the fact that they wanted an abortion primarily for matters of personal convenience. Second, the issue of whether or not the unborn was a person was irrelevant to them. And third, they recognized that, in their view, one and only one condition would ever justify their having a child—if they both wanted it. As Gail said at the end of the session: "I'm convinced that an unwanted baby should never be born." Mike agreed.

So preparations for the abortion were made. Shortly thereafter Gail had the abortion and the Belles returned to what they called "normal living."

Questions for Analysis

1. *Do you think abortions for reasons of personal convenience are morally justified?*

2. *Do you agree that an unwanted baby should never be born?*

3. *Suppose you were the counselor that interviewed the Belles. What points would you bring up that would be relevant to the Belles's situation?*

4. *Do you think that doctors have a moral obligation to set aside their own views on abortion and honor the wishes of their patients?*

5. *Do you think that the age of the unborn—the time since conception—in any way affects the morality of an abortion?*

Selections for Further Reading

Callahan, Daniel J. *Abortion: Law, Choice, and Morality.* New York: Macmillan, 1970.

Dickens, Bernard H. *Abortion and the Law.* Bristol, England: MacGibbon and Kee Ltd., 1966.

Ehrlich, Paul. *The Population Bomb.* New York: Ballantine, 1968.

Feinberg, Joel. *The Problem of Abortion.* Belmont, Calif.: Wadsworth, 1973.

Gebhard, Paul H., W. B. Pomeroy, C. E. Martin, and C. V. Christenson. *Pregnancy, Birth and Abortion.* New York: Harper & Row, 1958.

Granfield, David. *The Abortion Decision.* Garden City, N.Y.: Doubleday, 1969.

Group for the Advancement of Psychiatry: Committee on Psychiatry and Law. *The Right to Abortion: A Psychiatric View.* New York: Scribner's, 1970.

Guttmacher, Allan F., Ed. *The Case for Legalized Abortions Now.* Berkeley, Calif.: Diablo Press, 1967.

Hall, Robert E. *Abortion in a Changing World.* Vols. I and II. New York: Columbia University Press, 1970.

Huser, Roger J. *The Crime of Abortion in Common Law.* Canon Law Studies No. 162. Washington, D.C.: Catholic University Press, 1942.

Lader, Lawrence. *Abortion.* Indianapolis: Bobbs-Merrill, 1966.

Noonan, John T. *The Morality of Abortion: Legal and Historical Perspectives.* Cambridge, Mass.: Harvard University Press, 1970.

St. John-Stevas, Norman. *The Right to Life.* New York: Holt, Rinehart, and Winston, 1964.

6
EUTHANASIA

The case of Karen Ann Quinlan has probably done more than any other in recent years to rivet public attention on the legal and moral aspects of euthanasia, which generally refers to the act of painlessly putting to death a person suffering from an incurable disease. Although the Quinlan case was so widely publicized, it was not the only instance in which the question of euthanasia has been raised.

In fact, improvements in biomedical technology have made euthanasia an issue that more and more individuals and institutions must confront and that society must address. Respirators, artificial kidneys, intravenous feeding, new drugs—all have made it possible to sustain an individual's life artificially, that is, long after the individual has lost the capacity to sustain life independently. In cases like Quinlan's, individuals have fallen into a state of irreversible coma, what some term a vegetative state. In other instances, as for example after severe accidents or with congenital brain disease, the individual's consciousness has been so dulled and the personality has so deteriorated that the individual lacks the capacity for development and growth. In still other cases, such as with terminal cancer, individuals vacillate between agonizing pain and a drug-induced stupor, with no possibility of ever again enjoying life. Not too long ago, "nature would have taken its course"; such individuals would have died. Today we have the technological capacity to keep them alive artificially. Ought we? Or, at least in some instances, are we justified in not doing this, even obliged not to?

As with other issues we have discussed (that is, abortion and pornography), euthanasia raises two basic moral issues that must be distinguished. The first deals with the morality of euthanasia itself; the second concerns the morality of euthanasia legislation. We will consider both questions in this chapter.

Before discussing the arguments related to these questions, we must clarify a number of conceptual issues central to euthanasia. Among them are: the distinctions between "killing" and "allowing to die," the various meanings of *euthanasia*, and the difference between "voluntary" and "nonvoluntary" euthanasia. With these behind us, we can better understand the arguments concerning the morality of euthanasia and the legislation connected with it.

Killing vs. Allowing to Die

The first conceptual issue that we should try to clarify is what some consider to be the difference between "killing" a person and allowing a person to die. Presumably, "killing" a person refers to a definite action taken to end someone's life, as in the case of the physician who, out of mercy, injects a terminally ill patient with air or a lethal dose of a medication. Killing is an act of commission. In contrast, "allowing to die" presumably is an act of omission, whereby the steps needed to preserve someone's life simply are not taken. For example, a doctor, again out of mercy, fails to give an injection of antibiotics to a terminally ill patient who has contracted pneumonia. As a result of this omission, the patient dies.

Those making this distinction, such as the American Medical Association (AMA), say that the distinction is reasonable because in ordinary language and everyday life we distinguish between causing someone harm and permitting the harm to happen to them. If, in cases of euthanasia, the distinction is not made between killing and allowing to die, then we lose the important distinction between causing someone harm or permitting that harm to happen.

Proponents also claim that the distinction acknowledges cases in which additional curative treatment would serve no purpose, and in fact would interfere with a person's natural death. It recognizes that medical science will not initiate or sustain extraordinary means to preserve the life of a dying patient when such means would obviously serve no useful purpose for the patient or the patient's family.

Finally, some argue that the distinction is important in distinguishing causation of death, and ultimately responsibility. In instances where the patient dies following nontreatment, the proximate cause of the death is the patient's disease, not the treatment or the person who did not provide it. If we fail to distinguish between killing and allowing to die, we blur this distinction. If allowing to die is subsumed under the category of euthanasia, then the nontreatment is the cause of the death, not the disease.

Not everyone, however, agrees that the distinction is a logical one. Some argue that withholding extraordinary treatment or suspending heroic measures in terminal cases is tantamount to the intentional termination of the life of one human being by another; that is, it is an act of killing. Thus, they claim that no logical distinction can be made between killing and allowing to die.

Whether or not the distinction between the two can be sustained logically is only one question raised by the killing vs. letting die debate. Another is the moral relevancy of such a distinction. Even if the distinction is logical, does it have any bearing on the rightness or wrongness of acts commonly termed *euthanasia*?

On the one hand, for those making the distinction, allowing a patient to die under carefully circumscribed conditions could be moral. On the other hand, they seemingly would regard the killing of a patient, even out of mercy, an immoral act. But those opposing the killing/letting die distinction would not necessarily accept the close connection between killing a dying patient and an immoral act. For them, while killing may be wrong, in some cases it may be the right thing to do. What determines the morality of killing a patient, what is of moral relevance and importance, is not the manner of causing the death but the circumstances in which the death is caused.

In summary, those distinguishing killing and allowing to die claim that the distinction is logically and morally relevant. Generally, they would condemn any act of killing a patient, while recognizing that some acts of allowing a patient to die may be moral (as, for example, in cases where life is being preserved heroically and death is imminent). In contrast are those who hold that the killing/letting die distinction is not logical, that allowing to die is in effect killing. They claim that killing a patient may be morally justifiable depending on the *circumstances* and not the *manner* in which the death is caused. The debate that surrounds the killing vs. allowing to die question is basic to the very meaning of *euthanasia*.

Meaning of *Euthanasia:* Narrow vs. Broad Interpretations

Construing euthanasia narrowly, some philosophers have taken it to be the equivalent of killing. Since allowing someone to die does not involve killing, allowing to die would not actually be an act of euthanasia at all. By this account, then, there are acts of allowing to die, which may be moral; and acts of euthanasia, which are always wrong.

Other philosophers interpret the meaning of *euthanasia* more broadly. For them euthanasia includes not only acts of killing but also acts of allowing to die. In other words, euthanasia can take an active or a passive form. *Active* (sometimes termed *positive*) *euthanasia refers to the act of painlessly putting to death persons suffering from incurable conditions or diseases.* Injecting a lethal dosage of medication into a terminally ill patient would constitute active euthanasia. *Passive euthanasia*, in contrast, *refers to any act of allowing a patient to die.* Not providing a terminally ill patient the needed antibiotics to survive pneumonia would be an example of passive euthanasia.

It is tempting to view the debate between the narrow and the broad interpretations of *euthanasia* largely in terms of semantics. While the meaning of *euthanasia* certainly is a factor in the disagreement, the issue involves more than mere word definition.

One side, the narrow interpretation, considers killing a patient always morally wrong. Since euthanasia, by this definition, is killing a patient, euthanasia is always morally wrong. But allowing a patient to die does not involve killing a patient. Therefore, allowing a patient to die does not fall under the moral prohibition that euthanasia does. Thus, allowing a patient to die may be morally right.

The other side, the broad interpretation, considers acts of allowing patients to die acts of euthanasia, albeit passive euthanasia. They argue that if euthanasia is wrong, then so is allowing patients to die (since it is a form of euthanasia). But if allowing patients to die is not wrong, then euthanasia is not always wrong.

Generally, those favoring the broad interpretation, in fact, claim that allowing patients to die is not always wrong; that euthanasia, therefore, may be morally justifiable. With the possible moral justifiability of euthanasia established, it is conceivable that acts of active euthanasia, as well as passive, may be moral. What determines their morality are the conditions under which the death is caused, and not the manner in which it is caused.

Voluntary vs. Nonvoluntary Euthanasia

In addition to the distinctions between killing and allowing to die, and the meaning of the term *euthanasia*, there is another conceptual issue that arises in discussions of euthanasia. It concerns the difference between voluntary and nonvoluntary decisions about death.

Voluntary decisions about death refer to cases in which a competent adult patient requests or gives informed consent to a particular course of medical treatment or non-treatment. Voluntary decisions also include cases in which persons take their own lives either directly or by refusing treatment, and cases where patients deputize others to act in their behalf. For example, a woman who is terminally ill instructs her husband and family not to permit antibiotic treatment should she contract pneumonia, or not to use artificial support systems should she lapse into a coma and be unable to speak for herself. Similarly, a man requests that he be given a lethal injection after an industrial explosion has left him with third-degree burns over most of his body and no real hope of recovery. For a decision about death to be voluntary, the individual must give explicit consent.

A nonvoluntary decision about death refers to cases in which the decision is not made by the person who is to die. Such cases would include situations where, because of age, mental impairment, or unconsciousness, patients are not competent to give informed consent to life or death decisions and where others make the decisions for them. For example, suppose that as a result of an automobile accident, a woman suffers massive and irreparable brain damage, falls into unconsciousness, and can be maintained only by artificial means. Should she regain consciousness, she would likely be little more than a vegetable. Given this prognosis, the woman's family, in consultation with her physicians, decide to suspend artificial life-sustaining means and allow her to die.

In actual situations, the difference between voluntary and nonvoluntary decisions about death is not always clear. For example, take the case of a man who has heard his mother say that she would never want to be kept alive with "machines and pumps and tubes." Now that she is, in fact, being kept alive that way, and is unable to express a life or death decision, the man is not sure that his mother actually would choose to be allowed to die. Similarly, a doctor might not be certain that the tormented cries of a stomach-cancer patient to be "put out of my misery" is an expression of informed consent or of profound pain and momentary despair.

The voluntary/nonvoluntary distinction is relevant to both the narrow and the broad interpretations of the meaning of *euthanasia*. Each interpretation seem-

ingly distinguishes four kinds of death decisions, in which the voluntary/
nonvoluntary distinction plays a part. Thus, the narrow interpretation recognizes cases of:

1. Voluntary euthanasia
2. Nonvoluntary euthanasia
3. Voluntary allowing to die
4. Nonvoluntary allowing to die

By this account, the first two generally are considered immoral; instances of
the second two may be moral under carefully circumscribed conditions.

Recognizing no logical or morally relevant distinction between euthanasia
and allowing to die, the broad interpretation allows four forms of euthanasia:

1. Voluntary active euthanasia
2. Nonvoluntary active euthanasia
3. Voluntary passive euthanasia
4. Nonvoluntary passive euthanasia

By this account, any of these types of euthanasia may be morally justifiable
under carefully circumscribed conditions.

The narrow and the broad interpretations differ sharply in their moral
judgment of *deliberate* acts taken to end or shorten a patient's life, that is, acts
that the narrow interpretation terms voluntary or nonvoluntary euthanasia, and
that the broad interpretation terms voluntary or nonvoluntary *active* euthanasia.
Generally, the narrow interpretation considers such acts always morally repugnant; the broad interpretation views them as being morally justifiable under
carefully circumscribed conditions.

With these complicated conceptual issues behind us, we can now turn to the
arguments for and against death decisions. The most conservative death decisions involve cases of voluntary allowing to die, which we will take as circum-
stantially a rough equivalent to voluntary passive euthanasia.[1] Having raised the
relevant pro and con arguments, we will then see how they can be and are
applied to other forms of death decisions.

Arguments for Voluntary Allowing to Die

1. *Individuals have the right to decide about their own lives and deaths.*

POINT: "What more basic right is there than to decide whether or not you're
going to live? There is none. A person under a death sentence who's being kept
alive through so-called heroic measures certainly has a fundamental right to say,
'Enough's enough. The treatment's worse than the disease. Leave me alone. Let
me die!' Ironically, those who would deny the terminally ill this right do so out
of a sense of high morality. Don't they realize that in denying the gravely ill and

1. *For contrast, see the Steinbock essay, which rejects this assumption.*

the suffering the right to release themselves from pain they commit the arch villainy?''

COUNTERPOINT: "The way you talk you'd swear people have absolute rights over their bodies and lives. You know as well as I that just isn't true. No individual has absolute freedom. Even 'A Patient's Bill of Rights,' which was drawn up by the American Hospital Association, recognizes this. While acknowledging that patients have the right to refuse treatment, the document also recognizes that they have this right and freedom only to the extent permitted by law. Maybe people should be allowed to die if they want to. But if so, it's not because they have an absolute right to dispose of themselves if they so choose.''

2. *The period of suffering can be shortened.*

POINT: "Have you ever been in a terminal cancer ward? It's grim, but enlightening. Anyone who has knows how much people can suffer before they die. And not just physically. The emotional, even spiritual, agony is often worse. Today our medical hardware is so sophisticated that the period of suffering can be extended beyond the limit of human endurance. What's the point of allowing someone a few more months or days or hours of so-called life when death is inevitable? There's no point. In fact, it's downright inhumane. When someone under such conditions asks to be allowed to die, it's far more humane to honor that request than deny it.''

COUNTERPOINT: "Only a fool would minimize the agony that many terminally ill patients endure. And there's no question that by letting them die on request we shorten their period of suffering. But we also shorten their lives. Can you seriously argue that the saving of pain is a greater good than the saving of life? Or that the presence of pain is a greater evil than the loss of life? I don't think so. Of course nobody likes to see a creature suffer, especially when the creature has requested a halt to the suffering. But we have to keep our priorities straight. In the last analysis life is a greater value than freedom from pain; death is a worse evil than suffering.''

3. *People have a right to die with dignity.*

POINT: "Nobody wants to end up plugged into machines and wired to tubes. Who wants to spend his last days lying in a hospital bed wasting away to something that's hardly recognizable as a human being, let alone his former self? Nobody. And rightly so. Why, the very prospect insults the whole concept of what it means to be a human. People are entitled to dignity, in life *and* in death. Just as we respect the individual's right to live with dignity, so we must respect their right to die with dignity. In the case of the terminally ill, that means that people have the right to refuse life-sustaining treatment when it's obvious to them that the treatment is only eroding their dignity, destroying their self-concept and self-respect, and reducing them to some subhuman level of biological life.''

COUNTERPOINT: "Listening to you, someone would swear that the superhuman efforts often made to keep someone alive are not worthy of human beings. What could be more dignified, more respectful of human life, than to maintain life against all odds, against all hope? Why, in situations like those, humans live their finest hours. And that includes many patients. All of life is a struggle, and a gamble. At the gaming table of life nobody ever knows what the outcome will be. But on we go—dogged in our determination to see things through to a meaningful resolution. Indeed, humans are noblest when they persist in the face of the inevitable. Look at our literature. Reflect on our heroes. They are not those who have capitulated, but those who have endured. No, there's nothing undignified about being hollowed out by a catastrophic disease, about writhing in pain, about wishing it would end. The indignity lies in capitulation."

Arguments Against Voluntary Allowing to Die

1.   *We should not play God.*

POINT: "Our culture traditionally has recognized that only God gives life, and only God should take life away. When humans take it upon themselves to shorten their lives or have others do that by withdrawing life-sustaining apparatus, they play God. They usurp the divine function; they interfere with the divine plan."

COUNTERPOINT: "Well, I'm impressed! It's not everyday that I meet somebody who knows the mind of God. But you obviously do. How you can be so sure about the 'divine plan,' however, quite escapes me. Did it ever occur to you that the intervention of modern medicine to keep people alive who otherwise would have long since died, might itself be an interference with God's will? If there is a God and a divine plan, it seems pretty clear that God didn't intend that His creatures should live forever. Judging from history, God meant for all humans to die. Don't you think that modern medicine has interfered with this plan? What could be more like 'playing God' than keeping people alive artificially? Let's face it: Nobody knows what God's plan is for allowing people to die."

2.   *We cannot be sure consent is voluntary.*

POINT: "Many of those opposed to nonvoluntary death decisions are quick to approve of voluntary ones. What they overlook is that we can't ever be sure consent is voluntary. In fact, the circumstances that surround most terminal cases make voluntary consent impossible. Take the case of the terminal patient who's built up a tolerance to drugs and, as a result, is tortured by pain. Just when are we supposed to get this person's consent? If we get it when they're drugged, then they're not clearheaded enough for the consent to be voluntary. If we withdraw the drugs, then they'll probably be so crazed with pain that their free consent still will be in question. Since consent in such cases can't be voluntary, it can only be presumed. And to allow a death decision on the basis of presumed consent is wrong."

COUNTERPOINT: "Agreed, in the situations you set up rational free choice is in question. But you've overlooked cases where people facing a death due to a dreadful disease make a death request *before* they're suffering pain. Maybe you'll reply that the consent of people in such situations is uninformed and anticipatory, and that patients can't bind themselves to be killed in the future. Okay, but what about cases where patients not under pain indicate a desire for ultimate euthanasia and reaffirm that request when under pain? Surely, by any realistic criteria, this would constitute voluntary consent."

3. *Diagnoses may be mistaken.*

POINT: "Doctors aren't infallible, that's for sure. The American Medical Association readily admits that far too many medical procedures and operations aren't even necessary. This doesn't mean physicians are malicious, but only that they're human. They make mistakes in their diagnoses. Any instance of electing death runs the tragic risk of terminating a life unnecessarily, and for that reason it's wrong."

COUNTERPOINT: "Sure, physicians make mistakes, but not as often as you imply. In fact, in terminal cases mistaken diagnoses are as rare as the kiwi bird. But that fact probably won't satisfy you, because you claim that any risk makes a death decision wrong. Well, by the same token every diagnosis, from the simplest to most complex, carries a chance of error and with it the possibility of needless treatment. Sometimes the treatment involves operations, and operations always involve some jeopardy for the patient. So what are we to say— that it's wrong for people to opt for procedures that expert medical opinion says they need, because there's always a chance of mistaken diagnosis? Of course not. The fact of the matter is that the correctness of a diagnosis is a separate issue from the individual's right to request and receive treatment. This applies with equal force to death decisions."

4. *There is always a chance of a cure or of some new relief from pain.*

POINT: "People easily forget how final death is. That may sound silly, but it's pertinent to death decisions. After all, people can never be recalled from the grave to benefit from a cure to the diseases that ravage them, or from a new drug to relieve the pain they suffered. Instances of such 'wonder' drugs, even of spontaneous remissions of disease, are common enough to make a death decision precipitate, and therefore wrong."

COUNTERPOINT: "First of all, it's highly unlikely that some kind of cure will benefit those who are already ravaged by a disease. Ask physicians. They'll tell you that a cure is most likely in the early stages of a disease, and most unlikely in its final stages. But the issue of death decision pertains precisely to people in the final, torturous stages of a disease. So, even if a cure is discovered, its likelihood of helping these patients is virtually nonexistent. Another thing. You fail to distinguish between cases where a cure is imminent, cases where it's remote, and those where it falls somewhere in between. To treat all terminal diseases as if they had an equal probability of being cured is unrealistic. Generally speaking, there's a time lapse between a medical discovery and the general availability of a drug. I might agree that it would be 'precipitate' and even wrong to elect death in that interim between discovery and general availability of the drug. But I don't see why it would be precipitate and wrong for a person to elect death when suffering from a terminal disease for which no cure or relief has ever been discovered.''

5. *Allowing death decisions will lead to abuses.*

POINT: "Of course it's easy to think of death decisions as isolated instances of individuals electing to die. Looked at this way, those who make such decisions appear to be above moral reproach. But when individuals choose to die and are subsequently allowed to, their actions open the door for all sorts of abuses. The chief abuse is *nonvoluntary* death decisions. A terminal patient who elects to die at the very least brings individuals and society closer to accepting nonvoluntary killing, such as in cases of defective infants, old and senile people, and the hopelessly insane. Indeed, such 'private' decisions will likely set off a chain reaction that will lead to horrible abuses."

COUNTERPOINT: "The treatments of defective infants, old and senile people, and the hopelessly insane are issues separate and distinct from permitting death decisions. There is no causal connection between them and allowing death decisions, such that allowing death decisions will inevitably lead to the abuses you fear. But even if there were a connection, that wouldn't of itself demonstrate that voluntary death decisions are immoral, only that they shouldn't be legalized."

Arguments For and Against Other Forms of Death Decisions

The foregoing are the arguments generally marshalled for and against voluntary allowing to die or voluntary passive euthanasia. They, or variations of them, are commonly enlisted in discussions of other forms of death decisions as well.

For example, those arguing for voluntary active euthanasia often stress the inherent freedom of individuals to do as they choose, so long as their actions do not hurt anyone else. They also contend that it is cruel and inhuman to make people suffer when they have requested to have their lives ended. In contrast, those opposing voluntary active euthanasia appeal to the sanctity of human life, arguing that the intentional termination of an innocent human life is always immoral. They also express concern about mistaken diagnoses, the possibility of cure and relief, and especially about the potentially dangerous consequences resulting from such a lessening of respect for human life.

Similarly, those supporting nonvoluntary active or passive euthanasia generally appeal to principles of humanness and human dignity. Those opposing it marshall all the arguments that we have catalogued against a voluntary death decision, while stressing how morally objectionable it is to allow people to die or to kill people without voluntary consent.

Of course, various positions are possible, and likely, within this broad outline. For example, some who support voluntary decisions might well oppose the nonvoluntary. And many who support nonvoluntary allowing to die or nonvoluntary passive euthanasia might object to nonvoluntary active euthanasia. In other words, for some moralists the key factor in determining the morality of a death decision is whether or not it is voluntary. Thus, for many a death decision is moral if and only if it is voluntary. Others concern themselves primarily with the distinction between active and passive, not voluntary and nonvoluntary. In their view, the focus should not be on who makes the death decision, but on whether there is a morally significant difference between active and passive euthanasia, such that even if passive euthanasia is acceptable, the active form is not.

Legal Considerations

Even if we decide that some form of euthanasia is morally acceptable, another question arises: Should individuals have a legal right to euthanasia? Ought people be permitted under law to have their lives terminated?

Currently it is illegal to deliberately cause the death of another person. It is generally recognized, however, that people have a right to refuse life-sustaining treatment. In recent years numerous attempts have been made to legislate the individual's right to refuse life-sustaining treatment. By and large these efforts have been rebuffed. Some object to the proposed legislation because of inherent difficulties in trying to define phrases such as "death with dignity," "natural death," "extraordinary means," "heroic measures," and "informed consent." Others observe that such legislation is not needed, since there is already a widely recognized right to reject life-sustaining treatment. Still others express concern that legalizing such a right will lead to abuses.

In the absence of specific legislation, various documents and directives have been developed to allow people to inform others about the nature and extent of the treatment they wish to have should they become seriously ill. Such documents usually are termed *living wills*. While living wills do specify the person's wishes, and relieve others of having to make momentous life or death decisions, generally they are not legally binding. Thus, there is no guarantee that the person's wishes will be implemented.

In 1977 the State of California, as part of the "Natural Death Act," created a version of a living will called "Directive to Physicians." What makes this document unique is that it guarantees those who execute it the same legal power guaranteed by an estate will. Of course, as with estate wills, the "Directive to Physicians" can be contested. But the document takes a giant step toward according living wills legal status.

It is important to note that the morality of legalizing death decisions is a separate issue from the morality of euthanasia itself. While many of the arguments for and against the legalization of death decisions capitalize on the general arguments previously outlined, it is entirely possible that one could approve of individual death decisions but at the same time object to any systematic social policy permitting them. The objection could be based on a fear that such a policy would lead to abuses by physicians, families, and others, or that it would lead to more permissive legislation allowing, say, nonvoluntary or active euthanasia.

Ethical Theories

Egoism

As on all moral issues, egoism would approach the morality of death decisions from the viewpoint of self-interest. Such conceptual issues as the meaning of *euthanasia*, the distinction between killing and allowing to die, voluntary and nonvoluntary, and active and passive would not figure significantly in the egoist's calculation. Instead, the egoist would determine what would be the likely consequences for the self. For example, if a death decision would produce a net saving of pain, then a dying patient tortured by pain would be morally justified in making such a decision. Whether it is proper for an outside party to allow or help such a patient to die is a separate question, the answer to which depends on an application of the self-interest yardstick. Thus, if a doctor sees his or her best long-term self-interests served by allowing or helping such a patient to die, then the doctor ought to so assist the patient. Egoists simply would not be overly concerned with the difference between voluntary and nonvoluntary, or active and passive.

As for legalizing some form of euthanasia, again the egoist would determine whether or not the legislation likely would advance one's best long-term interests. Figuring prominently in the evaluation would be the possibility of one's ultimately facing a death decision. Without specific legislation acknowledging an individual's right to make a death decision and have it implemented, one might not be able to die with dignity. Egoists would consider other factors, such as the social impact of such a law, only insofar as they would affect the egoist's personal happiness.

Act Utilitarianism

Act utilitarians would examine each proposed act of euthanasia separately. If the act likely would produce the greatest total happiness, then it would be morally justifiable. By this account, no form of a death decision would be in and of itself objectionable. However, the act utilitarian would be sensitive to the possible long-range negative social effects of any act of euthanasia, particularly nonvoluntary euthanasia, which could have potentially sinister consequences for individuals and society. Nevertheless, if in the final analysis, any death decision—including cases of nonvoluntary euthanasia—would likely produce the most total good then it would be morally justifiable. (We should add that either the act or the rule utilitarian could argue that since life is a necessary condition for happiness, euthanasia would be wrong because the destruction of life would preclude the possibility of all future happiness.)

As for legalizing euthanasia, again if such an act likely would produce the greatest social good it would be justifiable. If not, it would be wrong. Act utilitarians who would agree that some acts of euthanasia are morally justifiable could object to any systematic social policy permitting even voluntary euthanasia if, for example, they foresaw abuses, needless deaths, or other undesirable consequences.

Rule Utilitarianism

Rule utilitarians would apply the utility principle to the rule under which the specific death decision falls. Thus, before applying the various forms of euthanasia to terminal patients who have no relief from torturous pain, the rule utilitarian would evaluate a variety of rules: (1) Allowing a human life to end is permissible when suffering is intense and the condition of the person permits no legitimate hope. (2) Even if not voluntary, allowing a human life to end is permissible when suffering is intense and the condition of the person permits no legitimate hope. (3) When a person requests it, the taking of a human life is permissible when suffering is intense, and the condition of the patient permits no legitimate hope. (4) Even when a person has not requested it, the taking of a human life is permissible when suffering is intense and the condition of the person permits no legitimate hope.

In theory the rule utilitarian could endorse any of these rules, if following the rule generally produced more total good than not following it. In evaluating the consequences of the proposed rule, rule utilitarians would be alert to the abuse to which a rule might be open. This is especially noteworthy with rules (3) and (4). But the caution would apply to all the rules.

Regarding the legalization of euthanasia, the rule utilitarian would evaluate the morality of any proposed law on the basis of its likely social consequences. If such a law appeared likely to produce the most total happiness, then it would be justifiable. Rule utilitarians would consider very carefully the implications for abuse of having a systematic social policy that acknowledged and vouchsafed the right to a death decision.

Divine Command

Divine command theorists generally would disapprove of any deliberate action taken to terminate a life. Whether the action is voluntary or nonvoluntary is irrelevant. The key factor is whether or not the action is positive. A positive, deliberate act to terminate a life is the killing of an innocent life, which violates the will and law of God.

Most religious positions distinguish between euthanasia and allowing to die. The former is killing and is never permissible, its voluntary nature notwithstanding. Allowing to die is not killing and may, under carefully circumscribed conditions, be moral. For most, the "carefully circumscribed conditions" probably would include consent or presumed consent. The Roman Catholic position on this issue is a good example of this distinction. Roman Catholicism expressly rejects all forms of euthanasia as equivalent to suicide or murder, which are considered contrary to the law of God. However, Roman Catholicism does not recognize any moral obligation to maintain hopeless cases through extraordinary means. Thus, by Roman Catholic moral theology, it would be justifiable for persons to refuse extraordinary treatment and let the will of God determine the outcome. This is precisely what occurred in the Quinlan case. The Quinlans, who are Roman Catholics, requested that life-sustaining treatment be discontinued, an action that was perfectly compatible with the moral tenets of their faith. Curiously, Karen Ann did not die when the extraordinary means were removed—God evidently did not want her to die. Had the Quinlans then initiated some direct action (active euthanasia) to terminate Karen Ann's life, they would have acted immorally, according to Roman Catholicism, for they would have interfered with the will of God. Had Karen Ann been conscious and tortured by pain, by Roman Catholic theology it would be perfectly all right to have administered drugs for the purpose of relieving the pain, even if the drugs indirectly happened to shorten her life. So long as a patient's death is not intended, such an action is not considered killing or a violation of God's will.

Of course, not all divine command applications would parallel the Roman Catholics. It is possible to argue, for example, that the divine command forbids even allowing someone to die or administering drugs that indirectly shorten their lives. Obviously, much depends on what one construes to be the "will of God.'

The same considerations would apply to legislation about death decisions. If a particular death decision, such as allowing persons to die, is considered consistent with the law of God, then seemingly there would be no reason to object to a law that would explicitly guarantee patients this right. Although the divine command theorist might conceivably still raise the issue of potential abuse or the "wedge argument," these consequential objections really seem inconsistent with an absolute divine command approach. Autonomous creatures should have the freedom to act in a way thought to be compatible with the will of God. Indeed, leaving the matter in a kind of legal limbo would seem at least indirectly to limit the freedom of self-determination that, presumably, God wills His creatures to have. Obviously much depends on an interpretation of God's will.

Categorial Imperative

A quick reading of Kant's theory might lead one to conclude that Kant would oppose all forms of euthanasia. After all, Kant claims that autonomous, rational beings have a duty to preserve their lives. Refusing needed medical care or committing suicide would be inconsistent with this obligation and therefore immoral.

Yet, Kant asserts that it is by the very fact that we are rational and autonomous that we have inherent worth and dignity. What happens when the status as rational and autonomous creatures is severely damaged or impaired, as it is when people are disoriented, comatose, or irrational due to severe and prolonged injury or illness? Since their status is damaged, even destroyed, they may have lost their inherent worth and dignity, and it is no longer clear that there is a moral imperative to sustain them. Even if such patients do maintain their status of rational, autonomous creatures, the obligation that humans have to accord one another the dignity they deserve may make it more consistent for loved ones or health care professionals to permit a patient to die or even to kill the patient rather than allow the patient to suffer in an undignified manner. In short, voluntary death decisions could be justified, even obligatory, under Kantian ethics.

Given the ambiguity of the Kantian position, it is impossible to predict accurately a Kantian ethicist's reaction to any proposed legislation about death decisions. If voluntary death decisions are moral, then it would seem that people ought to have a legal right to make them. To deny them that right or not expressly to grant them the right would appear to be incompatible with the freedom that rational, autonomous creatures are entitled to.

Prima Facie Duties

In applying the ethics of prima facie duties to death decisions, Ross would give the duty of noninjury paramount consideration. Ross holds that we have a prima facie duty not to kill any human being except in justifiable self-defense, *unless we have an even stronger prima facie duty to do something that can be accomplished only by killing.* What might that "stronger prima facie duty" be? Not to injure another person. It could be argued, therefore, that there may be times when only by killing can we meet an overriding prima facie obligation not to cause injury to another person. But this seems like a paradox, for is not killing someone causing someone injury? Perhaps not. In the cases of comatose or irrational terminal patients, if we treat them as they would want to be treated if they had all their faculties, then we might not be causing them injury at all. In fact, maybe people in such a state are beyond injury. In any event, if, while the patient is in that state, we can make a fair and honest presumption that the person would want to be allowed to die or even to be killed, then we cannot be said to be causing the person injury in implementing the implied request and consent. When patients have left specific instructions to that effect, as, say, in a "living will," then again we would not be injuring them in fulfilling their requests; seemingly we would even have a prima facie obligation to do so. In contrast, when it is clear that the person wants to be maintained at all costs, then, despite our own feelings, we would have a prima facie obligation to honor that preference. Not to do so would be to injure the person.

Apparently, then, the issue of voluntary consent could be crucial for Ross in determining whether the death decision involves injustice. When there is expressed or implied consent, then no injury seems to be involved and the death decision would be morally justifiable. Furthermore, people should have a legal right to make such decisions; for lacking appropriate legislation, patients easily could be prevented from embarking on a perfectly moral course of action in a matter of the greatest urgency.

Maximin Principle

Many of the observations about Ross's ethics apply equally to Rawls's maximin principle. Assuming the original position, behind the veil of ignorance, people likely would not want to be bound by a rule that would prohibit them from ending the sort of intense suffering under discussion. Thus, Rawls's ethics would appear to sanction at least voluntary death decisions. Moreover, Rawls's paternalism would allow, perhaps encourage, death decisions based on the presumption of consent, providing of course the evidence for presumption was overwhelming. In no instance, however, would Rawls approve of killing patients who wish to be maintained at all costs. And in all probability, Rawls would condemn a death decision where there was no evidence or not enough for presuming consent. Of course, what constitutes "enough" evidence is problematic. Again, as with Ross, the key issue seems to be whether the consent is voluntary. By this account, Rawls, like Ross, could support legislation that would permit voluntary death decisions. Such laws would maximize individual liberty in a way that is compatible with a like liberty for all.

Active and Passive Euthanasia

James Rachels

In "Active and Passive Euthanasia," professor of philosophy James Rachels begins by admitting that the distinction between active and passive euthanasia is thought crucial for medical ethics. He cites a statement by the American Medical Association that, in effect, condemns the intentional termination of a life but sanctions, under carefully circumscribed conditions, the cessation of treatment needed to preserve the life of a terminally ill patient. Rachels in the rest of his essay challenges this doctrine and the distinction between active and passive euthanasia. Indeed, he identifies the AMA doctrine with the active/passive distinction, a point with which some disagree (see the Steinbock essay that follows).

There are two essential points on which Rachels's argument turns. First, Rachels insists, and tries to show, that allowing someone to die may cause more pain and suffering than directly terminating the person's life. Second, Rachels claims that the conventional doctrine and distinction lead to life-or-death decisions that are made on irrelevant grounds.

If, as Rachels claims, the distinction between active and passive euthanasia is misguided, even pernicious, then why do people commonly make it? Rachels suggests it is because we generally regard killing as morally worse than letting someone die. He tries to show that there is no moral difference between the two. Another reason for the common distinction, he believes, is that people

From James Rachels, "Active and Passive Euthanasia," New England Journal of Medicine, 292 (January 9, 1975), 78–80. Reprinted by permission of the publisher.

confuse the issue with whether most cases of killing are more reprehensible than most cases of letting die. Again, Rachels does not believe that is necessarily so.

In short, Rachels opposes the distinction between active and passive euthanasia. If passive euthanasia is morally permissible under carefully circumscribed conditions, then in his view there is no compelling reason for the absolute prohibition against active euthanasia.

Abstract   The traditional distinction between active and passive euthanasia requires critical analysis. The conventional doctrine is that there is such an important moral difference between the two that, although the latter is sometimes permissible, the former is always forbidden. This doctrine may be challenged for several reasons. First of all, active euthanasia is in many cases more humane than passive euthanasia. Secondly, the conventional doctrine leads to decisions concerning life and death on irrelevant grounds. Thirdly, the doctrine rests on a distinction between killing and letting die that itself has no moral importance. Fourthly, the most common arguments in favor of the doctrine are invalid. I therefore suggest that the American Medical Association policy statement that endorses this doctrine is unsound.

The distinction between active and passive euthanasia is thought to be crucial for medical ethics. The idea is that it is permissible, at least in some cases, to withhold treatment and allow a patient to die, but it is never permissible to take any direct action designed to kill the patient. This doctrine seems to be accepted by most doctors, and it is endorsed in a statement adopted by the House of Delegates of the American Medical Association on December 4, 1973:

> The intentional termination of the life of one human being by another—mercy killing—is contrary to that for which the medical profession stands and is contrary to the policy of the American Medical Association.
>
> The cessation of the employment of extraordinary means to prolong the life of the body when there is irrefutable evidence that biological death is imminent is the decision of the patient and/or his immediate family. The advice and judgment of the physician should be freely available to the patient and/or his immediate family.

However, a strong case can be made against this doctrine. In what follows I will set out some of the relevant arguments, and urge doctors to reconsider their views on this matter.

To begin with a familiar type of situation, a patient who is dying of incurable cancer of the throat is in terrible pain, which can no longer be satisfactorily alleviated. He is certain to die within a few days, even if present treatment is continued, but he does not want to go on living for those days since the pain is unbearable. So he asks the doctor for an end to it, and his family joins in the request.

Suppose the doctor agrees to withhold treatment, as the conventional doctrine says he may. The justification for his doing so is that the patient is in terrible agony, and since he is going to die anyway, it would be wrong to prolong his suffering needlessly. But now notice this. If one simply withholds treatment, it may take the patient longer to die, and so he may suffer more than he would if more direct action were taken and a lethal injection given. This fact provides strong reason for thinking that, once the initial decision not to prolong his agony has been made, active euthanasia is actually preferable to passive euthanasia, rather than the reverse. To say otherwise is to endorse the option that leads to more suffering rather than less, and is contrary to the humanitarian impulse that prompts the decision not to prolong his life in the first place.

Part of my point is that the process of being "allowed to die" can be relatively slow and painful, whereas being given a lethal injection is relatively quick and painless. Let me give a different sort of example. In the United States about one in 600 babies is born with Down's syndrome. Most of these babies are otherwise healthy—that is, with only the usual pediatric care, they will proceed to an otherwise normal infancy. Some, however, are born with congenital defects such as intestinal obstructions that require operations if they are to live. Sometimes, the parents and the doctor will decide not to operate, and let the infant die. Anthony Shaw describes what happens then:

> . . . When surgery is denied [the doctor] must try to keep the infant from suffering

while natural forces sap the baby's life away. As a surgeon whose natural inclination is to use the scalpel to fight off death, standing by and watching a salvageable baby die is the most emotionally exhausting experience I know. It is easy at a conference, in a theoretical discussion, to decide that such infants should be allowed to die. It is altogether different to stand by in the nursery and watch as dehydration and infection wither a tiny being over hours and days. This is a terrible ordeal for me and the hospital staff—much more so than for the parents who never set foot in the nursery.[1]

I can understand why some people are opposed to all euthanasia, and insist that such infants must be allowed to live. I think I can also understand why other people favor destroying these babies quickly and painlessly. But why should anyone favor letting "dehydration and infection wither a tiny being over hours and days"? The doctrine that says that a baby may be allowed to dehydrate and wither, but may not be given an injection that would end its life without suffering, seems so patently cruel as to require no further refutation. The strong language is not intended to offend, but only to put the point in the clearest possible way.

My second argument is that the conventional doctrine leads to decisions concerning life and death made on irrelevant grounds.

Consider again the case of the infants with Down's syndrome who need operations for congenital defects unrelated to the syndrome to live. Sometimes, there is no operation, and the baby dies, but when there is no such defect, the baby lives on. Now, an operation such as that to remove an intestinal obstruction is not prohibitively difficult. The reason why such operations are not performed in these cases is, clearly, that the child has Down's syndrome and the parents and the doctor judge that because of that fact it is better for the child to die.

But notice that this situation is absurd, no matter what view one takes of the lives and potentials of such babies. If the life of such an infant is worth preserving, what does it matter if it needs a simple operation? Or, if one thinks it better that such a baby should not live on, what difference does it make that it happens to have an unobstructed intestinal tract? In either case, the matter of life and death is being decided on irrelevant grounds. It is the Down's syndrome, and not the intestines, that is the issue. The matter should be decided, if at all, on that basis, and not be allowed to depend on the essentially irrelevant question of whether the intestinal tract is blocked.

What makes this situation possible, of course, is the idea that when there is an intestinal blockage, one can "let the baby die," but when there is no such defect there is nothing that can be done, for one must not "kill" it. The fact that this idea leads to such results as deciding life or death on irrelevant grounds is another good reason why the doctrine should be rejected.

One reason why so many people think that there is an important moral difference between active and passive euthanasia is that they think killing someone is morally worse than letting someone die. But is it? Is killing, in itself, worse than letting die? To investigate this issue, two cases may be considered that are exactly alike except that one involves killing whereas the other involves letting someone die. Then, it can be asked whether this difference makes any difference to the moral assessments. It is important that the cases be exactly alike, except for this one difference, since otherwise one cannot be confident that it is this difference and not some other that accounts for any variation in the assessments of the two cases. So, let us consider this pair of cases:

In the first, Smith stands to gain a large inheritance if anything should happen to his six-year-old cousin. One evening while the child is taking his bath, Smith sneaks into the bathroom and drowns the child, and then arranges things so that it will look like an accident.

In the second, Jones also stands to gain if anything should happen to his six-year-old cousin. Like Smith, Jones sneaks in planning to drown the child in his bath. However, just as he enters the bathroom Jones sees the child slip and hit his head, and fall face down in the water. Jones is delighted; he stands by, ready to push the child's head back under if it is necessary, but it is not necessary. With only a little thrashing about, the child drowns all by himself, "accidentally," as Jones watches and does nothing.

Now Smith killed the child, whereas Jones "merely" let the child die. That is the only difference between them. Did either man behave better, from a moral point of view? If the difference between killing and letting die were in itself a morally important matter, one should say that Jones's behavior was less reprehensible than Smith's. But does one really want to say that? I think not. In the first place, both men acted from the same motive, personal gain, and both had exactly the same end in view when they acted. It may be inferred from Smith's conduct that he is a bad man, although that judgment may be withdrawn or modified if certain further facts are learned about him—for example, that he is mentally deranged. But would not the very same thing be inferred about Jones from his conduct? And would not the same further considerations also be relevant to any modification of this judgment? Moreover, suppose Jones pleaded, in his own defense, "After all, I didn't do anything except just stand there and watch the child drown. I didn't kill him; I only let him die." Again, if letting die were in itself less bad than killing, this defense should have at least some weight. But it does not. Such a "defense" can only be regarded as a grotesque perversion of moral reasoning. Morally speaking, it is no defense at all.

Now, it may be pointed out, quite properly, that the cases of euthanasia with which doctors are concerned are not like this at all. They do not involve personal gain or the destruction of normal healthy children. Doctors are concerned only with cases in which the patient's life is of no further use to him, or in which the patient's life has become or will soon become a terrible burden. However, the point is the same in these cases: the bare difference between killing and letting die does not, in itself, make a moral difference. If a doctor lets a patient die, for humane reasons, he is in the same moral position as if he had given the patient a lethal injection for humane reasons. If his decision was wrong—if, for example, the patient's illness was in fact curable—the decision would be equally regrettable no matter which method was used to carry it out. And if the doctor's decision was the right one, the method used is not in itself important.

The AMA policy statement isolates the crucial issue very well: The crucial issue is "the intentional termination of the life of one human being by another." But after identifying this issue, and forbidding "mercy killing," the statement goes on to deny that the cessation of treatment is the intentional termination of a life. This is where the mistake comes in, for what is the cessation of treatment, in these circumstances, if it is not "the intentional termination of the life of one human being by another"? Of course it is exactly that, and if it were not, there would be no point to it.

Many people will find this judgment hard to accept. One reason, I think, is that it is very easy to conflate the question of whether killing is, in itself, worse than letting die, with the very different question of whether most actual cases of killing are more reprehensible than most actual cases of letting die. Most actual cases of killing are clearly terrible (think, for example, of all the murders reported in the newspapers), and one hears of such cases everyday. On the other hand, one hardly ever hears of a case of letting die, except for the actions of doctors who are motivated by humanitarian reasons. So one learns to think of killing in a much worse light than of letting die. But this does not mean that there is something about killing that makes it in itself worse than letting die, for it is not the bare difference between killing and letting die that makes the difference in these cases. Rather, the other factors—the murderer's motive of personal gain, for example, contrasted with the doctor's humanitarian motivation—account for different reactions to the different cases.

I have argued that killing is not in itself any worse than letting die; if my contention is right, it follows that active euthanasia is not any worse than passive euthanasia. What arguments can be given on the other side? The most common, I believe, is the following:

"The important difference between active and passive euthanasia is that, in passive euthanasia, the doctor does not do anything to bring about the patient's death. The doctor does nothing, and the patient dies of whatever ills already afflict him. In active euthanasia, however, the doctor does something to bring about the patient's death: He kills him. The doctor who gives the patient with cancer a lethal injection has himself caused his patient's death; whereas if he merely ceases treatment, the cancer is the cause of the death."

A number of points need to be made here. The first is that it is not exactly correct to say that in passive euthanasia the doctor does nothing, for he does do one thing that is very important: He lets the patient die. "Letting someone die" is certainly different, in some respects, from other types of action—mainly in that it is a kind of action that one may perform by way of not performing certain other actions. For example, one may let a patient die by way of not giving medication, just as one may insult someone by way of not shaking his hand. But for any purpose of moral assessment, it is a type of action nonetheless. The decision to let a patient die is subject to moral appraisal in the same way that a decision to kill him would be subject to moral appraisal: It may be assessed as wise or unwise, compassionate or sadistic, right or wrong. If a doctor deliberately let a patient die who was suffering from a routinely curable illness, the doctor would certainly be to blame for what he had done, just as he would be to blame if he had needlessly killed the patient. Charges against him would then be appropriate. If so, it would be no defense at all for him to insist that he didn't "do anything." He would have done something very serious indeed, for he let his patient die.

Fixing the cause of death may be very important from a legal point of view, for it may determine whether criminal charges are brought against the doctor. But I do not think that this notion can be used to show a moral difference between active and passive euthanasia. The reason why it is considered bad to be the cause of someone's death is that death is regarded as a great evil—and so it is. However, if it has been decided that euthanasia—even passive euthanasia—is desirable in a given case, it has also been decided that in this instance death is no greater an evil than the patient's continued existence. And if this is true, the usual reason for not wanting to be the cause of someone's death simply does not apply.

Finally, doctors may think that all of this is only of academic interest—the sort of thing that philosophers may worry about but that has no practical bearing on their own work. After all, doctors must be concerned about the legal consequences of what they do, and active euthanasia is clearly forbidden by the law. But even so, doctors should also be concerned with the fact that the law is forcing upon them a moral doctrine that may well be indefensible, and has a considerable effect on their practices. Of course, most doctors are not now in the position of being coerced in this matter, for they do not regard themselves as merely going along with what the law requires. Rather, in statements such as the AMA policy statement that I have quoted, they are endorsing this doctrine as a central point of medical ethics. In that statement, active euthanasia is condemned not merely as illegal but as "contrary to that for which the medical profession stands," whereas passive euthanasia is approved. However, the preceding considerations suggest that there is really no moral difference between the two, considered in themselves (there may be important moral differences in some cases in their *consequences*, but, as I pointed out, these differences may make active euthanasia, and not passive euthanasia, the morally preferable option). So, whereas doctors may have to discriminate between active and passive euthanasia to satisfy the law, they should not do any more than that. In particular, they should not give the distinction any added authority and weight by writing it into official statements of medical ethics.

Note

1.   A. Shaw, "Doctor, Do We Have a Choice?" *The New York Times Magazine*, January 30, 1972, p. 54.

Questions for Analysis

1. *Early in his essay, Rachels sets up a familiar situation involving a throat-cancer patient. What is the point of the example? Do you think that suspending pain-relieving drugs is what people generally understand by "withholding treatment"?*

2. *Explain, through Rachels's own example of the infant with Down's syndrome, why he thinks the distinction between active and passive euthanasia leads to life or death decisions made on irrelevant grounds.*

3. *Do you agree with Rachels that the cessation of treatment is tantamount to the intentional termination of life?*

4.   *Rachels claims that killing is not necessarily any worse than allowing a person to die. What are the implications of this claim for the morality of active euthanasia?*

5.   *Rachels believes that it is inaccurate and misleading to say that a doctor who allows a patient to die does "nothing" to cause the death. Do you agree?*

The Intentional Termination of Life

Bonnie Steinbock

In "The Intentional Termination of Life," professor of philosophy Bonnie Steinbock argues that, contrary to the claims of James Rachels and others, such as Michael Tooley, the AMA statement does not at all imply support of an active/passive distinction. In fact, Steinbock claims, the statement rejects both forms of euthanasia as killing.

Steinbock believes the mistake that Rachels and Tooley make is to identify the cessation of life-supporting treatment with passive euthanasia. She points out that there are at least two situations in which the suspension of life-prolonging treatment cannot be identified with euthanasia. The first involves cases where patients exercise their right to refuse treatment. In her view, the right to refuse treatment does not at all imply the right to decide one's own death. The second situation involves cases where continued treatment has little chance of improving the patient's condition or actually brings greater discomfort. In such situations, Steinbock argues, intentionally stopping life-prolonging treatment is not identical to intentionally terminating life, unless, of course, the death of the patient is what is actually intended.

Does the mere fact that someone—for example, a doctor—foresees the result, say death, mean that the doctor brought about the result intentionally? No, says Steinbock. She believes that one of two conditions must be met in order to establish that the intentional cessation of life-prolonging treatment is tantamount to intentional killing. Either the death of the patient must actually be intended, or the reason for ceasing the treatment is irrelevant to its characterization as the intentional termination of life.

According to James Rachels and Michael Tooley, . . . a common mistake in medical ethics is the belief that there is a moral difference between active and passive euthanasia. This is a mistake, they argue, because the rationale underlying the distinction between active and passive euthanasia is the idea that there is a significant moral difference between intentionally killing and intentionally letting die. "This idea," Tooley says, "is admittedly very common. But I believe that it can be shown to reflect either confused thinking or a moral point of view unrelated to the interests of individuals." Whether or not the belief that there is a significant moral difference is mistaken is not my concern here. For it is far from clear that this distinction *is* the basis of the doctrine of the American Medical Association which Rachels attacks. And if the killing/letting die distinction is not the basis of the AMA doctrine, then arguments showing that the distinction has no moral force do not, in themselves, reveal in the doctrine's adherents either "confused thinking" or "a moral point of view unrelated to the interests of individuals." Indeed, as we examine the AMA doctrine, I think it will become clear that it appeals to and makes use of a number of overlapping distinctions, which may

I would like to express my thanks to Jonathan Bennett, Josiah Gould, Deborah Johnson, David Pratt, Bruce Russell, and David Zimmerman, all of whom provided helpful criticism and suggestions for this article.

have moral significance in particular cases, such as the distinction between intending and foreseeing, or between ordinary and extraordinary care. Let us then turn to the 1973 statement, from the House of Delegates of the American Medical Association, which Rachels cites:

> The intentional termination of the life of one human being by another—mercy killing—is contrary to that for which the medical profession stands and is contrary to the policy of the American Medical Association.
>
> The cessation of the employment of extraordinary means to prolong the life of the body when there is irrefutable evidence that biological death is imminent is the decision of the patient and/or his immediate family. The advice and judgment of the physician should be freely available to the patient and/or his immediate family.

Rachels attacks this statement because he believes that it contains a moral distinction between active and passive euthanasia. Tooley also believes this to be the position of the AMA, saying:

> Many people hold that there is an important moral distinction between passive euthanasia and active euthanasia. Thus, while the AMA maintains that people have a right "to die with dignity," so that it is morally permissible for a doctor to allow someone to die if that person wants to and is suffering from an incurable illness causing pain that cannot be sufficiently alleviated, the AMA is unwilling to countenance active euthanasia for a person who is in similar straits, but who has the misfortune not to be suffering from an illness that will result in a speedy death.

Both men, then, take the AMA position to prohibit active euthanasia, while allowing, under certain conditions, passive euthanasia.

I intend to show that the AMA statement does not imply support of the active/passive euthanasia distinction. In forbidding the intentional termination of life, the statement rejects both active and passive euthanasia. It does allow for "the cessation of the employment of extraordinary means" to prolong life. The mistake Rachels and Tooley make is in identifying the cessation of life-prolonging treatment with passive euthanasia, or intentionally letting die. If it were right to equate the two, then the AMA statement would be self-contradictory, for it would begin by condemning, and

end by allowing, the intentional termination of life. But if the cessation of life-prolonging treatment is not always or necessarily passive euthanasia, then there is no confusion and no contradiction.

Why does Rachels think that the cessation of life-prolonging treatment is the intentional termination of life? He says:

> The AMA policy statement isolates the crucial issue very well: The crucial issue is "the intentional termination of the life of one human being by another." But after identifying this issue, and forbidding "mercy killing," the statement goes on to deny that the cessation of treatment is the intentional termination of a life. This is where the mistake comes in, for what is the cessation of treatment, in these circumstances, if it is not "the intentional termination of the life of one human being of another"? Of course it is exactly that, and if it were not, there would be no point to it.

However, there *can* be a point (to the cessation of life-prolonging treatment) other than an endeavor to bring about the patient's death, and so the blanket identification of cessation of treatment with the intentional termination of a life is inaccurate. There are at least two situations in which the termination of life-prolonging treatment cannot be identified with the intentional termination of the life of one human being by another.

The first situation concerns the patient's right to refuse treatment. Both Tooley and Rachels give the example of a patient dying of an incurable disease, accompanied by unrelievable pain, who wants to end the treatment which cannot cure him but can only prolong his miserable existence. Why, they ask, may a doctor accede to the patient's request to stop treatment, but not provide a patient in a similar situation with a lethal dose? The answer lies in the patient's right to refuse treatment. In general, a competent adult has the right to refuse treatment, even where such treatment is necessary to prolong life. Indeed, the right to refuse treatment has been upheld even when the patient's reason for refusing treatment is generally agreed to be inadequate.[1] This right can be overridden (if, for example, the patient has dependent children) but, in general, no one may legally compel you to undergo treatment to which you have not consented. "Historically, surgical intrusion has always been considered a technical battery upon the person and one to be excused or justified by consent of the patient or justified by necessity created by the circumstances of the moment. . . ."[2]

At this point, an objection might be raised that if one has the right to refuse life-prolonging treatment, then consistency demands that one have the right to decide to end his or her life, and to obtain help in doing so. The idea is that the right to refuse treatment somehow implies a right to voluntary euthanasia, and we need to see why someone might think this. The right to refuse treatment has been considered by legal writers as an example of the right to privacy or, better, the right to bodily self-determination. You have the right to decide what happens to your own body, and the right to refuse treatment is an instance of that right. But if you have the right to determine what happens to your own body, then should you not have the right to choose to end your life, and even a right to get help in doing so?

However, it is important to see that the right to refuse treatment is not the same as, nor does it entail, a right to voluntary euthanasia, even if both can be derived from the right to bodily self-determination. The right to refuse treatment is not itself a "right to die"; that one may choose to exercise this right even at the risk of death, or even *in order to die*, is irrelevant. The purpose of the right to refuse medical treatment is not to give persons a right to decide whether to live or die, but to protect them from the unwanted interferences of others. Perhaps we ought to interpret the right to bodily self-determination more broadly, so as to include a right to die; but this would be a substantial extension of our present understanding of the right to bodily self-determination, and not a consequence of it. If we were to recognize a right to voluntary euthanasia, we would have to agree that people have the right not merely to be left alone but also the right to be killed. I leave to one side that substantive moral issue. My claim is simply that there can be a reason for terminating life-prolonging treatment other than "to bring about the patient's death."

The second case in which termination of treatment cannot be identified with intentional termination of life is where continued treatment has little chance of improving the patient's condition and brings greater discomfort than relief.

The question here is what treatment is appropriate to the particular case. A cancer specialist describes it in this way:

> My general rule is to administer therapy as long as a patient responds well and has the potential for a reasonably good quality of life. But when all feasible therapies have been administered and a patient shows signs of rapid deterioration, the continuation of therapy can cause more discomfort than the cancer. From that time I recommend surgery, radiotherapy, or chemotherapy only as a means of relieving pain. But if a patient's condition should once again stabilize after the withdrawal of active therapy and if it should appear that he could still gain some good time, I would immediately reinstitute active therapy. The decision to cease anticancer treatment is never irrevocable, and often the desire to live will push a patient to try for another remission, or even a few more days of life.[3]

The decision here to cease anticancer treatment cannot be construed as a decision that the patient die, or as the intentional termination of life. It is a decision to provide the most appropriate treatment for that patient at that time. Rachels suggests that the point of the cessation of treatment is the intentional termination of life. But here the point of discontinuing treatment is not to bring about the patient's death but to avoid treatment that will cause more discomfort than the cancer and has little hope of benefiting the patient. Treatment that meets this description is often called "extraordinary."[4] The concept is flexible, and what might be considered "extraordinary" in one situation might be ordinary in another. The use of a respirator to sustain a patient through a severe bout with a respiratory disease would be considered ordinary; its use to sustain the life of a severely brain-damaged person in an irreversible coma would be considered extraordinary.

Contrasted with extraordinary treatment is ordinary treatment, the care a doctor would normally be expected to provide. Failure to provide ordinary care constitutes neglect, and can even be construed as the intentional infliction of harm, where there is a legal obligation to provide care. The importance of the ordinary/extraordinary care distinction lies partly in its connection to the doctor's intention. The withholding of extraordinary care should be seen as a decision not to inflict painful treatment on a patient without reasonable hope of success. The withholding of ordinary care, by contrast, must be seen as neglect. Thus, one doctor says, "We have to draw a distinction between ordinary and extraordinary means. We never withdraw what's needed to make a baby comfortable, we would never withdraw the care a parent would provide. We never kill a baby. . . . But we may decide certain heroic intervention is not worthwhile."[5]

We should keep in mind the ordinary/extraordinary care distinction when considering an example given by both Tooley and Rachels to show the irrationality of the active/passive distinction with regard to infanticide. The example is this: A child is born with Down's syndrome and also has an intestinal obstruction that requires corrective surgery. If the surgery is not performed, the infant will starve to death, since it cannot take food orally. This may take days or even weeks, as dehydration and infection set in. Commenting on this situation in his article in this book, Rachels says:

> I can understand why some people are opposed to all euthanasia, and insist that such infants must be allowed to live. I think I can also understand why other people favor destroying these babies quickly and painlessly. But why should anyone favor letting "dehydration and infection wither a tiny being over hours and days"? The doctrine that says that a baby may be allowed to dehydrate and wither, but may not be given an injection that would end its life without suffering, seems so patently cruel as to require no further refutation.

Such a doctrine perhaps does not need further refutation; but this is not the AMA doctrine. The AMA statement criticized by Rachels allows only for the cessation of extraordinary means to prolong life when death is imminent. Neither of these conditions is satisfied in this example. Death is not imminent in this situation, any more than it would be if a normal child had an attack of appendicitis. Neither the corrective surgery to remove the intestinal obstruction nor the intravenous feeding required to keep the infant alive until such surgery is performed can be regarded as extraordinary means, for neither is particularly expensive, nor does either place an overwhelming burden on the patient or others. (The continued existence of the child might be thought to place an overwhelming burden on its parents, but that has nothing to do with the characterization of the means to prolong its life as extraordinary. If it had, then *feeding* a severely defective child who required a great deal of care could be regarded as extraordinary.) The chances of success if the operation is undertaken are quite good, though there is always a risk in operating on infants. Though the Down's syndrome will not be alleviated, the child will proceed to an otherwise normal infancy.

It cannot be argued that the treatment is withheld for the infant's sake, unless one is prepared to argue that all mentally retarded babies are better off dead. This is particularly implausible in the case of Down's syndrome babies, who generally do not suffer and are capable of giving and receiving love, of learning and playing, to varying degrees.

In a film on this subject entitled, "Who Should Survive?", a doctor defended a decision not to operate, saying that since the parents did not consent to the operation, the doctors' hands were tied. As we have seen, surgical intrusion requires consent, and in the case of infants, consent would normally come from the parents. But, as legal guardians, parents are required to provide medical care for their children, and failure to do so can constitute criminal neglect or even homicide. In general, courts have been understandably reluctant to recognize a parental right to terminate life prolonging treatment.[6] Although prosecution is unlikely, physicians who comply with invalid instructions from the parents and permit the infant's death could be liable to aiding and abetting, failure to report child neglect, or even homicide. So it is not true that, in this situation, doctors are legally bound to do as the parents wish.

To sum up, I think that Rachels is right to regard the decision not to operate in the Down's syndrome example as the intentional termination of life. But there is no reason to believe that either the law or the AMA would regard it otherwise. Certainly the decision to withhold treatment is not justified by the AMA statement. That such infants have been allowed to die cannot be denied; but this, I think, is the result of doctors misunderstanding the law and the AMA position.

Withholding treatment in this case is the intentional termination of life because the infant is deliberately allowed to die; that is the point of not operating. But there are other cases in which that is not the point. If the point is to avoid inflicting painful treatment on a patient with little or no reasonable hope of success, this is not the intentional termination of life. The permissibility of such withholding of treatment, then, would have no implications for the permissibility of euthanasia, active or passive.

The decision whether or not to operate, or to institute vigorous treatment, is particularly agonizing in the case of children born with spina bifida, an opening in the base of the spine usually accompanied by hydrocephalus and mental retardation. If left unoperated, these children usually die of meningitis or kidney failure within the first few years of life. Even if they survive, all affected children face a lifetime of illness, operations, and varying degrees of disability. The policy used to be to save as many as possible, but the trend now is toward selective treatment, based on the physician's estimate of the chances of success. If operating is not likely to improve significantly the child's condition, parents and doctors may agree not to operate. This is not the intentional termination of life, for again the purpose is not the termination of the child's life but the avoidance of painful and pointless treatment. Thus, the fact that withholding treatment is justified does not imply that killing the child would be equally justified.

Throughout the discussion, I have claimed that intentionally ceasing life-prolonging treatment is not the intentional termination of life unless the doctor has, as his or her purpose in stopping treatment, the patient's death.

It may be objected that I have incorrectly characterized the conditions for the intentional termination of life. Perhaps it is enough that the doctor intentionally ceases treatment, foreseeing that the patient will die.

In many cases, if one acts intentionally, foreseeing that a particular result will occur, one can be said to have brought about that result intentionally. Indeed, this is the general legal rule. Why, then, am I not willing to call the cessation of life-prolonging treatment, in compliance with the patient's right to refuse treatment, the intentional termination of life? It is not because such an *identification* is necessarily opprobrious; for we could go

on to *discuss* whether such cessation of treatment is a *justifiable* intentional termination of life. Even in the law, some cases of homicide are justifiable; e.g., homicide in self-defense.

However, the cessation of life-prolonging treatment, in the cases which I have discussed, is not regarded in law as being justifiable homicide, because it is not homicide at all. Why is this? Is it because the doctor "doesn't do anything," and so cannot be guilty of homicide? Surely not, since, as I have indicated, the law sometimes treats an omission as the cause of death. A better explanation, I think, has to do with the fact that in the context of the patient's right to refuse treatment, a doctor is not at liberty to continue treatment. It seems a necessary ingredient of intentionally letting die that one could have done something to prevent the death. In this situation, of course the doctor can physically prevent the patient's death, but since we do not regard the doctor as *free* to continue treatment, we say that there is "nothing he can do." Therefore he does not intentionally let the patient die.

To discuss this suggestion fully, I would need to present a full-scale theory of intentional action. However, at least I have shown, through the discussion of the above examples, that such a theory will be very complex, and that one of the complexities concerns the agent's reason for acting. The reason why an agent acted (or failed to act) may affect the characterization of what he did intentionally. The mere fact that he did *something* intentionally, foreseeing a certain result, does not necessarily mean that he brought about that *result* intentionally.

In order to show that the cessation of life-prolonging treatment, in the cases I've discussed, is the intentional termination of life, one would either have to show that treatment was stopped in order to bring about the patient's death, or provide a theory of intentional action according to which the reason for ceasing treatment is irrelevant to its characterization as the intentional termination of life. I find this suggestion implausible, but am willing to consider arguments for it. Rachels has provided no such arguments: Indeed, he apparently shares my view about the intentional termination of life. For when he claims that the cessation of life-prolonging treatment *is* the intentional termination of life, his reason for making the claim is that "if it were not, there would be no point to it." Rachels believes that the point of ceasing treatment, "in these cases," is to bring about the patient's death. If that were not the point, he suggests, why would the doctor cease treatment? I have shown, however, that there can be a point to ceasing treatment which is not the death of the patient. In showing this, I have refuted Rachels' reason for identifying the cessation of life-prolonging treatment with the intentional termination of life, and thus his argument against the AMA doctrine.

Here someone might say: Even if the withholding of treatment is not the intentional termination of life, does that make a difference, morally speaking? If life-prolonging treatment may be withheld, for the sake of the child, may not an easy death be provided, for the sake of the child, as well? The unoperated child with spina bifida may take months or even years to die. Distressed by the spectacle of children "lying around, waiting to die," one doctor has written, "It is time that society and medicine stopped perpetuating the fiction that withholding treatment is ethically different from terminating a life. It is time that society began to discuss mechanisms by which we can alleviate the pain and suffering for those individuals whom we cannot help."[7]

I do not deny that there may be cases in which death is in the best interests of the patient. In such cases, a quick and painless death may be the best thing. However, I do not think that, once active or vigorous treatment is stopped, a quick death is always preferable to a lingering one. We must be cautious about attributing to defective children *our* distress at seeing them linger. Waiting for them to die may be tough on parents, doctors, and nurses—it isn't necessarily tough on the child. The decision not to operate need not mean a decision to neglect, and it may be possible to make the remaining months of the child's life comfortable, pleasant, and filled with love. If this alternative is possible, surely it is more decent and humane than killing the child. In such a situation, withholding treatment, foreseeing the child's death, is not ethically equivalent to killing the child, and we cannot move from the permissibility of the former to that of the latter. I am worried that there will be a tendency to do precisely that if active euthanasia is regarded as morally equivalent to the withholding of life-prolonging treatment.

Conclusion

The AMA statement does not make the distinction Rachels and Tooley wish to attack, that between active and passive euthanasia. Instead, the statement draws a distinction between the intentional termination of life, on the one hand, and the cessation of the employment of extraordinary means to prolong life, on the other. Nothing said by Rachels and Tooley shows that this distinction is confused. It may be that doctors have misinterpreted the AMA statement, and that this has led, for example, to decisions to allow defective infants to starve slowly to death. I quite agree with Rachels and Tooley that the decisions to which they allude were cruel and made on irrelevant grounds. Certainly it is worth pointing out that allowing someone to die *can* be the intentional termination of life, and that it can be just as bad as, or worse than, killing someone. However, the withholding of life-prolonging treatment is not necessarily the intentional termination of life, so that if it is permissible to withhold life-prolonging treatment it does not follow that, other things being equal, it is permissible to kill. Furthermore, most of the time, other things are not equal. In many of the cases in which it would be right to cease treatment, I do not think that it would also be right to kill.

Notes

1. For example, *In re Yetter,* 62 Pa. D. & C. 2d 619 (C. P., Northampton County Ct. 1974).

2. David W. Meyers, "Legal Aspects of Voluntary Euthanasia," in *Dilemmas of Euthanasia,* ed. John Behnke and Sissela Bok (New York: Anchor Books, 1975), p. 56.

3. Ernest H. Rosenbaum, M.D., *Living With Cancer* (New York: Praeger, 1975), p. 27.

4. See Tristram Engelhardt, Jr., "Ethical Issues in Aiding the Death of Young Children," in *Beneficent Euthanasia,* ed. Marvin Kohl (Buffalo, N.Y.: Prometheus Books, 1975).

5. B. D. Colen, *Karen Ann Quinlan: Living and Dying in the Age of Eternal Life* (Los Angeles: Nash, 1976), p. 115.

6. See Norman L. Cantor, "Law and the Termination of an Incompetent Patient's Life-Preserving Care," in *Dilemmas of Euthanasia,* pp. 69–105.

7. John Freeman, "Is There a Right to Die—Quickly?", *Journal of Pediatrics,* 80, no. 5 (1972), 904–905.

Questions for Analysis

1. What is the mistake that Steinbock believes Rachels and Tooley make, which leads them to misinterpret the AMA statement?

2. Steinbock insists that there is a difference between the cessation of life-prolonging treatment and passive euthanasia. Do you agree?

3. Why does the right to refuse treatment not imply the right to voluntary euthanasia?

4. Why does Steinbock feel that the decision to suspend treatment when the treatment does no good cannot be construed as a decision that the patient die?

5. Explain what is meant by extraordinary as opposed to ordinary treatment.

6. On what basis does Steinbock criticize Rachels's example of the infant with Down's syndrome?

Some Non-Religious Views Against Proposed "Mercy-Killing" Legislation

Yale Kamisar

Even cases of patients requesting euthanasia to escape from incurable, unceasing pain are not easy to handle. One complication is that no two cases are ever precisely the same. As a result, general rules to cover all cases often raise additional problems. In the following essay, professor of law Yale Kamisar raises two such problems: (1) the possibility of a medical practitioner making a mistake when given a wide range of freedom in determining even voluntary euthanasia, and (2) the possibility that voluntary euthanasia could become a precedent for legalizing nonvoluntary euthanasia. For these consequential reasons, Kamisar objects to the state establishing a legal right to euthanasia. It is important to note, however, that one could support Kamisar's view while at the same time agreeing that some cases of voluntary euthanasia are morally justifiable. In other words, one might see nothing objectionable about individual acts of voluntary euthanasia, but object to any social policy that would permit any form of voluntary euthanasia for the same utilitarian reasons that Kamisar does.

A recent book, Glanville Williams' *The Sanctity of Life and the Criminal Law*, once again brings to the fore the controversial topic of euthanasia, more popularly known as "mercy-killing." In keeping with the trend of the euthanasia movement over the past generation, Williams concentrates his efforts for reform on the *voluntary* type of euthanasia, for example, the cancer victim begging for death; as opposed to the *involuntary variety*, that is, the case of the congenital idiot, the permanently insane, or the senile.

As an ultimate philosophical proposition, the case for voluntary euthanasia is strong. Whatever may be said for and against suicide generally, the appeal of death is immeasurably greater when it is sought not for a poor reason or just any reason, but for "good cause," so to speak; when it is invoked not on behalf of a "socially useful" person, but on behalf of, for example, the pain-racked "hopelessly incurable" cancer victim. If a person is *in fact* (1) presently incurable, (2) beyond the aid of any respite which may come along in his life ex-

From Yale Kamisar, "Some Non-Religious Views against Proposed 'Mercy-Killing' Legislation," Minnesota Law Review, 42 *(1958). Reprinted by permission of the publisher and the author. Footnotes omitted.*

pectency, suffering (3) intolerable and (4) unmitigable pain and of a (5) fixed and (6) rational desire to die, I would hate to have to argue that the hand of death should be stayed. But abstract propositions and carefully formed hypotheticals are one thing; specific proposals designed to cover everyday situations are something else again.

In essence, Williams' proposal is that death be authorized for a person in the above situation "by giving the medical practitioner a wide discretion and trusting to his good sense." This, I submit, raises too great a risk of abuse and mistake to warrant a change in the existing law. That a proposal entails risk of mistake is hardly a conclusive reason against it. But neither is it irrelevant. Under any euthanasia program the consequences of mistake, of course, are always fatal. As I shall endeavor to show, the incidence of mistake of one kind or another is likely to be quite appreciable. If this indeed be the case, unless the need for the authorized conduct is compelling enough to override it, I take it the risk of mistake *is* a conclusive reason against such authorization. I submit too, that the possible radiations from the proposed legislation, *e.g.*, involuntary euthanasia of idiots and imbeciles (the typical "mercy-killings" reported by the press) and the emergence of the legal precedent that there are lives not "worth living," give additional cause to pause.

I see the issue, then, as the need for voluntary euthanasia versus (1) the incidence of mistake and abuse; and (2) the danger that legal machinery initially designed to kill those who are a nuisance to themselves may someday engulf those who are a nuisance to others.

The "freedom to choose a merciful death by euthanasia" may well be regarded, as does Professor Harry Kalven in a carefully measured review of another recent book urging a similar proposal, as "a special area of civil liberties far removed from the familiar concerns with criminal procedures, race discrimination, and freedom of speech and religion." The civil liberties angle is definitely a part of Professor Williams' approach:

> If the law were to remove its ban on euthanasia, the effect would merely be to leave this subject to the individual conscience. This proposal would . . . be easy to defend, as restoring personal liberty in a field in which men differ on the question of conscience. . . .

> On a question like this there is surely everything to be said for the liberty of the individual.

I am perfectly willing to accept civil liberties as the battlefield, but issues of "liberty" and "freedom" mean little until we begin to pin down *whose* "liberty" and "freedom" and for *what* need and at *what* price. This paper is concerned largely with such questions.

> It is true also of journeys in the law that the place you reach depends on the direction you are taking. And so, where one comes out on a case depends on where one goes in.

So it is with the question at hand. Williams champions the "personal liberty" of the dying to die painlessly. I am more concerned about the life and liberty of those who would needlessly be killed in the process or who would irrationally choose to partake of the process. Williams' price on behalf of those who are *in fact* "hopeless incurables" and *in fact* of a fixed and rational desire to die is the sacrifice of (1) some few, who, though they know it not, because their physicians know it not, need not and should not die; (2) others, probably not so few, who, though they go through the motions of "volunteering," are casualties of strain, pain, or narcotics to such an extent that they really know not what they do. My price on behalf of those who, despite appearances to the contrary, have some relatively normal and reasonably useful life left in them, or who are incapable of making the choice, is the lingering on for awhile of those who, if you will, *in fact* have no desire and no reason to linger on.

A Close-Up View of Voluntary Euthanasia: The Euthanasiast's Dilemma and Williams' Proposed Solution

As if the general principle they advocate did not raise enough difficulties in itself, euthanasiasts have learned only too bitterly that specific plans of enforcement are often much less palatable than the abstract notions they are designed to effectuate. In the case of voluntary euthanasia, the means of implementation vary from (1) the simple proposal that mercy-killings by anyone, typically relatives, be immunized from the criminal law; to (2) the elaborate legal machinery contained in the bills of the Voluntary Euthanasia Legalisation Society

(England) and the Euthanasia Society of America for carrying out euthanasia.

The English Society would require the eligible patient, *i.e.*, one over twenty-one and "suffering from a disease involving severe pain and of an incurable and fatal character," to forward a specially prescribed application—along with two medical certificates, one signed by the attending physician, and the other by a specially appointed Euthanasia Referee "who shall satisfy himself by means of a personal interview with the patient and otherwise that the said conditions shall have been fulfilled and that the patient fully understands the nature and purpose of the application"; and, if so satisfied, shall then send a euthanasia permit to the patient; which permit shall, seven days after receipt, become "operative" in the presence of an official witness; unless the nearest relative manages to cancel the permit by persuading a court of appropriate jurisdiction that the requisite conditions have not been met.

The American Society would have the eligible patient, *i.e.*, one over twenty-one "suffering from severe physical pain caused by a disease for which no remedy affording lasting relief or recovery is at the time known to medical science," petition for euthanasia in the presence of two witnesses and file same, along with the certificate of an attending physician, in a court of appropriate jurisdiction; said court to then appoint a committee of three, of whom at least two must be physicians, "who shall forthwith examine the patient and such other persons as they deem advisable or as the court may direct and within five days after their appointment, shall report to the court whether or not the patient understands the nature and purpose of the petition and comes within the [act's] provisions"; whereupon, if the report is in the affirmative, the court shall—"unless there is some reason to believe that the report is erroneous or untrue"— grant the petition; in which event euthanasia is to be administered in the presence of the committee, or any two members thereof.

As will be seen, and as might be expected, the simple negative proposal to remove "mercy-killings" from the ban of the criminal law is strenuously resisted on the ground that it offers the patient far too little protection from not-so-necessary or not-so-merciful killings. On the other hand, the elaborate affirmative proposals of the euthanasia societies meet much pronounced eye-blinking, not a few guffaws, and sharp criticism that the legal machinery is so drawn-out, so complex, so formal, and so tedious as to offer the patient far too little solace. . . .

Nothing rouses Professor Williams' ire more than the fact that opponents of the euthanasia movement argue that euthanasia proposals offer either inadequate protection or overelaborate safeguards. Williams appears to meet this dilemma with the insinuation that because arguments are made in the antithesis *they must each be invalid, each be obstructionist, and each be made in bad faith.*

It just may be, however, that each alternative argument is quite valid, that the trouble lies with the euthanasiasts themselves in seeking a goal which is *inherently inconsistent:* a procedure for death which *both* (1) provides ample safeguards against abuse and mistake; and (2) is "quick" and "easy" in operation. Professor Williams meets the problem with more than bitter comments about the tactics of the opposition. He makes a brave try to break through the dilemma:

> The reformers might be well advised, in their next proposal, to abandon all their cumbrous safeguards and to do as their opponents wish, giving the medical practitioner a wide discretion and trusting to his good sense.
>
> The essence of the bill would then be simple. It would provide that no medical practitioner should be guilty of an offense in respect of an act done intentionally to accelerate the death of a patient who is seriously ill, unless it is proved that the act was not done in good faith with the consent of the patient and for the purpose of saving him from severe pain in an illness believed to be of an incurable and fatal character. Under this formula it would be for the physician, if charged, to show that the patient was seriously ill, but for the prosecution to prove that the physician acted from some motive other than the humanitarian one allowed to him by law. . . .

Evidently, the presumption is that the general practitioner is a sufficient buffer between the patient and the restless spouse or overwrought or overreaching relative, as well as a depository of enough general scientific know-how and enough information about current research developments and trends, to assure a minimum of error in diagnosis and anticipation of new measures of relief. Whether or not the general practitioner will accept the responsibility Williams would confer on him is itself a problem of major proportions. Putting that question aside, the soundness of the underlying premises of Williams' "legislative suggestion" will be examined in the course of the discussion of various aspects of the euthanasia problem.

The "Choice"

Under current proposals to establish legal machinery, elaborate or otherwise, for the administration of a quick and easy death, it is not enough that those authorized to pass on the question decide that the patient, in effect, is "better off dead." The patient must concur in this opinion. Much of the appeal in the current proposal lies in this so-called "voluntary" attribute.

But is the adult patient really in a position to concur? Is he truly able to make euthanasia a "voluntary" act? There is a good deal to be said, is there not, for Dr. Frohman's pithy comment that the "voluntary" plan is supposed to be carried out "only if the victim is both sane and crazed by pain."

By hypothesis, voluntary euthanasia is not to be resorted to until narcotics have long since been administered and the patient has developed a tolerance to them. *When*, then, does the patient make the choice? While heavily drugged? Or is narcotic relief to be withdrawn for the time of decision? But if heavy dosage no longer deadens pain, indeed, no longer makes it bearable, how overwhelming is it when whatever relief narcotics offer is taken away, too? . . .

Undoubtedly, some euthanasia candidates will have their lucid moments. How they are to be distinguished from fellow-sufferers who do not, or how these instances are to be distinguished from others when the patient is exercising an irrational judgment is not an easy matter. Particularly is this so under Williams' proposal, where no specially qualified persons, psychiatricially trained or otherwise, are to assist in the process.

Assuming, for purposes of argument, that the occasion when a euthanasia candidate possesses a sufficiently clear mind can be ascertained and that a request for euthanasia is then made, there remain other problems. The mind of the pain-racked

may occasionally be clear, but is it not also likely to be uncertain and variable? This point was pressed hard by the great physician, Lord Horder, in the House of Lords debate:

> During the morning depression he [the patient] will be found to favor the application under this Bill, later in the day he will think quite differently, or will have forgotten all about it. The mental clarity with which noble Lords who present this Bill are able to think and to speak must not be thought to have any counterpart in the alternating moods and confused judgments of the sick man.

The concept of "voluntary" in voluntary euthanasia would have a great deal more substance to it if, as is the case with voluntary admission statutes for the mentally ill, the patient retained the right to reverse the process within a specified number of days after he gives written notice of his desire to do so—but unfortunately this cannot be. The choice here, of course, is an irrevocable one. . . .

Even if the patient's choice could be said to be "clear and incontrovertible," do not other difficulties remain? Is this the kind of choice, assuming that it can be made in a fixed and rational manner, that we want to offer a gravely ill person? Will we not sweep up, in the process, some who are not really tired of life, but think others are tired of them; some who do not really want to die, but who feel they should not live on, because to do so when there looms the legal alternative of euthanasia is to do a selfish or a cowardly act? Will not some feel an obligation to have themselves "eliminated" in order that funds allocated for their terminal care might be better used by their families or, financial worries aside, in order to relieve their families of the emotional strain involved?

It would not be surprising for the gravely ill person to seek to inquire of those close to him whether he should avail himself of the legal alternative of euthanasia. Certainly, he is likely to wonder about their attitude in the matter. It is quite possible, is it not, that he will not exactly be gratified by any inclination on their part—however noble their motives may be in fact—that he resort to the new procedure? . . .

At such a time, . . . members of the family are not likely to be in the best state of mind, either, to make this kind of decision. Financial stress and conscious or unconscious competition for the family's estate aside:

> The chronic illness and persistent pain in terminal carcinoma may place strong and excessive stresses upon the family's emotional ties with the patient. The family members who have strong emotional attachment to start with are most likely to take the patient's fears, pains, and fate personally. Panic often strikes them. Whatever guilt feelings they may have toward the patient emerge to plague them.
>
> If the patient is maintained at home, many frustrations and physical demands may be imposed on the family by the advanced illness. There may develop extreme weakness, incontinence, and bad odors. The pressure of caring for the individual under these circumstances is likely to arouse a resentment and, in turn, guilt feelings on the part of those who have to do the nursing.

Nor should it be overlooked that while Professor Williams would remove the various procedural steps and the various personnel contemplated in the American and English Bills and bank his all on the "good sense" of the general practitioner, no man is immune to the fear, anxieties, and frustrations engendered by the apparently helpless, hopeless patient. Not even the general practitioner:

> Working with a patient suffering from a malignancy causes special problems for the physician. First of all, the patient with a malignancy is most likely to engender anxiety concerning death, even in the doctor. And at the same time, this type patient constitutes a serious threat or frustration to medical ambition. As a result, a doctor may react more emotionally and less objectively than in any other area of medical practice. . . . His deep concern may make him more pessimistic than is necessary. As a result of the feeling of frustration in his wish to help, the doctor may have moments of annoyance with the patient. He may even feel almost inclined to want to avoid this type of patient.

The only Anglo-American prosecution involving an alleged mercy-killing physician seems to be the case of Dr. Herman Sander. The state's testimony was to the effect that, as Sander had admitted on various occasions, he finally yielded to the persistent pleas of his patient's husband and pumped air into her veins "in a weak moment." Sander's version was that he finally "snapped" under the strain of caring for the cancer victim, bungled simple tasks, and became "obsessed" with the need to "do something" for her—if only to inject air into her *already* dead body. Whichever side one believes—and the jury evidently believed Dr. Sander—the case well demonstrates that at the moment of decision the tired practitioner's "good sense" may not be as good as it might be. . . .

The boldness and daring which characterizes most of Glanville Williams' book dims perceptibly when he comes to involuntary euthanasia proposals. As to the senile, he states:

> At present the problem has certainly not reached the degree of seriousness that would warrant an effort being made to change traditional attitudes toward the sanctity of life of the aged. Only the grimmest necessity could bring about a change that, however cautious in its approach, would probably cause apprehension and deep distress to many people, and inflict a traumatic injury upon the accepted code of behaviour built up by two thousand years of the Christian religion. It may be, however, that as the problem becomes more acute it will itself cause a reversal of generally accepted values.

To me, this passage is the most startling one in the book. On page 348 Williams invokes "traditional attitudes towards the sanctity of life" and "the accepted code of behaviour built up by two thousand years of the Christian religion" to check the extension of euthanasia to the senile, but for 347 pages he had been merrily rolling along debunking both. Substitute "cancer victim" for "the aged" and Williams' passage is essentially the argument of many of his *opponents* on the voluntary euthanasia question.

The unsupported comment that "the problem [of senility] has certainly not reached the degree of seriousness" to warrant euthanasia is also rather puzzling, particularly coming as it does after an observation by Williams on the immediately preceding page that "it is increasingly common for men and women to reach an age of 'second childishness and mere oblivion,' with a loss of almost all adult faculties except that of digestion."

How "serious" does a problem have to be to warrant a change in these "traditional attitudes?"

If, as the statement seems to indicate, "seriousness" of a problem is to be determined numerically, the problem of the cancer victim does not appear to be as substantial as the problem of the senile. For example, taking just the 95,837 first admissions to "public prolonged-care hospitals" for mental diseases in the United States in 1955, 23,561—or one fourth—were cerebral arteriosclerosis or senile brain disease cases. I am not at all sure that there are 20,000 cancer patients per year who die *unbearably painful* deaths. Even if there were, I cannot believe that among their ranks are some 20,000 per year who, when still in a rational state, so long for a quick and easy death that they would avail themselves of legal machinery for euthanasia.

If the problem of the incurable cancer victim "has reached the degree of seriousness that would warrant an effort being made to change traditional attitudes toward the sanctity of life," as Williams obviously thinks it has, then so has the problem of senility. In any event, the senility problem will undoubtedly soon reach even Williams' requisite degree of seriousness:

> A decision concerning the senile may have to be taken within the next twenty years. The numbers of old people are increasing by leaps and bounds. Pneumonia, "the old man's friend" is now checked by antibiotics. The effects of hardship, exposure, starvation, and accident are now minimized. Where is this leading us? . . . What of the drooling, helpless, disoriented old man or the doubly incontinent old woman lying loglike in bed? Is it here that the real need for euthanasia exists?

If, as Williams indicates, "seriousness" of the problem is a major criterion for euthanatizing a category of unfortunates, the sum total of mentally deficient persons would appear to warrant high priority, indeed.

When Williams turns to the plight of the "hopelessly defective infants," his characteristic vim and vigor are, as in the senility discussion, conspicuously absent:

> While the Euthanasia Society of England has never advocated this, the Euthanasia Society of America did include it in its original program. The proposal certainly escapes the chief objection to the similar proposal for senile dementia: it does not create a sense of

insecurity in society, because infants cannot, like adults, feel anticipatory dread of being done to death if their condition should worsen. Moreover, the proposal receives some support on eugenic grounds, and more importantly on humanitarian grounds—both on account of the parents, to whom the child will be a burden all their lives, and on account of the handicapped child itself. (It is not, however, proposed that any child should be destroyed against the wishes of its parents.) Finally, the legalization of euthanasia for handicapped children would bring the law into closer relation to its practical administration, because juries do not regard parental mercy-killing as murder. For these various reasons the proposal to legalize humanitarian infanticide is put forward from time to time by individuals. They remain in a very small minority, and the proposal may at present be dismissed as politically insignificant.

It is understandable for a reformer to limit his present proposals for change to those with a real prospect of success. But it is hardly reassuring for Williams to cite the fact that only "a very small minority" has urged euthanasia for "hopelessly defective infants" as the *only* reason for not pressing for such legislation now. If, as Williams sees it, the only advantage voluntary euthanasia has over the involuntary variety lies in the organized movements on its behalf, that advantage can readily be wiped out.

In any event, I do not think that such "a very small minority" has advocated "humanitarian infanticide." Until the organization of the English and American societies led to a concentration on the voluntary type, and until the byproducts of the Nazi euthanasia program somewhat embarrassed, if only temporarily, most proponents of involuntary euthanasia, about as many writers urged one type as another. Indeed, some euthanasiasts have taken considerable pains to demonstrate the superiority of defective infant euthanasia over incurably ill euthanasia. . . .

Nor do I think it irrelevant that while public resistance caused Hitler to yield on the adult euthanasia front, the killing of malformed and idiot children continued unhindered to the end of the war, the definition of "children" expanding all the while. Is it the embarrassing experience of the Nazi euthanasia program which has rendered destruction of defective infants presently "politically insignificant"? If so, is it any more of a jump from the incurably and painfully ill to the unorthodox political thinker than it is from the hopelessly defective infant to the same "unsavory character"? Or is it not so much that the euthanasiasts are troubled by the Nazi experience as it is that they are troubled that the public is troubled by the Nazi experience?

The Parade of Horrors

> Look, when the messenger cometh, shut the door, and hold him fast at the door; is not the sound of his master's feet behind him?

This is the "wedge principle," the "parade of horrors" objection, if you will, to voluntary euthanasia. Glanville Williams' peremptory retort is:

> This use of the "wedge" objection evidently involves a particular determination as to the meaning of words, namely the words "if raised to a general line of conduct." The author supposes, for the sake of argument, that the merciful extinction of life in a suffering patient is not in itself immoral. Still it is immoral, because if it were permitted this would admit "a most dangerous wedge that might eventually put all life in a precarious condition." It seems a sufficient reply to say that this type of reasoning could be used to condemn any act whatever, because there is no human conduct from which evil cannot be imagined to follow if it is persisted in when some of the circumstances are changed. All moral questions involve the drawing of a line, but the "wedge principle" would make it impossible to draw a line, because the line would have to be pushed farther and farther back until all action became vetoed.

I agree with Williams that if a first step is "moral" it is moral wherever a second step may take us. The real point, however, the point that Williams sloughs, is that whether or not the first step is precarious, is perilous, is worth taking, rests in part on what the second step is likely to be.

It is true that the "wedge" objection can always be advanced, the horrors can always be paraded. But it is no less true that on some occasions the objection is much more valid than it is on others. One reason why the "parade of horrors" cannot be too lightly dismissed in this particular instance is that Miss Voluntary Euthanasia is not likely to be going it alone for very long. Many of her admirers, as I have endeavored to show in the preceding section, would be neither surprised nor distressed to see her joined by Miss Euthanatize the Congenital Idiots and Miss Euthanatize the Permanently Insane and Miss Euthanatize the Senile Dementia. And these lasses—whether or not they themselves constitute a "parade of horrors"—certainly make excellent majorettes for such a parade:

> Some are proposing what is called euthanasia; at presently only a proposal for killing those who are a nuisance to themselves; but soon to be applied to those who are a nuisance to other people.

Another reason why the "parade of horrors" argument cannot be too lightly dismissed in this particular instance, it seems to me, is that the parade *has* taken place in our time and the order of procession has been headed by the killing of the "incurables" and the "useless":

> Even before the Nazis took open charge in Germany, a propaganda barrage was directed against the traditional compassionate nineteenth-century attitudes toward the chronically ill, and for the adoption of a utilitarian, Hegelian point of view. . . . Lay opinion was not neglected in this campaign. Adults were propagandized by motion pictures, one of which, entitled "I Accuse," deals entirely with euthanasia. This film depicts the life history of a woman suffering from multiple sclerosis; in it her husband, a doctor, finally kills her to the accompaniment of soft piano music rendered by a sympathetic colleague in an adjoining room. Acceptance of this ideology was implanted even in the children. A widely used high-school mathematics text . . . included problems stated in distorted terms of the cost of caring for and rehabilitating the chronically sick and crippled. One of the problems asked, for instance, how many new housing units could be built and how many marriage-allowance loans could be given to newly wedded couples for the amount of money it cost the state to care for "the crippled, the criminal, and the insane. . . ." The beginnings at first were merely a subtle shift in emphasis in the basic attitude of the physicians. *It started with the acceptance of the*

*attitude, basic in the euthanasia movement, that
there is such a thing as life not worthy to be lived.*
This attitude in its early stages concerned itself
merely with the severely and chronically sick.
Gradually the sphere of those to be included in
this category was enlarged to encompass the
socially unproductive, the ideologically
unwanted, the racially unwanted, and finally
all non-Germans. But it is important to realize
that the infinitely small wedged-in lever from
which this entire trend of mind receives its
impetus was the attitude toward the non-
rehabilitable sick.

The apparent innocuousness of Germany's "small
beginnings" is perhaps best shown by the fact that
German Jews were at first excluded from the program. For it was originally conceived that "the
blessing of euthanasia should be granted only to
[true] Germans."

Relatively early in the German program, Pastor Braune, Chairman of the Executive Committee
of the Domestic Welfare Council of the German
Protestant Church, called for a halt to euthanasia
measures "since they strike sharply at the moral
foundations of the nation as a whole. The inviolability of human life is a pillar of any social order."
And the pastor raised the same question which
euthanasia opponents ask today, as well they
might, considering the disinclination of many in
the movement to stop at voluntary "mercy-
killngs": Where do we, how do we, draw the line?
The good pastor asked:

> How far is the destruction of socially unfit
> life to go? The mass methods used so far have
> quite evidently taken in many people who are
> to a considerable degree of sound mind. . . . Is
> it intended to strike only at the utterly hopeless
> cases—the idiots and imbeciles? The
> instruction sheet, as already mentioned, also
> lists senile diseases. The latest decree by the
> same authorities requires that children with
> serious congenital disease and malformation of
> every kind be registered, to be collected and
> processed in special institutions. This
> necessarily gives rise to grave apprehensions.
> Will a line be drawn at the tubercular? In the
> case of persons in custody by court order
> euthanasia measures have evidently already
> been initiated. Are other abnormal or antisocial
> persons likewise to be included? Where is the
> borderline? Who is abnormal, antisocial,
> hopelessly sick?

Williams makes no attempt to distinguish or
minimize the Nazi Germany experience. Apparently he does not consider it worthy of mention in
a euthanasia discussion. There are, however, a
couple of obvious arguments by which the Nazi
experience can be minimized.

One goes something like this: It is silly to
worry about the prospects of a dictatorship utilizing euthanasia "as a pretext for putting inconvenient citizens out of the way. Dictatorships have no
occasion for such subterfuges. The firing squad is
less bother." One reason why this counter argument is not too reassuring, however, if again I may
be permitted to be so unkind as to meet speculation with a concrete example to the contrary, is
that Nazi Germany had considerable occasion to
use just such a subterfuge.

Thus, Dr. Leo Alexander observes:

> It is rather significant that the German people
> are considered by their Nazi leaders more
> ready to accept the exterminations of the sick
> than those for political reasons. It was for that
> reason that the first exterminations of the latter
> group were carried out under the guise of
> sickness. So-called "psychiatric experts" were
> dispatched to survey the inmates of camps
> with the specific order to pick out members of
> racial minorities and political offenders from
> occupied territories and to dispatch them to
> killing centers with specially made diagnoses
> such as that of "inveterate German hater"
> applied to a number of prisoners who had
> been active in the Czech underground.
>
> A large number of those marked for death
> for political or racial reasons were made
> available for "medical experiments involving
> the use of involuntary human subjects."

The "hunting season" in Germany officially
opened when Hitler signed on his own letterhead
a secret order dated September 1, 1939, which
read:

> Reichsleiter Bouhler and Dr. Brandt, M.D.,
> are charged with the responsibility of enlarging
> the authority of certain physicians, to be
> designated by name, in such a manner that
> persons who, according to human judgment,
> are incurable can, upon a more careful
> diagnosis of their condition of sickness, be
> accorded a mercy death.

Physicians asked to participate in the program
were told that the secrecy of the order was de-

signed to prevent patients from becoming "too agitated" and that it was in keeping with the policy of not publicizing home front measures in time of war.

About the same time that aged patients in some hospitals were being given the "mercy" treatment, the Gestapo was also "systematically putting to death the mentally deficient population of the Reich."

The courageous and successful refusal by a Protestant pastor to deliver up certain cases from his asylum well demonstrates that even the most totalitarian governments are not always indifferent to the feelings of the people, that they do not always feel free to resort to the firing squad. Indeed, vigorous protests by other ecclesiastical personalities and some physicians, numerous requests of various public prosecutors for investigation of the circumstances surrounding the mysterious passing away of relatives, and a generally aroused public opinion finally caused Hitler to yield, if only temporarily, and in August of 1941 he verbally ordered the discontinuance of the adult euthanasia program. Special gas chambers in Hadamar and other institutions were dismantled and shipped to the East for much more extensive use on Polish Jews.

Perhaps it should be noted, too, that even dictatorships fell prey to the inertia of big government:

> It is . . . interesting that there was so much talk against euthanasia in certain areas of Germany, particularly in the region of Wiesbaden, that Hitler in 1943 asked Himmler to stop it. But, it had gained so much impetus by 1943 and was such an easy way in crowded concentration camps to get rid of undesirables and make room for newcomers, that it could not be stopped. The wind had become a whirlwind.

Another obvious argument is that it just can't happen here. I hope not. I think not.

But then, neither did I think that tens of thousands of perfectly loyal native-born Americans would be herded into prison camps without proffer of charges and held there for many months,

even years, because they were of "Japanese blood" and, although the general who required these measures emitted considerable ignorance and bigotry, his so-called military judgment would be largely sustained by the highest court of the land. The Japanese-American experience of World War II undoubtedly fell somewhat short of first-class Nazi tactics, but we were getting warm. I venture to say it would not be too difficult to find American citizens of Japanese descent who would maintain we were getting very warm indeed.

A Final Reflection

There have been and there will continue to be compelling circumstances when a doctor or relative will violate The Law On The Books and, more often than not, receive protection from The Law In Action. But this is not to deny that there are other occasions when The Law On The Books operates to stay the hand of all concerned, among them situations where the patient is in fact (1) presently incurable, (2) beyond the aid of any respite which may come along in his life expectancy, suffering (3) intolerable and (4) unmitigable pain and of a (5) fixed and (6) rational desire to die. That any euthanasia program may only be the opening wedge for far more objectionable practices, and that even within the bounds of a "voluntary" plan such as Williams' the incidence of mistake or abuse is likely to be substantial, are not much solace to one in the above plight.

It may be conceded that in a narrow sense it is an "evil" for such a patient to have to continue to suffer—if only for a little while. But in a narrow sense, long-term sentences and capital punishment are "evils," too. If we can justify the infliction of imprisonment and death by the state "on the ground of the social interests to be protected" then surely we can similarly justify the postponement of death by the state. The objection that the individual is thereby treated not as an "end" in himself but only as a "means" to further the common good was, I think, aptly disposed of by Holmes long ago. "If a man lives in society, he is likely to find himself so treated."

Questions for Analysis

1. State precisely Glenville Williams's position that Kamisar is reacting to.

2. Kamisar joins the issue on the "battlefield" of civil rights. Whose liberties is Kamisar concerned with? And Williams?

3. Who, according to Kamisar, does Williams regard as a sufficient safeguard against euthanasia abuse? Does Kamisar agree? Do you?

4. Why does Kamisar question that consent can be voluntary?

5. What does Kamisar regard as the "most startling" passage in Williams's book? What point does Kamisar make in using this passage? Do you think that the passage makes Kamisar's point as well as he thinks?

6. What is the "parade of horrors" that Kamisar fears? Do you think that this argument is any more than a slippery-slope appeal? Kamisar feels that the "parade of horrors" cannot be dismissed lightly. Do you agree?

Euthanasia Legislation: Rejoinder to Non-Religious Objections

Glanville Williams

---

*Responding to Kamisar's charges, Glanville Williams, fellow of Jesus College and Rouse Ball
Professor of the Laws of England at the University of Cambridge, argues through nonconsequential
ethics that prohibiting voluntary euthanasia is cruel and inhumane. Williams concedes but
downplays the frightening scenarios that Kamisar sketches. In contrast, he argues for the inherent
liberty of individuals to choose euthanasia. Indeed, he claims that the argument for voluntary
euthanasia is an application of two values: the prevention of cruelty, and liberty.*

*Williams is careful to reply to each of Kamisar's objections: (1) the difficulty of ascertaining
consent, (2) the risk of mistaken diagnosis, (3) the possibility of cure, (4) the wedge argument.
Along the way he takes time to clarify and reinforce his own position, as, for example, when he
compares euthanasia to a medical procedure or operation.*

I welcome Professor Kamisar's reply to my argument for voluntary euthanasia, because it is on the whole a careful, scholarly work, keeping to knowable facts and accepted human values. It is, therefore, the sort of reply that can be rationally considered and dealt with. In this short rejoinder I shall accept most of Professor Kamisar's valuable notes, and merely submit that they do not bear out his conclusion.

The argument in favor of voluntary euthanasia in the terminal stages of painful diseases is a quite simple one, and is an application of two values that are widely recognized. The first value is the prevention of cruelty. Much as men differ in their ethical assessments, all agree that cruelty is an evil—the only difference of opinion residing in what is meant by cruelty. Those who plead for the legalization of euthanasia think that it is cruel to allow a human being to linger for months in the last stages of agony, weakness and decay, and to refuse him his demand for merciful release. There is also a second cruelty involved—not perhaps quite so compelling, but still worth consideration: the agony of the relatives in seeing

---

*From Glanville Williams, "Euthanasia Legislation: Rejoinder to Non-Religious Objections," Minnesota Law Review, 42 (1958).
Reprinted by permission of the publisher and the author.*

their loved one in his desperate plight. Opponents of euthanasia are apt to take a cynical view of the desires of relatives, and this may sometimes be justified. But it cannot be denied that a wife who has to nurse her husband through the last stages of some terrible disease may herself be so deeply affected by the experience that her health is ruined, either mentally or physically. Whether the situation can be eased for such a person by voluntary euthanasia I do not know; probably it depends very much upon the individuals concerned, which is as much as to say that no solution in terms of a general regulatory law can be satisfactory. The conclusion should be in favor of individual discretion.

The second value involved is that of liberty. The criminal law should not be invoked to repress conduct unless this is demonstrably necessary on social grounds. What social interest is there in preventing the sufferer from choosing to accelerate his death by a few months? What positive value does his life still possess for society, that he is to be retained in it by the terrors of the criminal law?

And, of course, the liberty involved is that of the doctor as well as that of the patient. It is the doctor's responsibility to do all he can to prolong worth-while life, or, in the last resort, to ease his patient's passage. If the doctor honestly and sincerely believes that the best service he can perform for his suffering patient is to accede to his request for euthanasia, it is a grave thing that the law should forbid him to do so.

This is the short and simple case for voluntary euthanasia, and, as Kamisar admits, it cannot be attacked directly on utilitarian grounds. Such an attack can only be by finding possible evils of an indirect nature. These evils, in the view of Professor Kamisar, are (1) the difficulty of ascertaining consent, and arising out of that the danger of abuse; (2) the risk of an incorrect diagnosis; (3) the risk of administering euthanasia to a person who could later have been cured by developments in medical knowledge; (4) the "wedge" argument. . . .

Kamisar's first objection, under the heading "The Choice," is that there can be no such thing as truly voluntary euthanasia in painful and killing diseases. He seeks to impale the advocates of euthanasia on an old dilemma. Either the victim is not yet suffering pain, in which case his consent is merely an uninformed and anticipatory one—and he cannot bind himself by contract to be killed in the future—or he is crazed by pain and stupefied by drugs, in which case he is not of sound mind. I have dealt with this problem in my book; Kamisar has quoted generously from it, and I leave the reader to decide. As I understand Kamisar's position, he does not really persist in the objection. With the laconic "perhaps," he seems to grant me, though unwillingly, that there are cases where one can be sure of the patient's consent. But having thus abandoned his own point, he then goes off to a different horror, that the patient may give his consent only in order to relieve his relatives of the trouble of looking after him.

On this new issue, I will return Kamisar the compliment and say: "Perhaps." We are certainly in an area where no solution is going to make things quite easy and happy for everybody, and all sorts of embarrassments may be conjectured. But these embarrassments are not avoided by keeping to the present law: We suffer from them already. If a patient, suffering pain in a terminal illness, wishes for euthanasia partly because of his pain and partly because he sees his beloved ones breaking under the strain of caring for him, I do not see how this decision on his part, agonizing though it may be, is necessarily a matter of discredit either to the patient himself or to his relatives. The fact is that, whether we are considering the patient or his relatives, there are limits to human endurance.

Kamisar's next objection rests on the possibility of mistaken diagnosis. . . . I agree with him that, before deciding on euthanasia in any particular case, the risk of mistaken diagnosis would have to be considered. Everything that is said in the essay would, therefore, be most relevant when the two doctors whom I propose in my suggested measure come to consult on the question of euthanasia; and the possibility of mistake might most forcefully be brought before the patient himself. But have these medical questions any true relevance to the legal discussion?

Kamisar, I take it, notwithstanding his wide reading in medical literature, is by training a lawyer. He has consulted much medical opinion in order to find arguments against changing the law. I ought not to object to this, since I have consulted the same opinion for the opposite purpose. But what we may well ask ourselves is this: Is it not a trifle bizarre that we should be doing so at all? Our profession is the law, not medicine. How does it come about that lawyers have to examine medical literature to assess the advantages and disadvantages of a medical practice?

If the import of this question is not immediately clear, let me return to my imaginary state of Ruritania. Many years ago, in Ruritania as elsewhere, surgical operations were attended with great risk. Lister had not discovered antisepsis, and surgeons killed as often as they cured. In this state of things, the legislature of Ruritania passed a law declaring all surgical operations to be unlawful in principle, but providing that each specific type of operation might be legalized by a statute specially passed for the purpose. The result is that, in Ruritania, as expert medical opinion sees the possibility of some new medical advance, a pressure group has to be formed in order to obtain legislative approval for it. Since there is little public interest in these technical questions, and since, moreover, surgical operations are thought in general to be inimical to the established religion, the pressure group has to work for many years before it gets a hearing. When at last a proposal for legalization is seriously mooted, the lawyers and politicians get to work upon it, considering what possible dangers are inherent in the new operation. Lawyers and politicians are careful people, and they are perhaps more prone to see the dangers than the advantages in a new departure. Naturally they find allies among some of the more timid or traditional or less knowledgeable members of the medical profession, as well as among the priesthood and the faithful. Thus it is small wonder that whereas appendectomy has been practised in civilized countries since the beginning of the present century, a proposal to legalize it has still not passed the legislative assembly of Ruritania.

It must be confessed that on this particular matter the legal prohibition has not been an unmixed evil for the Ruritanians. During the great popularity of the appendix operation in much of the civilized world during the 'twenties and 'thirties of this century, large numbers of these organs were removed without adequate cause, and the citizens of Ruritania have been spared this inconvenience. On the other hand, many citizens of that country have died of appendicitis, who would

have been saved if they had lived elsewhere. And whereas in other countries the medical profession has now learned enough to be able to perform this operation with wisdom and restraint, in Ruritania it is still not being performed at all. Moreover, the law has destroyed scientific inventiveness in that country in the forbidden fields.

Now, in the United States and England we have no such absurd general law on the subject of surgical operations as they have in Ruritania. In principle, medical men are left free to exercise their best judgment, and the result has been a brilliant advance in knowledge and technique. But there are just two—or possibly three—"operations" which are subject to the Ruritanian principle. These are abortion, euthanasia, and possibly sterilization of convenience. In these fields we, too, must have pressure groups, with lawyers and politicians warning us of the possibility of inexpert practitioners and mistaken diagnosis, and canvassing medical opinion on the risk of an operation not yielding the expected results in terms of human happiness and the health of the body politic. In these fields we, too, are forbidden to experiment to see if the foretold dangers actually come to pass. Instead of that, we are required to make a social judgment on the probabilities of good and evil before the medical profession is allowed to start on its empirical tests.

This anomaly is perhaps more obvious with abortion than it is with euthanasia. Indeed, I am prepared for ridicule when I describe euthanasia as a medical operation. Regarded as surgery it is unique, since its object is not to save or prolong life but the reverse. But euthanasia has another object which it shares with many surgical operations— the saving of pain. And it is now widely recognized, as Lord Dawson said in the debate in the House of Lords, that the saving of pain is a legitimate aim of medical practice. The question whether euthanasia will effect a net saving of pain and distress is, perhaps, one that we can attempt to answer only by trying it. But it is obscurantist to forbid the experiment on the ground that until it is performed we cannot certainly know its results. Such an attitude, in any other field of medical endeavor, would have inhibited progress.

The argument based on mistaken diagnosis leads into the argument based on the possibility of dramatic medical discoveries. Of course, a new medical discovery which gives the opportunity of remission or cure will almost at once put an end to mercy-killings in the particular group of cases for which the discovery is made. On the other hand, the discovery cannot affect patients who have already died from their disease. The argument based on mistaken diagnosis is therefore concerned only with those patients who have been mercifully killed just before the discovery becomes available for use. The argument is that such persons may turn out to have been 'mercy-killed' unnecessarily, because if the physician had waited a bit longer they would have been cured. Because of this risk for this tiny fraction of the total number of patients, patients who are dying in pain must be left to do so, year after year, against their entreaty to have it ended.

Just how real is the risk? When a new medical discovery is claimed, some time commonly elapses before it becomes tested sufficiently to justify large-scale production of the drug, or training in the techniques involved. This is a warning period when euthanasia in the particular class of case would probably be halted anyway. Thus it is quite probable that when the new discovery becomes available, the euthanasia process would not in fact show any mistakes in this regard.

Kamisar says that in my book I "did not deign this objection to euthanasia more than a passing reference." I still do not think it is worth any more than that.

He advances the familiar but hardly convincing arguments that the quantitative need for euthanasia is not large. As one reason for this argument, he suggests that not many patients would wish to benefit from euthanasia, even if it were allowed. I am not impressed by the argument. It may be true, but it is irrelevant. So long as there are *any* persons dying in weakness and grief who are refused their request for a speeding of their end, the argument for legalizing euthanasia remains. Next, he suggests that there is no great need for euthanasia because of the advances made with pain-killing drugs. He has made so many quotations from my book that I cannot complain that he has not made more, but there is one relevant point that he does not mention. In my book, recognizing that medical science does manage to save many dying patients from the extreme of physical pain, I pointed out that it often fails to save them from an artificial, twilight existence, with nausea, giddiness, and extreme restlessness, as well as the long hours of consciousness of a hopeless condition. A dear friend of mine, who died of cancer of the bowel, spent his last months in just this state, under the influence of morphine, which deadened pain, but vomiting incessantly, day in and day out. The question that we have to face is whether the unintelligent brutality of such an existence is to be imposed on one who wishes to end it. . . .

The last part of the essay is devoted to the ancient "wedge" argument which I have already examined in my book. It is the trump card of the traditionalist, because no proposal for reform, however strong the arguments in its favor, is immune from the wedge objection. In fact, the stronger the arguments in favor of a reform, the more likely it is that the traditionalist will take the wedge objection—it is then the only one he has. C. M. Cornford put the argument in its proper place when he said that the wedge objection means this: that you should not act justly today, for fear that you may be asked to act still more justly tomorrow.

We heard a great deal of this type of argument in England in the nineteenth century, when it was used to resist almost every social and economic change. In the present century we have had less of it, but it is still accorded an exaggerated importance in some contexts. When lecturing on the law of torts in an American university a few years ago, I suggested that just as compulsory liability insurance for automobiles had spread practically throughout the civilized world, so we should in time see the law of tort superseded in this field by a system of state insurance for traffic accidents, administered independently of proof of fault. The suggestion was immediately met by one student with a horrified reference to "creeping socialism." That is the standard objection made by many people to any proposal for a new department of state activity. The implication is that you must resist every proposal, however admirable in itself, because otherwise you will never be able to draw the line. On the particular question of socialism, the fear is belied by the experience of a number of countries which have extended state control of the economy without going the whole way to socialistic state regimentation.

Kamisar's particular bogey, the racial laws of Nazi Germany, is an effective one in the democratic countries. Any reference to the Nazis is a powerful weapon to prevent change in the traditional taboo on sterilization as well as euthanasia. The case of sterilization is particularly interesting on this; I dealt with it at length in my book, though Kamisar does not mention its bearing on the argument. When proposals are made for promoting voluntary sterilization on eugenic and other grounds, they are immediately condemned by most people as the thin end of a wedge leading to involuntary sterilization; and then they point to the practices of the Nazis. Yet a more persuasive argument pointing in the other direction can easily be found. Several American states have sterilization laws, which for the most part were originally drafted in very wide terms to cover desexualization as well as sterilization, and authorizing involuntary as well as voluntary operations. This legislation goes back long before the Nazis; the earliest statute was in Indiana in 1907. What has been its practical effect? In several American states it has hardly been used. A few have used it, but in practice they have progressively restricted it until now it is virtually confined to voluntary sterilization. This is so, at least, in North Carolina, as Mrs. Woodside's study strikingly shows. In my book I summed up the position as follows:

> The American experience is of great interest because it shows how remote from reality in a democratic community is the fear—frequently voiced by Americans themselves   that voluntary sterilization may be the "thin end of the wedge," leading to a large-scale violation of human rights as happened in Nazi Germany. In fact, the American experience is the precise opposite—starting with compulsory sterilization, administrative practice has come to put the operation on a voluntary footing.

But it is insufficient to answer the "wedge" objection in general terms; we must consider the particular fears to which it gives rise. Kamisar professes to fear certain other measures that the Euthanasia Societies may bring up if their present measure is conceded to them. Surely these other measures, if any, will be debated on their merits? Does he seriously fear that anyone in the United States or in Great Britain is going to propose the

extermination of people of a minority race or religion? Let us put aside such ridiculous fancies and discuss practical politics.

Kamisar is quite right in thinking that a body of opinion would favor the legalization of the involuntary euthanasia of hopelessly defective infants, and some day a proposal of this kind may be put forward. The proposal would have distinct limits, just as the proposal for voluntary euthanasia of incurable sufferers has limits. I do not think that any responsible body of opinion would now propose the euthanasia of insane adults, for the perfectly clear reason that any such practice would greatly increase the sense of insecurity felt by the borderline insane and by the large number of insane persons who have sufficient understanding on this particular matter.

Kamisar expresses distress at a concluding remark in my book in which I advert to the possibility of old people becoming an overwhelming burden on mankind. I share his feeling that there are profoundly disturbing possibilities here; and if I had been merely a propagandist, intent upon securing agreement for a specific measure of law reform, I should have done wisely to have omitted all reference to this subject. Since, however, I am merely an academic writer, trying to bring such intelligence as I have to bear on moral and social issues, I deemed the topic too important and threatening to leave without a word. I think I have made it clear, in the passages cited, that I am not for one moment proposing any euthanasia of the aged in present society; such an idea would shock me as much as it shocks Kamisar and would shock everybody else. Still, the fact that we may one day have to face is that medical science is more successful in preserving the body than in preserving the mind. It is not impossible that, in the foreseeable future, medical men will be able to preserve the mindless body until the age, say, of a thousand, while the mind itself will have lasted only a tenth of that time. What will mankind do then? It is hardly possible to imagine that we shall establish huge hospital-mausolea where the aged are kept in a kind of living death. Even if it is desired to do this, the cost of the undertaking may make it impossible.

This is not an immediately practical problem, and we need not yet face it. The problem of maintaining persons afflicted with senile dementia is well within our economic resources as the matter stands at present. Perhaps some barrier will be found to medical advance which will prevent the problem becoming more acute. Perhaps, as time goes on, and as the alternatives become more clearly realized, men will become more resigned to human control over the mode of termination of life. Or the solution may be that after the individual has reached a certain age, or a certain degree of decay, medical science will hold its hand, and allow him to be carried off by natural causes. But what if these natural causes are themselves painful? Would it not then be kinder to substitute human agency?

In general, it is enough to say that we do not have to know the solutions to these problems. The only doubtful moral question upon which we have to make an immediate decision in relation to involuntary euthanasia is whether we owe a moral duty to terminate the life of an insane person who is suffering from a painful and incurable disease. Such a person is left unprovided for under the legislative proposal formulated in my book. The objection to any system of involuntary euthanasia of the insane is that it may cause a sense of insecurity. It is because I think that the risk of this fear is a serious one that a proposal for the reform of the law must exclude its application to the insane.

Questions for Analysis

1. *What two cruelties does Williams see present in terminal cases where euthanasia is a possibility? Can you think of any other possible cruelties? Would the permissibility of euthanasia in any way add to these cruelties or produce new ones?*

2. *State precisely what Williams means by the liberty value. Would you agree with his formulation?*

3. *Whose liberty is involved in euthanasia decisions?*

4. *How does Williams reply to each of Kamisar's objections? Do you think that the replies are satisfactory, that they refute Kamisar's points?*

5. *What is Williams's point in setting up the fictitious state of Ruritania? Do you think that conditions as he describes them in Ruritainia are analogous to conditions surrounding the euthanasia debate, or are there significant differences?*

6. *What is Williams's basis for calling euthanasia a medical procedure?*

CASE PRESENTATION
The Last Haul

"I should have pulled the trigger, I really should have," the sandy-haired man said in a thick voice. He clutched a cup of black coffee between his heavily bandaged hands and shivered, though it was the middle of August. "I carry a pistol, you know."

In his five years at the burn center, Dr. Chamberlin thought he'd witnessed the gamut of human reactions to tragedy. But this one—well, what do you make of the hero who would be the scapegoat?

By all rights, the doctor thought, Barney should feel ten feet tall after what he did. Dr. Chamberlin had a point. After all it was Barney who'd got Dutch under the shoulders and pulled him halfway out of the tanker. And there he'd held him, though his own hands were ablaze, until help arrived to free Dutch's leg, which was pinched under the steering wheel.

What made the heroics even more remarkable was that Barney hardly knew Dutch. They'd hauled together a few times, as they had that night. Barney knew Dutch had no family except for a sister he'd lost contact with 15 year before. Apart from that, Barney knew little more about Dutch, just that he did his job and did it well.

"He begged me to, you know," Barney said, gazing into the coffee cup as if it were a crystal ball.

"To shoot him?" Doctor Chamberlin asked.

Barney nodded. "The pain, I guess. . . ." His voice trailed off.

"You can't blame yourself," the doctor told him.

But Barney didn't seem to hear him. "Funny," he said, his eyes never leaving the cup, "once we came up on an awful accident. The driver was trapped inside the cab. We could hardly see his face for the flames and smoke. But we could *hear* him real good. He was screaming something fierce, begging to be killed. . . . Later, on the road again, Dutch said to me, 'If I had a gun, I'd have obliged the poor bastard.' Then he made me promise to oblige him if the occasion ever 'rose. I said I would."

The two men were silent for a long time, neither even glancing at the other. Then Barney asked, "Will he live?"

Doctor Chamberlin deflected the question. "Much of his body is severely burned," he said, "and his lungs are damaged. We're giving him plasma and saline solutions to rehydrate him. The big threat, of course, is infection. We're loading him with antibiotics."

For the first time Barney looked the doctor squarely in the eyes. "You didn't answer my question, Doc," he said.

"Frankly," the doctor said, "I don't think he has much of a chance."

"And the pain," Barney said, "is there a lot of pain?"

Doctor Chamberlin eyed the floor and admitted, "There's just so much we can do."

Quick as a flash, Barney said, "Then help him die."

Doctor Chamberlin said he couldn't do that, but he could stop treating him and "let nature take its course."

"It doesn't seem right," Barney said, "to let a man fight for his life when there's no hope."

"There's always hope," the doctor said.

Barney didn't reply. His eyes had returned to the cup as if searching for something he'd lost in the steaming black coffee.

Questions for Analysis

1. *Do you think Barney would have been justified in shooting Dutch? Was he wrong in saving Dutch's life?*

2. *Should Doctor Chamberlin stop treating Dutch and "let nature take its course"?*

3. *Do you think Doctor Chamberlin would be morally justified in actively terminating Dutch's life?*

4. *Would you say that this is a case of voluntary consent or not?*

5. *How would each of the ethical theories evaluate the morality of (a) suspending all treatment of Dutch or (b) terminating his life by some direct action? Do you think any of them would suggest that it is immoral under the circumstances to treat him?*

CASE PRESENTATION
The Bitter End

A lot of people around here—doctors and nurses alike—think I should have acted differently. But some have come forth privately and confessed they thought I did the right thing. A few even said they thought it took "guts." I don't know about that. If anybody showed guts, it was Esther Minturn, not me.

Who would have thought such a gentle woman, who hardly ever spoke above a whisper, had the stuff to make a decision like that? But she bit the bullet all right; nobody can deny that. Maybe she'd bitten it earlier when she married Sam Minturn, I don't know. After all, she did know he had to undergo cancer surgery.

And a nasty bit of business it was, a radical neck dissection that left a gaping wound in Sam's throat and his right carotid artery vulnerable. But even during the long period in ICU that followed, Sam remained cheerful and optimistic. And Esther, well, she almost never left his bedside. The surgeon had taught Esther how to care for Sam's wound; and so she quickly became his private duty nurse.

At first Sam made good progress. Every day he got stronger and more self-sufficient. But then the abscess set in. We didn't know it at the time, but it foreshadowed the end. Grafts were started, but infection thwarted them. I guess it was sometime during those two weeks when Sam went to the operating room about six times that we realized he wouldn't make it. Even the attendents admitted that his chances were slim.

From then on, it was all downhill. Infection raged; treatment failed. Sam lost his will to live. He talked less and less. After awhile he spoke only to request Demerol. When he become disoriented, he had to be restrained.

We all felt for him. A nicer guy you'd never want to meet. And look how he was going out—not in the warmth and security of his own bed, but in a hospital drugged and restrained like some sort of dangerous beast.

Two days before the end, I went into Sam's room to take his vitals and discovered blood spurting upward from a spontaneous carotid rupture. I thought about just turning on my heels and returning later to take his blood pressure. And I would've, if the surgeons hadn't been nearby. But instead, I summoned the surgical resident, who patched him up and then admitted he couldn't do it again.

The next day Sam had to be put on a respirator. We told Esther. In a quiet, determined voice, she simply said, "I won't allow it." We followed her request.

From then on Esther never left Sam's side. She would see it through to the bitter end. She asked nothing for herself, not even a cup of coffee. All she wanted was for Sam not to suffer, for it to be over.

The hours hung like weeks. Then things happened fast. They always do at the end. Out in the hall the intern informed me that Esther had asked the resident to stop the I.V. The resident had refused. The intern said I should slow it until it was just open.

When I returned to Sam's room, I found Esther removing the I.V. I didn't know what to say. Every human instinct told me she had a right to do it. But the nurse in me spoke: "I can't condone what you're doing," I told her, ". . . I have my orders."

"Your orders be damned!" Esther said sharply. "He belongs to me, not to your hospital!"

With that she did what she had to do. I didn't stop her.

Questions for Analysis

1. *Was Esther morally justified in withdrawing Sam's I.V.?*

2. *Would you regard Esther's action as active or passive?*

3. *Did the narrator have a moral obligation to stop Esther?*

4. *Was the intern morally justified in ordering that the I.V. be slowed until it was just open?*

5. *Apply the act utilitarian, rule utilitarian, divine command, categorical imperative, and prima facie standards to Esther's action.*

Selections for Further Reading

Behnke, John A., and Sissela Bok. *The Dilemmas of Euthanasia.* New York: Doubleday Anchor, 1975.

Choron, Jacques. *Death and Western Thought.* New York: Collier, 1968.

Cutler, D. R., Ed. *Updating Life and Death.* Boston: Beacon Press, 1968.

Downing, A. B., Ed. *Euthanasia and the Right to Die.* New York: Humanities Press, 1969.

Gould, Jonathan, and Lord Craigmyle, Eds. *Your Death Warrant?* New York: Arlington House, 1971.

Kohn, Marvin, Ed. *Beneficent Euthanasia.* Buffalo, N.Y.: Prometheus Books, 1975.

Kubler-Ross, Elisabeth. *On Death and Dying.* New York: Macmillan, 1969.

_____. *Questions and Answers on Death and Dying.* New York: Macmillan, 1974.

Russell, O. Ruth. *Freedom To Die: Moral and Legal Aspects of Euthanasia.* New York: Human Sciences Press, 1975. (Also, New York: Dell Publishing Co., 1976).

Williams, Glanville. *The Sanctity of Life and the Criminal Law.* New York: Alfred A. Knopf, 1957.

Winter, Arthur, Ed. *The Moment of Death: A Symposium.* Springfield, Ill.: Thomas, 1969.

7
CAPITAL PUNISHMENT

Gary Gilmore, John Spenkelink, Jesse Walter Bishop—do these names ring a bell? Between 1977 and 1979 these men were executed for a variety of crimes. With their executions, capital punishment once again became an issue of national debate.

Currently about 550 men and a half-dozen women wait on death row. Who may die next is uncertain since none of these cases has exhausted its appeal. An added complication is that, as of now, the U.S. Supreme Court has not ruled comprehensively on whether capital punishment by its very nature is cruel and unusual punishment and thus violates the Eighth Amendment to the U.S. Constitution. However, in the case of *Furman* v. *Georgia* (1972), the Court did rule that capital punishment *as currently administered* was cruel and unusual punishment. In *Furman* v. *Georgia*, the Court actually was ruling on the constitutionality of the death penalty as imposed in three cases, one of murder, two of rape. Since nothing seemed atypical about those cases, the Court's ruling was taken to mean that the death penalty as currently administered violated the Eighth Amendment and, therefore, was unconstitutional. However, all this changed with the executions of Gilmore by firing squad, Spenkelink by electrocution, and Bishop by gas.

The death penalty is a form of punishment. Consequently, one's view of the morality of the death penalty usually is influenced by one's view of punishment generally. Thus, the specific moral question under discussion in this chapter is: Is capital punishment ever a justifiable form of punishment?

The Nature and Definition of Punishment

Generally, philosophers discuss punishment in terms of five elements. For something to be punishment it must (1) involve pain, (2) be administered for an

258

offense against a law or rule, (3) be administered to someone who has been judged guilty of an offense, (4) be imposed by someone other than the offender, and (5) be imposed by rightful authority. Whether or not a punishment is commensurate with an offense, whether it is fair and equitable—these are very important moral and legal questions. But they must be distinguished from the question of what is punishment.

1. *Punishment must involve pain, harm, or some other consequence normally considered unpleasant.* For example, if a convicted robber was sentenced to "five-to-twenty" in a Beverly Hills country club, this would not be considered punishment, since ordinarily it would not involve pain or other unpleasant consequences (unless the robber had to pick up the tab). If he were sentenced to have his hands cut off, this could constitute punishment, though draconian by many people's standards.

2. *The punishment must be administered for an offense against a law or rule.* While punishment involves pain, obviously not all pain involves punishment. Thus, if a robber broke into your house and stole your stereo, he is not "punishing" you even though his action satisfies element (1). Although it caused you pain, his action is not taken as an offense against a law or rule. However, should the robber subsequently be sent to prison for the crime, then *that* action would be administered for breaking a law and thus satisfy element (2).

3. *The punishment must be administered to someone who has been judged guilty of an offense.* Suppose the robber is apprehended and imprisoned, although never judged guilty of the robbery. This would not be punishment. However, if he is imprisoned after his conviction for stealing your stereo, then he is being punished.

4. *The punishment must be imposed by someone other than the offender.* It is true that people sometimes speak of "punishing themselves" for a transgression, for example, as a very religious or spiritual person might for a sin. This, however, is not punishment in the strict sense, but a self-imposed act of atonement. Thus, suffering from a twinge of conscience as he listens to the latest Willie Nelson album on your stereo, the robber decides to "punish" himself by listening to Robert Goulet, whom he detests, for two hours each day for a year. Properly speaking, this would not be punishment, although it might qualify as masochism.

5. *The punishment must be imposed by rightful authority.* In a strictly legal sense, "rightful authority" would be that constituted by a legal system against whom the offense is committed. In the case of the robber, "rightful authority" likely would be a court judge and jury. In a less legal sense, the authority might be a parent, a teacher, or some official who has a right to harm a person in a particular way for having done something or failed to do something.

These five elements, then, generally constitute the nature of punishment. Combining them produces a useful definition of *punishment*. Thus, a punishment is harm inflicted by a rightful authority on a person who has been judged to have violated a law or rule.[1]

The Moral Acceptability of Punishment

Is punishment ever morally acceptable? This may seem a foolish question to ask, since it is hard to imagine society functioning without an established legal system of punishment. In fact, philosophers generally agree that punishment is morally acceptable. They, like most others, view punishment as a part of rule and law—which announces to individuals that certain kinds of acts are forbidden—that it is necessary to minimize the occurrence of these acts. In short, law without punishment is toothless.

Still, there are people who do not share this view. They argue that society should be restructured so that a legal system of punishment is unnecessary. Just how this can or should be done remains problematic. The method most often proposed involves some form of therapeutic treatment or behavioral modification for antisocial behavior, rather than a traditional form of punishment. Among the most morally controversial procedures for modifying undesirable social behavior are those associated with some startling advances in biomedicine. Such cases rarely can be resolved by a simple appeal to the individual's right to obtain appropriate treatment on request, and are even less likely to be resolved by an appeal to society's right to order such treatment.

To highlight the moral problems involved, consider one case provided by a leading research scientist in the field, Dr. J. R. Delgado. A number of years ago, Delgado recalls, an attractive 24-year-old woman of average intelligence and education and a long record of arrests for disorderly conduct approached him and his associates. The patient explained how she had been repeatedly involved in bar brawls in which she would entice men to fight over her. Having spent a number of years in jail and mental institutions, the woman expressed a strong desire but inability to change her behavior. Because past psychological therapy had proved ineffective, both she and her mother urgently requested that some sort of brain surgery be performed to control her antisocial and destructive behavior. As Delgado said: "They asked specifically that electrodes be implanted to orient a possible electrocoagulation of a limited cerebral area; and if that wasn't possible, they wanted a lobotomy."[2]

At that time, medical knowledge could not determine whether such procedures could help resolve the woman's problem. So, the physicians rejected surgical intervention. When Delgado and his colleagues explained their decision to the woman and her mother, the two reacted with disappointment and anxiety: "What is the future? Only jail or the hospital?"[3]

1. *See Burton M. Lesier,* Liberty, Justice, and Morals *(New York: Macmillan, 1973), pp. 195–197.*

2. *J. R. Delgado,* Physical Control of the Mind: Toward a Psycho-Civilized Society *(New York: Harper & Row, 1969), p. 85.*

3. *Delgado,* Physical Control of the Mind, *p. 85.*

What is the future, indeed? The day could very well come when such therapeutic treatment renders traditional kinds of punishment obsolete, perhaps barbaric. But even then, pressing moral questions will remain concerning society's right to alter an individual's personality against his or her will. For now, most agree that punishment is a morally acceptable practice. What they do not agree on, however, is the aim of punishment.

Aims of Punishment

The aims of punishment can be divided into two categories: (1) according to whether punishment is viewed in terms of giving people what they deserve, or (2) in terms of its desirable consequences. The first category includes retributive theories of punishment; the second includes preventive, deterrent, and rehabilitative theories.

Retribution

The term *retribution* refers to punishment given in return for some wrong done. Thus, the retributive view of punishment holds that we should punish people simply because they deserve it. Traditionally retributive theorists have considered punishment a form of revenge, whereby offenders are made to suffer in kind for the harm they have caused others. Arguments in favor of capital punishment commonly make this point.

But another version of retribution associates punishment not with revenge, but with respect for persons, both noncriminals and criminals. Thus, proponents of this theory argue that the robber, for example, like everyone else in society, ought to live under the same limitations of freedom. When the robber steals your stereo, he is taking unfair advantage of you, disrupting the balance of equal limitations. When the state subsequently punishes him, the punishment is viewed as an attempt to restore this disrupted balance, to reaffirm society's commitment to fair treatment for all. This version of retribution focuses on the noncriminal generally and the victim in particular, claiming that respect for the parties who abide by society's limitations requires punishment of those who flout those limitations.

The other side of the respect-retribution theory concerns respect for the offender. Proponents of retribution sometimes argue that failure to punish is tantamount to treating offenders with disrespect because it denies them autonomy and responsibility for their actions. Thus, showing respect entails giving people what they deserve, whether that be reward or punishment. To deny praise to a deserving person is disrespectful. By the same token, to deny punishment to a deserving person is equally as disrespectful. Both views of respect-retribution can be used in defense of capital punishment.

Prevention

The prevention view of punishment holds that we should punish to ensure that offenders do not repeat their offense and so further injure society. Thus, the robber should be punished, perhaps imprisoned, so that he will not steal anything else. Prevention is one of the most common justifications for capital punishment.

Deterrence

The deterrence view holds that we should punish in order to discourage others from committing similar offenses. Like the prevention theory, it aims to minimize the crime rate. Thus, when other potential thieves see that the robber has been punished for his crime, they will be less likely to rob and steal. Deterrence is perhaps the most common argument made on behalf of capital punishment, and thus is the one that those against capital punishment often focus on. For the moment, we will simply observe that if a punishment is to function effectively as a deterrent, it must be severe enough to be undesirable and, just as important, it must be known and certain. Thus, potential offenders must be aware of the kind and severity of the punishment that awaits them, and they must be convinced that they will receive it, if they commit the offense.

Rehabilitation

The rehabilitation theory holds that we should punish in order to reform or restore the offender to society as a contributing member. Thus, deterrent theorists might argue that if imprisoned, the robber should be provided educational and vocational services that will equip him to find a useful place in society when released. Obviously, capital punishment could not be justified on grounds of rehabilitation. Indeed, sometimes it is opposed because it precludes any hope of rehabilitating the offenders and restoring them to society as constructive members.

Retentionist and *Abolitionist* Defined

Having briefly examined some aspects of punishment, including its nature and definition, its moral acceptability, and its aims, let us now turn to the particular form of punishment that is the concern of this chapter: capital punishment. The central moral question that concerns us is: Is capital punishment ever a justifiable form of punishment?

Those who support retaining or reinstituting capital punishment can be termed *retentionists*. Retentionists are not agreed that all the arguments supporting capital punishment are acceptable or on the conditions under which capital punishment should be imposed. But they do agree that capital punishment is at least sometimes morally justifiable. Those who oppose capital punishment are commonly termed *abolitionists*. Like retentionists, abolitionists disagree among themselves about which arguments against capital punishment are acceptable. But all abolitionists share the belief that capital punishment is never morally justifiable.

Abolitionist Arguments (Against Capital Punishment)

1. *Life is sacred.*

POINT: "Life is sacred—a fact that our religious and moral institutions traditionally have upheld. The sanctity of life precludes any person taking another's life, whatever the circumstances or provocations."

COUNTERPOINT: Yes, generally speaking, life is sacred. But the life of a murderer shares only accidental features with the life of an innocent person. What makes the murderer's life materially different is that the murderer has taken an innocent life. Furthermore, how can you seriously argue that all killing is morally objectionable? Is killing in self-defense morally objectionable?"

2. *Capital punishment does not deter crime.*

POINT: "A comparative analysis of states that have capital punishment and those that don't indicates that the murder rate in capital-punishment states frequently is no lower than in those states that have capital punishment. In some cases, it's higher. It's obvious, therefore, that capital punishment simply doesn't deter crime. And since capital punishment does not function as an effective deterrent to crime, it should be abolished."

COUNTERPOINT: "A statistical correlation does not establish a causal connection. Many things influence the commission of crimes, including economic, political, sociological, and psychological factors. A high crime rate in a non-capital-punishment state may be accounted for in a variety of ways, none of which bears on the absence of capital punishment. Conversely, a low crime rate in a non-capital-punishment state doesn't in itself disprove the deterrent value of capital punishment."

3. *Capital punishment is implemented with a class bias.*

POINT: "Statistics indicate that the poor, the underprivileged, and members of minority groups are executed in far greater numbers than the rich, the influential, and white people. Thus, capital punishment actually serves to oppress the most disadvantaged in our society. This is patently unfair and must be stopped."

COUNTERPOINT: "Your point is irrelevant because it addresses the inequity of the penalty's distribution, not whether it's a justifiable form of punishment. If the rich, white, or influential escape capital punishment for crimes that other people are executed for, then the problem lies with our judicial system, not with the punishment. Of course it's unfair that comparable crimes don't get the same penalties, no matter who the offender is. But let's remedy the system that allows this injustice, and not throw out the penalty."

4. *The innocent may die.*

POINT: "It's no secret that innocent people are often convicted of crimes. This is always tragic. Such a deplorable occurrence is reversible with every kind of punishment except capital punishment. Obviously we can't call the innocent back from their graves, make our apologies, and offer reparation, once we've executed them. Even if only one innocent person is executed, that's inexcusable. The very existence of capital punishment allows for such a heinous possibility, and therefore it should be abolished."

COUNTERPOINT: "Actually, very few innocent people are ever executed. True, the execution of even one innocent person is tragic and diminishes all of us and our system of justice. But no institution is perfect, certainly not the judicial system. Laws and the institutions that enforce them are made and run by humans, and human factor always spells potential error. This doesn't mean that we shouldn't minimize the possibility that someone will be executed for something he or she didn't do. Of course we should, and the death penalty ought never be given casually. But at the same time, we must recognize the fallibility of people and their institutions, and consequently view the rare execution of an innocent person in that sobering light."

5. *Retribution is uncivilized.*

POINT: "Putting someone to death can't bring back the victim or in any meaningful way repay the victim's loved ones. So what's the function of capital punishment? Clearly, it is to satisfy the primitive and apparently irrepressible urge for revenge. Such a motive is not worthy of a society that considers itself civilized."

COUNTERPOINT: "Your argument focuses on only one aspect of retributive justice. Even if the desire for revenge is an unwholesome basis for punishment, one can still make a case for respect-retribution. Furthermore, your argument assumes that capital punishment can be only retributive. But punishment can have aims other than that, for example, deterrence."

6. *Capital punishment precludes rehabilitation.*

POINT: "When someone is put to death, the chance that they can ever be restored to a useful place in society dies with them. How tragic that society should compound one heinous deed by committing another. The fact is that society bears as much responsiblity for crime as do criminals. After all, societal influences help shape individuals into the criminals they subsequently become."

COUNTERPOINT: "Why assume that the sole or at least primary function of punishment is rehabilitation? And I categorically reject that societal influence can be so strong that persons lose their sense of right and wrong, or have their will so constrained that they cannot help committing heinous crimes. Such a degree of societal influence over individuals has never been established. In fact, many individuals who function as admirable citizens have been exposed to more sinister environmental influences than those who commit murder. Finally, your argument confuses social responsibility with personal responsibility. Where personal responsibility is involved, one can rightly assign blame. But to speak of 'social responsibility' is to blame everyone and no one. Pushed far enough, the concept of social responsiblity ends up holding no one personally responsible for anything."

7. *Capital punishment injures the judicial system.*

POINT: "Capital punishment actually has the effect of making judges and juries soft on crime. It makes a mockery of the judicial system. Where capital punishment has been a mandatory sentence, judges and juries have been known to strain the evidence to acquit rather than sentence to death. And to make matters worse, cases of capital punishment inevitably involve years of costly appeals. This not only delays justice but subjects the people who are directly and indirectly involved to cruel and inhuman punishment."

COUNTERPOINT: "If judges and juries would rather acquit a guilty party than sentence the person to death, then the trouble lies not with capital punishment but with judges and juries. The same applies to the duration of capital offense cases: The trouble isn't with capital punishment but with the judicial system. Yes, make the system more responsive, efficient, and accountable. But don't throw out capital punishment. That would be like throwing the baby out with the bathwater."

Retentionist Arguments (For Capital Punishment)

1. *Capital punishment is the only prevention against certain crimes.*

POINT: "Certain major crimes cannot be deterred in any way other than by capital punishment. Take, for example, the cases of political revolutionaries or traitors. These people won't be deterred from violent acts by threats of life imprisonment, because in their view they'll eventually gain freedom, even acclaim when their cause succeeds. Then there are those who are prone to violence, unreformable individuals whose very existence constitutes a potential threat to society. The only way society can protect itself from the possibility that such persons will strike again is to execute them."

COUNTERPOINT: "Your argument assumes that those bent on murder or revolution will be deterred by capital punishment. But there's no evidence for this. In fact, it's more sensible to believe that the fanatical mind is indifferent to any potential punishment, no matter how severe. As for the unreformable, since society has never unflinchingly committed itself to a concept of punishment as rehabilitation, we have no way of knowing who, if anyone, is unreformable. This aside, protecting ourselves through executing people seems to be treating the symptoms not the disease. The root causes of crime are social: poverty, prejudice, sickness, despair. Thinking that we're protecting ourselves through capital punishment is an illusion. The real way to protect ourselves is to root out the conditions that breed crime.''

2. *Capital punishment balances the scales of justice.*

POINT: ''When someone wantonly takes another's life, that person upsets the balance of equal limitations under which everyone in society ought to live. This disruption must be balanced. The only way to do this is to impose a punishment equal to the offense that upset the balance. Let the punishment fit the crime. Thus, those who murder forfeit their own claim to life. The state has the right and the duty to execute them.''

COUNTERPOINT: ''Why do you take for granted the retributive view of punishment? Surely, that theory is at least questionable. Just what is this 'balance of equal limitations' you talk about? The fact is that for no other crime except a capital offense is there a one-to-one correspondence between the crime and the punishment. Thieves aren't punished by having something stolen from them; blackmailers aren't punished by being blackmailed; muggers aren't punished by being mugged. Why should murderers necessarily be punished by being executed? It's true that, generally, punishment is given according to the crime committed. The robber is punished differently from the drunken driver, and the murderer should be punished differently from the robber. But 'difference' doesn't necessarily entail capital punishment for the murderer.''

3. *Capital punishment deters crime.*

POINT: ''When potential murderers realize that they may have to pay for their crimes with their lives, they'll think twice before killing. There's no telling how many potential murderers have been deterred from murdering because of capital punishment. It's just common sense to think that people will think more seriously about committing a murder if they know that they can lose their own lives as a result. And they'll be more likely to kill if their own necks aren't on the line.''

COUNTERPOINT: ''The statistics on this point are inconclusive. We just don't know for sure that capital punishment does or doesn't deter crime. Until we know for sure, your assumption is unsupported.''

4. *Capital punishment is an economical way to manage offenders.*

POINT: ''There's no conclusive evidence that murderers can be rehabilitated. That means that society is faced with having to foot the bill for their incarceration. But is this fair? Why should innocent people be made to pay for the care of those who have wantonly violated society's conventions when there's no evidence that such care will rehabilitate them?''

COUNTERPOINT: ''That is a crass disregard for the value of human life. How can you seriously measure the worth of life, even a criminal's, in dollars and cents? Surely such considerations are beneath the dignity of a society that considers itself civilized. Rehabilitation or not, destroying a human life, even a murderer's, because it's the most economical thing to do is an outrage.''

Ethical Theories

Egoism

Only those aspects of punishment and capital punishment with consequential overtones would be relevant in an egoistic calculation. Thus, the egoist theory of punishment would draw from an amalgam of prevention, deterrence, and rehabilitation (the latter, of course, would be irrelevant in the case of capital punishment). Regarding capital punishment, egoists would focus on consequential considerations of prevention, deterrence, and economics. Nonconsequential considerations such as the sacredness of life or balancing of the scales of justice would not figure in their assessment. They would relate the consequential aspects of the issue to long-term self-interest. If in the final calculation, capital punishment would likely produce more long-term self-benefit than its abolition, egoists would be in favor of it.

Act Utilitarianism

Considerations of social utility traditionally have played a key role in discussions of punishment and capital punishment. Whether act or rule, utilitarians believe the primary justification of any kind of punishment lies in its social utility. As for any particular kind of punishment, such as capital punishment, act utilitarians would examine each situation as it arose. If in a particular case, the act of capital punishment likely would produce more common good than any other alternative, then it would be moral. Figuring prominently in the act utilitarian's calculation would be such consequential aspects of capital punishment as prevention and deterrence.

Act utilitarians would reject the proposition that capital punishment is never morally justifiable. To endorse such a proposition would be to undermine their own theory, which calls for a case by case analysis. Like egoists, act utilitarians would affirm that capital punishment may sometimes be morally justifiable. Taking that position allows them to evaluate each proposed act of capital punishment in the light of its social consequences.

Rule Utilitarianism

Like act utilitarians, rule utilitarians would be concerned with social utility as applied to capital punishment. But rule utilitarians would apply the utility standard not to each individual act of capital punishment but to the rule under which the particular act falls. Is the rule more or less productive of the common good than its contradiction? (The rule here presumably would be: Capital punishment is never morally justifiable.) The answer to the question would determine the rule utilitarian's position on individual acts of capital punishment.

Most probably, the rule utilitarian would reject unconditional prohibition against capital punishment, and thus endorse limited capital punishment. After all, accepting a rule of unconditional prohibition would be far more restricting than endorsing limited capital punishment. That is, a rule endorsing limited capital punishment would have all the social advantages of an unconditional prohibition, plus one: It would allow the imposition of capital punishment where it was determined to operate in a preventive or deterrent way, whereas an unconditional prohibition would disallow capital punishment even in those cases.

Divine Command

Like the preceding consequential views, divine command also could provide a theoretical foundation for an endorsement of limited capital punishment. Divine command theorists could argue from a retributive viewpoint, for example, that murderers forfeit their own right to life, that the scales of justice must be balanced, that the sanctity of human life must be upheld by imposing capital punishment on those who have wantonly taken life. For these reasons, capital punishment traditionally has been viewed as an exception to the religious prohibition against killing. It would be possible, however, to interpret "Thou shalt not kill" in a far narrower sense, as indeed some of the abolitionists have. Thus, they have argued that God disapproves of all forms of killing, including capital punishment. While this view does not represent mainstream religious thinking or all views on divine command, it does show that divine command frequently is open to different, even conflicting, interpretations.

Categorical Imperative

An application of Kant's theory would require a determination of the universalizability of the maxim implied in any act of capital punishment. This maxim might be expressed: Never impose capital punishment. Can this maxim be universalized? If it can, then capital punishment is never morally justifiable; if it cannot, then capital punishment is at least sometimes morally justifiable.

From Kant's view the maxim is internally inconsistent. To understand why requires some understanding of Kant's retributive concept of punishment. For Kant the only justification for punishment is desert. Punishment is not a matter of prevention, deterrence, or rehabilitation; it is a question of giving people what they deserve. Thus, punishing people who deserve it ensures justice. As Kant states:

> Judicial punishment can never be used as a means to promote one other good for the criminal himself or for civil society, but instead must in all cases be imposed on him only on the ground that he has committed a crime; for a human being can never be manipulated merely as a means to the purposes of someone else and can never be confused with the objects of the law of things. . . . He must first be found to be deserving of punishment before any consideration is given to the utility of this punishment for himself or for his fellow citizens. The law concerning punishment is a categorical imperative, and woe to him who rummages around in the winding paths of a theory of happiness looking for some advantage to be gained by releasing the criminal from punishment or by reducing the amount of it.[4]

4.   *Immanuel Kant*, The Metaphysical Elements of Justice, *trans. John Ladd (Indianapolis: Bobbs-Merrill, 1965), p. 100.*

The end of the preceding quote gives us an insight into Kant's view on capital punishment. By Kant's reasoning the proper kind and degree of retribution is based on an equality between punishment and offense. While he admits that it is not always obvious what constitutes equality, he has no doubt that a murderer must die: "There is no substitute that will satisfy the requirements of legal justice."[5] Kant would also require such a severe penalty out of respect for the rights of the offender. Free and autonomous agents should get what they deserve; to treat them otherwise is to show contempt for their inherent worth and dignity.

Thus, taking a retributive viewpoint, Kant argues that when the moral order is upset by an offense, it is only proper that the imbalance be corrected by punishment equal in intensity to the seriousness of the offense. A maxim that would disallow capital punishment would be inconsistent with the nature of punishment. Thus, for Kant, capital punishment is not only morally justifiable, in some cases it is morally obligatory.

Prima Facie Duties

Ross's concept of punishment is essentially retributive. According to Ross, retributive punishment may involve redress. Thus, a robber may be forced to make restitution, as for example by being made to return the stereo he stole from you. Or he may be forced to provide compensation, as by giving you something of equal value. This concept of punishment springs from the state's duty of fidelity, justice, and noninjury to its citizens. In short, the state has a tacit agreement with its citizens to enforce redress when the citizen is wronged. Should the state fail to punish by not enforcing redress, it violates its agreement with its citizens, and consequently wrongs the victim. The only way the state can protect the citizen's right of redress is to force offenders to redress their wrongs, that is, to punish them.

Maximim Principle

Rawls's theory of social justice could provide a defense of capital punishment, if the following line of reasoning is pursued. How would rational, self-interested creatures operating behind a veil of ignorance react to the prospect of capital punishment? Remember, each person is ignorant of his or her sex, race, natural endowments, social position, economic conditions, and so on. Also, keep in mind that the ignorance of the participants means that they cannot try to seek advantages for themselves.

We might imagine some individuals in the original position would argue against capital punishment, reasoning that if they committed murder they would then escape execution. But even so, they would have to admit that they would still experience immense suffering and loss in the form of some other kind of punishment, such as a life in prison.

5. *Kant,* The Metaphysical Elements of Justice, *p. 102.*

These same rational, self-interested creatures, however, would realize that they might end up as the victim of a murderer who was not executed. They would also realize that if they themselves were not victims, then loved ones, friends, associates, or even perfect strangers could be. In any event, the loss would be immense.

Presumably, these rational, self-interested creatures would recognize that the chance of their being murderers and thus "benefiting" from the abolition of capital punishment would be far less than the chance of their being victimized directly or indirectly by murder. Since the veil of ignorance prevents them from knowing their actual position in society, it would not seem rational for people to endorse the abolition of capital punishment when the likelihood of their experiencing immense loss is far greater than if capital punishment was retained. If this account is correct, then the maximin principle could provide a theoretical basis for supporting capital punishment.

The Death Sentence

Sidney Hook

In "The Death Sentence," professor of philosophy Sidney Hook suggests that much of the debate about capital punishment suffers from vindictiveness and sentimentality. For example, abolitionists often argue that capital punishment is no more than an act of revenge, that it is the ultimate inhumanity. Hook is no more sympathetic, however, to the thrust of retentionist arguments. He points out that capital punishment has never been established as a deterrent to crime. Furthermore, he rejects as question begging the retentionist argument that capital punishment is justified because it fulfills a community need, or that it is the only appropriate punishment for certain unspeakable offenses.

So where does Hook stand on the issue? Despite his feelings that no valid case for capital punishment has thus far been made, Hook is not categorically opposed to it. Indeed, he cites two conditions under which he believes capital punishment is justified. The first is in cases where criminals facing a life-imprisonment sentence request it. The second involves cases of convicted murderers who murder again. Hook regards the abolitionist objections to these exceptions as expressions of sentimentalism, even cruelty.

Is there anything new that can be said for or against capital punishment? Anyone familiar with the subject knows that unless extraneous issues are introduced a large measure of agreement about it can be, and has been, won. For example, during the last 150 years the death penalty for criminal offenses has been abolished, or remains unenforced, in many countries; just as important, the number of crimes punishable by death has been sharply reduced in all countries. But while the progress has been encouraging, it still seems to me that greater clarity on the issues involved is desir-

From Sidney Hook, "The Death Sentence," The New Leader, vol. 44 (April 3, 1961). Copyright © The American Labor Conference on International Affairs, Inc. Reprinted, with three paragraphs added, by permission of the publisher. Cf. the original version which appeared in The New York Law Forum (August 1961), pp. 278–283, as an address before the New York State District Attorneys' Association.

able: Much of the continuing polemic still suffers from one or the other of the twin evils of vindictiveness and sentimentality.

Sentimentality, together with a great deal of confusion about determinism, is found in Clarence Darrow's speeches and writings on the subject. Darrow was an attractive and likeable human being but a very confused thinker. He argued against capital punishment on the ground that the murderer was always a victim of heredity and environment—and therefore it was unjust to execute him. ("Back of every murder and back of every human act are sufficient causes that move the human machine beyond their control.") The crucifiers and the crucified, the lynch mob and its prey are equally moved by causes beyond their control and the relevant differences between them is therewith ignored. Although Darrow passionately asserted that no one knows what justice is and that no one can measure it, he nonetheless was passionately convinced that capital punishment was unjust.

It should be clear that if Darrow's argument were valid, it would be an argument not only against capital punishment but against all punishment. Very few of us would be prepared to accept this. But the argument is absurd. Even if we are all victims of our heredity and environment, it is still possible to alter the environment by meting out capital punishment to deter crimes of murder. If no one can help doing what he does, if no one is responsible for his actions, then surely this holds just as much for those who advocate and administer capital punishment as for the criminal. The denunciation of capital punishment as unjust, therefore, would be senseless. The question of universal determinism is irrelevant. If capital punishment actually were a deterrent to murder, and there existed no other more effective deterrent, and none as effective but more humane, a case could be made for it.

Nor am I impressed with the argument against capital punishment on the ground of its inhumanity. Of course it is inhumane. So is murder. If it could be shown that the inhumanity of murder can be decreased in no other way than by the inhumanity of capital punishment acting as a deterrent, this would be a valid argument for such punishment.

I have stressed the hypothetical character of these arguments because it makes apparent how crucially the wisdom of our policy depends upon the alleged facts. Does capital punishment serve as the most effective deterrent we have against murder? Most people who favor its retention believe that it does. But any sober examination of the facts will show that this has never been established. It seems plausible, but not everything which is plausible or intuitively credible is true.

The experience of countries and states which have abolished capital punishment shows that there has been no perceptible increase of murders after abolition—although it would be illegitimate to infer from this that the fear of capital punishment never deterred anybody. The fact that "the state with the very lowest murder rate is Maine, which abolished capital punishment in 1870," may be explained by the hypothesis that fishermen, like fish, tend to be cold-blooded, or by some less fanciful hypothesis. The relevant question is: What objective evidence exists which would justify the conclusion that if Maine had not abolished capital punishment, its death rate would have been higher? The answer is: No evidence exists.

The opinion of many jurists and law enforcement officers from Cesare Beccaria (the eighteenth century Italian criminologist) to the present is that swift and certain punishment of some degree of severity is a more effective deterrent of murder than the punishment of maximum severity when it is slow and uncertain. Although this opinion requires substantiation, too, it carries the weight which we normally extend to pronouncements by individuals who report on their life experience. And in the absence of convincing evidence that capital punishment is a more effective and/or humane form of punishment for murder than any other punishment, there remains no other reasonable ground for retaining it.

This is contested by those who speak of the necessity for capital punishment as an expression of the "community need of justice," or as the fulfillment of "an instinctive urge to punish injustice." Such views lie at the basis of some forms of the retributive theory. It has been alleged that the retributive theory is nothing more than a desire for revenge, but it is a great and arrogant error to assume that all who hold it are vindictive. The theory has been defended by secular saints like G. E. Moore and Immanuel Kant, whose dispassionate interest in justice cannot reasonably be challenged. Even if one accepted the retributive theory or believed in the desirability of meeting the community need of justice, it doesn't in the least follow that this justifies capital punishment. Other forms of punishment may be retributive, too.

I suppose that what one means by community need or feeling and the necessity of regarding it, is that not only must justice be done, it must be seen to be done. A requirement of good law is that it must be consonant with the feeling of the community, something which is sometimes called "the living law." Otherwise it is unenforceable and brings the whole system of law into disrepute. Meeting community feeling is a necessary condition for good law, but not a sufficient condition for good law. This is what Justice Holmes meant when he wrote in *The Common Law* that "The first requirement of a sound body of law is that it should correspond with the actual feelings and demands of the community, whether right or wrong." But I think he would admit that sound law is sounder still if in addition to being enforceable it is also just. Our moral obligation as citizens is to build a community feeling and demand which is right rather than wrong.

Those who wish to retain capital punishment on the ground that it fulfills a community need or feeling must believe either that community feeling *per se* is always justified, or that to disregard it in any particular situation is inexpedient because of the consequences, *viz.*, increase in murder. In either case they beg the question—in the first case, the question of justice, and in the second, the question of deterrence.

One thing is incontestable. From the standpoint of those who base the argument for retention of capital punishment on the necessity of satisfying community needs there could be no justification whatsoever for any *mandatory* death sentence. For a mandatory death sentence attempts to determine in advance what the community need and feeling will be, and closes the door to fresh inquiry about the justice as well as the deterrent consequences of any proposed punishment.

Community need and feeling are notoriously fickle. When a verdict of guilty necessarily entails a death sentence, the jury may not feel the sentence warranted and may bring in a verdict of not guilty

even when some punishment seems to be legally and morally justified. Even when the death sentence is not mandatory, there is an argument, not decisive but still significant, against any death sentence. This is its incorrigibility. Our judgment of a convicted man's guilt may change. If he has been executed in the meantime, we can only do him "posthumous justice." But can justice ever really be posthumous to the victim? Rarely has evidence, even when it is beyond reasonable doubt, the same finality about its probative force as the awful finality of death. The weight of this argument against capital punishment is all the stronger if community need and feeling are taken as the prime criteria of what is just or fitting.

What about heinous political offenses? Usually when arguments fail to sustain the demand for capital punishment in ordinary murder cases, the names of Adolf Hitler, Adolf Eichmann, Joseph Stalin and Ilse Koch are introduced and flaunted before the audience to inflame their feelings. Certain distinctions are in order here. Justice, of course, requires severe punishment. But why is it assumed that capital punishment is, in these cases, the severest and most just of sentences? How can any equation be drawn between the punishment of one man and the sufferings of his numerous victims? After all, we cannot kill Eichmann six million times or Stalin twelve million times (a conservative estimate of the number of people who died by their order).

If we wish to keep alive the memory of political infamy, if we wish to use it as a political lesson to prevent its recurrence, it may be educationally far more effective to keep men like Eichmann in existence. Few people think of the dead. By the same token, it may be necessary to execute a politically monstrous figure to prevent him from becoming the object of allegiance of a restoration movement. Eichmann does not have to be executed. He is more useful alive if we wish to keep before mankind the enormity of his offense. But if Hitler had been taken alive, his death would have been required as a matter of political necessity, to prevent him from becoming a living symbol or rallying cry of Nazi die-hards and irreconcilables.

There is an enormous amount of historical evidence which shows that certain political tyrants, after they lose power, become the focus of restoration movements that are a chronic source of bloodshed and civil strife. No matter how infamous a tyrant's actions, there is usually some group which has profited by it, resents being deprived of its privileges, and schemes for a return to power. In difficult situations, the dethroned tyrant also becomes a symbol of legitimacy around which discontented elements rally who might otherwise have waited for the normal processes of government to relieve their lot. A *mystique* develops around the tyrant, appeals are made to the "good old days," when his bread and circuses were used to distract attention from the myriads of his tortured victims, plots seethe around him until they boil over into violence and bloodshed again. I did not approve of the way Mussolini was killed. Even he deserved due process. But I have no doubt whatsoever that had he been sentenced merely to life imprisonment, the Fascist movement in Italy today would be a much more formidable movement, and that sooner or later, many lives would have been lost in consequence of the actions of Fascist legitimists.

Where matters of ordinary crime are concerned these political considerations are irrelevant. I conclude, therefore, that no valid case has so far been made for the retention of capital punishment, that the argument from deterrence is inconclusive and inconsistent (in the sense that we do not do other things to reinforce its deterrent effect if we believe it has such an effect), and that the argument from community feeling is invalid.

However, since I am not a fanatic or absolutist, I do not wish to go on record as being categorically opposed to the death sentence in all circumstances. I should like to recognize two exceptions. A defendant convicted of murder and sentenced to life should be permitted to choose the death sentence instead. Not so long ago a defendant sentenced to life imprisonment made this request and was rebuked by the judge for his impertinence. I can see no valid grounds for denying such a request out of hand. It may sometimes be denied, particularly if a way can be found to make the defendant labor for the benefit of the dependents of his victim as is done in some European countries. Unless such considerations are present, I do not see on what reasonable ground the request can be denied, particularly by those who

believe in capital punishment. Once they argue that life imprisonment is either a more effective deterrent or more justly punitive, they have abandoned their position.

In passing, I should state that I am in favor of permitting *any* criminal defendant, sentenced to life imprisonment, the right to choose death. I can understand why certain jurists, who believe that the defendant wants thereby to cheat the state out of its mode of punishment, should be indignant at the idea. They are usually the ones who believe that even the attempt at suicide should be deemed a crime—in effect saying to the unfortunate person that if he doesn't succeed in his act of suicide, the state will punish him for it. But I am baffled to understand why the absolute abolitionist, dripping with treacly humanitarianism, should oppose this proposal. I have heard some people actually oppose capital punishment in certain cases on the ground that: "Death is too good for the vile wretch! Let him live and suffer to the end of his days." But the absolute abolitionist should be the last person in the world to oppose the wish of the lifer, who regards this form of punishment as torture worse than death, to leave our world.

My second class of exceptions consists of those who having been sentenced once to prison for premeditated murder, murder again. In these particular cases we have evidence that imprisonment is not a sufficient deterrent for the individual in question. If the evidence shows that the prisoner is so psychologically constituted that, without being insane, the fact that he can kill again with impunity may lead to further murderous behavior, the court should have the discretionary power to pass the death sentence if the criminal is found guilty of a second murder.

In saying that the death sentence should be *discretionary* in cases where a man has killed more than once, I am *not* saying that a murderer who murders again is more deserving of death than the murderer who murders once. Bluebeard was not twelve times more deserving of death when he was finally caught. I am saying simply this: that in a sub-class of murderers, i.e., those who murder several times, there may be a special group of sane murderers who, knowing that they will not be executed, will not hesitate to kill again and again. For *them* the argument from deterrence is obviously valid. Those who say that there must be no exceptions to the abolition of capital punishment cannot rule out the existence of such cases on *a priori* grounds. If they admit that there is a reasonable probability that such murderers will murder again or attempt to murder again, a probability which usually grows with the number of repeated murders, and still insist they would *never* approve of capital punishment, I would conclude that they are indifferent to the lives of the human beings doomed, on their position, to be victims. What fancies itself as a humanitarian attitude is sometimes an expression of sentimentalism. The reverse coin of sentimentalism is often cruelty.

Our charity for all human beings must not deprive us of our common sense. Nor should our charity be less for the future or potential victims of the murderer than for the murderer himself. There are crimes in this world which are, like acts of nature, beyond the power of men to anticipate or control. But not all or most crimes are of this character. So long as human beings are responsible and educable, they will respond to praise and blame and punishment. It is hard to imagine it but even Hitler and Stalin were once infants. Once you *can* imagine them as infants, however, it is hard to believe that they were already monsters in their cradles. Every confirmed criminal was once an amateur. The existence of confirmed criminals testifies to the defects of our education—where they can be reformed—and of our penology—where they cannot. That is why we are under the moral obligation to be intelligent about crime and punishment. Intelligence should teach us that the best educational and penological system is the one which prevents crimes rather than punishes them; the next best is one which punishes crime in such a way as to prevent it from happening again.

Questions for Analysis

1. Why does Hook say that if Darrow's argument were valid, it would be an argument not against capital punishment but against all punishment?

2. Why is Hook not impressed by the claim that capital punishment is inhumane? Do you agree with him?

3. Why does Hook feel that those who justify capital punishment by appeal to community feeling beg the question? Do you accept his argument?

4. How does Hook respond to the retentionist claim that capital punishment is justified for politically heinous offenses?

5. Do you agree that a "lifer's" request for capital punishment ought to be honored? Is Hook's justification for his position consequential or nonconsequential? Explain.

6. Why does Hook believe that capital punishment is justified when a convicted murderer murders again? Is his defense utilitarian? Explain.

7. Do you agree with Hook that what are called "humanitarian" objections to his two exceptions are really expressions of sentimentalism, even cruelty?

8. Do you think that Rawls's maximin principle could be used to justify Hook's two exceptions?

On Deterrence and the Death Penalty

Ernest Van Den Haag

Professor of social philosophy Ernest Van Den Haag begins his essay, "On Deterrence and the Death Penalty," by conceding that capital punishment cannot be defended on grounds of rehabilitation or protection of society from unrehabilitated offenders. But he does believe that the ultimate punishment can be justified on grounds of deterrence.

To make his point, Van Den Haag at some length provides a psychological basis for deterrence. He associates deterrence with human responses to danger. Law functions to change social dangers into individual ones: Legal threats are designed to deter individuals from actions that threaten society. Most of us, Van Den Haag argues, transfer these external penalty dangers into internal ones; that is, we each develop a conscience that threatens us if we do wrong. But this conscience is and needs to be reinforced by external authority, which imposes penalties for antisocial behavior.

Van Den Haag then critically examines the reason that punishment has fallen into disrepute as a deterrent to crime: the claim that slums, ghettos, and personality disorders are the real causes of crime. He dismisses these as spurious explanations, and insists that only punishment can deter crime. In Van Den Haag's view, whether or not individuals will commit crimes depends exclusively on whether they perceive the penalty risks as worth it.

While he concedes that the death penalty cannot be proved to deter crime, Van Den Haag observes that this in no way means that capital punishment lacks a deterrent value. Indeed, it is this very uncertainty about its deterrence that impels Van Den Haag to argue for its retention. In the last analysis, he believes that retaining capital punishment leads to a net gain for society, notwithstanding the occasional abuse of it. In arguing for capital punishment, then, Van Den Haag takes a utilitarian viewpoint.

I

If rehabilitation and the protection of society from unrehabilitated offenders were the only purposes of legal punishment the death penalty could be abolished: It cannot attain the first end, and is not needed for the second. No case for the death penalty can be made unless "doing justice," or "deterring others," are among our penal aims.[1] Each of these purposes can justify capital punishment by itself; opponents, therefore, must show that neither actually does, while proponents can rest their case on either.

Although the argument from justice is intellectually more interesting, and, in my view, decisive enough, utilitarian arguments have more appeal: The claim that capital punishment is useless because it does not deter others, is most persuasive. I shall, therefore, focus on this claim. Lest the argument be thought to be unduly narrow, I shall show, nonetheless, that some claims of injustice rest on premises which the claimants reject when arguments for capital punishment are derived therefrom; while other claims of injustice have no independent standing: Their weight depends on the weight given to deterrence.

II

Capital punishment is regarded as unjust because it may lead to the execution of innocents, or because the guilty poor (or disadvantaged) are more likely to be executed than the guilty rich.

Regardless of merit, these claims are relevant only if "doing justice" is one purpose of punishment. Unless one regards it as good, or, at least, better, that the guilty be punished rather than the

From *Ernest Van Den Haag, "On Deterrence and the Death Penalty,"* Journal of Criminal Law, Criminology and Police Science, ©*1969 by Northwestern University School of Law, vol. 60, no. 2. Reprinted by special permission of the publisher.*

innocent, and that the equally guilty be punished equally,[2] unless, that is, one wants penalties to be just, one cannot object to them because they are not. However, if one does include justice among the purposes of punishment, it becomes possible to justify any one punishment—even death—on grounds of justice. Yet, those who object to the death penalty because of its alleged injustice, usually deny not only the merits, or the sufficiency, of specific arguments based on justice, but the propriety of justice as an argument: They exclude "doing justice" as a purpose of legal punishment. If justice is not a purpose of penalties, injustice cannot be an objection to the death penalty, or to any other; if it is, justice cannot be ruled out as an argument for any penalty.

Consider the claim of injustice on its merits now. A convicted man may be found to have been innocent; if he was executed, the penalty cannot be reversed. Except for fines, penalties never can be reversed. Time spent in prison cannot be returned. However a prison sentence may be remitted once the prisoner serving it is found innocent; and he can be compensated for the time served (although compensation ordinarily cannot repair the harm). Thus, though (nearly) all penalties are irreversible, the death penalty, unlike others, is irrevocable as well.

Despite all precautions, errors will occur in judicial proceedings: The innocent may be found guilty,[3] or the guilty rich may more easily escape conviction, or receive lesser penalties than the guilty poor. However, these injustices do not reside in the penalties inflicted but in their maldistribution. It is not the penalty—whether death or prison—which is unjust when inflicted on the innocent, but its imposition on the innocent. Inequity between poor and rich also involves distribution, not the penalty distributed.[4] Thus injustice is not an objection to the death penalty but to the distributive process—the trial. Trials are more likely to be fair when life is at stake—the death penalty is probably less often unjustly inflicted than others. It requires special consideration not because it is more, or more often, unjust than other penalties, but because it is always irrevocable.

Can any amount of deterrence justify the possibility of irrevocable injustice? Surely injustice is unjustifiable in each actual individual case; it must

be objected to whenever it occurs. But we are concerned here with the process that may produce injustice, and with the penalty that would make it irrevocable—not with the actual individual cases produced, but with the general rules which may produce them. To consider objections to a general rule (the provision of any penalties by law) we must compare the likely net result of alternative rules and select the rule (or penalty) likely to produce the least injustice. For however one defines justice, to support it cannot mean less than to favor the least injustice. If the death of innocents because of judicial error is unjust, so is the death of innocents by murder. If some murders could be avoided by a penalty conceivably more deterrent than others—such as the death penalty—then the question becomes: Which penalty will minimize the number of innocents killed (by crime and by punishment)? It follows that the irrevocable injustice, sometimes inflicted by the death penalty would not significantly militate against it, if capital punishment deters enough murders to reduce the total number of innocents killed so that fewer are lost than would be lost without it.

In general, the possibility of injustice argues against penalization of any kind only if the expected usefulness of penalization is less important than the probable harm (particularly to innocents) and the probable inequities. The possibility of injustice argues against the death penalty only inasmuch as the added usefulness (deterrence) expected from irrevocability is thought less important than the added harm. (Were my argument specifically concerned with justice, I could compare the injustice inflicted by the courts with the injustice—outside the courts—avoided by the judicial process. *I.e.*, "important" here may be used to include everything to which importance is attached.)

We must briefly examine now the general use and effectiveness of deterrence to decide whether the death penalty could add enough deterrence to be warranted.

III

Does any punishment "deter others" at all? Doubts have been thrown on this effect because it is thought to depend on the incorrect rationalistic psychology of some of its 18th and 19th century proponents. Actually deterrence does not depend on rational calculation, on rationality or even on capacity for it; nor do arguments for it depend on rationalistic psychology. Deterrence depends on the likelihood and on the regularity—not on the rationality—of human responses to danger; and further on the possibility of reinforcing internal controls by vicarious external experiences.

Responsiveness to danger is generally found in human behavior; the danger can, but need not, come from the law or from society; nor need it be explicitly verbalized. Unless intent on suicide, people do not jump from high mountain cliffs, however tempted to fly through the air; and they take precautions against falling. The mere risk of injury often restrains us from doing what is otherwise attractive; we refrain even when we have no direct experience, and usually without explicit computation of probabilities, let alone conscious weighing of expected pleasure against possible pain. One abstains from dangerous acts because of vague, inchoate, habitual and, above all, preconscious fears. Risks and rewards are more often felt than calculated; one abstains without accounting to oneself, because "it isn't done," or because one literally does not conceive of the action one refrains from. Animals as well refrain from painful or injurious experiences presumably without calculation; and the threat of punishment can be used to regulate their conduct.

Unlike natural dangers, legal threats are constructed deliberately by legislators to restrain actions which may impair the social order. Thus legislation transforms social into individual dangers. Most people further transform external into internal danger: They acquire a sense of moral obligation, a conscience, which threatens them, should they do what is wrong. Arising originally from the external authority of rulers and rules, conscience is internalized and becomes independent of external forces. However, conscience is constantly reinforced in those whom it controls by the coercive imposition of external authority on recalcitrants and on those who have not acquired it. Most people refrain from offenses because they feel an obligation to behave lawfully. But this obligation would scarcely be felt if those who do not feel or follow it were not to suffer punishment.

Although the legislators may calculate their threats and the responses to be produced, the ef-

fectiveness of the threats neither requires nor depends on calculations by those responding. The predictor (or producer) of effects must calculate; those whose responses are predicted (or produced) need not. Hence, although legislation (and legislators) should be rational, subjects, to be deterred as intended, need not be: They need only be responsive.

Punishments deter those who have not violated the law for the same reasons—and in the same degrees (apart from internalization: moral obligation) as do natural dangers. Often natural dangers—all dangers not deliberately created by legislation (e.g., injury of the criminal inflicted by the crime victim) are insufficient. Thus, the fear of injury (natural danger) does not suffice to control city traffic; it must be reinforced by the legal punishment meted out to those who violate the rules. These punishments keep most people observing the regulations. However, where (in the absence of natural danger) the threatened punishment is so light that the advantage of violating rules tends to exceed the disadvantage of being punished (divided by the risk), the rule is violated (i.e., parking fines are too light). In this case the feeling of obligation tends to vanish as well. Elsewhere punishment deters.

To be sure, not everybody responds to threatened punishment. Non-responsive persons may be (a) self-destructive or (b) incapable of responding to threats, or even of grasping them. Increases in the size, or certainty, of penalties would not affect these two groups. A third group (c) might respond to more certain or more severe penalties.[5] If the punishment threatened for burglary, robbery, or rape were a $5 fine in North Carolina, and 5 years in prison in South Carolina, I have no doubt that the North Carolina treasury would become quite opulent until vigilante justice would provide the deterrence not provided by law. Whether to increase penalties (or improve enforcement) depends on the importance of the rule to society, the size and likely reaction of the group that did not respond before, and the acceptance of the added punishment and enforcement required to deter it. Observation would have to locate the points—likely to differ in different times and places—at which diminishing, zero, and negative returns set in. There is no reason to believe that all present and future offenders belong to the *a priori* non-responsive groups, or that all penalties have reached the point of diminishing, let alone zero returns.

IV

Even though its effectiveness seems obvious, punishment as a deterrent has fallen into disrepute. Some ideas which help explain this progressive heedlessness were uttered by Lester Pearson, then Prime Minister of Canada, when, in opposing the death penalty, he proposed that instead "the state seek to eradicate the causes of crime—slums, ghettos and personality disorders."[6]

"Slums, ghettos and personality disorders" have not been shown, singly or collectively, to be "the causes" of crime.

(1) The crime rate in the slums is indeed higher than elsehwere; but so is the death rate in hospitals. Slums are no more "causes" of crime, than hospitals are of death; they are locations of crime, as hospitals are of death. Slums and hospitals attract people selectively; neither is the "cause" of the condition (disease in hospitals, poverty in slums) that leads to the selective attraction.

As for poverty which draws people into slums, and, sometimes, into crime, any relative disadvantage may lead to ambition, frustration, resentment and, if insufficiently restrained, to crime. Not all relative disadvantages can be eliminated; indeed very few can be, and their elimination increases the resentment generated by the remaining ones; not even relative poverty can be removed altogether. (Absolute poverty—whatever that may be—hardly affects crime.) However, though contributory, relative disadvantages are not a necessary or sufficient cause of crime: Most poor people do not commit crimes, and some rich people do. Hence, "eradication of poverty" would, at most, remove one (doubtful) cause of crime.

In the United States, the decline of poverty has not been associated with a reduction of crime. Poverty measured in dollars of constant purchasing power, according to present government standards and statistics, was the condition of 1/2 of all our families in 1920; of 1/5 in 1962; and of less than 1/6 in 1966. In 1967, 5.3 million families out of 49.8 million were poor—1/9 of all families in the United States. If crime has been reduced in a similar manner, it is a well kept secret.

Those who regard poverty as a cause of crime often draw a wrong inference from a true proposition: The rich will not commit certain crimes—Rockefeller never riots; nor does he steal. (He mugs, but only on T.V.) Yet while wealth may be the cause of not committing (certain) crimes, it does not follow that poverty (absence of wealth) is the cause of committing them. Water extinguishes or prevents fire; but its absence is not the cause of fire. Thus, if poverty could be abolished, if everybody had all "necessities" (I don't pretend to know what this would mean), crime would remain, for, in the words of Aristotle, "the greatest crimes are committed not for the sake of basic necessities but for the sake of superfluities." Superfluities cannot be provided by the government; they would be what the government does not provide.

(2) Negro ghettos have a high, Chinese ghettos have a low crime rate. Ethnic separation, voluntary or forced, obviously has little to do with crime; I can think of no reason why it should.[7]

(3) I cannot see how the state could "eradicate" personality disorders even if all causes and cures were known and available. (They are not.) Further, the known incidence of personality disorders within the prison population does not exceed the known incidence outside—though our knowledge of both is tenuous. Nor are personality disorders necessary, or sufficient causes for criminal offenses, unless these be identified by means of (moral, not clinical) definition with personality disorders. In this case, Mr. Pearson would have proposed to "eradicate" crime by eradicating crime—certainly a sound, but not a helpful idea.

Mr. Pearson's views are part as well of the mental furniture of the former U.S. Attorney General, Ramsey Clark, who told a congressional committee that ". . . only the elimination of the causes of crime can make a significant and lasting difference in the incidence of crime." Uncharitably interpreted, Mr. Clark revealed that only the elimination of causes eliminates effects—a sleazy cliche and wrong to boot. Given the benefit of the doubt, Mr. Clark probably meant that the causes of crime are social; and that therefore crime can be reduced "only" by non-penal (social) measures.

This view suggests a fireman who declines

fire-fighting apparatus by pointing out that "in the long run only the elimination of the causes" of fire "can make a significant and lasting difference in the incidence" of fire, and that fire-fighting equipment does not eliminate "the causes"— except that such a fireman would probably not rise to fire chief. Actually, whether fires are checked, depends on equipment and on the efforts of the firemen using it no less than on the presence of "the causes": inflammable materials. So with crimes. Laws, courts and police actions are no less important in restraining them than "the causes" are in impelling them. If firemen (or attorneys general) pass the buck and refuse to use the means available, we may all be burned while waiting for "the long run" and "the elimination of the causes."

Whether any activity—be it lawful or unlawful—takes place depends on whether the desire for it, or for whatever is to be secured by it, is stronger than the desire to avoid the costs involved. Accordingly people work, attend college, commit crimes, go to the movies—or refrain from any of these activities. Attendance at a theatre may be high because the show is entertaining and because the price of admission is low. Obviously the attendance depends on both—on the combination of expected gratification and cost. The wish, motive or impulse for doing anything—the experienced, or expected, gratification—is the cause of doing it; the wish to avoid the cost is the cause of not doing it. One is no more and no less "cause" than the other. (Common speech supports this use of "cause" no less than logic: "Why did you go to Jamaica!" *"Because* it is such a beautiful place." "Why didn't you go to Jamaica?" *"Because* it is too expensive."—"Why do you buy this?" *"Because* it is so cheap." Why don't you buy that?" *"Because* it is too expensive.") Penalties (costs) are causes of lawfulness, or (if too low or uncertain) of unlawfulness, of crime. People do commit crimes because, given their conditions, the desire for the satisfaction sought prevails. They refrain if the desire to avoid the cost prevails. Given the desire, low cost (penalty) causes the action, and high cost restraint. Given the cost, desire becomes the causal variable. Neither is intrinsically more causal than the other. The crime rate increases if the cost is reduced or the desire raised. It can be decreased by raising the cost or by reducing the desire.

The cost of crime is more easily and swiftly changed than the conditions producing the inclination to it. Further, the costs are very largely within the power of the government to change, whereas the conditions producing propensity to crime are often only indirectly affected by government action, and some are altogether beyond the control of the government. Our unilateral emphasis on these conditions and our undue neglect of costs may contribute to an unnecessarily high crime rate.

V

The foregoing suggests the question posed by the death penalty: Is the deterrence added (return) sufficiently above zero to warrant irrevocability (or other, less clear, disadvantages)? The question is not only whether the penalty deters, but whether it deters more than alternatives and whether the difference exceeds the cost of irrevocability. (I shall assume that the alternative is actual life imprisonment so as to exclude the complication produced by the release of the unrehabilitated.)

In some fairly infrequent but important circumstances the death penalty is the only possible deterrent. Thus, in case of acute *coups d' état*, or of acute substantial attempts to overthrow the government, prospective rebels would altogether discount the threat of any prison sentence. They would not be deterred because they believe the swift victory of the revolution will invalidate a prison sentence and turn it into an advantage. Execution would be the only deterrent because, unlike prison sentences, it cannot be revoked by victorious rebels. The same reasoning applies to deterring spies or traitors in wartime. Finally, men who, by virtue of past acts, are already serving, or are threatened, by a life sentence, could be deterred from further offenses only by the threat of the death penalty.[8]

What about criminals who do not fall into any of these (often ignored) classes? Prof. Thorsten Sellin has made a careful study of the available statistics: He concluded that they do not yield evidence for the deterring effect of the death penalty.[9] Somewhat surprisingly, Prof. Sellin seems to think that this lack of evidence for deterrence is evidence for the lack of deterrence. It is not. It means that deterrence has not been demonstrated statistically—not that non-deterrence has been.

It is entirely possible, indeed likely (as Prof. Sellin appears willing to concede), that the statistics used, though the best available, are nonetheless too slender a reed to rest conclusions on. They indicate that the homicide rate does not vary greatly between similar areas with or without the death penalty, and in the same area before and after abolition. However, the similar areas are not similar enough; the periods are not long enough; many social differences and changes, other than the abolition of the death penalty, may account for the variation (or lack of) in homicide rates with and without, before and after abolition; some of these social differences and changes are likely to have affected homicide rates. I am unaware of any statistical analysis which adjusts for such changes and differences. And logically, it is quite consistent with the postulated deterrent effect of capital punishment that there be less homicide after abolition: With retention there might have been still less.

Homicide rates do not depend exclusively on penalties any more than do other crime rates. A number of conditions which influence the propensity to crime, demographic, economic or generally social changes or differences—even such matters as changes of the divorce laws or of the cotton price—may influence the homicide rate. Therefore variation or constancy cannot be attributed to variations or constancy of the penalties, unless we know that no other factor influencing the homicide rate has changed. Usually we don't. To believe the death penalty deterrent does not require one to believe that the death penalty, or any other, is the only, or the decisive causal variable; this would be as absurd as the converse mistake that "social causes" are the only, or always the decisive factor. To favor capital punishment, the efficacy of neither variable need be denied. It is enough to affirm that the severity of the penalty may influence some potential criminals, and that the added severity of the death penalty adds to deterrence, or may do so. It is quite possible that such a deterrent effect may be offset (or intensified) by non-penal factors which affect propensity; its presence or absence therefore may be hard, and perhaps impossible to demonstrate.

Contrary to what Prof. Sellin *et al.* seem to presume, I doubt that offenders are aware of the absence or presence of the death penalty state by state or period by period. Such unawareness argues against the assumption of a calculating murderer. However, unawareness does not argue against the death penalty if by deterrence we mean a preconscious, general response to a severe, but not necessarily specifically and explicitly apprehended, or calculated threat. A constant homicide rate, despite abolition, may occur because of unawareness and not because of lack of deterrence: People remain deterred for a lengthy interval by the severity of the penalty in the past, or by the severity of penalties used in similar circumstances nearby.

I do not argue for a version of deterrence which would require me to believe that an individual shuns murder while in North Dakota, because of the death penalty, and merrily goes to it in South Dakota since it has been abolished there; or that he will start the murderous career from which he had hitherto refrained, after abolition. I hold that the generalized threat of the death penalty may be a deterrent, and the more so, the more generally applied. Deterrence will not cease in the particular areas of abolition or at the particular times of abolition. Rather, general deterrence will be somewhat weakened, through local (partial) abolition. Even such weakening will be hard to detect owing to changes in many offsetting, or reinforcing, factors.

For all of these reasons, I doubt that the presence or absence of a deterrent effect of the death penalty is likely to be demonstrable by statistical means. The statistics presented by Prof. Sellin *et al.* show only that there is no statistical proof for the deterrent effect of the death penalty. But they do not show that there is no deterrent effect. Not to demonstrate presence of the effect is not the same as to demonstrate its absence; certainly not when there are plausible explanations for the non-demonstrability of the effect.

It is on our uncertainty that the case for deterrence must rest.[10]

VI

If we do not know whether the death penalty will deter others, we are confronted with two uncertainties. If we impose the death penalty, and achieve no deterrent effect thereby, the life of a convicted murderer has been expended in vain (from a deterrent viewpoint). There is a net loss. If we impose the death sentence and thereby deter some future murderers, we spared the lives of some future victims (the prospective murderers gain too; they are spared punishment because they were deterred). In this case, the death penalty has led to a net gain, unless the life of a convicted murderer is valued more highly than that of the unknown victim, or victims (and the non-imprisonment of the deterred non-murderer).

The calculation can be turned around, of course. The absence of the death penalty may harm no one and therefore produce a gain—the life of the convicted murderer. Or it may kill future victims of murderers who could have been deterred, and thus produce a loss—their life.

To be sure, we must risk something certain—the death (or life) of the convicted man, for something uncertain—the death (or life) of the victims of murderers who may be deterred. This is in the nature of uncertainty—when we invest, or gamble, we risk the money we have for an uncertain gain. Many human actions, most commitments—including marriage and crime—share this characteristic with the deterrent purpose of any penalization, and with its rehabilitative purpose (and even with the protective).

More proof is demanded for the deterrent effect of the death penalty than is demanded for the deterrent effect of other penalties. This is not justified by the absence of other utilitarian purposes such as protection and rehabilitation; they involve no less uncertainty than deterrence.[11]

Irrevocability may support a demand for some reason to expect more deterrence than revocable penalties might produce, but not a demand for more proof of deterrence, as has been pointed out above. The reason for expecting more deterrence lies in the greater severity, the terrifying effect inherent in finality. Since it seems more important to spare victims than to spare murderers, the burden of proving that the greater severity inherent in irrevocability adds nothing to deterrence lies on those who oppose capital punishment. Proponents of the death penalty need show only that there is no more uncertainty about it than about greater severity in general.

The demand that the death penalty be proved more deterrent than alternatives can not be satisfied any more than the demand that six years in prison be proved to be more deterrent than three. But the uncertainty which confronts us favors the death penalty as long as by imposing it we might save future victims of murder. This effect is as plausible as the general idea that penalties have deterrent effects which increase with their severity. Though we have no proof of the positive deterrence of the penalty, we also have no proof of zero, or negative effectiveness. I believe we have no right to risk additional future victims of murder for the sake of sparing convicted murderers; on the contrary, our moral obligation is to risk the possible ineffectiveness of executions. However rationalized, the opposite view appears to be motivated by the simple fact that executions are more subjected to social control than murder. However, this applies to all penalties and does not argue for the abolition of any.

Notes

1. Social solidarity of "community feeling" (here to be ignored) might be dealt with as a form of deterrence.

2. Certainly a major meaning of *suum cuique tribue*

3. I am not concerned here with the converse injustice, *which I regard as no less grave.*

4. Such inequity, though likely, has not been demonstrated. Note that, since there are more poor than rich, there are likely to be more guilty poor; and, if poverty contributes to crime, the proportion of the poor who are criminals also should be higher than of the rich.

5. I neglect those motivated by civil disobedience or, generally, moral or political passion. Deterring them depends less on penalties than on the moral support they receive, though penalties play a role. I also neglect those who may belong to all three groups listed, some successively, some even simultaneously, such as drug addicts. Finally, I must altogether omit the far-from-negligible role that problems of apprehension and conviction play in deterrence—beyond saying that, by reducing the government's ability to apprehend and convict, courts are able to reduce the risks of offenders.

6. I quote from the *New York Times* (November 24, 1967, p. 22). The actual psychological and other factors which bear on the disrepute—as distinguished from the rationalizations—cannot be examined here.

7. Mixed areas, incidentally, have higher crime rates than segregated ones (see, e.g., R. Ross and E. van den Haag, *The Fabric of Society* (New York: Harcourt, Brace & Co., 1957), pp. 102–4. Because slums are bad (morally) and crime is, many people seem to reason that "slums spawn crime"—which confuses some sort of moral with a causal relation.

8. Cautious revolutionaries, uncertain of final victory, might be impressed by prison sentences—but not in the acute stage, when faith in victory is high. And one can increase even the severity of a life sentence in prison. Finally, harsh punishment of rebels can intensify rebellious impulses. These points, though they qualify it, hardly impair the force of the argument.

9. Sellin considered mainly homicide statistics. His work may be found in his *Capital Punishment* (New York: Harper & Row, 1967); or, most conveniently, in H. A. Bedau, *The Death Penalty in America* (Garden City, N.Y.: Doubleday & Co., 1964), which also offers other material, mainly against the death penalty.

10. In view of the strong emotions aroused (itself an indication of effectiveness to me: Might not murderers be as upset over the death penalty as those who wish to spare them?) and because I believe penalties must reflect community feeling to be effective, I oppose mandatory death sentences and favor optional, and perhaps binding, recommendations by juries after their finding of guilt. The opposite course risks the non-conviction of guilty defendants by juries who do not want to see them executed.

11. Rehabilitation or protection are of minor importance in our actual penal system (though not in our theory). We confine many people who do not need rehabilitation and against whom we do not need protection (e.g., the exasperated husband who killed his wife); we release many unrehabilitated offenders against whom protection is needed. Certainly rehabilitation and protection are not, and deterrence is, the main actual function of legal punishment if we disregard non-utilitarian ones.

Questions for Analysis

1. *Van Den Haag claims that injustice is an objection not to the death penalty but to the distributive process. What does he mean? Is his distinction between penalty and distribution germane?*

2. *What does deterrence depend on, in Van Den Haag's view?*

3. *How does punishment differ from natural dangers?*

4. *What kinds of people do not respond to threatened punishment? Would you be persuaded by the anti-capital-punishment argument that insists the death penalty simply does not deter certain people?*

5. *What determines whether penalties ought to be increased? Explain how this is a utilitarian argument.*

6. *Does Van Den Haag convince you that slums, ghettos, and personality disorders are "no more 'causes' of crimes, than hospitals are of death"?*

7. *In Van Den Haag's view, what is the sole determinant of whether persons will or will not commit crimes? Do you agree?*

8. *Why does Van Den Haag not believe that the presence or absence of a deterrent effect of the death penalty is likely to be proved statistically? Does this weaken, strengthen, or have no effect on his own retentionist position?*

9. *Explain why Van Den Haag believes that there is more to be gained by retaining the death penalty than by abolishing it.*

The Death Penalty as a Deterrent: Argument and Evidence

Hugo Adam Bedau

The following article, "The Death Penalty as a Deterrent: Argument and Evidence," was written by a leading abolitionist, philosophy professor Hugo Adam Bedau. Bedau applies the scalpel of logical analysis to the contentions made by Van Den Haag in the preceding essay.

Bedau isolates five main points made by Van Den Haag, and then critically analyzes each of them. First, Bedau objects to Van Den Haag's claim that the utilitarian abolitionist considers capital punishment useless because it does not deter crime. Bedau says that Van Den Haag's point founders on the concept of "deterrence," which is "too ill-formulated to be of any serious use." Second, Bedau rejects Van Den Haag's claim that the death penalty is the only way to deter certain classes of criminals.

Third, Bedau spends considerable time critically analyzing Van Den Haag's contention that no statistical case can be made for capital punishment as a nondeterrent. Bedau points out that the issue of abolishing the death penalty is not whether the death penalty is a deterrent but whether it is a superior deterrent to life imprisonment. There is no evidence, in Bedau's view, that points to the superiority of the death penalty as a deterrent. Indeed, he suggests, there is evidence that capital punishment is not a superior deterrent to life imprisonment.

Fourth, therefore, Bedau rejects the claim that the death penalty should be favored to life imprisonment because it may add to deterrence. And fifth, he likewise rejects the contention that abolitionists must prove that capital punishment does not add to deterrence.

Apart from further advancing the debate on capital punishment, Bedau's essay well illustrates the rigorous analysis that philosophers apply to moral questions and positions on them.

Professor Van Den Haag's recent article, "On Deterrence and the Death Penalty,"[1] raises a number of points of that mixed (i.e., empirical-and-conceptual-and-normative) character which typifies most actual reasoning in social and political controversy but which (except when its purely formal aspects are in question) tends to be ignored by philosophers. I pass by any number of tempting points in his critique in order to focus in detail only on those which affect his account of what he says is the major topic, namely, the argument for retaining or abolishing the death penalty as that issue turns on the question of *deterrence*.

On this topic, Van Den Haag's main contentions seem to be these five: (I) Abolitionists of a utilitarian persuasion "claim that capital punishment is useless because it does not deter others" (p. 280, col. 1). (II) There are some classes of criminals and some circumstances in which "the death penalty is the only possible deterrent" (p. 284, col. 2). (III) As things currently stand, "deterrence [namely, of criminal homicide by the death penalty] has not been demonstrated statistically"; but it is mistaken to think that "non-deterrence" has been demonstrated statistically (p. 285, col. 1). (IV) The death penalty is to be favored over imprisonment, because "the added severity of the death penalty adds to deterrence, or may do so" (p. 285, col. 2; cf. p. 286, col. 1). (V) "Since it seems more important to spare victims than to spare murderers, the burden of proving that the greater severity inherent in irrevocability adds nothing to deterrence lies on those who oppose capital punishment" (p. 287, col. 1).

Succinctly, I shall argue as follows: (I) is not reasonably attributable to abolitionists, and in any case it is false; (II) is misleading and, in the interesting cases, is empirically insignificant; (III),

From Hugo Adam Bedau, "The Death Penalty as a Deterrent: Argument and Evidence," Ethics 80 (1970): 205–217. Copyright ©1970 by The University of Chicago. Reprinted by permission of the publisher and the author.

which is the heart of the dispute, is correct in what it affirms but wrong and utterly misleading in what it denies; (IV) is unempirical and one-sided as well; and (V) is a muddle and a dodge.

The reasons for pursuing in some detail what at first might appear to be mere polemical controversy is not that Professor Van Den Haag's essay is so persuasive or likely to be of unusual influence. The reason is that the issues he raises, even though they are familiar, have not been nearly adequately discussed, despite a dozen state, congressional, and foreign government investigations into capital punishment in recent years. In Massachusetts, for example, several persons under sentence of death have been granted stays of execution pending the final report of a special legislative commission to investigate the death penalty. The exclusive mandate of this commission is to study the question of deterrence.[2] Its provisional conclusions, published late in 1968, though not in the vein of Van Den Haag's views, are liable to the kind of criticism he makes. This suggests that his reasoning may be representative of many who have tried to understand the arguments and research studies brought forward by those who would abolish the death penalty, and therefore that his errors are worth exposure and correction once and for all.

I

The claim Van Den Haag professes to find "most persuasive," namely, "capital punishment is useless because it does not deter others," is strange, and it is strange that he finds it so persuasive. Anyone who would make this claim must assume that only deterrent efficacy is relevant to assessing the utility of a punishment. In a footnote, Van Den Haag implicitly concedes that deterrence may not be the only utilitarian consideration, when he asserts that whatever our penal "theory" may tell us, "deterrence is . . . the *main actual* function of legal punishment if we disregard non-utilitarian ones" (italics added). But he does not pursue this qualification. Now we may concede that if by "function" we mean intended or professed function, deterrence is the main function of punishment. But what is deterrence? Not what Van Den Haag says it is, namely, "a preconscious, general response to a severe but not neces-

sarily specifically and explicitly apprehended or calculated threat" (pp. 285–86). How can we count as evidence of deterrence, as we may under this rubric of "general response," the desire of persons to avoid capture and punishment for the crimes they commit? Some criminologists have thought this is precisely what severe punishments tend to accomplish; if so, then they accomplish this effect only if they have failed as a deterrent. Van Den Haag's conception of deterrence is too ill-formulated to be of any serious use, since it does not discriminate between fundamentally different types of "general response" to the threat of punishment.

Let us say (definition 1) that a given punishment (P) is a *deterrent* for a given person (A) with respect to a given crime (C) at a given time (t) if and only if A does not commit C at t because he believes he runs some risk of P if he commits C, and A prefers, *ceteris paribus*, not to suffer P for committing C. This definition does not presuppose that P really is the punishment for C (a person could be deterred through a mistaken belief); it does not presuppose that A runs a high risk of incurring P (the degree of risk could be zero); or that A consciously thinks of P prior to t (it is left open as to the sort of theory needed to account for the operation of A's beliefs and preferences on his conduct). Nor does it presuppose that anyone ever suffers P (P could be a "perfect" deterrent), or that only P could have deterred A from C (some sanction less severe than P might have worked as well); and, finally, it does not presuppose that because P deters A at t from C, therefore P would deter A at any other time or anyone else at t. The definition insures that we cannot argue from the absence of instances of C to the conclusion that P has succeeded as a deterrent: The definition contains conditions (and, moreover, contains them intentionally) which prevent this. But the definition does allow us to argue from occurrences of C to the conclusion that P has failed on each such occasion as a deterrent.

Definition 1 suggests a general functional analogue appropriate to express scientific measurements of *differential deterrent efficacy* of a given punishment for a given crime with respect to a given population (definition 2). Let us say that a given Punishment, P, deters a given population, H, from a crime, C, to the degree, D, that the members of H do not commit C because they believe that they run some risk of P if they commit C and, *ceteris paribus,* they prefer not to suffer P for committing C. If $D = 0$, then P has completely failed as a deterrent, whereas if $D = 1$, P has proved to be a perfect deterrent. Given this definition and the appropriate empirical results for various values of P, C, and H, it should be possible to establish on inductive grounds the relative effectiveness of a given punishment as a deterrent.

Definition 2 in turn leads to the following corollary for assertions of relative superior deterrent efficacy of one punishment over another. A given Punishment, P_1, is a superior deterrent to another punishment, P_2, with respect to some crime, C, and some population, H, if and only if: If the members of H, believing that they are liable to P_1, upon committing C, commit C to the degree D_1; whereas if the members of H believe that they are liable to P_2 upon committing C, they commit C to the degree D_2, and $D_1 > D_2$. This formulation plainly allows that P_1 may be a more effective deterrent than P_2 for C_1 and yet less effective as a deterrent than P_2 for a different crime C_2 (with H constant), and so forth, for other possibilities. When speaking about deterrence in the sections which follow, I shall presuppose these definitions and this corollary. For the present, it is sufficient to notice that they have, at least, the virtue of eliminating the vagueness in Van Den Haag's definition complained of earlier.

Even if we analyze the notion of deterrence to accommodate the above improvements, we are left with the central objection to Van Den Haag's claim. Neither classic nor contemporary utilitarians have argued for or against the death penalty *solely* on the ground of deterrence, nor would their ethical theory entitle them to do so. One measure of the non-deterrent utility of the death penalty derives from its elimination (through death of a known criminal) of future possible crimes from that source; another arises from the elimination of the criminal's probable adverse influence upon others to emulate his ways; another lies in the generally lower budgetary outlays of tax moneys needed to finance a system of capital punishment as opposed to long-term imprisonment. There are still further consequences apart from deterrence which the scrupulous utilitarian must weigh, along with the three I have mentioned. Therefore,

it is incorrect, because insufficient, to think that if it could be demonstrated that the death penalty is not a deterrent then we would be entitled to infer, on utilitarian assumptions, that "the death penalty is useless" and therefore ought to be abolished. The problem for the utilitarian is to make commensurable such diverse social utilities as those measured by deterrent efficacy, administrative costs, etc., and then to determine which penal policy in fact maximizes utility. Finally, inspection of sample arguments actually used by abolitionists[3] will show that Van Den Haag has attacked a straw man: There are few if any contemporary abolitionists (and Van Den Haag names none) who argue solely from professedly utilitarian assumptions, and it is doubtful whether there are any nonutilitarians who would abolish the death penalty solely on grounds of its deterrent inefficacy.

II

Governments faced by incipient rebellion or threatened by a coup d'état may well conclude, as Van Den Haag insists they should, that rebels (as well as traitors and spies) can be deterred, if at all, by the threat of death, since "swift victory" of the revolution "will invalidate [the deterrent efficacy] of a prison sentence" (pp. 284–85).[4] This does not yet tell us how important it is that such deterrence be provided, any more than the fact that a threat of expulsion is the severest deterrent available to university authorities tells them whether they ought to insist on expelling campus rebels. Also, such severe penalties might have the opposite effect of inducing martyrdom, of provoking attempts to overthrow the government to secure a kind of political sainthood. This possibility Van Den Haag recognizes, but claims in a footnote that it "hardly impair[s] the force of the argument" (p. 288). Well, from a logical point of view it impairs it considerably; from an empirical point of view, since we are wholly without any reliable facts or hypotheses on politics in such extreme situations, the entire controversy remains quite speculative.

The one important class of criminals deterrable, if at all, by the death penalty consists, according to Van Den Haag, of those already under "life" sentence or guilty of a crime punishable by "life."

In a trivial sense, he is correct; a person already suffering a given punishment, P, for a given crime, C_1 could not be expected to be deterred by anticipating the reinfliction of P were he to commit C_2. For if the anticipation of P did not deter him from committing C_1, how could the anticipation of P deter him from committing C_2, given that he is already experiencing P? This generalization seems to apply whenever P = "life" imprisonment. Actually, the truth is a bit more complex, because in practice (as Van Den Haag concedes, again in a footnote) so-called "life" imprisonment always has its aggravations (e.g., solitary confinement) and its mitigations (parole eligibility). These make it logically possible to deter a person already convicted of criminal homicide and serving "life" imprisonment from committing another such crime. I admit that the aggravations available are not in practice likely to provide much added deterrent effect; but exactly how likely or unlikely this effect is remains a matter for empirical investigation, not idle guesswork. Van Den Haag's seeming truism, therefore, relies for its plausibility on the false assumption that "life" imprisonment is a uniform punishment not open to further deterrence-relevant aggravations and mitigations.

Empirically, the objection to his point is that persons already serving a "life" sentence do not in general constitute a source of genuine alarm to custodial personnel. Being already incarcerated and integrated into the reward structure of prison life, they do not seem to need the deterrent controls allegedly necessary for other prisoners and the general public.[5] There are exceptions to this generalization, but there is no known way of identifying them in advance, their number has proved to be not large, and it would be irrational, therefore, to design a penal policy (as several states have)[6] which invokes the death penalty in the professed hope of deterring such convicted offenders from further criminal homicide. Van Den Haag cites no evidence that such policies accomplish their alleged purpose, and I know of none. As for the real question which Van Den Haag's argument raises—is there any class of actual or potential criminals for which the death penalty exerts a marginally superior deterrent effect over every less severe alternative?—we have no evidence at all, one way or the other. Until this proposition, or some corollary, is actually tested

and confirmed, there is no reason to indulge Van Den Haag in his speculations.

III

It is not clear why Van Den Haag is so anxious to discuss whether there is evidence that the death penalty is a deterrent, or whether—as he thinks—there is no evidence that it is not a deterrent. For the issue over abolishing the death penalty, as all serious students of the subject have known for decades, is not whether (1) *the death penalty is a deterrent*, but whether (2) *the death penalty is a superior deterrent to "life" imprisonment*, and consequently the evidential dispute is also not over (1) but only over (2). As I have argued elsewhere,[7] abolitionists have reason to contest (1) only if they are against *all* punitive alternatives to the death penalty; since few abolitionists (and none cited by Van Den Haag) take this extreme view, it may be ignored here. We should notice in passing, however, that if it were demonstrated that (1) were false, there would be no need for abolitionists to go on to marshal evidence against (2), since the truth of (1) is a presupposition of the truth of (2). Now it is true that some abolitionists may be faulted for writing as if the falsity of (1) followed from the falsity of (2), but this is not a complaint Van Den Haag makes nor is it an error vital to the abolitionist argument against the death penalty. Similar considerations inveigh against certain pro-death-penalty arguments. Proponents must do more than establish (1), they must also provide evidence in favor of (2); and they cannot infer from evidence which establishes (1) that (2) is true or even probable (unless, of course, that evidence would establish [2] independently). These considerations show us how important it is to distinguish (1) and (2) and the questions of evidence which each raises. Van Den Haag never directly discusses (2), except when he observes in passing that "the question is not only whether the death penalty deters but whether it deters more than alternatives" (p. 284, col. 2). But since he explicitly argues only over the evidential status of (1), it is unclear whether he wishes to ignore (2) or whether he thinks that his arguments regarding (1) also have consequences for the evidential status of (2). Perhaps Van Den Haag thinks that if there is no evidence disconfirming (1), then there can be no evidence disconfirming (2); or perhaps he thinks that none of the evidence disconfirming (2) also disconfirms (1). (If he thinks either, he is wrong.) Or perhaps he is careless, conceding on the one hand that (2) is important to the issue of abolition of the death penalty, only to slide back into a discussion exclusively about (1).

He writes as if his chief contentions were these two: We must not confuse (a) the assertion that there is no evidence that not-(1) (i.e., evidence that [1] is false); and abolitionists have asserted (b) whereas all they are entitled to assert is (a).[8] I wish to proceed on the assumption that since (1) is not chiefly at issue, neither is (a) nor (b) (though I grant, as anyone must, that the distinction between [a] and [b] is legitimate and important). What is chiefly at issue, even though Van Den Haag's discussion obscures the point, is whether abolitionists must content themselves with asserting that there is no evidence against (2), or whether they may go further and assert that there is evidence that not-(2) (i.e., evidence that [2] is false). I shall argue that abolitionists may make the stronger (latter) assertion.

In order to see the issue fairly, it is necessary to see how (2) has so far been submitted to empirical tests. First of all, the issue has been confined to the death penalty for criminal homicide; consequently, it is not (2) but a subsidiary proposition which critics of the death penalty have tested namely, (2a) *the death penalty is a superior deterrent to "life" imprisonment for the crime of criminal homicide.* The falsification of (2a) does not entail the falsity of (2); the death penalty could still be a superior deterrent to "life" imprisonment for the crime of burglary, etc. However, the disconfirmation of (2a) is obviously a partial disconfirmation of (2). Second, (2a) has not been tested directly but only indirectly. No one has devised a way to count or estimate directly the number of persons in a given population who have been deterred from criminal homicide by the fear of the penalty. The difficulties in doing so are plain enough. For instance, it would be possible to infer from the countable numbers who have not been deterred (because they did commit a given crime) that everyone else in the population was deterred, but only on the assumption that the only reason why a person did not commit a given crime is because he was deterred. Unfortunately for this argument (though

happily enough otherwise) this assumption is almost certainly false. Other ways in which one might devise to test (2a) directly have proved equally unfeasible. Yet it would be absurd to insist that there can be no *evidence* for or against (2a) unless it is *direct* evidence for or against it. Because Van Den Haag nowhere indicated what he thinks would count as evidence, direct or indirect, for or against (1), much less (2), his insistence upon the distinction between (a) and (b) and his rebuke to abolitionists is in danger of implicitly relying upon just this absurdity.

How, then, has the indirect argument over (2a) proceeded? During the past generation, at least six different hypotheses have been formulated, as corollaries of (2a), as follows:[9]

i) death-penalty jurisdictions should have a lower annual rate of criminal homicide than abolition jurisdictions;

ii) jurisdictions which abolished the death penalty should show an increased annual rate of criminal homicide after abolition;

iii) jurisdictions which reintroduced the death penalty should show a decreased annual rate of criminal homicide after reintroduction;

iv) given two contiguous jurisdictions differing chiefly in that one has the death penalty and the other does not, the latter should show a higher annual rate of criminal homicide;

v) police officers on duty should suffer a higher annual rate of criminal assault and homicide in abolition jurisdictions than in death-penalty jurisdictions;

vi) prisoners and prison personnel should suffer a higher annual rate of criminal assault and homicide from life-term prisoners in abolition jurisdictions than in death-penalty jurisdictions.

It could be objected to these six hypotheses that they are, as a set, insufficient to settle the question posed by (2a) no matter what the evidence for them may be (i.e., that falsity of [i]–[vi] does not entail the falsity of [2]). Or it could be argued that each of (i)–(vi) has been inadequately tested or insufficiently (dis)confirmed so as to establish any (dis)confirmation of (2a), even though it is conceded that if these hypotheses were highly (dis)confirmed they would (dis)confirm (2*a*). Van Den Haag's line of attack is not entirely clear as between these two alternatives. It looks as if he ought to take the former line of criticism in its most extreme version. How else could he argue his chief point, that the research used by abolitionists has so far failed to produce *any* evidence against (1)—we may take him to mean (2) or (2*a*). Only if (i)–(vi) were *irrelevant* to (2a) could it be fairly concluded from the evidential disconfirmation of (i)–(vi) that there is still no disconfirmation of (2*a*). And this is Van Den Haag's central contention. The other ways to construe Van Den Haag's reasoning are simply too preposterous to be considered: He cannot think that the evidence is indifferent to or *confirms* (i)–(vi); nor can he think that there has been no *attempt* at all to disconfirm (2*a*); nor can he think that the evidence which disconfirms (i)–(vi) is not therewith also evidence which confirms the negations of (i)–(vi). If any of these three was true, it would be a good reason for saying that there is "no evidence" against (2*a*); but each is patently false. If one inspects (i)–(vi) and (2*a*), it is difficult to see how one could argue that (dis)confirmation of the former does not constitute (dis)confirmation of the latter, even if it might be argued that verification of the former does not constitute verification of the latter. I think, therefore, that there is nothing to be gained by pursuing further this first line of attack.

Elsewhere, it looks as though Van Den Haag takes the other alternative of criticism, albeit rather crudely, as when he argues (against [iv], I suppose, since he nowhere formulated [i]–[vi]) that "the similar areas are not similar enough" (p. 285, col. 1). As to why, for example, the rates of criminal homicide in Michigan and in Illinois from 1920 to 1960 are not relevant because the states aren't "similar enough," he does not try to explain. But his criticism does strictly concede that if the jurisdictions *were* "similar enough," then it would be logically possible to argue from the evidence against (iv) to the disconfirmation of (2*a*). And this seems to be in keeping with the nature of the case; it is this second line of attack which needs closer examination.

Van Den Haag's own position and objections apart, what is likely to strike the neutral observer who studies the ways in which (i)–(vi) have been tested and declared disconfirmed is that their dis-

confirmation, and, a fortiori, the disconfirmation of (2*a*), is imperfect for two related reasons. First, all the tests rely upon *unproved empirical assumptions;* second, it is not known whether there is any *statistical significance* to the results of the tests. It is important to make these concessions, and abolitionists and other disbelievers in the deterrent efficacy of the death penalty have not always done so.

It is not possible here to review all the evidence and to reach a judgment on the empirical status of (i)–(vi). But it is possible and desirable to illustrate how the two qualifications cited above must be understood, and then to assess their effect on the empirical status of (2*a*). The absence of statistical significance may be illustrated by reference to hypothesis (v). According to the published studies, the annual rate of assaults upon on-duty policemen in abolition jurisdictions is lower than in death-penalty jurisdictions (i.e., a rate of 1.2 attacks per 100,000 population in the former as opposed to 1.3 per 100,000 in the latter). But is this difference statistically significant or not? The studies do not answer this question because the data were not submitted to tests of statistical significance. Nor is there any way to my knowledge, that these data could be subjected to any such tests. This is, of course, no reason to suppose that the evidence is really not evidence after all, or that though it is evidence against (i) it is not evidence against (2*a*). Statistical significance is, after all, only a measure of the strength of evidence, not a *sine qua non* of evidential status.

The qualification concerning unproved assumptions is more important, and is worth examining somewhat more fully (though, again, only illustratively). Consider hypothesis (i). Are we entitled to infer that (i) is disconfirmed because in fact a study of the annual homicide rates (as measured by vital statistics showing cause of death) unquestionably indicates that the rate in all abolition states is consistently lower than in all death-penalty states? To make this inference we must assume that (A1) homicides as measured by vital statistics are in a generally constant ratio to criminal homicides, (A2) the years for which the evidence has been gathered are representative and not atypical, (A3) however much fluctuations in the homicide rate owe to other factors, there is a nonnegligible proportion which is a function of the penalty, and (A4) the deterrent effect of a penalty is not significantly weakened by its infrequent imposition. (There are, of course, other assumptions, but these are central and sufficiently representative here.) Assumption A1 is effectively unmeasurable because the concept of a criminal homicide is the concept of a homicide which *deserves* to be criminally prosecuted.[10] Nevertheless, A1 has been accepted by criminologists for over a generation. A2 is confirmable, on the other hand, and bit by bit, a year at a time, seems to be being confirmed. Assumption A3 is rather more interesting. To the degree to which it is admitted or insisted that other factors than the severity of the penalty affect the volume of homicide, to that degree A3 becomes increasingly dubious; but at the same time testing (2a) by (i) becomes increasingly unimportant. The urgency of testing (2a) rests upon the assumption that it is the deterrent efficacy of penalties which is the chief factor in the volume of crimes, and it is absurd to hold that assumption and at the same time doubt A3. On the other hand, A4 is almost certainly false (and has been believed so by Bentham and other social theorists for nearly two hundred years). The falsity of A4, however, is not of fatal harm to the disconfirmation of (i) because it is not known how frequently or infrequently a severe penalty such as death or life imprisonment needs to be imposed in order to maximize its deterrent efficacy. Such information as we do have on this point leads one to doubt that for the general population the frequency with which the death sentence is imposed makes any significant different to the volume of criminal homicide.[11]

I suggest that these four assumptions and the way in which they bear upon interpretation and evaluation of the evidence against (i), and therefore the disconfirmation of (2a), are typical of what one finds as one examines the work of criminologists as it relates to the rest of these corollaries of (2a). Is it reasonable, in the light of these considerations, to infer that we have no evidence against (i)–(vi), or that although we do have evidence against (i)–(vi), we have none against (2a)? I do not think so. Short of unidentified and probably unobtainable "crucial experiments," we shall never be able to marshal evidence for (2a) or for (i)–(vi) except by means of certain additional assumptions such as A1–A4. To reason otherwise is

to rely on nothing more than the fact that it is logically possible to grant the evidence against (i)–(vi) and yet deny that (2a) is false; or it is to insist that the assumptions which the inference relies upon are not plausible assumptions at all (or though plausible are themselves false or disconfirmed) and that no other assumptions can be brought forward which will both be immune to objections and still preserve the linkage between the evidence and the corollaries and (2a). The danger now is that one will repudiate assumptions such as A1–A4 in order to guarantee the failure of efforts to disconfirm (2a) via disconfirmation of (i)–(vi); or else that one will place the standards of evidence too high before one accepts the disconfirmation. In either case one has begun to engage in the familiar but discreditable practice of "protecting the hypothesis" by making it, in effect, immune to any kind of disconfirmation.

On my view things stand in this way. An empirical proposition not directly testable, (2), has a significant corollary, (2a), which in turn suggests a number of corollaries, (i)–(vi), each of which is testable with varying degrees of indirectness. Each of (i)–(vi) has been tested. To accept the results as evidence disconfirming (i)–(vi) and as therefore disconfirming (2a), it is necessary to make certain assumptions, of which A1–A4 are typical. These assumptions in turn are not all testable, much less directly tested; some of them, in their most plausible formulation, may even be false (but not in that formulation necessary to the inference, however). Since this structure of indirect testing, corollary hypotheses, unproved assumptions, is typical of the circumstances which face us when we wish to consider the evidence for or against any complex empirical hypothesis such as (2), I conclude that while (2) has by no means been disproved (whatever that might mean), it is equally clear that (2) has been disconfirmed, rather than confirmed or left untouched by the inductive arguments we have surveyed.

I have attempted to review and appraise the chief "statistical" arguments (as Van Den Haag calls them) marshaled during the past fifteen years or so in this country by those critical of the death penalty. But in order to assess these arguments more adequately, it is helpful to keep in mind two other considerations. First, most of the criminologists skeptical of (1) are led to this attitude not by the route we have examined—the argument against (2)—but by a general theory of the causation of crimes of personal violence. Given their confidence in that theory, and the evidence for it, they tend not to credit seriously the idea that the death penalty deters (very much), much less the idea that it is a superior deterrent to a severe alternative such as "life" imprisonment (which may not deter very much, either). The interested reader should consult in particular Professor Marvin Wolfgang's monograph, *Patterns of Criminal Homicide* (1958). Second, very little of the empirical research purporting to establish the presence or absence of deterrent efficacy of a given punishment is entirely reliable because almost no effort has been made to isolate the relevant variables. Surely, it is platitudinously true that *some* persons in *some* situations considering *some* crimes can be deterred from committing them by *some* penalties. To go beyond this, however, and supplant these variables with a series of well-confirmed functional hypotheses about the deterrent effect of current legal sanctions is not possible today.

Even if one cannot argue, as Van Den Haag does, that there is no evidence against the claim that the death penalty is a better deterrent than life imprisonment, this does not yet tell us how good this evidence is, how reliable it is, how extensive, and how probative. Van Den Haag could, after all, give up his extreme initial position and retreat to the concession that although there is evidence against the superior deterrent efficacy of the death penalty, still, the evidence is not very good, indeed, not good enough to make reasonable the policy of abolishing the death penalty. Again, it is not possible to undertake to settle this question short of a close examination of each of the empirical studies which confirm (i)–(vi). The reply, so far as there is one, short of further empirical studies (which undoubtedly are desirable—I should not want to obscure that), is twofold: The evidence, such as it is, for (i)–(vi) is uniformly confirmatory in all cases; and the argument of Section IV which follows.

IV

Van Den Haag's "argument" rests considerable weight on the claims that "the added severity of the death penalty adds to deterrence, or may do

so"; and that "the generalized threat of the death penalty may be a deterrent, and the more so, the more generally applied." These claims are open to criticism on at least three grounds.

First, as the modal auxiliaries signal, Van Den Haag has not really committed himself to any affirmative empirical claim, but only to a truism. It is always logically possible, no matter what the evidence, that a given penalty which is *ex hypothesi* more severe than an alternative, may be a better deterrent under some conditions not often realized, and be proven so by evidence not ever detectable. For this reason, there is no possible way to prove that Van Den Haag's claims are false, no possible preponderance of evidence against his conclusions which must, logically, force him to give them up. One would have hoped those who believe in the deterrent superiority of the death penalty could, at this late date, offer their critics something more persuasive than logical possibilities. As it is, Van Den Haag's appeal to possible evidence comes perilously close to an argument from ignorance: The possible evidence we might gather is used to offset the actual evidence we have gathered.

Second, Van Den Haag rightly regards his conclusion above as merely an instance of the general principle that, *ceteris paribus*, "the Greater the Severity the Greater the Deterrence," a "plausible" idea, as he says (p. 287). Yet the advantage on behalf of the death penalty produced by this principle is a function entirely of the evidence for the principle itself. But we are offered no evidence at all to make this plausible principle into a confirmed hypothesis of contemporary criminological theory of special relevance to crimes of personal violence. Until we see evidence concerning specific crimes, specific penalties, specific criminal populations, which show that in general the Greater the Severity the Greater the Deterrence, we run the risk of stupifying ourselves by the merely plausible. Besides, without any evidence for this principle we will find ourselves at a complete standoff with the abolitionist (who, of course, can play the same game), because he has his own equally plausible first principle: The Greater the Severity of Punishment the Greater the Brutality Provoked throughout Society. When at last, exhausted and frustrated by mere plausibilities, we once again turn to study the evidence, we will find that the current literature on deterrence in criminology does not encourage us to believe in Van Den Haag's principle.[12]

Third, Van Den Haag has not given any reason why, in the quest for deterrent efficacy, one should fasten (as he does) on the severity of the punishments in question, rather than (as Bentham long ago counseled) on the relevant factors, notably the ease and speed and reliability with which the punishment can be inflicted. Van Den Haag cannot hope to convince anyone who has studied the matter that the death penalty and "life" imprisonment differ only in their severity, and that in all other respects affecting deterrent efficacy they are equivalent; and if he believes this himself it would be interesting to have seen his evidence for it. The only thing to be said in favor of fastening exclusively upon the question of severity in the appraisal of punishments for their relative deterrent efficacy is that augmenting the severity of a punishment in and of itself usually imposes little if any added direct cost to operate the penal system; it even may be cheaper. This is bound to please the harried taxpayer, and at the same time gratify the demand on government to "do something" about crime. Beyond that, emphasizing the severity of punishments as the main (or indeed the sole) variable relevant to deterrent efficacy is unbelievably superficial.

V

Van Den Haag's final point concerning where the burden of proof lies is based, he admits, on playing off a certainty (the death of the persons executed) against a risk (that innocent persons, otherwise the would-be victims of those deterrable only by the death penalty, would be killed).[13] This is not as analogous as he seems to think it is to the general nature of gambling, investment, and other risk-taking enterprises. In none of them do we deliberately cause anything to be killed, as we do, for instance, when we weed out carrot seedlings to enable those remaining to grow larger (a eugenic analogy, by the way, which might be more useful to Van Den Haag's purpose). In none, that is, do we venture a sacrifice in the hope of a future net gain; we only *risk* a present loss in that hope. Moreover, in gambling ventures we recoup what we risked if we win, whereas in executions we

must lose something (the lives of persons executed) no matter if we lose or win (the lives of innocents protected). Van Den Haag's attempt to locate the burden of proof by appeal to principles of gambling is a failure.

Far more significantly, Van Den Haag frames the issue in such a way that the abolitionist has no chance of discharging the burden of proof once he accepts it. For what evidence could be marshaled to prove what Van Den Haag wants proved, namely, that "the greater severity inherent in irrevocability [of the death penalty] . . . adds nothing to deterrence"? The evidence alluded to at the end of Section IV does tend to show that this generalization (the negation of Van Den Haag's own principle) is indeed true, but it does not prove it. I conclude, therefore, that either Van Den Haag is wrong in his argument which shows the locus of burden of proof to lie on the abolitionist, or one must accept less than proof in order to discharge this burden (in which case, the very argument Van Den Haag advances shows that the burden of proof now lies on those who would retain the death penalty).

"Burden of proof" in areas outside judicial precincts where evidentiary questions are at stake tends to be a rhetorical phrase and nothing more. Anyone interested in the truth of a matter will not defer gathering evidence pending a determination of where the burden of proof lies. For those who do think there is a question of burden of proof, as Van Den Haag does, they should consider this: Advocacy of the death penalty is advocacy of a rule of penal law which empowers the state to deliberately take human life and in general to threaten the public with the taking of life. *Ceteris paribus*, one would think anyone favoring such a rule would be ready to offer considerable evidence for its necessity and efficacy. Surely, some showing of necessity, some evidentiary proof, is to be expected to satisfy the skeptical. Exactly when and in what circumstances have the apologists for capital punishment offered evidence to support their contentions? Where is that evidence recorded for us to inspect, comparable to the evidence cited in Section III against the superior deterrent efficacy of the death penalty? Van Den Haag conspicuously cited no such evidence, and so it is with all other proponents of the death penalty. The insistence that the burden of proof lies on abolitionists, therefore, is nothing but the rhetorical demand of every defender of the status quo who insists upon evidence from those who would effect change, while reserving throughout the right to dictate criteria and standards of proof and refusing to offer evidence for his own view.[14]

I should have thought that the death penalty was a sufficiently momentous matter and of sufficient controversy that the admittedly imperfect evidence assembled over the past generation by those friendly to abolition would have been countered by evidence tending to support the opposite, retentionist, position. It remains a somewhat sad curiosity that nothing of the sort has happened; no one has ever published research tending to show, however inconclusively, that the death penalty after all is a deterrent, and a superior deterrent to "life" imprisonment. Among scholars at least, if not among legislators and other politicians, the perennial appeal to burden of proof really ought to give way to offering of proof by those interested enough to argue the issue.

TUFTS UNIVERSITY

Notes

1. *Ethics* 78 (July 1968):280–88. Van Den Haag later published a "revised version" under the same title in *Journal of Criminal Law, Criminology and Police Science* 60 (1969):141–47. I am grateful to Professor Van Den Haag for providing me with a reprint of each version. I should add that his revisions in the later version were minimal, especially in his Section V which is mainly what I shall criticize. All page references in the text are to the version published in *Ethics.*

2. See Massachusetts Laws, chap. 150, Resolves of 1967; "Interim Report of the Special Commission Established to Make an Investigation and Study Relative to the Effectiveness of Capital Punishment as a Deterrent to Crime," mimeographed (Boston: Clerk, Great and General Court, State House, 1968).

3. See the several essays reprinted in Bedau, ed., *The Death Penalty in America,* rev. ed. (New York, 1967), chap. 4 and the articles cited therein at pp. 166–70.

4. The same argument has been advanced earlier by Sidney Hook (see the *New York Law Forum* [1961], pp. 278–83, and the revised version of this argument published in Bedau, pp. 150–51).

5. See, e.g., Thorsten Sellin, "Prison Homicides," in *Capital Punishment,* ed. Sellin (New York, 1967), pp. 154–60.

6. Rhode Island (1852), North Dakota (1915), New York (1965), Vermont (1965), and New Mexico (1969), have all qualified their abolition of the death penalty in this way; for further details, see Bedau, p. 12.

7. Bedau, pp. 260–61.

8. Van Den Haag accuses Professor Thorsten Sellin, a criminologist "who has made a careful study of the available statistics," of seeming to "think that this lack of evidence for deterrence is evidence for the lack of deterrence" (p. 285, col. 1), that is, of thinking that (*a*) is (*b*)! In none of Sellin's writings which I have studied (see, for a partial listing, note 9, below) do I see any evidence that Sellin "thinks" the one "is" the other. What will be found is a certain vacillation in his various published writings, which span the years from 1953 to 1967, between the two ways of putting his conclusions. His most recent statement is unqualifiedly in the (*b*) form (see his *Capital Punishment,* p. 138). Since Van Den Haag also cited my *Death Penalty in America* (though not in this connection), I might add that there I did distinguish between (*a*) and (*b*) but did not insist, as I do now, that the argument entitles abolitionists to assert (*b*) (see Bedau, pp. 264–65). It is perhaps worth noting here some other writers, all criminologists, who have recently stated the same or a stronger conclusion. "Capital punishment does not act as an effective deterrent to murder" (William J. Chambliss, "Types of Deviance and the Effectiveness of Legal Sanctions," *Wisconsin Law Review* [1967], p. 706); "The capital punishment controversy has produced the most reliable information on the general deterrent effect of a criminal sanction. It now seems established and accepted that . . . the death penalty makes no difference to the homicide rate" (Norval Morris and Frank Zimring, "Deterrence and Corrections," *Annals* 381 [January 1969]:143); "the evidence indicates that it [namely, the death penalty for murder] has no discernible effects in the United States" (Walter C. Reckless, "The Use of the Death Penalty," *Crime and Delinquency* 15 [January 1969]:52); "Capital punishment is ineffective in deterring murder" (Eugene Doleschal, "The Deterrent Effect of Legal Punishment," *Information Review on Crime and Delinquency* 1 [June 1969]:7).

9. The relevant research, regarding each of the six hypotheses in the text, is as follows: (i) Karl Schuessler, "The Deterrent Influence of the Death Penalty," *Annals* 284 (November 1952): 57; Walter C. Reckless, "The Use of the Death Penalty—a Factual Statement," *Crime and Delinquency* 15 (1969):52, table 9. (ii) Thorsten Sellin, *The Death Penalty* (Philadelphia: American Law Institute, 1959), pp. 19–24, reprinted in Bedau, pp. 274–84; updated in Sellin, *Capital Punishment,* 135–38. (iii) Sellin, *The*

Death Penalty, pp. 34–38; reprinted in Bedau, pp. 339–43. (iv) See works cited in (iii), above. (v) Canada, *Minutes and Proceedings of Evidence,* Joint Committee of the Senate and House of Commons on Capital Punishment and Corporal Punishment and Lotteries (1955), appendix F, pt. 1, pp. 718–28; "The Death Penalty and Police Safety," reprinted in Bedau, pp. 284–301, and in Sellin, *Capital Punishment,* pp. 138–54, with postscript (1967); Canada, "The State Police and the Death Penalty," pp. 729–35, reprinted in Bedau, pp. 301–15. (vi) *Massachusetts, Report and Recommendations of the Special Commission . . . [on] the Death Penalty . . .* (1958), pp. 21–22, reprinted on Bedau, p. 400; Thorsten Sellin, "Prison Homicides," in Sellin, *Capital Punishment,* pp. 154–60.

10. See, for discussion surrounding this point, Bedau, pp. 56–74.

11. See Robert H. Dann, *The Deterrent Effect of Capital Punishment* (Philadelphia, 1935); Leonard H. Savitz, "A Study in Capital Punishment," *Journal of Criminal Law, Criminology and Police Science* 49 (1958): 338–41, reprinted in Bedau, pp. 315–32; William F.

Graves, "A Doctor Looks at Capital Punishment," *Medical Arts and Sciences* 10 (1956):137–41, reprinted in Bedau, pp. 322–32, with addenda (1964).

12. See, for a general review, Eugene Doleschal, "The Deterrent Effect of Legal Punishment: A Review of the Literature," *Information Review on Crime and Delinquency* 1 (June 1969): 1–17, and the many research studies cited therein, especially the survey by Norval Morris and Frank Zimring, "Deterrence and Corrections," *Annals* 381 (January 1969):137–46; also Gordon Hawkins, "Punishment and Deterrence," *Wisconsin Law Review* (1969), pp. 550–65.

13. The same objection has been raised earlier by Joel Feinberg (see his review of Bedau in *Ethics* 76 (October 1965):63.

14. For a general discussion which is not inconsistent with the position I have taken, and which illuminates the logicorhetorical character of the appeal to burden of proof in philosophical argument, see Robert Brown, "The Burden of Proof," *American Philosophical Quarterly* 7 (1970):74–82.

Questions for Analysis

1. Explain why Bedau believes that Van Den Haag's definition of deterrence is "too ill-formulated to be of any serious use." Do you agree?

2. On what grounds does Bedau dismiss Van Den Haag's contention that the death penalty is the only possible deterrent for some classes of criminals?

3. Why does Bedau feel it is so important to distinguish (1) the death penalty as a deterrent from (2) the death penalty as a superior deterrent to life imprisonment? Does the falsity of (1) necessarily follow from the falsity of (2)? Does the establishment of (1) thereby establish (2)?

4. What hypotheses have been formulated to test the proposition that the death penalty is a superior deterrent to life imprisonment for the crime of criminal homicide? What have been the results? What are Van Den Haag's objections to these tests, and how does Bedau respond to the objections? Do you feel that Bedau has adequately met the objections?

5. Regarding the same hypotheses, Bedau concedes that their disconfirmation is imperfect for two related reasons. What are those reasons? Does Bedau go on to turn these concessions to his own advantage? If so, how?

6. Why does Bedau reject Van Den Haag's argument that the severity of the death penalty may add to deterrence?

7. How does Bedau respond to Van Den Haag's claim that abolitionists must prove that capital punishment adds nothing to deterrence?

Reflections on Hanging

Arthur Koestler

Arthur Koestler, one of society's outstanding social critics, is perhaps best known for his novel and play, Darkness at Noon. *But his* Reflections on Hanging *is the work that continues to interest abolitionists—understandably so. Although Koestler wrote* Reflections *as an impassioned and eloquent plea for the abolition of hanging in England, it has provided considerable ammunition for abolitionists on both sides of the Atlantic.*

In the following selection from Reflections, *Koestler tests three common arguments against life imprisonment as an alternative to capital punishment: (1) that capital punishment is "unsafe," (2) that it is inhumane, (3) that it is not cruel enough.*

Koestler attacks the first claim by examining murderers as a class and their behavior both in prison and outside after their release. He then questions the legitimacy of the second claim by examining prison life. While Koestler does not believe the facts justify the charge that life imprisonment constitutes cruel and unusual punishment, at the same time he does not accept the third claim that it is not harsh enough for the murderer.

In the last analysis, Koestler sees the real punishment not in the prison environment but in the facts of going to prison and being in prison, as well as in the loss of liberties. To support his position, he quotes the testimony of those most familiar with prison life—those serving time and those watching them do it.

The alternative to capital punishment is imprisonment "for life." This really means imprisonment for a length of period determined by the demands of public safety and the rehabilitation of the prisoner.

The arguments most often heard against this alternative can be classified as follows:

(a) It is *unsafe*. The murderer serving a life sentence is usually let out after a number of years and may commit another murder.

(b) To keep a murderer, who cannot be reformed, in prison to the end of his life is *more cruel* than a quick death.

(c) Imprisonment is *not cruel enough*; modern prisons pamper the criminal instead of punishing him—plus the subsidiary arguments about the burden to the taxpayer, the strain on prison warders, the danger of escape.

1. Murderers as a Class

That it would be *unsafe* to let murderers live is an argument in which many well-meaning people

believe, though they loathe the idea of hanging and would rather do away with it. But the public's idea of the murderer is modelled on exceptional and untypical cases (Heath, Haig, Crippen, Christie), which receive the widest publicity and are part of the national folklore. The murderer is either thought of as a homicidal maniac, or a hardened criminal, or a monster planning the "perfect murder." But these popular figures who impress themselves on the public imagination are no more typical of murderers as a class, than Lawrence of Arabia was of British subalterns as a class.

The figures quoted in Chapter II [of *Reflections on Hanging*] show that during the fifty years 1900–49 only in one out of twelve cases was the murderer found so dangerous for public safety or his crime so "unpardonable" that he was executed—that means only 8% of the total. In Scotland, the proportion was even lower: 4%. Every analysis of the motive and circumstances under which the crime was committed, shows the extreme rarity of the cold-blooded type of murder. Half a century ago, Sir John Macdonell, Master of the Supreme Court, analyzed the criminal statistics from 1866 to

---

From Arthur Koestler, Reflections on Hanging. ©*1957 by Arthur Koestler. Reprinted by permission of The Sterling Lord Agency, Inc. and A. D. Peters & Co. Ltd. Sections and footnotes renumbered.*

1905 and found the following result: 90% of the murders were committed by men, and nearly two-thirds of their victims were their wives, mistresses or sweethearts. The peak day for murder is Saturday, and the peak hours 8 p.m. to 2 a.m. Approximately 30% of the murders were caused by drink, quarrels and violent rage, another 40% by jealousy, intrigues and sexual motives, and only 10% by financial motives. Sir John Macdonell concludes his survey in the following words (my italics):

> I hesitate to draw any conclusions from imperfect data as to matters of great complexity, but I am inclined to think that this crime is *not generally the crime of the so-called criminal classes* but is in most cases rather an *incident in miserable lives in which disputes, quarrels, angry words and blows are common*. The short history of the large number of cases which have been examined might be summed up thus: Domestic quarrels and brawls; much previous ill-treatment; drinking, fighting, blows; a long course of brutality and continued absence of self-restraint. This crime is generally the last of a series of acts of violence.[1]

Half a century later, the Royal Commission examined the statistics of the years 1900–49 and came to the conclusion that they "confirm Sir John Macdonell's statement that murder is not in general a crime of the so-called criminal classes."[2]

2. The Behavior of Murderers in Prison

Next, let us examine, from the point of view of public safety, the conduct of murderers who have been convicted and reprieved. The people best qualified to decide this question are evidently the prison governors, warders, prison chaplains and Home Office experts. These were heard both by the Select Committee and by the Royal Commission. Their opinions are quoted below; they were unanimous and without dissent. Since this point is of great importance in correcting popular misbeliefs about murderers as a class, I am quoting in full the relevant passages from both reports. First, the Select Committee of 1930:

> High tribute was paid to the general conduct in prison, and on release, of reprieved murderers. . . . The testimony of the Home Office witnesses was as follows:
> "A very large number of murderers are, in other respects, perfectly decent people, and a very large proportion of them, if they were let out, would be very unlikely to commit any other murder or any other crime. They are really a class by themselves; they are quite different from the ordinary criminal as a rule. . . . It is certainly not common experience that a murderer who has been released after serving part of a life sentence returns to prison . . . as to . . . committing further murders on release, that might be entirely ruled out."

Lord Brentford [Home Secretary, 1924–29] said of the reprieved murderer that he was a man who had committed one crime and, not being of a criminal type or of a criminal mind, he made a very good prisoner. He did not think he had come across a single case of a reprieved murderer committing another murder.

Colonel Hales, Governor of Parkhurst Prison, could not recall one who, from the moment he was discharged, had not made good. The same testimony was given by Revd. William Lewis Cottrell, M.A., Chaplain at Wormwood Scrubs, by Mr. Walter Middleton, Chief Officer of Pentonville Prison, and by Captain Clayton, Governor of Dartmoor.[3]

None of the prison governors or officials dissented from this opinion, although the majority were probably anti-abolitionist. Twenty years later the Royal Commission came to the same conclusion:

> There is a popular belief that prisoners serving a life sentence after conviction of murder form a specially troublesome and dangerous class. That is not so. Most find themselves in prison because they have yielded to temptation under the pressure of a combination of circumstances unlikely to recur. "Taking murderers as a class," said one witness [Major Benke, Governor of Wandsworth Prison and Chairman of the Panel of Prison Governors] "there are a considerable number who are first offenders and who are not people of criminal tendencies. The murder is in many cases their first offence against the law. Previous to that they were law-abiding citizens and their general tenor of life is still to be law-abiding. . . ."[4]

In August, 1952, there was a total of 91 reprieved murderers among the prison population of England and Wales, out of which 82, that is, more than 90%, belonged to the star class.[5] Thus the large majority of reprieved murderers are unusually well-behaved model prisoners. What happens when they are let loose on society after serving their sentence? Do the reformed lambs turn into wolves again?

3. Murderers Turned Loose

The answer is given in the statistics of the Home Office, of Scotland Yard and the Central After Care Association. During the twenty-year period 1928–48, 174 people were sentenced to life, and of these 112 had been released at the end of the period in question.[6] Of these 112, only one was alleged to have committed a second murder: Walter Graham Rowland; and he was, as we saw, one of the most probable victims of mistaken identity. Yet Rowland is, as far as one can gather from existing reports, the only case of a "sane" reprieved murderer being convicted of a second murder in the United Kingdom in the course of the twentieth century.[7] None of the other released "lifers" during the twenty-year period ending in 1948 committed crimes of violence against the person; and only five committed offences against property. In Scotland, eleven reprieved murderers were released during the same period: Only two of these were re-convicted, one for theft and one for "lewd practices."[8]

The evidence before the Royal Commission from the Commonwealth countries and the U.S.A. was as follows:

> *New South Wales:* In general such prisoners after release behave well. Very occasionally . . . the murderer with a previous record of criminality . . . will again come into conflict with the law, but seldom for a serious offence.
> *Queensland* (capital punishment abolished): In the fifty years 1900–50, four released murderers committed subsequent offences: one attempt to kill, one indecent assault, one infliction of bodily harm, one cattle stealing.
> *South Australia:* No prisoner released after life sentence has been returned for breach of conditions.
> *Candada:* The average of failures is estimated to have fluctuated around 3%.
> *Ceylon:* No accurate information available, but cases where murderers returned to prison are exceptional.
> *New Zealand:* So far as memory goes, no prisoner released after a conviction of murder has broken any of the conditions of his release

or committed any offence or been returned to prison.
> *South Africa:* Recommittals of this class of prisoner are extremely rare occurrences.
> *U.S.A.:* Generally speaking, I doubt if there are any facts which would indicate that persons originally convicted and later commuted and released under parole have any higher degree of failure on parole than any other group. There have been a few notorious cases where persons have lapsed into delinquency again, but it is usually a comparatively minor sort of crime as compared to the one which originally got them into trouble. Cases of murder committed by persons pardoned from the death-penalty are rare if not almost unknown.[9]

It may be objected that this unanimous body of evidence refers only to the more harmless type of murderers who were reprieved precisely because they were considered harmless. But the experience of countries which have abolished capital punishment and where, therefore, every murderer is automatically reprieved, whether considered "harmless" or not, is exactly the same as in countries where murderers are still being executed.

Regarding the Dominions, we have already seen that in Queensland and New Zealand, both abolitionist during the period in question, only one case is known of a reprieved man attempting murder in the last fifty years. In Europe, the Royal Commission's inquiry embraced six countries: Belgium, Denmark, the Netherlands, Norway, Sweden and Switzerland. *In these six countries altogether six convicted murderers have committed crimes of violence after their release in the course of the last thirty years.*[10] The Royal Commission concludes:

"Even in countries which have abolished capital punishment the protection of society is rarely thought to require that murderers who are mentally normal should be detained in prison for the remainder of their life or even for very long periods. . . . The evidence that we ourselves received in these countries was also to the effect that released murderers who commit further crimes of violence are rare, and those who become useful citizens are common."[11]

These facts are so amazing and contrary to public belief that they call for some explanation. It is partly contained in the statements of the prison governors and Home Office experts which I have quoted: Namely, that with rare exceptions, murder is not a crime of the criminal classes, and that the average murderer is *not* an "enemy of society" in the broad sense. This general statement was borne out by the statistics on the motives and circumstances of murder. It was confirmed by the experience of abolitionist countries which show that released murderers are less apt to relapse into crime than other offenders. Broadly speaking, it boils down to this: that the vast majority of murderers are either "crazy" in the elastic, non-legal sense of the word, or momentarily "crazed" ("mad" in American parlance); because a normal person in a normal state of mind just doesn't commit murder. Hence murderers are, by and large, either mentally abnormal, or acting under abnormal circumstances. The former belong not to prison but to an institution; the latter are easier to reform than any other type of criminal.

There remain the rare exceptions—the Christies and Haigs—who, in all likelihood, cannot be reformed and would have to be kept safely locked away to the end of their natural lives. But these "monsters" who so much agitate public imagination, form such a small percentage as to be almost negligible as a social problem. Moreover, they do not affect the question we are discussing—life imprisonment as an alternative to the death-penalty—because they do not belong to prison but to an institution. The Royal Commission says about them: "We agree with the Home Office that any convicted murderers whom it would be unsafe ever to release are likely to be in the category of the mentally abnormal."[12] They belong to a category apart, since the protection of society against them becomes the responsibility not of the legal but of the medical profession.

The practical consequences of abolition would in fact hardly be felt or noticed by the country. The cessation of the death-penalty would simply mean that on an average thirteen persons per year would be added to the British prison population. Even the Home Office, traditionally opposed to abolition, agrees that these people "would not be likely to give any exceptional trouble to prison officers."[13] And furthermore, that those who could not be safely released in due time would form a very small proportion of the whole, and would be found in the category of the mentally abnormal and in that category alone.[14]

For the thirteen men and women who are annually hanged with the nation's tacit consent are by no means "monsters" and "irretrievables." We saw how the rigidity of the law and the anachronism of the M'Naghten Rules transform justice into an unholy roulette game. Mrs. Ellis, Mrs. Thompson, the boy Bentley, all of whom were hanged, were no more "irretrievable" than Macebearer Martin, who was spared. The late Sir Alexander Paterson, Director of Convict Prisons, had this to say about the thirteen whom we annually hang: "If the estimate of [the condemned person's] character, formed by those who have to look after him for several weeks while awaiting sentence, could be taken into account by those who have to advise the Secretary of State, a considerable number might be respited."[15] And the Chaplain at Wormwood Scrubs Prison, the Rev. W. L. Cottrell, summed up his experience as follows:

> Of the 15 men whom I have seen executed I have felt very much indeed that a proportion of those men, perhaps half of them or even more, might really have been allowed to live, and had they been allowed to live I have felt that they would really turn into decent honest citizens. That is not emotional sentiment that has carried me away, but it is the real hard facts of the men whom I have known, because a chaplain gets very intimate with these men before they die, and I have felt that many of them, like so many reprieved murderers have done of whom I know today, would really have been quite decent honest citizens and could have taken their place in the world and in Society.[16]

The precautions taken by the Home Office before a man sentenced to life is released, will be discussed later. But the evidence of the extreme rarity of the cases where a murderer found fit for release committed a second crime, is in itself sufficient to show that the risk run by the community through the substitution of life for death sentences, is almost entirely an imaginary one. It is certainly smaller than the joint risks of executing innocent people and of letting guilty people off because the jury is not certain enough to hang the man, but would send him to prison in the knowledge that the case can be reopened. We have seen that these are the inevitable consequences of an outdated law, and the chances are that there are more murderers at large for this reason in England than in countries where capital punishment was abolished.

4. The Length of a Life Sentence

We now come to the argument that a quick death is less cruel than a long prison sentence. It comes from two categories of people: those who rationalize their sadistic tendencies by a pious "break his neck for his own good," and from genuine humanitarians who, ignorant of conditions in modern prisons, base their apprehensions on vague notions of gaol-life in Dickensian days.

The person best qualified to judge whether prison is preferable to execution is evidently the prisoner himself. Sir Basil Thomson, an outstanding authority, wrote that "no Governor has ever yet met a condemned prisoner who would refuse a reprieve or who did not ardently long for one."[17] Calvert quotes another ex-prison official as stating "that of the thirty reprieved murderers whom, in the course of his duties, he had come to know intimately, there was not one but had testified, after years of imprisonment, to his thankfulness for the respite."[18] Yet at that time prison routine was much grimmer and more depressing than nowadays.

The actual length of a "life" sentence is determined by the Home Office. It is not decided in advance, but according to the reports received on the prisoner's character and conduct. Each case is reviewed at least every four years. In exceptional cases the reprieved prisoner may be released almost instantaneously. Home Office statistics[19] show that during the decade 1940–49, 93 people were released from serving commuted life sentences. Of these, 6 had served less than a year— among them a woman who had gassed her son, a hopeless imbecile of thirty who had to be nursed like a baby; and a Jewish refugee woman from Nazi Germany who, together with her mother, tried to poison herself during the war for fear of a German invasion. The mother died, the daughter survived and was convicted of murder as a survivor of a suicide pact.

Of the others, on an average 5 persons were released each year between their second and sixth year in prison. This makes a total of 32 persons out of 93, released after serving less than seven years. All of these were obviously pathetic cases, who could not be of the remotest danger to society. The peak years of release were between the seventh and eighth years after conviction—36 cases, amounting to 40% of the total. Of the remainder, 10 persons were made to serve nine years, 8 persons ten years, 2 eleven years, 3 twelve years, 1 thirteen years and 1 fourteen years. Nobody was released who had served more than fourteen years. The table does not say how many prisoners there were who had served more than fourteen years and were *not* released; but the Home Office states that "only most exceptionally would anybody serve more than fifteen years under the present practice; the normal is much less than that."[20] From this we must conclude, that most of the "over-fifteen-years," i.e. the irretrievables, are in Broadmoor. Yet, as we saw, there was only one case in England, Wales or Scotland, during the last fifty years, of a released "lifer" committing an act of violence—and that was the enigmatic case of Rowland.

5. How a Life Sentence Is Spent

So much for the length of time spent in prison by reprieved murderers before they are considered to have expiated their crime, and safe to be released. How is that time spent?

Long-term prisoners in England are divided into two classes: "star" and "ordinary." The star class comprises all first offenders unless they are considered a bad influence, but also prisoners with previous convictions if they are supposed to become a good influence; there is no rigid rule.

In August, 1952, the prison population included, as previously mentioned, 91 reprieved murderers, 82 of whom were in the star class. The men of the star class were serving their term partly at Wakefield, partly at the new "open prison" at Leyhill; the women, either at Aylesbury or at the "open prison" at Askam Grange. Others were undergoing hospital treatment, or waiting for their transfer from local prisons.[21]

The "open prisons" are a recent experiment, dating back to 1946. There are no walls around the prison, no bars on the windows, no locks on the doors, and no guards are posted. Leyhill houses on the average 250 to 300 prisoners, of whom, in 1952, 20 were reprieved murderers. Escape is, of course, child's play—but it is not in the interests of the type of prisoner sent to an "open prison." In

1947, the first year after the experiment was started, fourteen escaped; in 1948, eight; in 1949, five; in 1950, one; in 1951, one; in 1952, nil.[22]

Yet the great majority of reprieved murderers serve part of their sentences—often a large part—in "open prisons."

The major part of the day—seven to eight hours—is spent by the prison population much in the same manner as by the ordinary free population: on work. "Work" for the prisoner under the old regime meant "the treadmill, the shot drill and the crank, of which the deliberate intention was to be irksome, fatiguing and—because totally unproductive—degrading."[23] Today "work' means nearly anything in the prisoner's own trade or a trade learnt in prison: from farming and market gardening to printing and bookbinding. At Wakefield, prisoners are engaged in: weaving, tailoring, precision engineering, bricklaying, foundry work, painting and decorating. At Leyhill: in carpentry, shoemaking, printing and binding. Some Leyhill prisoners work on local farms, or at road-mending, or as bricklayers and builders. They bicycle to their places of employment without any escort, and work without prison supervision. Other prisons send out parties of up to twenty prisoners with a single officer accompanying them, to do agricultural or forestry work. In women's prisons, the main trades are needlework, dressmaking, knitting, cleaning, painting, gardening and laundering. Some prisoners manufacture fishermen's nets, others footballs, others gloves and pullovers. The customers of their produce are the prison administration itself, other Government departments, public and local bodies and, to a small extent, private firms.

All prisons in which long sentences are served have vocational courses for those prisoners who had no skill or trade, or who wish to acquire a new one. They take the form of a six-months course of both practical and theoretical instruction based on a Ministry of Labour syllabus. They include, for men: precision engineering, carpentry, fitting, bricklaying, painting and decorating, foundry work, weaving, printing, bookbinding. For women, there are courses in cookery and general housewifery, tailoring, and so forth.

The pay is very small. It normally does not exceed four shillings a week. The idea behind this seems to be that the surplus value of the prisoner's work should pay for his upkeep. On the Continent the rates of pay are generally much higher: In Belgium, prisoners earn up to thirty shillings, in Denmark up to two pounds a week, half of which can be spent in prison, the other half kept until release. However that may be, the system answers the old idiotic argument that abolition of the death-penalty would increase the taxpayer's burden. The average of thirteen broken necks per annum costs the taxpayer ten pounds per neck to Mr. Pierrepoint, plus the fee to his assistant, to which have to be added travelling expenses for both; not to mention the outlay for warders going sick after each operation; maintenance of the apparatus, wear and tear of the rope, and so forth. The reprieved convict, on the other hand, earns his keep, plus a surplus for the prison administration. The costly prisoners are those who serve short sentences in local prisons, such as vagabonds and petty thieves. From the anxious taxpayer's point of view, it would be more logical to hang these.

Outside working hours there is a large and growing program for various activities in both the field of education and entertainment. There are lectures, theatre performances, film shows and concerts. In some prisons the prisoners have their own orchestras and dramatic societies. All have libraries, but prisoners may also receive books and periodicals from outside and subscribe to correspondence courses for any trade or hobby. Games are played at weekends, and physical training is given to younger prisoners. At Wakefield there are five courts; at Leyhill, the cricket and football teams play against the local clubs; the inmates can have their own gardens, competing in the annual flower show; they have a putting course, a deck-tennis court, a swimming pool, ping-pong, billiards and a wireless room.

It can hardly be said that detention under these conditions is "a doom far worse than death," as the Lord Chancellor of the day, Lord Jowitt, and the previous Lord Chancellor, Viscount Simon, said in the House of Lords debate in 1948. These worthies, whom I had occasion to quote before, were referring to some long bygone horrors of the Belgian and Italian prison systems as the only conceivable alternative to hanging. It is worth a digression to listen to the Lord Chancellor:

> In Belgium the position is that a murderer
> who is sentenced nominally to imprisonment
> for life is usually allowed out after some

twenty-five years, but he serves the first ten of the twenty-five in solitary confinement. . . . Speaking for myself, I do not for a moment doubt that these are fates worse than death, and I am quite certain that nobody in this House or in another place would for one moment tolerate the conception of any such penalty as that.[24]

The facts are that even in Belgium, which has a harsher prison regime than any other European country, solitary confinement "has been gradually abandoned since 1920. . . . It must be emphatically stated that solitary confinement in Belgium . . . no longer exists."[25]

But even if the Lord Chancellor's information had been correct, and not outdated by twenty years, why on earth would England have to imitate just that one example? Lord Jowitt had thought of this objection, and had the following answer to it:

> Logically, one is perfectly entitled to say, "Look at what has happened in Belgium." One can say, "Well, you see, the abolition of the death-penalty had no ill-effects; there are no more murderers." On the other hand, if one says that, then, logically [sic], one must be prepared to say, "I will accept the Belgian remedy." Yet none of us would accept that. Therefore, I come to the conclusion that, logically, it is fallacious to rely on the experience of foreign countries, unless one is to accept the remedy which they propound.[26]

I have said before that the strongest case for the abolition of the death-penalty is to be found in the arguments of its upholders.

6. Pampering the Murderer

The majority in the House of Lords which in 1948 defeated abolition for a trial period was based on a holy alliance between those who proclaimed with the Lord Chancellor that a life sentence was a cruelty "worse than death," and those who thought with Lord Sandhurst that it was not cruel enough.

> Unless we look out (that noble Lord warned the House), prison will become a home from home, and the next thing will be that they will be giving the beggars weekend leave. . . . We have to remember that quite a large proportion of the criminal population come from, and are the result of, bad housing and bad homes. The

effect would be to make prison more comfortable than home, and even now such people know that when they go to prison—and the magistrates' courts produce evidence of this—at least they will be warm throughout the winter. . . . The general view of the police is dead against this suggestion [suspension of the death-penalty]. I think it was well summed up by the Commissioner when he said that it is safer to commit murder than to cross the road. At the present moment, that is perfectly true. If you commit murder, you know that you will be out of danger of everything except of a natural death for the next ten or fifteen years. Not one of us in this House can say that. So long as we are free to roam about the streets freely, as some people do, we are liable to come to a sudden and abrupt end at any moment.[27]

Which proves that Hansard can be funnier than P. G. Wodehouse. For if there are people in this nation living under such wretched conditions that even prison is preferable to them, then decency demands that housing conditions should be improved and not that prison conditions should be made more wretched. Fortunately, people attracted to prison on these grounds exist mainly in the noble Lord's imagination, and among picturesque characters in Dickens's and Joyce Cary's novels.

But this kind of nonsense apart, it may still be thought that the swimming pool and dramatic society of Leyhill mean going too far towards coddling the criminal. The answer is that conditions even in the most modern prison seem more idyllic when one reads about them than if one has to live in them. A quarter-century ago, before the great prison reform got under way, Sir Alexander Patterson told the Select Committee:

> Whatever means of education, stimulation and recreation may be employed, however you may seek to ring the changes on handicrafts and literature, skittles or chess or ping-pong, despite the invaluable labours of most devoted voluntary workers, it requires a superman to survive 20 years of imprisonment with character and soul intact.[28]

Since this was said, prison conditions have been radically changed, and terms of detention shortened. Yet even so, detention for six, eight or ten years is a very dreadful thing. It is a modern purgatory with welfare services, skittles and ping-pong, yet a purgatory nevertheless which those who never lay in gaol cannot really visualize even if endowed with sympathy and imagination.[29] In its matter-of-fact language, the Royal Commission says that:

> The deterrent effect of imprisonment on the individual offender lies primarily in the shame of being sent to prison and the fact of being in prison, with all that that fact in itself implies—complete loss of personal liberty; separation from home, family and friends; subjection to disciplinary control and forced labour; and deprivation of most of the ordinary amenities and intercourse of everyday life. An offender is sent to prison *as* a punishment and not *for* punishment.[30]

However terrible the act that landed him in limbo was: the cracking of a human skull or the stopping of a human breath, the delinquent is chewing the cud of his deed and vomiting it out and swallowing it again at least once a day, multiplied by 365, multiplied by 5, 6, 7, 8, 9, 10, repeating to him or herself "if only at that moment I hadn't. . . ." Atonement consists in the knowledge, or the illusion, that one could have acted otherwise than one did; purgatory is the internal combustion of the missed chance. It is not a continuous process. It may stop after a while, or diminish and then start again in a furious crescendo: "if only . . . then I wouldn't be here." Until gradually, with ups and downs, periods of depression and periods of excitement, which are all in a day's, week's, year's work, gradually the past is burnt out and the future becomes real again; and the "I wouldn't be here" is replaced by "when I get out." At its worst, prison is limbo; at its best, it is a forced residence for adult, full-blooded and mostly temperamental people in a kind of boarding-school-cum-Y.M.C.A.-cum-Salvation-Army-doss-house, mitigated by lectures, skittles and games on Sunday.

The worst of it is not the absence of sex, or drink, or even of the family. The first two lose their sting after a while, and at times surprisingly quickly; and the intense friendships and tensions of a convict community substitute for the third. The worst is the loss of one's adult manhood or womanhood—in the non-sexual, purely human sense. A prisoner feels as if he were castrated—not because he can't sleep with women, but because he has been deprived of the dignity of his manhood and reduced to a schoolboy or ward, to an infantile and helpless state, no longer the master of his destiny but its victim, deprived of responsibility, under constant observation: a marionette in a fair and enlightened puppet-player's hands, yet still a marionette. Even when working without supervision or playing soccer, convict team against village team, he feels that he is not quite human—a man not exactly despised, yet not exactly trusted, crippled in his rights, diminished in his self-esteem—a star prisoner, treated with benevolence, in a word a creature *almost* human.

Whatever reforms are introduced, even if the bars vanish and the prison is an open one, this basic defect cannot be remedied because it is the essence of the prisoner's condition, the irreducible core of his punishment. That is why that very wise White Paper says: "An offender is sent to prison *as* a punishment and not *for* punishment."

That is also the reason why "lifers" are so reasonable and well behaved, and give less trouble than the small fry. The primary motive is not the hope for privileges and remissions—though, of course, the earning of privilege and remission is for the prisoner the equivalent of the freeman's pursuit of career and material gains. The true reason is that the only way open to the prisoner to save the remainder of his human dignity, and to avoid further humiliation, is to be a model prisoner. That means not only outwardly obeying the rules, but inwardly accepting them as a condition of existence; or, which amounts to the same thing, to treat the rules as if they were non-existent by conforming to them, thus avoiding that they be enforced. Moreover, well-behavedness among long-termers is not regarded as "sissy," nor is unruliness and showing off regarded with approval, for it makes life more difficult for everybody, and because every disciplinary action makes a prison more grim and prison-like. On the other hand, correct and disciplined behavior will, apart from its practical benefits, gradually earn the prisoner the respect of the warders. This, in turn, will raise his self-respect and diminish the span between the almost-human and the human condition—which he will only re-attain when he is set free.

To quote the saying about the repentant sinner who causes more rejoicing, and so forth, would be sentimental and out of place. But it is no exaggeration to say of a man who has been condemned to die and has worked himself through purgatory and finally regained his freedom, that he has earned every moment of it at a much higher price than ordinary mortals, born under kinder stars.

Notes

1. Quoted by Calvert, op. cit., p. 32.
2. R.C.R., Appendix 6, p. 4.
3. S.C.R., 237–40.
4. R.C.R., 617.
5. R.C.R., 627. The text says that there were 79 prisoners of the Star Class, but the subsequent figures in the same paragraph seem to indicate that the Commissioners made a mistake in adding up.
6. R.C.R., 650.
7. Straffen was not released; he escaped from Broadmoor.
8. R.C.R., 650. R.C.R., Appendix 15, pp. 486–7.
9. R.C.R., Appendix 15, 487–8.
10. Two in Belgium and four in Denmark.
11. R.C.R., 651.
12. R.C.R., 652.
13. S.C.R., 246.
14. R.C.R., 658.
15. S.C.R., 244.
16. S.C.M., 844.
17. While awaiting trial, many prisoners are indifferent to their fate. But after sentence of death has been passed on them, the instinct of survival seems to reassert itself with a vengeance.
18. Calvert, op. cit., p. 194.
19. R.C.R., Appendix III, table XII.
20. R.C.R., 646.
21. R.C.R., 627.
22. R.C.R., 626.
23. R.C.R., 624.
24. Hansard, April 27th, 1948, column 397.
25. R.C.R., Appendix XIV, p. 4.
26. Hansard, April 27th, 1948, columns 397–8.
27. Hansard, April 27th, 1948, columns 454–5.
28. R.C.R., 653.
29. This writer has only spent a little more than a year in prisons in various countries (as described elsewhere), yet this short taste of limbo was sufficient to alter his whole outlook on life.
30. R.C.R., 622.

Questions for Analysis

1. According to Koestler, what is the public's idea of the murderer modeled on? What does Koestler provide that disputes the popular concept of the murderer?

2. What appears to be the consensus view about the behavior of murderers in prison? What is the significance of this view for Koestler's argument against those who reject life imprisonment as an alternative to capital punishment?

3. One of the common arguments against life imprisonment as an alternative to death is that a murderer may be released, whereupon the person may kill again. Do the statistics bear out this social threat scenario?

4. What evidence does Koestler offer to refute the claim that life imprisonment is excessively cruel? Suppose that in some cases it really is: Would this fact be germane to the issue of abolition?

5. Why does Koestler say that "the strongest case for the abolition of the death penalty is to be found in the arguments of its upholders"?

6. Explain what Koestler means when he says: "Atonement consists in the knowledge, or the illusion, that one could have acted otherwise than one did; purgation is the internal combustion of the missed chance." How does this observation apply to the charge that life imprisonment is "too good" for the murderer? Do you agree with Koestler's characterization of atonement?

CASE PRESENTATION
A Death Wish

The judge had received all sorts of letters from prisoners and their attorneys, but none to compare with this. Never before had she received a letter from a convicted murderer requesting that he be put to death.

The judge recalled the case of Robert Weatherman vividly. It had involved thirteen gruesome murders that Weatherman openly admitted to having committed "for the thrill of it." So, there was never any question of Weatherman's guilt. The only issue the court had to assure itself of was Weatherman's sanity when he committed the murders. When that was determined, the jury deliberated only long enough to poll its members. Weatherman was found guilty and sentenced to life in prison with no chance of parole. Still ringing in her ears was the cry that had erupted somewhere in the gallery when sentence was passed: "Good! Death is too good for him!"

That had been three years ago. Now Weatherman was asking for the death penalty.

While his letter was impassioned, it nonetheless presented a well-reasoned argument for death. Weatherman mentioned the "unfair financial burden" that his imprisonment was placing on the taxpayers. "Why," he asked, "ought the taxpayers be made to support someone who has wantonly violated society's standards of behavior and human decency?" Why, indeed, the judge thought. Then there was a veiled threat, a fear really, that desperate as he was, Weatherman might kill again—and he didn't want to do that.

But mostly the letter was an appeal to what Weatherman termed "Your Honor's humaneness." "I implore you, Your Honor," Weatherman wrote at one point, "to put me out of my misery, to end the sleepless nights that are haunted by the fearful faces and the tortured screams of those I brutalized." Elsewhere Weatherman wrote: "Allow me to atone for the lives I've taken by giving up my own." And the convicted murderer even suggested that in keeping him alive— "to wallow in his own misery and self-accusation, in the knowledge that I will never again have the dignity of a free, untroubled man"—the state was making him suffer in ways that it could never have anticipated, and could never understand. "Death is not the ultimate punishment," Weatherman closed his letter. "Living as I am is."

The judge folded the letter and returned it to its envelope. Already her head was swimming with the many conflicting obligations that she knew she must consider.

Questions for Analysis

1. *If you were the judge, what would you do? Why?*
2. *What arguments can you think of for refusing a "lifer's" request to die?*

3.   *Apply the divine command theory to the dilemma facing the judge.*

4.   *Apply Kant's ethical theory to the dilemma facing the judge.*

5.   *Do you think the claim that "death is too good" for an offender is nothing more than an expression of vindictiveness?*

CASE PRESENTATION
Death of a Foreman

"Well, you're what they call an *anomaly*, Jake," the waiter told the grizzled old man trying to blow the heat from his navy-bean soup.

That's all Jake ever ordered—soup. Judging from his tattered clothes, the waiter figured soup was all the old-timer could afford. So, once in a while, because he felt sorry for the old man, he gave him some extra crackers, which the old man would stuff into the pockets of his oversized overcoat—to eat later, the waiter guessed.

"What's that?" the old man asked. He'd been called lots of things before, but never an "anomaly."

"You know," the waiter said, "the exception to the rule."

"What rule?"

The waiter replied without hesitation: "The rule that says an old sod like you ought to want all the protection he can get—especially in a neighborhood like this."

The old man understood. "I see," he said, and cursed his soup because it was still too hot. "You figure that makes me nuts, huh? For saying I think the death penalty stinks?"

Old people are funny, the waiter thought. You have to be careful what you say to them; they always take things the wrong way. "I didn't mean it that way, Jake."

"Forget it, forget it," the old man told him. Then he tapped his fingers on the counter, impatient for his soup to cool. "Let me tell you something. You ever hear of the Griffin Delivery Truck case?" The waiter hadn't, so Jake explained.

The case involved a man named Griffin who went to the electric chair for a crime he didn't commit. His case was tried back in 1934. Eight undisputed eyewitnesses had identified the defendant, Emmett Griffin, a delivery-truck driver, as the man who had murdered an employee of a local movie house. The case was "open-and-shut." Griffin was convicted and executed within the year.

Some months after Griffin's execution, a man named Watham, eaten with guilt, came forward and admitted to the murder. Further investigation proved beyond any reasonable doubt that Watham was, in fact, the murderer.

"Ah!" the waiter said, with a contemptuous wave of a towel. "There must have been more to it than that."

"Believe me," said the old man, "there wasn't."

The waiter wasn't convinced. "How can you be so sure?"

The old man poured a little ice water into his soup before saying, "I was the foreman on that jury."

When the old man finished his soup, he stuffed some extra crackers into his pockets and disappeared into the night.

"Imagine that!" the waiter said the next morning, as he read of the murder of an unidentified old man in an alley not far from the cafe. "Imagine that!" He wondered if the police had found crackers in the victim's pockets, and what the old man would have said now about the death penalty.

Questions for Analysis

1. *There is always the possibility that an innocent person will be put to death. How strong do you think this abolitionist argument is?*

2. *How do retentionists respond to this argument of the miscarriage of capital punishment?*

3. *How might proponents of retribution justify capital punishment for the old man's murderer?*

4. *Do you think that the state has any duty of reparation arising out of a miscarriage of the death penalty? If it does, what would the reparation be?*

Selections for Further Reading

Bedau, Hugo. *The Death Penalty in America.* Rev. Ed. Garden City, N.Y.: Doubleday, 1965.

Black, Charles L., Jr. *Capital Punishment: The Inevitability of Caprice and Mistake.* New York: W. W. Norton, 1974.

Camus, Albert. *Reflections on the Guillotine: An Essay on Capital Punishment.* Richard Howard, Trans. Michigan City, Ind.: Fridtjof-Karla Press, 1959.

Gowers, Sir Ernest. *A Life for a Life.* London: Chatto and Windus, 1956.

Hale, Leslie. *Hanged in Error.* Baltimore: Penguin, 1961.

Joyce, J. A. *Capital Punishment: A World View.* New York: Thomas Nelson & Sons, 1961.

Koestler, Arthur. *Reflections on Hanging.* New York: Macmillan, 1957.

Koestler, Arthur, and C. H. Ralph. *Hanged by the Neck.* Baltimore: Penguin, 1961.

McCafferty, James A., Ed. *Capital Punishment.* New York: Lieber-Atherton, 1972.

8
REVERSE DISCRIMINATION

In recent years laws have been passed and programs formulated to ensure fair and equal treatment of all persons in employment practices. Nevertheless, unequal practices still exist. To help remedy these, the federal government in the early 1970s instituted an affirmative action program.

Before affirmative action, many institutions already followed nondiscriminatory as well as merit-hiring employment practices to equalize employment opportunities. In proposing the affirmative action program, the government recognized the worth of such endeavors, but said that it did not think that they were enough. Affirmative action, therefore, refers to positive measures beyond neutral nondiscriminatory and merit-hiring employment practice. It is an aggressive program intended to identify and remedy discrimination practiced against many people who are qualified for jobs.

One of the most controversial aspects of affirmative action are its preferential and quota-hiring systems. *Preferential hiring* is an employment practice designed to give special consideration to persons from groups that traditionally have been victimized by racism, sexism, or other forms of discrimination. *Quota hiring* is the policy of hiring and employing people in direct proportion to their numbers in society or in the community. According to affirmative action guidelines, preferential and quota hiring go hand in glove; thus, for simplicity, we will refer to both by the phrase *quota hiring*. Courts are increasingly requiring companies and unions to provide apprentice and reapprentice training to hire, promote, and train minorities and women in specified numerical ratios, in specified job categories, until specified remedial goals are reached. But critics charge that at least in some instances, implementing affirmative action guidelines has led to *reverse discrimination—that is, the unfair treatment of a majority member (usually a white male)*.

To illustrate how a quota-hiring system might work, suppose that an equally qualified man and woman are applying for a single job. The employer, conscious of affirmative action guidelines, realizes that the company historically has discriminated against women. So, the employer plugs in a quota-hiring factor that clearly serves the female's interests. She gets the job. Problem: Is the employer's action moral? Has the male applicant been treated unfairly? Would it have been fairer had their names been thrown into a hat from which one was drawn? Obviously a quota-hiring system raises questions of social justice.

Undoubtedly some will wonder: Why not focus directly on the morality of sexism? By *sexism* we mean the unequal treatment of a person exclusively on the basis of sex. Perhaps we should focus on it, but consider that in all our discussions so far we have made reasonable cases for at least two sides of an issue. True, perhaps one side was more flawed than another, but in all cases reasonable people could disagree. But the fact is that no one seriously argues anymore that sexism, as defined, is moral. So, if we focused on sexism we would be inviting a most lopsided discussion. This would be unfortunate in the light of so many aspects of sexism that genuinely deserve moral debate. One of these aspects involves such proposed remedies as quota hiring.

Another reason for not considering sexism exclusively is that this chapter, as well as the next, naturally raises questions of social justice. Many discussions of social justice founder because they remain abstract, content to theorize while scrupulously avoiding practice. For example, it is easy and safe to argue that a government must remedy racial injustice. It is far more controversial to argue that a government must implement forced busing to do so. The same applies to sexism. Most would agree that the government has an obligation to correct the social injustice of sexism, but how?

It is one thing to recognize, deplore, and want to correct any injustice. It is entirely another thing to remedy the injustice fairly. Sadly, too many discussions of social justice ignore means entirely, often offering the defense that the means vary from situation to situation. Undoubtedly. But the debate that flies around so many social justice questions today concerns proposed means. We should learn to examine every situation's means and also the common but agonizing predicament of applauding the intention and even the probable consequences of an action, but deploring the action itself. For many people, quota hiring is just such a problem.

Justice

One undeniable fact about human beings is that we are social animals. We work with, depend on, and relate to each other for our survival and prosperity. The totality of the relationships among people is known as society. A specific society consists of a group of human beings broadly distinguished from other groups by similar interests, shared institutions, and a common culture. The relationships that exist between an individual and society are often ill-defined and fraught with moral conflict.

One element of this relationship is justice. Social and political philosophers since Plato have spoken of the need for a just society and have offered their concepts of it. Our political and social structures seek to attain justice through a contract between the individual and the state, by which is meant municipal, state, and federal governments in general. In evaluating a state we invariably wonder how fairly it treats its citizens. We probably think that the just state is the one that tries to treat its citizens fairly; the unjust one the one that does not. But what are justice and fair play?

This question plays a prominent role in women's fight for equality. Historically women have been one of the most oppressed and exploited social groups. This has been particularly true in the area of employment and in too many instances remains true. Too often, only because of their sex, women are denied jobs that they can easily perform. Even more often they receive lower pay than men who perform the same work. And when promotion time comes around, females are frequently passed over.

A quota-hiring system as previously defined is a direct effort to remedy this unequal treatment. But whether a government has the right to tell persons whom they must hire is a question that is hotly debated. Some say that the government has no right to invade what is clearly the realm of individual privacy. Others say that the government not only has the right but the obligation to redress blatant inequality when it directly violates the rights of its citizens, in this case women. What is at issue is the proper line of demarcation between individual and society; and this line, wherever it lies, involves the question of justice. It also directly affects our lives and personal morality.

Today some white males feel that affirmative action guidelines have the effect of treating them unjustly. When we speak of someone being treated unjustly, we usually mean that the person's rights are being violated. The meaning and nature of rights are difficult to establish precisely. For our purposes we will define *a right as an area of decision that other persons do or should respect and that the law does or should protect.*[1] Thus, the white male feels that he has the right to be considered for a job solely on the criteria that apply directly to it, what are commonly called job specifications. When his sex is not directly related to the performance of the job for which he is applying, he feels that he is being treated unfairly.

When we speak of the "just state," we usually mean the one that ensures a person's rights, whereas the unjust state violates them. Almost all would agree that the just state must ensure the individual's general rights, such as the freedom of expression rights, which include freedom of speech, religion, press, and assembly. Similarly, there is little dispute that the state must ensure certain human or natural rights, such as the right to life, as well as respect for and guarantee of the individual's right to be treated equally with other citizens, regardless of religion, race, and sex. But in order to ensure these individual rights, the state must have certain rights or powers of its own.

We tend to think that the state derives these rights as a kind of regulatory agency, with which individuals have entered into a contract whereby they foresake certain individual freedoms in return for the protection of certain rights. The theory behind this contractual relationship is complex, but it is necessary to understand it in order to perceive the dimensions of social justice, which is at the root of the reverse discrimination issue.

1.   *Carl Wellman,* Morals & Ethics *(Glenview, Ill.: Scott, Foresman, 1975), p. 252.*

Contract Theory

The so-called contract theory does not refer to a Mafia-sponsored method of erasing certain social problems. Rather, contract theory is an explanation of the origin of the state and a defense of its authority. We see evidence of this contract theory as far back as Plato, but its most noteworthy proponents were Thomas Hobbes (1588–1679) and John Locke (1632–1704). Jean Jacques Rousseau (1712–1778) further advanced the theory.

Hobbes based his political philosophy on the principles of the scientific materialism of the seventeenth century. According to scientific materialism, the world is a mechanical system that can be explained by laws of motion. Even the behavior of humans or complex societies, it was argued, were subject to geometric and physical explanations. Hobbes accepted this view of reality and from it deduced how things must necessarily occur.

In his most famous work, *Leviathan*, Hobbes portrays humans as selfish, unsocial creatures driven by two needs, survival and personal pleasure—a view undoubtedly shared today by the advertising moguls of Madison Avenue. This state is characterized by constant struggle, strife, and war, in which individual is pitted against individual in a battle of self-preservation and gain. As Hobbes writes in *Leviathan*:

> To this, war of every man against every man, this also is consequent: that
> nothing can be unjust. . . . It is consequent also to the same conditions,
> that there be no propriety, no dominion, no mine and thine distinct; but
> only that to be every man's, that he can get; and for so long, as he can keep it.

Granting that the instinct for self-preservation was the basic drive behind human behavior, Hobbes also believed that humans had the capacity to reason.

Although Hobbes never viewed reason to be as energizing a force as self-preservation, he believed that reason could regulate human actions and anticipate their results. So, Hobbes pictures humans as self-centered but rational. This rationality enables them to evaluate the long-term results of behavior originally motivated by self-interest.

Rational concern for their own survival and best long-term interests impel humans to enter into a contract with each other that creates society. Because they recognize that they are destined to be "solitary, poor, nasty, brutish," humans agree to accept an authority outside themselves that has the power to force all to act in the best interests of the majority. For Hobbes this authority is irrevocable. Once set up, the political body with this power exercises complete authority over its subjects and remains in power as long as it is able to compel them to do what they otherwise would not.

So, although individuals contract for society, the society is superior to the individuals, who owe complete allegiance to it. For Hobbes, the state cannot bear any resistance to its rule; however, if such resistance becomes effective, then the state proves itself unable to govern, in which case the established officials no longer rule and the people are no longer subjects. At that point the people revert to their natural state of self-preservation and gain, where they remain until they form another contract.

In contrast with Hobbes's rather pessimistic view of humans, John Locke viewed them as essentially moral beings who ought to obey natural moral rules. Where Hobbes saw the human's natural state characterized by warfare, Locke saw it characterized, at least partially, by a system of natural moral laws. As a result, Locke viewed humans as inherently free and equal, regardless of the existence of any government. It is not, he argued, a government that decrees mutual respect for the freedom and liberties of all, but nature itself.

Nevertheless, like Hobbes, Locke saw a need for a contract. Although he maintained that humans are by nature free, rational, and social creatures, he said that they establish governments because three things are missing in the state of nature: (1) a firm, clearly understood interpretation of natural law, (2) unbiased judges to resolve disputes, and (3) personal recourse in the face of injustices. So, to maintain their *natural rights*, individuals enter into a social contract, whereby they create a political entity capable of preserving the inherent rights of "life, liberty and estate." This contract is based on the consent of the majority, and all willingly agree to obey the decisions of the majority. The state's authority, according to Locke, is limited by the terms of the contract, which is continuously reviewed by the citizenry. So, unlike Hobbes's authoritarian state, Locke's is specific and limited. Most important, one of the fundamental moral rights that humans retain in the political state is the right to resist and to challenge authority. While Hobbes believed that resistance to authority was never justified except for self-preservation, Locke regarded rebellion as an inherent human right.

Although the contrast between Hobbes and Locke is sharp, they do agree that humans are rational and that this rationality enables them to perceive the necessity of forming a social contract. This contract theory, especially as enunciated by Locke, has heavily influenced our own concept of government, as these lines from the Declaration of Independence suggest:

> To secure these rights (life, liberty and the pursuit of happiness),
> governments are instituted among Men, deriving their just powers from the
> consent of the governed. That whenever any Form of Government becomes
> destructive of these ends, it is the Right of the People to alter or to abolish it,
> and to institute a new Government, laying its foundation on such principles
> and organizing its powers in such form, as to them shall seem most likely to
> effect their safety and Happiness.

The Declaration and the contract theory agree that when a government "becomes destructive of" the individual rights of life, liberty, and the pursuit of happiness ("estate" for Locke), the people have the right to dismiss it. Problems of social justice arise, however, in interpreting and applying the contract.

Interpreting the Contract

Precisely when is a government destroying individual rights? Perhaps it would not be hard to define when it is depriving us of our lives, but what about liberty and the pursuit of happiness? It could be argued that the liberties referred to are political and civil in nature and thus can be spelled out constitutionally. Still, it is one thing for a constitution to guarantee the right of assembly, it is quite another for the mayor of a city to interpret an assembly as a mob, and for a court to uphold the forceful action the mayor took to disperse that mob. In other words, the U.S. Constitution, like the contract theory on which it is based, provides a general framework to ensure liberties but rightly leaves great latitude for the interpretation and possible restriction of those liberties.

However, it is difficult to determine when a government has become destructive of the pursuit of happiness. For example, some might argue that a graduated income tax destroys the pursuit of happiness. When affluent persons' earnings and holdings are taxed considerably more than lower-income earning persons, some contend that the government is violating the wealthy's pursuit of happiness. A white male might argue that his pursuit of happiness has been lessened by the affirmative action program. His job possibilities are diminished, and worse, his pride, sense of self-worth, and concept of fair play have been damaged. In contrast, a female or minority member might defend not only the right of the government to intervene, but its duty as well.

Under the social contract, then, we give up certain rights to get others. Specifically, under our political system we are guaranteed the rights of life, liberty, and the pursuit of happiness. The problem with remedies for inequality such as quota hiring is whether the government is actually securing these rights. Put another way: Is the government acting in such a way that it is actually depriving us of these rights?

There is no simple answer to this question. Obviously, what makes it especially nettlesome is that the issue involves a conflict of rights. On the one hand, there is the right of all job applicants to be treated equally insofar as they will be evaluated only on criteria directly related to their ability to perform the job. On the other hand, it seems that the only way to ensure that persons are not discriminated against on sexual or racial grounds and to remedy this existent problem as quickly as possible is to compel employers to hire a certain number of females and minority members. Indeed, this has been the thrust of affirmative action. The issue here is when, if at all, a government may violate individual rights in order to redress a social problem that involves inequity. Thus, affirmative action, which we will now consider, raises problems of liability, equality, and justice—all subjects that social philosophers traditionally have debated.

Affirmative Action: Preferential Treatment

As amended by the Equal Employment Opportunity Act of 1972, the Civil Rights Act of 1964 requires that businesses that have substantial dealings with the federal government undertake affirmative action programs. *Affirmative action programs are plans designed to correct imbalances in employment that exist directly as a result of past discrimination against women and minority groups.* Even though these acts do not technically require companies to undertake affirmative action programs, in recent years courts have responded to acts of discrimination in the work place by ordering the offending firms to undertake affirmative action programs to combat the effects of past discrimination. In effect, then, all business institutions must adopt affirmative action programs either in theory or in fact. They must be able to prove that they have not been practicing institutional sexism or racism, and if they cannot prove this, they must undertake programs to ensure against racism or sexism.

What do affirmative action programs involve? The U.S. Equal Employment Opportunity Commission lists general guidelines as steps to affirmative action. Under these steps, firms must issue a written equal employment policy and an affirmative action commitment. They must appoint a top official with responsibility and authority to direct and implement their program and to publicize their policy and affirmative action commitment. In addition, firms must survey current female and minority employment by department and job classification. Where underrepresentation of these groups is evident, firms must develop goals and timetables to improve utilization of women and minorities in each area of underrepresentation. They then must develop specific programs to achieve these goals, establish an internal audit system to monitor them, and evaluate progress in each aspect of the program. Finally, companies must develop supportive in-house and community programs to combat sexual and racial discrimination.

In implementing such programs, some companies have adopted a policy of preferential treatment for women and minorities. *Preferential treatment refers to the practice of giving individuals favored consideration in hiring or promotions for other than job-related reasons* (such as the person is female or black). Those espousing preferential treatment argue that such a policy is the only way to remedy traditional sexism and racism, or at least that it is the most expeditious and fairest way to do it. In some instances preferential treatment for women and minorities takes the form of a *quota system, that is, an employment policy of representing women and minorities in the firm in direct proportion to their numbers in society or in the community at large.* Thus a firm operating in a community which has a 20 percent black population might try to ensure that 20 percent of its work force be black.[2]

To unravel some of the complex moral issues that affirmative action programs can raise, let us look at a specific instance of quota hiring. Suppose that an equally qualified man and woman are applying for a job. The employer, conscious of affirmative action guidelines and realizing that the company has historically discriminated against women in its employment policies, adopts a quota-hiring system. Since males are already disproportionately well-represented and females underrepresented, the quota system functions to give the female applicant a decided advantage over the male simply because she is a woman. As a result the employer hires the female. Is this action moral? Are affirmative action programs that operate in the preferential way moral?

Many persons argue that affirmative action programs are inherently discriminatory and therefore unjust. In this context, *discriminatory* should be understood to refer to policies that favor individuals on non-job-related grounds (for example, on the basis of sex, color, or ethnic heritage). It has been argued that

2.   *Some institutions simply reserve a number of places for women and minority members. The University of California at Davis, for example, had such a policy in its medical school when it denied Alan Bakke admission. Bakke appealed to the Supreme Court, which—in a five-to-four decision—found in his favor. He was presumably more qualified than some "minority" students who had been admitted.*

quota hiring is unjust because it involves giving preferential treatment to women and minorities over equally qualified white males, a practice that is clearly discriminatory, albeit reverse discrimination.

Those in favor of affirmative action, however, generally attempt to rebut this objection by appealing to principles of *compensatory justice. In other words, since women and minorities clearly continue to be victimized directly and indirectly by traditional discrimination in the work place, they are entitled to some compensation.* This is the basis for preferential treatment. The soundness of this contention seems to rely on at least two factors: (1) that affirmative action programs involving preferential treatment will in fact provide adequate compensation; (2) that they will provide compensation more fairly than any other alternative.[3] Since the justice and the morality of affirmative action programs depend to a large degree on these assumptions, we should examine them.

The question that comes to mind in regard to the first assumption is: adequate compensation for whom? The answer seems obvious: for women and minorities. But does this answer mean *individual* women and minority-group members, or women and minorities taken *collectively?* University of Tampa Professor Herman J. Saatkamp, Jr., has demonstrated that this question, far from being merely a technical one, bears directly on the morality of affirmative action programs and how they are implemented.[4]

Saatkamp points out that the question of the conflict between individual and collective merit is one that typifies the debate between government agencies and business over employment policies. On the one hand, business is ordinarily concerned with the individual merit and deserts of its employees. On the other hand, government agencies primarily focus on the relative status of groups within the population at large. To put the conflict in perspective, employment policies based solely on individual merit would try to ensure that only those individuals who could prove they deserved compensation would benefit and only those proved to be the source of discrimination would suffer. Of course, such a focus places an almost unbearable burden on the resources of an individual to provide sufficient, precise data to document employment discrimination, which is commonly acknowledged to exist at times in subtle forms at imperceptible organizational levels. Indeed, social policies recognize this difficulty by focusing on discrimination on an aggregate level. Individuals, then, need not prove that they themselves were discriminated against, only that they are members of groups that have traditionally suffered because of discrimination.

Taking the collective approach to remedying work-place discrimination is not without its own disadvantages.

1. Policies based on collective merit tend to pit one social group against another. Thus white males face off against all nonwhite males; women find themselves jockeying with other disadvantaged groups for priority employment status; even black females can end up contesting with white

---

3. *Albert W. Flores, "Reverse Discrimination: Towards a Just Society,"* Business & Professional Ethics, *a quarterly newsletter/report (Troy N.Y.: Center for the Study of the Human Dimensions of Science & Technology, Rensselaer Polytechnic Institute, Jan. 1978), p. 4.*

4. *Flores, "Reverse Discrimination: Towards a Just Society," pp. 5–6.*

Hispanic males for preferred treatment. This factionalizing aspect of policies based on collective merit can prove detrimental to society.

2. Policies based on collective merit victimize some individuals. The individual white male who loses out on a job because of preferential treatment given a woman or minority is penalized.

3. In many cases the women and minority members selected under preferential treatment are, in fact, less deserving of compensation than those women and minorities who are not selected. In short, those most in need may not benefit at all.

4. Some members of nonfavored groups may be just as deserving or more deserving of compensation than some women or members of minority groups. Many white males, for example, are more seriously limited in seeking employment than some women and minority-group members are.

5. From the viewpoint of business investment, policies based on collective merit can be prohibitively expensive. In order to enforce such programs, businesses must hire people to collect data, process forms, deal with government agencies, and handle legal procedures. From business's viewpoint this additional time, energy, and expense could have been channeled into more commercially productive directions.

In sum, those who argue that affirmative action programs will provide adequate compensation for the victims of discrimination must grapple with the problems of determining the focus of the compensation: on the individual or on the group. While both focuses have merit, neither is without disadvantages. Furthermore, it seems that neither approach can be implemented without first resolving a complex chain of moral concerns.

But even if we assume that affirmative action programs will provide adequate compensation, it is still difficult to demonstrate the validity of the second assumption of those who endorse affirmative action by appealing to principles of compensatory justice: that such programs will provide compensation more fairly than any other alternative. By nature affirmative action programs provide compensation at the expense of the white males' right to fair and equal employment treatment. In other words, affirmative action programs in the form of preferential treatment or quota systems undermine the fundamental principle of just employment practice that a person should be hired or promoted only on job-related grounds. Apparently, then, it presents an awesome undertaking to defend the proposition that affirmative action will provide compensation more fairly than any other alternative when such a proposition makes a non-job-related factor (membership in a group) a relevant employment criterion.

Although it would appear that reverse discrimination may not be justified on grounds of compensation, we should not conclude that it cannot be justified. In fact, some persons contend that a more careful examination of the principles of justice suggests an alternative defense. As we have mentioned, those who argue against affirmative action programs do so because such programs allegedly involve unequal treatment and are therefore unjust. The clear assumption here is that whatever involves unequal treatment is in and of itself unjust. But, as Professor Albert W. Flores points out, while justice would demand that equals receive equal treatment, it is likewise true that unequals should receive treatment appropriate to their differences. Hence, he concludes that "unfair or differential treatment may be required by the principles of justice."[5] In other words, unequal treatment is unfair in the absence of any characteristic difference between applicants which, from the viewpoint of justice, would constitute relevant differences. Following this line of reasoning, we must wonder whether being a female or a minority member would constitute a "relevant difference" that would justify unequal treatment.

To illustrate, let us ask how one could justify giving preferential consideration to a female job applicant over an equally qualified white male. Flores contends that while sex may be irrelevant to the job, it may be a relevant consideration as to who should be selected. In effect, he distinguishes between criteria relevant to a job and those relevant to candidate selection. He clearly bases this distinction on a concept of business's social responsibilities. As has been amply demonstrated elsewhere, business does not exist in a commercial vacuum. It is part of a social system and, as such, has obligations that relate to the welfare and integrity of society at large. Thus Flores argues that when a firm must decide between two equally qualified applicants, say a white male and a female, it is altogether justified in introducing as a selection criterion some concept of social justice, which in this case takes cognizance of a fair distribution of society's resources and scarcities among competing groups. From the viewpoint of justice, business may be correct in hiring the qualified female or minority member. Notice, however, that this contention is based primarily not on principles of compensatory justice but on a careful examination of the nature of justice.

The moral issues that affirmative action programs raise with respect to justice are profound and complex. In this brief overview, we have been able to raise only a few, but these demonstrate that the morality of preferential treatment through affirmative action cuts to our basic assumptions about the nature of human beings and the principles of justice. Any moral resolution to the problem of reverse discrimination in the work place will not only betray these assumptions but must justify them.

Arguments Against Reverse Discrimination

1. *Reverse discrimination is unequal treatment.*

POINT: "By definition reverse discrimination means that one sex or race will receive preferential treatment over the other solely for biological reasons. This is inherently unfair because it means unequal treatment. Equality can exist only where all individuals are treated the same, where they are rewarded or punished to the same degree for the same behavior, regardless of their sex or race. But reverse discrimination precludes this. That's why it's wrong."

5.   Flores, *"Reverse Discrimination: Towards a Just Society," p. 4.*

COUNTERPOINT: "If your argument was directed at sexism and racism, I'd totally agree with you. Both practices are morally repugnant. But reverse discrimination is different in purpose. First, unlike sexism or racism, reverse discrimination is designed to provide equal opportunity for all, not to ensure unequal opportunity. Second, reverse discrimination is a case not so much of preferring people because of sex or race, but of trying to compensate certain classes of people for the wrongs they've suffered."

2.   *Reverse discrimination injures white males.*

POINT: "Surely two of the basic aspects of one's self-concept are the sexual and the racial. In individuals who have what psychologists call a "healthy self-concept," you will inevitably find a healthy sense of sexual and racial self-identity. Conversely, where self-image is damaged, you will likely find serious identity problems. When people have poor self-concepts, they experience anxiety and frustration and cannot attain happiness; indeed, they can hardly pursue happiness. By making individuals feel inferior, inadequate, or incomplete because of their sex or race, we do them incalculable harm by violating their right to a positive self-image. This, I think, is one of the most potent arguments against sexism and racism. But it also applies to reverse discrimination. After all, doesn't the white male have a right to a positive self-image, which reverse discrimination can only undermine?"

COUNTERPOINT: "Why do you focus exclusively on the white male? Considered from the viewpoint of women and minorities, reverse discrimination could have a quite positive effect on self-image. It could help restore to those people the dignity and sense of self-worth that years of sexism and racism have sullied. I doubt very seriously that the occasional white male who may lose an opportunity because of reverse discrimination will be irreparably damaged. After all he is a member of a class that for centuries has held a preferred position in this society and, consequently, he has considerable resources to draw on when 'wronged.' "

3.   *Reverse discrimination wastes the best human resources.*

POINT: "A most insidious part of reverse discrimination is that it wastes human resources. Just think of all the qualified individuals who will not be admitted to medical, dental, or law schools; or given entry into other areas where our nation and the world could use all the human power they can muster. In business, the picture is even bleaker. Under pressure to satisfy governmental standards, employers sometimes must overlook the one best qualified for a job—who just happens to be a white male. This is fair to neither the employer, the white male, nor society generally."

COUNTERPOINT: "There is no necessary connection between reverse discrimination and the waste of human resources. If anything, reverse discrimination, by increasing the selection pool, should maximize our chances of securing the most competent people in all human endeavors. I don't doubt that there have been abuses in the administration of affirmative action programs. But I think it's important to distinguish between the unqualified and the minimally qualified. I agree that nothing would justify employing an unqualified person, no matter the sex or color. But if a person is minimally qualified to do a job, then I don't see any reason that other factors can't be introduced. Indeed, they already are: institutions often consider regional 'qualifications'; businesses and schools have been known to consider 'who you know.' The point is that in the scramble for opportunities, the spoils don't always go to the person who on paper is 'best qualified.' So, why not introduce sex and race as two considerations among many in evaluating a candidate?"

Arguments for Reverse Discrimination

1. *Compensatory justice demands reverse discrimination.*

POINT: "Nobody denies that as groups women and minorities traditionally have been discriminated against, often viciously. As individuals and as a nation, we can't ignore the sins of our fathers and mothers. In fact, we have an obligation to do something to help repair the wrongs of the past. Giving women and minorities preferential treatment in things like employment is one sound way to do this."

COUNTERPOINT: "If the living were made to pay for the sins of the dead, we'd be spending all our time making restitution. What's more, we wouldn't even be compensating those who rightly deserved it. So, to the people who say, "You must pay for the past," I say, "Why?" I didn't do the wrong; why should I be held accountable for it? And why should I be held accountable to someone who wasn't even the party wronged? What you're proposing will result in the ludicrous situation of an innocent individual being made to compensate a party who wasn't even wronged!"

2. *Reverse discrimination defuses the bomb of social unrest.*

POINT: "Conditions in our society today are volatile. Blacks are pitched against whites, females against males. At the root of class tensions is the fact that women and minorities don't share in the economic bounty of this land to the same degree as white males. Furthermore, women and minorities perceive white males and the establishment they man—no pun intended—as bent on preserving the white male's preferred social and economic position. Whether or not this perception is accurate is irrelevant. One thing's for sure: Women and minorities do, in fact, see it that way. Moreover, the economic gap between white males and others is widening, which can only deepen this perception and increase the chances of serious social unrest, even class warfare. The way to defuse this social bomb is through reverse discrimination. At least in that way, the white male establishment will have gone on record as recognizing and being sympathetic to the plight of the disenfranchised. Also, of course, by introducing women and minorities into the economic mainstream, reverse discrimination will thereby give them a vested interest in the system. This, in turn, will have the effect of getting women and minorities to work constructively within the system and not destructively outside it."

COUNTERPOINT: "I'm not sure I accept the ominous picture you draw of the relations between the sexes and races, but I'll concede it. Still, I doubt that reverse discrimination is going to bring us all together. Indeed, have you contemplated the impact that reverse discrimination will have on white males who perceive it as reverse sexism and racism? Already several white males have gone to court claiming 'Foul!' And more probably will. How can this be good for society? How can it draw us closer together? If anything I think it's forcing people to take sides. And no wonder—can any program that attempts to fight injustice with injustice possibly succeed?"

3.   *Reverse discrimination is the only way to eradicate sexism and racism."*

POINT: "If there were any other way to root out sexism and racism in our society, I'd favor it over reverse discrimination. But there isn't. While neither sexism nor racism may be as flagrant as it used to be, each is still of virulent proportions in our society. In fact, some would say they are more pernicious today because they're more subtle. Sure, I'd like to count on the good graces of the white male power elite to rid us of these inequities. But there's nothing to suggest that the white male will, in fact, do that. Quite the opposite. Until the passage of various civil rights acts and the equal employment opportunity act, very little had been done. The lesson of history is clear: Until people are forced to change, they won't; until people are forced to play fair, they will not relinquish their preferred positions."

COUNTERPOINT: "It's funny you mention the civil rights acts and the equal employment opportunity act. Out of these grew the Equal Employment Opportunity Commission (EEOC) and affirmative action programs, which I believe represent a viable alternative to reverse discrimination. The fact is that already numerous cases of sexism and racism have been argued successfully before the EEOC. Already millions of dollars have been awarded in reparations. All of which leads me to believe that reverse discrimination isn't the way to eradicate sexism and racism. Strict, vigorous, uncompromising enforcement of the law is. If change isn't happening fast enough for some people, then the problem lies with how we're implementing the law, and we should do something about that."

Ethical Theories

One can approach the issue of the morality of reverse discrimination by first asking if sexism or racism is ever morally justifiable. By *sexism* we mean the deliberate discrimination of one person against another solely on the basis of sex; by *racism* we mean the deliberate discrimination of one person against another solely on the basis of race. Whether or not sexism and racism are ever morally justifiable seems an important question, for if not, then programs that give one sex or race preferential job or educational consideration over the others (reverse discrimination) would appear to be unjustifiable.

Egoism

In theory egoism could defend sexist or racist practices on the basis of best long-term self-interests. However, the same consideration might lead to a condemnation of a specific act of sexism or racism. In general, though, given the current social and legal climate, egoists might condemn the practices since an individual stands to lose so much in approving of and practicing sexism and racism.

As for preferential hiring programs, egoists could not approve or disapprove of them without introducing the interests of the particular agent in question. But who would this be? From the viewpoint of a woman or a black, quota systems might be justified egoistically. From the viewpoint of the white male, they might not. Of course, it is true that the kind of society they live in will affect the happiness of egoists, and thus egoists could consistently introduce social considerations. But in the last analysis, egoism seems to lack the theoretical means to provide some principles of social justice. In fact, it is in areas of social justice that egoism appears most inadequate to provide moral direction.

Act Utilitarianism

Like egoism, act utilitarianism would not take an unqualified position on sexism and racism. If a sexist or racist practice was calculated to produce more social good than any other alternative, then it would be good and right. If not, then it would be bad and wrong. If act utilitarians object to a particular discriminatory act, their reason would not be that the act violates a basic human right or that it inherently treats people unfairly. The utilitarian calculus is based not on any inherent characteristic of an act but on its social productivity. When human rights and unfair treatment enter into the calculation, they do so on the basis of the likely consequences that follow upon supporting them and abridging them. Thus, any appeal to principles of justice would take root in efficiency, not in fair play.

For example, if the issue is whether or not to give Mary Smith an equal chance as any male to get a job, the ultimate decision would be based on the comparative value in terms of total social good of giving or denying her an equal opportunity. If more total good would result from denying Smith an equal opportunity, then the act utilitarian would argue that she should be denied equality of opportunity.

Act utilitarians would evaluate acts of preferential treatment in, say, affirmative action programs the same way. Where they would object to preferential treatment, they would do so not because of the violation of any basic human right or concept of fair play, but because the specific act was not as productive of total happiness as some other alternative. Of course, act utilitarians could support acts of reverse discrimination by appealing to the social good. Again, the criterion would be justice considered as efficiency. So, in theory, act utilitarianism could support both discrimination and particular acts calculated to remedy discrimination.

Rule Utilitarianism

While rule utilitarianism also would base its moral decision about sexism and racism on the social good, it would do so by appealing to the rule under which the particular practice or act fell. Thus, if Mary Smith is excluded from job consideration because she is a female, this action might fall under a rule formulated to proscribe an employer ever excluding a person from a job on the basis of sex. If following this rule likely would produce more favorable consequences for more people than breaking it, then the employer who denies Smith job consideration would be acting immorally.

Similarly, the morality of preferential hiring programs would have to be determined on the basis of the probable consequences of following a rule that enjoins an employer from providing preferential treatment to members of groups traditionally discriminated against. If the probable consequences likely would produce more total good, then one must follow the rule; if not, then one must not follow the rule. Of course, determining the total good of such programs would not be easy. Thus, while in theory rule utilitarianism provides a moral direction, in practice that direction remains unclear and uncertain.

It is important to note that rule utilitarianism, like egoism and act utilitarianism, is motivated by a concept of justice as efficiency, that is, the greatest good for the greatest number. Thus, rule utilitarians might consider affirmative action programs just only insofar as they make better use of human resource, advance societal harmony, and produce more social good than any other alternative rule. In effect, such a concept of justice reduces the efficacy of a rule to a cost-benefit analysis.

Divine Command

A Christian interpretation of divine command likely would condemn sexism and racism. Divine command theorists might point out that all humans are equal in the sense of having been made in God's image, of having inherent worth and dignity, of deserving respect and basic rights. One of these basic rights is the right to be given equal consideration, not to be discriminated against unfairly. In most cases, sexism would be viewed as unfair discrimination, and therefore a violation of God's will. It would follow, then, that divine command theorists also must condemn reverse discrimination. They would acknowledge that intending to give advantage to the most disadvantaged is wholesome enough. But, at the same time, preferential treatment on the basis of race or sex remains a form of unfair discrimination, and therefore is wrong. However, we should hasten to qualify this analysis in the light of some Biblical interpretations that, in fact, appear to sanction some forms of sexism, as in the oft-quoted injunction that wives be subject to their husbands. This notwithstanding, it seems inconceivable that divine command in the Western tradition could be used today to justify sexist discrimination against women in employment and educational opportunities.

Categorical Imperative

Kant would look at the practice of sexism or racism as incompatible with the inherent worth, dignity, and equality of all rational creatures. Any maxim that would legitimize such practices would not be universalizable because it would be inconsistent with the nature of rational, autonomous creatures. More important for our purposes, any rule that is self-contradictory and therefore immoral does not become logical and moral in the presence of qualifiers. Thus, since sexism is immoral, any form it takes—no matter what the social goal—also would be immoral. Looked at another way, Kant's theory always prohibits the individual being made a means to a social end. Thus, any social policy that attempted to use white males as a means of achieving a desirable social end would violate a foundational principle of Kant's moral theory. Thus, Kant's categorical imperative would condemn affirmative action programs that institutionalize preferential treatment, and, of course, it would disallow any private acts of sexism.

Prima Facie Duties

Undoubtedly Ross would condemn traditionally practiced sexism and racism as injuring individuals and groups, as well as insulting the individual's basic right to fair and equal treatment. It would be considerably more difficult, however, to apply his theory decisively to the issue of preferential treatment in affirmative action programs, because the duties of justice and noninjury could be applied to conflicting interests. Ross's moral principles would not necessarily lead to a condemnation of reverse discrimination. In fact, they could be used to justify it, in view of the multiple duties involved. For example, the issues and policies of preferential treatment inevitably involve prima facie duties of reparation, stemming from the obligation to help repair the past damage done through institutional sexism and racism. There are also duties of beneficence: Society generally, and institutions in particular, are in a position, through preferential treatment programs, to improve materially the lots of those least well-off. In addition, there are duties of self-improvement, arising from the possibility that individually and collectively we are in a position to improve our own moral stature by actively pursuing equal opportunity. In contrast, there are obvious duties of noninjury and justice relating to those who will not benefit from reverse discrimination, who may even be hurt by it.

In short, Ross's theory could allow reverse discrimination. At the same time, it would recognize as deplorable that such policies need be implemented and that some sort of reparation may be due those who are injured by them.

Maximin Principle

There is no doubt that Rawls's maximin principle would condemn traditional forms of sexism and racism. Just consider the original position. Knowing that they could be victimized by such practices, rational, self-interested creatures would hardly condone them.

As with Ross, however, the question of preferential treatment—reverse discrimination—raises more complex problems. Still, as a bona fide theory of social justice, Rawls's maximin principle generally provides more distinct direction. On the one hand, one could argue that in the original position reverse discrimination would be condemned as a species of sexism or racism. On the other hand, Rawls's difference principle allows for unequal treatment as long as everyone benefits by it, or at least those most disadvantaged. Since those most disadvantaged—women and minority members—would likely benefit from reverse discrimination, it seems that at least in theory Rawls's maximin principle could condone the practice.

This conclusion is strengthened when one introduces Rawls's principle of paternalism, by which he obliges those in a position of authority to introduce the interests of those unable to foster their own interests. This principle presumably would obligate governmental and institutional leaders to pursue aggressively the equal employment and treatment of women and minorities, though not necessarily in the form of reverse discrimination.

The Justification of Reverse Discrimination

Tom L. Beauchamp

In "The Justification of Reverse Discrimination," philosophy professor Tom L. Beauchamp argues that reverse discrimination can be morally justified. But Beauchamp does not defend reverse discrimination on grounds of compensation owed for past wrongs. On the contrary, he holds that reverse discrimination is justified in order to eliminate present discriminatory practices. Clearly, then, Beauchamp must demonstrate that discrimination exists and that it can be eradicated only through methods of reverse discrimination.

Beauchamp approaches his task first by showing that reverse discrimination is compatible with principles of justice and utility. He then turns away from moral considerations to strictly factual ones. The principal factual matter is whether or not seriously discriminatory conditions exist in our society. To establish this, Beauchamp offers an array of statistical and linguistic evidence. Not only does discrimination exist, Beauchamp claims, it is intractable. Moreover, reverse discrimination is the only way it can be rooted out.

In recent years government policies intended to ensure fairer employment and educational opportunities for women and minority groups have engendered alarm. Although I shall in this paper argue in support of enlightened versions of these policies, I nonetheless think there is much to be said for the opposition arguments. In general I would argue that the world of business is now overregulated by the federal government, and I therefore hesitate to support an extension of the regulative arm of government into the arena of hiring and firing. Moreover, policies that would eventuate in reverse discrimination in present North American society have a heavy presumption against them, for both justice-regarding and utilitarian reasons: The introduction of such preferential treatment on a large scale could well produce a series of injustices, economic advantages to

---

Adapted from Tom L. Beauchamp, "The Justification of Reverse Discrimination," in Social Justice and Preferential Treatment, *William T. Blackstone and Robert Heslep (eds.), ©1977 by University of Georgia Press. Reprinted by permission of the publisher, Robert Heslep, and Tom L. Beauchamp.*

some who do not deserve them, protracted court battles, jockeying for favored position by other minorities, congressional lobbying by power groups, a lowering of admission and work standards in vital institutions, reduced social and economic efficiency, increased racial hostility, and continued suspicion that well-placed women and minority group members received their positions purely on the basis of quotas. Conjointly these reasons constitute a powerful case against the enactment of policies productive of reverse discrimination in hiring.

I find these reasons against allowing reverse discrimination to occur both thoughtful and tempting, and I want to concede from the outset that policies of reverse discrimination can create serious and perhaps even tragic injustices. One must be careful, however, not to draw an overzealous conclusion from this admission. Those who argue that reverse discrimination creates injustices often say that, because of the injustice, such policies are *unjust.* I think by this use of "unjust" they generally mean "not justified" (rather than "not sanctioned by justice"). But a policy can create and even perpetuate injustices, as violations of the principle of formal equality, and yet be justified by other reasons. It would be an injustice in this sense to fire either one of two assistant professors with exactly similar professional credentials, while retaining the other of the two; yet the financial condition of the university or compensation owed the person retained might provide compelling reasons which justify the action. The first reason supporting the dismissal is utilitarian in character, and the other derives from the principle of compensatory justice. This shows both that there can be conflicts between different justice-regarding reasons and also that violations of the principle of formal equality are not in themselves sufficient to render an action unjustifiable.

A proper conclusion, then—and one which I accept—is that all discrimination, including reverse discrimination, is prima facie immoral, because a basic principle of justice creates a prima facie duty to abstain from such treatment of persons. But no absolute duty is created come what may, for we might have conflicting duties of sufficient weight to justify such injustices. The latter is the larger thesis I wish to defend: Considerations of compensatory justice and utility are conjointly of sufficient weight in contemporary society to neutralize and overcome the quite proper presumption of immorality in the case of some policies productive of reverse discrimination.

I

It is difficult to avoid accepting two important claims: (a) that the law ought never to sanction any discriminatory practices (whether plain old unadorned discrimination or reverse discrimination), and (b) that such practices can be eradicated by bringing the full weight of the law down on those who engage in discriminatory practices. The first claim is a moral one, the second a factual one. I contend in this section that it is unrealistic to believe, as *b* suggests, that in contemporary society discriminatory practices *can* be eradicated by legal measures which do not permit reverse discrimination. And because they cannot be eradicated, I think we ought to relax our otherwise unimpeachably sound reservations (as recorded in *a* and discussed in the first section) against allowing any discriminatory practices whatever.

My argument is motivated by the belief that racial, sexual, and no doubt other forms of discrimination are not antique relics but are living patterns which continue to warp selection and ranking procedures. In my view the difference between the present and the past is that discriminatory treatment is today less widespread and considerably less blatant. But its reduction has produced apathy; its subtleness has made it less visible and considerably more difficult to detect. Largely because of the reduced visibility of racism and sexism, I suggest, reverse discrimination now strikes us as all too harsh and unfair. After all, quotas and preferential treatment have no appeal if one assumes a just, primarily non-discriminatory society. Since the presence or absence of seriously discriminatory conditions in our society is a factual matter, empirical evidence must be adduced to show that the set of discriminatory attitudes and selection procedures I have alleged to exist do in fact exist. The data I shall mention derive primarily from historical, linguistic, sociological, and legal sources.

Statistical Evidence

Statistican imbalances in employment and admission are often discounted because so many variables can be hypothesized to explain why, for non-discriminatory reasons, an imbalance exists. We can all think of plausible non-discriminatory reasons why 22% of Harvard's graduate students in 1969 were women but its tenured Arts and Sciences Faculty in the Graduate School consisted of 411 males and 0 females.[1] But sometimes we are able to discover evidence which supports the claim that skewed statistics are the result of discrimination. Quantities of such discriminatory findings, in turn, raise serious questions about the real reasons for suspicious statistics in those cases where we have *not* been able to determine these reasons—perhaps because they are so subtle and unnoticed. I shall discuss each factor in turn: (a) statistics which constitute prima facie but indecisive evidence of discrimination; (b) findings concerning discriminatory reasons for some of these statistics; and (c) cases where the discrimination is probably undetectable because of its subtleness, and yet the statistical evidence is overwhelming.

a. A massive body of statistics constituting prima facie evidence of discrimination has been assembled in recent years. Here is a tiny but diverse fragment of some of these statistical findings.[2] (1) Women college teachers with identical credentials in terms of publications and experience are promoted at almost exactly one-half the rate of their male counterparts. (2) In the United States women graduates of medical schools in 1965 stood at 7%, as compared with 36% in Germany. The gap in the number of women physicians was similar. (3) Of 3,000 leading law firms surveyed in 1957 only 32 reported a woman partner, and even these women were paid much less (increasingly so for every year of employment) than their male counterparts. (4) 40% of the white-collar positions in the United States are presently held by women, but only 10% of the management positions are held by women, and their pay again is significantly less (70% of clerical workers are women). (5) 8,000 workers were employed in May 1967 in the construction of BART (Bay Area Rapid Transit), but not a single electrician, ironworker, or plumber was black. (6) In the population as a whole in the United States, 3 out of 7 employees hold white-collar positions, but only 1 of 7 blacks holds such a position, and these latter jobs are clustered in professions which have the fewest jobs to offer in top-paying positions. (7) In the well-known A. T. & T. case, this massive conglomerate signed a set-

tlement giving tens of millions of dollars to women and minority employees. A. T. & T. capitulated to this settlement based on impressive statistics indicating discriminatory treatment.

b. I concede that such statistics are far from decisive indicators of discrimination. But when further evidence concerning the reasons for the statistics is uncovered, they are put in a perspective affording them greater power—clinching power in my view. Consider (3)—the statistics on the lack of women lawyers. A survey of Harvard Law School alumnae in 1970 provided evidence about male lawyers' attitudes.[3] It showed that business and legal firms do not generally expect the women they hire to become lawyers, that they believe women cannot become good litigators, and that they believe only limited numbers of women should be hired since clients generally prefer male lawyers. Surveys of women applicants for legal positions indicate they are frequently either told that a woman will not be hired, or are warned that "senior partners" will likely object, or are told that women will be hired to do only probate, trust, and estate work. (Other statistics confirm that these are the sorts of tasks dominantly given to women.) Consider also (5)—a particular but typical case of hiring in non-white-collar positions. Innumerable studies have shown that most of these positions are filled by word-of-mouth recruitment policies conducted by all-white interviewers (usually all-male as well). In a number of decisions of the Equal Employment Opportunity Commission, it has been shown that the interviewers have racially biased attitudes and that the applications of blacks and women are systematically handled in unusual ways, such as never even being filed. So serious and consistent have such violations been that the EEOC has publicly stated its belief that word-of-mouth recruitment policies without demonstrable supplementary and simultaneous recruitment in minority group communities is in itself a "prima facie violation of Title VII."[4] Gertrude Ezorsky has argued, convincingly I believe, that this pattern of "special ties" is no less present in professional white collar hiring, which is neither less discriminatory nor more sensitive to hiring strictly on the basis of merit.[5]

c. Consider, finally, (1)—statistics pertaining to the treatment of women college teachers. The Carnegie Commission and others have assembled statistical evidence to show that in even the most favorable construal of relevant variables, women teachers have been discriminated against in hiring, tenuring, and ranking. But instead of summarizing this mountain of material, I wish here to take a particular case in order to illustrate the difficulty in determining, on the basis of statistics and similar empirical data, whether discrimination is occurring even where courts have been forced to find satisfactory evidence of discrimination. In December 1974 a decision was reached by the Commission against Discrimination of the Executive Department of the State of Massachusetts regarding a case at Smith College where the two complainants were women who were denied tenure and dismissed by the English Department.[6] The women claimed sex discrimination and based their case on the following: (1) Women at the full professor level in the college declined from 54% in 1958 to 21% in 1972, and in the English department from 57% in 1960 to 11% in 1972. These statistics compare unfavorably at all levels with Mt. Holyoke's, a comparable institution (since both have an all female student body and are located in Western Massachusetts). (2) Thirteen of the department's fifteen associate and full professorships at Smith belonged to men. (3) The two tenured women had obtained tenure under "distinctly peculiar experiences," including a stipulation that one be only part-time and that the other not be promoted when given tenure. (4) The department's faculty members conceded that tenure standards were applied subjectively, were vague, and lacked the kind of precision which would avoid discriminatory application. (5) The women denied tenure were at no time given advance warning that their work was deficient. Rather, they were given favorable evaluations of their teaching and were encouraged to believe they would receive tenure. (6) Some stated reasons for the dismissals were later demonstrated to be rationalizations, and one letter from a senior member to the tenure and promotion committee contradicted his own appraisal of teaching ability filed with the department. (7) The court accepted expert testimony that any deficiencies in the women candidates were also found in male candidates promoted and given tenure during this same period, and that the women's positive credentials were at least as good as the men's.

The commissioner's opinion found that "the Complainants properly used statistics to demonstrate that the Respondents' practices operate with a discriminatory effect." Citing *Parham* v. *Southwestern Bell Telephone Co.*,[7] the commissioner argued that "in such cases extreme statistics may establish discrimination as a matter of law, without additional supportive evidence." But in this case the commissioner found abundant additional evidence in the form of "the historical absence of women," "word-of-mouth recruitment policies" which operate discriminatorily, and a number of "subtle and not so subtle, societal patterns" existing at Smith.[8] On December 30, 1974 the commissioner ordered the two women reinstated with tenure and ordered the department to submit an affirmative action program within 60 days.

This case is interesting because there is little in the way of clinching proof that the members of the English Department actually held discriminatory attitudes. Yet so consistent a pattern of *apparently* discriminatory treatment must be regarded, according to this decision, as *de facto* discrimination. The commissioner's ruling and other laws are quite explicit that "intent or lack thereof is of no consequence." If a procedure constitutes discriminatory treatment, then the parties discriminated against must be recompensed. Here we have a case where irresistible statistics and other sociological evidence of "social exclusion" and "subtle societal patterns" provide convincing evidence that strong, court backed measures must be taken because nothing short of such measures is sufficiently strong to overcome the discriminatory pattern, as the Respondents' testimony in the case verifies.[9]

Some understanding of the attitudes underlying the statistical evidence thus far surveyed can be gained by consideration of some linguistic evidence now to be mentioned. It further supports the charge of widespread discrimination in the case of women and of the difficulty in changing discriminatory attitudes.

Linguistic Evidence

Robert Baker has assembled some impressive linguistic evidence which indicates that our language is male-slanted, perhaps male chauvinistic, and that language about women relates something of fundamental importance concerning the males' most fundamental conceptions of women.[10] Baker argues that as the term "boy" once expressed a paternalistic and dominating attitude toward blacks (and was replaced in our conceptual structure because of this denigrating association), so are there other English terms which serve similar functions in regard to women (but are not replaced because not considered by men as in need of replacement). Baker assembles evidence both from the language itself and from surveys of users of the language to show the following.

The term "woman" is broadly substitutable for and frequently interchanged in English sentences such as "Who is that _____ over there?" by terms such as those in the following divisions:

A. Neutral Categories	B. Animal Categories	C. Plaything Categories
lady	chick	babe
gal	bird	doll
girl	fox	cuddly thing
broad	vixen	
(sister)	filly	
	bitch	

D. Gender Categories	E. Sexual Categories
skirt	snatch
hem	cunt
	ass
	twat
	piece
	lay
	pussy

Baker notes that (1) while there are differences in the frequency of usage, all of these terms are standard enough to be recognizable at least by most male users of the language; (2) women do not typically identify themselves in sexual categories; and (3) typically only males use the nonneutral categories (B-E). He takes this to be evidence—and I agree—that the male conception of women differs significantly from the female conception and that the categories used by the male in classifying women are "prima facie denigrating." He then argues that it is clearly and not merely prima facie denigrating when categories such as C and E are used, as they are either derived from playboy male images or are outright vulgarities. Baker argues that it is most likely that B and D are similarly used in denigrating ways. His arguments center

on the metaphorical associations of these terms, but the evidence cannot be further pursued here.

Although Baker does not remark that women do not have a similar language for men, it seems to me important to notice this fact. Generally, any negative categories used by women to refer to men are as frequently or more frequently used by men to apply to women. This asymmetrical relation does not hold, of course, for the language used by whites and blacks for denigrating reference. This fact perhaps says something about how blacks have caught onto the impact of the language as a tool of denigrating identification in a way women have yet to do, at least in equal numbers. It may also say something about the image of submissiveness which many women still bear about themselves—an image blacks are no longer willing to accept.

Baker concludes from his linguistic studies that "sexual discrimination permeates our conceptual structure. Such discrimination is clearly inimical to any movement toward sexual egalitarianism and virtually defeats its purpose at the outset."[11] His conclusion may somewhat overreach his premises, but when combined with the corroborating statistical evidence previously adduced, it seems apt. Linguistic dispositions lead us to categorize persons and events in discriminatory ways which are sometimes glaringly obvious to the categorized but accepted as "objective" by the categorizer. My contention, derived from Baker's and to be supported as we proceed, is that cautious, good faith movements toward egalitarianism such as affirmative action guidelines *cannot* succeed short of fundamental conceptual and ethical revisions. And since the probability of such revisions approximates zero (because discriminatory attitudes are covertly embedded in language and cultural habit), radical expedients are required to bring about the desired egalitarian results, expedients which may result in reverse discrimination.

Conclusions

Irving Thalberg has argued, correctly I believe, that the gravest contemporary problems with racism stem from its "protectively camouflaged" status, which he calls "visceral." Thalberg skillfully points to a number of attitudes held by those whites normally classified as unprejudiced which indicate that racism still colors their conception of social facts.[12] My alliance with such a position ought to be obvious by now. But my overall intentions and conclusions are somewhat different. I hold that because of the peculiarly concealed nature of the protective camouflage under which sexism and racism have so long thrived, it is not a reasonable expectation that the lightweight programs now administered under the heading of affirmative action will succeed in overcoming discriminatory treatment. I turn now directly to this topic.

II

The rawest nerve of the social and political controversy concerning reverse discrimination is exposed by the following question: What government policies are permissible and required in order to bring about a society where equal treatment of persons is the rule rather than the exception? Fair-minded opponents of any government policy which might produce reverse discrimination—Carl Cohen and William Blackstone, for example—seem to me to oppose them largely because and perhaps only because of their *factual belief* that present government policies not causing reverse discrimination will, if seriously and sincerely pursued, prove sufficient to achieve the goal of equal consideration of persons.

Once again a significant factual disagreement has emerged: What means are not only fair but also sufficient? I must again support my contentions by adducing factual data to show that my pessimism is sustained by the weight of the evidence. The evidence cited here comes from government data concerning affirmative action programs. I shall discuss the affirmative action program in order to show that on the basis of present government guidelines (which, to my knowledge, are the best either in law or proposed as law by those who oppose reverse discrimination), discriminatory business as usual will surely prevail.

Affirmative Action

I begin with a sample of the affirmative action guidelines, as understood by those who administer them. I use the example of HEW guidelines for educational institutions receiving federal financial aid. These guidelines are not radically different from those directed at hiring practices throughout the world of business. Specifically, these guidelines cover three areas: admission, treatment of students, and employment. A sample of the sorts of requirements universities are under includes: (1) They may not advertise vacant positions as open only to or preferentially to a particular race or sex, except where sex is a legitimate occupational requirement. (2) The university sets standards and criteria for employment, but if these effectively work to exclude women or minorities as a class, the university must justify the job requirements. (3) An institution may not set different standards of admission for one sex, race, etc. (4) There must be active recruitment where there is an underrepresentation of women and minorities, as gauged by the availability of qualified members of these classes. However, the relevant government officials have from time to time made it clear that (1) quotas are unacceptable, either for admission or employment, though target goals and timetables intended to correct deficiencies are acceptable and to be encouraged. (2) A university is never under any obligation to dilute legitimate standards, and hence there is no conflict with merit hiring. (3) Reserving positions for members of a minority group (and presumably for the female sex) is "an outrageous and illegal form of reverse bias" (as one former director of the program wrote).[13] By affirmative action requirements I mean this latter interpretation and nothing stronger (though I have given only a sample set of qualifications, of course).

The question I am currently asking is whether these guidelines, assuming they will be vigorously pursued, can reasonably be expected to bring about their goal, which is the social circumstance of non-discriminatory treatment of persons. If they *are* strong enough, then Cohen, Blackstone, and others are right: Reverse discrimination is not under such circumstances justified. Unfortunately the statistical and linguistic evidence previously adduced indicates otherwise. The *Smith College* case is paradigmatic of the concealed yet serious discrimination which occurs through the network of subtle distortions, old-boy procedures, and prejudices we have accumulated. Only when the statistics become egregiously out of proportion is action taken or a finding of mistreatment possible.

And that is one reason why it seems unlikely that substantial progress can be made, in any realistic sense of "can," by current government measures not productive of reverse discrimination. According to Peter Holmes, once the Director of HEW's Office for Civil Rights and in charge of interpreting affirmative action guidelines: "It has been our policy that it is the institutions' responsibility to determine non-discriminatory qualifications in the first instance, and that such qualifications, in conjunction with other affirmative action steps, should yield results."[14] This is the received HEW view, but the last sentence contains an ambiguous use of the word "should." If the "should" in this statement is a moral "should," none will disagree. But if it is an empirical, predictive "should," as I take Mr. Holmes to intend, we are back to the core of the difficulty. I now turn to a consideration of how deficient such affirmative action steps have proven to be.

Government Data

The January 1975 Report of the United States Commission on Civil Rights contains a section on "compliance reviews" of various universities. These are government assessments of university compliance with Executive Orders pertaining to affirmative action plans. The report contains a stern indictment of the Higher Education Division (HED) of HEW—the division in charge of overseeing all HEW civil rights enforcement activities in the area of higher education. It concludes that "HED has, in large part, failed to follow the procedures required of compliance agencies under the Executive order regulations."[15] But more interesting than this mere failure to enforce the law is the report's discussion of how very difficult it is to obtain compliance even when there is a routine attempt to enforce the law. The Commission reviewed four major campuses in the United States (Harvard, University of Michigan, University of Washington, Berkeley). They concluded that there is a pattern of inadequate compliance reviews, inordinate delays, and inexcusable failures to take enforcement action where there were clear violations of the Executive order regulations.[16]

Consider the example of the "case history of compliance contacts" at the University of California at Berkeley. According to HED's own staff a "conciliation agreement" with this university "is now being used as a model for compliance activities with other campuses." When the Office for Civil Rights of HEW determined to investigate Berkeley (April 1971), after several complaints, including a class action sex discrimination complaint, the university refused to permit access to its personnel files and refused to permit the interviewing of faculty members without an administrator present. Both refusals are, as the report points out, "direct violations of the Executive order's equal opportunity clause," under which Berkeley held contracts. Despite this clear violation of the law, no enforcement action was taken. A year and one-half later, after negotiations and more complaints, the university was instructed to develop a written affirmative action plan to correct "documented deficiencies" of "pervasive discrimination." The plan was to include target goals and timetables wherever job underutilization had been identified.[17]

In January 1973 the university, in a letter from Chancellor Albert H. Bowker, submitted a draft affirmative action plan which was judged "totally unacceptable." Throughout 1973 Berkeley received "extensive technical assistance" from the government to aid it in developing a better plan. No such plan emerged, and OCR at the end of the year began to question "the university's commitment to comply with the executive order." The university submitted other unacceptable plans, and finally in March 1974 "a conciliation agreement was reached." However, "the document suffered from such extreme vagueness that, as of August 1974, the university and OCR were in substantial disagreement on the meaning of a number of its provisions," and "the agreement specifically violated OFCC regulations in a number of ways." These violations are extensive and serious, and the report characterizes one part as "outrageous." Four years after this "model" compliance case began, it was unresolved and no enforcement proceedings had been taken against the university. The report concludes: "In its Title VI reviews of colleges and universities, HEW routinely finds noncompliance, but it almost never imposes sanctions; instead HEW responds by making vague recommendations. Moreover, HEW does not routinely require the submission of progress reports or conduct sufficient followup to determine if its recommendations have been followed."

III

No one could be happy about the conclusions I have reached or about the depressing and disturbing facts on which they are based. But I do take it to be a *factual* and not an *evaluative* conclusion both (1) that the camouflaged attitudes I have discussed exist and affect the social position of minority groups and women and (2) that they will in all likelihood continue to have this influence. It is, of course, an evaluative conclusion that we are morally permitted and even required to remedy this situation by the imposition of quotas, target goals, and timetables. But anyone who accepts my *interpretation* of the facts bears a heavy burden of moral argument to show that we ought not to use such means to that end upon which I take it we all agree, viz., the equal consideration of persons irrespective of race, sex, religion, or nationality.

By way of conclusion, it is important to set my arguments in the framework of a distinction between real reverse discrimination and merely apparent reverse discrimination. My evidence demonstrates present, ongoing barriers to the removal of discriminatory practices. My contentions set the stage for showing that *because* of the existence of what Thalberg calls "visceral racism," and because of visceral sexism as well, there will be many occasions on which we can only avoid inevitable discrimination by policies productive of reverse discrimination. Sometimes, however, persons will be hired or admitted—on a quota basis, for example—who appear to be displacing better applicants, but the appearance is the result of visceral discriminatory perceptions of the person's qualifications. In this case there will certainly appear to the visceral racist or sexist to be reverse discrimination, and this impression will be reinforced by knowledge that quotas were used; yet the allegation of reverse discrimination will be a mistaken one. On other occasions there will be genuine reverse discrimination, and on many occasions it will be impossible to determine whether or not this consequence is occurring. The evidence I have adduced is, of course, intended to support the contention that real and not merely apparent reverse discrimination is justified. But it is justified only as a means to the end of ensuring genuinely nondiscriminatory treatment of all persons.

Notes

1. From "Statement of Dr. Bernice Sandler," *Discrimination Against Women: Congressional Hearings on Equal Rights in Education and Employment*, ed. Catharine R. Stimpson (New York: R. R. Bowker Company, 1973), pp. 61, 415. Hereafter *Discrimination Against Women*.

2. All of the statistics and quotations cited are taken from the compilations of data in the following sources: (1) Kenneth M. Davidson, Ruth B. Ginsburg, and Herma H. Kay, eds., *Sex-Based Discrimination: Text, Cases, and Materials* (Minneapolis: West Publishing Company, 1974), esp. Ch. 3. Hereafter *Sex-Based Discrimination*. (2) *Discrimination Against Women*, esp. pp. 397–441 and 449–502. (3) Alfred W. Blumrosen, *Black Employment and the Law* (New Brunswick, N.J.: Rutgers University Press, 1971), esp. pp. 107, 122f. (4) *The Federal Civil Rights Enforcement Effort—1971*, A Report of the United States Commission on Civil Rights.

3. *Discrimination Against Women*, pp. 505f.

4. *Sex-Based Discrimination*, p. 516.

5. "The Fight Over University Women," *The New York Review of Books*, May 16, 1974, pp. 32–39.

6. *Maurianne Adams and Mary Schroeder v. Smith College*, Massachusetts Commission Against Discrimination, Nos. 72-S-53, 72-S-54 (December 30, 1974). Hereafter *The Smith College Case*.

7. 433 F.2d 421, 426 (8 Cir. 1970).

8. *The Smith College Case*, pp. 23, 26.

9. *Ibid.*, pp. 26f.

10. Robert Baker, "'Pricks' and 'Chicks': A Plea for Persons," in Richard Wasserstrom, ed., *Today's Moral Problems* (New York: Macmillan Publishing Company, 1975), pp. 152–170.

11. *Ibid.*, p. 170.

12. "Visceral Racism," *The Monist*, 56 (1972), 43–63, and reprinted in Wasserstrom.

13. J. Stanley Pottinger, "Race, Sex, and Jobs: The Drive Towards Equality," *Change Magazine*, 4 (Oct. 1972), 24–29.

14. Peter E. Holmes, "HEW Guidelines and 'Affirmative Action,'" *The Washington Post*, Feb. 15, 1975.

15. *The Federal Civil Rights Enforcement Effort—1974*, 3:276.

16. *Ibid*, p. 281.

17. *Ibid*, all subsequent references are from pp. 281–286.

Questions for Analysis

1. What obligations, if any, does Beauchamp draw from claims of compensatory justice?

2. Why does Beauchamp construe reverse discrimination as primarily a factual matter?

3. When Beauchamp says that reverse discrimination is compatible with principles of justice, does he mean that no injustice results from reverse discrimination or that these injustices can be justified? Explain the difference, and why the latter claim is a utilitarian one.

4. What are the two minimal principles of justice that Beauchamp uses to support the claim that reverse discrimination is compatible with justice? Compare and contrast these principles with Rawls's equality and difference principles.

5. Beauchamp says: ". . . all discrimination, including reverse discrimination, is prima facie immoral." Explain why this admission is not inconsistent with his claim that reverse discrimination can be morally justified.

6. What statistical and linguistic evidence does Beauchamp provide to prove that discrimination still exists?

7. Do you think that Beauchamp has established that reverse discrimination is the only way to eradicate intractable discrimination?

A Defense of Programs of Preferential Treatment

Richard Wasserstrom

In "A Defense of Programs of Preferential Treatment," philosophy professor Richard Wasserstrom provides a limited defense of quota hiring by attacking two of the opposition's major arguments. First, opponents of preferential treatment often charge proponents with "intellectual inconsistency." Thus, they argue that those now supporting preferential treatment opposed it in the past. But Wasserstrom feels that social realities in respect to the distribution of resources and opportunities make present preferential treatment programs enormously different from quotas of the past.

The second argument commonly raised against preferential treatment programs is that such programs, by introducing sex and race, compromise what really should matter: individual qualifications. Wasserstrom counters this charge on both an operational and a theoretical level. He feels that, to be decisive, this argument must appeal, not to efficiency, but to desert: Those who are most qualified deserve to receive the benefits. But Wasserstrom sees no necessary connection between qualifications and desert.

From Richard Wasserstrom "A Defense of Programs of Preferential Treatment," Phi Kappa Phi Journal, LVIII (Winter 1978); originally Part II of "Racism, Sexism, and Preferential Treatment: An Approach to the Topics," 24 U.C.L.A. Law Review, 581 (1977). Reprinted by permission of the author.

Many justifications of programs of preferential treatment depend upon the claim that in one respect or another such programs have good consequences or that they are effective means by which to bring about some desirable end, e.g., an integrated, equalitarian society. I mean by "programs of preferential treatment" to refer to programs such as those at issue in the *Bakke* case—programs which set aside a certain number of places (for example, in a law school) as to which members of minority groups (for example, persons who are non-white or female) who possess certain minimum qualifications (in terms of grades and test scores) may be preferred for admission to those places over some members of the majority group who possess higher qualifications (in terms of grades and test scores).

Many criticisms of programs of preferential treatment claim that such programs, even if effective, are unjustifiable because they are in some important sense unfair or unjust. In this paper I present a limited defense of such programs by showing that two of the chief arguments offered for the unfairness or injustice of these programs do not work in the way or to the degree supposed by critics of these programs.

The first argument is this. Opponents of preferential treatment programs sometimes assert that proponents of these programs are guilty of intellectual inconsistency, if not racism or sexism. For, as is now readily acknowledged, at times past employers, universities, and many other social institutions did have racial or sexual quotas (when they did not practice overt racial or sexual exclusion), and many of those who were most concerned to bring about the eradication of those racial quotas are now untroubled by the new programs which reinstitute them. And this, it is claimed, is inconsistent. If it was wrong to take race or sex into account when blacks and women were the objects of racial and sexual policies and practices of exclusion, then it is wrong to take race or sex into account when the objects of the policies have their race or sex reversed. Simple considerations of intellectual consistency—of what it means to give racism or sexism as a reason for condemning these social policies and practices—require that what was a good reason then is still a good reason now.

The problem with this argument is that despite appearances, there is no inconsistency involved in holding both views. Even if contemporary preferential treatment programs which contain quotas are wrong, they are not wrong for the reasons that made quotas against blacks and women pernicious. The reason why is that the social realities do make an enormous difference. The fundamental evil of programs that discriminated against blacks or women was that these programs were a part of a larger social universe which systematically maintained a network of institutions which unjustifiably concentrated power, authority, and goods in the hands of white male individuals, and which systematically consigned blacks and women to subordinate positions in the society.

Whatever may be wrong with today's affirmative action programs and quota systems, it should be clear that the evil, if any, is just not the same. Racial and sexual minorities do not constitute the dominant social group. Nor is the conception of who is a fully developed member of the moral and social community one of an individual who is either female or black. Quotas which prefer women or blacks do not add to an already relatively overabundant supply of resources and opportunities at the disposal of members of these groups in the way in which the quotas of the past did maintain and augment the overabundant supply of resources and opportunities already available to white males.

The same point can be made in a somewhat different way. Sometimes people say that what was wrong, for example, with the system of racial discrimination in the South was that it took an irrelevant characteristic, namely race, and used it systematically to allocate social benefits and burdens of various sorts. The defect was the irrelevance of the characteristic used—race—for that meant that individuals ended up being treated in a manner that was arbitrary and capricious.

I do not think that was the central flaw at all. Take, for instance, the most hideous of the practices, human slavery. The primary thing that was wrong with the institution was not that the particular individuals who were assigned the place of slaves were assigned there arbitrarily because the assignment was made in virtue of an irrelevant characteristic, their race. Rather, it seems to me that the primary thing that was and is wrong with slavery is the practice itself—the fact of some individuals being able to own other individuals and all that goes with that practice. It would not matter by what criterion individuals were assigned; human slavery would still be wrong. And the same can be said for most if not all of the other discrete practices and institutions which comprised the system of racial discrimination even after human slavery was abolished. The practices were unjustifiable—they were oppressive—and they would have been so no matter how the assignment of victims had been made. What made it worse, still, was that the institutions and the supporting ideology all interlocked to create a system of human oppression whose effects on those living under it were as devastating as they were unjustifiable.

Again, if there is anything wrong with the programs of preferential treatment that have begun to flourish within the past ten years, it should be evident that the social realities in respect to the distribution of resources and opportunities make the difference. Apart from everything else, there is simply no way in which all of these programs taken together could plausibly be viewed as capable of relegating white males to the kind of genuinely oppressive status characteristically bestowed upon women and blacks by the dominant social institutions and ideology.

The second objection is that preferential treatment programs are wrong because they take race or sex into account rather than the only thing that does matter—that is, an individual's qualification. What all such programs have in common and what makes them all objectionable, so this argument goes, is that they ignore the persons who are more qualified by bestowing a preference on those who are less qualified in virtue of their being black or female.

There are, I think, a number of things wrong with this objection based on qualifications, and not the least of them is that we do not live in a society in which there is even the serious pretense of a qualification requirement for many jobs of substantial power and authority. Would anyone claim, for example, that the persons who comprise the judiciary are there because they are the most qualified lawyers or the most qualified persons to be judges? Would anyone claim that Henry Ford II is

the head of the Ford Motor Company because he is the most qualified person for the job? Part of what is wrong with even talking about qualifications and merit is that the argument derives some of its force from the erroneous notion that we would have a meritocracy were it not for programs of preferential treatment. In fact, the higher one goes in terms of prestige, power and the like, the less qualifications seem ever to be decisive. It is only for certain jobs and certain places that qualifications are used to do more than establish the possession of certain minimum competencies.

But difficulties such as these to one side, there are theoretical difficulties as well which cut much more deeply into the argument about qualifications. To begin with, it is important to see that there is a serious inconsistency present if the person who favors "pure qualifications" does so on the ground that the most qualified ought to be selected because this promotes maximum efficiency. Let us suppose that the argument is that if we have the most qualified performing the relevant tasks we will get those tasks done in the most economical and efficient manner. There is nothing wrong in principle with arguments based upon the good consequences that will flow from maintaining a social practice in a certain way. But it is inconsistent for the opponent of preferential treatment to attach much weight to qualifications on this ground, because it was an analogous appeal to the good consequences that the opponent of preferential treatment thought was wrong in the first place. That is to say, if the chief thing to be said in favor of strict qualifications and preferring the most qualified is that it is the most efficient way of getting things done, then we are right back to an assessment of the different consequences that will flow from different programs, and we are far removed from the considerations of justice or fairness that were thought to weigh so heavily against these programs.

It is important to note, too, that qualifications—at least in the educational context—are often not connected at all closely with any plausible conception of social effectiveness. To admit the most qualified students to law school, for example—given the way qualifications are now determined—is primarily to admit those who have the greatest chance of scoring the highest grades at law school. This says little about efficiency except perhaps that these students are the easiest for the faculty to teach. However, since we know so little about what constitutes being a good, or even successful lawyer, and even less about the correlation between being a very good law student and being a very good lawyer, we can hardly claim very confidently that the legal system will operate most effectively if we admit only the most qualified students to law school.

To be at all decisive, the argument for qualifications must be that those who are the most qualified deserve to receive the benefits (the job, the place in law school, etc.) because they are the most qualified. The introduction of the concept of desert now makes it an objection as to justice or fairness of the sort promised by the original criticism of the programs. But now the problem is that there is no reason to think that there is any strong sense of "desert" in which it is correct that the most qualified deserve anything.

Let us consider more closely one case, that of preferential treatment in respect to admission to college or graduate school. There is a logical gap in the inference from the claim that a person is most qualified to perform a task, e.g., to be a good student, to the conclusion that he or she deserves to be admitted as a student. Of course, those who deserve to be admitted should be admitted. But why do the most qualified deserve anything? There is simply no necessary connection between academic merit (in the sense of being most qualified) and deserving to be a member of a student body. Suppose, for instance, that there is only one tennis court in the community. Is it clear that the two best tennis players ought to be the ones permitted to use it? Why not those who were there first? Or those who will enjoy playing the most? Or those who are the worst and, therefore, need the greatest opportunity to practice? Or those who have the chance to play least frequently?

We might, of course, have a rule that says that the best tennis players get to use the court before the others. Under such a rule the best players would deserve the court more than the poorer ones. But that is just to push the inquiry back one stage. Is there any reason to think that we ought to have a rule giving good tennis players such a preference? Indeed, the arguments that might be given for or against such a rule are many and varied. And few if any of the arguments that might

support the rule would depend upon a connection between ability and desert.

Someone might reply, however, that the most able students deserve to be admitted to the university because all of their earlier schooling was a kind of competition, with university admission being the prize awarded to the winners. They deserve to be admitted because that is what the rule of the competition provides. In addition, it might be argued, it would be unfair now to exclude them in favor of others, given the reasonable expectations they developed about the way in which their industry and performance would be rewarded. Minority-admission programs, which inevitably prefer some who are less qualified over some who are more qualified, all possess this flaw.

There are several problems with this argument. The most substantial of them is that it is an empirically implausible picture of our social world. Most of what are regarded as the decisive characteristics for higher education have a great deal to do with things over which the individual has neither control nor responsibility: such things as home environment, socioeconomic class of parents, and, of course, the quality of the primary and secondary schools attended. Since individuals do not deserve having had any of these things vis à vis other individuals, they do not, for the most part, deserve their qualifications. And since they do not deserve their abilities they do not in any strong sense deserve to be admitted because of their abilities.

To be sure, if there has been a rule which connects say, performance at high school with admission to college, then there is a weak sense in which those who do well at high school deserve, for that reason alone, to be admitted to college. In addition, if persons have built up or relied upon their reasonable expectations concerning performance and admission, they have a claim to be admitted on this ground as well. But it is certainly not obvious that these claims of desert are any stronger or more compelling than the competing claims based upon the needs of or advantages to women or blacks from programs of preferential treatment. And as I have indicated, all rule-based claims of desert are very weak unless and until the rule which creates the claim is itself shown to be a justified one. Unless one has a strong preference for the status quo, and unless one can defend that preference, the practice within a system of allocating places in a certain way does not go very far at all in showing that that is the right or the just way to allocate those places in the future.

A proponent of programs of preferential treatment is not at all committed to the view that qualifications ought to be wholly irrelevant. He or she can agree that, given the existing structure of any institution, there is probably some minimal set of qualifications without which one cannot participate meaningfully within the institution. In addition, it can be granted that the qualifications of those involved will affect the way the institution works and the way it affects others in the society. And the consequences will vary depending upon the particular institution. But all of this only establishes that qualifications, in this sense, are relevant, not that they are decisive. This is wholly consistent with the claim that race or sex should today also be relevant when it comes to matters such as admission to college or law school. And that is all that any preferential treatment program—even one with the kind of quota used in the *Bakke* case—has ever tried to do.

I have not attempted to establish that programs of preferential treatment are right and desirable. There are empirical issues concerning the consequences of these programs that I have not discussed, and certainly not settled. Nor, for that matter, have I considered the argument that justice may permit, if not require, these programs as a way to provide compensation or reparation for injuries suffered in the recent as well as distant past, or as a way to remove benefits that are undeservedly enjoyed by those of the dominant group. What I have tried to do is show that it is wrong to think that programs of preferential treatment are objectionable in the centrally important sense in which many past and present discriminatory features of our society have been and are racist and sexist. The social realities as to power and opportunity do make a fundamental difference. It is also wrong to think that programs of preferential treatment could, therefore, plausibly rest both on the view that such programs are not unfair to white males (except in the weak, rule-dependent sense described above) and on the view that it is unfair to continue the present set of unjust—often racist and sexist—institutions that comprise the social reality. And the case for these programs could rest as well on the proposition that, given the distribution of power and influence in the United States today, such programs may reasonably be viewed as potentially valuable, effective means by which to achieve admirable and significant social ideals of equality and integration.

Questions for Analysis

1. What does it mean to claim that proponents of preferential treatment are guilty of "intellectual inconsistency"?

2. Do you think that Wasserstrom convincingly refutes this charge? Would Kant accept his rationale?

3. Would you agree that Wasserstrom's objection to slavery is nonconsequential? Explain.

4. How does Wasserstrom respond to the charge that preferential treatment programs compromise the only thing that really matters: individual qualifications?

5. Describe the inconsistency present for the person who favors "pure qualifications" on grounds of maximum efficiency.

6. Do you agree that there is no necessary connection between qualifications and desert?

7. Do you think Wasserstrom's tennis analogy is a sound one?

8. Would it be accurate to say that Wasserstrom unequivocally supports preferential treatment programs? Explain.

Reverse Discrimination and Compensatory Justice

William T. Blackstone

In "Reverse Discrimination and Compensatory Justice," philosophy professor William T. Blackstone is concerned with a single question: Is reverse discrimination ever justified on grounds of repairing past wrongs done to women and minorities? Blackstone thinks not. In his view, reverse discrimination cannot be so justified either morally or legally.

Blackstone builds his case primarily on a utilitarian foundation. In short, he believes that more harm than good would result from a systematic policy of reverse discrimination. (Curiously, as he points out, reverse discrimination often is justified on an appeal to utility.) Since reverse discrimination is not justified on utilitarian or justice-regarding grounds, Blackstone concludes that compensation through reverse discrimination is not justifiable. Indeed, he argues that affirmative action programs, despite how they have sometimes been implemented, not only oppose reverse discrimination but forbid it.

Is reverse discrimination justified as a policy of compensation or of preferential treatment for women and racial minorities? That is, given the fact that women and racial minorities have been invidiously discriminated against in the past on the basis of the irrelevant characteristics of race and sex—are we now justified in discriminating in their favor on the basis of the same characteristics? This is a central ethical and legal question today, and it is one which is quite unresolved. Philosophers, jurists, legal scholars, and the man-in-the-street line up on both sides of this issue. These differences are plainly reflected (in the Supreme Court's majority opinion and Justice Douglas's dissent) in *DeFunis* v. *Odegaard.*[1] . . .

I will argue that reverse discrimination is improper on both moral and constitutional grounds, though I focus more on moral grounds. However, I do this with considerable ambivalence, even "existential guilt." Several reasons lie behind that ambivalence. First, there are moral and constitutional arguments on both sides. The ethical waters are very muddy and I simply argue that the balance of the arguments are against a policy of reverse discrimination.[2] My ambivalence is further due not only to the fact that traditional racism is still a much larger problem than that of reverse discrimination but also because I am sympathetic

to the *goals* of those who strongly believe that reverse discrimination as a policy is the means to overcome the debilitating effects of past injustice. Compensation and remedy are most definitely required both by the facts and by our value commitments. But I do not think that reverse discrimination is the proper means of remedy or compensation. . . .

I

Let us now turn to the possibility of a utilitarian justification of reverse discrimination and to the possible conflict of justice-regarding reasons and those of social utility on this issue. The category of morally relevant reasons is broader, in my opinion, than reasons related to the norm of justice. It is broader than those related to the norm of utility. Also it seems to me that the norms of justice and utility are not reducible one to the other. We cannot argue these points of ethical theory here. But, if these assumptions are correct, then it is at least possible to morally justify injustice or invidious discrimination in some contexts. A case would have to be made that such injustice, though regrettable, will produce the best consequences for society and that this fact is an overriding or weightier moral reason than the temporary injus-

From William T. Blackstone, "Reverse Discrimination and Compensatory Justice," in Social Justice and Preferential Treatment, *William T. Blackstone and Robert Heslep (eds.). ©1977 by University of Georgia Press, Athens. Reprinted by permission of the publisher and Robert Heslep.*

tice. Some arguments for reverse discrimination have taken this line. Professor Thomas Nagel argues that such discrimination is justifiable as long as it is "clearly contributing to the eradication of great social evils."[3] . . .

Another example of what I would call a utilitarian argument for reverse discrimination was recently set forth by Congressman Andrew Young of Georgia. Speaking specifically of reverse discrimination in the context of education, he stated: "While that may give minorities a little edge in some instances, and you may run into the danger of what we now commonly call reverse discrimination, I think the educational system needs this. Society needs this as much as the people we are trying to help . . . a society working toward affirmative action and inclusiveness is going to be a stronger and more relevant society than one that accepts the limited concepts of objectivity. . . . I would admit that it is perhaps an individual injustice. But it might be necessary in order to overcome an historic group injustice or series of group injustices."[4] Congressman Young's basic justifying grounds for reverse discrimination, which he recognizes as individual injustice, are the results which he thinks it will produce: a stronger and more relevant education system and society, and one which is more just overall. His argument may involve pitting some justice-regarding reasons (the right of women and racial minorities to be compensated for past injustices) against others (the right of the majority to the uniform application of the same standards of merit to all). But a major thrust of his argument also seems to be utilitarian.

Just as there are justice-regarding arguments on both sides of the issue of reverse discrimination, so also there are utilitarian arguments on both sides. In a nutshell, the utilitarian argument in favor runs like this: Our society contains large groups of persons who suffer from past institutionalized injustice. As a result, the possibilities of social discord and disorder are high indeed. If short-term reverse discrimination were to be effective in overcoming the effects of past institutionalized injustice and if this policy could alleviate the causes of disorder and bring a higher quality of life to millions of persons, then society as a whole would benefit.

There are moments in which I am nearly convinced by this argument, but the conclusion that such a policy would have negative utility on the whole wins out. For although reverse discrimination might appear to have the effect of getting more persons who have been disadvantaged by past inequities into the mainstream quicker, that is, into jobs, schools, and practices from which they have been excluded, the cost would be invidious discrimination against majority group members of society. I do not think that majority members of society would find this acceptable, i.e., the disadvantaging of themselves for past inequities which they did not control and for which they are not responsible. If such policies were put into effect by government, I would predict wholesale rejection or noncooperation, the result of which would be negative not only for those who have suffered past inequities but also for the justice-regarding institutions of society. Claims and counter-claims would obviously be raised by other ethnic or racial minorities—by Chinese, Chicanos, American Indians, Puerto Ricans—and by orphans, illegitimate children, ghetto residents, and so on. Literally thousands of types or groups could, on similar grounds as blacks or women, claim that reverse discrimination is justified on their behalf. What would happen if government attempted policies of reverse discrimination for all such groups? It would mean the arbitrary exclusion or discrimination against all others relative to a given purpose and a given group. Such a policy would itself create an injustice for which those newly excluded persons could then, themselves, properly claim the need for reverse discrimination to offset the injustice to them. The circle is plainly a vicious one. Such policies are simply self-destructive. In place of the ideal of equality and distributive justice based on relevant criteria, we would be left with the special pleading of self-interested power groups, groups who gear criteria for the distribution of goods, services, and opportunities to their special needs and situations, primarily. Such policies would be those of special privilege, not the appeal to objective criteria which apply to all.[5] They would lead to social chaos, not social justice.

Furthermore, in cases in which reverse discrimination results in a lowering of quality, the consequences for society, indeed for minority victims of injustice for which reverse discrimination is designed to help, may be quite bad. It is no easy matter to calculate this, but the recent report sponsored by the Carnegie Commission on Higher Education points to such deleterious consequences.[6] If the quality of instruction in higher education, for example, is lowered through a policy of primary attention to race or sex as opposed to ability and training, everyone—including victims of past injustice—suffers. Even if such policies are clearly seen as temporary with quite definite deadlines for termination, I am skeptical about their utilitarian value. . . .

II

The inappropriateness of reverse discrimination, both on utilitarian and justice-regarding grounds, in no way means that compensation for past injustices is inappropriate. It does not mean that those who have suffered past injustices and who have been disadvantaged by them are not entitled to compensation or that they have no moral right to remedy. It may be difficult in different contexts to translate that moral right to remedy into practice or into legislation. When has a disadvantaged person or group been compensated enough? What sort of allocation of resources will compensate without creating additional inequities or deleterious consequences? There is no easy answer to these questions. Decisions must be made in particular contexts. Furthermore, it may be the case that the effects of past injustices are so severe (poverty, malnutrition, and the denial of educational opportunities) that genuine compensation—the balancing of the scales—is impossible. The effects of malnutrition or the lack of education are often non-reversible (and would be so even under a policy of reverse discrimination). This is one of the tragedies of injustice. But if reverse discrimination is inappropriate as a means of compensation and if (as I have argued) it is unjust to make persons who are not responsible for the suffering and disadvantaging of others to suffer for those past injuries, then other means must be employed unless overriding moral considerations of another type (utilitarian) can be clearly demonstrated. That compensation must take a form which is consistent with our constitutional principles and with reasonable principles of justice. Now it seems to me that the Federal Government's Equal Opportunity and Affirmative Action Programs are consistent with these principles, that they are not only not committed to reverse discrimination but rather absolutely forbid

it.[7] However, it also seems to me that some officials authorized or required to implement these compensatory efforts have resorted to reverse discrimination and hence have violated the basic principles of justice embodied in these programs. I now want to argue both of these points: first, that these federal programs reject reverse discrimination in their basic principles; secondly, that some implementers of these programs have violated their own principles.

Obviously our country has not always been committed constitutionally to equality. We need no review of our social and political heritage to document this. But with the Fourteenth Amendment, equality as a principle was given constitutional status. Subsequently, social, political, and legal practices changed radically and they will continue to do so. The Fourteenth Amendment declares that states are forbidden to deny any person life, liberty, or property without due process of law or to deny to any person the equal protection of the laws. In my opinion the principles of the Equal Opportunity and Affirmative Action Programs reflect faithfully this constitutional commitment. I am more familiar with those programs as reflected in universities. In this context they require that employers "recruit, hire, train, and promote persons in all job classifications without regard to race, color, religion, sex or national origin, except where sex is a bona fide occupational qualification."[8] They state explicitly that "goals may not be rigid and inflexible quotas which must be met, but must be targets reasonably attainable by means of good faith effort."[9] They require the active recruitment of women and racial minorities where they are "underutilized," this being defined as a context in which there are "fewer minorities or women in a particular job classification than would reasonably be expected by their availability."[10] This is sometimes difficult to determine; but some relevant facts do exist and hence the meaning of a "good faith" effort is not entirely fluid. In any event the Affirmative Action Program in universities requires that "goals, timetables and affirmative action commitment, must be designed to correct any identifiable deficiencies," with separate goals and timetables for minorities and women.[11] It recognizes that there has been blatant discrimination against women and racial minorities in universities and elsewhere, and it assumes that there are "identifiable deficiencies." But it does not require that blacks be employed because they are black or women employed because they are women; that is, it does not require reverse discrimination with rigid quotas to correct the past. It requires a good faith effort in the present based on data on the availability of qualified women and racial minorities in various disciplines and other relevant facts. (Similar requirements hold, of course, for non-academic employment at colleges and universities.) It does not mandate the hiring of the unqualified or a lowering of standards; it mandates only equality of opportunity for all which, given the history of discrimination against women and racial minorities, requires affirmative action in recruitment.

Now if this affirmative action in recruitment, which is not only consistent with but required by our commitment to equality and social justice, is translated into rigid quotas and reverse discrimination by those who implement equal opportunity and affirmative action programs in the effort to get results immediately—and there is no doubt in my mind that this has occurred—then such action violates the principles of those programs.

This violation—this inconsistency of principle and practice—occurs, it seems to me, when employers hire with *priority emphasis* on race, sex, or minority-group status. This move effectively eliminates others from the competition. It is like pretending that everyone is in the game from the beginning while all the while certain persons are systematically excluded. This is exactly what happened recently when a judge declared that a certain quota or number of women were to be employed by a given agency regardless of their qualifications for the job,[12] when some public school officials fired a white coach in order to hire a black one,[13] when a DeFunis is excluded from law school on racial grounds, and when colleges or universities announce that normal academic openings will give preference to female candidates or those from racial minorities.

If reverse discrimination is prohibited by our constitutional and ethical commitments, what means of remedy and compensation are available? Obviously, those means which are consistent with those commitments. Our commitments assure the right to remedy to those who have been treated unjustly, but our government has not done enough to bring this right to meaningful fruition in practice. Sound progress has been made in recent years, especially since the Equal Employment Opportunity Act of 1972 and the establishment of the Equal Employment Opportunities Commission. This Act and other laws have extended anti-discrimination protection to over 60% of the population.[14] The Commission is now authorized to enforce anti-discrimination orders in court and, according to one report, it has negotiated out-of-court settlements which brought 44,000 minority workers over 46 million dollars in back-pay.[15] Undoubtedly this merely scratches the surface. But now the framework exists for translating the right to remedy into practice, not just for sloughing off race and sex as irrelevant criteria of differential treatment but other irrelevant criteria as well—age, religion, the size of hips (I am thinking of airline stewardesses), the length of nose, and so on.

Adequate remedy to overcome the sins of the past, not to speak of the present, would require the expenditure of vast sums for compensatory programs for those disadvantaged by past injustice in order to assure equal access. Such programs should be racially and sexually neutral, benefiting the disadvantaged of *whatever sex or race*. Such neutral compensatory programs would have a high proportion of blacks and other minorities as recipients, for they as members of these groups suffer more from the injustices of the past. But the basis of the compensation would be that fact, not sex or race. Neutral compensatory policies have definite theoretical and practical advantages in contrast to policies of reverse discrimination: Theoretical advantages, in that they are consistent with our basic constitutional and ethical commitments whereas reverse discrimination is not; practical advantages, in that their consistency, indeed their requirement by our constitutional and ethical commitments, means that they can marshall united support in overcoming inequalities whereas reverse discrimination, in my opinion, can not.

Notes

1. 94 S. Ct. 1704 (1974).
2. I hasten to add a qualification—more ambivalence!—resulting from discussion with Tom Beauchamp of Georgetown University. In cases of extreme recalcitrance to equal employment by

certain institutions or businesses some quota requirement (reverse discrimination) may be justified. I regard this as distinct from a general policy of reverse discrimination.

3. "Equal Treatment and Compensatory Discrimination," *Philosophy and Public Affairs*, 2 (Summer 1974).

4. *The Atlanta Journal and Constitution*, Sept. 22, 1974, p. 20-A.

5. For similar arguments see Lisa Newton, "Reverse Discrimination as Unjustified," *Ethics*, 83 (1973).

6. Richard A. Lester, *Antibias Regulation of Universities* (New York, 1974); discussed in *Newsweek*, July 15, 1974, p. 78.

7. See The Civil Rights Act of 1964, especially Title VII (which created the Equal Employment Opportunity Commission), amended by The Equal Employment Opportunity Act of 1972, found in *ABC's of The Equal Employment Opportunity Act*, prepared by the Editorial Staff of The Bureau of National Affairs, Inc., 1972. Affirmative Action Programs came into existence with Executive Order 11246. Requirements for affirmative action are found in the rules and regulations 41-CFR Part 60-2, Order #4 (Affirmative Action Programs) generally known as Executive Order #4 and Revised Order #4 41-CFT 60-2 B. For discussion see Paul Brownstein, "Affirmative Action Programs," in *Equal Employment Opportunities Compliance*, Practising Law Institute, New York City (1972), pp. 73–111.

8. See Brownstein, "Affirmative Action Programs" and, for example, *The University of Georgia Affirmative Action Plan*, Athens, Ga., 1973–74, viii, pp. 133, 67.

9. Brownstein and *The University of Georgia Affirmative Action Plan*, Athens, Ga., 1973–74, p. 71.

10. *Ibid.*, p. 69.

11. *Ibid.*, p. 71.

12. See the *Atlanta Journal and Constitution*, June 9, 1974, p. 26-D.

13. See *Atlanta Constitution*, June 7, 1974, p. 13-B.

14. *Newsweek*, June 17, 1974, p. 75.

15. *Ibid.*, p. 75.

Questions for Analysis

1. Why does Blackstone argue his case with a certain amount of "existential guilt"?

2. State the utilitarian argument for reverse discrimination.

3. Would it be accurate to say that Blackstone rejects utility as a legitimate standard for determining the morality of reverse discrimination?

4. Consider this proposition: "Blackstone is opposed to compensating those who have suffered past injustices." Is this statement true or false? Explain.

5. What are some of the problems that compensation raises?

6. Some people would claim that it is wrong to hold people today responsible for the wrongs of their ancestors; and that it is equally as wrong to compensate people today for the wrongs that their ancestors may have experienced. Do you agree? Explain your answers by appeal to some concept of justice.

7. What reasons does Blackstone offer for saying that affirmative action programs actually forbid reverse discrimination? Do you think his argument is persuasive? What objections to his interpretations might you raise?

8. Granted that reverse discrimination is prohibited by our constitution and ethical commitments, what means of redress are available? Do you agree that a vigorous and unflinching implementation of these means will satisfy the obligation to eradicate discrimination?

9. Explain the following statement: "Kant would agree with Blackstone's conclusion about reverse discrimination, but he would question the moral legitimacy of at least some of Blackstone's premises."

Reverse Discrimination as Unjustified

Lisa Newton

Professor of philosophy Lisa Newton delivered a version of the following essay, "Reverse Discrimination as Unjustified," at a meeting of the Society for Women in Philosophy in 1972. She argues that reverse discrimination cannot be justified by an appeal to the ideal of equality. Indeed, according to Newton, reverse discrimination does not advance but actually undermines equality because it violates the concept of equal justice under law for all citizens.

Specifically, Newton attacks the defense for reverse discrimination on grounds of equality. She contends that no violation of justice can be justified by an appeal to the ideal of equality, for the idea of equality is logically dependent on the notion of justice.

In addition to this theoretical objection to reverse discrimination, Newton opposes it because she believes it raises insoluble problems. Among them are: determining what groups have been sufficiently discriminated against in the past to deserve preferred treatment in the present; and determining the degree of reverse discrimination that will be compensatory. Newton concludes that reverse discrimination destroys justice, law, equality, and citizenship itself.

I have heard it argued that "simple justice" requires that we favor women and blacks in employment and educational opportunities, since women and blacks were "unjustly" excluded from such opportunities for so many years in the not so distant past. It is a strange argument, an example of a possible implication of a true proposition advanced to dispute the proposition itself, like an octopus absentmindedly slicing off his head with a stray tentacle. A fatal confusion underlies this argument, a confusion fundamentally relevant to our understanding of the notion of the rule of law.

Two senses of justice and equality are involved in this confusion. The root notion of justice, progenitor of the other, is the one that Aristotle (*Nichomachean Ethics* 5. 6; *Politics* 1.2; 3.1) assumes to be the foundation and proper virtue of the political association. It is the condition which free men establish among themselves when they "share a common life in order that their association bring them self-sufficiency"—the regulation of their relationship by law, and the establishment, by law, of equality before the law. Rule of law is the name and pattern of this justice; its equality stands against the inequalities—of wealth, talent, etc.—otherwise obtaining among its participants, who

by virtue of that equality are called "citizens." It is an achievement—complete, or, more frequently, partial—of certain people in certain concrete situations. It is fragile and easily disrupted by powerful individuals who discover that the blind equality of rule of law is inconvenient for their interests. Despite its obvious instability, Aristotle assumed that the establishment of justice in this sense, the creation of citizenship, was a permanent possibility for men and that the resultant association of citizens was the natural home of the species. At levels below the political association, this rule-governed equality is easily found; it is exemplified by any group of children agreeing together to play a game. At the level of the political association, the attainment of this justice is more difficult, simply because the stakes are so much higher for each participant. The equality of citizenship is not something that happens of its own accord, and without the expenditure of a fair amount of effort it will collapse into the rule of a powerful few over an apathetic many. But at least it has been achieved, at some times in some places; it is always worth trying to achieve, and eminently worth trying to maintain, wherever and to whatever degree it has been brought into being.

From Lisa H. Newton, *"Reverse Discrimination as Unjustified,"* Ethics 83 (1973): 308–312. Copyright ©1973 by The University of Chicago. Reprinted by permission of the publisher and the author.

Aristotle's parochialism is notorious; he really did not imagine that persons other than Greeks could associate freely in justice, and the only form of association he had in mind was the Greek *polis*. With the decline of the *polis* and the shift in the center of political thought, his notion of justice underwent a sea change. To be exact, it ceased to represent a political type and became a moral ideal: the ideal of equality as we know it. This ideal demands that all men be included in citizenship—that one Law govern all equally, that all men regard all other men as fellow citizens, with the same guarantees, rights, and protections. Briefly, it demands that the circle of citizenship achieved by any group be extended to include the entire human race. Properly understood, its effect on our associations can be excellent: It congratulates us on our achievement of rule of law as a process of government but refuses to let us remain complacent until we have expanded the associations to include others within the ambit of the rules, as often and as far as possible. While one man is a slave, none of us may feel truly free. We are constantly prodded by this ideal to look for possible unjustifiable discrimination, for inequalities not absolutely required for the functioning of the society and advantageous to all. And after twenty centuries of pressure, not at all constant, from this ideal, it might be said that some progress has been made. To take the cases in point for this problem, we are now prepared to assert, as Aristotle would never have been, the equality of sexes and of persons of different colors. The ambit of American citizenship, once restricted to white males of property, has been extended to include all adult free men, then all adult males including ex-slaves, then all women. The process of acquisition of full citizenship was for these groups a sporadic trail of half-measures, even now not complete; the steps on the road to full equality are marked by legislation and judicial decisions which are only recently concluded and still often not enforced. But the fact that we can now discuss the possibility of favoring such groups in hiring shows that over the area that concerns us, at least, full equality is presupposed as a basis for discussion. To that extent, they are full citizens, fully protected by the law of the land.

It is important for my argument that the moral ideal of equality be recognized as logically distinct from the condition (or virtue) of justice in the political sense. Justice in this sense exists *among* a citizenry, irrespective of the number of the populace included in that citizenry. Further, the moral ideal is parasitic upon the political virtue, for "equality" is unspecified—it means nothing until we are told in what respect that equality is to be realized. In a political context, "equality" is specified as "equal rights"—equal access to the public realm, public goods and offices, equal treatment under the law—in brief, the equality of citizenship. If citizenship is not a possibility, political equality is unintelligible. The ideal emerges as a generalization of the real condition and refers back to that condition for its content.

Now, if justice (Aristotle's justice in the political sense) is equal treatment under law for all citizens, what is injustice? Clearly, injustice is the violation of that equality, discriminating for or against a group of citizens, favoring them with special immunities and privileges or depriving them of those guaranteed to the others. When the southern employer refuses to hire blacks in white-collar jobs, when Wall Street will only hire women as secretaries with new titles, when Mississippi high schools routinely flunk all the black boys above ninth grade, we have examples of injustice, and we work to restore the equality of the public realm by ensuring that equal opportunity will be provided in such cases in the future. But of course, when the employers and the schools *favor* women and blacks, the same injustice is done. Just as the previous discrimination did, this reverse discrimination violates the public equality which defines citizenship and destroys the rule of law for the areas in which these favors are granted. To the extent that we adopt a program of discrimination, reverse or otherwise, justice in the political sense is destroyed, and none of us, specifically affected or not, is a citizen, a bearer of rights—we are all petitioners for favors. And to the same extent, the ideal of equality is undermined, for it has content only where justice obtains, and by destroying justice we render the ideal meaningless. It is, then, an ironic paradox, if not a contradiction in terms, to assert that the ideal of equality justifies the violation of justice; it is as if one should argue, with William Buckley, that an ideal of humanity can justify the destruction of the human race.

Logically, the conclusion is simple enough: All

discrimination is wrong prima facie because it violates justice, and that goes for reverse discrimination too. No violation of justice among the citizens may be justified (may overcome the prima facie objection) by appeal to the ideal of equality, for that ideal is logically dependent upon the notion of justice. Reverse discrimination, then, which attempts no other justification than an appeal to equality, is wrong. But let us try to make the conclusion more plausible by suggesting some of the implications of the suggested practice of reverse discrimination in employment and education. My argument will be that the problems raised there are insoluble, not only in practice but in principle.

We may argue, if we like, about what "discrimination" consists of. Do I discriminate against blacks if I admit none to my school when none of the black applicants are qualified by the tests I always give? How far must I go to root out cultural bias from my application forms and tests before I can say that I have not discriminated against those of different cultures? Can I assume that women are not strong enough to be roughnecks on my oil rigs, or must I test them individually? But this controversy, the most popular and well-argued aspect of the issue, is not as fatal as two others which cannot be avoided: If we are regarding the blacks as a "minority" victimized by discrimination, what is a "minority"? And for any group—blacks, women, whatever—that has been discriminated against, what amount of reverse discrimination wipes out the initial discrimination? Let us grant as true that women and blacks were discriminated against, even where laws forbade such discrimination, and grant for the sake of argument that a history of discrimination must be wiped out by reverse discrimination. What follows?

First, are there other groups which have been discriminated against? For they should have the same right of restitution. What about American Indians, Chicanos, Appalachian Mountain whites, Puerto Ricans, Jews, Cajuns, and Orientals? And if these are to be included, the principle according to which we specify a "minority" is simply the criterion of "ethnic (sub) group," and we're stuck with every hyphenated American in the lower-middle class clamoring for special privileges for *his* group—and with equal justification. For be it noted, when we run down the Harvard roster, we find not only a scarcity of blacks (in comparison with the proportion in the population) but an even more striking scarcity of those second-, third-, and fourth-generation ethnics who make up the loudest voice of Middle America. Shouldn't they demand *their* share? And eventually, the WASPs will have to form their own lobby; for they too are a minority. The point is simply this: There is no "majority" in America who will not mind giving up just a bit of their rights to make room for a favored minority. There are only other minorities, each of which is discriminated against by the favoring. The initial injustice is then repeated dozens of times, and if each minority is granted the same right of restitution as the others, an entire area of rule governance is dissolved into a pushing and shoving match between self-interested groups. Each works to catch the public eye and political popularity by whatever means of advertising and power politics lend themselves to the effort, to capitalize as much as possible on temporary popularity until the restless mob picks another group to feel sorry for. Hardly an edifying spectacle, and in the long run no one can benefit: The pie is no larger—it's just that instead of setting up and enforcing rules for getting a piece, we've turned the contest into a free-for-all, requiring much more effort for no larger a reward. It would be in the interests of all the participants to reestablish an objective rule to govern the process, carefully enforced and the same for all.

Second, supposing that we do manage to agree in general that women and blacks (and all the others) have some right of restitution, some right to a privileged place in the structure of opportunities for a while, how will we know when that while is up? How much privilege is enough? When will the guilt be gone, the price paid, the balance restored? What recompense is right for centuries of exclusion? What criterion tells us when we are done? Our experience with the Civil Rights movement shows us that agreement on these terms cannot be presupposed: A process that appears to some to be going at a mad gallop into a black takeover appears to the rest of us to be at a standstill. Should a practice of reverse discrimination be adopted, we may safely predict that just as some of us begin to see "a satisfactory start toward righting the balance," others of us will see that we "have already gone too far in the other direction" and will suggest that the discrimination ought to be reversed again. And such disagreement is inevitable, for the point is that we could not *possibly* have any criteria for evaluating the kind of recompense we have in mind. The context presumed by any discussion of restitution is the context of the rule of law: Law sets the rights of men and simultaneously sets the method for remedying the violation of those rights. You may exact suffering from others and/or damage payments for yourself if and only if the others have violated your rights; the suffering you have endured is not sufficient reason for them to suffer. And remedial rights exist only where there is law: Primary human rights are useful guides to legislation but cannot stand as reasons for awarding remedies for injuries sustained. But then, the context presupposed by any discussion of restitution is the context of preexistent full citizenship. No remedial rights could exist for the excluded; neither in law nor in logic does there exist a right to *sue* for a standing to sue.

From these two considerations, then, the difficulties with reverse discrimination become evident. Restitution for a disadvantaged group whose rights under the law have been violated is possible by legal means, but restitution for a disadvantaged group whose grievance is that there was no law to protect them simply is not. First, outside of the area of justice defined by the law, no sense can be made of "the group's rights," for no law recognizes that group or the individuals in it, qua members, as bearers of rights (hence *any* group can constitute itself as a disadvantaged minority in some sense and demand similar restitution). Second, outside of the area of protection of law, no sense can be made of the violation of rights (hence the amount of the recompense cannot be decided by any objective criterion). For both reasons, the practice of reverse discrimination undermines the foundation of the very ideal in whose name it is advocated; it destroys justice, law, equality, and citizenship itself, and replaces them with power struggles and popularity contests.

Questions for Analysis

1. What is the "fatal confusion" underlying the argument that "simple justice" requires *preferential treatment*?

2. Can you describe how justice under Aristotle moved from a "political type" to a "moral ideal"?

3. Why is it important for Newton's argument that she distinguish the moral ideal of equality from the condition of justice in the political sense?

4. Central to Newton's argument is her definition of justice and her assumptions about the relationship between justice and equality. Do you agree with her? Would you say her views are essentially nonconsequential?

5. Do you think that Rawls would agree with Newton's analysis? Explain.

6. Would you agree that in part Newton objects to reverse discrimination on utilitarian grounds? Explain.

7. Do you agree that the problems Newton says surround reverse discrimination really are "insoluble"?

CASE PRESENTATION
Cutback

Manuel Ortega was manager of the design department of Quilling Engineering, a division of Universal Business Equipment (UBE). Although business for Quilling had been brisk, UBE was feeling the pinch of a sluggish economy. So, UBE management had asked all its divisions to cut back costs by 12.5 percent.

Wanting to ensure that his company made this goal, the president of Quilling raised the cutback costs to 15 percent. Manuel didn't think this was right, and he told the president so. But the president insisted. So, like the "good soldier" he was, Manuel promised to implement the president's decision.

On the very day that he received his orders, Manuel informed his section heads to draw up plans reflecting the proposed cutback.

A few days later the plans came in, each listing project cuts and employees to be laid off. A note on one plan caught Manuel's eye: "One of the five engineers to be laid off is Barbara Marshall, the *only* female working in the design department."

"Oh, hell!" Manuel said to himself. Then, without hesitation, he removed from his desk a booklet containing UBE's policy about hiring women and minority group members. It read: "Managers should realize that they are expected to meet the equal opportunity goals within their departments, while at the same time meeting profit goals."

Manuel smiled. "Easier said than done," he muttered to himself.

Manuel took out Barbara Marshall's personnel file. A glance told him she was a 32-year-old divorced mother of two. Her progress reports indicated that she was cooperative, competent, and eager to learn. But they also pegged her as, at present, the least effective of the engineers in the design department.

In the days ahead, Manuel tried every way he could to transfer Marshall to another department without having to bump someone else. But it was impossible. He knew that, in the end, he'd have to either discharge Marshall and thus violate UBE policy, or keep her and dismiss a more valuable employee.

If she were a man, Manuel Ortega thought to himself, there wouldn't be any question. She'd be picking up her severance pay by now.

Questions for Analysis

1. *Given Ortega's two alternatives, which do you think is fairer? Explain.*

2. *Do you think a business like UBE has a moral obligation to help redress social inequities? If so, how far does that obligation extend? For example, would it go so far as to oblige Quilling to keep Barbara Marshall and allow an apparently more productive worker to go?*

3. *How would utilitarians—both act and rule—approach this problem?*

4. *Do you think that Kant would consider it morally justifiable to keep Barbara Marshall in order to satisfy affirmative action guidelines?*

CASE PRESENTATION
First Hired, First Fired

Marvin Alcott knew it was foolish. But, as a personnel director faced with a sticky decision, he couldn't help wishing that Frank Stimson were anything but a white male.

Things had been going so well with the firm's pilot program for training the hard-core unemployed for positions as assistant machinists. Just a month before, Alcott had placed 16 workers in the program, one of whom—indeed the first—was Frank Stimson. Having been out of work for the better part of a year and having no specific skills, Stimson had easily met the program's minimal qualifications for training.

A number of things about Stimson had impressed Alcott. It seemed that since returning from his two-year stint in Vietnam, Stimson had found nothing but tough employment sledding. In fact, as Stimson told it, if it hadn't been for the meager income his wife earned waitressing, he would have had to apply for welfare, something he strongly objected to on principle. As Stimson had said in the interview, "I was brought up to believe that you should carry your own weight. Anything less was being a leech, if you know what I mean." Then Stimson had explained how he didn't think it was right to expect society to bear the burden of what he termed a "misspent youth." Stimson had put it quite graphically: "Why should I expect others to pay for my screw-ups?" Predictably enough, when Alcott informed Stimson that he was the first trainee to be selected, Stimson was elated and expressed every desire to seize this opportunity to make something of himself.

Alcott chuckled on the first day of training when Stimson showed up for work a half-hour before the prescribed time. He appreciated Stimson's enthusiasm especially since it contrasted sharply with the apparent indifference of some other trainees.

After the first week of training, several instructors went out of their way to compliment Alcott on his selection of Stimson, while at the same time indicating that they'd had to admonish several other employees for being tardy, nonchalant, and generally uninterested in the opportunity that the program was providing them.

It's little wonder, then, that Marvin Alcott considered Frank Stimson his top job trainee. This is precisely what made the decision he faced so painful.

It seems that when the firm launched the program, it did so with the government's implicit promise to fund 16 positions. When the grant was actually issued, it covered only 15 trainees. Alcott was faced with having to drop one.

Being a thoughtful, sensitive, and fair man, Alcott was trying to determine the most equitable way to manage the cut. One possibility was a lottery. He'd simply put the names of the candidates into a hat and draw one to be dropped. He had also considered making the drop on the basis of apparent job potential.

But whatever method he contemplated, Alcott was haunted by the fact that Stimson was a white male. The other 15 trainees were members of minority groups and women, and Alcott was keenly aware of affirmative action guidelines that prescribed benefits for members of traditionally disadvantaged groups. In short, there was a real question in his mind whether he'd endanger the entire program should he decide to drop one of the 15 disadvantaged members.

Above all else Alcott wanted to be fair. There was no doubt in his mind that from what he and other company officials had observed, Stimson was the most promising trainee in the program. At the same time, he felt the press of fairness to members of groups traditionally discriminated against, which left him questioning the fairness of perhaps the most obvious solution: Drop the last selected.

Questions for Analysis

1. *What should Alcott do?*

2. *What moral directions do the ethical theories provide?*

3. *In the event that Alcott decides to drop Stimson, does he have an obligation to make a case to the firm for underwriting Stimson's training? Do you think the firm has a moral obligation to do this?*

Selections for Further Reading

Amundsen, Kirsten. *The Silenced Majority: Women and American Democracy.* Englewood Cliffs, N.J.: Prentice-Hall, 1971.

Beauvoir, Simone de. *The Second Sex.* H. M. Parshley, Trans. New York: Knopf, 1953.

Bier, Caroline. *Women in Modern Life.* Bronx, N.Y.: Fordham University Press, 1968.

Bird, Caroline, and Briller, Sara Welles. *Born Female: The High Cost of Keeping Women Down.* New York: McKay, 1970.

Doriot, George, Ed. *The Management of Racial Integration in Business.* New York: McGraw-Hill, 1965.

Kothe, Charles A. *A Tale of Twenty-Two Cities: Report on Title VII of the Civil Rights Act of 1964.* Washington, D.C.: National Association of Manufacturers, 1965.

Mill, John Stuart, and Mill, Harriet T. *Essays on Sex Equality.* Alice C. Rossi, Ed. Chicago: University of Chicago Press, 1970.

9
WORLD HUNGER AND ECONOMIC INJUSTICE

There is no question that much of the world population literally are starving to death. Recent figures estimate that at least 10,000 people die of starvation every day, that as many as two billion more are malnourished; that annually 14,000 children in India alone go blind because of insufficient protein. In short, two-thirds of the world's population are caught on a seemingly irreversible treadmill of hunger-sickness-death.

We in the other one-third, in the West, are lucky. Rarely, if ever, do any of us directly experience the unkind fate of the world's starving masses. Fortunate to have been born in a land of plenty, we seldom realize that altogether we feed our house pets each day enough protein to meet the daily nutritional needs of hundreds of thousands of people, that we throw away in one week more food than countless people will see in a year. Even for those who are aware of massive world starvation, the problem remains remote, even abstract, to many. But to those facing starvation, the problem is not only real, immediate, and paramount, it also appears to have no escape, except in death.

With the disparity between those who have and those who have not, a moral question of considerable importance emerges: Do the affluent nations of the world have any moral obligation to help the world's starving masses? If we answer affirmatively, then precisely how should these nations go about sharing their wealth? Stated in more global terms: How should the world's goods be distributed? This last question makes explicit the issue of economic justice, which is implied in the issue of moral obligation and world hunger.

In this final chapter, then, we confront two questions of considerable moral importance. The first is whether the affluent nations have an obligation to help the starving nations; the second concerns the fairest distribution of the world's wealth. While these questions are distinct, they are not easily separated. Indeed, as we will see, many of the arguments for an obligation to help are rooted in a concept of economic justice. For this reason, we will consider first the issue of economic justice, then relate it to the problem of moral obligation and world hunger.

Initial Considerations

A whole cluster of moral problems surrounds the issues of world hunger and economic justice. Let us catalogue some of them before turning to this chapter's main concerns.

One of these problems concerns the right to our own property or holdings. Often it is argued, for example, that the right to property functions as a quasi-absolute right, which in effect means that I can do with my holdings virtually whatever I please. If I choose to squander my wealth while others need it to survive, presumably I am free to do that. But am I? Is the property right so extensive? Many think not. They argue that my right to my holdings is limited by the satisfaction of the basic needs of other people. Yes, they say, I may do with my wealth whatever I choose, but only after the basic needs of others have been satisfied. But what "others" are intended? Relatives, friends, neighbors, fellow citizens, everyone? There seems no clear answer to this.

Related to our property rights is how we obtained our holdings. Many argue that if property rights exist, they apply only to what an owner has acquired legally and morally. Suppose a particular man is made wealthy by inheriting a fortune, much of which was amassed in the distant past through the dishonesty and ruthless exploitation of others. While the person himself may be virtuous as a monk, his holdings are tainted. What are we to say about his rights to what he "owns"? The same question may be asked about a nation's wealth acquired through years of dubious moral conduct. Does the nation, therefore, have no claim to its wealth, or no right to determine how it shall spend the riches? Indeed, how can we separate "clean" from "dirty" money anyway?

Clearly the issue of how far property rights extend bears on the question of world hunger. For if I have a quasi-absolute right to dispose of my property however I choose—no matter the source of that property, then I have no obligation to help the starving masses. But if that right is subordinate to the claims of those seeking to satisfy maintenance needs, then I could have an obligation to help them.

Also bearing on moral obligation and world hunger are the likely effects of massive food relief. What will happen if the affluent nations continue to feed the peoples of destitute nations? Many claim that the long-term results will spell catastrophe. These Neo-Malthusians,[1] as they are sometimes called, predict that food relief will only swell the populations of nations already bursting with more people than they can support. By this account, food relief will increase the net suffering and deprivation not only of recipients but of donors as well. Not everyone agrees, however. Many claim that such dire projections are exaggerated. More important, they say that such a horrifying scenario could develop only if food relief is not coupled with developmental assistance aimed at improving productivity through modernizing agriculture. All this raises still another issue.

If the rich nations have an obligation to help the poor ones, just what sort of

---

1. *Named after the English economist John Malthus (1766–1834), who argued that population tends to increase faster than the means of subsistence, unless checked by such factors as war and famine.*

help are they obliged to provide? It is possible to identify at least three kinds of aid that affluent nations such as the United States give to poor nations. The first is developmental assistance, aid designed to help underdeveloped countries educationally and technologically to accumulate capital and raise their standards of living. A second is emergency famine or disaster relief, given in the wake of natural disasters such as drought, flood, and earthquake. A third is relief for countries suffering chronic famine because their birth rate far exceeds their actual or potential productivity. If rich nations are obliged to help, just which, if any, of these categories of aid are they obliged to provide?

Some would argue that affluent nations should give only emergency aid; others that they should give only emergency and developmental aid; still others that they should give all three. One common position among Neo-Malthusians is that rich nations should not provide any aid in the third category.

The issue of which kind of aid is to be given is clearly inseparable from the question of who should receive the aid. Perhaps we should dole out aid by *triage*, a method of allocating resources used first by the French during World War I. The French sorted their wounded into three categories and allocated scarce medical resources and medical aid on that basis. Those with superficial injuries were given immediate emergency attention; those beyond hope were allowed to die; and those with serious wounds who could be helped to survive were given the lion's share of intensive care. Applied to the starving nations of the world, the method of triage might classify the nations as: (1) those with slight food problems who will survive even without aid; (2) those with serious food problems who can benefit from help because they are ready to take steps to control their populations and increase their productivity; (3) those whose problems cannot be solved because they are not prepared to take any measures to help themselves. Given these classifications, some would say, "Yes, affluent nations have an obligation to provide help, but only to those nations falling into categories (1) and (2)." Indeed, they might and sometimes do argue that rich nations have an obligation *not* to help nations in category (3). Opposed to these positions are those who say the worst-off nations should receive immediate and massive aid. Such appears to be the United States' position. Of course, the question of who, if anyone, ought to receive help grows ever darker as resources dwindle.

Finally, if there is an obligation to help, whose obligation is it? Is it the obligation of an individual, you and I personally? A nation, such as the United States? A group of nations, perhaps through an international organization such as the United Nations? Our discussion here of world hunger and economic justice focuses on possible obligations that richer nations have to poorer ones. But it is also perfectly reasonable to ask: Can a nation have obligations? Is it sensible to attribute rights, duties, and obligations to some disembodied entity called a nation? And if it is, to whom do nations have responsibilities and against whom do they have claims—other nations, individuals, a combination?

These are only some of the questions that make world hunger and economic justice extraordinarily complex issues. They are questions that can be investigated thoroughly only in a study of social philosophy. Given the narrow scope of our present study, we can merely draw these issues to the reader's attention and encourage a deeper investigation of them elsewhere.

Economic Justice

Economic justice refers to what people deserve economically. The question of moral obligation regarding world hunger is inseparable from the issue of economic justice. To see why, consider this simple example.

Suppose you are walking down a big-city street with a friend. You are approached by a beggar who asks, "You got some change for a meal, pal?" You fish into your pocket for a couple of quarters and hand them to the man. The man thanks you and moves on.

Your friend is outraged. "Why did you do that?" she asks you, in a most disapproving tone.

"Because the guy needed to eat," you reply.

"But the guy was a bum!" she points out. "Let him get a job, not a handout!"

Presumably you feel you have an obligation to help the beggar, but your friend does not. In fact, she seems to think she has an obligation *not* to help him. But notice the reasons behind these judgments, reasons that imply full-blown views on what people deserve economically. On the one hand, you feel the beggar deserves something simply because he *needs* it. Your friend believes you should not give the beggar anything because of the kind of person he is (a "bum") and because he has done nothing to help himself. For her, *need* is not as much a determinant of economic desert as are *merit* and *effort*. For both of you, economic justice is associated with some view of distributive justice.

Distributive Justice

The subject of economic desert touches numerous areas, from jobs to income to taxes to world resources. Thus, questions of economic justice would include: How ought jobs be awarded? How should income and taxes be determined? What is the fairest way to allocate the wealth of the world? Any answer to these questions inevitably implies a working principle of *distributive justice, that is, an assumption about what is the proper way of passing out the wealth of a society.* For example, people commonly say: "Jobs should be awarded on the basis of merit." "Income should be determined on the basis of contribution to society or on the degree of preparation for a job." "Taxes should be assessed on the basis of ability to pay." Each statement implies some standard that should be considered in the distribution of society's wealth: merit, contribution and effort, capacity. Whether or not these or other principles should be taken into account is a basic concern of economic justice.

Such a question is also basic to the issue of worldwide hunger. To illustrate, some argue that the affluent nations have a moral obligation to help feed the hungry nations simply because the latter need help. Others argue that the affluent nations do not have an obligation to share what they have because they have a proprietary right to what they have earned and may dispose of it however they choose. Still others argue that only starving nations that attempt to help themselves (as, for example, by controlling their populations) should receive help. Again, underlying each of these positions is a principle of distributive justice. Thus, in the matter of world hunger, some believe *need* ought to determine the distribution of aid; others feel that *merit* should; and still others that *effort* should.

Whether the entity under consideration is a business, a society, or the world, serious questions of distributive and economic justice arise as soon as we begin to speculate about how—on what basis—the wealth of the entity ought to be parceled out. Well, just what are the options? What are the vying principles on the basis of which we can mete out economic justice? There appear to be five likely candidates, which bear on world hunger: (1) equality, (2) need, (3) merit or achievement, (4) contribution, and (5) effort. The first two can be viewed as equalitarian principles, the last three as desert principles.

EQUALITY.   The principle of equality would give each individual an equal share in the distribution, for, it is claimed, as human beings they deserve to be treated equally. By this account, every individual in a society would be entitled to the same portion of a society's goods as every other individual in the society.

Notice that the principle of equality ignores individual merit, contribution, and effort. Most importantly, claim its critics, it overlooks need. Is a pattern of distribution that ignores individual differences fair? Is any distribution that results from it equitable?

To see the thrust of this criticism, consider that I may need more food than you; and you may need more money than I; and both of us may need less medical attention than somebody else. Under strict equality distribution, each of us would receive identical shares of the goods and services available. Clearly, there would be no guarantee that any one of us would receive all that we need.

Applied to world hunger, the equality principle would lead to equal shares of the world's food for all the peoples of the world, presumably on a person-by-person basis. Conceivably, as a result of such equal distribution, some individuals who need more food than others might be left malnourished. Or possibly, those starving to death might, as a result of a greater share of food, not only live but add to their nation's population problems, which in turn would reduce the individual share. Operational problems such as these have caused some people, who want some sort of equalitarian principle, to turn to a different consideration.

NEED.   The principle of need would give to each individual according to his or her needs. Notice that this principle is, like the preceding, an equalitarian principle, in that it treats everyone equally. By the principle of need, each of us should get exactly what we require. Clearly, this principle, unlike the first, squarely faces the problem of differences among individuals. However, it too has several operational challenges.

In a world of limited resources, priorities must be set. Needs must be ranked. But what needs are to receive top priority? After we answer that question, how do we establish whose needs shall be met among those with similar needs when there is not enough to satisfy the needs of all? For example, suppose we give top priority to the need for enough food to maintain life. Taking a global view, let us suppose that a very needy nation will survive if given enough food because it is prepared to take population control measures. In contrast, another even needier nation probably will not survive even with massive food aid, because it is not prepared to take any population control measures. Now, let us say that if we fully satisfy the needs of the more desperate nation, we will not be able to satisfy the food needs of the less desperate one. Should we, nevertheless, give the lion's share of the available food to the nation that appears doomed?

As indicated, both the principle of equality and of need rest on considerations of equality, on treating people the same way. The first claims that everyone should receive an equal share; the second holds that everyone should get the share they need. In contrast, the next three principles emphasize desert, not equal treatment.

MERIT OR ACHIEVEMENT.   The principle of merit or achievement would give to each individual according to the kind of person he or she is or the characteristics he or she has. But just what types of characteristic should we consider? Skill, some say. But what kind of skills? If we introduce native skills or inherited aptitude as a basis of desert, then we seem to reward and punish individuals for their genetic inheritances. But, since none of us has an opportunity to choose our genes, is it fair that we should be judged on them? Perhaps we should consider acquired or learned skills. While perhaps a fairer consideration than the genetic calculus, acquired skills to a large degree depend on native skills. True, the degree to which we develop our skills is greatly influenced by individual effort: practice, drill, perseverance. But to introduce *effort* as a principle of justice is to depart from the principle of merit or achievement. After all, effort refers to labor; merit to productivity.

Others who advocate merit or achievement want to evaluate merit in terms of virtue. Thus, those individuals who show character qualities such as kindness, courage, diligence, reliability, and the like should receive a greater share of the economic pie than those who do not or who are cruel, cowardly, careless, and irresponsible. But by what standard are these traits to be isolated and measured? And even if we can locate and calculate them, are such qualities the sort of things that we want to make economic allotments for? Critics argue that by definition acts of virtue must result from motives other than pecuniary ones, that tying virtue to material rewards undermines the nature of virtue itself.

Others who espouse principles based on desert focus their nonequalitarian theories not on what one is, but on what one has done. The final two principles typify these views.

CONTRIBUTION.   The principle of contribution would give each individual precisely that portion of a society's wealth that he or she has produced. But in as complex a society and economy as ours, this is extraordinarily difficult to determine, if possible at all. It requires not only a precise measurement of the contribution, but an evaluation of its significance toward creating a society's wealth. In the production, say, of a car, what is the comparable worth of the contribution of the designer, the engineer, the assembler, the retailer, the stockholder, and the numerous others involved in the production and sale of the automobile? Or, how is the artist's contribution to society to be measured? What about the persons who collect our garbage, wash our laundry, cut our hair?

It might be easier to evaluate the contribution of nations to the world's wealth. Just look at their gross national products. Maybe the world resources should be distributed on that basis: Nations will get back exactly the proportion of the world's food supply that they themselves have created. But is this fair? Surely there is a measure of fortune, of chance, in the development of nations. Like individuals, some nations appear to have begun with a head start; they have had more to work with, to develop and exploit. Also, there is always a line of social factors stretching far back into a nation's history that help account for its present economic stature. In short, individuals have no say over the society or nations they are born into. To expect them to reverse in their lifetimes the historical interplay of natural and social forces, or to penalize them by neglect for the decisions and actions of those long since dead, hardly seems fair.

EFFORT.   The principle of effort would give to each according to the degree of his or her labor. Like the principle of contribution, effort focuses on what people have done, not on what they are. But unlike contribution, the principle of effort is not concerned with what individuals have produced, but on the effort they make. By this account, the nature of one's job is irrelevant to justice. Equal effort requires equal remuneration. But how is effort to be measured? Effort appears to be relative to the individual who is doing the work. The effort you expend in writing an essay might be far greater than someone else's because that person happens to be a more "gifted" writer. Also, the degree to which we extend ourselves is largely determined by genetic and early environmental factors.

As with compensation, we might apply the effort principle more easily to nations than to individuals. For example, we might distribute food according to the effort a nation has made to become self-sufficient, as, for example, by controlling its population, utilizing its natural resources, and modernizing its agriculture. Having identified nations who have made the greatest effort, we might evaluate individuals within those nations by the same criteria. It is difficult, however, in instances such as these to separate effort from results. In some cases, the results are appalling; but that does not necessarily mean that the effort was lacking. After all, birth control programs often are required to take hold in the soil of superstition, social taboos, and invincible ignorance. True, a country may fail to control its population, but perhaps not for the lack of effort. The effort simply may be no match for the gargantuan obstacles to be overcome.

These, then, are some common candidates for principles of economic justice. Some people base their views of proper distribution on a single principle. Others appeal to a combination. Whatever one's approach, it will underlie one's position on the issue of moral obligation and world hunger.

Arguments for an Obligation to Help

1. *All human beings have equal rights to the necessities of life.*

POINT: "Where people are treated differently, the different treatment should be based on their freely chosen actions and not on accidents of their birth. But look around you and what do you see? Millions of people who are starving, not because of some action of their own but because they were unlucky enough to be born in a most hostile and unforgiving environment. To ignore their plight is the height of moral callousness. We have an obligation to help the starving for one reason and one reason only: They are human beings, and as human beings they have the same rights that we all do to the necessities of life."

COUNTERPOINT: "What you say sounds fine until one realizes that it flies in the face of fact. Don't you see that if we equally shared what we have with the starving people of the world, then all of us would end up suffering? There simply isn't enough food to go around. So, if we did what you propose we must, everybody would end up malnourished."

2. *People are required to help prevent suffering.*

POINT: "I agree that it's irrational to ask people to help others when such help is going to create great hardship for the 'good samaritans' themselves. But it's altogether reasonable to expect people to help if by so doing they don't seriously injure themselves. This is precisely the situation with world hunger. Two-thirds of the world's people—the so-called Third World—are malnourished. The remaining one-third—the West—are consuming two-thirds of the world's resources. Now, surely that affluent one-third could share their resources and help feed the starving masses, without imperiling themselves. They could and they are obliged to—at least up to the point where any more help would cause them as much suffering as it would prevent. We in the West are far from having reached that point. Just where that point is, it's impossible to say. But surely, since we're dealing with millions of human lives, we are obligated to extend ourselves, even if it means great personal sacrifice and a radical change in our life styles. After all, by no measure of decency can it be seriously and respectably argued that we are justified in feeding our cats and dogs each day enough protein to meet the daily requirements of thousands of people, who, for lack of protein, are contracting horrible diseases and even dying. We must give, and give until it hurts, to the degree commensurate with the suffering of those starving."

COUNTERPOINT: "I know I must sound like an arch villain to criticize an argument in behalf of the starving masses, but criticize I must. Let's assume for argument's sake that the affluent Western nations share their food until every Westerner is just well-nourished, no more. At that point the surplus of food is distributed equally to the remaining two-thirds of the world's population. Even then the Third World peoples would still be malnourished. My point is that there simply isn't enough food currently available to feed everyone on an equal basis. And if you're suggesting that the affluent nations should share to the point of leaving themselves malnourished, what's the logic behind that? Is the world better off having four-fifths, five-sixths, maybe even 100 percent of its population malnourished rather than two-thirds? All this aside, why do you focus exclusively on the 'rights' of the starving? What about the rights of the affluent? They're human beings, too, you know. On what grounds is it justifiable to expect them to 'give until it hurts, to a degree commensurate with the suffering of the starving'?"

3.   *Human beings have a right to be saved from starvation.*

POINT: "Those who claim that the affluent nations have no obligation to help the starving forget what we're dealing with: individual, flesh-and-blood human beings. Human beings who have the same needs, fears, and pains as you or I do. When they ask for help, they're not merely begging for charity or pleading for us to be benevolent. To insist that they are is to elevate their plight to the level of a street-corner beggar and to reduce the urgency of their plea to the level of backalley panhandling. But don't kid yourself—the need of these people is neither trivial nor manufactured. Their need is real and dire, and desperate need creates obligations and rights. The starving person has a moral right to get help from those in a position to provide it. This right derives from a more general right to be saved from preventible death due to deprivation, and this general right is based on human need. The bottom line is that anyone starving to death has a right to the goods and services that will prevent his or her death by deprivation. And if you or I happen to have the necessary goods and services, then we have an obligation to prevent the person's death. So, it's quite clear that the affluent nations are obliged to help the world's starving masses. Should they fail to try to meet this obligation, they will be guilty of an act as morally reprehensible as if they had taken a direct action to kill these people."

COUNTERPOINT: "Although I can sympathize with the sincerity, even urgency, of your appeal, I can't get a handle on what you mean by a 'right based on need.' I can understand moral rights resulting from promises, or from special roles and relationships. But when you talk of a right based on need, you lose me. But I'll grant that there could be such a category of 'need rights.' Even so, the whole concept is terribly vague. For example, I have a tough time distinguishing 'needs' from 'wants' or 'wishes.' Then there's the matter of how intense a need must be to be considered a right. Some people undoubtedly have a profound 'need' to be loved, and if this need is not met, they seem to languish. Does that mean they have a right to be loved, and that someone has an obligation to provide that love? Another thing: Assuming that a need can be the basis of a right, whom, if anyone, is this right correctly claimed against? Suppose, for example, that we consider a person's need for medical care a right. Precisely whom is this claim made against? If I didn't put the person in the condition of need, why should I be obligated? Then there's the matter of conflicting rights. It's generally acknowledged that individuals and nations have a right to control their resources and property. Does a right based on need automatically take precedence over such ownership rights? If so, why? It could very well be that your central argument is cogent. But until you clear up this concept of 'need right,' I'll remain unconvinced.''

Arguments for an Obligation Not to Help

1.   *Helping will actually damage some recipient nations.*

POINT: ''There's no question that a number of Third World countries have exceeded their 'carrying capacity.' In simple English, that means their populations exceed their productivity. They neither are nor can be self-sufficient. So, if we give aid to countries whose reproduction has outstripped their productivity, all we do is increase their population without increasing their rate of productivity. The ironic result is that we increase the number of starving people and produce a net loss of life and a net increase in human misery. Now don't misunderstand. I'm not objecting to our helping countries in biological balance, countries whose populations haven't so outpaced their production that they can never be self-sufficient. On the contrary, I think we ought to help such countries, and also of course those in need of emergency famine or disaster relief. But I don't think we have an obligation to help if by helping we actually increase the net suffering of a recipient country. And this is precisely what we will do in the case of many countries. In fact, it would be immoral to help, since by 'helping' we would create more pain.''

COUNTERPOINT: ''First of all, how does one determine precisely the point at which a country has exceeded its 'carrying capacity'? What criteria do you use to determine that a country can never be self-sufficient? Your whole argument assumes that we can clearly identify population trends that indicate major worldwide population growth. And it also assumes that these trends are irreversible. But why couldn't immediate food assistance together with developmental assistance aimed at improved food production contain and even wipe out widespread hunger? India is a case in point. Far from being hopelessly overpopulated, India actually reduced its population growth rate in many areas as a result of a well-planned birth control effort. Specifically, during India's third 'Five Year Plan' (1961–1966), the birth rate in Bombay actually declined to only 27 per 1000 population, which is only slightly higher than the U.S. rate, 23 per 1000.[2] True, this was the most impressive result in the country, but there were other promising signs. For example, in one rural district of West Bengal the birth rate dropped from 43 to 36 per 1000. Such results suggest that the hopeless picture you paint grossly distorts the plights of these countries.''

2.   *Helping would ultimately threaten the human species.*

POINT: ''Consider a couple of sobering facts. The population of the two-thirds of the world that we call the 'Third World' is increasing more than twice as fast as the population of the one-third we call 'affluent.' What's more, if you

2.   B. L. Raina, ''India,'' *in* Family Planning and Populations Programs: A Review of World Developments, *ed. Bernard Berelson (Chicago: University of Chicago Press, 1966), pp. 111–122.*

compare most Third World countries with just the United States, you'll find that their populations are doubling *three* or *four* times as fast as the U.S. population! Now, suppose we decide to share what we have with these starving nations. What do you think things would be like by the end of this century? Each one of us in the United States would be sharing our resources with about a dozen people. Even if there were still enough to go around, contemplate the miserable conditions we'd all be living under. Of course, ultimately it wouldn't be a question of quality of life; there simply wouldn't be any life left! That's right, the human species would die out. So, not only do the affluent nations have *no* obligation to help the starving peoples of the world, they *must not* share their food or even provide developmental assistance. Their moral obligation is to the species, to future generations. Above everything else, we, the affluent, must ensure our own survival by retaining a safety factor of surplus and by preserving the environment for posterity."

COUNTERPOINT: "Again, you assume not only that population trends are identifiable but that they're not reversible. I remind you of India's experiences, and caution you about such distortive population projections as the ones you make. It wasn't too long ago, you know, that China faced widespread starvation problems. Many people termed China's plight 'hopeless.' But today China's huge population is adequately fed. What happened? To put it in the vernacular, China got its agricultural act together. So, your doomsday forecasts are very misleading. Even worse, they do a dreadful, and potentially fatal, disservice to the world's poor by making their plight appear hopeless and, thus, futile to address. I'll give you an example of what I mean. Remember the starvation problem that Bangladesh faced a few years ago? Well, recall how the media represented it. The only pictures that ever appeared in our newspapers and on our television screens were of children and adults with bellies swollen with hunger. No wonder a lot of people in this country got the impression that Bangladesh was beyond hope. But the fact of the matter is that the majority of Bangladeshi have enough to get by and that Bangladesh potentially has one of the world's richest croplands. 'Potentially'—it all depends on whether a well-formulated aid program is forthcoming. But judging from the reporting on Bangladesh, we understandably considered their plight hopeless. In the last analysis, short-term relief programs coupled with long-range population control programs and assistance to improve local agriculture could minimize if not eradicate starvation."

Argument for Helping as Morally Permissible But Not Obligatory

1. *Helping is an act of charity.*

POINT: "Helping the starving people of the world isn't something we must or must not do. It's something we can do, if we choose. In other words, we should look on such help as charity or benevolence. As with any act of charity, we are not obligated to perform it. Sure, it might be nice if we did, even desirable, noble. But it's not required of us. After all, we have a right to our property and can dispose of it pretty much however we choose. If we choose to share what we have, fine; but we have no duty to do so. The difference between a duty and an option to help is that with a duty we may be required to help even if we don't want to. With an option we may help if we want to, but we're not required to if we don't want to. So, helping to feed the world's needy is an option that the well-fed have. In the last analysis, it's an act of charity or benevolence, but not a duty."

COUNTERPOINT: "Your argument ignores important aspects of the other two positions—(1) that we have a duty to help, (2) that we have a duty not to help. I think those people supporting position (1) can legitimately ask: Why do you relegate something as important as preventing massive starvation to 'charity'? If we don't have a duty to help prevent human misery and death, just what duties do we have? To leave such a momentous issue to the benevolent urges of individuals and nations is wholly unrealistic. Furthermore, you imply that personal property rights are extensive, if not unlimited. Maybe they are, but I find it hard to argue that I have a right to something that is not necessary, such as a second car or a swimming pool, even when others will die unless they have the food that can otherwise be purchased with the money used to buy these things. If an affluent nation could save millions of people from starvation by diverting a fraction of its GNP into developmental assistance or hunger relief, would that country be morally justified in retaining that wealth? Besides, you don't for a minute consider how the affluent obtained their wealth, which may be morally suspect. Do we have moral rights to what we've acquired nefariously? Similarly, I think those supporting position (2) are justified in pointing out that whether the help springs from charity or duty, the result is the same. And, according to the Neo-Malthusians, the result isn't good; in fact it's calculated to cause overpopulation and increase human misery for recipients and donors alike. Are these dire futuristic projections mistaken, or irrelevant? You're going to have to deal with this question before you can convince any Neo-Malthusian of the merit of your argument."

Ethical Theories

Egoism

Any egoistic concept of justice would be tied to consequences for self. Thus, what is "fair" is what is most productive of the egoist's best long-term interests. By this account, the affluent egoist would likely, but not necessarily, associate economic justice with one or more of the principles of desert, since these appear more productive of his or her own best interests than either of the equalitarian principles. Following this line, the affluent egoist certainly would not recognize any prima facie obligation to help that springs from consideration of an individual's right to the necessities of life or to be saved from starvation. But egoists would consider very seriously the futuristic projections of those who argue for an obligation not to help, since these arguments involve consequences that may have impact for the egoist.

It is tempting to conclude from this assessment that affluent egoists likely would oppose helping the starving. While in many cases they would, an egoistic calculation does not necessarily lead to this conclusion. In cases where their own interests are served, egoists would feel justified in helping, even obliged to help. But, again, they would not recognize any outstanding *duty* to help those starving. According to egoism, if we do have an obligation to help, we do only because helping will advance our best long-term interests.

Act Utilitarianism

Both versions of utilitarianism associate justice with efficiency or the utility principle. What is fair is what is productive of the common good. For the act utilitarian what is productive of the greatest happiness can vary from situation to situation, and thus so can what is considered fair. In some cases, the fair act may be to give an equal share to everyone; in other cases it may be fair to give to each according to his or her needs; in still other cases, what is fair may be to give to each according to individual contribution. The key factor is that the act utilitarian's endorsement of any pattern of distribution is contingent, that is, dependent on which pattern will likely produce the most common good in a particular situation.

Act utilitarians presumably would address world hunger on a case-by-case basis. In all instances they would use the utility principle to determine whether help ought to be given. Of utmost importance in this calculation would be Neo-Malthusian forecasts, since these suggest that aid might in the long run produce a net increase in pain and suffering. If that is true, then the act utilitarian would feel justified and obliged in not providing help.

Rule Utilitarianism

Much of the foregoing discussion about act utilitarianism also applies to rule utilitarianism, except of course the rule utilitarian is concerned with the rule under which an act falls. There seem to be essentially two rules involved in the issue of moral obligation and world hunger. The first deals with whether help should be given. Thus, the rule utilitarian must evaluate whether the rule that says "Rich nations ought to help poor nations satisfy basic needs" generally produces more total good than its contradiction, which would allow for at least discriminate aid. The answer largely depends on the projected consequences of giving aid. If the doomsday forecasters are correct, then the consequences of following that rule probably would not produce the greatest happiness. If the forecasts are inaccurate, then following the rule may be of greater benefit. Since the accuracy of the forecasts is still undetermined, it is impossible to calculate the relative merit of the rule. If a rule allowing at least discriminate aid to starving peoples promises the most collective benefit, the rule utilitarian then must determine how the goods ought to be distributed. This would entail formulating a second rule stating which pattern or patterns of distribution are calculated to produce the most common good. Just what the pattern or patterns would be is impossible to say. In terms of utility, no single principle seems necessarily the most productive of the common good. Perhaps a combination of principles would be in order.

One way the rule utilitarian could possibly approach both problems—whether help ought to be given and, if so, how—is to categorize the candidates for aid by the triage method. The rule utilitarian might then formulate a rule such that help is given only to those with the best chance of survival. Such a rule would respond not only to the question of whether help ought to be given, but also imply some principles of distribution—need and effort. But, of course, the rule would have to be shown the most productive of the common good.

Divine Command

Generally, nonconsequential theories would give far greater weight to equalitarian principles than to desert principles in distributing the goods of the world. Thus, divine command theorists would argue that basic needs take priority over other concerns. They might argue that when there is economic abundance, then an individual's claims to life and to the conditions necessary to maintain life are claims that all individuals as creatures of God make with perfect equality. Thus, on personal and collective levels we have an obligation to help the starving peoples of the world. In fact, divine command theorists would argue that this obligation increases as the gap between those who have and those who have not widens. After everyone's basic needs have been met, however, then the basis for sharing what we have—that is, the basis of human need—dissolves. At that point, the principles of contribution and effort would be acceptable bases for distributing goods. Thus, once basic needs have been met, considerations of desert, especially contribution and effort, would play an increasing role in the distribution of economic surplus or luxury goods. The reason for this is that while we all share a common God-given nature, at the same time we are divinely created *individuals*. Distributing goods equally, after all maintenance needs have been satisfied, seemingly flouts this individuality; distributing them on the basis of desert recognizes, even encourages, what makes each of us as individuals unique.

Categorical Imperative

Kant's view of justice is based on a consideration of giving people what they are due by reason of their being rational, autonomous creatures. Certainly, people need whatever is necessary to preserve their status as rational, autonomous creatures. Food would be paramount. Thus, Kant would support the proposition that we have an obligation to help satisfy the basic maintenance needs of others. He would endorse the three chief arguments for such an obligation: (1) that all human beings have an equal right to the necessities of life, (2) that people are required to help prevent suffering, (3) that human beings have a right to be saved from starvation. As maxims of behavior, these propositions constitute moral imperatives. Violating any of them is always immoral. Once these maintenance needs are satisfied, however, then principles of justice based on desert would be more in keeping with the nature of a rational, autonomous being.

With this said, we should quickly add a postscript. Kant's ethics put no one under obligation to help prevent suffering and death at the cost of one's own health or life. Indeed, taken with full knowledge, such an action would be self-destructive, tantamount to suicide. Thus, if we knew beyond doubt that aiding or helping the starving masses, in effect, would spell the end of the species as we know it or would directly lead to even more deaths than not helping would, then we would be obliged to refrain from giving the aid. We can infer from this that the accuracy of Neo-Malthusian forecasts would be most important in the Kantian analysis, not from the view of desirable or undesirable consequences, but from the standpoint of acting in a way consistent with the nature of rational, autonomous beings, and of treating people with the respect and dignity they deserve.

In short, while we are obliged to "help the starving," in Kant's view, we are not obliged to "help the starving, *even at the cost of our own lives.*"

Prima Facie Duties

Ross would agree that individuals have a right to have their basic needs satisfied, and that those in a position to help satisfy those needs ought to do so. Certainly, no need is more basic than the need for physical sustenance, food. Thus, those with more than they need have a prima facie duty (of justice, noninjury, and benevolence) to share what they have with those who do not have what they need to survive or maintain health. Of course, it is possible to imagine cases where other considerations might override this prima facie obligation to share. If by sharing we create more injury and death, then the overriding obligation might be to prevent the greater injury by refraining from helping. But the key point is that, unlike consequential theorists, Ross considers as *prima facie* duties the duties to prevent suffering and starvation and to help provide others the necessities of life. These duties may be overridden only by more pressing duties, and then only with considerable compunction translated into an effort to improve the conditions that would lead to the hellish decision to let some people starve to death.

Maximin Principle

While Rawls believes that it is neither just nor unjust that individuals are born into circumstances of relative wealth or poverty, he also recognizes that social policies affect opportunity to alter one's lot in life. Thus, social policies can make it easier or harder for individuals, rich or poor, to meet their needs and pursue their aims. A just social policy, therefore, is one that acknowledges the equality of desert arising out of basic common needs and the difference in abilities to meet those needs due to social circumstances. Clearly, then, as with other nonconsequentialists, the principle of need figures prominently in Rawls's view of economic justice, certainly at the maintenance level. The poor nations need food; the wealthy nations have more food than they need. Rawls would consider the affluent nations morally obligated to adopt a social policy of sharing this food with those who are starving. Such a policy, combined, say, with developmental assistance in agriculture, would be designed to work to the advantage of those who are disadvantaged. It would aid the poor in overcoming their economic disadvantages.

Lifeboat Ethics: The Case Against Helping the Poor

Garrett Hardin

In "Lifeboat Ethics: The Case Against Helping the Poor," biologist Garrett Hardin rejects the claim, and the ethic entailing it, that affluent nations have an obligation to help the world's starving masses. Indeed, Hardin argues that the duty of the affluent nations is not to help. And he implies that this duty includes not providing even developmental assistance.

After criticizing the environmentalists' metaphor of the earth as a spaceship, Hardin sets up an extended metaphor of his own. He asks us to regard each rich nation as a lifeboat with limited capacity and full of relatively rich people. Outside the lifeboat, the sea is full of the poor and needy, who want to get in the boat. Hardin claims that unless the lifeboat's occupants maintain a safety factor—that is, keep people out—the boat will swamp.

But "swamping" is precisely what the "spaceship" or sharing ethic will lead to, Hardin believes. A good example, he feels, can be seen in the international food bank, which he considers nothing more than a device for moving the wealth of the rich, productive nations over to the poor, unproductive ones. Eventually, Hardin predicts, there will be nothing left to "withdraw." In the end, the sharing ethic will undo us all.

Thus, Hardin concludes that we must reject the sharing ethic. We owe it to future generations, to the species, not to help the starving masses.

Environmentalists use the metaphor of the earth as a "spaceship" in trying to persuade countries, industries and people to stop wasting and polluting our natural resources. Since we all share life on this planet, they argue, no single person or institution has the right to destroy, waste, or use more than a fair share of its resources.

But does everyone on earth have an equal right to an equal share of its resources? The spaceship metaphor can be dangerous when used by misguided idealists to justify suicidal policies for sharing our resources through uncontrolled immigration and foreign aid. In their enthusiastic but unrealistic generosity, they confuse the ethics of a spaceship with those of a lifeboat.

A true spaceship would have to be under the control of a captain, since no ship could possibly survive if its course were determined by committee. Spaceship Earth certainly has no captain; the United Nations is merely a toothless tiger, with little power to enforce any policy upon its bickering members.

If we divide the world crudely into rich nations and poor nations, two thirds of them are desperately poor, and only one third comparatively rich, with the United States the wealthiest of all. Metaphorically each rich nation can be seen as a lifeboat full of comparatively rich people. In the ocean outside each lifeboat swim the poor of the world, who would like to get in, or at least to share some of the wealth. What should the lifeboat passengers do?

From Garrett Hardin, "Lifeboat Ethics: The Case Against Helping the Poor," Psychology Today, 8 (1974), 36–43, 123–126. Copyright © 1974 Ziff-Davis Publishing Company. Reprinted by permission of the publisher.

First, we must recognize the limited capacity of any lifeboat. For example, a nation's land has a limited capacity to support a population and as the current energy crisis has shown us, in some ways we have already exceeded the carrying capacity of our land.

Adrift in a Moral Sea

So here we sit, say fifty people in our lifeboat. To be generous, let us assume it has room for ten more, making a total capacity of sixty. Suppose the fifty of us in the lifeboat see 100 others swimming in the water outside, begging for admission to our boat or for handouts. We have several options: We may be tempted to try to live by the Christian ideal of being "our brother's keeper," or by the Marxist ideal of "to each according to his needs." Since the needs of all in the water are the same, and since they can all be seen as "our brothers," we could take them all into our boat, making a total of 150 in a boat designed for sixty. The boat swamps, everyone drowns. Complete justice, complete catastrophe.

Since the boat has an unused excess capacity of ten more passengers, we could admit just ten more to it. But which ten do we let in? How do we choose? Do we pick the best ten, the neediest ten, "first come, first served"? And what do we say to the ninety we exclude? If we do let an extra ten into our lifeboat, we will have lost our "safety factor," an engineering principle of critical importance. For example, if we don't leave room for excess capacity as a safety factor in our country's agriculture, a new plant disease or a bad change in the weather could have disastrous consequences.

Suppose we decide to preserve our small safety factor and admit no more to the lifeboat. Our survival is then possible, although we shall have to be constantly on guard against boarding parties.

While this last solution clearly offers the only means of our survival, it is morally abhorrent to many people. Some say they feel guilty about their good luck. My reply is simple: "Get out and yield your place to others." This may solve the problem of the guilt-ridden person's conscience, but it does not change the ethics of the lifeboat. The needy person to whom the guilt-ridden person yields his place will not himself feel guilty about his good luck. If he did, he would not climb aboard. The net result of conscience-stricken people giving up their unjustly held seats is the elimination of that sort of conscience from the lifeboat.

This is the basic metaphor within which we must work out our solutions. Let us now enrich the image, step by step, with substantive additions from the real world, a world that must solve real and pressing problems of overpopulation and hunger.

The harsh ethics of the lifeboat become even harsher when we consider the reproductive differences between the rich nations and the poor nations. The people inside the lifeboats are doubling in numbers every eighty-seven years; those swimming around outside are doubling, on the average, every thirty-five years, more than twice as fast as the rich. And since the world's resources are dwindling, the difference in prosperity between the rich and the poor can only increase.

As of 1973, the U.S. had a population of 210 million people, who were increasing by 0.8 percent per year. Outside our lifeboat, let us imagine another 210 million people, (say the combined populations of Colombia, Ecuador, Venezuela, Morocco, Pakistan, Thailand and the Philippines) who are increasing at a rate of 3.3 percent per year. Put differently, the doubling time for this aggregate population is twenty-one years, compared to eighty-seven years for the U.S.

Multiplying the Rich and the Poor

Now suppose the U.S. agreed to pool its resources with those seven countries, with everyone receiving an equal share. Initially the ratio of Americans to non-Americans in this model would be one-to-one. But consider what the ratio would be after eighty-seven years, by which time the Americans would have doubled to a population of 420 million. By then, doubling every twenty-one years, the other group would have swollen to 354 billion. Each American would have to share the available resources with more than eight people.

But, one could argue, this discussion assumes that current population trends will continue, and they may not. Quite so. Most likely the rate of population increase will decline much faster in the U.S. than it will in the other countries, and there does not seem to be much we can do about it. In sharing with "each according to his needs," we must recognize that needs are determined by population size, which is determined by the rate of reproduction, which at present is regarded as a sovereign right of every nation, poor or not. This being so, the philanthropic load created by the sharing ethic of the spaceship can only increase.

The Tragedy of the Commons

The fundamental error of spaceship ethics, and the sharing it requires, is that it leads to what I call "the tragedy of the commons." Under a system of private property, the men who own property recognize their responsibility to care for it, for if they don't they will eventually suffer. A farmer, for instance, will allow no more cattle in a pasture than its carrying capacity justifies. If he overloads it, erosion sets in, weeds take over, and he loses the use of the pasture.

If a pasture becomes a commons open to all, the right of each to use it may not be matched by a corresponding responsibility to protect it. Asking everyone to use it with discretion will hardly do, for the considerate herdsman who refrains from overloading the commons suffers more than a selfish one who says his needs are greater. If everyone would restrain himself, all would be well; but it takes only one less than everyone to ruin a system of voluntary restraint. In a crowded world of less than perfect human beings, mutual ruin is inevitable if there are no controls. This is the tragedy of the commons.

One of the major tasks of education today should be the creation of such an acute awareness of the dangers of the commons that people will recognize its many varieties. For example, the air and water have become polluted because they are treated as commons. Further growth in the population or per-capita conversion of natural resources into pollutants will only make the problem worse. The same holds true for the fish of the oceans. Fishing fleets have nearly disappeared in many parts of the world, technological improvements in the art of fishing are hastening the day of complete ruin. Only the replacement of the system of the commons with a responsible system of control will save the land, air, water and oceanic fisheries.

The World Food Bank

In recent years there has been a push to create a new commons called a World Food Bank, an international depository of food reserves to which nations would contribute according to their abilities and from which they would draw according to their needs. This humanitarian proposal has received support from many liberal international groups, and from such prominent citizens as Margaret Mead, U.N. Secretary General Kurt Waldheim, and Senators Edward Kennedy and George McGovern.

A world food bank appeals powerfully to our humanitarian impulses. But before we rush ahead with such a plan, let us recognize where the greatest political push comes from, lest we be disillusioned later. Our experience with the "Food for Peace program," or Public Law 480, gives us the answer. This program moved billions of dollars worth of U.S. surplus grain to food-short, population-long countries during the past two decades. But when P.L. 480 first became law, a headline in the business magazine *Forbes* revealed the real power behind it: "Feeding the World's Hungry Millions: How It Will Mean Billions for U.S. Business."

And indeed it did. In the years 1960 to 1970, U.S. taxpayers spent a total of $7.9 billion on the Food for Peace program. Between 1948 and 1970, they also paid an additional $50 billion for other economic-aid programs, some of which went for food and food-producing machinery and technology. Though all U.S. taxpayers were forced to contribute to the cost of P.L. 480, certain special interest groups gained handsomely under the program. Farmers did not have to contribute the grain; the Government, or rather the taxpayers, bought it from them at full market prices. The increased demand raised prices of farm products generally. The manufacturers of farm machinery, fertilizers and pesticides benefited by the farmers' extra efforts to grow more food. Grain elevators profited from storing the surplus until it could be shipped. Railroads made money hauling it to ports, and shipping lines profited from carrying it overseas. The implementation of P.L. 480 required the creation of a vast Government bureaucracy, which then acquired its own vested interest in continuing the program regardless of its merits.

Extracting Dollars

Those who proposed and defended the Food for Peace program in public rarely mentioned its importance to any of these special interests. The public emphasis was always on its humanitarian effects. The combination of silent selfish interests and highly vocal humanitarian apologists made a powerful and successful lobby for extracting money from taxpayers. We can expect the same lobby to push now for the creation of a World Food Bank.

However great the potential benefit to selfish interests, it should not be a decisive argument against a truly humanitarian program. We must ask if such a program would actually do more good than harm, not only momentarily but also in the long run. Those who propose the food bank usually refer to a current "emergency" or "crisis" in terms of world food supply. But what is an emergency? Although they may be infrequent and sudden, everyone knows that emergencies will occur from time to time. A well-run family, company, organization or country prepares for the likelihood of accidents and emergencies. It expects them, it budgets for them, it saves for them.

Learning the Hard Way

What happens if some organizations or countries budget for accidents and others do not? If each country is solely responsible for its own well-being, poorly managed ones will suffer. But they can learn from experience. They may mend their ways, and learn to budget for infrequent but certain emergencies. For example, the weather varies from year to year, and periodic crop failures are certain. A wise and competent government saves out of the production of the good years in anticipation of bad years to come. Joseph taught this policy to Pharaoh in Egypt more than 2,000 years ago. Yet the great majority of the governments in the world today do not follow such a policy. They lack either the wisdom or the competence, or both. Should those nations that do manage to put something aside be forced to come to the rescue each time an emergency occurs among the poor nations?

"But it isn't their fault!" some kindhearted liberals argue. "How can we blame the poor people who are caught in an emergency? Why must they suffer for the sins of their governments?" The concept of blame is simply not relevant here. The real question is, what are the operational consequences of establishing a world food

bank? If it is open to every country every time a need develops, slovenly rulers will not be motivated to take Joseph's advice. Someone will always come to their aid. Some countries will deposit food in the world food bank, and others will withdraw it. There will be almost no overlap. As a result of such solutions to food shortage emergencies, the poor countries will not learn to mend their ways, and will suffer progressively greater emergencies as their populations grow.

Population Control the Crude Way

On the average, poor countries undergo a 2.5 percent increase in population each year; rich countries, about 0.8 percent. Only rich countries have anything in the way of food reserves set aside, and even they do not have as much as they should. Poor countries have none. If poor countries received no food from the outside, the rate of their population growth would be periodically checked by crop failures and famines. But if they can always draw on a world food bank in time of need, their population can continue to grow unchecked, and so will their "need" for aid. In the short run, a world food bank may diminish that need, but in the long run it actually increases the need without limit.

Without some system of worldwide food sharing, the proportion of people in the rich and poor nations might eventually stabilize. The overpopulated poor countries would decrease in numbers, while the rich countries that had room for more people would increase. But with a well-meaning system of sharing, such as a world food bank, the growth differential between the rich and the poor countries will not only persist, it will increase. Because of the higher rate of population growth in the poor countries of the world, 88 percent of today's children are born poor, and only 12 percent rich. Year by year the ratio becomes worse, as the fast-reproducing poor outnumber the slow-reproducing rich.

A world food bank is thus a commons in disguise. People will have more motivation to draw from it than to add to any common store. The less provident and less able will multiply at the expense of the abler and more provident, bringing eventual ruin upon all who share in the commons. Besides, any system of "sharing" that amounts to foreign aid from the rich nations to the poor nations will carry the taint of charity, which will contribute little to the world peace so devoutly desired by those who support the idea of a world food bank.

As past U.S. foreign-aid programs have amply and depressingly demonstrated, international charity frequently inspires mistrust and antagonism rather than gratitude on the part of the recipient nation.

Chinese Fish and Miracle Rice

The modern approach to foreign aid stresses the export of technology and advice, rather than money and food. As an ancient Chinese proverb goes: "Give a man a fish and he will eat for a day; teach him how to fish and he will eat for the rest of his days." Acting on this advice, the Rockefeller and Ford Foundations have financed a number of programs for improving agriculture in the hungry nations. Known as the "Green Revolution," these programs have led to the development of "miracle rice" and "miracle wheat," new strains that offer bigger harvests and greater resistance to crop damage. Norman Borlaug, the Nobel Prize winning agronomist who, supported by the Rockefeller Foundation, developed "miracle wheat," is one of the most prominent advocates of a world food bank.

Whether or not the Green Revolution can increase food production as much as its champions claim is a debatable but possibly irrelevant point. Those who support this well-intended humanitarian effort should first consider some of the fundamentals of human ecology. Ironically, one man who did was the late Alan Gregg, a vice president of the Rockefeller Foundation. Two decades ago he expressed strong doubts about the wisdom of such attempts to increase food production. He likened the growth and spread of humanity over the surface of the earth to the spread of cancer in the human body, remarking that "cancerous growths demand food; but, as far as I know, they have never been cured by getting it."

Overloading the Environment

Every human born constitutes a draft on all aspects of the environment: food, air, water, forests, beaches, wildlife, scenery and solitude. Food can, perhaps, be significantly increased to meet a growing demand. But what about clean beaches, unspoiled forests, and solitude? If we satisfy a growing population's need for food, we necessarily decrease its per capita supply of the other resources needed by men.

India, for example, now has a population of 600 million, which increases by 15 million each year. This population already puts a huge load on a relatively impoverished environment. The country's forests are now only a small fraction of what they were three centuries ago, and floods and erosion continually destroy the insufficient farmland that remains. Every one of the 15 million new lives added to India's population puts an additional burden on the environment, and increases the economic and social costs of crowding. However humanitarian our intent, every Indian life saved through medical or nutritional assistance from abroad diminishes the quality of life for those who remain, and for subsequent generations. If rich countries make it possible, through foreign aid, for 600 million Indians to swell to 1.2 billion in a mere twenty-eight years, as their current growth rate threatens, will future generations of Indians thank us for hastening the destruction of their environment? Will our good intentions be sufficient excuse for the consequences of our actions?

My final example of a commons in action is one for which the public has the least desire for rational discussion—immigration. Anyone who publicly questions the wisdom of current U.S. immigration policy is promptly charged with bigotry, prejudice, ethnocentrism, chauvinism, isolationism or selfishness. Rather than encounter such accusations, one would rather talk about other matters, leaving immigration policy to wallow in the crosscurrents of special interests that take no account of the good of the whole, or the interests of posterity.

Perhaps we still feel guilty about things we said in the past. Two generations ago the popular press frequently referred to Dagos, Wops, Polacks, Chinks and Krauts, in articles about how America was being "overrun" by foreigners of supposedly inferior genetic stock. But because the implied inferiority of foreigners was used then as justification for keeping them out, people now assume that restrictive policies could only be based on such misguided notions. There are other grounds.

A Nation of Immigrants

Just consider the numbers involved. Our Government acknowledges a net inflow of 400,000 immigrants a year. While we have no hard data on the extent of illegal entries, educated guesses put the figure at about 600,000 a year. Since the natural increase (excess of births over deaths) of the resident population now runs about 1.7 million per year, the yearly gain from immigration amounts to at least 19 percent of the total annual increase, and may be as much as 37 percent if we include the estimate for illegal immigrants. Considering the growing use of birth-control devices, the potential effect of educational campaigns by such organizations as Planned Parenthood Federation of America and Zero Population Growth, and the influence of inflation and the housing shortage, the fertility rate of American women may decline so much that immigration could account for all the yearly increase in population. Should we not at least ask if that is what we want?

For the sake of those who worry about whether the "quality" of the average immigrant compares favorably with the quality of the average resident, let us assume that immigrants and nativeborn citizens are of exactly equal quality, however one defines that term. We will focus here only on quantity; and since our conclusions will depend on nothing else, all charges of bigotry and chauvinism become irrelevant.

Immigration vs. Food Supply

World food banks *move food to the people*, hastening the exhaustion of the environment of the poor countries. Unrestricted immigration, on the other hand, *moves people to the food*, thus speeding up the destruction of the environment of the rich countries. We can easily understand why poor people should want to make this latter transfer, but why should rich hosts encourage it?

As in the case of foreign-aid programs, immigration receives support from selfish interests and humanitarian impulses. The primary selfish interest in unimpeded immigration is the desire of employers for cheap labor, particularly in industries and trades that offer degrading work. In the past, one wave of foreigners after another was brought into the U.S. to work at wretched jobs for wretched wages. In recent years the Cubans,

Puerto Ricans and Mexicans have had this dubious honor. The interests of the employers of cheap labor mesh well with the guilty silence of the country's liberal intelligentsia. White Anglo-Saxon Protestants are particularly reluctant to call for a closing of the doors to immigration for fear of being called bigots.

But not all countries have such reluctant leadership. Most educated Hawaiians, for example, are keenly aware of the limits of their environment, particularly in terms of population growth. There is only so much room on the islands, and the islanders know it. To Hawaiians, immigrants from the other forty-nine states present as great a threat as those from other nations. At a recent meeting of Hawaiian government officials in Honolulu, I had the ironic delight of hearing a speaker, who like most of his audience was of Japanese ancestry, ask how the country might practically and constitutionally close its doors to further immigration. One member of the audience countered: "How can we shut the doors now? We have many friends and relatives in Japan that we'd like to bring here some day so that they can enjoy Hawaii too." The Japanese-American speaker smiled sympathetically and answered: "Yes, but we have children now, and someday we'll have grandchildren too. We can bring more people here from Japan only by giving away some of the land that we hope to pass on to our grandchildren some day. What right do we have to do that?"

At this point, I can hear U.S. liberals asking: "How can you justify slamming the door once you're inside? You say that immigrants should be kept out. But aren't we all immigrants, or the descendents of immigrants? If we insist on staying, must we not admit all others?" Our craving for intellectual order leads us to seek and prefer symmetrical rules and morals: a single rule for me and everybody else; the same rule yesterday, today, and tomorrow. Justice, we feel, should not change with time and place.

We Americans of non-Indian ancestry can look upon ourselves as the descendants of thieves who are guilty morally, if not legally, of stealing this land from its Indian owners. Should we then give back the land to the now living American descendants of those Indians? However morally or logically sound this proposal may be, I, for one, am unwilling to live by it and I know no one else who is. Besides, the logical consequence would be absurd. Suppose that, intoxicated with a sense of pure justice, we should decide to turn our land over to the Indians. Since all our wealth has also been derived from the land, wouldn't we be morally obliged to give that back to the Indians too?

Pure Justice vs. Reality

Clearly, the concept of pure justice produces an infinite regression to absurdity. Centuries ago, wise men invented statutes of limitations to justify the rejection of such pure justice, in the interest of preventing continual disorder. The law zealously defends property rights, but only relatively recent property rights. Drawing a line after an arbitrary time has elapsed may be unjust, but the alternatives are worse.

We are all the descendants of thieves, and the world's resources are inequitably distributed. But we must begin the journey to tomorrow from the point where we are today. We cannot remake the past. We cannot safely divide the wealth equitably among all peoples so long as people reproduce at different rates. To do so would guarantee that our grandchildren, and everyone else's grandchildren, would have only a ruined world to inhabit.

To be generous with one's own possessions is quite different from being generous with those of posterity. We should call this point to the attention of those who, from a commendable love of justice and equality, would institute a system of the commons, either in the form of a world food bank, or of unrestricted immigration. We must convince them if we wish to save at least some parts of the world from environmental ruin.

Without a true world government to control reproduction and the use of available resources, the sharing ethic of the spaceship is impossible. For the foreseeable future, our survival demands that we govern our actions by the ethics of a lifeboat, harsh though they may be. Posterity will be satisfied with nothing less.

Questions for Analysis

1. Why does Hardin object to the environmentalists' metaphor of the earth as a spaceship?

2. Hardin seems opposed even to developmental assistance. Why?

3. What does the merit of Hardin's argument depend on?

4. In Hardin's view, "pure justice" is not compatible with survival. What does he mean? Do you agree?

5. Do you agree that future generations have a claim against us? If they do, what is the nature of this claim?

6. Explain why Hardin's argument can be called utilitarian.

Famine, Affluence, and Morality

Peter Singer

Unlike Garrett Hardin, professor of philosophy Peter Singer believes that the affluent nations of the world have an obligation to help the poor nations. Singer opens his argument with what he considers are two uncontroversial principles. The first is that suffering and death from lack of food,

---

From Peter Singer, "Famine, Affluence, and Morality," Philosophy and Public Affairs, I, no. 3 (Spring 1972), pp. 229–243. *Copyright ©1972 by Princeton University Press. Reprinted by permission of Princeton University Press.*

shelter, and medical care are bad. The second is that if we can prevent something bad from happening "without thereby sacrificing anything of comparable moral importance," then we should do it. (While Singer believes that this principle is correct, he does offer a "weaker" version of it as well: We ought to prevent something bad from happening unless we have to sacrifice something morally significant.)

Basing his argument on these principles, Singer concludes that help or relief for the starving masses is a duty, not charity. Affluent nations are morally obliged to help; to refrain from helping is not merely uncharitable, it is immoral.

In addition to drawing a philosophical distinction between charity and duty, Singer raises a number of practical concerns. One is whether help to poor nations should be a government responsibility and not a personal one. Another is whether relief to countries lacking effective population control measures merely postpones starvation. Still another concern is just how much individually and collectively we ought to be giving away.

In the postscript to his essay, written several years afterward, Singer concedes that there is a serious case to be made for denying aid to countries that refuse to take any population control measures. He also admits definitional problems with the phrase "moral significance," which, of course, is crucial in his second principle.

As I write this, in November 1971, people are dying in East Bengal from lack of food, shelter, and medical care. The suffering and death that are occurring there now are not inevitable, not unavoidable in any fatalistic sense of the term. Constant poverty, a cyclone, and a civil war have turned at least nine million people into destitute refugees; nevertheless, it is not beyond the capacity of the richer nations to give enough assistance to reduce any further suffering to very small proportions. The decisions and actions of human beings can prevent this kind of suffering. Unfortunately, human beings have not made the necessary decisions. At the individual level, people have, with very few exceptions, not responded to the situation in any significant way. Generally speaking, people have not given large sums to relief funds; they have not written to their parliamentary representatives demanding increased government assistance; they have not demonstrated in the streets, held symbolic fasts, or done anything else directed toward providing the refugees with the means to satisfy their essential needs. At the government level, no government has given the sort of massive aid that would enable the refugees to survive for more than a few days. Britain, for instance, has given rather more than most countries. It has, to date, given £14,750,000. For comparative purposes, Britain's share of the nonrecoverable development costs of the Anglo-French Concorde project is already in excess of £275,000,000, and on present estimates will reach £440,000,000. The implication is that the British government values a supersonic transport more than thirty times as highly as it values the lives of the nine million refugees. Australia is another country which, on a per capita basis, is well up in the "aid to Bengal" table. Australia's aid, however, amounts to less than one-twelfth of the cost of Sydney's new opera house. The total amount given, from all sources, now stands at about £65,000,000. The estimated cost of keeping the refugees alive for one year is £464,000,000. Most of the refugees have now been in the camps for more than six months. The World Bank has said that India needs a minimum of £300,000,000 in assistance from other countries before the end of the year. It seems obvious that assistance on this scale will not be forthcoming. India will be forced to choose between letting the refugees starve or diverting funds from her own development program, which will mean that more of her own people will starve in the future.[1]

These are the essential facts about the present situation in Bengal. So far as it concerns us here, there is nothing unique about this situation except its magnitude. The Bengal emergency is just the latest and most acute of a series of major emergencies in various parts of the world, arising both from natural and from man-made causes. There are also many parts of the world in which people die from malnutrition and lack of food independent of any special emergency. I take Bengal as my example only because it is the present concern, and because the size of the problem has ensured that it has been given adequate publicity. Neither individuals nor governments can claim to be unaware of what is happening there.

What are the moral implications of a situation like this? In what follows, I shall argue that the way people in relatively affluent countries react to a situation like that in Bengal cannot be justified; indeed, the whole way we look at moral issues—our moral conceptual scheme—needs to be altered, and with it, the way of life that has come to be taken for granted in our society.

In arguing for this conclusion I will not, of course, claim to be morally neutral. I shall, however, try to argue for the moral position that I take, so that anyone who accepts certain assumptions, to be made explicit, will, I hope, accept my conclusion.

I begin with the assumption that suffering and death from lack of food, shelter, and medical care are bad. I think most people will agree about this, although one may reach the same view by different routes. I shall not argue for this view. People can hold all sorts of eccentric positions, and perhaps from some of them it would not follow that death by starvation is in itself bad. It is difficult, perhaps impossible, to refute such positions, and so for brevity I will henceforth take this assumption as accepted. Those who disagree need read no further.

My next point is this: If it is in our power to prevent something bad from happening, without thereby sacrificing anything of comparable moral importance, we ought, morally, to do it. By "without sacrificing anything of comparable moral importance" I mean without causing anything else comparably bad to happen, or doing something that is wrong in itself, or failing to promote some moral good, comparable in significance to the bad thing that we can prevent. This principle seems almost as uncontroversial as the last one. It requires us only to prevent what is bad, and not to promote what is good, and it requires this of us only when we can do it without sacrificing anything that is, from the moral point of view, comparably important. I could even, as far as the application of my argument to the Bengal emergency is concerned, qualify the point so as to make it: If it is in our power to prevent something very bad from happening, without thereby sacrificing anything morally significant, we ought, morally, to do it. An

application of this principle would be as follows: If I am walking past a shallow pond and see a child drowning in it, I ought to wade in and pull the child out. This will mean getting my clothes muddy, but this is insignificant, while the death of the child would presumably be a very bad thing.

The uncontroversial appearance of the principle just stated is deceptive. If it were acted upon, even in its qualified form, our lives, our society, and our world would be fundamentally changed. For the principle takes, firstly, no account of proximity or distance. It makes no moral difference whether the person I can help is a neighbor's child ten yards from me or a Bengali whose name I shall never know, ten thousand miles away. Secondly, the principle makes no distinction between cases in which I am the only person who could possibly do anything and cases in which I am just one among millions in the same position.

I do not think I need to say much in defense of the refusal to take proximity and distance into account. The fact that a person is physically near to us, so that we have personal contact with him, may make it more likely that we *shall* assist him, but this does not show that we *ought* to help him rather than another who happens to be further away. If we accept any principle of impartiality, universalizability, equality, or whatever, we cannot discriminate against someone merely because he is far away from us (or we are far away from him). Admittedly, it is possible that we are in a better position to judge what needs to be done to help a person near to us than one far away, and perhaps also to provide the assistance we judge to be necessary. If this were the case, it would be a reason for helping those near to us first. This may once have been a justification for being more concerned with the poor in one's town than with famine victims in India. Unfortunately for those who like to keep their moral responsibilities limited, instant communication and swift transportation have changed the situation. From the moral point of view, the development of the world into a "global village" has made an important, though still unrecognized, difference to our moral situation. Expert observers and supervisors, sent out by famine relief organizations or permanently stationed in famine-prone areas, can direct our aid to a refugee in Bengal almost as effectively as we could get it to someone in our own block. There would seem, therefore, to be no possible justification for discriminating on geographical grounds.

There may be a greater need to defend the second implication of my principle—that the fact that there are millions of other people in the same position, in respect to the Bengali refugees, as I am, does not make the situation significantly different from a situation in which I am the only person who can prevent something very bad from occurring. Again, of course, I admit that there is a psychological difference between the cases; one feels less guilty about doing nothing if one can point to others, similarly placed, who have also done nothing. Yet this can make no real difference to our moral obligations.[2] Should I consider that I am less obliged to pull the drowning child out of the pond if on looking around I see other people, no further away than I am, who have also noticed the child but are doing nothing? One has only to ask this question to see the absurdity of the view that numbers lessen obligation. It is a view that is an ideal excuse for inactivity; unfortunately most of the major evils—poverty, overpopulation, pollution—are problems in which everyone is almost equally involved.

The view that numbers do make a difference can be made plausible if stated in this way: If everyone in circumstances like mine gave £5 to the Bengal Relief Fund, there would be enough to provide food, shelter, and medical care for the refugees; there is no reason why I should give more than anyone else in the same circumstances as I am; therefore I have no obligation to give more than £5. Each premise in this argument is true, and the argument looks sound. It may convince us, unless we notice that it is based on a hypothetical premise, although the conclusion is not stated hypothetically. The argument would be sound if the conclusion were: if everyone in circumstances like mine were to give £5, I would have no obligation to give more than £5. If the conclusion were so stated, however, it would be obvious that the argument has no bearing on a situation in which it is not the case that everyone else gives £5. This, of course, is the actual situation. It is more or less certain that not everyone in circumstances like mine will give £5. So there will not be enough to provide the needed food, shelter, and medical care. Therefore by giving more than £5 I will prevent more suffering than I would if I gave just £5.

It might be thought that this argument has an absurd consequence. Since the situation appears to be that very few people are likely to give substantial amounts, it follows that I and everyone else in similar circumstances ought to give as much as possible, that is, at least up to the point at which by giving more one would begin to cause serious suffering for oneself and one's dependents—perhaps even beyond this point to the point of marginal utility, at which by giving more one would cause oneself and one's dependents as much suffering as one would prevent in Bengal. If everyone does this, however, there will be more than can be used for the benefit of the refugees, and some of the sacrifice will have been unnecessary. Thus, if everyone does what he ought to do, the result will not be as good as it would be if everyone did a little less than he ought to do, or if only some do all that they ought to do.

The paradox here arises only if we assume that the actions in question—sending money to the relief funds—are performed more or less simultaneously, and are also unexpected. For if it is to be expected that everyone is going to contribute something, then clearly each is not obliged to give as much as he would have been obliged to had others not been giving too. And if everyone is not acting more or less simultaneously, then those giving later will know how much more is needed, and will have no obligation to give more than is necessary to reach this amount. To say this is not to deny the principle that people in the same circumstances have the same obligations, but to point out that the fact that others have given, or may be expected to give, is a relevant circumstance: Those giving after it has become known that many others are giving and those giving before are not in the same circumstances. So the seemingly absurd consequence of the principle I have put forward can occur only if people are in error about the actual circumstances—that is, if they think they are giving when others are not, but in fact they are giving when others are. The result of everyone doing what he really ought to do cannot be worse than the result of everyone doing less than he ought to do, although the result of everyone doing what he reasonably believes he ought to do could be.

If my argument so far has been sound, neither our distance from a preventable evil nor the number of other people who, in respect to that evil, are in the same situation as we are, lessens our obligation to mitigate or prevent that evil. I shall therefore take as established the principle I asserted earlier. As I have already said, I need to assert it only in its qualified form: If it is in our power to prevent something very bad from happening, without thereby sacrificing anything else morally significant, we ought, morally, to do it.

The outcome of this argument is that our traditional moral categories are upset. The traditional distinction between duty and charity cannot be drawn, or at least, not in the place we normally draw it. Giving money to the Bengal Relief Fund is regarded as an act of charity in our society. The bodies which collect money are known as "charities." These organizations see themselves in this way—if you send them a check, you will be thanked for your "generosity." Because giving money is regarded as an act of charity, it is not thought that there is anything wrong with not giving. The charitable man may be praised, but the man who is not charitable is not condemned. People do not feel in any way ashamed or guilty about spending money on new clothes or a new car instead of giving it to famine relief. (Indeed, the alternative does not occur to them.) This way of looking at the matter cannot be justified. When we buy new clothes not to keep ourselves warm but to look "well-dressed" we are not providing for any important need. We would not be sacrificing anything significant if we were to continue to wear our old clothes, and give the money to famine relief. By doing so, we would be preventing another person from starving. It follows from what I have said earlier that we ought to give money away, rather than spend it on clothes which we do not need to keep us warm. To do so is not charitable, or generous. Nor is it the kind of act which philosophers and theologians have called "supererogatory"—an act which it would be good to do, but not wrong not to do. On the contrary, we ought to give the money away, and it is wrong not to do so.

I am not maintaining that there are no acts which are charitable, or that there are no acts which it would be good to do but not wrong not to do. It may be possible to redraw the distinction between duty and charity in some other place. All I am arguing here is that the present way of draw-

ing the distinction, which makes it an act of charity for a man living at the level of affluence which most people in the "developed nations" enjoy to give money to save someone else from starvation, cannot be supported. It is beyond the scope of my argument to consider whether the distinction should be redrawn or abolished altogether. There would be many other possible ways of drawing the distinction—for instance, one might decide that it is good to make other people as happy as possible, but not wrong not to do so.

Despite the limited nature of the revision in our moral conceptual scheme which I am proposing, the revision would, given the extent of both affluence and famine in the world today, have radical implications. These implications may lead to further objections, distinct from those I have already considered. I shall discuss two of these.

One objection to the position I have taken might be simply that it is too drastic a revision of our moral scheme. People do not ordinarily judge in the way I have suggested they should. Most people reserve their moral condemnation for those who violate some moral norm, such as the norm against taking another person's property. They do not condemn those who indulge in luxury instead of giving to famine relief. But given that I did not set out to present a morally neutral description of the way people make moral judgments, the way people do in fact judge has nothing to do with the validity of my conclusion. My conclusion follows from the principle which I advanced earlier, and unless that principle is rejected, or the arguments shown to be unsound, I think the conclusion must stand, however strange it appears.

It might, nevertheless, be interesting to consider why our society, and most other societies, do judge differently from the way I have suggested they should. In a well-known article, J. O. Urmson suggests that the imperatives of duty, which tell us what we must do, as distinct from what it would be good to do but not wrong not to do, function so as to prohibit behavior that is intolerable if men are to live together in society.[3] This may explain the origin and continued existence of the present division between acts of duty and acts of charity. Moral attitudes are shaped by the needs of society, and no doubt society needs people who will observe the rules that make social existence tolerable. From the point of view of a particular society, it is essential to prevent violations of norms against killing, stealing, and so on. It is quite inessential, however, to help people outside one's own society.

If this is an explanation of our common distinction between duty and supererogation, however, it is not a justification of it. The moral point of view requires us to look beyond the interests of our own society. Previously, as I have already mentioned, this may hardly have been feasible, but it is quite feasible now. From the moral point of view, the prevention of the starvation of millions of people outside our society must be considered at least as pressing as the upholding of property norms within our society.

It has been argued by some writers, among them Sidgwick and Urmson, that we need to have a basic moral code which is not too far beyond the capacities of the ordinary man, for otherwise there will be a general breakdown of compliance with the moral code. Crudely stated, this argument suggests that if we tell people that they ought to refrain from murder and give everything they do not really need to famine relief, they will do neither, whereas if we tell them that they ought to refrain from murder and that it is good to give to famine relief but not wrong not to do so, they will at least refrain from murder. The issue here is: Where should we draw the line between conduct that is required and conduct that is good although not required, so as to get the best possible result? This would seem to be an empirical question, although a very difficult one. One objection to the Sidgwick-Urmson line of argument is that it takes insufficient account of the effect that moral standards can have on the decisions we make. Given a society in which a wealthy man who gives 5 percent of his income to famine relief is regarded as most generous, it is not surprising that a proposal that we all ought to give away half our incomes will be thought to be absurdly unrealistic. In a society which held that no man should have more than enough while others have less than they need, such a proposal might seem narrow-minded. What it is possible for a man to do and what he is likely to do are both, I think, very greatly influenced by what people around him are doing and expecting him to do. In any case, the possibility that by spreading the idea that we ought to be doing very much more than we are to relieve famine we shall bring about a general breakdown of moral behavior seems remote. If the stakes are an end to widespread starvation, it is worth the risk. Finally, it should be emphasized that these considerations are relevant only to the issue of what we should require from others, and not to what we ourselves ought to do.

The second objection to my attack on the present distinction between duty and charity is one which has from time to time been made against utilitarianism. It follows from some forms of utilitarian theory that we all ought, morally, to be working full time to increase the balance of happiness over misery. The position I have taken here would not lead to this conclusion in all circumstances, for if there were no bad occurrences that we could prevent without sacrificing something of comparable moral importance, my argument would have no application. Given the present conditions in many parts of the world, however, it does follow from my argument that we ought, morally, to be working full time to relieve great suffering of the sort that occurs as a result of famine or other disasters. Of course, mitigating circumstances can be adduced—for instance, that if we wear ourselves out through overwork, we shall be less effective than we would otherwise have been. Nevertheless, when all considerations of this sort have been taken into account, the conclusion remains: We ought to be preventing as much suffering as we can without sacrificing something else of comparable moral importance. This conclusion is one which we may be reluctant to face. I cannot see, though, why it should be regarded as a criticism of the position for which I have argued, rather than a criticism of our ordinary standards of behavior. Since most people are self-interested to some degree, very few of us are likely to do everything that we ought to do. It would, however, hardly be honest to take this as evidence that it is not the case that we ought to do it.

It may still be thought that my conclusions are so wildly out of line with what everyone else thinks and has always thought that there must be something wrong with the argument somewhere. In order to show that my conclusions, while certainly contrary to contemporary Western moral standards, would not have seemed so extraordinary at other times and in other places, I would like to quote a passage from a writer not normally thought of as a way-out radical, Thomas Aquinas.

> Now, according to the natural order instituted by divine providence, material goods are provided for the satisfaction of human needs. Therefore the division and appropriation of property, which proceeds from human law, must not hinder the satisfaction of man's necessity from such goods. Equally, whatever a man has in superabundance is owed, of natural right, to the poor for their sustenance. So Ambrosius says, and it is also to be found in the *Decretum Gratiani*: "The bread which you withhold belongs to the hungry; the clothing you shut away, to the naked; and the money you bury in the earth is the redemption and freedom of the penniless."[4]

I now want to consider a number of points, more practical than philosophical, which are relevant to the application of the moral conclusion we have reached. These points challenge not the idea that we ought to be doing all we can to prevent starvation, but the idea that giving away a great deal of money is the best means to this end.

It is sometimes said that overseas aid should be a government responsibility, and that therefore one ought not to give to privately run charities. Giving privately, it is said, allows the government and the noncontributing members of society to escape their responsibilities.

This argument seems to assume that the more people there are who give to privately organized famine relief funds, the less likely it is that the government will take over full responsibility for such aid. This assumption is unsupported, and does not strike me as at all plausible. The opposite view—that if no one gives voluntarily, a government will assume that its citizens are uninterested in famine relief and would not wish to be forced into giving aid—seems more plausible. In any case, unless there were a definite probability that by refusing to give one would be helping to bring about massive government assistance, people who do refuse to make voluntary contributions are refusing to prevent a certain amount of suffering without being able to point to any tangible beneficial consequence of their refusal. So the onus of showing how their refusal will bring about government action is on those who refuse to give.

I do not, of course, want to dispute the contention that governments of affluent nations should be giving many times the amount of genuine, no-strings-attached aid that they are giving now. I agree, too, that giving privately is not enough, and that we ought to be campaigning actively for entirely new standards for both public and private contributions to famine relief. Indeed, I would sympathize with someone who thought that campaigning was more important than giving oneself, although I doubt whether preaching what one does not practice would be very effective. Unfortunately, for many people the idea that "it's the government's responsibility" is a reason for not giving which does not appear to entail any political action either.

Another, more serious reason for not giving to famine relief funds is that until there is effective population control, relieving famine merely postpones starvation. If we save the Bengal refugees now, others, perhaps the children of these refugees, will face starvation in a few years' time. In support of this, one may cite the now well-known facts about the population explosion and the relatively limited scope for expanded production.

This point, like the previous one, is an argument against relieving suffering that is happening now, because of a belief about what might happen in the future; it is unlike the previous point in that very good evidence can be adduced in support of this belief about the future. I will not go into the evidence here. I accept that the earth cannot support indefinitely a population rising at the present rate. This certainly poses a problem for anyone who thinks it important to prevent famine. Again, however, one could accept the argument without drawing the conclusion that it absolves one from any obligation to do anything to prevent famine. The conclusion that should be drawn is that the best means of preventing famine, in the long run, is population control. It would then follow from the position reached earlier that one ought to be doing all one can to promote population control (unless one held that all forms of population control were wrong in themselves, or would have significantly bad consequences). Since there are organizations working specifically for population control, one would then support them rather than more orthodox methods of preventing famine.

A third point raised by the conclusion reached

earlier relates to the question of just how much we all ought to be giving away. One possibility, which has already been mentioned, is that we ought to give until we reach the level of marginal utility—that is, the level at which, by giving more, I would cause as much suffering to myself or my dependents as I would relieve by my gift. This would mean, of course, that one would reduce oneself to very near the material circumstances of a Bengali refugee. It will be recalled that earlier I put forward both a strong and a moderate version of the principle of preventing bad occurrences. The strong version, which required us to prevent bad things from happening unless in doing so we would be sacrificing something of comparable moral significance, does seem to require reducing ourselves to the level of marginal utility. I should also say that the strong version seems to me to be the correct one. I proposed the more moderate version—that we should prevent bad occurrences unless, to do so, we had to sacrifice something morally significant—only in order to show that even on this surely undeniable principle a great change in our way of life is required. On the more moderate principle, it may not follow that we ought to reduce ourselves to the level of marginal utility, for one might hold that to reduce oneself and one's family to this level is to cause something significantly bad to happen. Whether this is so I shall not discuss, since, as I have said, I can see no good reason for holding the moderate version of the principle rather than the strong version. Even if we accepted the principle only in its moderate form, however, it should be clear that we would have to give away enough to ensure that the consumer society, dependent as it is on people spending on trivia rather than giving to famine relief, would slow down and perhaps disappear entirely. There are several reasons why this would be desirable in itself. The value and necessity of economic growth are now being questioned not only by conservationists, but by economists as well.[5] There is no doubt, too, that the consumer society has had a distorting effect on the goals and purposes of its members. Yet looking at the matter purely from the point of view of overseas aid, there must be a limit to the extent to which we should deliberately slow down our economy; for it might be the case that if we gave away, say, 40 percent of our Gross National Product, we would slow down the economy so much that in absolute terms we would be giving less than if we gave 25 percent of the much larger GNP that we would have if we limited our contribution to this smaller percentage.

I mention this only as an indication of the sort of factor that one would have to take into account in working out an ideal. Since Western societies generally consider one percent of the GNP an acceptable level for overseas aid, the matter is entirely academic. Nor does it affect the question of how much an individual should give in a society in which very few are giving substantial amounts.

It is sometimes said, though less often now than it used to be, that philosophers have no special role to play in public affairs, since most public issues depend primarily on an assessment of facts. On questions of fact, it is said, philosophers as such have no special expertise, and so it has been possible to engage in philosophy without committing oneself to any position on major public issues. No doubt there are some issues of social policy and foreign policy about which it can truly be said that a really expert assessment of the facts is required before taking sides or acting, but the issue of famine is surely not one of these. The facts about the existence of suffering are beyond dispute. Nor, I think, is it disputed that we can do something about it, either through orthodox methods of famine relief or through population control or both. This is therefore an issue on which philosophers are competent to take a position. The issue is one which faces everyone who has more money than he needs to support himself and his dependents, or who is in a position to take some sort of political action. These categories must include practically every teacher and student of philosophy in the universities of the Western world. If philosophy is to deal with matters that are relevant to both teachers and students, this is an issue that philosophers should discuss.

Discussion, though, is not enough. What is the point of relating philosophy to public (and personal) affairs if we do not take our conclusions seriously? In this instance, taking our conclusion seriously means acting upon it. The philosopher will not find it any easier than anyone else to alter his attitudes and way of life to the extent that, if I am right, is involved in doing everything that we ought to be doing. At the very least, though, one can make a start. The philosopher who does so will have to sacrifice some of the benefits of the consumer society, but he can find compensation in the satisfaction of a way of life in which theory and practice, if not yet in harmony, are at least coming together.

Postscript

The crisis in Bangladesh that spurred me to write the above article is now of historical interest only, but the world food crisis is, if anything, still more serious. The huge grain reserves that were then held by the United States have vanished. Increased oil prices have made both fertilizer and energy more expensive in developing countries, and have made it difficult for them to produce more food. At the same time, their population has continued to grow. Fortunately, as I write now, there is no major famine anywhere in the world; but poor people are still starving in several countries, and malnutrition remains very widespread. The need for assistance is, therefore, just as great as when I first wrote, and we can be sure that without it there will, again, be major famines.

The contrast between poverty and affluence that I wrote about is also as great as it was then. True, the affluent nations have experienced a recession, and are perhaps not as prosperous as they were in 1971. But the poorer nations have suffered as least as much from the recession, in reduced government aid (because if governments decide to reduce expenditure, they regard foreign aid as one of the expendable items, ahead of, for instance, defense or public construction projects) and in increased prices for goods and materials they need to buy. In any case, compared to the difference between the affluent nations and the poor nations, the whole recession was trifling; the poorest in the affluent nations remained incomparably better off than the poorest in the poor nations.

So the case for aid, on both a personal and a governmental level, remains as great now as it was in 1971, and I would not wish to change the basic argument that I put forward then.

There are, however, some matters of emphasis that I might put differently if I were to rewrite the article, and the most important of these concerns the population problem. I still think that, as I wrote then, the view that famine relief merely postpones starvation unless something is done to check population growth is not an argument against aid, it is only an argument against the *type* of aid that should be given. Those who hold this view have the same obligation to give to prevent starvation as those who do not; the difference is that they regard assisting population control schemes as a more effective way of preventing starvation in the long run. I would now, however, have given greater space to the discussion of the population problem; for I now think that there is a serious case for saying that if a country refuses to take any steps to slow the rate of its population growth, we should not give it aid. This is, of course, a very drastic step to take, and the choice it represents is a horrible choice to have to make; but if, after a dispassionate analysis of all the available information, we come to the conclusion that without population control we will not, in the long run, be able to prevent famine or other catastrophes, then it may be more humane in the long run to aid those countries that are prepared to take strong measures to reduce population growth, and to use our aid policy as a means of pressuring other countries to take similar steps.

It may be objected that such a policy involves an attempt to coerce a sovereign nation. But since we are not under an obligation to give aid unless that aid is likely to be effective in reducing starvation or malnutrition, we are not under an obligation to give aid to countries that make no effort to reduce a rate of population growth that will lead to catastrophe. Since we do not force any nation to accept our aid, simply making it clear that we will not give aid where it is not going to be effective cannot properly be regarded as a form of coercion.

I should also make it clear that the kind of aid that will slow population growth is not just assistance with the setting up of facilities for dispensing contraceptives and performing sterilizations. It is also necessary to create the conditions under which people do not wish to have so many children. This will involve, among other things, providing greater economic security for people, particularly in their old age, so that they do not need the security of a large family to provide for them. Thus, the requirements of aid designed to reduce population growth and aid designed to eliminate starvation are by no means separate; they overlap, and the latter will often be a means to the former.

The obligation of the affluent is, I believe, to do both. Fortunately, there are now so many people in the foreign aid field, including those in the private agencies, who are aware of this.

One other matter that I should now put forward slightly differently is that my argument does, of course, apply to assistance with development, particularly agricultural development, as well as to direct famine relief. Indeed, I think the former is usually the better long-term investment. Although this was my view when I wrote the article, the fact that I started from a famine situation, where the need was for immediate food, has led some readers to suppose that the argument is only about giving food and not about other types of aid. This is quite mistaken, and my view is that the aid should be of whatever type is most effective.

On a more philosophical level, there has been some discussion of the original article which has been helpful in clarifying the issues and pointing to the areas in which more work on the argument is needed. In particular, as John Arthur has shown in "Rights and the Duty to Bring Aid" (included in this volume), something more needs to be said about the notion of "moral significance." The problem is that to give an account of this notion involves nothing less than a full-fledged ethical theory; and while I am myself inclined toward a utilitarian view, it was my aim in writing "Famine, Affluence, and Morality" to produce an argument which would appeal not only to utilitarians, but also to anyone who accepted the initial premises of the argument, which seemed to me likely to have a very wide acceptance. So I tried to get around the need to produce a complete ethical theory by allowing my readers to fill in their own version—within limits—of what is morally significant, and then see what the moral consequences are. This tactic works reasonably well with those who are prepared to agree that such matters as being fashionably dressed are not really of moral significance; but Arthur is right to say that people could take the opposite view without being obviously irrational. Hence, I do not accept Arthur's claim that the weak principle implies little or no duty of benevolence, for it will imply a significant duty of benevolence for those who admit, as I think most nonphilosophers and even off-guard philosophers will admit, that they spend considerable sums on items that by their own standards are of no moral

significance. But I do agree that the weak principle is nonetheless too weak, because it makes it too easy for the duty of benevolence to be avoided.

On the other hand, I think the strong principle will stand, whether the notion of moral significance is developed along utilitarian lines, or once again left to the individual reader's own sincere judgment. In either case, I would argue against Arthur's view that we are morally entitled to give greater weight to our own interests and purposes simply because they are our own. This view seems to me contrary to the idea, now widely shared by moral philosophers, that some element of impartiality or universalizability is inherent in the very notion of a moral judgment. (For a discussion of the different formulations of this idea, and an indication of the extent to which they are in agreement, see R. M. Hare, "Rules of War and Moral Reasoning," *Philosophy and Public Affairs* I, no. 2 [1972].) Granted, in normal circumstances, it may be better for everyone if we recognize that each of us will be primarily responsible for running our own lives and only secondarily responsible for others. This, however, is not a moral ultimate, but a secondary principle that derives from consideration of how a society may best order its affairs, given the limits of altruism in human beings. Such secondary principles are, I think, swept aside by the extreme evil of people starving to death.

Notes

1. There was also a third possibility: that India would go to war to enable the refugees to return to their lands. Since I wrote this paper, India has taken this way out. The situation is no longer that described above, but this does not affect my argument, as the next paragraph indicates.

2. In view of the special sense philosophers often give to the term, I should say that I use "obligation" simply as the abstract noun derived from "ought," so that "I have an obligation to" means no more, and no less, than "I ought to." This usage is in accordance with the definition of "ought" given by the *Shorter Oxford English Dictionary*: "the general verb to express duty or obligation." I do not think any issue of substance hangs on the way the term is used; sentences in which I use "obligation" could all be rewritten, although somewhat clumsily, as sentences in which a clause containing "ought" replaces the term "obligation."

3. J. O. Urmson, "Saints and Heroes," in *Essays in Moral Philosophy*, ed. Abraham I. Melden (Seattle: University of Washington Press, 1958), p. 214. For a related but significantly different view see also Henry Sidgwick, *The Methods of Ethics*, 7th edn. (London: Dover Press, 1907), pp. 220–21, 492–93.

4. *Summa Theologica*, II-II, Question 66, Article 7, in *Aquinas, Selected Political Writings*, ed. A. P. d'Entreves, trans. J. G. Dawson (Oxford: Basil Blackwell, 1948), p. 171.

5. See, for instance, John Kenneth Galbraith, *The New Industrial State* (Boston: Houghton Mifflin, 1967); and E. J. Mishan, *The Costs of Economic Growth* (New York: Praeger, 1967).

Questions for Analysis

1. What is the difference between the strong and weak versions of the principle of preventing bad occurrences?

2. What does Singer mean by "without sacrificing anything of comparable importance"?

3. Why does Singer say that the world would be fundamentally different if we followed his two principles?

4. Suppose someone said to Singer: "But I'm not responsible for the starvation that people experience. So why do I have a duty to prevent it?" How might Singer reply?

5. Why does Singer not regard helping as charity?

6. Suppose one accepts the argument that relief to countries without population control measures merely postpones starvation. Does this absolve one of the obligation to do anything to prevent starvation?

7. Is it accurate to say that, while Singer is inclined to the utilitarian view, his principles are essentially nonconsequential or at least could appeal to nonconsequentialists? Explain.

8. Does Singer's postscript undercut his original argument?

Reason and Morality in a World of Limited Food

Richard A. Watson

The principle of equity is central to philosophy professor Richard A. Watson's thesis in his "Reason and Morality in a World of Limited Food." The principle of equity refers to equal sharing. Watson's thesis is that, with respect to world hunger, there should be an equal sharing of food.

Watson is aware of the most trenchant objection to his position: Sharing food may turn out to be futile. Indeed, what if, as a result of sharing, the human species perishes? So be it, Watson answers. No matter how horrendous the consequences, the moral action is to share and share equally. As Watson says, "No principle of morality absolves one of behaving immorally simply to save one's life or nation."

From Richard A. Watson, "Reason and Morality in a World of Limited Food," in World Hunger and Moral Obligation, William Aiken and Hugh LaFollette, eds. (Englewood Cliffs, N.J.: Prentice-Hall, 1977). Reprinted by permission of the author.

Watson grants that such a suicidal course may be irrational. Nevertheless, he argues that the claims of morality supersede those of conflicting reason. In other words, the moral action may not necessarily be the reasonable or practical action. Where in fact the moral action is unreasonable, one nevertheless has an obligation to behave morally.

Watson believes that his conclusion that we must equally share what we have follows inexorably from the assumption that every human life is equal in value. Accepting this assumption, then presumably we must conclude that everyone deserves an equal share—no matter what the consequences, even if they be extinction.

Obviously Watson subordinates the principle of survival to the principle of equity. He feels that this is justified because "in the milieu of morality, it is immaterial whether or not the human species survives as a result of individual moral behavior."

Like Singer, Watson is arguing for an obligation to share. But, while Singer's basis is utilitarian, Watson's is decidedly nonconsequential, even Kantian in its rejection of any consequential considerations as a basis for morality.

A few years ago, President Johnson said:

> There are 200 million of us and 3 billion of them and they want what we've got, but we're not going to give it to them.

In this essay I examine the conflict between reasonable and moral behavior in a world of limited food. It appears to be unreasonable—and conceivably immoral—to share all food equally when this would result in everyone's being malnourished. Arguments for the morality of unequal distribution are presented from the standpoint of the individual, the nation, and the human species. These arguments fail because, although it is unreasonable to share limited food when sharing threatens survival, the moral principle of equity ranks sharing above survival. I accept the principle of equity, and conclude by challenging the ideological basis that makes sharing unreasonble.

The contrast of the moral with the reasonable depends on distinguishing people from things. Moral considerations pertain to behavior of individuals that affects other people by acting on them directly or by acting on things in which they have an interest. The moral context is broad, for people have interests in almost everything, and almost any behavior may affect someone.

If reasonable and moral behavior were coextensive, then there would be no morality. Thus, there is no contrast at the extremes that bound the moral milieu, reason and morality being the same at one pole, and morality not existing at the other. These extremes meet in evolutionary naturalism: If it is moral to treat people as animals surviving, then reason augmenting instinct is the best criterion for behavior, and a separate discipline of morality is extraneous. Only between the extremes can reason and morality conflict.

Between the extremes, some moralists use "rational" to indicate conclusions that tend toward moral behavior, and "practical" for conclusions that excusably do not. The use of these terms often constitutes special pleading, either to gain sympathy for a position that is not strictly reasonable but is "rational" (because it is "right"), or that is not strictly moral but is "practical" (because it "should" be done). These hedges hide the sharp distinction between people and things in the context of reason and morality. The rational and the practical are obviously reasonable in a way that they are not obviously either moral or immoral. Reasonable behavior is either moral, immoral, or amoral. When reason and morality conflict, there can be confusion, but no compromise.

Attacks on morality by reason disguised in practical dress are so common as to go almost without notice. The practical ousts morality as a determinant of behavior, particularly in industrialized nations. Many argue that the practical imperatives of survival preclude moral behavior even by those who want to be moral. If only it were practical to be moral, then all would gladly be so.

It is difficult to be moral in a world of limited food because the supreme moral principle is that of equity. The principle of equity is based on the belief that all human beings are moral equals with equal rights to the necessities of life. Differential treatment of human beings thus should be based only on their freely chosen actions and not on accidents of their birth and environment. Specific to this discussion, everyone has a right to an equal share of available food.

However, we find ourselves in a world about which many food and population experts assert the following:

1.   One-third of the world's people (the West) consume two-thirds of the world's resources.

2.   Two-thirds of the world's people (the Third World) are malnourished.

3.   Equal distribution of the world's resources would result in everyone's being malnourished.

There is ample evidence that these statements are true, but for this discussion it is enough that many people in the West—particularly those who occupy positions of responsibility and power—understand and accept them.

These moral and factual beliefs drive one to this practical conclusion: Although morally we should share all food equally, and we in the West eat more than we need, equal sharing would be futile (unreasonable), for then no one would be well nourished. Thus, any food sharing is necessarily symbolic, for no practical action would alleviate the plight of the malnourished.

For example, practical action—moral as far as it goes—might be to reduce food consumption until every Westerner is just well-nourished. But if the surplus were distributed equally to the other two-thirds of the world's people, they would still be malnourished. Thus, an easy excuse for not sharing at all is that it would neither solve the nourishment problem nor change the moral situation. Two-thirds would still be malnourished, and one-third would still be consuming more than equal shares of the world's food, to which everyone has equal rights.

Another argument for unequal distribution is as follows: All people are moral equals. Because everyone has a right to be well nourished, it would be immoral to take so much food from someone who has enough as to leave him without enough. Anyone who takes the food would be acting immorally, even if the taker is starving. This argument can go two ways. One could simply say that it would be immoral to deprive oneself of what one has. But if one wanted to discredit morality itself,

one could claim that morality in this instance is self-contradictory. For if I behave morally by distributing food equally, I behave immorally by depriving someone (myself) of enough food to remain well-nourished. And noticing that if all food were shared equally, everyone would be malnourished instead of just some, one might argue that it cannot be moral to deprive one person of his right to enough food so that two people have less than enough. Proper moral action must be to maintain the inequity, so at least one person can enjoy his rights.

Nevertheless, according to the highest principles of traditional Western morality, available food should be distributed equally even if everyone then will be malnourished. This is belabored by everyone who compares the earth to a lifeboat, a desert island, or a spaceship. In these situations, the strong are expected to take even a smaller share than the weak. There is no need for us to go overboard, however. We shall soon be as weak as anyone else if we just do our moral duty and distribute the food equally.

Given this, the well-nourished minority might try to buttress its position morally by attempting to solve the nourishment problem for everyone, either by producing enough food for everyone, or by humanely reducing the world's population to a size at which equal distribution of food would nourish everyone adequately. The difficulty with this is that national survival for the food-favored industrial nations requires maintenance of political and economic systems that depend on unequal distribution of limited goods.[1] In the present world context, it would be unreasonable (disastrous) for an industrialized nation to attempt to provide food for everybody. Who would pay for it? And after all, well-nourished citizens are obviously important to the survival of the nation. As for humanely reducing the world's population, there are no practical means for doing it. Thus, the practical expediencies of national survival preclude actions that might justify temporary unequal distribution with the claim that it is essential for solving the nourishment problem. Equal distribution is impossible without total (impractical) economic and political revolution.

These arguments are morally spurious. That food sufficient for well-nourished survival is the equal right of every human individual or nation is a specification of the higher principle that everyone has equal right to the necessities of life. The moral stress of the principle of equity is primarily on equal sharing, and only secondarily on what is being shared. The higher moral principle is of human *equity per se*. Consequently, the moral action is to distribute all food equally, *whatever the consequences*. This is the hard line apparently drawn by such moralists as Immanuel Kant and Noam Chomsky—but then, morality is hard. The conclusion may be unreasonable (impractical and irrational in conventional terms), but it is obviously moral. Nor should anyone purport surprise; it has always been understood that the claims of morality—if taken seriously—supersede those of conflicting reason.

One may even have to sacrifice one's life or one's nation to be moral in situations where practical behavior would preserve it. For example, if a prisoner of war undergoing torture is to be a (perhaps dead) patriot even when reason tells him that collaboration will hurt no one, he remains silent. Similarly, if one is to be moral, one distributes available food in equal shares (even if everyone then dies). That an action is necessary to save one's life is no excuse for behaving unpatriotically or immorally if one wishes to be a patriot or moral. No principle of morality absolves one of behaving immorally simply to save one's life or nation. There is a strict analogy here between adhering to moral principles for the sake of being moral, and adhering to Christian principles for the sake of being Christian. The moral world contains pits and lions, but one looks always to the highest light. The ultimate test always harks to the highest principle—recant or die—and it is pathetic to profess morality if one quits when the going gets rough.

I have put aside many questions of detail—such as the mechanical problems of distributing food—because detail does not alter the stark conclusion. If every human life is equal in value, then the equal distribution of the necessities of life is an extremely high, if not the highest, moral duty. It is at least high enough to override the excuse that by doing it one would lose one's own life. But many people cannot accept the view that one must distribute equally even if the nation collapses or all people die.

If everyone dies, then there will be no realm of morality. Practically speaking, sheer survival comes first. One can adhere to the principle of equity only if one exists. So it is rational to suppose that the principle of survival is morally higher than the principle of equity. And though one might not be able to argue for unequal distribution of food to save a nation—for nations can come and go—one might well argue that unequal distribution is necessary for the survival of the human species. That is, some large group—say one-third of present world population—should be at least well-nourished for human survival.

However, from an individual standpoint, the human species—like the nation—is of no moral relevance. From a naturalistic standpoint, survival does come first; from a moralistic standpoint—as indicated above—survival may have to be sacrificed. In the milieu of morality, it is immaterial whether or not the human species survives as a result of individual moral behavior.

A possible way to resolve this conflict between reason and morality is to challenge the view that morality pertains only to the behavior of individual human beings. One way to do this is to break down the distinction between people and things. It would have to be established that such abstract things as "the people," "the nation," and "the human species" in themselves have moral status. Then they would have a right to survival just as human beings have a right to life: We should be concerned about the survival of these things not merely because human beings have an interest in them, but because it would be immoral *per se* to destroy them.

In the West, corporation law provides the theoretical basis for treating things as people.[2] Corporate entities such as the State, the Church, and trading companies have long enjoyed special status in Western society. The rights of corporate entities are precisely defined by a legal fiction, the concept of the corporate person. Christopher D. Stone says that corporate persons enjoy as many legal rights as, and sometimes more than, do individual human persons.[3] Thus, while most of us are not tempted to confuse ordinary things like stones and houses with people, almost everyone concurs with a legal system that treats corporate entities as people. The great familiarity and usefulness of this system supports the delusion that corporate entities have rights in common with, and are the moral equals of, individual human beings.

On these grounds, some argue that because of the size, importance, and power of corporate entities, institutional rights have priority over the rights of individuals. Of course, to the extent that society is defined by the economy or the State, people are dependent on and subordinate to these institutions. Practically speaking, institutional needs come first; people's needs are satisfied perhaps coextensively with, but secondarily to, satisfying institutional needs. It is argued that to put individual human needs first would be both illogical and impractical, for people and their needs are defined only in the social context. Institutions come first because they are prerequisite to the very existence of people.

A difficulty with the above argument as a support for any given institution is that it provides merely for the priority of *some* institutions over human individuals, not, say, for the priority of the United States or the West. But it does appear to provide an argument for the priority of the human species.

Given that the human species has rights as a fictional person on the analogy of corporate rights, it would seem to be rational to place the right of survival of the species above that of individuals. Unless the species survives, no individual will survive, and thus an individual's right to life is subordinate to the species' right to survival. If species survival depends on the unequal distribution of food to maintain a healthy breeding stock, then it is morally right for some people to have plenty while others starve. Only if there is enough food to nourish everyone well does it follow that food should be shared equally.

This might be true if corporate entities actually do have moral status and moral rights. But obviously, the legal status of corporate entities as fictional persons does not make them moral equals or superiors of actual human persons. Legislators might profess astonishment that anyone would think that a corporate person is a *person* as people are, let alone a moral person. However, because the legal rights of corporate entities are based on individual rights, and because corporate entities are treated so much like persons, the transition is often made.

Few theorists today would argue that the state or the human species is a personal agent.[4] But all this means is that idealism is dead in theory. Unfortunately, its influence lives, so it is worth giving an argument to show that corporate entities are not real persons.

Corporate entities are not persons as you and I are in the explicit sense that we are self-conscious agents and they are not. Corporate entities are not *agents* at all, let alone moral agents. This is a good reason for not treating corporate entities even as fictional persons. The distinction between people and other things, to generalize, is that people are self-conscious agents, whereas things are not.

The possession of rights essentially depends on an entity's being self-conscious, i.e., on its actually being a person. If it is self-conscious, then it has a right to life. Self-consciousness is a necessary, but not sufficient, condition for an entity's also being a responsible moral agent as most human beings are. A moral agent must have the capacity to be responsible, i.e., the capacity to choose and to act freely with respect to consequences that the agent does or can recognize and accept as its own choice and doing. Only a being who knows himself as a person, and who can effect choices and accept consequences, is a responsible moral agent.

On these grounds, moral equality rests on the actuality of moral agency based on reciprocal rights and responsibilities. One is responsible to something only if it can be responsible in return. Thus, we have responsibilities to other people, and they have reciprocal rights. We have no responsibilities to things as such, and they have no rights. If we care for things, it is because people have interests in them, not because things in themselves impose responsibilities on us.

That is, as stated early in this essay, morality essentially has to do with relations among people, among persons. It is nonsense to talk of things that cannot be moral agents as having responsibilities; consequently, it is nonsense to talk of whatever is not actually a person as having rights. It is deceptive even to talk of legal rights of a corporate entity. Those rights (and reciprocal responsibilities) actually pertain to individual human beings who have an interest in the corporate entity. The State or the human species have no rights at all, let alone rights superior to those of individuals.

The basic reason given for preserving a nation or the human species is that otherwise the milieu of morality would not exist. This is false so far as specific nations are concerned, but it is true that the existence of individuals depends on the existence of the species. However, although moral behavior is required of each individual, no principle requires that the realm of morality itself be preserved. Thus, we are reduced to the position that people's interest in preserving the human species is based primarily on the interest of each in individual survival. Having shown above that the principle of equity is morally superior to the principle of survival, we can conclude again that food should be shared equally even if this means the extinction of the human race.

Is there no way to produce enough food to nourish everyone well? Besides cutting down to the minimum, people in the West might quit feeding such nonhuman animals as cats and dogs. However, some people (e.g., Peter Singer) argue that mere sentience—the capacity to suffer pain—means that an animal is the moral equal of human beings.[5] I argue that because nonhuman animals are not moral agents, they do not share the rights of self-conscious responsible persons. And considering the profligacy of nature, it is rational to argue that if nonhuman animals have any rights at all, they include not the right to life, but merely the right to fight for life. In fact, if people in the West did not feed grain to cattle, sheep, and hogs, a considerable amount of food would be freed for human consumption. Even then, there might not be enough to nourish everyone well.

Let me remark that Stone and Singer attempt to break down the distinction between people on the one hand, and certain things (corporate entities) and nonhuman animals on the other, out of moral concern. However, there is another, profoundly antihumanitarian movement also attempting to break down the distinction. All over the world, heirs of Gobineau, Goebbels, and Hitler practice genocide and otherwise treat people as nonhuman animals and things in the name of the State. I am afraid that the consequences of treating entities such as corporations and nonhuman animals—that are not moral agents—as persons with rights will not be that we will treat national parks and chickens the way we treat people, but that we will have provided support for those who would treat people the way we now treat nonhuman animals and things.

The benefits of modern society depend in no small part on the institution of corporation law.

Even if the majority of these benefits are to the good—of which I am by no means sure—the legal fiction of corporate personhood still elevates corporate needs above the needs of people. In the present context, reverence for corporate entities leads to the spurious argument that the present world imbalance of food and resources is morally justified in the name of the higher rights of sovereign nations, or even of the human species, the survival of which is said to be more important than the right of any individual to life.

This conclusion is morally absurd. This is not, however, the fault of morality. We *should* share all food equally, at least until everyone is well-nourished. Besides food, *all* the necessities of life should be shared, at least until everyone is adequately supplied with a humane minimum. The hard conclusion remains that we should share all food equally even if this means that everyone starves and the human species becomes extinct. But, of course, the human race would survive even equal sharing, for after enough people died, the remainder could be well-nourished on the food that remained. But this grisly prospect does not show that anything is wrong with the principle of equity. Instead, it shows that something is profoundly wrong with the social institutions in which sharing the necessities of life equally is "impractical" and "irrational."

In another ideological frame, moral behavior might also be practical and rational. As remarked above, equal sharing can be accomplished only through total economic and political revolution. Obviously, this is what is needed.

Notes

1. See Richard Watson, "The Limits of World Order," *Alternatives: A Journal of World Policy*, I (1975), 487–513.

2. See Christopher D. Stone, *Should Trees Have Standing? Toward Legal Rights for Natural Objects* (Los Altos, Calif.: William Kaufman, 1974). Stone proposes that to protect such things as national parks, we should give them legal personhood as we do corporations.

3. Ibid., p. 47: "It is more and more the individual human being, with his consciousness, that is the legal fiction." Also: "The legal system does the best it can to maintain the illusion of the reality of the individual human being." (footnote 125) Many public figures have discovered that they have a

higher legal status if they incorporate themselves than they do as individual persons.

4. Stone (ibid., p. 47) does say that "institutions . . . have wills, minds, purposes, and inertias that are in very important ways their own, i.e., that can transcend and survive changes in the consciousness of the individual humans who supposedly comprise them, and whom they supposedly serve," but I do not think Stone actually believes that corporate entities are persons like you and me.

5. See Peter Singer, *Animal Liberation* (New York: The New York Review of Books/Random House, 1975).

Questions for Analysis

1. Describe the conflict between the "reasonable" and the "moral."

2. At one point in the essay, Watson invokes Kant to fortify his position. But surely Kant saw no conflict between the "reasonable" and the "moral." Do you think that Watson is using the term reasonable in the sense of what is practical, useful, or productive of happiness; and not in the sense of what is logically consistent? Explain.

3. Why does Watson feel that arguments for the morality of unequal distribution fail?

4. Why does Watson say: "It is difficult to be moral in a world of limited food because the supreme moral principle is that of equity"? Do you accept the supremacy of equity as a moral principle?

5. From what higher principle does Watson say that people have a right to food sufficient for well-nourished survival?

6. Do you agree with Watson that morality in some cases may be irrational? Is it necessary first to clarify Watson's use of the term irrational?

7. If morality may be unreasonable, does this create any special problems for the moralist?

8. Do you think that Kant would agree that "if one is to be moral, one distributes available food in equal shares (even if everyone then dies)"?

Equality, Entitlements, and the Distribution of Income

John Arthur

As indicated in the chapter, an alternative to the positions that argue for an obligation to share or not to share food is the position that views sharing as morally permissible but not obligatory. In his "Equality, Entitlements, and the Distribution of Income," professor of philosophy John Arthur argues that sharing ultimately is an act of benevolence. At the same time, he claims that there may be times when we have a duty to be so benevolent.

Thanks to Aleta Arthur Clement Dore, and William Shaw for helpful comments on an earlier version of this paper, and especially to Richard B. Brandt, whose influence is apparent throughout.

Arthur begins by observing an ambivalence in our moral code. Sometimes we feel obliged to help the needy; other times we feel justified in keeping what we have, even though our sacrifice might cause greater evil to be avoided. How can we resolve the tension?

Singer in his essay suggested a principle of greater moral evil. Thus, any time we can prevent something bad without sacrificing anything of comparable moral significance, we ought to do it. Arthur rejects this response, arguing that it ignores the essential role of entitlements in our moral code. Arthur then goes on to discuss entitlements in terms of rights and desert and demonstrates how they are embedded in our moral outlook. Indeed, by dissecting the nature of morality, with special attention to the kind of morality we want to endorse, Arthur champions entitlements as a necessary part of an ideal moral code.

Be careful not to misconstrue Arthur. He is not *making entitlements absolute; he is* not *saying that individuals never have an obligation to help the needy. Quite the opposite, he acknowledges that we likely have obligations to help* where there is no substantial cost to ourselves. *By the same token, in Arthur's view it is at least sometimes moral to invoke rights and duties as justification for not giving aid.*

Introduction

My guess is that everyone who reads these words is wealthy by comparison with the poorest millions of people on our planet. Not only do we have plenty of money for food, clothing, housing, and other necessities, but a fair amount is left over for far less important purchases like phonograph records, fancy clothes, trips, intoxicants, movies, and so on. And what's more we don't usually give a thought to whether or not we ought to spend our money on such luxuries rather than to give it to those who need it more; we just assume it's ours to do with as we please.

Peter Singer, "Famine, Affluence, and Morality," and Richard Watson, "Reason and Morality in a World of Limited Food" (both reprinted in this volume) argue that our assumption is wrong, that we should not buy luxuries when others are in severe need. But are they correct? In the first two sections of this paper my aim is to get into focus just what their arguments are, and to evaluate them. Both Singer and Watson, it seems to me, ignore an important feature of our moral code, namely that it allows people who deserve or have rights to their earnings to keep them.

But the fact that our code encourages a form of behavior is not a complete defense, for it is possible that our current moral attitudes are mistaken. Sections 3 and 4 consider this possibility from two angles: universalizability and the notion of an ideal moral code. Neither of these approaches, I argue, requires that desert and rights be sacrificed in the name of redistribution.

1. Equality and the Duty to Aid

What does our moral code have to say about helping people in need? Watson emphasizes what he calls the "principle of equity." Since "all human life is of equal value," and difference in treatment should be "based on freely chosen actions and not accidents of birth or environment," he thinks that we have "equal rights to the necessities of life." To distribute food unequally assumes that some lives are worth more than others, an assumption which, he says, we do not accept. Watson believes, in fact, that we put such importance on the "equity principle" that it should not be violated even if unequal distribution is the only way for anybody to survive. (Leaving aside for the moment whether or not he is correct about our code, it seems to me that if it really did require us to commit mass suicide rather than allow inequality in wealth, then we would want to abandon it for a more suitable set of rules. But more on that later.)

Is Watson correct in assuming that all life is of equal value? Did Adolph Hitler and Martin Luther King, for example, lead two such lives? Clearly one did far more good and less harm than the other. Nor are moral virtues like courage, kindness, and trustworthiness equally distributed among people. So there are at least two senses in which people are not morally equal.

Yet the phrase "All men are equal" has an almost platitudinous ring, and many of us would not hesitate to say that equality is a cornerstone of our morality. But what does it mean? It seems to me that we might have in mind one of two things.

First is an idea that Thomas Jefferson expressed in the *Declaration of Independence*. "All men are created equal" meant, for him, that no man is the moral inferior of another, that, in other words, there are certain rights which all men share equally, including life and liberty. We are entitled to pursue our own lives with a minimum of interference from others, and no person is the natural slave of another. But, as Jefferson also knew, equality in that sense does not require equal distribution of the necessities of life, only that we not interfere with one another, allowing instead every person the liberty to pursue his own affairs, so long as he does not violate the rights of his fellows.

Others, however, have something different in mind when they speak of human equality. I want to develop this second idea by recounting briefly the details of Singer's argument in "Famine, Affluence, and Morality." He first argues that two general moral principles are widely accepted, and then that those principles imply an obligation to eliminate starvation.

The first principle is simply the "suffering and death from lack of food, shelter and medical care are bad." Some may be inclined to think that the mere existence of such an evil in itself places an obligation on others, but that is, of course, the problem which Singer addresses. I take it that he is not begging the question in this obvious way and will argue from the existence of evil to the obligation of others to eliminate it. But how, exactly, does he establish this? The second principle, he thinks, shows the connection, but it is here that controversy arises.

This principle, which I will call the greater moral evil rule, is as follows:

> If it is in our power to prevent something bad from happening, without thereby sacrificing anything of comparable moral importance, we ought, morally, to do it.[1]

In other words, people are entitled to keep their earnings only if there is no way for them to prevent a greater evil by giving them away. Providing others with food, clothing, and housing would generally be of more importance than buying luxuries, so the greater moral evil rule now requires substantial redistribution of wealth.

Certainly there are few, if any, of us who live by that rule, although that hardly shows we are *justified* in our way of life; we often fail to live up

to our own standards. Why does Singer think our shared morality requires that we follow the greater moral evil rule? What arguments does he give for it?

He begins with an analogy. Suppose you came across a child drowning in a shallow pond. Certainly we feel it would be wrong not to help. Even if saving the child meant we must dirty our clothes, we would emphasize that those clothes are not of comparable significance to the child's life. The greater moral evil rule thus seems a natural way of capturing why we think it would be wrong not to help.

But the argument for the greater moral evil rule is not limited to Singer's claim that it explains our feelings about the drowning child or that it appears "uncontroversial." Moral equality also enters the picture. Besides the Jeffersonian idea that we share certain rights equally, most of us are also attracted to another type of equality, namely that like amounts of suffering (or happiness) are of equal significance, no matter who is experiencing them. I cannot reasonably say that, while my pain is no more severe than yours, I am somehow special and it's more important that mine be alleviated. Objectivity requires us to admit the opposite, that no one has a unique status which warrants such special pleading. So equality demands equal consideration of interests as well as respect for certain rights.

But if we fail to give to famine relief and instead purchase a new car when the old one will do, or buy fancy clothes for a friend when his or her old ones are perfectly good, are we not assuming that the relatively minor enjoyment we or our friends may get is as important as another person's life? And that a form of prejudice; we are acting as if people were not equal in the sense that their interests deserve equal consideration. We are giving special consideration to ourselves or to our group, rather like a racist does. Equal consideration of interests thus leads naturally to the greater moral evil rule.

2. Rights and Desert

Equality, in the sense of giving equal consideration to equally serious needs, is part of our moral code. And so we are led, quite rightly I think, to the conclusion that we should prevent harm to others if in doing so we do not sacrifice anything of comparable moral importance. But there is also another side to the coin, one which Singer and Watson ignore. This can be expressed rather awkwardly by the notion of entitlements. These fall into two broad categories, rights and desert. A few examples will show what I mean.

All of us could help others by giving away or allowing others to use our bodies. While your life may be shortened by the loss of a kidney or less enjoyable if lived with only one eye, those costs are probably not comparable to the loss experienced by a person who will die without any kidney or who is totally blind. We can even imagine persons who will actually be harmed in some way by your not granting sexual favors to them. Perhaps the absence of a sexual partner would cause psychological harm or even rape. Now suppose that you can prevent this evil without sacrificing anything of comparable importance. Obviously such relations may not be pleasant, but according to the greater moral evil rule that is not enough; to be justified in refusing, you must show that the unpleasantness you would experience is of equal importance to the harm you are preventing. Otherwise, the rule says you must consent.

If anything is clear, however, it is that our code does not *require* such heroism, you are entitled to keep your second eye and kidney and not bestow sexual favors on anyone who may be harmed without them. The reason for this is often expressed in terms of rights; it's your body, you have a right to it, and that weighs against whatever duty you have to help. To sacrifice a kidney for a stranger is to do more than is required, it's heroic.

Moral rights are normally divided into two categories. Negative rights are rights of non-interference. The right to life, for example, is a right not to be killed. Property rights, the right to privacy, and the right to exercise religious freedom are also negative, requiring only that people leave others alone and not interfere.

Positive rights, however, are rights of recipience. By not putting their children up for adoption, parents give them various positive rights, including rights to be fed, clothed, and housed. If I agree to share in a business venture, my promise creates a right of recipience, so that when I back out of the deal, I've violated your right.

Negative rights also differ from positive in that the former are natural; the ones you have

depend on what you are. If lower animals lack rights to life or liberty it is because there is a relevant difference between them and us. But the positive rights you may have are not natural; they arise because others have promised, agreed, or contracted to give you something.

Normally, then, a duty to help a stranger in need is not the result of a right he has. Such a right would be positive, and since no contract or promise was made, no such right exists. An exception to this would be a lifeguard who contracts to watch out for someone's children. The parent whose child drowns would in this case be doubly wronged. First, the lifeguard should not have cruelly or thoughtlessly ignored the child's interests, and second, he ought not to have violated the rights of the parents that he help. Here, unlike Singer's case, we can say there are rights at stake. Other bystanders also act wrongly by cruelly ignoring the child, but unlike the lifeguard they do not violate anybody's rights. Moral rights are one factor to be weighed, but we also have other obligations; I am not claiming that rights are all we need to consider. That view, like the greater moral evil rule, trades simplicity for accuracy. In fact, our code expects us to help people in need as well as to respect negative and positive rights. But we are also entitled to invoke our own rights as justification for not giving to distant strangers or when the cost to us is substantial, as when we give up an eye or kidney.

Rights come in a variety of shapes and sizes, and people often disagree about both their shape and size. Can a woman kill an unborn child because of her right to control her body? Does mere inheritance transfer rights to property? Do dolphins have a right to live? While some rights are widely accepted, others are controversial.

One more comment about rights, then we'll look at desert. Watson's position, which I criticized for other reasons earlier, is also mistaken because he ignores important rights. He claims that we must pay no attention to "accidents of birth and environment" and base our treatment of people on "what they freely choose." But think about how you will (or did) select a spouse or lover. Are you not entitled to consider such "accidents of birth and environment" as attractiveness, personality, and intelligence? It is, after all, your future, and it is certainly a part of our shared moral code that you have a right to use those (or whatever) criteria you wish in selecting a mate. It is at best an exaggeration to say we must always "ignore accidents of birth and environment" in our treatment of people.

Desert is a second form of entitlement. Suppose, for example, an industrious farmer manages through hard work to produce a surplus of food for the winter while a lazy neighbor spends his summer fishing. Must our industrious farmer ignore his hard work and give the surplus away because his neighbor or his family will suffer? What again seems clear is that we have more than one factor to weigh. Not only should we compare the consequences of his keeping it with his giving it away; we also should weigh the fact that one farmer deserves the food, he earned it through his hard work. Perhaps his deserving the product of his labor is outweighed by the greater need of his lazy neighbor, or perhaps it isn't, but being outweighed is in any case not the same as weighing nothing!

Desert can be negative, too. The fact that the Nazi war criminal did what he did means he deserves punishment, that we have a reason to send him to jail. Other considerations, for example the fact that nobody will be deterred by his suffering, or that he is old and harmless, may weigh against punishment and so we may let him go; but again that does not mean he doesn't still deserve to be punished.

Our moral code gives weight to both the greater moral evil principle and entitlements. The former emphasizes equality, claiming that from an objective point of view all comparable suffering, whoever its victim, is equally significant. It encourages us to take an impartial look at all the various effects of our actions; it is thus forward-looking. When we consider matters of entitlement, however, our attention is directed to the past. Whether we have rights to money, property, eyes, or whatever, depends on how we came to possess them. If they were acquired by theft rather than from birth or through gift exchange, then the right is suspect. Desert, like rights, is also backward-looking, emphasizing past effort or past transgressions which now warrant reward or punishment.

Our commonly shared morality thus requires that we ignore neither consequences nor entitlements, neither the future results of our action nor relevant events in the past. It encourages people to help others in need, especially when it's a friend or someone we are close to geographically, and when the cost is not significant. But it also gives weight to rights and desert, so that we are not usually obligated to give to strangers.

One path is still open as a defense of the greater moral evil rule, and it deserves comment. I have assumed throughout that Singer wants to emphasize the great disparity in the amount of enjoyment someone may get from, say, a new car, as compared with the misery that could be prevented by using the money to save another's life. The fact that the two are not comparable means that the money should not be spent on the car. It is possible to interpret the rule differently, however. By admitting that having rights and deserving things are also of moral significance Singer could accept what I have said so that the greater moral evil rule would survive intact.

The problem with this response, however, is that the greater moral evil rule has now become an almost empty platitude, urging nothing more than that we should prevent something bad unless we have adequate moral reason not to do so. Since rights and desert often provide such reasons, the rule would say nothing useful about our obligation to help others, and it certainly would not require us to "reduce ourselves to the level of marginal utility" so that the "consumer society" would "slow down and perhaps disappear" as Singer claims. I will therefore assume he would not accept such an interpretation of his view, that entitlements are not among the sacrifices which could balance off the suffering caused by failing to help people in need.

But unless we are moral relativists, the mere fact that entitlements are an important part of our moral code does not in itself justify such a role. Singer and Watson can perhaps best be seen as moral reformers, advocating the rejection of rules which provide for distribution according to rights and desert. Certainly the fact that in the past our moral code condemned suicide and racial mixing while condoning slavery should not convince us that a more enlightened moral code, one which we would want to support, would take such positions. Rules which define acceptable behavior are continually changing, and we must allow for the replacement of inferior ones.

Why should we not view entitlements as

examples of inferior rules we are better off without? What could justify our practice of evaluating actions by looking backward to rights and desert instead of just to their consequences? One answer is that more fundamental values than rights and desert are at stake, namely fairness, justice, and respect. Failure to reward those who earn good grades or promotions is wrong because it's *unfair;* ignoring past guilt shows a lack of regard for *justice;* and failure to respect rights to life, privacy, or religious choice suggests a lack of *respect for other persons.*

Some people may be persuaded by those remarks, feeling that entitlements are now on an acceptably firm foundation. But an advocate of equality may well want to question why fairness, justice, and respect for persons should matter. But since it is no more obvious that preventing suffering matters than that fairness, respect, and justice do, we again seem to have reached an impasse.

3. Universalizability

It is sometimes thought that we can choose between competing moral rules by noting which ones are compatible with some more fundamental rule. One such fundamental standard is attributed to Kant, though it is also rooted in traditional Christian thought. "Do unto others as you would have them do unto you" and the Kantian categorical imperative, "Act only on maxims that you can will would become universal laws," express an idea some think is basic to *all* moral rules. The suggestion is that if you think what you're doing is right, then you have got to be willing to universalize your judgment, that is, to acknowledge that anyone in similar circumstances would be correct if he were to follow the same rule.

Such familiar reasoning can be taken in two very different ways. The first requires only that a person not make himself an exception, that he live up to his own standard. This type of universalizability, however, cannot help choose between the two rules. An advocate of rights and desert would surely agree that whether he were the deserving or undeserving one, whether he had the specific right or did not have it, entitlements still should not be ignored. Nothing about the position of those supporting rights and desert suggests that they must make exceptions for themselves; such

rules are in that sense universalizable. But the advocate of the greater moral evil rule can also be counted on to claim that he too should not be made an exception, and that *ignoring* entitlements in favor of the greater moral evil rule is the proper course whether or not he would benefit from the policy. Both views, then, could be universalized in the first sense.

But if we understand universalizability in another sense, neither of the rules passes the test. If being "willing to universalize the judgment" means that a supporter of a particular moral rule would be equally happy with the result were the roles reversed, then there is doubt whether either is universalizable. The rights advocate cannot promise always to like the outcome; he probably would *prefer,* were the tables turned and his life depended on somebody not keeping his rightfully owned income, that entitlements be ignored in that instance. But his opponent cannot pass the test either, since he would likely prefer that rights and desert *not* be ignored were he in a position to benefit from them. But in any case it is not at all clear why we should expect people who make moral judgments to be neutral as to which position they occupy. Must a judge who thinks justice requires that a murderer go to jail agree that he would prefer jail if he were the murderer? It seems that all he must do to universalize his judgment is agree that it would be *right* that he go to jail if the tables were turned, that, in other words, he is not exempt from the rules. But that is a test, as I said, which supporters of entitlements can pass.

So the test of universalizability does not provide grounds for rejecting entitlement rules, and we are once again at an impasse. A second possibility is to view the egalitarian as a moral reformer. Then, perhaps, the criticism of entitlements can be defended as part of a more reasonable and effective moral system. In the final section I look in detail at the idea that rights and desert would not be part of a such ideal moral code, one which we would support if we were fully rational.

4. Entitlements and the Ideal Moral Code

The idea I want now to consider is that part of our code should be dropped, so that people could no longer invoke rights and desert as justification for not making large sacrifices for strangers. In place of entitlements would be a rule requiring that any time we can prevent something bad without sacrificing anything of comparable moral significance we ought to do it. Our current code, however, allows people to say that, while they would do more good with their earnings, still they have rights to the earnings, the earnings are deserved, and so need not be given away. The crucial question is whether we want to have such entitlement rules in our code, or whether we should reject them in favor of the greater moral evil rule.

Universalizability, I argued, gives no clear answer to this. Each position also finds a certain amount of support within our code, either from the idea of equal consideration of interests or from our concerns about fairness, justice, and respect for other persons. The problem to be resolved, then, is whether there are other reasons to drop entitlement rules in favor of the greater moral evil rule.

I believe that our best procedure is not to think about this or that specific rule, drawing analogies, refining it, and giving counter-examples, but to focus instead on the nature of morality as a whole. What is a moral code? What do we want it to do? What type of code do we want to support? These questions will give us a fresh perspective from which to consider the merits of rules which allow people to appeal to rights and desert and to weigh the issue of whether our present code should be reformed.

We can begin with the obvious: A moral code is a system of rules designed to guide people's conduct. As such, it has characteristics in common with other systems of rules. Virtually every organization has rules which govern the conduct of members; clubs, baseball leagues, corporations, bureaucracies, profession associations, even *The* Organization all have rules. Another obvious point is this: What the rules are depends on why the organization exists. Rules function to enable people to accomplish the goals which lead them to organize in the first place. Some rules, for example, "Don't snitch on fellow mafioso," "Pay dues to the fraternity," and "Don't give away trade secrets to competing companies," serve in obvious ways. Other times the real purposes of rules are controversial, as when doctors do not allow advertising by fellow members of the AMA.

Frequently rules reach beyond members of a specific organization, obligating everyone who is capable of following them to do so. These include costs of civil and criminal law, etiquette, custom, and morality. But before discussing the specific purposes of moral rules, it will be helpful to look briefly at some of the similarities and differences between these more universal codes.

First, the sanctions imposed on rule violators vary among different types of codes. While in our legal code, transgressions are punished by fines, jail, or repayment of damages, informal sanctions of praise, blame, or guilt encourage conformity to the rules of morality and etiquette. Another difference is that while violation of a moral rule is always a serious affair, this need not be so for legal rules of etiquette and custom. Many of us think it unimportant whether a fork is on the left side of a plate or whether an outmoded and widely ignored Sunday closing law is violated, but violation of a moral rule is not ignored. Indeed, that a moral rule has lost its importance is often shown by its demotion to status of mere custom.

A third difference is that legal rules, unlike rules of morality, custom, and etiquette, provide for a specific person or procedure that is empowered to alter the rules. If Congress acts to change the tax laws, then as of the date stated in the statute the rules are changed. Similarly for the governing rules of social clubs, government bureacracies, and the AMA. Rules of custom, morals, and etiquette also change, of course, but they do so in a less precise and much more gradual fashion, with no person or group specifically empowered to make changes.

This fact, that moral rules are *in a sense* beyond the power of individuals to change, does not show that rules of morality, any more than those of etiquette, are objective in the same sense that scientific laws are. All that needs to happen for etiquette or morality to change is for people to change certain practices, namely the character traits they praise and blame, or the actions they approve or disapprove. Scientific laws, however, are discovered, not invented by society, and so are beyond human control. The law that the boiling point of water increases as its pressure increases cannot be changed by humans, either individually or collectively. Such laws are a part of the fabric of nature.

But the fact that moral rules, like legal ones, are not objective in the same sense as scientific ones does not mean that there is no objective standard of right or wrong, that one code is as good as another, or even that the "right thing to do" is just what the moral code currently followed in our society teaches is right. Like the rules of a fraternity or corporation, legal and moral rules can serve their purposes either well or poorly, and whether they do is a matter of objective fact. Further, if a moral code doesn't serve its purpose, we have good reason to criticize all or part of it, to ignore it, and to think of a way to change it, just as its serving us well provides a good reason to obey. In important respects morality is not at all subjective.

Take for example a rule which prohibits homosexual behavior. Suppose it serves no useful purpose, but only increases the burdens of guilt, shame, and social rejection borne by 10% of our population. If this is so, we have good reason to ignore the rule. On the other hand, if rules against killing and lying help us to accomplish what we want from a moral code, we have good reason to support those rules. Morality is created, and as with other systems of rules which we devise, a particular rule may or may not further the shared human goals and interests which motivated its creation. There is thus a connection between what we ought to do and how well a code serves its purposes. If a rule serves well the general purposes of a moral code then we have reason to support it, and if we have reason to support it we also have reason to obey it. But if, on the other hand, a rule is useless, or if it frustrates the purposes of morality, we have reason neither to support nor to follow it. All of this suggests the following conception of a right action: Any action is right which is approved by an ideal moral code, one which it is rational for us to support. Which code we would want to support would depend, of course, on which one is able to accomplish the purposes of morality.

If we are to judge actions in this way, by reference to what an ideal moral code would require, we must first have a clear notion of just what purposes morality is meant to serve. And here again the comparison between legal and moral rules is instructive. Both systems discourage certain types of behavior—killing, robbing, and beating—while encouraging others—repaying debts, keeping important agreements, and providing for one's children. The purpose which both have in discouraging various behaviors is obvious.

Such negative rules help keep people from causing harm. Think for example of how we are first taught it is wrong to hit a baby brother or sister. Parents explain the rule by emphasizing that it hurts the infant when we hit him. Promoting the welfare of ourselves, our friends and family, and to a lesser degree all who have the capacity to be harmed is the primary purpose of negative moral rules. It's how we learn them as children and why we support them as adults.

The same can be said of positive rules, rules which encourage various types of behavior. Our own welfare, as well as that of friends, family, and others, depends on general acceptance of rules which encourage keeping promises, fulfilling contracts, and meeting the needs of our children. Just try to imagine a society in which promises or agreements mean nothing, or where family members took no concern for one another. A life without positive or negative rights would be as Thomas Hobbes long ago observed: nasty, brutish, and short.

Moral rules thus serve two purposes. They promote our own welfare by discouraging acts of violence and promoting social conventions like promising and paying debts, and second, they perform the same service for our family, friends, and others. We have reason to support a moral code because we care about our own welfare, and because we care about the well-being of others. For most of us the ideal moral code, the one we would support because it best fulfills these purposes, is the code which is most effective in promoting general welfare.

But can everyone be counted on to share these concerns? Think, for example, of an egoist, who only desires that *he* be happy. Such a person, if he existed, would obviously like a code which maximizes his own welfare. How can we hope to get agreement about which code it is rational to support, if different people expect different things from moral rules?

Before considering these questions, I want to mention two preliminary points. First, the problem with egoism is that it tends to make morality relative. If we are going to decide moral disputes by considering what would be required by the code which it is rational for people to support, then we must reach agreement about what that code is. Otherwise the right action for an altruist, the one which is required by the code which it's rational for him to support, may be the wrong act for the egoist. Yet how can the very same act done in identical circumstances be wrong for one person yet right for another? Maybe morality is relative in that way, but if so the prospects for peaceful resolution of important disputes is lessened, a result not to be hoped for.

My second point is that while we certainly do not want to assume people are perfect altruists, we also do not want to give people less credit than they deserve. There is some evidence, for example, that concern for others in our species is part of our biological heritage. Some geneticists think that many animals, particularly higher ones, take an innate interest in the welfare of other members of their species.[3] Other researchers argue that feelings of benevolence originate naturally, through classical conditioning; we develop negative associations with our own pain behavior (since we are then in pain) and this attitude becomes generalized to the pain behavior of others.[4] If either of these is true, egoism might be far more unusual than is commonly supposed, perhaps rare enough that it can be safely ignored.

There is also a line of reasoning which suggests that disagreement about which moral code to support need not be as deep as is often thought. What sort of code in fact *would* a rational egoist support? He would first think of proposing one which allows him to do anything whatsoever that he desires, while requiring that others ignore their own happiness and do what is in his interests. But here enters a family of considerations which will bring us back to the merits of entitlements versus the greater moral evil rule. Our egoist is contemplating what code to *support*, which means going before the public and trying to win general acceptance of his proposed rules. Caring for nobody else, he might secretly prefer the code I mentioned, yet it would hardly make sense for him to work for its public adoption since others are unlikely to put his welfare above the happiness of themselves and their families. So it looks as if the code an egoist would actually support might not be all that different from the ideal (welfare maximizing) code; he would be wasting his time to advocate rules that serve only his own interests because they have no chance of public acceptance.

The lesson to be learned here is a general one: The moral code it is rational for us to support must be practical; it must actually work. This means,

among other things, that it must be able to gain the support of almost everyone.

But the code must be practical in other respects as well. I have emphasized that it is wrong to ignore the possibilities of altruism, but it is also important that a code not assume people are more unselfish than they are. Rules that would work only for angels are not the ones it is rational to support for humans. Second, an ideal code cannot assume we are more objective than we are; we often tend to rationalize when our own interests are at stake, and a rational person will also keep that in mind when choosing a moral code. Finally, it is not rational to support a code which assumes we have perfect knowledge. We are often mistaken about the consequences of what we do, and a workable code must take that into account as well.

I want now to bring these various considerations together in order to decide whether or not to reject entitlements in favor of the greater moral evil rule. I will assume that the egoist is not a serious obstacle to acceptance of a welfare maximizing code, either because egoists are, like angels, merely imaginary, or because a practical egoist would only support a code which can be expected to gain wide support. We still have to ask whether entitlements would be included in a welfare maximizing code. The initial temptation is to substitute the greater moral evil rule for entitlements, requiring people to prevent something bad whenever the cost to them is less significant than the benefit to another. Surely, we might think, total welfare would be increased by a code requiring people to give up their savings if a greater evil can be prevented.

I think, however, that this is wrong, that an ideal code would provide for rights and would encourage rewarding according to desert. My reasons for thinking this stem from the importance of insuring that a moral code really does, in fact, work. Each of the three practical considerations mentioned above now enter the picture. First, it will be quite difficult to get people to accept a code which requires that they give away their savings, extra organs, or anything else merely because they can avoid a greater evil for a stranger. Many people simply wouldn't do it, they aren't that altruistic. If the code attempts to require it anyway, two results would likely follow. First, because many would not live up to the rules, there would be a tendency to create feelings of guilt in those who keep their savings in spite of having been taught it is wrong, as well as conflict between those who meet their obligations and those who do not. And, second, a more realistic code, one which doesn't expect more than can be accomplished, may actually result in more giving. It's a bit like trying to influence how children spend their money. Often they will buy less candy if rules allow them to do so occasionally but they are praised for spending on other things than if its purchase is prohibited. We cannot assume that making a charitable act a requirement will always encourage such behavior. Impractical rules not only create guilt and social conflict, they often tend to encourage the opposite of the desired result. By giving people the right to use their savings for themselves, yet praising those who do not exercise the right but help others instead, we have struck a good balance; the rules are at once practical yet reasonably effective.

Similar practical considerations would also influence our decision to support rules that allow people to keep what they deserve. For most people, working is not their favorite activity. If we are to prosper, however, goods and services must be produced. Incentives are therefore an important motivation, and one such incentive for work is income. Our code encourages work by allowing people to keep a large part of what they earn, indeed that's much the point of entitlements. "I worked hard for it, so I can keep it" is an oft-heard expression. If we eliminate this rule from our code and ask people to follow the greater moral evil rule instead, the result would likely be less work done and so less total production. Given a choice between not working and continuing to work knowing the efforts should go to benefit others, many would choose not to work.

Moral rules should be practical in a third sense, too. They cannot assume people are either more unbiased or more knowledgeable than they are. This fact has many implications for the sorts of rules we would want to include in a welfare maximizing code. For example, we may be tempted to avoid slavish conformity to counterproductive rules by allowing people to break promises whenever they think doing so would increase total welfare. But again we must not ignore human nature, in this case our tendency to give special weight to our own welfare and our inability to be always objective in tracing the ef-

fects of our actions. While we would not want to teach that promises must never be broken no matter what the consequences, we also would not want to encourage breaking promises any time a person can convince himself the results of doing so would be better than if he kept his word.

Similar considerations apply to the greater moral evil rule. Imagine a situation where someone feels he can prevent an evil befalling himself by taking what he needs from a large store. The idea that he's preventing something bad from happening (to himself) without sacrificing anything of comparable moral significance (the store won't miss the goods) would justify robbery. Although sometimes a particular act of theft really is welfare maximizing, it does not follow that we should support a *rule* which allows theft whenever the robber is preventing a greater evil. Such a rule, to work, would require more objectivity and more knowledge of long-term consequences than we have. Here again, including rights in our moral code serves a useful role, discouraging the tendency to rationalize our behavior by underestimating the harm we may cause to others or exaggerating the benefits that may accrue to ourselves.

The first sections of this paper attempted to show that our moral code is a bit schizophrenic. It seems to pull us in opposite directions, sometimes toward helping people who are in need, other times toward the view that rights and desert justify keeping things we have even if greater evil could be avoided were we to give away our extra eye or our savings account. This apparent inconsistency led us to a further question: Is the emphasis on entitlements really defensible, or should we try to resolve the tension in our own code by adopting the greater moral evil rule and ignoring entitlements? In this section I considered the idea that we might choose between entitlements and the greater moral evil rule by paying attention to the general nature of a moral code, and in particular to the sort of code we might want to support. I argued that all of us, including egoists, have reason to support a code which promotes the welfare of everyone who lives under it. That idea, of an ideal moral code which it is rational for everyone to support, provides a criterion for deciding which rules are sound and which ones we should support.

My conclusion is a conservative one: Concern that our moral code encourages production and not fail because it unrealistically assumes people are more altruistic or objective than they are means that our rules giving people rights to their possessions and encouraging distribution according to desert should be part of an ideal moral code. And since this is so, it is not always wrong to invoke rights or claim that money is deserved as justification for not giving aid, even when something worse could be prevented by offering help. The welfare maximizing moral code would not require us to maximize welfare in each individual case.

I have not yet discussed just how much weight should be given to entitlements, only that they are important and should not be ignored as Singer and Watson suggest. Certainly an ideal moral code would not allow people to overlook those in desperate need by making entitlements absolute, any more than it would ignore entitlements. But where would it draw the line?

It's hard to know, of course, but the following seems to me to be a sensible stab at an answer. Concerns about discouraging production and the general adherence to the code argue strongly against expecting too much; yet on the other hand, to allow extreme wealth in the face of grinding poverty would seem to put too much weight on entitlements. It seems to me, then, that a reasonable code would require people to help when there is no substantial cost to themselves, that is, when what they are sacrificing would not mean *significant* reduction in their own or their families' level of happiness. Since most people's savings accounts and nearly everybody's second kidney are

not insignificant, entitlements would in those cases outweigh another's need. But if what is at stake is trivial, as dirtying one's clothes would normally be, then an ideal moral code would not allow rights to override the greater evil that can be prevented. Despite our code's unclear and sometimes schizophrenic posture, it seems to me that these judgments are not that different from our current moral attitudes. We tend to blame people who waste money on trivia when they could help others in need, yet not to expect people to make large sacrifices to distant strangers. An ideal moral code thus might not be a great deal different from our own.

Notes

1. Singer also offers a "weak" version of this principle which, it seems to me, is *too* weak. It requires giving aid only if the gift is of *no* moral significance to the giver. But since even minor embarrassment or small amounts of happiness are not completely without moral importance, this weak principle implies little or no obligation to aid, even to the drowning child.

2. This difficulty leads many to think the choice of a code should be made behind a "veil of ignorance" about one's particular station in life, talents, class, and religious or other moral values. The major proponent of this view is John Rawls, *A Theory of Justice* (Cambridge: Harvard University Press, 1971).

3. Stephen Jay Gould, "So Cleverly Kind an Animal" in *Ever Since Darwin* (New York: W. W. Norton Co., 1977).

4. Richard B. Brandt, *Theory of Right and Good* (New York: Oxford University Press, 1979).

Questions for Analysis

1. *What is the "greater moral evil principle"?*

2. *What does Arthur mean by "entitlements"?*

3. *What is the difference between negative and positive rights?*

4. *Arthur claims that the greater moral evil principle is forward-looking, while matters of entitlement are directed to the past. What does he mean?*

5. *In what sense can both the greater moral evil rule and the rights-and-desert rule be universalized? In what sense can they not?*

6. *Explain how a consideration of the nature of morality demonstrates the need for entitlements.*

7. *According to Arthur, what two purposes do moral rules serve?*

8. *Are there features of Arthur's presentation that remind you of Ross's or Rawls's ethics? Explain.*

CASE PRESENTATION
To Aid or Not to Aid

The conference on world hunger had promised to be uneventful. Such conferences had convened periodically over the past 40 years. Invariably they did little more than tell everyone what they already knew: World hunger is still with us.

The first hint that this conference would be different was when the secretary of the U.S. Commission on World Hunger injected a political note. He suggested that the declining trend in U.S. foreign assistance had to be reversed if American leadership in the world was to continue.

"Intelligently administering foreign aid," the secretary pointed out, "is in America's self-interest and in the interest of world security." Then, as if to reinforce his point, he added, "Make no mistake about it. The purpose of our international aid program is self-serving. It's an approach that makes sense not only in international relations, but also in managing our families, businesses, and other aspects of our lives. That approach recognizes that it's safer and cheaper to anticipate a problem than to wait for it to become a crisis."

Thus, the secretary concluded that it was in our national interests to do all we could to combat the conditions that will otherwise likely drive people to desperation. By slashing international programs, he said finally, we're not saving money but merely postponing, even raising the costs that we'll one day have to pay.

Not everyone agreed, however. In fact, one panel member strongly objected to the secretary's remarks. She suggested that our international aid might actually be hurting the very people we want to help.

"Our aid fails to help," she argued, "because it assumes that aid can reach the powerless, even though it's funneled through the powerful. Well, it can't." She went on to insist that our aid to those countries where economic control is concentrated in the hands of a few merely underwrites the local, national, and international elites whose control over the land and other productive resources is generating the poverty and hunger we are trying to eradicate.

The secretary listened attentively to her remarks. When she finished, he said, "What would you propose we do?"

"Cut aid to all countries where a genuine redistribution of control over productive resources isn't under way," she shot back.

"Do you know how many countries that would involve?" the secretary asked her.

"Dozens," she said. "Perhaps scores."

The secretary agreed. "And do you know how many people would starve?"

"Millions," she said without hesitation. Then she asked the secretary, "Do you know how many people we're sentencing to a life of suffering and to a death by starvation through our well-intentioned but tragically misguided aid?"

Questions for Analysis

1. *How would Kant evaluate aid given primarily out of self-interest?*

2. *Do you think it would be moral to allow people to starve so long as a nation was not taking measures to redistribute control of its productive resources?*

3. *Would it be accurate to describe both the secretary's and the panel member's positions as consequential?*

4. *If the secretary agreed that the panel member is correct in her assessment of the impact of U.S. aid, could he continue to argue that it is still in our best interest to provide aid?*

5. *Do you think a rich nation such as the United States is morally justified in using its aid program as a weapon for molding the social and economic infrastructures of recipient nations?*

CASE PRESENTATION
The Way Out

"You know the worst of it?" Lila Robbins asked her companion Walter Moore, who was decrying the greyish-brown poison that passed for air in the Los Angeles basin.

"Sure," said Walt, "it's killing us." With that he honked the car's horn. Not that it would do any good. As usual during "rush hour," the freeway traffic had backed up. Walt knew that at best they'd crawl at a snail's pace for the next 30 minutes or so. But it always made him feel better to honk the horn, as if he still had some control over things.

"No," Lila said. "The worst thing is that there is absolutely nothing anyone of us can do to stop its spread."

"How depressing!"

"Depressing but true. An individual act of renunciation would be meaningless."

"Unless everyone else did the same thing," Walt said.

Lila wagged her head from side to side and said, "It'll never happen."

The young couple took on the gloom of the day. Unconsciously they checked to see if their windows were sealed.

"So what's the solution?" Walt asked with a sigh.

"Control the behavior that's causing the problem," Lila answered firmly.

"You mean get people off the roads?"

"I'm not just talking about smog," Lila said. "The smog's just a symptom of a far more serious problem."

"Which is?"

"The pursuit of private gratification. That's what's responsible for pollution, world hunger, dwindling resources—what environmentalists call *ecological scarcity*."

She went on to explain that ecological scarcity is upon us. We live on a finite planet containing limited resources, and we appear to be approaching those limits at breakneck speed. In short, "We're about to overtax the carrying capacity of our planet."

Walt disagreed. "What you fail to take note of," he told Lila, "is that technology is simultaneously expanding the limits."

Lila shook her head. "Look," she said, "we're like fish in a pond where all life is rapidly being suffocated by a water lily that doubles in size every day and will cover the whole pond in a month."

"I don't deny that the lily—to use your metaphor—is growing really fast. But the pond can be made to grow even faster. We'll never run out of resources because economics and technology will always keep finding ways for us to meet our needs."

"You miss the point."

"What point?"

"That either way we lose." Walt didn't catch her drift. "Look," Lila said, "if I'm right, then sooner or later—probably sooner—we'll reach the physical limits and all hell will break loose. It'll be every person for himself, dog-eat-dog, sheer anarchy. The only way to restore order will be through a dictatorship."

"And if I'm right?" Walt asked her.

"If you're right, the result will be much the same. Think about it. If we can save ourselves technologically, we'll still have to vigilantly guard our resources, and that means we must control human behavior—through strong-armed tactics, if necessary. In the end the measures we'll have to adopt to survive won't be much different from the future that I'm predicting when we reach our physical limits."

The traffic inched forward and then stopped. Walt craned his head out his window, but he couldn't see much. Up ahead the smog hung thicker. He rolled his window up again and dabbed his stinging eyes. "So what's the way out?"

"We have to abandon our political corruption. We must stop using liberty as a license for self-indulgence. We must recognize that we can lead a very good life, even an affluent one, without wasteful use of our resources. When we recognize that the pursuit of happiness doesn't mean an insane, lustful quest for material gain, then we'll start dealing with the crisis of ecological scarcity. Then we'll seriously start dealing with problems like world poverty, sickness, and starvation."

Walt mulled over what Lila had said. After several minutes he spoke, "You make it sound like our real shortage is in moral resources."

"Exactly!" Lila was quick to agree. "There's no real scarcity in nature. It's just that our wants have outstripped nature's bounty. If we're to avoid a grim future, we must assume full moral responsibilities."

"Thank God!" Walt blurted out as the traffic bolted forward. He turned on the headlights and started to think about something to eat. "I'm famished!" he said.

But Lila wasn't listening. She was recalling a quotation from the Chinese sage Lao-tzu:

Nature sustains itself through three precious principles, which one does well to embrace and follow.
These are gentleness, frugality, and humility.

Questions for Analysis

1. *Do you agree with Lila?*
2. *What do you think Lila means by "assuming full moral responsibilities"?*
3. *What connection, if any, do you see between our alleged failure to assume moral responsibilities, and ecological scarcity?*
4. *How is ecological scarcity related to world hunger?*
5. *An essay entitled "The Scarcity Society" inspired this case presentation. In it the author, William Ophuls, writes: "If this inexorable process is not controlled by prudent and, above all, timely political restraints on the behavior that causes it, then we must resign ourselves to ecological self-destruction."[3] What political restraints do you think are necessary?*

Selections for Further Reading

Bedau, H. A., Ed. *Justice and Equality.* Englewood Cliffs, N.J.: Prentice-Hall, 1971.

Brown, Lester R., and Erik P. Eckholm. *By Bread Alone.* Praeger, 1974.

Brunner, E. *Justice and the Social Order.* M. Huttinger, Trans. London: Lutterworth Press, 1946.

Ehrlich, Paul. *The Population Bomb.* New York: Ballantine, 1971.

Paddock, Paul, and William Paddock. *Famine—1975.* Boston: Little, Brown, 1968.

Simon, Arthur. *Bread for the World.* New York: Paulist Press, 1975.

Simon, Arthur, and Paul Simon. *The Politics of World Hunger.* New York: Harper's Magazine Press, 1973.

---

3.   *William Ophuls, "The Scarcity Society,"* Harper's Magazine *(April 1974), pp. 29–37.*

Index